W9-DFB-502

780.15
Gil

98536

Gillespie.
The musical experience.

Date Due

JUL 2 9 '79			
SEP 9 '79			
RESERVE			
11-9-75			
[illegible]			
12-9-75			

WITHDRAWN

The Library
Nazareth College of Rochester, N. Y.

PRINTED IN U.S.A.

WADSWORTH MUSIC SERIES

Advanced Music Reading by William Thomson

Basic Concepts in Music by Gary M. Martin

Basic Piano for Adults by Helene Robinson

Basic Resources for Learning Music by Alice Snyder Knuth and William E. Knuth

English Folk Song: Some Conclusions, 4th edition, by Cecil J. Sharp (edited by Maud Karpeles)

Five Centuries of Keyboard Music by John Gillespie

Foundations in Music Theory, Regular edition by Leon Dallin

Foundations in Music Theory, 2nd edition, with Programed Exercises by Leon Dallin

Harmony and Melody, Volumes I and II, and *A Workbook for Harmony and Melody, Volumes I and II,* by Elie Siegmeister

Introduction to Ear Training by William E. Thomson and Richard P. DeLone

An Introduction to Musical Understanding and Musicianship by Ethel G. Adams

Introduction to Music Reading by William Thomson

Keyboard Harmony: A Comprehensive Approach to Musicianship by Isabel Lehmer

Keyboard Skills: Sight Reading, Transposition, Harmonization, Improvisation by Winifred K. Chastek

Music Essentials by Robert Pace

Music Fundamentals by Howard A. Murphy with John F. Park

Music Reading through Singing by Charles W. Walton and Harry R. Wilson

Talking about Symphonies by Antony Hopkins

The Understanding of Music by Charles R. Hoffer

The Musical Experience

JOHN GILLESPIE

University of California, Santa Barbara

The Musical Experience

Wadsworth Publishing Company, Inc.
Belmont, California

Cover illustration: Boy Playing a Lyre. End of three-sided relief from Greek altar (the "Ludovisi Throne"), marble, 5th century B.C. *Photo courtesy of Museum of Fine Arts, Boston, Henry L. Pierce Residuary Fund.*

Endpaper illustration: Tintoretto (1518–1594). Apollo and Marsyas. Photo courtesy of Wadsworth Atheneum, Hartford.

Frontispiece: Frans Hals (c.1580–1666). Boys Singing and Playing Music. Photo courtesy of Marburg-Art Reference Bureau.

98536

Third printing: July 1969

© 1968 by Wadsworth Publishing Company, Inc., Belmont, California. All rights reserved. No part of this book may be reproduced in any form, by mimeograph or any other means, without permission in writing from the publisher.

L. C. Cat. Card No.: 68–15396
Printed in the United States of America

780.15
Fil

To My Students

Preface

A major feature of this book is its flexibility. Some instructors do not like to discuss music history, styles, and forms in chronological sequence, while other instructors absolutely prefer the chronological method. Although the historical material in Part II of this text is arranged chronologically (my own preference), I have taken pains to make it flexible. Each chapter is independent to allow the instructor to begin with whatever period he chooses. Also, for the instructor who prefers to progress by forms (that is, the development of the symphony, the string quartet, or other form), the text contains subheadings, with page references for each form listed in the index. In addition, I have tried to provide sufficient musical analyses so that each instructor can find examples suitable for his particular course. Whenever practical, I have included enough material so that the instructor can choose and arrange according to his own preferences, selecting some portions of the book for reading assignments and some for class lectures, and omitting some sections.

Other salient features of this book derive either from personal interviews with instructors who teach music appreciation and similar courses or from questionnaires sent to such teachers. The tabulated results of these interviews and questionnaires served as a valuable reference for current ideas about teaching music appreciation.

The interviews and questionnaires—coincident with my own views—indicated that both teachers and students want more emphasis on contemporary music. I have therefore covered this field as thoroughly as space permits, discussing the music and composers by country. In order to make the contemporary material as up-to-date as possible and to give each composer an opportunity to present his own ideas about his music, I sent questionnaires to living composers. This direct information on contemporary music has not to my knowledge been offered in previous music-appreciation texts.

While preparing the text, I kept in mind certain guidelines to make the book as useful as I could for both student and teacher. These guidelines are:

1. Whenever feasible, I have let each composer—beginning with the Baroque period—speak for himself, so that he is no longer just a name but a person giving firsthand information about himself, his style, and at times his views on music in general.

2. I have tried to bear in mind that students using this book will be young people from approximately 17 to 20 years of age, many of whom will have had no previous music study.

3. I have included discussions of folk song, jazz, and Eastern music because each type contributes enjoyment and knowledge to the listening experience. Since hearing these different types of music depends greatly on records, Chapter 27 contains a short discography.

4. I have tried to maintain an even balance between opera, symphony, solo works, and chamber music, and I have deliberately chosen standard items of musical repertoire for analysis. Even though most of the teachers interviewed consider such standby works as Beethoven's *Fifth Symphony* overused, they usually agree that many of their students have never heard such familiar works.

5. I have tried to make the book self-contained. Part I introduces the student to the basic factors of the musical language: sound, rhythm, meter, melody, elementary form, texture, instruments, and aesthetics. Part II covers the historical development of music through its various styles and periods. For the purposes of his course, the student should not have to look elsewhere for explanations and information. At the end of each chapter, however, there is a short annotated bibliography for those students who desire to pursue the subject further. I have listed paperback books (designated as PB) when possible for the practical reason that they cost less.

6. I have made liberal use of photographs. Some show how musical periods relate to those of the other arts; others illustrate textual descriptions (of instruments, for example); and some relate to music inspired by a nonmusical work of art, such as a painting or sculpture.

7. I have inserted a number of musical examples. Although Chapter 3—*Reading Music*—will not teach students to read music fluently, it will help them to acquire a general feeling for note progressions, melodic contour, rhythmic subtlety, and dynamic indications. For the most part, the musical examples illustrate the development and transformation of themes used in well-known compositions. The student should find it easier to retain themes and melodies if he has a graphic illustration as a frame of reference.

8. In order to draw the student personally into the musical experience, I have added several discussion questions and assignments to each chapter. In addition, several examples of early music (ancient Greek song, organum, etc.) are simple enough to be learned and executed by a class.

Class lectures and reading can accomplish just so much. The student must be encouraged to devote time to active listening through radio, recordings, and live concerts. Then he can relate what he has learned about music to what he hears in a complete aural experience.

I am beholden to many people for many things. The timely character of the book is due largely to the composers whose personal remarks appear in the chapters on contemporary music—I am in debt and grateful to them. A sincere word of thanks is due those teachers who granted me an interview or else took the time to give careful answers to my detailed questionnaire: William Austin, Cornell University; Mahlon Balderston, Santa Barbara City College; Paul B. Banham, University of Utah; Nelson Bonar, Fullerton Junior College; John Bresnahan, Yuba College; Theodore Brunson, San Diego State College; Vada Butcher, Howard University; Andrew Charlton, California State College at Fullerton; Harold Confer, San Bernardino Valley College; Salvatore Ferrantelli, San Diego State College; Robert Fisher, East Los Angeles College; Darwin Fredrickson, Fullerton Junior College; Rita Fuszek, California State College at Fullerton; Daniel Goode, University of Minnesota; Lionel Greenberg, Los Angeles Pierce College; Marie Henderson, University of Florida at Gainesville; Truitt Hollis, East Los Angeles College; Charles Hubbard, California State College at Los Angeles; Earle Immel, Lost Angeles Valley College; Larry Jarvis, San Fernando Valley State College; Ronald R. Kidd, Purdue University; Kenneth Mack, Barstow College; Frank Macomber, Syracuse University; Frank Magliocco, Citrus College; Elizabeth R. Nelson, Pasadena College; Mario Oneglia, Montclair State College; Carolyn Powell, Santa Ana College; Myron Roberts, University of Nebraska; Marjorie Rohfleisch, San Diego State College; Jack Sacher, Montclair State College; Frank Salazar, Ventura College; Edward Szabo, Montclair State College; Rowan Taylor, Los Angeles Pierce College; Roger Vaughn, California State College at Fullerton; Stennis Waldon, Pasadena City College; Don Lee White, California State College at Los Angeles.

I also give special thanks to the reviewers who read the manuscript and offered constructive, pertinent criticism: Maynard C. Anderson, Wartberg College; Alice Catalyne, Los Angeles Valley College; John K. Galm, University of Colorado; Lawrence Intravaia, Southern Illinois University; John R. King, University of Massachusetts; James E. Richards, East Texas State University; Wallace D. Rushkin, Sacramento State College; Royal Stanton, De Anza College.

Two personal friends and music historians, Dr. Arthur Moorefield, California Lutheran College, and Peter Gano, University of California, Santa Barbara, helped immeasurably by carefully and critically reading the entire manuscript.

Finally—but first and foremost—I thank my wife Anna, who has read the entire manuscript countless times and whose experienced editorial hand is discernable on every page of the printed text.

John Gillespie

Contents

Part One

Music's Vocabulary

1 The Ingredients for the Musical Experience

Those composers are exemplars who unite nature and art in their works.

LUDWIG VAN BEETHOVEN (1824)

In Egypt, where ancient pyramids and temples still dominate the landscape, a priest chants highly ornate melodies as he celebrates a ritual Mass for Coptic Christians. In a basement café located on Omonia Square in Athens, a small instrumental band delights customers with the oriental-tinged strains of Greek folk songs. In India, a sitar player sits cross-legged on the ground surrounded by a group of admirers as he improvises endlessly on a melody. In a Japanese temple, an orchestra of flutes, lutes, drums, gongs, and mouth organs plays ceremonial music whose origins are lost in time. In New York's Carnegie Hall, a famous pianist plays the music of Chopin to a rapt audience. And throughout the United States, thousands of guitars are being sold as high school and college students experience the joy of making their own music.

Music in different manifestations exists all over the world, and each type has its special value. Although we will examine music deriving from non-Western cultures briefly in this book, our attention will be directed primarily to Western music. The quantity of this music alone is staggering, for each European and American country has its unique musical history and development.

Music in our hemisphere is typically classified into one of three categories. Folk music expresses basic human emotions—love, sorrow, fear, revenge—in simple, direct musical language. Popular music, in one of its many phases, assisted in the birth and development of jazz. Finally there is that other form of music, called variously "classical," "serious," "concert," or "art" music—all rather inadequate but familiar terms.

The adjectives "classical," "serious," "concert," and "art" attest to the inadequacy of present-day musical terminology. If one type of music is serious, are all other types frivolous? And do we not have jazz concerts as well as chamber-music concerts? The term "art" cannot be applied to just one type of music, for there are several kinds of music that qualify as art music. So we are left with "classical" music, a term likely to be confused with music from the Classic period of the eighteenth century; but since most people use this term and know to which type of music it refers, we shall use it in this book.

Folk music offers no listening problems for even a musically uninformed individual, because this music speaks directly and naturally and is easily understood. Most people grow up with folk music: nursery ditties, campfire songs, historical songs, patriotic songs; almost all such familiar songs are in some way related to folk song. Thus folk music is an important part of our cultural heritage and must be given due recognition in any discussion of music as a total experience. Folk songs also help us learn about melody and grasp the basic elements of musical structure.

Sometimes the word "jazz" creates a mild shock among well-intentioned classical-music lovers, almost as though the term were taboo, whereas in truth jazz is an art in itself and must not be ignored. It is a distinctive product of American musical culture, and its origins and growth provide an exciting, intriguing story. Apart from its intrinsic qualities, jazz has noticeably influenced other kinds of music, particularly contemporary classical music. (But since "contemporary classical" seems to be an anachronism, we shall call twentieth-century "classical" music simply "contemporary music.")

Folk music offers an almost spontaneous experience to the average person. With much jazz, understanding comes readily. However, some of the best jazz can pose considerable listening problems, and we have to understand at least a few basic techniques in order to experience its full impact.

Complications arise when the listener attempts Western classical music, because this music is not always easily assimilated. In fact, one of its attractions is that full understanding comes only after repeated, concentrated hearings. Unlike folk music, which has varied its style only slightly during a centuries-old existence, and jazz, which is still very young, classical music has been subjected to almost continuous stylistic changes for more than a thousand years. Classical music thus offers the greatest listening challenge, and we will concentrate principally on such music.

WHAT IS MUSIC?

There are numerous definitions of music, from naïve to scientific, from picturesque to scholarly. The following, written about 200 years ago, still furnishes an objective general explanation and is charming besides.

> Music is the Gift of God, and bestow'd on Man, to edulcorate [sweeten], and heighten the Pleasures of human Life; and to alleviate, and dispel its Cares in this World: and is the principal Entertainment of God, and the Souls of the Blessed hereafter.[1]

Alexander Pope in his *Essay on Criticism* (1711) compared music to the more palpable art of poetry.

> Music resembles Poetry, in each
> Are nameless graces which no methods teach,
> And which a master-hand alone can reach.[2]

[1] William Tans'ur, *The Elements of Musick Display'd* (London: Stanley Crowder, 1772), p. iii.

[2] *The Works of Alexander Pope, Esq.* (London: A. Millar *et al.*, 1766), Vol. 1, p. 108.

The Shorter Oxford English Dictionary defines music as "that one of the fine arts which is concerned with the combination of sounds with a view to beauty of form and the expression of thought or feeling: also the science of the laws or principles by which this art is regulated."[3]

Obviously there is no one absolute definition of music, for music is such a personal experience—a quality to be grateful for in our mass-production age—that each listener draws a different benefit from it. There is nothing to see or grasp while listening to music; the imagination has complete freedom to create for the listener whatever his natural sensibilities require. No wonder music is difficult to define!

LEARNING THE LANGUAGE

If we first of all accept the premise that musical intelligence, awareness, and appreciation are worth attaining, we arrive at a crucial question: How does one achieve them? Simply by becoming an intelligent listener. Music is a language, as natural a mode of expression as speech. It is a subtle language, delicate yet powerful, capable of infinite extension and development. It is an emotional language, yet premised on natural psychological laws and lasting principles of styles and construction.

Proper introduction to the language begins with learning the basic elements of music and the essentials of technique and style. We shall examine these elements in the first part of this book.

One point must be emphasized here: from the beginning to the end of your study you are expected to take time to listen, listen, and listen! Television, radio, recordings—all offer ample opportunity for listening, but live concerts are best because the listener participates more fully in the musical experience.

Although there are various avenues leading to intelligent listening, no single approach is exclusively desirable; rather a combination of approaches should be sought. What the potentially perceptive listener must avoid is purely passive hearing: music to study by, music to eat by, music to garden by. Although this kind of musical encounter is very pleasant, in all probability the music is not often absorbed, for hearing and listening are two different things. In most instances of passive hearing the hearer can't even remember what he has heard, not to mention how he felt about it.

Any one of several basic approaches may be used to prepare for the listening experience. The intellectual approach presupposes a perceptive listener, one who consciously strives to use his innate faculties to extract meaning from what he hears, to achieve a responsive experience through mental awareness and inquisitiveness. He familiarizes himself with background information about the composer and the composition. In other words, even before approaching the music, the intelligent listener prepares himself with guides, with a frame of reference. He then turns his attention to the auditory experience, concentrating to develop a habit of listening attentively. He must recognize elements of musical structure, listen for melodies and follow their transformations, and mentally note the rhythm and the harmonic variety. Doing all this requires studied attention.

Perceptive listeners know that listening to a composition once never

[3] *The Shorter Oxford English Dictionary* (Oxford: Clarendon Press, 1933), Vol. 1, p. 1300.

results in a total experience. Classical music demands repeated hearings before it divulges all the components contributing to the total experience.

While the intellectual or perceptive approach is superior, there are other methods. At the opposite end of the spectrum lies the sensuous—or nonintellectual—attitude. A listener can enjoy some music while remaining blissfully ignorant about it. Few people understand oriental music, yet many are attracted by its unusual sound combinations, its improvisatory mood, and the exotic instruments called for. The thunderous tones drawn from a pipe organ can be exciting, even inspiring. Unfortunately, such emotional responses are not durable, and the chances are that the nonintellectual hearer will become less excited and less inspired when he hears the same pipe organ a second time. The sensuous experience merely arouses surface emotions; it cannot do justice to the music or to the listener's mental capacities.

A more reasonable approach combines intellectual and emotional elements. The total effect of music by composers such as Chopin or Schubert or Brahms is revealed only by a blending of mental and emotional experiences. As sheer sound, their works are delightfully diverting. In their total perceptive-emotional context, they are exquisite.

A final word concerning the important item of time: there is no such thing as instant music appreciation. To become a perceptive listener takes time and ambition: time to investigate musical problems and to absorb the various elements that synthesize to create a musical image; ambition to learn the musical vocabulary and to acquire the tools of learning and listening. These are the requirements for becoming an intelligent listener. The rewards are rich and they are permanent.

THE FOUR MAJOR INGREDIENTS

A good way to begin your understanding and appreciation of music is to get acquainted with the elements of music, such as the characteristics of sound, the dimensions of musical form (melody, rhythm, counterpoint, harmony, texture), and the various musical instruments. These are the subjects of the first six chapters of this book. Once you have assimilated these technical aspects at least partially, you will be ready to learn about the different periods in music history, the forms and styles associated with each period, and the representative music illustrating these styles.

There is another exceptionally helpful preliminary to your study of music appreciation: determining exactly how much you know before you start. Some of the general facts about music are clearly self-evident, but discussing these facts now as a kind of prologue will save confusion later on.

There are four major ingredients in the recipe for making this intangible art: the composer, who begins the creative process; the music resulting from his talent and efforts; the performer or performers; and the listener or audience, who must evaluate and judge the final product.

The Composer

Let us begin with the composer, since music in our own civilization begins with him. What, after all, do we listen for when we listen to a composer? He

> need not tell us a story like the novelist; he need not "copy" nature like the sculptor; his work need have no immediate practical function like the architect's drawings. What is it that he gives us, then? Only one answer seems possible to me: He gives us himself. Every artist's work is, of course, an expression of himself, but none so direct as that of the creative musician. He gives us, without relation to exterior "events," the quintessential part of himself—that part which embodies the fullest and deepest expression of himself as a man and of his experience as a fellow being.
>
> Always remember that when you listen to a composer's creation you are listening to a man, to a particular individual, with his own special personality. For a composer, to be of any value, must have his own personality. It may be of greater or lesser importance, but, in the case of significant music, it will always mirror that personality. No composer can write into his music a value that he does not possess as a man. His character may be streaked with human frailties—like Lully's or Wagner's, for example—but whatever is fine in his music will come from whatever is fine in him as a man.[4]

Thus Aaron Copland, one of America's fine composers, indicates that music reflects the nature of its creator.

Music has very likely been created by someone since mankind's beginnings. Originally each man was his own composer, creating songs spontaneously while he worked, prayed, and played. We know, although most of the music has disappeared, that in ancient Greece author and composer were one, with the dramatist composing music to accompany his prose. Most composers from the Middle Ages remain anonymous for the reason that they were mainly clerics who wrote music to glorify God. Such a prideful act as signing their names to their music perhaps never occurred to them. Not until the later Middle Ages did it become customary for composers to sign their works.

Renaissance society created a need for professional musicians, and it was during this time that composers attained a highly desirable position: cardinals and other prelates employed composer-musicians in their private chapels, and music-loving monarchs retained them at court. This respectable status continued into the Baroque era, when even the wealthy bourgeoisie of eighteenth-century society competed to hire the best musicians. By the nineteenth century the composer had become more independent, existing on the merits of his music rather than the whim of a patron.

Within the composer lies the initial creative impulse to write music. It is he who conceives the design, fills in the outline, and produces the written work. A composer cannot really be taught how to compose; the talent for composition is an inborn gift. He can master writing techniques and study past traditions; he can observe and sometimes imitate; but there is no standard formula for him to follow. He must study, observe, and practice—and then let his talent develop with experience.

What makes a composer want to compose? Is he urged to do so by some unexplainable something within himself? The answer varies according to social and cultural customs in successive societies. Before the nineteenth century, a composer attached to a court or wealthy household worked on command. Would-be composers approached the art of composition as they would any other craft. During the nineteenth century, when composers were no longer dependent on patronage, they allowed their emotions to dictate what they wrote, thus making their work more personal.

[4] From *What to Listen for in Music* by Aaron Copland. Copyright © 1957 by McGraw-Hill, Inc. Used by permission of McGraw-Hill Book Company.

Today composers generally seem to preserve a little of each era in their thinking about musical creativity. Although the prime requisite for composition is talent, the artist must also feel a need for artistic self-expression; in other words, he must feel compelled to create a work of art through music. This desire embodies his instinctive emotions, yet the modern composer is also careful about structure and clarity.

Once a man has a desire to compose, how does he go about it? Immediately the word inspiration comes to mind. Despite the fact that this term is considered outmoded by many contemporary composers, creative musicians have always attested to the existence of something called inspiration, perhaps for lack of a better word. To some people inspiration means a spiritual gift mysteriously bestowed by God. Such an explanation is unacceptable to others, who prefer to regard inspiration as an idea stimulated by an acute sensation or as a suggestion "breathed" into the mind from atmosphere or events, thereby arousing the intellect or emotions.

Inspiration is handled differently by different artists. Some composers seek stimulus in the music of other composers, without any thought of imitating them. César Franck, the French organist and composer, professed to be inspired by playing the works of Wagner or Bach on the piano. The eighteenth-century symphonist Joseph Haydn sought stimulus by improvising at the piano before attempting to write.

In some instances composers rely on a mental vision, creating inspiration through an imaginary picture or story, but they rarely divulge the exact nature of these mental fantasies. Other artists find their senses quickened under pressure and compose best that way. The Italian composer Gioacchino Rossini once advised a young opera composer never to write his overture until the evening before the first performance. This method may have been successful for Rossini; it might prove disastrous for others.

The creative process may germinate with a flash of feeling. Reading a poem could suggest a musical setting to Franz Schubert, and he frequently reacted by spontaneously composing a song. Beethoven, on the other hand, jotted down ideas as they occurred to him and then waited, giving his thoughts time to mature. Bach could compose on demand, and he was often obliged to do just that because his position depended on his production.

In addition to inspiration—no matter how it originates or how we describe it—a composer needs technical proficiency, for inspiration alone cannot create a work of art. The composer must know how to put his ideas into usable form. If he is serious about his work, he will keep in mind its eventual performance. That is, he will remember that a song should be confined within the range of a specific voice type; that a sonata for violin should not demand impossible gymnastics for the instrument; that a piano composition should not require abnormal stretches for the hands; that an orchestral work should not call for an unrealistic orchestral apparatus. Such considerations are important. Music must be playable to be heard, and it is only through performance that it can be appraised.

The Music

Music as a listening experience is the end result of a rather unusual chain of events: the creative artist, working alone, becomes inspired and writes down the sound patterns he hears within his mind; the finished product is usually read for performance by a person or persons unknown to the composer; the performer's interpretation of the music is then heard by still another group of strangers. To help you understand and appreciate music coming from such unrelated sources, let us examine some of the terms used over and over again in conversations about music. These terms may very well be self-explanatory, but they are discussed here in the interest of consistency and clarity.

The term *work* is frequently used to describe something produced by creative talent and effort. It is not a precise definition, for it is applied equally to a book, an etching, a poem, a symphony, or any other "work of art." The term also refers to an individual artist's total creative products, such as Bach's or Rembrandt's "work."

Piece (or *piece of music*) is commonly employed to describe a musical work even though this expression is totally undescriptive. A piece may be a creative musical work, it is true, but the term has come to have many other meanings in the artistic sense. Currently it applies to almost any artistic endeavor—a picture, painting, play, drama, and even a passage to be recited.

The term *composition* (or, better still, *musical composition*) is a far more selective and logical choice for describing a composer's finished product. It is an exact term: a composition is a written musical work, especially an original work of some magnitude to whose formal structure appropriate attention has been given.

A musical work may be a single composition or several contrasting compositions combined to form a larger structure. Each contrasting composition is called a *movement,* from the fact that one chief element contributing to the contrast is the rate of speed (*tempo*) in each composition. The movements are more or less independent, yet definitely related to the whole.

Another word often heard in music discussion is *score,* which is a generic term used to identify written music that shows all the instrumental or vocal parts of a particular composition. A *part,* therefore, refers to the music for a particular voice or instrument in the score. There are various types of scores. A *full score* supplies all parts but displays each orchestral and vocal part separately, one above the other. An *orchestral score* presents individual instrumental parts. A *vocal score* for a choral or operatic work shows vocal parts but has the orchestral parts arranged for piano. A *piano score* is an orchestral score reduced to a piano version. A *miniature score* is a pocket-sized full score.

Another thought that comes to mind when an inquisitive listener hears music is the intent of the composition. What is the composer trying to say or illustrate? This in turn brings up the subject of program music versus absolute music.

The term *program music* originated in the mid-nineteenth century with the composer-pianist Franz Liszt, that flamboyant musician who frequently prefaced his compositions with a verbal description of their dramatic content. He defined this as "any preface in intelligible language added to a piece of instrumental music, by means of which the composer intends to guard the listener against a wrong poetical interpretation, and to direct his attention to the poetical idea of the whole or to a particular part of it."[5] In our day composers deem it unnecessary to explain their work by including a detailed program or plot,

[5] Quoted in Percy Scholes, *The Oxford Companion to Music,* 9th Edition (London: Oxford University Press, 1960), "Programme Music," p. 839.

although sometimes they depend on a title or explanatory motto to convey their message. Generally speaking, program music is descriptive music. It is supposed to draw mental pictures for the listener or to touch his emotions. Program music emphasizes dramatics and emotions, yet some kind of formal structure is always present.

Although Liszt originated the term "program music," the idea dates back much further. Clément Jannequin's (*c.*1475–*c.*1560) storytelling compositions for chorus, with titles such as *The Battle* and *The Song of the Birds,* are excellent examples of early program music even though the term itself had not then been invented. During the eighteenth century François Couperin delighted audiences with picturesque harpischord pieces having such titles as *The Little Windmills, French Follies,* and *Tender Nanette.* The nineteenth century, that battlefield of Romanticism, reveled in programmatic compositions of all kinds. Numerous composers used descriptive titles such as *Dance of Death* and *Pictures at an Exhibition.*

Program music continues to be written and in the twentieth century has produced some happy results. Ottorino Respighi has written delightful music describing his native Italy in *Pines of Rome* and *Fountains of Rome.* Arthur Honegger's orchestral music in this vein is also highly effective: *Pacific 231* is a musical description of a locomotive, and *Rugby* offers a musical picture of football.

Although the dividing line is at times thinly drawn, the implied opposite of program music is *absolute music,* sometimes called *abstract music.* (There also exists a grey area between program and absolute music. Such works as Beethoven's *Pastoral Symphony* and Elgar's *Enigma Variations* are difficult to classify as either program or absolute music.) Absolute music speaks for itself without a descriptive title, story, or preconceived mental picture. The composer concentrates his efforts to create a work of formal design and intrinsic beauty. Because absolute music is self-sufficient, concerned only with pure sound, it leaves the listener free to find in it whatever suits his personal mood or need. Most sonatas, symphonies, and fugues are typical examples of absolute music, for here the composer uses thematic development to impress musical ideas on the listener. In one way this music offers a greater challenge to the listener: lacking a dramatic program to follow or interpret, he is forced to listen seriously in order to make the most of the musical experience.

The sounding body—instruments or voices—that translates written music into sound is known as the *medium.* In the music field the term *solo* applies to a composition intended for one voice or principal instrument, with accompaniment usually by piano. Keyboard instruments, as well as the harp, are traditionally heard in solo performance, without accompaniment. Almost all orchestral instruments possess a solo repertoire. When the solo instrument is accompanied by an orchestra instead of a piano, the result is usually a *concerto.*

The term *chamber music* has taken on various meanings in the course of music history. Dr. Charles Burney in his *History of Music* (1789) speaks of chamber music in general as "cantatas, single songs, solos and trios, quartets, concertos and symphonies of few parts." Today our use of the term chamber music is somewhat different. First, as a term it is restricted primarily to classical and contemporary music. Second, although this fact is not adhered to in actual practice, chamber music is designed for performance in an intimate drawing room, whereas concert music is meant for a large auditorium or hall. Third, the term "chamber music" includes all instrumental ensemble music for two or more instruments, performed with one player on each part.

It is customary to classify chamber music according to the number of players, or parts. Thus a *trio* is for three players, a *quartet* for four, a *quintet* for five. Even a sonata for violin and piano qualifies as chamber music so long as the piano part is not an accompaniment but maintains equal importance with the violin part.

Although chamber music now typically refers to instrumental ensembles, it can also pertain to small vocal groups, especially madrigal singers, where the group is small and each singer has a separate part.

A *trio* may consist of any three instruments; the most usual combinations are the string trio (violin, viola, and cello) and the piano trio (piano, violin, and cello). A *quartet* is usually a string quartet (two violins, viola, and cello). If the quartet is not intended for this combination, the title indicates the substituted instruments required for performance; thus a piano quartet calls for piano, violin, viola, and cello.

There is great variety in orchestral music, the most familiar, of course, being the *symphony,* typically an elaborate composition for full orchestra. A *symphonic poem* is a programmatic composition. An *overture* may be an introductory composition or an independent work. A *symphonic suite* or *orchestral suite* is an extended composition consisting of a number of individual movements but not conforming to the accepted idea of a symphony.

Opera covers a broad field of talents: orchestra, soloists, chorus, conductor, stage director, prompter. A *chorus* is a large singing group with numerous voices singing each part, while a *choir* is usually a smaller vocal ensemble. (Colloquially, the word "chorus" is often substituted for the term *refrain* in the recurring melody of a popular song.) Frequently the word "choir" refers to an organized body of singers in a church service.

The Performer

The performer is the essential link in the chain connecting composer to audience. Without the performer to interpret and re-create the composer's intent, music would indeed be a sterile art.

The performer cannot depend on artistic talent alone. He must put in years of technical practice to be able to create the right sound; he must train almost as an athlete trains. He needs disciplined reflexes and a keen awareness of all the capabilities and technical problems of his instrument.

Besides technique and agility, the performer has to have a sound musical background. The more he knows about the traditions of his profession, the more convincing he will be in interpreting the composer's ideas. Taste and opinion are also essential. Certain accepted traditions of musical interpretation have become unwritten laws. The performer attempts to follow these traditions as authentically as he can; at the same time, he injects his own personality into the performance to give it vitality and excitement.

The Listener

The listener has before him a twofold musical experience: hearing a composer's music and analyzing the performer's interpretation of it. Composer and performer imperceptibly blend into one whole, yet a perceptive listener can automatically separate the two in his mental appraisal. He will be conscious of whether it is the music itself or the quality or authenticity of the performance that pleases or displeases him.

In addition to the immense pleasure and spiritual satisfaction that he can derive from music, the listener has a duty to fulfill. He must distinguish good music from bad, fine performances from poor ones, for in the end it is usually the listeners who determine the value of an artistic work (although conductors and performers can decide the fate of a composition with a superb or an inadequate interpretation of it). Listeners are sometimes mistaken in their judgment, as proved by the forgotten composers who once were idols and the master composers who were misjudged by their contemporaries. But in listening to music, and while still experiencing its inherent emotional and intellectual appeal, one should try to make honest appraisals.

SUMMARY

Thus the total musical experience involves many people doing many things. The composer acquires technical facility and musical background; he is inspired, stimulated, or otherwise induced to create within his mind the elements of a composition, which he puts into written form. When the performer obtains the composition, he reads it, studies it, practices it until he is satisfied with his interpretation; then he plays it to an unknown audience.

It is the intelligent listener who gains the greatest benefit and pleasure from this total effort, and it is he who frequently decides the music's fate.

FOR DISCUSSION AND ASSIGNMENT

1. Do you think a composer's life and times can influence the music he writes? In what ways would reading a composer's biography help in understanding his music?
2. What advantages and disadvantages came to a composer under the patronage of a prince or a cardinal? Compare these with the privileges and drawbacks of the nineteenth-century "free" composer.
3. Compare the problems confronting the solo performer with those facing a chamber-music ensemble or an orchestra.
4. Listen to two different recordings of the same composition. Can you detect any differences? Describe them.
5. Listen to an unidentified piece of programmatic music. What does the music suggest to you? Now read the composer's specified intent. Does your reaction agree with the composer's program? How definitely descriptive do you think music can be?

FOR FURTHER READING

Barzun, Jacques. *Music in American Life.* Bloomington, Ind.: Indiana University Press, 1956. A Midland PB. This discerning look at our musical culture should be read by everyone interested in furthering the cause of good music in America.

———, ed. *Pleasures of Music.* New York: The Viking Press, 1951. A Compass Books PB. This delightful anthology contains great writing about music and musicians by authors ranging from Benvenuto Cellini to George Bernard Shaw. It includes fictional tales, music criticism, essays on music and drama, a section on composers and performers, discussions on politics and patronage, some remarks on musical instruments, and a selection of letters.

Copland, Aaron. *Copland on Music.* New York: W. W. Norton & Co., Inc., 1960. PB. The first chapter in Section One of this selection from Copland's writings on music is called "The Pleasures of Music." The eminent composer has written here a personal, meaningful essay on the musical experience and its attendant joys.

———. *Music and Imagination.* New York: The New American Library, 1952. A Mentor PB. A highly readable book that examines the role of the imaginative mind in composing, performing, and listening to music. Mr. Copland's emphasis on twentieth-century music significantly relates us as listeners to the music of our time.

Portnoy, Julius. *Music in the Life of Man.* New York: Holt, Rinehart and Winston, Inc., 1963. PB. In defining music's role as a fine art and highlighting its importance as a driving force in the history of mankind, the author has contributed a book that should be read from cover to cover.

Sessions, Roger. *The Musical Experience of Composer, Performer, Listener.* New York: Atheneum Publishers, 1950. PB. One of America's outstanding composers has written six fine essays in which he discusses some basics of music. The book is difficult for those who do not read music, but even so almost everyone will find it stimulating.

Shaw, George Bernard. *Shaw on Music,* edited by Eric Bentley. New York: Doubleday and Co., Inc., 1955. An Anchor PB. A series of essays and observations by one of England's most famous, brilliant, and provocative critics.

2 Sound

The man that hath no music in himself,
Nor is not mov'd with concord of sweet sounds,
Is fit for treasons, stratagems, and spoils.

WILLIAM SHAKESPEARE
The Merchant of Venice, Act V, Scene 1

Music *is* sound, but how do we decide what kind of sound it is that the listener hears? That is a difficult question, for a general investigation into the subject of sound really belongs in a physics class. However, a simple explanation of how sound is made and what its characteristics are will provide a foundation for studying musical sound patterns and relationships.

The phenomenon of sound is a sensation caused by an impact on the ear made by regular air vibrations (that is, alternate compressions and rarefactions) set in motion by various media (irregular vibrations produce noise). Expressed in another way, sound is the effect of *vibration.* Vibration can be felt and even seen in an object such as a tuning fork. Anyone who has heard a loud explosion realizes that sound often produces vibrating air waves powerful enough to break windows. Mountain climbers in the vicinity of perilous glaciers speak softly so that sound vibrations will not cause a crack in the ice and start a slide. When a church organist plays loudly in the lower registers of his instrument, the resultant vibrations often make windows rattle.

Vibrating an elastic material—such as gut string or wire—produces sound. The violinist draws a bow across the strings on his instrument or he plucks the strings with his fingers to create sound. In a harpsichord, small tongues of leather or quill pluck the strings; in a clavichord, metal tangents strike the strings; in a piano, felt-tipped wooden hammers strike the strings. In all these instruments sound is produced by activated strings that send vibrations (invisible but very real) to the ear. Elastic membranes also cause vibrations; when the kettledrum—a metal bowl with a piece of skin stretched over the top—is struck, the hide vibrates, sending out vibrations.

Sound can also be produced by a vibrating column of air; for example, when an organist presses a key on his instrument, he forces a wind-chest to shoot columns of air through the organ pipes. Flutes and other wind instruments also emit sound via an air column (Ill. 2:1).

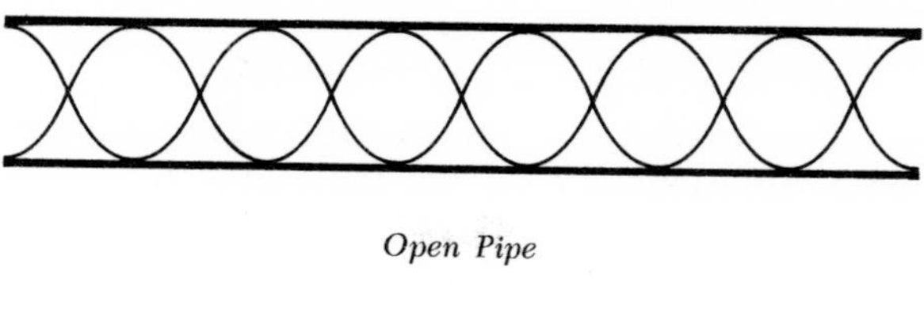

Open Pipe

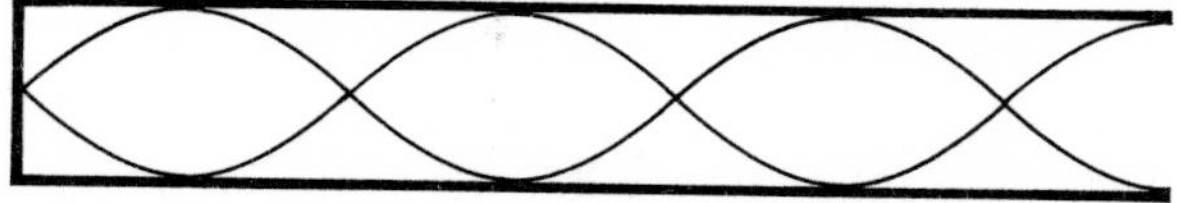

Stopped Pipe

Ill. 2:1. ***Diagram of air columns.***

Sound vibrations can be manufactured synthetically as well; in an electric organ, vibrations are transmitted electrically, and the sound is thus artificially created.

Regardless of its source, once sound is produced it must be amplified—reinforced to make it clearly audible. The piano's sounding board and the bellies and backs of stringed instruments act as amplifiers of a sort. These so-called general resonators react to all sounds and reinforce them by resonance; that is, they enhance sounds and project them into the air.

Sound travels at approximately 1100 feet per second. Thus, at the back of a large auditorium or concert hall, a sound reaches the listener about a second after it has been produced. Sound waves bounce away from hard surfaces. If a concert in a large hall has a small audience, the sound will be comparatively bright; brightness diminishes when more people fill the hall, since their bodies will absorb some sound.

The walls of a room, hall, or auditorium also affect the duration of sound. In an enclosed room a given sound may bounce from one surface to another. If the walls are hard there may be several hundred rapid, successive, overlapping sound reflections from walls, ceiling, floor, and furniture before the sound becomes inaudible. The resulting sensation of a continuous roll of sound is called *reverberation*. The length of time that a sound continues to be heard in a room, through reflections, after its source has stopped sounding is called the *reverberation time:* as a general rule, a reverberation time of from one to two seconds is best for music. Thus the material of walls, ceiling, and floor becomes very important in determining the acoustics of a room.

This general introduction to vibration and sound leads to the consideration of one single sound. When we strike a piano key, bow a string on a violin, blow a tone on a clarinet, or simply make a sound with our voice, we are creating a basic component of music. By learning what this single tone has to tell and what its characteristics are, we prepare for a more extended study of music.

CHARACTERISTICS OF A MUSICAL TONE

A musical tone has four primary characteristics: pitch, intensity, tone quality, and duration.

Pitch

Pitch indicates whether a sound is high, low, or somewhere in between. It is determined by the vibration frequency of the sound waves striking the ear. The more vibrations per second, the higher the pitch. When the string belonging to *middle C* on the piano is struck, it vibrates at the rate of 256 vibrations per second. The *C* located an octave (8 white keys) above middle *C* vibrates at the rate of 512 per second.

In general, flute sounds are high and cello and bassoon sounds are low, but the question arises, particularly in reference to a single sound, of how high or how low? Fortunately, a system of notation (discussed in Chapter 3) has been devised, making it possible to write on paper the notes representing certain pitches. Notation enables the composer to write down his music so that it can be read and translated into a tonal performance.

Physically, pitch is determined by the fundamental vibration frequency of the medium in use (string, air column, membrane). With a vibrating string, frequency in turn depends on the length of the string, its thickness, and the tension and density involved. A short string produces a higher sound than does a long string; a thick string produces a lower sound than does a thin string of the same length. Increased tension on a string creates higher pitch. If a string is submitted to heat, it expands, causing a lower pitch.

With an air column like that in the flute or organ pipe, frequency of vibration depends on the length of the column, the nature of the tube enclosing it, and the density of the atmosphere. A short air column creates a higher pitch than does a long column. Any atmospheric change alters the pitch of an air column; therefore most wind (or air) instruments require retuning when the density of the atmosphere changes.

The phonograph is a good example of the relation between frequency and pitch. If we speed up the turntable, we increase the rate of revolutions. The needle, tracing the record grooves, transmits this acceleration of vibrations to the sound mechanism, and the pitch is raised.

To summarize, pitch depends on the predominating frequency of vibration. High pitches are caused by rapid frequencies and are usually produced by small instruments. Low pitches are caused by slower frequencies and are usually produced by large instruments.

Intensity (Volume)

Whereas vibration frequency determines pitch, intensity—loudness or softness—depends on the extent or *amplitude* of vibration. As the force operating the generating agent (string, air column, membrane) becomes greater, the volume of sound increases. The less force applied, the softer the sound.

The string and air column both have a set vibration speed, which is not affected by any change in the extent or amplitude of the vibrations. If a violin or cello string is plucked gently, it vibrates perhaps one-sixteenth of an inch on each side of its normal position of repose and makes a soft sound. If it is plucked more violently, it vibrates about one-eighth of an inch on each side of that position and produces a louder sound. The pitch, however, remains the same in both experiments (Ill. 2:2).

So it is with a reed, tube, or stretched membrane in a wind or percussion

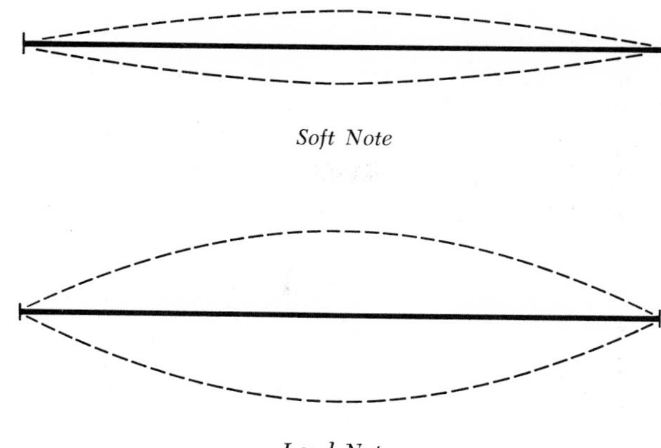

Ill. 2:2. *Intensity change in a string having fixed pitch.*

instrument. Intensity can be controlled by applying more or less force with the breath or striking agent. (As long as vibrating agents possess the same vibrating length and tension, the pitches remain constant.)

How does a composer notate the desired degree of this intensity (volume) in his music? By using dynamic marks—signs placed close to the written notes or musical passages—to indicate a degree of *relative* intensity. Some of the most common dynamic markings are:

pp	pianissimo (very soft)
p	piano (soft)
mp	mezzo piano (moderately soft)
mf	mezzo forte (moderately loud)
f	forte (loud)
ff	fortissimo (very loud)

Traditionally, words indicating dynamics have always been written in Italian, but modern writers are adopting the vernacular. In addition to these marks, composers use expression marks to indicate gradations in intensity:

crescendo: gradual increase in intensity, also shown by the sign <

diminuendo: gradual decrease in intensity, also shown by the sign >

To summarize, intensity depends on the amplitude of vibration. Loud tones are caused by vibrations of considerable force and extent. Soft tones are caused by vibrations of small force and extent.

Tone Quality (Timbre)

How can the various instruments give off such unique sounds? Why is a violin's sound different from a harp's? For the answers, we must return to the theory of the vibrating string. Almost all vibrations are compound. From its whole length, a vibrating string produces a sound known as the fundamental note of the string; simultaneously, various portions along the length of that string also vibrate to produce higher sounds, a few of which can be detected by the trained ear. The same thing occurs in a wind instrument, with an air column acting as the main vibrating agent. Thus, while the entire string or air column is vibrating to produce a fundamental sound, half the length is also vibrating, producing an octave, two-thirds is vibrating to produce a fifth above the fundamental, and so on. The presence or absence (in varying intensities) of particular members among these higher sounds (called partials, overtones, or harmonics) determines the tone quality (timbre) of a sound (Ex. 2:1).

Ex. 2:1. ***A fundamental note (C) with its upper partials or harmonics***

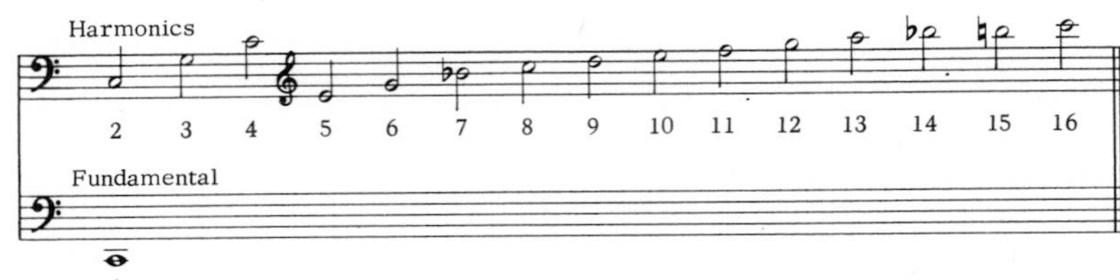

In other words, any distinctive sound consists of many sounds blended together. A tuning fork has almost no harmonics. The pure sound of the flute results from a lack of practically all harmonics except the first (the octave); on the other hand, the cello is capable of rich sound because its vibrating strings create assorted harmonics.

To summarize, tone quality depends on the vibrating medium (string, air column, membrane) and the number and intensity of overtones or harmonics produced. Pure tones emanate from relatively simple vibration forms; richer tones require more complex vibration forms; brilliant tones need very complex vibration forms. It may be interesting to look at one author's rough classification of sounds according to their increasing complexity. As the author points out, the classes have no sharp dividing lines:

Relatively simple . . .
("Hooty," smooth, dark, dull at low pitches)

Moderate complexities . . .
(Richer, normally most pleasant)

Greater complexities . . .
(Rich, bright, brilliant, cutting, blaring, or even strident)

Tuning forks
Falsetto "oo"
Blown bottles
Wide, stopped, organ flue-pipes
Female and boy soprano voices
Flutes
Female mezzo or alto voices
Open organ flue-pipes
Soft horns
Soft male voices
Pianos
Strings
Wood-winds except flutes
Organ reed-pipes
Loud male voices
Loud brass
Chimes and bells
Ensembles
Noise[1]

[1] For the classification of sounds and other sound concepts found in this chapter, I am indebted to Wilmer T. Bartholomew, *Acoustics of Music,* © 1942. Reprinted by permission of Prentice-Hall, Inc., Englewood Cliffs, N.J.

Duration

Duration refers to the time elapsing between the beginning and end of a sound. It is a time factor that measures—or attempts to measure—the length of a tone, and it is influenced by the capabilities of the medium involved; for example, wind instrumentalists and singers can sustain a tone only for the length of one breath, violinists can hold a tone only for a bow length, and pianists sustain a sound only as long as the strings vibrate.

The time factor pertaining to one sound leads to a discussion of comparative durations of tones, and that subject involves rhythm and meter (see Chapter 4). Music notation simultaneously indicates pitch and duration, or at least *relative* duration.

SUMMARY

These characteristics—*pitch, intensity, tone quality,* and *duration*—are the elements that combine in varying degrees to create musical tones. When one tone is added to another and still another, consecutively or simultaneously, these elements fall into logical rhythmic and structural patterns. Note patterns are devised from the scale system (see Chapter 3). The succession of sounds—which becomes melody—takes on vitality and interest when the tones fit into a rhythmic pattern and the resultant melody conforms to a harmonic framework. Further manipulations, such as extending melody or changing harmony, develop the elemental materials into a finished musical composition.

FOR DISCUSSION AND ASSIGNMENT

1. It is a well-known fact that many deaf people are good dancers and enjoy dancing. Can you explain the reason?
2. If music sounds unpleasantly loud in a concert hall, the walls are sometimes re-covered with acoustical tile. What does this accomplish?
3. Listen to one sound. Try to describe it by means of its four characteristics.
4. Strike the octave below middle *C* on the piano rather vigorously and hold it. Now depress the *G* above middle *C* silently and hold it also. Still holding down the *G,* release the first key (*C*). What do you hear and how do you explain it?

FOR FURTHER READING

Bartholomew, Wilmer T. *Acoustics of Music.* Englewood Cliffs, N.J.: Prentice-Hall, Inc., 1942. An excellent book for musically informed laymen and music students. Although not a large volume, it treats each element of sound in considerable detail.

Benade, Arthur H. *Horns, Strings and Harmony: The Science of Enjoyable Sounds.* Garden City, N.Y.: Doubleday and Co., Inc., 1960. An Anchor PB. This is an interesting, readable account of instruments and their scientific sound components.

Dinn, Freda. *The Observer's Book of Music.* Revised Edition. New York: Frederick Warne & Co., Inc., 1959. The first chapter of this pocket-sized guide deals with "Sound and How We Hear It." The discussion, though brief, is clear and to the point.

Hall, Jody C., and Earle L. Kent. *The Language of Musical Acoustics.* Elkhart, Indiana: C. G. Conn, Ltd., 1957. PB. The well-known instrument manufacturer has published this helpful booklet about basic factors governing the phenomenon of sound.

Reading Music 3

From harmony, from heavenly harmony,
  This universal frame began:
  From harmony to harmony
Through all the compass of the notes it ran,
The diapason closing full in Man.

JOHN DRYDEN
A Song for St. Cecilia's Day

You will find music appreciation more rewarding if you understand at least the basics of music notation and music reading. These basics can be acquired in comparatively little time, and they are important, for they will help you perceive musical concepts and processes. The simplest way to explain notation is to show how piano-keyboard pitches are notated. The diagram shown in Ex. 3:1 will help.

Ex. 3:1. ***Keyboard diagram with corresponding pitch notation***

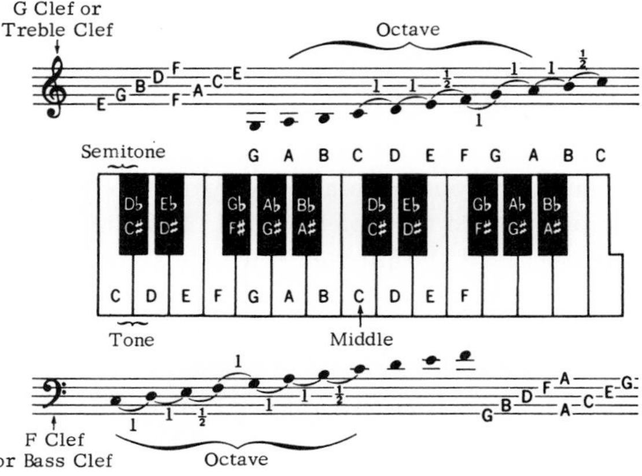

The standard piano keyboard has 88 keys arranged in patterns of twelve—seven white keys and five black keys. The five black keys within each group are divided into two sets, one set having two keys and the other set having three. A single white key separates the black keys within each set, but two consecutive white keys divide the sets from each other. Each black key is known either as the *sharp* (♯) of the white key directly below it or the *flat* (♭) of the white key just above it. Sharps and flats are alterations fitted to a tone.

In two places—between *E* and *F* and between *B* and *C*—there are no black keys. The two white notes at these positions are a half step apart; therefore, if *C* flat were desired, the correct key would be *B;* if *B* sharp were called for, *C* would be the correct key. In the same manner, *E* sharp is the key corresponding to *F,* and *F* flat is equivalent to *E.*

Pitches on the piano progress from the lowest (an *A*) at the extreme left end of the keyboard to the highest (a *C*) at the right end. The six white keys following after the low *A* are called in order *B, C, D, E, F,* and *G,* thus providing names for the seven white keys in the pattern of twelve. The key following *G* (the eighth key from the left end) is an octave higher than the first *A,* so this eighth key is also named *A,* thereby eliminating the need for additional alphabetical letters to name the white keys.

There are two ways to describe an octave. It is the physical distance from any alphabetically named white or black key up (right) or down (left) to the next white or black key having that same alphabetical letter name, a distance of eight white keys or six black keys on the piano. An octave is also the distance in pitch between these same keys. The eighth white key away from any specified white key sounds a tone similar to that of the first key because the octave above vibrates exactly twice as fast as the lower note. For example, middle *C*—located in approximately the center of the keyboard—vibrates at the rate of 256 vibrations per second; the *C* eight white keys above middle *C* vibrates at exactly twice that rate, or 512 vibrations per second, and each *C* above that vibrates at double the rate of the *C* just before it. In reverse, each *C* below middle *C* vibrates at one-half the rate of the *C* just above it.

The piano keyboard has seven complete octaves or, to put it another way, seven patterns containing seven white keys (named with alphabetical letters) and five black keys (commonly called sharps and flats). Other instruments, except for other keyboard instruments, usually have a much smaller number of patterns.

NOTATION

A *staff* having five horizontal lines is used to show on paper the pitches produced by these various keys on the piano. A sign placed at the beginning of each staff indicates the position of the notes named. This sign, called a *clef,* is the symbol that unlocks the secret of the pitches. Two clefs are most common: the *G* (or *treble*) clef and the *F* (or *bass*) clef. The *G* clef—with a circle flourish cutting through the *G* line on the staff—is used for music that is pitched relatively high. The *F* clef—with two dots enclosing the line belonging to the pitch *F*—is used for music that is pitched relatively low. A movable clef (*C* clef) appears occasionally. It establishes the position of middle *C* on the staff. When used on the third line, it is called the *alto* clef; when placed on the fourth line, it is referred to as the *tenor* clef (Ex. 3:2).

Both lines and spaces are used on the staff. The position of a written symbol—called a note—on any one of these lines or spaces determines the pitch. These notes are the visible signs of tones. Notes are seen, tones are heard.

Ex. 3:2. ***Illustration of clef signs on a staff***

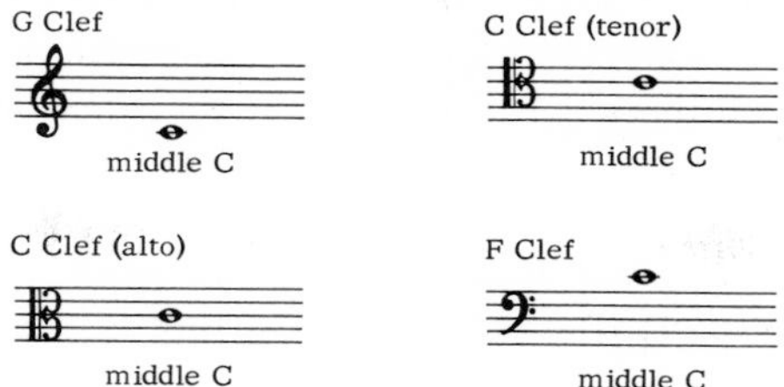

When the indicated pitch corresponds to a black-key alteration, sharp or flat signs must be inserted before each note as they are necessary, for staff lines and spaces are reserved for the pitches of the white piano keys. A *double sharp* (𝄪) or a *double flat* (♭♭) appears occasionally. When the alterations are no longer needed, a *natural sign* (♮) must be used to show that the sharp or flat, or the double sharp or double flat, is no longer in effect.

Pitches requiring notes above or below the staffs are notated on short extra lines or in the spaces created by the extra lines. These additional lines are known as *ledger lines,* vestiges of lines once incorporated into the staff but now used in abbreviated form only as pitch demands them.

In music written for piano and other keyboard instruments, the staff with treble clef and that with bass clef are joined by an extended vertical line and brace (Ex. 3:3), forming a *great staff.* The example shows that at one time an extra or eleventh line used to run through the center, accommodating middle *C* and making it a pivot note between the two staffs; but now that line has disappeared, leaving only a small ledger line running through *C.*

Ex. 3:3. ***Great staff***

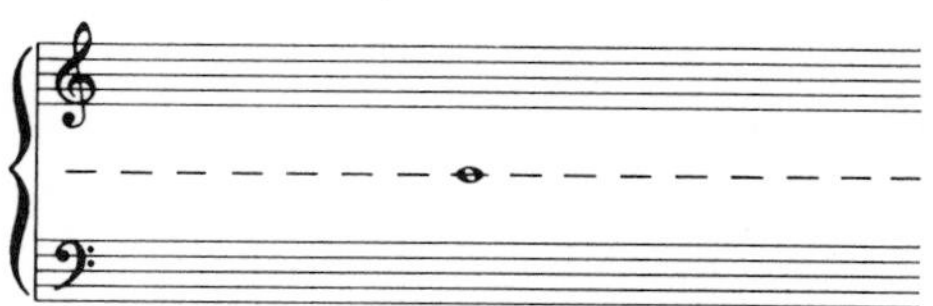

When several successive notes occur above or below the staff, a change of clef eliminates the necessity of writing extra ledger lines. This change is often found in piano music; for example, the *F* clef may appear on the upper staff for a short time or the *G* clef on the lower staff. The clef to be used is always printed at the beginning of each staff. A new clef is inserted to indicate a change of pitch relationships, and then the original clef is reinstated when that change is completed (Ex. 3:4).

Ex. 3:4. ***Illustration of clef change***

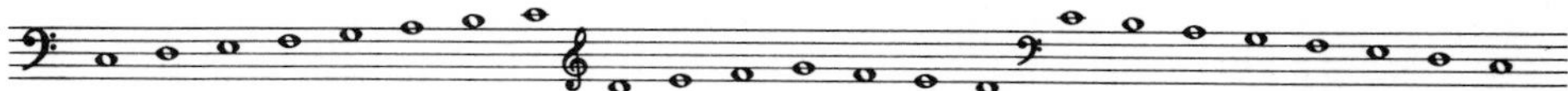

INTERVALS

We have established the fact that an octave is a pattern of twelve tones corresponding to the twelve white and black keys on the piano. When heard or played in sequence, these tones are known as the *chromatic scale. Intervals*—the distance from one tone to another—are named and identified in three ways. They may be calculated according to the number of *semitones* and *whole tones* they contain. The smallest interval on the piano is the semitone or half step, which comes between any white key and an adjacent black key, or else between *E* and *F* or *B* and *C* among the white keys. A whole tone comprises two semitones. Intervals may also be classified according to the numerical distance between the two tones forming the interval. Example 3:5 clarifies this second nomenclature.

Ex. 3:5. ***Table of intervals***

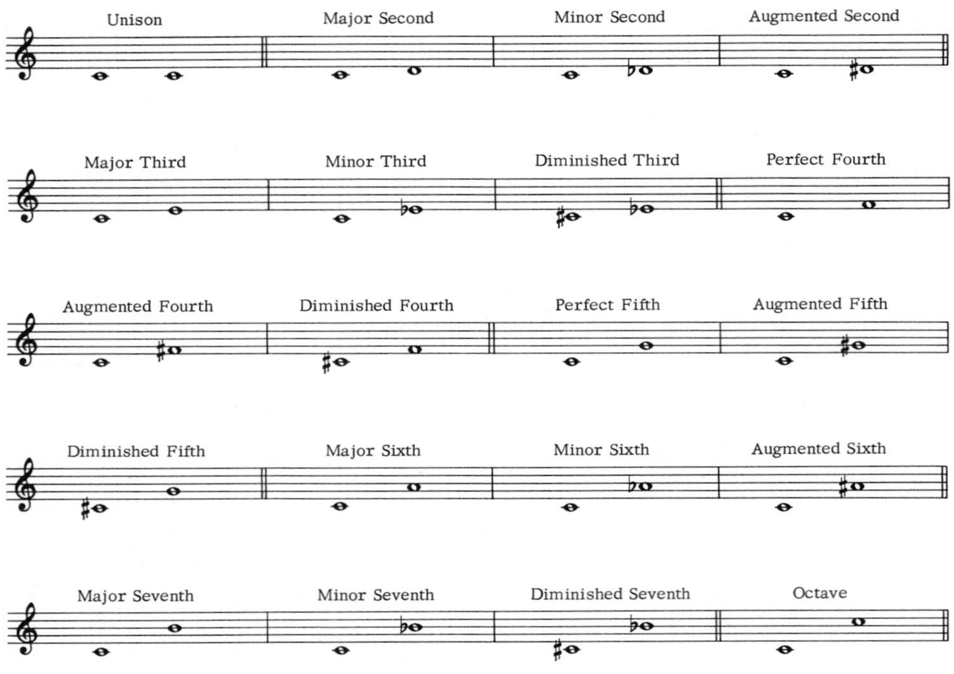

Intervals are also classified as either *consonant* or *dissonant*. Consonance results from a satisfying blending of two tones—from an interval that gives an agreeable effect. When the two tones of an interval refuse to blend, when the effect is one of tension, the result is called dissonance. Such a classification admittedly calls for some subjective judgments. However, for the most part, the unison (Ex. 3:5), perfect fourth and fifth, octave, and major and minor thirds and sixths are granted the status of consonant intervals. All others are dissonant (the perfect fourth, depending on the context in which it is found, may be either consonant or dissonant).

SCALES

For the past three hundred years our Western musical system has been based on *major* and *minor scales*, the word "scale" referring to various patterns of semitones and tones within an octave. The major scale, which may begin with any one of the twelve tones in the octave, consists of the following intervals in ascending order (1 equals a whole tone; ½ equals a semitone):

1 – 1 – ½ – 1 – 1 – 1 – ½

Or a regrouping gives a sequence that may be easier to remember. Two tetrachords (a tetrachord is a group of four consecutive notes), whose three intervals form the pattern 1–1–½, are connected by a whole tone:

1–1–½ 1 1–1–½

The *C*-major scale is the easiest to formulate, consisting as it does of white keys exclusively: *C–D–E–F–G–A–B–C* (*see* Ex. 3:1). To construct a major scale on any tone (or key) other than *C*, we must use some black keys to maintain the major-scale pattern. For example, the scale of *G* major calls for *F* sharp instead of *F* (Ex. 3:6):

Ex. 3:6. ***Scale pattern for* G *major***

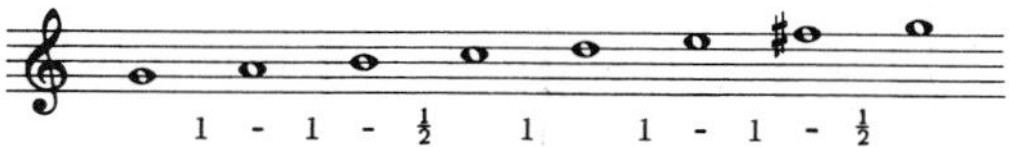

And the scale of *F* major calls for *B* flat instead of *B* (Ex. 3:7):

Ex. 3:7. ***Scale pattern for* F *major***

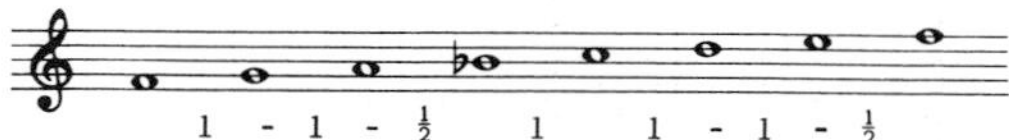

The sharps or flats pertinent to any given scale are written on the staff just after the clef and are known in that position as the *key signature*. Thus an *F* sharp in the key signature means that whenever an *F* is encountered during the composition being read (played), it is automatically sharped or raised a semitone.

The term "key" should not be confused with the physical keys on the piano and woodwind instruments. In musical notation, "key" is used to designate the arrangement of a scale pattern in which all tones bear a strong and easily recognized allegiance to a basic tone called the *keynote* or *tonic*. This affinity of different tones for one in particular is also called *tonality*. Mozart's *Sonata in F Major* (*K.332*) (that is, the key or tonality of *F* major) is an example of the meaning of the two terms "key" and "tonality." This composition is said to be written in the key of *F* major because it is based on the notes found in the *F*-major scale *and* because it recognizes and employs *F* as the principal note or tone.

The tones of the *F*-major scale (*F–G–A–B♭–C–D–E–F*), then, constitute the repertory of pitches used as the basis for Mozart's *Sonata in F Major*. Those passages in the sonata that are more restricted to these pitches are said to be *diatonic*. Those passages that indulge in numerous *accidentals* (sharps or flats not appearing in the key signature) are said to be *chromatic*. The attributes diatonic and chromatic constitute important factors in musical composition.

To facilitate the study of ear training (or *solfeggio*), we apply characteristic syllables to each pitch of a scale. Thus a *C*-major scale could be sung *C–D–E–F–G–A–B–C* or, more simply, do–re–mi–fa–sol–la–ti–do.

Example 3:8 shows the sharps and flats included in each major scale.

Each major scale has two corresponding minor scales. These minor scales keep the same signature but begin and end two scale degrees (one and a half tones) below the major scale. The *C*-major scale has the scale of *a* minor as its relative scale, *F* major has *d* minor, and so on. (For clarity, minor key designations are usually written with lower-case letter names; major, with capital letters.)

Ex. 3:8. ***Table of sharps and flats for major scales***

F Bb Eb Ab Db Gb Cb

The two kinds of minor scales are *harmonic* and *melodic,* and the construction of each necessitates some pitch alterations, or *accidentals.* The *harmonic minor* has the following pattern:

1–½–1 1 ½–1½–½

For example, the harmonic minor scale of *a* minor is (Ex. 3:9) :

Ex. 3:9. ***Relation of relative minor scale***

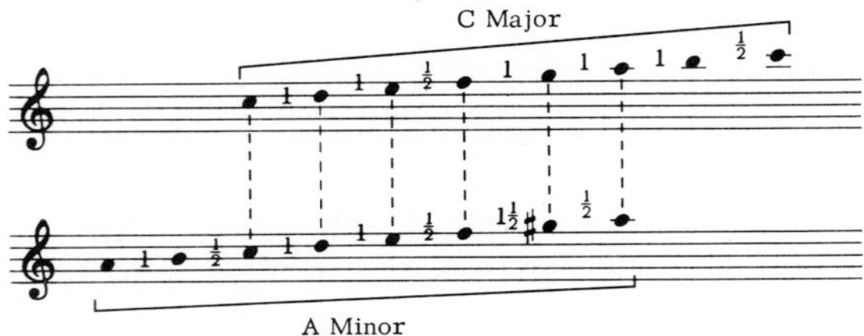

The only alteration necessary to shift from a major scale to its "relative" harmonic minor is to raise the seventh tone of the latter (in the example, *G* to *G* sharp) .

The *melodic minor* scale is somewhat different in structure because there are two patterns involved. Its ascending intervals are:

1–½–1 1 1–1–½

and the descending intervals are:

1–1–½ 1 1–½–1

This sense of character—individuality due to the mutual relation of tones within a given scale, major or minor—is often called tonality. Thus, by listening to a scale and without knowing on what tone it is constructed, you can discern its tonality from the uniqueness of the tonal relationships.

Besides major and minor scales there are other scales, such as the whole-tone scale and the pentatonic scale; these have been used at times, and they will be discussed as we meet them in particular types of music.

FOR DISCUSSION AND ASSIGNMENT

1. Sit at a piano. Choose any key and find the octave above and below it.
2. Listen to a short musical composition and decide whether it is written in a major or a minor key.

3. Look at the music for a simple folk-song melody. In what key is it written? Either write down the pitch name of each note or say it out loud. Then try to find the corresponding key on the piano.
4. Take a composition such as Rameau's *Le Tambourin* or Schubert's *Moment Musical, Op. 94, No. 3* or *Serenade*. Look at the music and listen to it. What is the key signature? In what key is the composition written? How do you know?

FOR FURTHER READING

Cooper, Grosvenor W. *Learning to Listen: A Handbook for Music.* Chicago: University of Chicago Press, 1957. A Phoenix PB. The first chapter of this music handbook interestingly incorporates musical notation with pitch, dynamics, etc. under the title "Rudiments."

Károlyi, Ottó. *Introducing Music.* Baltimore, Md.: Penguin Books, Inc., 1965. A Pelican PB. Part One, called "Sounds and Symbols," contains a well-written section on musical notation, although English terminology is used.

Shanet, Howard. *Learn to Read Music.* New York: Simon & Schuster, 1956. PB. A complete guide to elementary music reading. Although one could feasibly use this as a self-teacher, it is more effective when studied under guidance.

4 Music's Dimensions

Only when the form is quite clear to you will the spirit become clear to you.

ROBERT SCHUMANN

House-Rules and Maxims for Young Musicians

The word "dimensions," which refers to measurements or proportions, may strike you as a strange musical term, but dimensions are just what we must investigate if we want to analyze the musical listening experience at close range. It is one thing to describe sound in abstract terms; it is something else entirely to know what elements go into the making of a composition and in what proportions they are used. To get the most benefit from the music you hear, you must be able to recognize the basic elements that account for the dimensions of a musical composition.

RHYTHM AND METER

Rhythm and meter, so important in any study of music, can mean different things to different people. Even books on music appreciation and music essentials present diverse explanations of these two subjects. Perhaps the best way to understand what they are is to begin with dictionary definitions.

Rhythm is defined in Merriam-Webster as "the temporal pattern produced by the grouping and balancing of various stresses and tone lengths in relation to an underlying steady and persisting succession of beats." Rhythm is created from sound *plus* silence. It arises from a need to relate one tone to another in order to give motion and vitality to an otherwise lifeless series of tones.

In its larger sense, rhythm is essentially the art of time expressed in a succession of beats. For some reason the human ear demands that music convey a perceptible sensation of a unit of time. These inaudible time units are called beats, and the ear inevitably places them in groups of twos or threes. Sounds made by a ticking clock or clicking train wheels are heard in groups—a throbbing pattern—with an accent or stress on one member of the group. Even though physically *no* accent is involved, the ear imagines a pulsation.

To indicate musical beats on paper, we must have a time unit capable of subdivision. This time unit is a relative matter and is inextricably linked with speed (*tempo*). The unit most commonly used is the *whole note,* which may be split into two *half notes* or four *quarters.* Each quarter note may be reduced to two *eighth notes,* and the process further extended to *sixteenth notes.* Thus we have the following breakdown (Ex. 4:1), which could be continued down through *thirty-second* and *sixty-fourth notes.*

Ex. 4:1. ***Table of note values***

The value of any given note is augmented when a dot is placed to the right of it. This dot increases the note's value by half: since a quarter note equals two eighth notes, a dotted quarter note equals three eighth notes.

Since rhythm is created from the relation of sound to silence, there is a silence symbol corresponding to each note symbol. These silence symbols are called *rests* (Ex. 4:2).

Ex. 4:2. ***Table of rests***

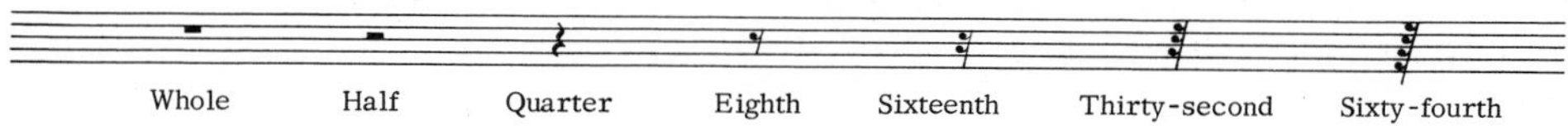

Besides having relative time values, individual notes and rests can be momentarily prolonged. A sign (𝄐), called a *hold, pause,* or *fermata,* above a note or rest indicates that the composer wants to lengthen the time value of that note or rest; the degree of prolongation is left to the discretion of the performer.

The rhythm created by a persistent succession of beats may be either *unmeasured* rhythm (sometimes incorrectly called "free" rhythm) or *measured* rhythm. Unmeasured rhythm is heard in plainsong, the traditional ritual melody of Western Christianity, and it is most ideally realized in the plainsong of the Roman Catholic Church. To comprehend unmeasured rhythm, think of it as prose rhythm. When fine prose is read aloud, there is a decided rhythm in the groupings of words and phrases, but it is not poetical rhythm. So it is with plainsong. The beats are grouped in twos, threes, and combinations of twos and threes, but the groups do not occur in any regular pattern (Ex. 4:3).

Ex. 4:3. ***Example of plainsong***

For the last 500 years nearly all Western music has been expressed through measured rhythm—that is, *meter.* Merriam-Webster defines meter as "the part of rhythmical structure concerned with the division of a musical composition into measures by means of *regularly* recurring accents, with each measure consisting of a uniform number of beats or time units, the first of which has the strongest accent."

When sounds are grouped into identical units of stressed and unstressed equal beats, they create meter. These units are separated by *measures* marked off by vertical lines (*bar lines*) cutting through the staff. There are basically two types of meter—two-beat and three-beat (*duple meter* and *triple meter*)—but the metrical units often combine to form larger measures of four, five, six, seven, or more beats. In the smaller groups, the regularly recurring accents usually fall on the first beat:

A four-beat unit also has a slight accent on the third:

The appropriate meter for a musical composition, or a passage of a composition, is usually indicated at the beginning of the music—to the right of the clef sign—with a *time signature,* which looks like a fraction without a bar (Ex. 4:4). The two numbers of this time signature, reading from top to bottom, explain how many of what kind of notes (or beats) will be found per measure. The time signature $\substack{2\\4}$ explains that there should be the equivalent of two beats—two quarter notes—in each measure. A signature of $\substack{3\\4}$ indicates three quarter notes or beats to each measure, and so on. Sometimes the sign **C** is used instead of a $\substack{4\\4}$ signature. Similarly, the sign **₵** indicates a $\substack{2\\2}$ meter, with a half note rather than a quarter note as the beat.

Ex. 4:4. ***Illustration of bar lines and time signatures***

When simple meters combine to produce five or more beats and two or more principal accents within the measure, they become compound meters. Regular compound meters have six, nine, or twelve beats. Thus $\substack{6\\8}$ meter has six beats per measure and two accents, on beats one and four. Irregular compound meters, such as five, seven, eleven, etc., are made by combining different meters. An example would be $\substack{5\\4}$ meter, achieved by combining triple and duple meters.

Occasionally a composer may want to use a group of three notes having equal time value where ordinarily two (or four) notes would be found. To indicate this substitution of a *triplet* figure, he groups the notes with a curved line and places a small number 3 above or below the group. Thus in a measure with a meter signature of $\substack{2\\4}$, ♩♩♩ (3) equals ♩ ♩

The definition of meter states that the first accent in a unit of beats is the strongest, which is usually true, but for the sake of variety this accent is occasionally displaced, and *syncopation*—an unexpected accent—results (Ex. 4:5). Syncopation is indicated by rests placed on strong beats or by accent signs (>) or abbreviations (*sf* or *sfz* are abbreviations for *sforzando*, "forcing").

Ex. 4:5. *Example of syncopation*

Neither the time signature nor the notes used tell at what speed a musical composition is to be performed. For this there are *tempo marks*—words written in Italian (or sometimes English, French, or German). Below are a few of the more common tempo marks.

Largo—very slowly and stately
Lento—slowly
Adagio—slowly, with great expression
Andante—in tranquil time but moving steadily
Moderato—moderately
Allegro—lively, animated
Vivace—vivaciously, with more rapid movement than allegro
Presto—with great rapidity

For fluctuations in tempo, the following expressions are the most common:

Accelerando—a gradual increase in speed
Rallentando }
Ritardando } —becoming gradually slower

Even tempo markings indicate speed only in a *relative* sense. For example, how fast is "moderately"? To obtain more precise tempo, composers (since about 1830) frequently indicate the use of a mechanical instrument, the *metronome*. It has a clockwork apparatus that counts the number of beats per minute by means of a ticking inverted pendulum on its front. Some metronomes have a bell that can be made to strike at the accented beat. The instrument made by Maelzel is the standard metronome: the indication M. M. ♩ = 100 means that the Maelzel metronome (M. M.) will tick off one hundred quarter-note beats per minute.

To see more clearly the basic relationship between rhythm and meter, let us consider some standard dance rhythms (Ex. 4:6), for here rhythm is one thing,

Ex. 4:6. *Examples of rhythm and meter*

meter is another, and both contribute to the character of the dance. Keep in mind that meter pertains to regularly recurring patterns of beats, whereas rhythm results from "the grouping and balancing of varying stresses and tone lengths."

MELODY

Like rhythm, melody is interpreted variously by different individuals, with each concept having some element of logic to it. Once again Merriam-Webster's description proves best: "a rhythmically organized and meaningful succession of single musical notes or tones having a definite relationship one with the other and forming an aesthetic whole." A point-by-point analysis of this definition will help to explain melody.

1. A melody is *rhythmically organized.* This statement reveals that rhythm is an important factor in melody, whether it is unmeasured plainsong rhythm or clipped, measured martial rhythm. Within its own contours a melody may contain a rhythmical motive that can be used independently—that is, when the melody itself is not present. The opening rhythmic motive of Beethoven's *Symphony No. 5*

first appears with its accompanying melodic motive:

Then later on it is used in company with other melodic material. Basically, rhythmic character in music is determined by metric signature and rhythmic note values, but both are rather inflexible rhythmic devices; melody is susceptible to greater enhancement through more elastic directions, such as *rubato* (flexibility of tempo), *accelerando* (becoming faster), *ritardando* (slackening in speed), and other interpretive suggestions.

2. A melody is composed of a *meaningful succession of single notes or tones.* Here the subjective element enters, for whether or not there is "meaningful succession" depends on each composer's idea of artistic creativity; the succession may not necessarily be meaningful to the individual listener. However, to arrive at his succession of notes, meaningful or otherwise, the composer—at least until quite recently—has relied on one of the major or minor scales discussed in Chapter 3. If he extracts these notes from the *C*-major scale, his melody will be in the key of *C* major; for example, the song "Swanee River" has a melody taken from the *C*-major scale (Ex. 4:7).

Ex. 4:7. Foster: "Swanee River"

Or the composer may construct his melody by using various notes from any scale plus some accidentals; for example, a Bach fugue in *d* minor uses notes from the *d*-minor scale plus *B* natural and *F* sharp to form its principal melody (Ex. 4:8).

Ex. 4:8. Bach: ***Chromatic Fantasy and Fugue: Fugue***

3. The notes in this meaningful succession have a *definite relationship one with the other.* The element binding the notes together may be a brief *motive,* which is used to create and preserve unity throughout the composition—one requisite for good melody.

Motives require repetition. The ear can follow, and will do so with interest, any phrase or motive that it has once heard. When used with restraint and discretion (Ex. 4:9), repetition is valuable for maintaining emotional recollections.

Ex. 4:9. Mozart: ***Sonata in A Major, K.331: Andante grazioso***

Or the succession may be designed to progress toward a climax—either a high or low tonal point—in order to hold the listener's interest and create a sense of movement through alternation of tension and relaxation (Ex. 4:10). The combination of tension and relaxation—in melody, in dynamics, in harmonic progressions—constitutes one of the very important concepts in effective musical composition.

Ex. 4:10. Chopin: ***Nocturne, Opus 27, No. 2***

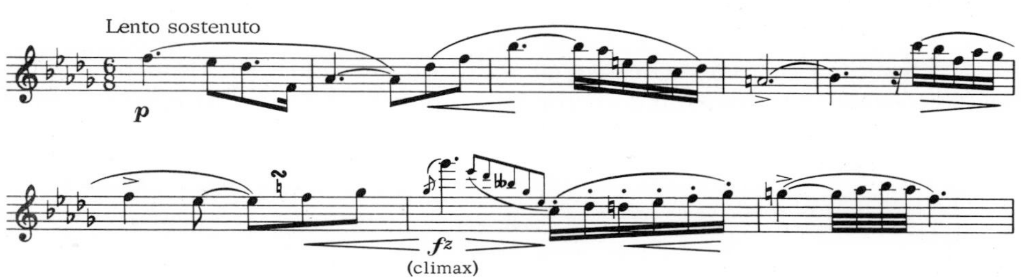

A composer must provide variety in the tone succession to avoid losing the listener's attention and to keep vitality in the melody. The composer can achieve diversity by altering rhythmic patterns, introducing syncopation, or inserting unusual skips and intervals, but he must manipulate such devices according to some plan; if not, musical chaos might result. A good melody should always imply a sense of direction, should always give the impression that it begins incisively and advances logically to its termination.

4. The succession of notes forms *an aesthetic whole.* A talented composer is able to weave his personal artistry and sensitivity into melodic inventions. Each listener hearing these melodies receives his own impression. There are melodies that appeal strongly to some listeners because their outlines indicate a basically vocal (lyric) character, regardless of the composer's intended medium; for instance, the cello melody from Schubert's *Symphony in B Minor* has a clear vocal character (Ex. 4:11). On the other hand, melodies like that shown in Ex. 4:12 are instrumentally oriented.

Ex. 4:11. Schubert: *Symphony No. 8 in B Minor: Allegro moderato*

Ex. 4:12. Bach: *Fantasy and Fugue in G Minor: Fugue*

From another point of view, melodies are either active or passive. The melody in Ex. 4:13 is inert and lacks direction. But the melody in Ex. 4:14 is brisk and lively.

Ex. 4:13. Sullivan: "The Lost Chord"

Ex. 4:14. Smith: "The Star Spangled Banner"

Some melodies are effective enough to stand alone, secure in their independent, original contours and rhythmic outlines (Ex. 4:15). By contrast, other

Ex. 4:15. "To Celia"

melodies unmistakably belong to a larger harmonic framework on which they depend for character and strength. When removed from that framework, such melodies, like that of Ex. 4:16, become vapid and dull. Yet this same melody,

Ex. 4:16. Chopin: *Prélude, Opus 28, No. 4*

when woven into Chopin's unique harmonic system with its unusual chord structure (Ex. 4:17), is beautiful, lyrical, and intense.

Ex. 4:17. Chopin: *Prélude, Opus 28, No. 4*

So to define a melody or to describe what constitutes a good melody ultimately resolves into individual preference concerning what is beautiful, logical, effective, and sensitive.

HARMONY AND COUNTERPOINT

So far we have discussed the properties, qualities, and characteristics of one tone and of a progressive series of tones. When two or more tones are heard simultaneously, they present another facet of music—*harmony* and *counterpoint.*

Harmony and counterpoint are often viewed as two distinct entities. This distinction is misleading, for they are actually two aspects of simultaneous tone combinations. Neither is completely independent, and neither can be wholly effective alone; in fact, harmony and counterpoint have been called, respectively, the vertical and horizontal considerations of note combinations.

Even Merriam-Webster's definition of counterpoint recognizes its tangible relationship to harmony: "The combination of two or more related but independent melodies into a single harmonic texture in which each retains its linear or horizontal character."

In writings on musical styles it is not uncommon to find the terms *counterpoint* and its adjective *contrapuntal* used almost interchangeably with *polyphony* and *polyphonic*. If one wished to make a differentiation, it would be that the former are often employed in a more academic sense—that is, used in connection with the study of polyphonic writing technique—whereas the latter refer to compositions and the style based on contrapuntal techniques.

In linear (horizontal) writing, the composer usually starts with a melody, borrowed or original. He then adds a counterpoint—a second melody heard simultaneously. The result is two-part counterpoint. In a like manner, a composer may create a composition with three-part counterpoint, four-part counterpoint, and so on. His concern is not only with the melodic lines themselves but with the intervals formed by the simultaneous sounding of various melodic tones at accent points. In Ex. 4:18, note the individual, independent quality in each vocal melody. At the same time, the intervals between the voices are calculated so as to produce a pleasing aural sensation. When dissonances occur, they are immediately resolved, smoothed into consonances.

Ex. 4:18. Guerrero: *Pange Lingua*

The great periods of contrapuntal writing were the Middle Ages, the Renaissance, and to a considerable extent the Baroque (see Chapters 8 through 10). Harmony and counterpoint came into effective use around the ninth century, and for eight hundred years the two remained inextricably enmeshed, with special emphasis on counterpoint. The ideal was to write beautiful melodies capable of blending together—a feat possible only if the composer paid attention to their vertical relationships.

Eventually certain contrapuntal writing traditions resulted in harmonic relationships so commonplace that they came to exist in their own right. Thus harmony as a full-blown technique and compositional approach came about as a by-product of counterpoint.

After the seventeenth century, when the "science" of harmony appeared, many composers accented harmony at the expense of counterpoint. Although they still exercised care when employing tones in their horizontal (melodic) relationships, their delight in manipulating chords naturally led to an emphasis on harmony.

The study of traditional harmony (*c.*1650–1900) centers on the *chord*—three or more tones arranged vertically in thirds and sounded simultaneously. Such a study is based on the *triad,* a chord of three tones. Within a specified tonality (major or minor), a triad can be built on any of the seven scale degrees. The triads derived from the *C*-major scale are shown in Ex. 4:19.

Ex. 4:19. ***Triads derived from the* C*-major scale***

Depending on their intervals, these chords (triads) are classified as major, minor, or diminished; according to their position on a certain degree of the scale, each receives a characteristic name (Ex. 4:20).

Ex. 4:20. ***Nomenclature of triads***

The most important chord is the tonic, which is constructed on the first degree of the scale, or key, in which a composition is written. Harmony results from the progression of chords, most of which revolve around this tonic chord and are eventually attracted to it by various means. Next in importance are the triads constructed on the fifth above the tonic—the dominant—and on the fifth below (or fourth above)—the subdominant.

Chords, like intervals, are either *consonant* or *dissonant* (see page 24). A consonant chord consists entirely of consonant intervals, while a dissonant chord contains one or more dissonant intervals. Thus the chord *C–E–G* contains a perfect fifth, a major third, and a minor third: it is consonant. The chord *B–D–F* contains a diminished fifth and two minor thirds: it is dissonant.

Chord study is complex, and you will find it helpful to have some basic knowledge of what is possible with chords.

1. Obviously music based exclusively on a series of three-tone chords would not be very expressive or useful. Standard harmony, like that in a mixed chorus (soprano, alto, tenor, bass) or string quartet, is premised on *four-tone* chords—that is, four-part harmony. The fourth tone is usually obtained by doubling one of the others. Thus *C–E–G* may expand to the chord *C–E–G–C*.

2. There are several methods by which four-tone chords and triads can be *inverted* (rearranged). The inversions shown in Ex. 4:21 are merely different arrangements of *C–E–G–C*. When four-tone chords and triads are not inverted, they are said to be in *root position*.

Ex. 4:21. ***Examples of chord inversion***

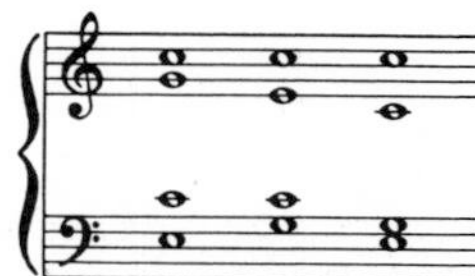

3. Chords may be diffused or spread horizontally. For example, when a series of chords is spread from bottom to top, the result can be music such as this delightful keyboard *Prelude* by Bach (Ex. 4:22).

Ex. 4:22. Bach: *Well-Tempered Clavier, Book I: Prelude in C Major*

4. When an additional third is added above a triad in root position, the result is called a chord of the seventh because the highest note is a seventh above the lowest (Ex. 4:23). Chords of the ninth, eleventh, thirteenth, and so on are fashioned in the same manner. (Obviously when a chord of the ninth is used for four-part harmony, one tone must be omitted).

Ex. 4:23. *Examples of seventh, ninth, and eleventh chords*

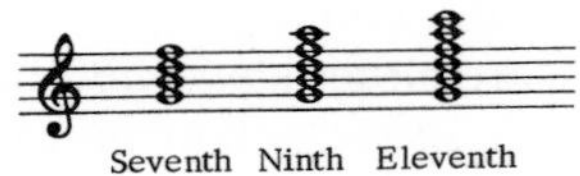

5. Chords should not proceed in haphazard sequence. When they do, the listener feels that the music is aimless, incomplete. To achieve artistic harmonic progressions, the composer must determine the "attraction" of one chord for another—that is, the smoothness or ease with which one chord member leads to a corresponding member in a new chord. Remember in this connection that dissonance is one of the main sources of musical movement, because it creates tensions that demand resolution to the consonant. (Compositions conventionally end with a consonant chord.)

The chords in Ex. 4:24a are not mutually dependent, whereas those in Ex. 4:24b are a classic illustration of chords that attract other chords or that consort easily with them.

6. A melody can be predominantly diatonic or chromatic, and so can harmonic progressions. In diatonic harmony, there are comparatively few accidentals. But chromatic harmony (Ex. 4:25) makes great use of altered tones or accidentals.

Ex. 4:24a. *Series of unrelated chords*

Ex. 4:24b. Chopin: *Prélude, Opus 28, No. 20*

Ex. 4:25. Wagner: *Die Walküre*

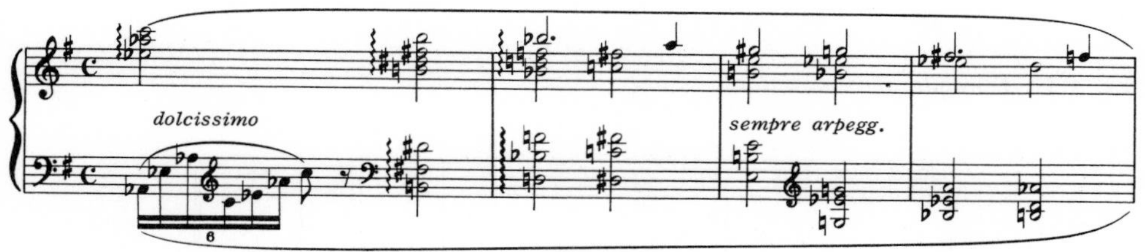

7. Punctuation is indispensable to music, just as it is to literature. The *cadence* is the musical equivalent of punctuation. It is a procession of chords (two or three) giving an effect of closing a section or movement. In other words, cadences are used as resting places during and at the end of a composition. The most common cadential formulas are shown in Ex. 4:26. Choice depends on how final the composer wants to be.

Ex. 4:26. *Cadential formulas in the key of* C *major*

Perfect cadences

Authentic cadence: dominant to tonic

Plagal cadence: subdominant to tonic

Imperfect cadence: tonic to dominant

Interrupted cadence: **dominant to some chord other than the tonic**

8. Chords are an important means of achieving *modulation*. Modulation, the art of key change, means passing from one key (tonality) to another so that the original keynote (tonic) is replaced by another as the center of the tonal structure. There are various ways of modulating. Example 4:27 shows a typical one.

Ex. 4:27. ***Example of modulation***

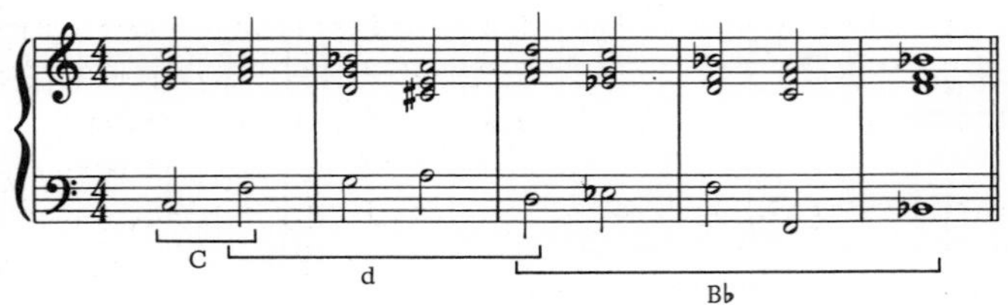

FORM

Since the Renaissance, musical composition has grown ever more complex. Individual instrumental works have become increasingly longer, new harmonic resources have opened up, and musical techniques have become more daring. The listener's bewilderment in facing these complexities is understandable; experience proves, however, that when the listener possesses some knowledge of *form,* he is less confused by irregular or intricate compositions.

Form refers to the design selected by the composer to express his musical ideas. In other words, musical form represents the structure of a composition. Some kind of form is a psychological necessity. It keeps an audience from becoming bored; even the most imaginative composer finds that if his music lacks form his audience becomes restless. As listeners we are not by nature prepared to assimilate a composition consisting only of new, inconclusive ideas. We require repetition and development of these ideas to keep us interested. Of course a long composition reiterating the same little musical idea throughout also provides a dismal listening experience. The composer must maintain a good balance between these extremes. Let us see how composers create repetition and variety.

Motives and Figures

Communication in any medium is achieved by the reduction of ideas into short units capable of being easily assimilated. These short units must then be logically combined to create a unified, organized entity. In music this brief unit is called a *motive*—the briefest intelligible and self-sufficient melodic or rhythmic fragment of a melody or musical theme. The motive's importance cannot be overestimated. A motive may appear in sequence or may combine with other motives to form melodies and themes; in fact, motives provide essential building material for thematic development.

Almost any good melody, when examined, reveals that it is based on one or several motives. Some of the best examples are in hymn tunes and folk songs (Ex. 4:28).

Ex. 4:28. "All Through the Night"

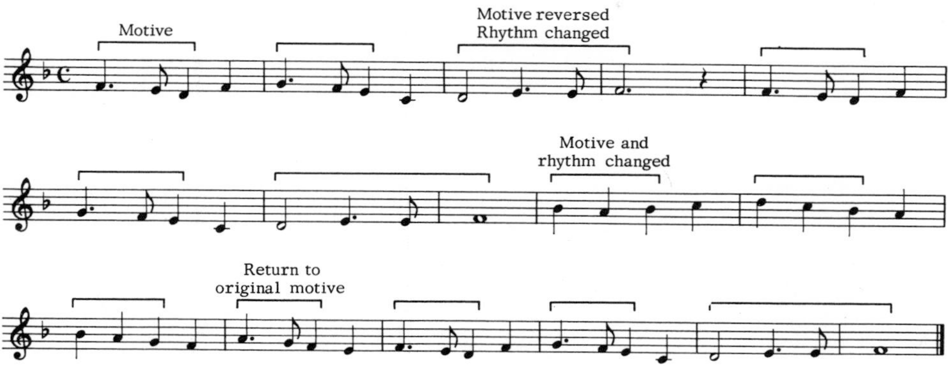

The motive plays an essential role in classical music. For example, Beethoven's *Symphony No. 3* begins with two motives that are expanded and developed throughout the first movement (Ex. 4:29).

Ex. 4:29. Beethoven: *Symphony No. 3 in E-Flat Major: Allegro con brio*

One also encounters the term *figure* in music. In contrast to a motive, a figure is not a component of a theme. It is a less important fragment serving principally as material for accompaniment in nonthematic passages (Ex. 4:30).

Ex. 4:30. Mozart: *String Quartet in C Major, K.465: Allegro*

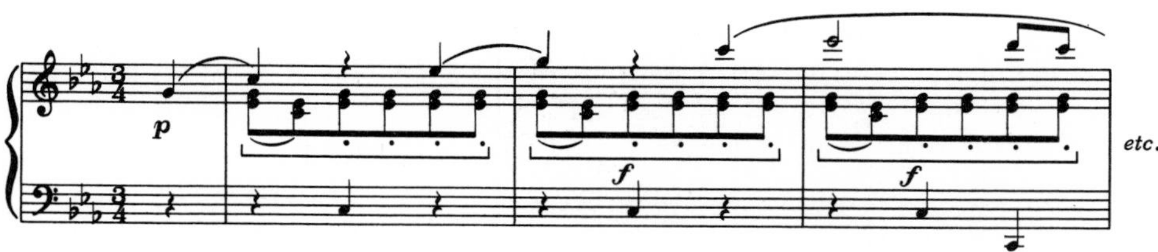

Phrases and Periods

The constituent structural elements in music can be isolated for the purposes of analysis. Just as words, phrases, sentences, paragraphs, and chapters are the formal elements in literary efforts, so motives, phrases, sections, and periods (or sentences) are structural elements in music.

"A *phrase* is the shortest passage of music which, having reached a point of relative repose, has expressed a more or less complete musical thought."[1] A normal phrase is four measures in length. It can end with a suggestion of either incompleteness or fulfillment (Ex. 4:31). A phrase can be broken into two

Ex. 4:31. ***Example of a phrase***

two-measure *sections* (Ex. 4:32). Two phrases combined make a *period* (*sentence*). The construction of the second phrase may be *parallel* ("To Celia"), *similar* ("Annie Laurie"), or *contrasting* ("Auld Lang Syne").

Ex. 4:32. ***Two-part phrase***

Ex. 4:33. ***Examples of musical periods***

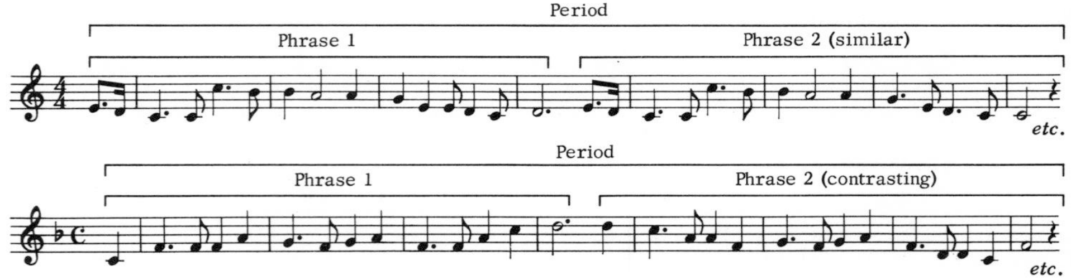

In a *double period* the construction is said to be parallel when the third phrase duplicates or even just begins like the first ("Flow Gently, Sweet Afton").

We have been speaking of standard phrases and phrase groupings, but we must not indulge in oversimplification: there are other sizes and shapes. For example, a long phrase with eight measures (two or three beats per measure) may be encountered in a fast tempo. Sixteen-measure periods are found in Johann Strauss's *Waltzes*. A short two-measure phrase may occur when the measures have many notes or when the measures are long and have $\frac{4}{2}$ meter (Ex. 4:34).

Ex. 4:34. "Battle Hymn of the Republic"

In general, phrases can be of any length, including three, five, six, seven, or any reasonable number of measures, as well as those described above. If phrases are longer than four measures, they usually contain some type of repetition. Thus three two-measure sections constitute the first phrase of "America" (Ex. 4:35).

[1] Douglass Green, *Form in Tonal Music,* p. 7. Copyright © 1965 by Holt, Rinehart and Winston, Inc., New York. Reprinted by permission.

Ex. 4:35. "America"

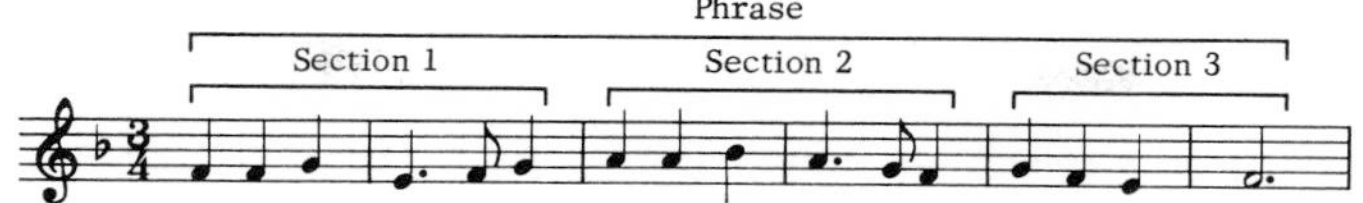

Basic Musical Forms

In addition to combining figures and motives into sections, sections into phrases, phrases into periods, and so on, the composer gives form to a work by organizing his thematic material and his keys or tonal scheme. This overall organization creates interest through repetition, variation, and contrast.

The seemingly endless types of musical forms can be classified into one of six categories, each capable of limitless diversity.

1. A two-section form: *simple binary*.
2. A three-section form: *simple ternary*.
3. *Sonata-allegro* form (also called *first-movement* form and *sonata* form).
4. An elaboration of simple ternary: the *rondo*.
5. *Air and variations*.
6. The *canon* and *fugue*.

The first two are the most basic forms and should be discussed now; the others are discussed in later chapters, in connection with particular musical periods.

Binary Form

Binary form is more indigenous to classical music than to folk music. It is a musical structure separated approximately into two sections (A and B), each section marked for repetition at the discretion of the performer or performers. The first section has one theme—sometimes fragments of a second—and toward the end of this first section there occurs a shift to a new tonal area (modulation). The second section begins either with new musical material or with some brief development or variation of the theme; it returns to the original key through modulation.

Seventeenth-century composers used binary form for many kinds of compositions, and it is typically associated with the dance suites of this era. However, the form persisted through the eighteenth and nineteenth centuries as part of a larger structural framework. When listening to the two parts of binary form, keep in mind that they are often melodically and stylistically related; that is, contrast is not the only objective. Also, there are different sizes and shapes of binary form: *symmetrical* binary exists when each half of the composition has the same length (*Gavotte II* from Bach's *Orchestral Suite No. 3* illustrates this type). When one half, usually the second, is longer, the result is *asymmetrical* binary—found in the *Air* from Bach's *Orchestral Suite No. 3*. *Rounded* binary means that the second section is longer than the first and features a return of all or part of the first section in the original key—a type found in *Gavotte I, Bourrée,* and *Gigue* from this same Bach suite.

Ternary Form

Ternary form is also favored by composers for short compositions. It consists of a tune or self-contained melody, a second melody almost always in a new key but frequently related to the first key, and a repeat of the first melody.

There are striking differences between binary and ternary form. Ternary is more sectional: the second theme is quite distinct from the first. In binary, the tonality of the second section is introduced at the end of the first; in ternary, the first section often closes in its own key. In other words, binary form seems more unified, whereas ternary form is noticeably divided into three separate sections.

Many folk songs have ternary form—its history reaches back into the late Middle Ages—and it is therefore one form that has remained in almost constant use. The best examples of ternary form in classical music occur in minuets, such as Beethoven's *Minuet in G* and, in a more extended vein, Chopin's *Prélude, Opus 28, No. 15.*

TEXTURE

Texture usually describes the way some physical object feels when touched: we speak of coarse-textured burlap or fine-textured silk. Texture can also convey a visual impression: we might refer to the thick texture of a Van Gogh painting.

With music we hear instead of physically feel or see, yet we still use the word "texture." When listening to music, we ask ourselves about the texture, meaning how does it "hear"? There are three generally recognized textures: monophonic, polyphonic, and homophonic.

Music is called *monophonic* when it consists of one line of unaccompanied melody. The finest example is Gregorian chant (plainsong), which, according to its official interpretation, has no accompaniment and has all participants singing the same melodic line (Ex. 4:36). Any type of unaccompanied solo on a single-voiced instrument also has monophonic texture.

Ex. 4:36. *Gregorian Kyrie*

Polyphonic (contrapuntal) texture best fits the analogy to a fabric, for the music is made up of *many* (Greek "poly") *voices* or *sounds* (Greek "phonos")—that is, melodies moving in a horizontal direction but connected with each other by a vertical (intervallic or harmonic) relationship.

Texture that is predominantly chordal is called *homophonic.* Here the substance is mainly a series of block chords connected horizontally by a melodic line soaring above them. Listen for this texture in Handel's *Largo* or Chopin's *Prélude, Opus 28, No. 7.*

Again we must guard against oversimplification, however, because between polyphonic and homophonic music there are numerous intermediate textures. One delightful characteristic of Bach's music is his skillful synthesizing of contrapuntal and harmonic elements into a texture that creates great musical variety and interest. Many fine nineteenth-century composers, such as Beethoven and Brahms, were able to blend the two elements not only successfully but beautifully.

SUMMARY

Now that the various aspects of music's dimensions have been examined, let us look at a short musical composition (Ex. 4:37) to see what we can find.

Ex. 4:37. Mozart: *Minuet in F Major* (*for harpsichord*)

1. This minuet is written in the key of *F* major—a fact indicated by the *B* flat in the signature and by the beginning and ending *F* in both treble and bass clefs.

2. The time signature indicates that each measure contains the equivalent of three quarter notes.

3. Although the meter is triple, the rhythmic motive of the whole composition is a pattern of two eighth notes followed by two quarter notes in each measure.

4. The composition appears to comprise two lines of music (one in the treble and one in the bass), yet the texture is homophonic: the chords are spread

out—some members are found in the melody, others in the bass line. Thus the notes used in the first measure are *F–A–C,* a tonic triad or chord in the key of *F* major; those in the second measure spell out *B♭–D–F,* a subdominant chord in the same key.

5. The accidentals in the second section (measures 9, 11, and 12) are used for modulation. The first section had already concluded (measures 7 and 8) in the dominant (*C–E–G–B♭*) of the principal key (*F*). The second section moves on to *g* minor and eventually modulates back to the home key of *F* major (measure 14).

6. The melody has an instrumental character. It is very active, with some large intervals, and covers a wide range (from high *A* in measure 1 to middle *C* in measure 5). The melodic line frequently outlines chords (the melody in measure 5 is *C–E–G,* a triad on the dominant). The triplet in measure 3 is used for variety. Notice the fermata in measure 20.

7. The first section (measures 1 to 8) is a period composed of two four-measure phrases. The second section (measures 9 to 24) has four phrases containing four measures each. Notice the repeat marks (:) at each end of the two sections (measures 8, 9, and 24). The overall form is asymmetrical binary: there are two sections, the second being larger. The use of similar material throughout provides continuity from beginning to end.

FOR DISCUSSION AND ASSIGNMENT

1. How many errors can you find in the following example?

2. Class project: Divide the group into a four-part chorus, and learn a straightforward hymn. Each student will be singing a horizontal melody, yet what will be heard is four-part harmony.
3. Listen to the predominant melody in each of several short compositions. How would you describe these individual melodies?
4. Listen to several characteristic folk songs and try to discover the design in each. Use letter names for each musical phrase and jot down a letter when you hear a new phrase.

FOR FURTHER READING

Miller, Hugh M. *Introduction to Music.* New York: Barnes & Noble, Inc., 1958. A College Outline Series PB. Recommended for those who wish to pursue the question of musical form in some detail. Professor Miller devotes almost 50 pages of his book to the principles of musical structure.

Randolph, David. *This Is Music.* New York: The New American Library, 1964. A Mentor PB. This interesting, useful book offers five chapters on musical forms and their purpose.

Smith, Warren S. *A Handbook of Musical Form.* Boston: Bruce Humphries, 1964. PB. In just 32 pages Mr. Smith outlines the basic elements of form as he sees them. Although designed for the student with some musical knowledge, this handbook could be of use to everyone with access to a phonograph.

5 Musical Instruments

All music is what awakes from you when you are reminded by the instruments.

WALT WHITMAN
A Song for Occupations

In Chapter 2, on sound, we saw that tone quality (*timbre*) depends mainly on the presence or absence of various overtones called harmonics or partials and that the harmonics themselves emanate from various vibrating segments of a sounding medium. This chapter continues the subject of tone quality by analyzing briefly the various sounding media capable of creating harmonics. These sounding agents are the musical instruments.

THE VOICE

The human voice is as true an instrument as, say, a clarinet or a violin. It has a sound-producing agent in the vocal cords—two vibrating strips of cartilage; it has an apparatus for wind supply in the lungs, which are connected to the vocal cords by a tube; and it has a resonating cavity—mouth, nose, and upper throat—wherein sounds are absorbed, amplified, and projected outside of the medium. The voice possesses an extra ability because it can frame sounds called words and pronounce them simultaneously with the tones.

Since the human voice is naturally produced, it is the most perfect musical instrument from an aesthetic point of view; however, it is also the most imperfect of all musical instruments, for it is susceptible to colds, laryngitis, and the nervous excitation of stage fright.

The singing voice is classified by its compass—that is, how high and how low it can function properly. There are six commonly accepted voice categories, three female and three male. From high to low, these are *soprano, mezzo-soprano* (literally half-soprano), and *alto* (*contralto*) among the female voices and *tenor, baritone,* and *bass* in the male group.

Some of these voice ranges have their own subdivisions according to quality or facility. For instance, a soprano voice with *coloratura* timbre can manage the highest singing range with spectacular agility. The powerful *dramatic* soprano voice is ideally equipped for declamatory and histrionic roles. In contrast to dramatic soprano, the *lyric* soprano voice, as the name suggests, achieves a smooth vocal line with grace and ease.

The *mezzo-soprano* voice is not concerned with displaying an extravagantly high vocal range. Instead of using vocal acrobatics or stunning vocalises, the trained mezzo-soprano displays her artistry through pure musicianship. On the other hand, the *contralto* voice delights the listener with its distinctive low pitch. Nature has endowed the contralto with a sensuous throaty quality that is thrilling to hear, and yet this voice is also flexible enough to attain a rather high pitch range.

The following *arias* (*airs*) from operas and oratorios illustrate the various female-voice qualities:

Coloratura Soprano: Delibes—"Bell Song," from *Lakmé;* Donizetti—"Mad Scene," from *Lucia di Lammermoor;* Mozart—"Der Hölle Rache kocht in meinem Herzen," from *The Magic Flute.*

Dramatic Soprano: Mendelssohn—"Hear Ye, Israel," from *Elijah;* Strauss—"Du wolltest mich nicht deinem Mund küssen lassen," from *Salome;* Wagner—"Liebestod," from *Tristan und Isolde.*

Lyric Soprano: Bizet—"Je dis que rien m'épouvante," from *Carmen;* Handel—"Come unto Him," from *Messiah;* Puccini—"Mi chiammano Mimi," from *La Bohème.*

Mezzo-Soprano: Bizet—"Habanera" and "Seguidilla," from *Carmen;* Saint-Saëns—"Mon coeur s'ouvre à ta voix," from *Samson et Dalila;* Verdi—"O don fatale," from *Don Carlos.*

Contralto: Brahms—*Alto Rhapsody;* Falla—Songs from *El amor brujo;* Wagner—"Weiche, Wotan," from *Das Rheingold.*

Among male voices, *lyric tenor* corresponds in quality and range to lyric soprano, and traditionally these two voices have been musically wedded for more than two centuries. Except for German operas, heroine and hero roles typically belong to a lyric soprano and a lyric tenor. The *tenor robusto* or *Heldentenor* (heroic tenor) is a full, powerful voice, possessing all the vigor needed for expressing strong emotions; this voice finds numerous roles in Wagner and Strauss operas.

The *baritone* voice, male counterpart of the mezzo-soprano, has a medium scope covering the lower tenor and upper bass ranges. The *bass* may be either *basso cantante,* a low-pitched, sonorous voice with the agility of the lyric soprano and tenor, or *basso profundo*—the lowest male voice—which is deep, heavy, and somberly expressive. Not very much music has been written expressly for the basso profundo.

Two other male voice types should be mentioned. The *countertenor* (male alto) is produced by the singer's use of his falsetto register. Composers of the late seventeenth and eighteenth centuries (Handel and Purcell, for example) wrote music for this voice, particularly choral music. In the nineteenth century the female contralto largely supplanted the countertenor, although male altos are still found in some English church choirs.

The popularity of the male soprano (*castrato*) during the seventeenth and eighteenth centuries, especially in Italy, noticeably influenced the concept of opera. An operation performed on the sexual organs before puberty permitted the singer to develop a powerful soprano. Handel, Gluck, and many other composers used the castrato voice for the male leads in operas. Castration to produce male sopranos was discontinued in the early nineteenth century.

The following arias from operas and oratorios illustrate the various male-voice qualities:

Lyric Tenor: Handel—"Every valley," from *Messiah;* Puccini—"Che gelida manina," from *La Bohème;* Rossini—"Ecco ridente," from *The Barber of Seville.*

Dramatic Tenor: Beethoven—"In des Lebens Frühlingstagen," from *Fidelio;* Wagner—"Lohengrin's Narrative," from *Lohengrin;* Wagner—"Walter's Prize Song," from *Die Meistersinger.*

Baritone: Bizet—"Chanson du Toreador," from *Carmen;* Gounod—"Avant de quitter ces lieux," from *Faust;* Leoncavallo—"Prologue," from *Pagliacci.*

Bass: Handel—"Why do the nations," from *Messiah;* Mozart—"In diesen heiligen Hallen," from *The Magic Flute;* Mussorgsky—"Farewell of Boris," from *Boris Godounov.*

INSTRUMENTS

The usual way to classify instruments is to group them under four headings: *string, wind, percussion,* and *keyboard.* A more graphic description is to say that instruments are (1) bowed or plucked, (2) blown, (3) struck, or (4) sounded via a keyboard.

Bowed Strings

Viol and violin sounds are generated by means of a bow consisting of a wood shaft with a sheath of horsehair attached to it. At one end a nut serves to hold the hair in place and also to adjust its tension. The bow stick curves out from the hairs. When the hair touches the strings, friction sets up vibrations that produce sound. For viol playing, the bow is held with the fingers curved upward. The violin bow is held with the fingers pointing downward.

The *viol family* enjoyed its greatest popularity during the sixteenth and seventeenth centuries. In the latter century the violin family began to eclipse the viols; and from the eighteenth century to the present, violins have held the favored position.

The viol (Ill. 5:1) has a flat back, its shoulders slope to the neck, and the whole body is made from rather thin wood with deep ribs. Usually it has six strings and a fretted fingerboard—most frets are raised strips of wood or metal —to indicate the position of semitones. The sound holes on the front are in the shape of a C. The bridge holding the strings in place is quite flat, making chords easier to play than on violins.

Standard viol sizes include *treble, tenor,* and *bass.* In the sixteenth century the term "chest of viols" referred to an actual chest used for storing the instruments necessary for a chamber ensemble—usually two trebles, two tenors, and two basses.

The viol tone is less incisive, less brilliant than that of the violin family, but it possesses a sweet, plaintive character that the latter does not have.

The *violin family* contains four standard instruments, of which the *violin* itself is the soprano and the one most often heard in solo. It has a basically bright tone so adaptable that it can be molded to express almost every emotion. The *viola* (alto), about one-seventh larger than the violin, gives off a more somber, sometimes melancholy tone. The *violoncello,* frequently abbreviated to *cello,* is exceptionally versatile, possessing both a high range and considerable possibility for depth in the lower range. Its tone is masculine, with flexibility like that of the violin. The *double bass* is the largest bowed string instrument in use today; when it plays the same written note as a cello, the tone sounds one octave lower. Violin, viola, and cello all have their four strings tuned at intervals of the fifth, but the double bass is tuned at the fourth to facilitate fingering on its large fingerboard. Actually, the double bass is not a true member of the violin family; it retains a number of characteristics of the viols (sloping shoulders, flat back), causing it sometimes to be called the bass viol.

Instruments of the violin family have a curved back, shoulders at right angles to the neck, no fretted fingerboard, four strings instead of six, and a curved bridge (Ill. 5:2).

98536

Ill. 5:1. ***Viols. Left to right, bass viol, tenor viol, treble viol. Courtesy of Arnold Dolmetsch Ltd.***
Ill. 5:2. ***Violin. Courtesy of Roth Violins, Cleveland, Ohio.***

With their wonderful flexibility, violins are indispensable to an orchestra or ensemble. As a family they cover a wide sound range—seven octaves—and permit endless variations in bow technique. The bow can be bounced loosely over the strings, producing *spiccato.* Short, quick bow strokes result in clear-cut, detached *staccato* notes, while brusque bow strokes in a "hammered" manner are called *martellato.* The bow played close to the bridge (*sul ponticello*) produces a nasal, brittle tone. *Tremolo* results when the bow is moved rapidly back and forth on one tone. The bow can even be turned over and the strings tapped with the wood instead of the hair, a technique described as playing *col legno.* Or the bow can be dispensed with and the fingers used to pluck the strings, thus producing *pizzicato.*

Other interesting effects can be accomplished with this versatile violin family. These instruments are capable of double-stopping—playing double notes and chords—which means that two (sometimes three) strings are played simultaneously. Also, violins can create harmonics; a finger placed lightly on the string at the fingerboard blocks out the fundamental tone and sounds a harmonic instead. When a device called a mute is clamped on the bridge, a silvery, muffled tone emerges.

Distinctive qualities identifying individual members of the violin family can be detected in the following compositions:

Violin: Lalo—*Symphonie Espagnole, for Violin and Orchestra, Op. 21;* Mendelssohn—*Concerto in e for Violin, Op. 64;* Saint-Saëns—*Introduction and Rondo Capriccioso, Op. 28.*

Viola: Bartók—*Concerto for Viola and Orchestra;* Berlioz—*Harold in Italy, for Viola and Orchestra, Op. 16;* Mozart—*Duo No. 2 in B♭, K. 424.*

Cello: Bach—*Suites for Cello Unaccompanied;* Haydn—*Concerto in D for Cello, Op. 101;* Saint-Saëns—"The Swan," from *Carnival of the Animals.*

Double Bass: Beethoven—*Symphony No. 5 in C, Op. 67,* third movement; Saint-Saëns—"The Elephant," from *Carnival of the Animals.*

String Ensemble: Bach—*Brandenburg Concerto No. 3 in G;* Barber—*Adagio for Strings* (from *Quartet, Op. 11*); Vaughan Williams—*Fantasia on "Greensleeves."*

Plucked Strings

Harps of various shapes were among the first instruments to serve in ritual music, a fact well documented in both pictorial and written history.

The modern harp's main visible features are the vertical pillar, curved neck, diagonal soundboard, and pedal box (Ill. 5:3). There are 47 strings—each having its own length and pitch—stretched over a large, open, triangular frame. The strings are tuned diatonically (seven strings to the octave) in the key of *C*-flat major (with a signature of seven flats). There are seven foot pedals, each equipped with two notches and each affecting one basic pitch of each octave by raising it a semitone or a whole tone. Thus the *C* pedal produces in normal position the pitch *C* flat in all octaves, in the first notch *C* natural, and in the second notch *C* sharp. The *D* pedal controls the *D* pitches in a like manner, and so on. By the manipulation of these foot devices, a harp can literally be pedalled from one key to another—the harpist can play in any major or minor key.

Besides plucking the strings—the standard technique—the harpist can

Ill. 5:3. ***Harp. Courtesy of Lyon and Healy.***

achieve many other effects. He can glide his fingers over the strings in a rippling motion, producing unique tone clusters called *glissandos.* Or he can play *arpeggios,* the result of playing chord tones successively rather than simultaneously. (Arpeggios can be played on other instruments, but the term [h]arpeggio stresses the fact that this effect is particularly associated with the harp.) The harpist can also play harmonics by pressing a string lightly at the desired position and then plucking it. In addition, there are numerous special effects possible on the harp.

There are many other plucked string instruments. The *lute,* highly favored during the sixteenth and seventeenth centuries for solo performance and for song accompaniment, is rarely heard today. Even though lute technique was and is difficult to master, a huge lute repertoire exists. The instrument has a large pear-shaped body, a neck with a fretted fingerboard, a rounded back, and no bridge. It is double-strung; that is, there are two strings for each of its from four to seven open pitches (Ill. 5:4). The lute belongs to an unusual instrument family, but it is the only member still active.

The *guitar,* a very popular stringed instrument with a flat back and a long fretted neck, was brought to Spain by the Moors in the Middle Ages. In addition to possessing a classical repertoire, the guitar is much in demand for Spanish flamenco music, traditional folk music, Western music, and the like. The electric guitar, used in certain types of popular music and jazz, is basically a guitar connected to an electric apparatus that modifies and amplifies the sound.

The *zither* is basically a wooden box with from 30 to 45 strings stretched over its open surface. A few of these strings are placed over a fretted board and

NAZARETH COLLEGE LIBRARY

Ill. 5:4. ***Hans Brosamer*** **(c.** ***1500–1554*****), Lute Player.** ***Courtesy of Prints Division, The New York Public Library.***

are used for playing melodies; the rest are used for chording. The player's left thumb adjusts the length of the melody strings on the fretted board, his right-hand thumb plays them with a plectrum, and three fingers on his right hand pluck the accompanying chords.

The *banjo* probably originated in Africa. It resembles a guitar except that it has a small body, and parchment rather than wood serves as its resonating medium. This parchment is stretched over a metal hoop open at the back, like a tambourine. On its surface five or six strings are strung over a low bridge, and frets are provided along the neck to indicate pitches.

Two other instruments complete the list of the more familiar plucked string instruments. The *mandolin* is similar to the lute but is infinitely easier to play. It has from eight to ten wire strings, which are played with a plectrum, and its tremolo sound creates useful and unusual sonorities. The common *ukulele*—sometimes called the Hawaiian guitar—falls far below other plucked string instruments in quality and beauty of sound. It has four strings and a very long fingerboard. After brief instruction, almost anyone can learn the strumming technique that makes the ukulele so easy to use for song accompaniment.

The distinctive qualities of some of these instruments can be heard in the following works:

Harp: Boieldieu—*Concerto in C for Harp;* Ravel—*Introduction and Allegro for Harp, Flute, Clarinet, and String Quartet;* Rodrigo—*Concert-Serenade for Harp and Orchestra.*

Lute: Dowland—*Dances for Lute;* Telemann—*Sonata for Viola da Gamba and Lute.*

Guitar: Castelnuovo-Tedesco—*Quintet for Guitar and String Quartet, Op. 143;* Rodrigo—*Concierto de Aranjuez for Guitar and Orchestra.*

Woodwind Instruments

The name "woodwind" applies collectively to those wind instruments originally made of wood; however, some are now manufactured in either wood or metal. They may be blown directly (flute), or else sounded by means of a reed, either single (clarinet) or double (oboe). In general, a woodwind instrument is a tube with holes. By closing the holes or leaving them open, the player lengthens or shortens the air column and obtains variety in pitch.

The Flute Family

There are two main types of flutes: the vertical flute and the horizontal or transverse flute. Formerly all flutes were wood, but metal transverse flutes are more frequent today. The vertical flute, known as a *recorder* or *fipple flute,* comes in several sizes. Many references to the recorder appear in literary as well as music history. Composers in the seventeenth and eighteenth centuries often wrote music especially for solo recorder and for recorder ensemble. In the nineteenth century the recorder followed other so-called ancient instruments into near oblivion, but it has been rescued during the last thirty years, so that recorder ensembles are now common and instrument makers are again manufacturing these instruments.

A recorder has eight holes and a whistle mouthpiece. The different sizes (Ill. 5:5) are *descant, treble, tenor,* and *bass* (in Germany the equivalent names are *soprano, alto, tenor,* and *bass*). Recorder ensembles usually have three, four, or five performers.

The side-blown or horizontal flute (commonly referred to simply as a *flute*) is basically a soprano instrument. It consists of a tube (usually metal), stopped at one end, near which a mouth hole is placed at the side. The player blows across this mouth hole so that his breath impinges on the edge of the hole and vibrates the air column. Richer tone color emerges from the upper flute range because the upper range contains more harmonics than the lower. The cool, suave flute sound is in great demand for orchestral coloring. Composers appreciate the instrument because of its agility in maneuvering rapidly.

Three horizontal flutes exist today. The *concert* flute (Ill. 5:6) is of course standard for orchestra and ensemble work, but the *flauto piccolo*—small flute—which sounds one octave higher than its larger sister, gives off the brightest tones in the orchestra when it participates. Military band music often requires a piccolo. Another member of the family, the *alto* flute, has a range a fourth lower than the concert flute. It is used frequently in contemporary music.

In the nineteenth century, when audiences delighted in vocal and instrumental acrobatics, the flute was able to oblige characteristically and uniquely. An operatic tour de force of that era was the coloratura soprano aria with flute obbligato; since the flute, more than any other instrument, resembles the voice, this combination became a true duet. Modern composers perhaps scorn this theatrical union, but it was effective and successful then.

Special qualities of the recorder and flute can be heard in the following compositions:

Recorder: Bach—*Brandenburg Concerto No. 4 in G;* Telemann—*Sonatas for Recorder and Harpsichord.*

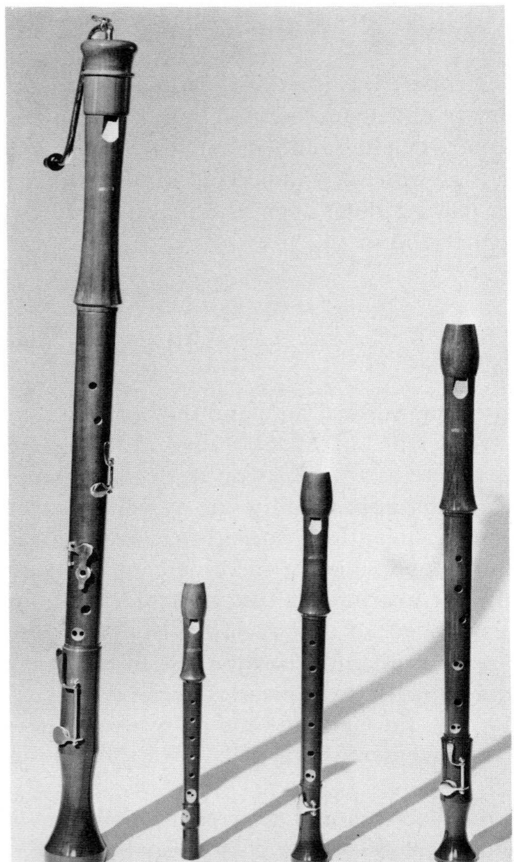

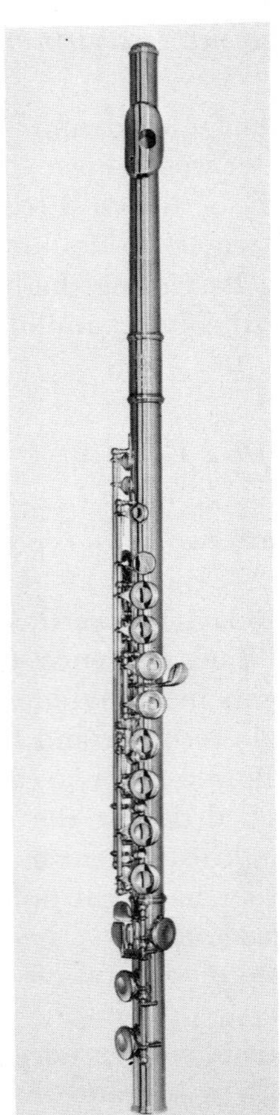

Ill. 5:5. *Recorders. Left to right, bass, soprano, alto, tenor. Courtesy of H. & A. Selmer, Inc.*
Ill. 5:6. *Flute. Courtesy of H. & A. Selmer, Inc.*

Flute: Debussy—*Syrinx for Flute Unaccompanied;* Griffes—*Poem for Flute and Orchestra;* Mozart—*Concerto No. 2 in D for Flute, K. 314.*

Piccolo: Sousa—*The Stars and Stripes Forever;* Tchaikovsky—"Chinese Dance," from *Nutcracker Suite, Op. 71A.*

The Double-Reed Family

The woodwind instruments classified as "double reed" are easily identified by their double reeds (two reeds placed together with a slight orifice between) and conical tubes. The *oboe* (Ill. 5:7)—soprano of the family—has an open, flaring bell. A distinctive instrument with a penetrating but not shrill tone, its plaintive sounds can be heard in the orchestra, in ensemble, and in solo performance.

The alto oboe or *English horn* (the name is misleading, since it is not a true member of the horn family) is longer than the soprano oboe, its bell is pear-shaped, and its reed is fitted into a metal tube bent back to the player's mouth. The English horn is not usually an independent solo instrument, but it is used extensively in orchestral music.

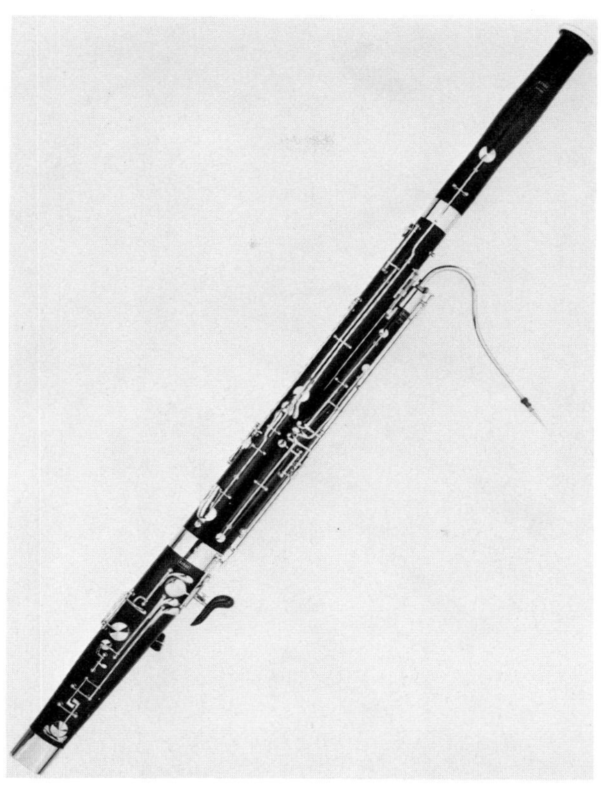

Ill. 5:7. ***Oboe. Courtesy of G. Leblanc Corporation.***
Ill. 5:8. ***Bassoon. Courtesy of H. & A. Selmer, Inc.***

The next double-reed instrument in descending order of pitch is the *bassoon* (Ill. 5:8), a long, wooden tube doubled back on itself into a "U" shape. Like the English horn, the bassoon has its reed attached to a curved metal tube. Although a bass instrument, the bassoon can sustain melodic lines, and it blends well with other orchestral instruments, particularly the horns. A deeper bassoon—the *double bassoon* or *contrabassoon*—sometimes is called on to provide deep, grumbly sounds in the orchestra.

There are also lesser-known members in this double-reed family. The *oboe da caccia, oboe d'amore,* and *heckelphone* are only occasionally used, and the *sarrusophone,* made of brass, is found in some European military bands.

Qualities distinguishing double-reed family instruments can be heard in the following selections:

Oboe: Handel—*Concerto No. 3 in g for Oboe;* Mozart—*Quartet in F for Oboe and Strings, K. 370;* Telemann—*Concertos for Oboe and Orchestra.*

English Horn: Dvořák—*Symphony No. 9 in e, Op. 95,* second movement; Franck—*Symphony in d,* second movement; Sibelius—*Swan of Tuonela* (from *Four Legends, Op. 22*).

Bassoon: Dukas—*The Sorcerer's Apprentice;* Mozart—*Concerto in B♭ for Bassoon, K. 191;* Rimsky-Korsakov—*Scheherazade, Op. 35,* second movement.

Double Bassoon: Ravel—"Conversations of Beauty and the Beast," from *Mother Goose Suite.*

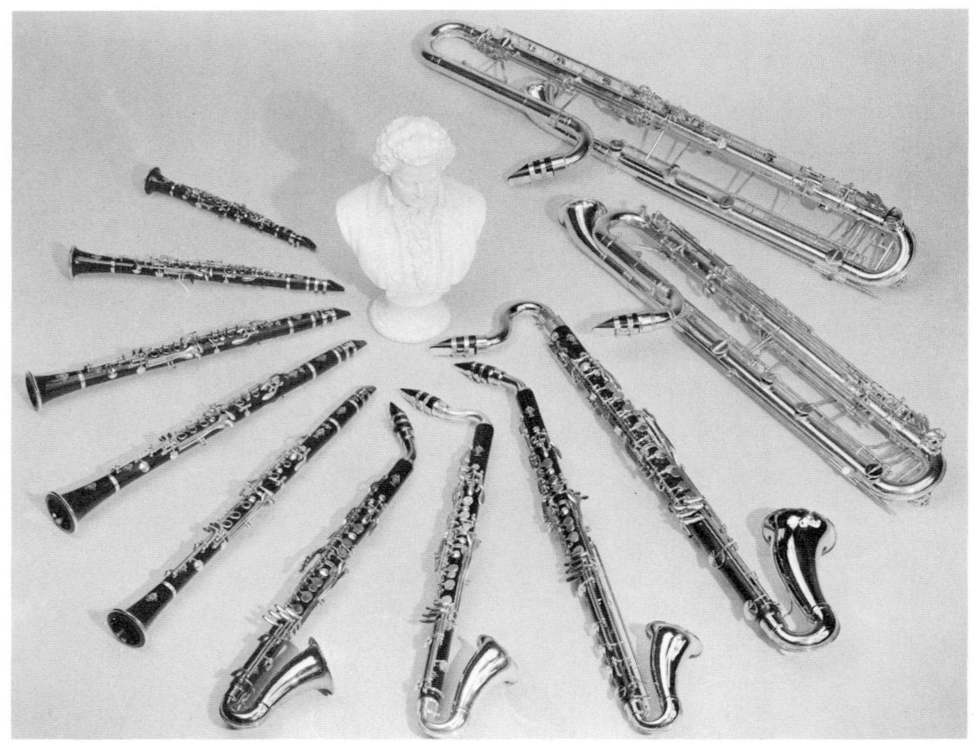

Ill. 5:9. *Clarinet family: A♭ sopranino to B♭ contrabass. Courtesy of G. Leblanc Corporation.*

The Single-Reed Family

A cylindrical tube and single reed characterize the *clarinet* family, whose smooth tone and flexible dynamic contrasts have kept it active since its perfection in the early nineteenth century. At the present time it serves in classical, popular, and folk music (folk ensembles in Greece often use the clarinet). The soprano or treble instrument is the clarinet in *B flat;*[1] the *bass* clarinet plays the lower ranges. The latter has a tubular body, its lower end curves up into a bell, and the upper end has a tube bent down to the player's mouth.

Other members of this family (Ill. 5:9) are the *E-flat* clarinet, capable of a very high range; the *alto* clarinet in *E* flat; the less sensitive *basset horn;* and the *double-bass* clarinet, used in military bands.

Distinctive qualities of the two principal clarinets can be heard in the following compositions:

> *Clarinet:* Brahms—*Quintet in b for Clarinet and Strings, Op. 115;* Mozart—*Concerto in A for Clarinet, K. 622;* Weber—*Concertino for Clarinet and Orchestra, Op. 26.*
>
> *Bass Clarinet:* Tchaikovsky—"Dance of the Sugar Plum Fairy," from *Nutcracker Suite, Op. 71A;* Wagner—"Liebestod," from *Tristan und Isolde.*

[1] Certain instruments on which the player produces a note different from the written note are called *transposing* instruments. Thus a clarinet in *B* flat produces the pitch of *B* flat when the written note *C* is played.

The Saxophone Family

Invented in 1846, the *saxophone* is the newest member of the reed group. It is a hybrid: it has a conical tube like the oboe, it is fashioned of brass like some other wind instruments, and it uses a single reed like the clarinet. Although originally regarded as a concert instrument in Europe, the saxophone arrived in the United States during the early jazz period and became indispensable to jazz. Many twentieth-century composers now include it in their orchestrations, and at least one clarinetist in every symphony orchestra is expected to be able to play the saxophone. Among the many different sizes, the most common are the *B-flat tenor* and *E-flat alto* saxophones (Ill. 5:10). Outstanding features of the saxophone and other woodwinds can be heard in the following works:

Saxophone: Debussy—*Rhapsodie for Saxophone and Orchestra;* Ibert—*Concertino da Camera for Saxophone and Orchestra;* Ravel—*Boléro.*

Woodwind Ensemble: Dittersdorf—*Partitas for Winds;* Stravinsky—*Octet for Wind Instruments;* Schoenberg—*Woodwind Quintet.*

Brass Instruments

The brasses include those instruments formed by a long, coiled metal tube through which the air column travels. The mouthpiece is like a cup or funnel pressed against the player's lips, which function somewhat like a double reed, or like the double vocal chords in the human throat. By varying the tension in his lips, the player causes the air column to vibrate in halves or thirds so as to produce various harmonics. Either valves or a slide changes the length of the air column, making it possible to play a complete scale.

The Horn

The *horn,* or *French horn,* is a long (more than eleven feet) coiled tube, very narrow at its mouthpiece end and flaring into a large bell at the opposite end. Valves control the length of the air column. The French horn (Ill. 5:11) is valuable both as a solo instrument and as an ensemble member. It is capable of great intensity and demands considerable technique for mastery. Horns have a medium pitch range with a lot of flexibility; therefore orchestral compositions often include parts for four horns, which on their own can play chordal harmony varying from forceful intensity to delicate softness.

The Trumpet

The *trumpet's* origins go back to antiquity: Biblical passages tell how it served in religious ceremonies, and Homer describes its function in battle. For one purpose or another, the trumpet has had steady employment since its first primitive appearance.

The modern trumpet (in *B* flat), oblong in appearance, displays a narrow cylindrical tube widening to a bell (Ill. 5:12). It has a cup-shaped mouthpiece and valves to facilitate playing. With its high sound range it delivers a bright, ringing tone.

Ill. 5:10. ***Alto saxophone. Courtesy of G. Leblanc Corporation.***
Ill. 5:11. ***French horn. Courtesy of H. & A. Selmer, Inc.***

To encompass the extremely high notes demanded by Bach in some of his compositions—the *Brandenburg Concerto No. 2* for one—performers frequently use trumpets pitched in *C* or *D*.

A *cornet* is similar to the trumpet in size, range, sound, and form. The cornet bore is a combination of conical and cylindrical tubing. The percentage of conical tubing is greater in the cornet than in the trumpet, and the tone produced by the cornet is less incisive, less penetrating. Cornets appear most often in concert bands and marching bands.

The Trombone

The *trombone* (Ill. 5:13) is unique among the brasses. Like the trumpet it has a tube (or tubes) of cylindrical bore, a cup-shaped mouthpiece, and a medium-sized bell; but in contrast to the trumpet, the trombone utilizes a larger mouthpiece and more tubing, which help to produce the solemn, noble qualities characteristic of this instrument. To shorten and lengthen the air column, the standard trombone uses sliding tubes, not valves. Valve trombones are made but seldom used, perhaps because their tone quality is inferior to that of the slide trombone.

The power and intensity possible with the trombone make it useful for specialized performance. It has been used in churches to support the plainsong of

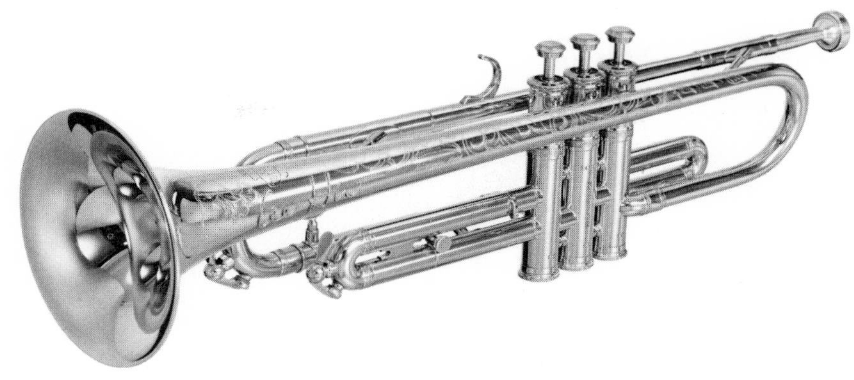

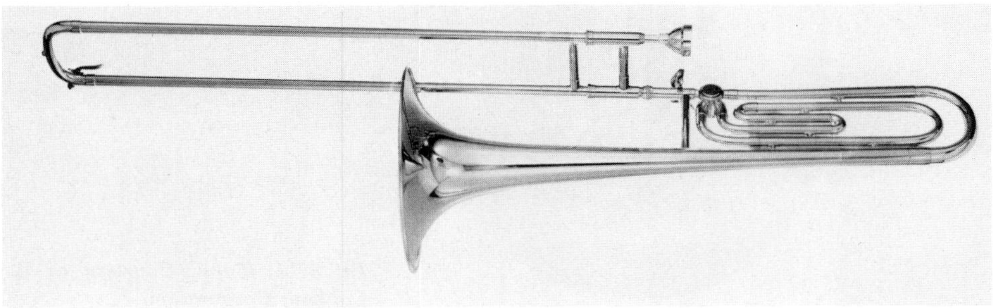

Ill. 5:12. ***Trumpet. Courtesy of G. Leblanc Corporation.***
Ill. 5:13. ***Trombone. Courtesy of The Wurlitzer Company.***

the choristers. In Germany, trombone ensembles used to play hymns from church towers. Now it is a stable member of both orchestra and band. There are several sizes, the *tenor* trombone being most important and best known. Others are the *tenor-bass* trombone and the *contrabass* (or *double-bass*) trombone.

The Tuba

It is almost impossible to define the word *tuba* (Ill. 5:14). So many types of instruments have been placed in this category that a tuba could mean any bass-pitched brass instrument other than a trombone. Most real tubas, however, have a wide conical bore and a cup-shaped mouthpiece.

Instruments included in the tuba class have various shapes, possibly because they are made by many makers in different countries. This widespread manufacturing attests to the popularity of military bands and other bands throughout the Western hemisphere, for the tuba is primarily a band instrument. Some of the different varieties are named *euphonium, helicon, sousaphone,* and *baritone.*

An orchestral tuba has the conical bore of a French horn and the oblong shape and cupped mouthpiece of a trumpet. Usually it has three or four valves.

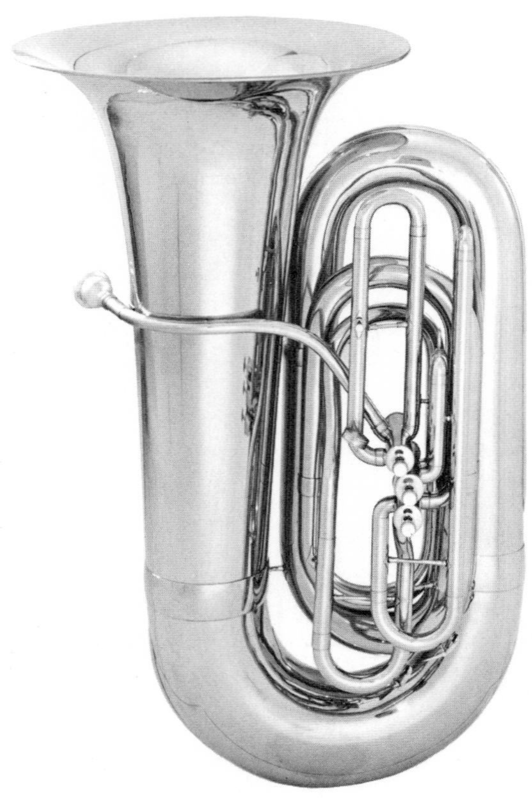

Ill. 5:14. *Tuba. Courtesy of G. Leblanc Corporation.*

Three sizes are standard: *tenor* in *B* flat, *bass* in *E* flat or *F,* and *double-bass,* pitched an octave below the tenor tuba.

The special sounds of the brass family can be heard in the following compositions:

Horn: Britten—*Serenade for Tenor, Horn, and Strings, Op. 31;* Mozart—*Concertos for Horn;* Wagner—"Prelude to Act III" of *Die Meistersinger.*

Trumpet: Haydn—*Concerto in E♭ for Trumpet and Orchestra;* Hindemith—*Sonata for Trumpet and Piano;* Verdi—"Grand March," from *Aida.*

Cornet: Stravinsky—"The Royal March," from *L'Histoire du Soldat* (Part 2).

Trombone: Beethoven—*Three Equali for Four Trombones;* Hindemith—*Sonata for Trombone and Piano;* Rimsky-Korsakov—*Concerto for Trombone and Band.*

Tuba: Strauss—*Don Quixote, Op. 35;* Stravinsky—"Suite" from *Petrouchka;* Wagner—"Prelude" to *Siegfried.*

Brass Choir: Gabrieli—*Canzoni for Brass Choirs;* Pezel—*Sonatas for Five Brass Instruments;* Pezel—*Tower and Festive Music.*

Percussion Instruments

There are numerous percussion instruments (Ill. 5:15), for this category includes any instrument that sounds by being struck; even the piano is sometimes used as a percussion instrument in the orchestra. Percussion instruments are more or less limited to orchestra and band performance, although some contemporary

Ill. 5:15. ***Symphonic percussion instruments. Courtesy of Ludwig Drum Co.***

composers have written ensemble music featuring them. They are classified in two groups: those that possess a definite pitch and those that do not.

Percussion Instruments with Definite Pitch

Kettledrum. The kettledrum (in a group they are called *timpani*) looks like a metal bowl with a membrane stretched over the top and held taut by screws set around the bowl's rim. These screws can be tightened or loosened, thus raising or lowering the drum's pitch. Pitch control is further maintained with a foot pedal. The drum is normally played with two felt-headed sticks.

Tubular Chimes. These are cylindrical metal tubes hung on a wooden frame and tuned to a diatonic scale. There are usually 18 bells in a set, with a range of 1½ octaves, and they are struck with a wooden hammer.

Orchestral Bells. Orchestral bells (*glockenspiel*) consist of a set of steel plates either fixed on a metal frame in the form of the ancient Greek lyre or arranged in a case in two rows corresponding to the white and black notes of the keyboard. They are played with two little hammers and have a bright, penetrating tone.

Celesta. Invented in 1880, the celesta superficially resembles a small piano. Inside is a set of steel plates, each plate having a wooden resonator attached to it, which accounts for the ethereal quality and sustaining power of the instrument. The plates are struck with hammers similar to those in a piano.

Xylophone. A xylophone is a graduated series of hard wooden bars mounted on a frame. The player uses two hard hand mallets and stands while performing. The xylophone's dry, wooden tone quality is applied for various orchestral effects.

Marimba. The marimba looks like a xylophone, but it has a wider tonal range, its wood bars are thinner, and each bar has a tuned metal resonator attached. The marimba's tone is softer than that of the xylophone, and it is played with soft mallets. The *vibraphone* (or *vibra-harp*), a type of marimba, has metal bars rather than wooden ones. Motor-driven discs revolving in the end of each resonator produce the vibraphone's characteristic tremolo.

Percussion Instruments with Indefinite Pitch

Most of the indefinite-pitch percussion instruments were introduced to Europe by Islamic army bands during the Crusades and by Turkish bands during the invasion of Western Europe.

Side or Snare Drum. This small drum consists of a circular metal frame with a membrane, or head, stretched across top and bottom. The upper head is struck with two drumsticks. The lower head has taut snares (strings somewhat like violin strings) stretched across it. The drum's brilliant sound depends on the vibrations of the lower head against these snares. The tremolo, or roll, is only one of its impressive effects.

Tenor Drum. Larger than a side drum, the tenor drum has a wooden frame instead of metal, and it does not have snares. This drum is infrequently used in the orchestra.

Bass Drum. This is the largest drum, and Mozart first used it as an orchestral instrument in his opera *Die Entführung aus dem Serail* (*The Abduction from the Seraglio*). The drummer can play single notes and rolls on it; he can produce effects ranging from a thunderous roar down to a mere whisper.

Tambourine. The tambourine—known as far back as the time of the Roman Empire—is a small, shallow wooden drum covered with one parchment head. Set around its wooden frame are loosely inserted small metal discs called "jingles," generally mounted in pairs. The percussionist plays a tambourine by striking the parchment with his knuckle, or by rubbing his thumb over the parchment to cause a tremolo of the jingles, or merely by shaking it.

Triangle. This instrument consists solely of a small steel tube bent into a triangular shape but open slightly at one corner. The player strikes the triangle with a small metal rod to produce one clear tone. It serves to create exotic effects, and its delicate tinkle blends agreeably with any harmonies heard in the orchestra.

Cymbals. These are two large, circular brass plates equipped with leather handles. The player manipulates them in various ways. Most of the time he holds one in each hand and clashes them together with a sideward movement; sometimes he strikes a single cymbal with a hard snare-drum stick or a soft timpani stick.

Gong or Tam-Tam. As the name suggests, this is a large broad disc made from heavy metal, slightly convex. It is suspended in a frame and struck with a heavy bass-drum beater.

Other percussion instruments occasionally used are castanets, rattle, anvil, thunder machine, Chinese wood blocks, and the wind machine.

The distinctive qualities of various percussion instruments can be heard in the following selections:

Kettledrums (Timpani) : Strauss (R.) —*Burleske in d for Piano and Orchestra.*

Tubular bells or chimes: Tchaikovsky—*1812 Overture, Op. 49.*

Orchestral Bells: Delibes—"Bell Song," from *Lakmé.*

Celesta: Tchaikovsky—*Nutcracker Suite, Op. 71A.*

Xylophone: Shostakovich—"Polka," from *Age of Gold.*

Marimba: Hanson—*Merry Mount Suite;* Puccini—*Turandot.*

Vibraphone: Berg—*Lulu Suite.*

Snare drum: Ravel—*Boléro.*

Tenor drum: Honegger—*Pacific 231.*

Bass drum: Copland—*El Salón México.*

Tambourine: Tchaikovsky—*Nutcracker Suite, Op. 71A.*

Triangle: Liszt—*Concerto No. 1 in E♭ for Piano and Orchestra.*

Cymbals: Mussorgsky—"The Great Gate at Kiev," from *Pictures at an Exhibition.*

Tam-Tam: Respighi—*The Pines of Rome.*

Keyboard Instruments

Clavichord, harpsichord, piano—each is a stringed keyboard instrument, yet each one as it appears in various shapes and sizes possesses its own merits and strengths as well as weaknesses. A flowing melodic line is most beautifully expressed by the clavichord, whose strings are activated by gentle pressure strokes from metal tangents; its lack of tonal power, however, limits its enjoyment to a small audience. The harpsichord, whose strings are plucked, is admirably suited to the quasi-polyphonic lines of Baroque music; however, the more lyric pieces of the early eighteenth century are less effective on the harpsichord due to its lack of flexibility in creating nuances. The piano—that dynamic instrument whose strings are struck by hammers—possesses extraordinary expressive possibilities but lacks the clarity of the harpsichord. These three instruments—together with their more elaborate companion, the pipe organ—form a keyboard dynasty that remains unchallenged.

Clavichord

The *clavichord* is the earliest type of stringed keyboard instrument about which specific information is available. Its known ancestry goes back to the sixth century B.C., when Pythagoras used a *monochord* for his experiments in musical mathematics. The monochord consisted of an oblong hollow box—the sounding board—above which stretched a string tuned by means of a peg. A movable bridge varied the length of the string. Later on, more strings were added.

The *dulcimer,* another precursor of the clavichord, has a series of strings that fit over two stationary bridges and are tuned by movable pins. The dulcimer is played by means of hammers that strike the strings from above. The Hungarian *cimbalom* is a special type of dulcimer.

The clavichord had a long period of development, but by the seventeenth century the instrument had achieved its classic form. The mechanism is enclosed in an oblong case from three to four feet long and two feet wide (Ill. 5:16). Sound is produced by means of small metal tangents attached to the ends of the keys; these tangents strike the strings gently from below. A certain nuance is possible, but only within a limited range. One technique peculiar to this instrument is the *Bebung* or tremolo, which produces a slight vibrato, or fluctuation in pitch. The clavichord served throughout Western Europe during the sixteenth

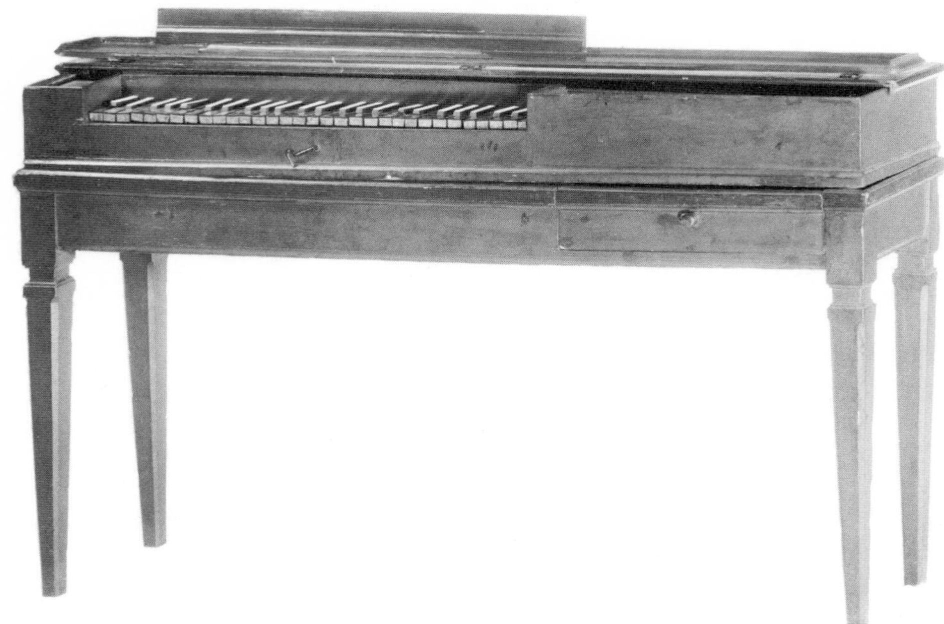

Ill. 5:16. *Clavichord. Courtesy of The Smithsonian Institution.*

and seventeenth centuries but went out of fashion during the eighteenth century, except in Germany, where it remained a favorite until the close of that century.

Harpsichord

The *harpsichord* (French *clavecin,* Italian *cembalo* or *clavicembalo*) played a primary role in eighteenth-century music; it enjoyed prestige similar to that of the concert grand piano during the nineteenth century. Yet today harpsichords are not considered obsolete; this instrument, shaped like a horizontal harp or wing, has undergone an unprecedented revival during the present century, and harpsichord factories are now flourishing.

Harpsichord history can be traced at least as far back as the Middle Ages, when the *psaltery,* a stringed instrument similar to the modern zither, appeared in various shapes; the strings were plucked by the fingers. It was comparatively simple to adjust a primitive keyboard to the psaltery and in turn to supply each key with a plucking mechanism.

During the seventeenth and eighteenth centuries, in addition to its virtuoso role, the harpsichord was indispensable as a sustaining and accompanying medium: it was heard in church, lending its support to the choir; it was seen in the salon, where it accompanied sonatas and played an important part in other chamber music; and it was found in the orchestra, as an integral part of the orchestral apparatus.

The harpsichord varies from six to eight feet in length and ideally has two keyboards, each with about five octaves (Ill. 5:17). There are three or four

Ill. 5:17. ***Harpsichord. Courtesy of Hugo Worch Collection, The Smithsonian Institution.***

sets of strings sounded by means of small quills or leather plectra hinged on wooden jacks. Each set of strings varies in pitch and tone quality. These strings are operated by means of stops placed above the keyboard or by foot pedals. Frequently there is a lute stop, a device that dampens individual strings by means of small pieces of cloth or felt in imitation of the lute sound. Since crescendo and diminuendo are impossible on this plucked instrument, different timbres have to be produced by the sets of strings.

The *spinet* is a modest harpsichord, usually in a triangular or pentagonal case, with its strings strung at acute angles to the keyboard. The *virginal* (sometimes called "virginals" or "pair of virginals") became the preferred instrument in England during the sixteenth and early seventeenth centuries; during the latter century it was replaced by the larger continental-type harpsichord. A small rectangular instrument, the virginal has only one set of strings, strung parallel to the keyboard.

Pianoforte

The large harpsichord had sparkling clarity but lacked expressive power. As keyboard manufacturers learned how to make instruments capable of greater nuance, the harpsichord began to lose favor. In 1709 the Florentine instrument maker Bartolomeo Cristofori realized a significant objective—a harpsichord with hammers. The Italian gave his instrument the shape of a large harpsichord and called it a *gravicembalo col piano e forte* (harpsichord with soft and loud). So began the era of the piano.

The new harpsichord with hammers was baptized in Germany at the court of Saxony, where two instruments made by Gottfried Silbermann in 1726 came to the attention of Johann Sebastian Bach. Aided by Bach's helpful advice, Silbermann in 1745 built the first pianoforte with perfectly equal sonority along its range of keys. Another builder, Silbermann's apprentice Johann Stein, converted Mozart to the piano through his superior instruments.

In the nineteenth century, improvements continued to be made. In 1821 Pierre Érard secured a patent for an action (key and hammer) mechanism that had been perfected by his uncle Sébastien, founder of the Érard piano firm. This mechanism made possible quicker, subtler note repetitions, thus encouraging virtuoso displays by such agile performers as Sigismund Thalberg and Franz Liszt. The Érard invention transformed finger technique and revealed unheard-of possibilities of execution.

The modern piano developed between 1830 and 1850, and by 1890 the instrument had attained its present form in all important particulars. Piano manufacturers mass-produced the two basic models, upright and grand, a tradition that has continued to the present day.

Despite various sizes and shapes, all pianos have characteristics in common. The keyboard has a normal compass of 88 keys—seven octaves plus three keys. The penetrating sonority results from the fact that each key usually strikes three unison strings (sometimes two are used for the lower bass tones). The striking is achieved by felt-tipped hammers attached to the key mechanism. After the string has been struck and the key released, a felt damper is automatically pushed against the string, stopping the vibrations and extinguishing the sound.

There are two foot pedals (Ill. 5:18). When the one to the right (*sostenuto*) is depressed, all the dampers rise and remain disengaged from the strings,

Ill. 5:18. ***Concert grand piano. Courtesy of Baldwin Piano & Organ Company.***

thus permitting sustained sounds (until the vibrations cease). The *una corda* pedal, located on the left, shifts the hammer mechanism slightly so that only two strings will be struck. The resultant sounds are somewhat softer. If a third (middle) pedal is present (mostly in American instruments), it is the prolongation pedal, making it possible to sustain a given chord but not the strings struck subsequently.

Organ

The *pipe organ* (Ill. 5:19) is actually a combination of many instrumental sounds and tone colors. As a mechanism, an organ consists of numerous rows of graduated pipes (like large whistles) connected to a wind-chest that supplies air for the pipes. Bellows driven by an electric motor keep an even air flow in the wind-chest.

A complete set of pipes having one particular timbre, with one pipe assigned to each note on the keyboard, is called a *rank.* A *slider* at each rank prevents all ranks from sounding at once. Each slider has a series of holes that match the mouths of the pipes. When the sliders are pushed in, the holes no longer coincide with the mouths, and the pipes are "stopped." Each individual slider is controlled by a *stop,* so the term "stop" is sometimes used to designate a rank of pipes. Stops are located in close proximity to the keyboard, either at the side or along the top of the keys.

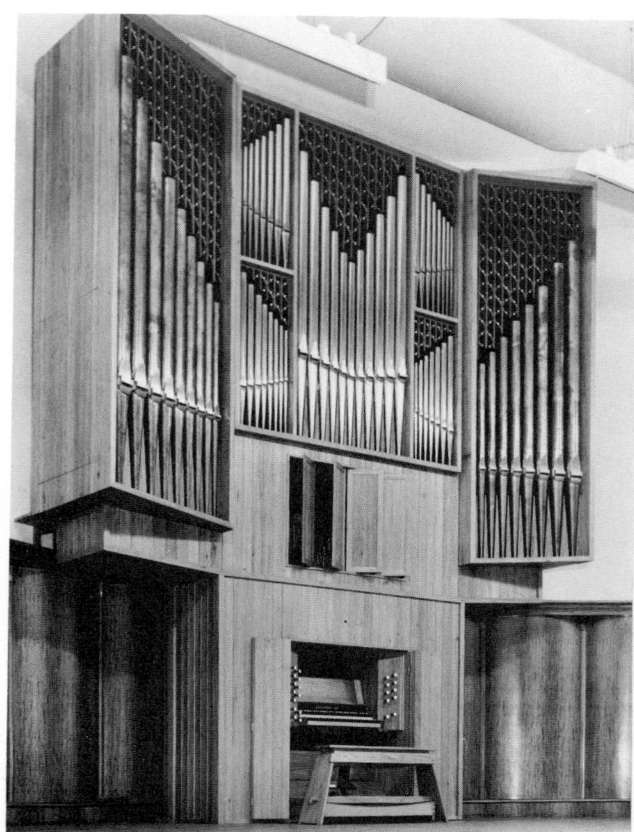

Ill. 5:19. ***Pipe organ. Leiden, Stadsgehoorzaal. Courtesy of Flentrop Orgelbouw.***

Within the organ chambers (the enclosures housing the pipes), the ranks are traditionally located in groups or divisions, each with a definite name and function, each controlled from its own keyboard, or *manual*. Organs usually have from two to four manuals, depending on the size of the instrument.

In addition to ranks sounded by the various keyboard manuals, there is a foot keyboard controlling a *pedal organ*. The pedal organ contains pipe ranks whose normal pitch is an octave below that of the keyboard manuals.

Pipe-organ history goes back to about the second century B.C., when Ktesibios of Alexandria fashioned a water organ, known as the *hydraulos* because water was used as weight to create the constant wind pressure necessary to make the pipes speak evenly. Since the organ was initially a secular instrument, used for public entertainment at games, spectacles, and gladiator fights, early Christians rejected it as a pagan instrument. Churches in the East still do not use organs, but Western churches accepted them about the eighth century.

By the sixteenth century, the organ had evolved into a complex mechanism containing manuals, stops, and a wide choice of tone colors. In the eighteenth century the so-called *Bach* or *classic* organ came into existence: it had at least two keyboards, a pedal board, about 30 stops, and an elegant, mellow tone.

From 1750 to about 1900 organ builders experimented to get more expression and grandeur from their instruments. Unfortunately, the Romantic period regarded the organ as an orchestra and exploited it as such by adding overpoweringly dramatic and sentimental ranks of pipes. Today, however, builders concentrate on re-creating the tasteful Bach organ.

THE ORCHESTRA

Many instruments discussed in this chapter find their most congenial role in the orchestra, and because the orchestra has undergone many transformations since its beginnings, we should briefly discuss this development.

The word *orchestra* means "dancing place" in Greek. It applied to that part of the ancient Greek theatre between the stage and the audience: the semicircular area where the chorus performed. The term was applied, during the early seventeenth century, to the instrumental ensembles that accompanied Italian operas; the name distinguished these ensembles from the more intimate chamber groups. The first orchestras called for several players for each part. Orchestral structure changed as obsolete instruments were replaced by new ones, a process that continued into the nineteenth century.

The early-eighteenth-century orchestra was comparatively modest: a

Ill. 5:20. ***Symphony orchestra. Courtesy of Los Angeles Philharmonic Orchestra.***

small body of strings, a few wind instruments, and kettledrums, all held together by a harpsichord (or organ), which played chords. The art of orchestration[2] as we now know it had not yet reached maturity.

The orchestra expanded during the Classic period (*c.*1750–1800): the string choir enlarged, and the wind instruments appeared in pairs. In the nineteenth century an additional complement of wind and percussion instruments necessitated more strings. So the story of the orchestra shows continual growth—in size and in types of instruments. Present-day orchestras vary in their makeup. An average large orchestra—capable of playing almost any orchestral composition—might consist of the following instruments:

Woodwinds: 1 piccolo; 3 flutes; 3 oboes plus an English horn; 2 clarinets in *B*♭, 1 in *E*♭, and 1 bass clarinet; 2 or 3 bassoons and 1 double bassoon.

[2] *Orchestration* may be defined as the art of writing for the orchestra. It is principally concerned with the color, technical capacity, and effective range of orchestral instruments—how they can be most effectively combined with one another and how the score should be designed.

Brass: 4 to 8 horns; 3 to 5 trumpets; 3 trombones and 1 bass trombone; 1 tuba.

Percussion (one timpani player and three percussion players constitute the personnel of this section): 4 or 5 timpani; 1 side drum; 1 triangle; 1 pair of cymbals; 1 bass drum.

Strings: 16 first violins; 16 second violins; 12 violas; 12 cellos; 8 double basses; 2 harps.

The conductor decides where all the players forming a modern symphony orchestra are to be located on the stage. Most conductors have decided that the

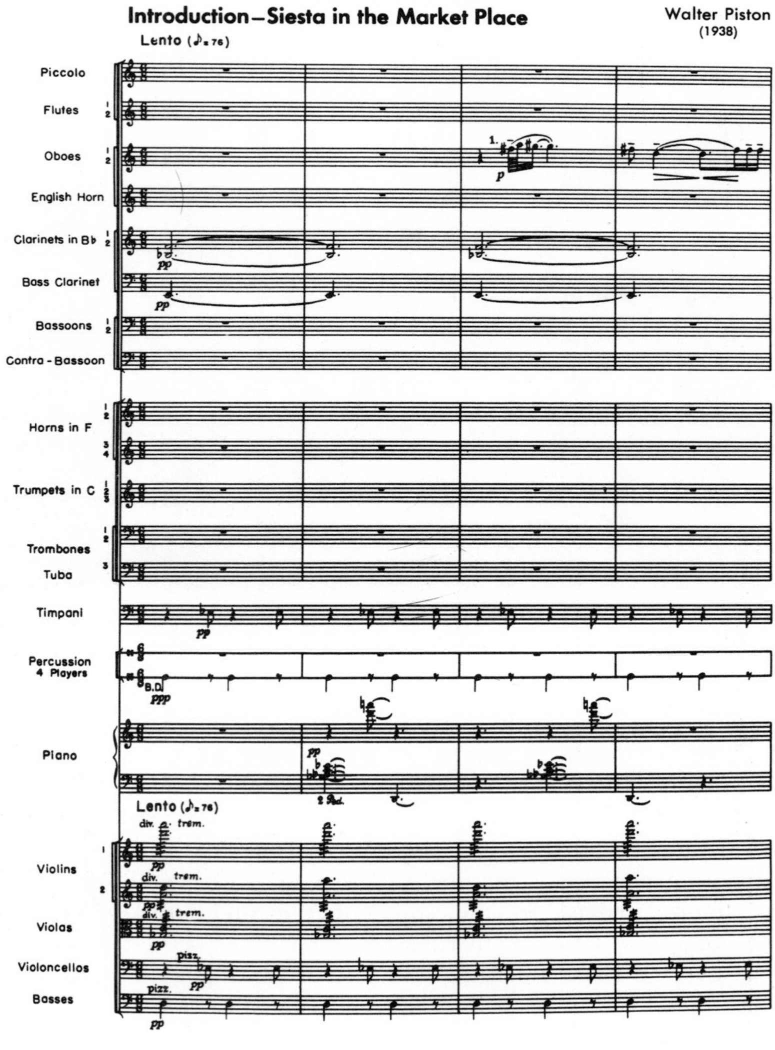

Ill. 5:21. ***Page of orchestral score. © Copyright 1938 by Associated Music Publishers, Inc., New York. Used by permission.***

best arrangement places the strings nearest him (Ill. 5:20). The first violins sit on his left; beside them are the second violins. Violas and cellos sit to the right (and center right) of the conductor. Double basses are located just behind the cellos. The wind section sits behind the strings—woodwinds to the left, brass to the right. Percussion instruments line up at the rear of the orchestra.

In eighteenth-century opera, the conductor led the orchestra from a harpsichord, on which he played the recitatives. Orchestras presenting symphonic music were often led by the principal first violinist. Today we are reminded of this fact by the title given to this violinist: in England he is called the "leader" and in America the "concertmaster." The baton (a short stick used by conductors to indicate tempo, expression, etc.) was introduced in 1820; since then the conductor has controlled the orchestra from his present position (see Ill. 5:20).

A conductor literally "plays" the orchestra as he stands before the musicians, using hand and body motions to coordinate all instruments and achieve a collective interpretation of the music. It is he who must exercise control over technical and artistic aspects of the work being played. He has to be a superb musician. His beat—with or without baton—must be reliable and distinct. He needs a good musical ear to discover and correct any faults during rehearsal. He must have a working knowledge of all instruments and a skill in reading and absorbing orchestral scores (Ill. 5:21). He must understand all musical styles, and if he is to persuade the musicians to accept his interpretations he needs a strong individuality and personal magnetism.

The only way to learn conducting is to conduct, which requires an apprenticeship period under an established conductor. The background, knowledge, and practice necessary to a good conductor obviously requires long years of hard work. The efforts expended, however, are well repaid, for a good conductor has the respect of all musicians as well as the admiration and appreciation of his audience.

FOR DISCUSSION AND ASSIGNMENT

1. Listen to some of the arias listed in this chapter until you can differentiate a soprano from a contralto, a tenor from a baritone.
2. Listen to the opening section of the third movement from Berlioz' *Symphonie fantastique*. Notice the differences and similarities in the oboe and English horn.
3. Look at the score reproduced in Ill. 5:21. Listen to the music and try to follow the movement of the different instruments.
4. Most music was composed with certain instruments in mind. Listen to a dance or two from a Bach harpsichord suite. Then listen to the same music on the piano. Do you find it equally effective?

FOR FURTHER READING

Baines, Anthony, ed. *Musical Instruments Through the Ages*. Baltimore, Md.: Penguin Books, 1961. A Pelican PB. Essays on instruments and instrumental families compose this valuable book, to which sixteen specialists have contributed. It is doubtlessly the most complete and readable handbook of musical instruments in existence.

Geiringer, Karl. *Musical Instruments.* New York: Oxford University Press, 1945. Dr. Geiringer's book proceeds within a historical framework. He discusses the development of various instruments through the centuries.

Sachs, Curt. *The History of Musical Instruments.* New York: W. W. Norton & Co., Inc., 1940. This book remains one of the most valuable—and readable—surveys on musical instruments, their construction, and their history.

The Aesthetics of Music 6

For beauty being the best of all we know
Sums up the unsearchable and secret aims
Of Nature.

ROBERT BRIDGES
The Growth of Love

Throughout the rest of this book—as a matter of fact throughout your entire listening experience—you will have to face some persistent, sometimes aggravating questions that properly should be introduced now. What makes music great? Why does one piece of music survive for centuries and another fade away within months? Why is one composer's music better than another's? How do you listen to a musical composition? Just *what* do you listen for? Can you organize a plan of approach?

Obviously these questions are interdependent. You can never discover what it is that makes music great or what its value is unless you know how to listen. And you cannot undertake the listening process without first realizing that while some musical standards have been set by tradition, personal taste and judgment will always be important factors.

AESTHETICS

The word *aesthetics* can be variously interpreted. Merriam-Webster defines it as "the branch of philosophy dealing with the beautiful, chiefly with respect to theories of its essential character, tests by which it may be judged, and its relation to the human mind; also, the branch of psychology treating of the sensations and emotions evoked by the fine arts and belle-lettres."

Aesthetics thus encompasses philosophy *and* psychology, and its two-sided character becomes especially significant in music. Willi Apel recognizes this fact when he succinctly defines musical aesthetics as "the study of the relationships of music to the human senses and intellect."[1]

Professional musical aestheticians have evolved two theories about mu-

[1] Willi Apel, *Harvard Dictionary of Music* (Cambridge, Mass.: Harvard University Press, 1944), p. 17. Reprinted by permission.

sic's inherent nature. The *autonomist* school maintains that music is a self-sufficient realm of sounds that have no meaning beyond their own intrinsic worth. The *heteronomous* partisans feel that music is a language of specific emotions, one that can be used to refer to and to describe anything.

Many who have lived with music for a long while agree with the philosopher Schopenhauer:

> Music stands quite alone. It is cut off from all the other arts. It does not express this or that particular and definite joy, this or that sorrow, or pain, or horror, or delight, or merriment, or peace of mind: but joy, sorrow, pain, horror, delight, merriment, peace of mind *themselves,* to a certain extent in the abstract, their essential nature, without accessories, and therefore without their motives. Yet it enables us to grasp and share them in their full quintessence.[2]

Naturally the musical notes written on paper do not in themselves "contain emotion." It is when the notes are translated into sound that they in some intangible way recall familiar emotions. The musical psychologist Carroll C. Pratt explains this experience:

> Each sense department has its own unique material. The material of the bodily senses is the stuff of emotion. The forms of tonal material, especially when designed by great artists, are so similar to those of the bodily senses that they are best described by using the same words that are also used to describe emotions. Tonal forms therefore seem to have emotional qualities, but these qualities must not be confused with real emotions. The latter exist only in the bodily senses.[3]

These quotes expose some of the issues raised—although not resolved—by musical aesthetics, so let us now briefly consider more practical questions. What constitutes greatness? Why is one composer considered finer than another? Any reasonable answer in either case depends on each individual's concept of value and taste.

EVALUATING THE LISTENING EXPERIENCE

Every cultural era sets its own style and each composer must be judged according to the standards of his own period. Eventually his intrinsic worth and ultimate contribution to music must also be evaluated. Has he added to man's artistic achievements or has he simply imitated the style of a superior talent?

Taste changes. Although we judge the music of our times according to the standards of our cultural era, remember that we do not judge music from past centuries with the same set of standards used by its contemporary critics. If we did, we should probably now be listening to the music of Graupner and Buononcini instead of Bach and Handel. Graupner was highly esteemed during the late Baroque era; now we feel that Bach is the most representative composer of that period.

Every composer desires artistic greatness. Repeated performances of a work achieve permanent recognition for its composer. A composer can pass from

[2] Arthur Schopenhauer, *The World as Will and Idea,* translated by R. B. Haldane and J. Kemp (London: Routledge and Kegan Paul Limited, 1948), Vol. 1, p. 338.

[3] Carroll C. Pratt, *Music as the Language of Emotion* (Washington, D.C.: The Library of Congress, 1952), pp. 24–25.

artistic greatness to historical greatness if his talent is acknowledged but his music is never performed. Once in this category, it is hard for a composer to regain an audience—unless some champion comes along to spur a revival of his music.

Why does some music wear for centuries, while other works die within a short time? For an obvious and perhaps oversimplified answer, compare a work like the *Air* from Bach's *Orchestral Suite in D Major* with a popular song current some 30 years ago (such as "Amapola"). Both are about the same length. One is enjoyed with undiminished enthusiasm. The other has faded away. Why?

To begin with, no listener was ever obliged to exert himself in order to grasp the *content* of a popular song. Its attractiveness is obvious and it can be a flash success from the start. It has no hidden meaning or message. In five minutes one knows it for what it is, and repeated hearings can make one tired of it.

But Bach's *Air!* It is original, and the freshness of its melodic curve stamps it forever as unique. Although the *Air* is perfectly simple, it is rich in nobility, spiritual content, and formal perfection. The *Air* is beautiful, whereas the popular song was merely pretty.

What makes anything beautiful? That argument will never be resolved, but the following brief table might help the listener to formulate his ideas about the music he hears.

MUSICAL QUALITIES

POSITIVE	*NEGATIVE*
Subtlety	Obviousness
Reserve	Exaggeration
Variety	Monotony
Originality	Triteness
Dignity	Flamboyance
Balance between intellectual and emotional elements	Imbalance between intellectual and emotional elements
Beauty	Prettiness
Sentiment	Sentimentality
Consistency	Inconsistency
Skill in formal design	Slipshod formal qualities
Simplicity and clarity	Pretentiousness

There are still the persistent questions about listening procedure. What do you listen for? If you are an untrained listener, you cannot be aware of all that is taking place musically. However, you can develop the ability to hear and listen for many things at once. To start, concentrate on two essentials: melody and rhythm; then with repeated hearings, fill in more detail. The following summary of questions may help you to organize your approach to listening.

Melody: Is it simple or ornate? Is it a brief melody with only a few phrases, or is there a feeling of continuous melody? Does it create interest and, if so, how? What instruments play the melody? Is it heard again and again, or is it varied or replaced by another melody? Is it a self-contained melody, or does its effect depend on harmony? If it is accompanied by words, do words and melody seem compatible?

Rhythm: Is it a consistent rhythm? What is the meter? Is the rhythm a vital element in the composition? Is it a driving, energetic rhythm, or is it unobtrusive and scarcely noticeable? Do you notice any rhythmic motives that are used throughout? Is just one rhythm in evidence, or are there two or more juxtaposed rhythms?

Harmony: Is the composition harmonically oriented, or does the music sound predominantly contrapuntal? Or do the two styles seem to be equally coexistent? Is the harmony itself interesting, or is it merely accompaniment for a melody? Is the harmony simply stated in chords, or is it complex? Does the harmony seem to belong to the melody?

Counterpoint and Polyphony: Is the work for voices and instruments or for just one of these? How many voice parts do you hear? Is there just one person to a part? Do you hear one voice or part imitating another part? In what language is the music sung? Is the music sacred or secular? Does the music enhance or attempt to interpret the words?

Tone Color: Is the composition for full orchestra or for a smaller instrumental group? What instruments are assigned solo passages? Does the composer seem to highlight some instruments? Does he feature particular voices or instrumental families from time to time? Can you recognize certain instrumental effects, such as pizzicato?

Form: In many cases the composition's title—symphony, prelude, symphonic variations, scherzo, fugue—gives a clue to the music's formal design. In addition to considering the suggestions above, you should listen for musical motives and be on the lookout for a characteristic musical phrase. Is it repeated numerous times in different guises? Is it heard several times intact but separated by new musical material? Is it initially developed a little and then superseded by another characteristic melodic phrase? It will take you time to learn how to recognize form. Other factors, such as the era and the composer's style, further complicate the picture. However, an active listener can learn to follow the composer as he lays out his design and creates variety within unity.

FOR DISCUSSION AND ASSIGNMENT

1. For many people, a composition's worth depends on its being beautiful. Do you think music that elicits other descriptions—shocking, ugly, hysterical, unmelodic—can have validity and meaning?
2. Listen to recordings of a folk song, some jazz, and a slow movement from a Tchaikovsky symphony. Which has the greatest direct emotional appeal? Can you explain why?
3. Debussy's *La Mer* supposedly evokes impressions of the sea. Listen to a portion of it. What do you think? To which school do you belong at present—autonomist or heteronomous—and why?

FOR FURTHER READING

Copland, Aaron. *What to Listen for in Music,* Revised Edition. New York: The New American Library, 1963. A Mentor PB. Copland's small book has become a classic of its kind. The chapters on "How We Listen" and "The Creative Process in Music" are most relevant to our discussion here.

Hanslick, Eduard. *The Beautiful in Music,* translated by G. Cohen and M. Weitz. Indianapolis, Ind.: The Bobbs-Merrill Co., Inc., 1957. A Library of Liberal Arts PB. This influential nineteenth-century music critic discusses his views on music as an expressive art. The book is important in the field of musical aesthetics.

Pratt, Carroll C. *Music as the Language of Emotion.* Washington, D.C.: The Library of Congress, 1952. A published paperbound lecture. The author, a psychologist, gives his profession's concept of music's basic qualities. The brief essay is readable and interesting.

Schopenhauer, Arthur. *The World as Will and Idea,* translated by R. B. Haldane and J. Kemp. New York: Humanities Press, Inc., 1948. 3 Vols. In the fourth book of this treatise, the eminent philosopher includes a superb essay, "The Object of Art." As part of this essay, he offers his ideas on the essence of music.

Part Two

Music's Historical Development

The Legacy of Greece and Rome

7

Heard melodies are sweet, but those unheard
Are sweeter.

JOHN KEATS
Ode on a Grecian Urn

Music has been essential to man since the very earliest times. If we wished to start at the beginning, we could go back to prehistoric eras and the primitive musical scenes drawn on cave walls—indications that man has always used music for his rituals. Or we might begin some 4,000 years ago with the ancient peoples of Egypt or Sumer, for we know that they had simple instruments to accompany their singing and dancing. But although we know that music existed long ago, we have discovered very little about what kind of music it was.

Since our approach to musical understanding is oriented principally toward Western music, the most logical historical starting point is ancient Greece, the superior civilization that linked the East to the West and left its unmistakable imprint on the art and intellect of the Western world.

The splendor of Greece is visible in her cultural, social, and political history. In all her achievements, several common denominators of Greek thought stand out. There is, for instance, *humanism*, which studies man and his environment and views life as something to be enjoyed here and now. This theme dominated Greek thought and action. In political and social life, democratic institutions—existing for the benefit of *man*—maintained a balance between aristocratic conservatism, with its austerity, stylization, and restraint, and liberal individualism, which favored emotionalism and naturalism. Sculptors brought the gods to earth and gave them idealized human form. The human body itself took on new dignity through movement in the dance and musical drama.

Rationalism was another significant element in Greek doctrine. Balance, clarity, and logic were considered requisites for a well-ordered mind. This concept particularly influenced the sciences and arts.

Both physical and spiritual beauty were bound to the moral order. *Idealism* prevailed, for the Greeks felt that if a subjective balance between body and spirit could harmonize with the objective order of the real and ideal worlds, the results would enable man to achieve moral grandeur. The Greek temples, the nobly proportioned sculptured figures, the heroes of epic poetry and drama, and the orderly relationship of the melodic intervals in music—all are embodiments of this ideal.

THE MUSIC OF ANCIENT GREECE

The Archaic Period

The earliest known references to Greek music appear in the Homeric poems, which are thought to have been composed about the ninth century B.C. In these epics the central character is the minstrel, always ready to entertain with a traditional ballad or one improvised on the spot to suit the occasion. Minstrels were responsible for transmitting orally the great epic poems and often assisted patriotic and government causes through their singing. Even Greek heroes turned minstrel when the occasion warranted it. The *Odyssey* tells us that Odysseus sometimes took the lyre in hand to sing a rhapsody about his own adventures, and many passages in the *Odyssey* refer to music.

> Silent all
> They sat and listened to the illustrious bard
> Who sang of the calamitous return
> Of the Greek host from Troy, at the command
> Of Pallas.[1]

The later (eighth century B.C.) poet Hesiod reveals more details about musical activities. The *Shield of Hercules* describes a Greek festive procession engraved on Hercules' shield.

> There men in dances and in festive joys
> Held revelry. Some on the smooth-wheel'd car
> A virgin bride conducted: then burst forth
> Aloud the marriage-song; and far and wide
> Long splendours flash'd from many a quivering torch
> Borne in the hands of slaves. Gay-blooming girls
> Preceded, and the dancers follow'd blithe:
> These, with shrill pipe indenting the soft lip,
> Breath'd melody, while broken echoes thrill'd
> Around them; to the lyre with flying touch
> Those led the love-enkindling dance. A group
> Of youths was elsewhere imag'd, to the flute
> Disporting: some in dances and in song.[2]

In the sixth century B.C., a philosopher-mathematician named Pythagoras applied his mathematical knowledge to music. By experimenting he was able to formulate and define the mathematical laws governing vibrating strings. Pythagoras's belief in music as an aesthetic is equally important in music history. This unusual man urged his followers to sing a hymn before retiring in order to compose their spirits and prepare them for rest.

[1] *The Odyssey of Homer,* translated by William Cullen Bryant (Boston: Houghton Mifflin Company, 1871), Book 1, p. 15.

[2] *The Works of Hesiod, Callimachus and Theognis,* translated by the Rev. J. Banks (London: George Bell & Sons, 1882), p. 330.

The Golden Age

A dozen musical fragments, some literary and philosophical commentaries, and a few theoretical treatises are all we have today for reconstructing ancient Greek music. But we have a far richer legacy, better than any melodic repertoire: an aesthetic (the idea that music is necessary and beneficial) and a technique (a system of scales), both developed to a high degree during Greece's Golden Age, in the fifth century B.C. When Western civilization many centuries later needed a strong foundation upon which to base its music, it discovered that foundation in this period of Greece's civilization, where there had been a concept of music's dignity and a logical approach to music theory. We go back to Greece even for our word "music," which at that time meant any art or science protected by the muses, those nine agreeable divinities who presided over the nobler activities of the Greek mind.

Music's close affiliation with poetry, drama, and literature is discussed in Plato's *Republic,* where the philosopher maintains that poetry becomes less effective when deprived of music.

> So mighty is the spell that these adornments naturally exercise; though when they are stripped bare of their musical colouring and taken by themselves, I think you know what sort of a showing these sayings of the poets make. For you, I believe, have observed them. . . . Do they not resemble the faces of adolescents, young but not really beautiful, when the bloom of youth abandons them?[3]

The Golden Age dramatists Aeschylus, Sophocles, and Euripides all made music an essential component in their tragedies. Music played a natural part in these dramas, since Greek tragedy originated in the dithyrambic choral hymn sung in honor of the god Dionysus. This choral hymn was not like our modern choral part singing, for the singing or chanting was done in unison. From the early performances given by one leader and a chorus—presenting song, dance, and pantomime—tragedy eventually developed into the polished art form of the master dramatists. Tragedy, therefore, was partly a musical experience: dialogue was delivered in a musical voice and commentary was sung by a chorus. Unfortunately the sole surviving relic of Greek music from the fifth century is the first stationary song of the chorus (*stasimon*) from Euripides' tragedy *Orestes,* written on papyrus and fragmentary.

Singers were accompanied by a *kithara,* not in our sense of accompaniment but mostly to strengthen the melodic line. Because the kithara was the instrument of Apollo, it was considered the national instrument, representing the Greek ideal of harmonious moderation. It consisted of a wooden sound box, a U-shaped frame, and a crossbar. A number of strings—from five to eleven—were stretched between the sound box and the crossbar.

From earliest times the *lyre* (Ill. 7:1) has been associated with Greek music. Smaller than the kithara, a lyre usually has a sound box made from a turtle shell. Lyric poetry to the Greeks meant verse sung to lyre accompaniment.

The *aulos,* the favorite wind instrument in ancient Greece, was an oboe-like instrument (sometimes incorrectly called a flute) having a double reed and from four to fourteen holes. The pictorial evidence extant shows that the

[3] Plato, *The Republic,* II, translated by Paul Shorey (London: William Heinemann Ltd., 1930), Vol. 1, p. 443.

Ill. 7:1. ***Boy playing a lyre. End of three-sided marble relief from Greek altar (the "Ludovisi Throne"), 5th century* B.C. *Courtesy of Museum of Fine Arts, Boston, Henry L. Pierce Residuary Fund.***

aulos consisted of two pipes (Ill. 7:2); perhaps the larger pipe provided a few tones missing from the other. Some authorities think that the second pipe served as a drone, producing a single persistent tone.

Aeschylus, Sophocles, and Euripides themselves wrote the music for their dramas, but later dramatists were neither as ambitious nor as interested in music's significance in drama. In the end it was music theory, the Greeks' technical contributions to music, that proved durable.

The origins of our modern scale system can be traced to the Greeks, who devised various tetrachords (see p. 25) and joined them together to form modes (scales) named Dorian, Phrygian, and Lydian, after different Greek provinces. They even developed a quite readable musical notation. However, all the Greek manuscripts have come down to us through the hands of medieval scribes, who omitted the musical notation of the earlier copies because they could not comprehend it.

Music's influence in Greece also proved important to later civilizations reflecting that culture. Medieval teachers leaned heavily on Greek musical theory. Baroque opera was premised on a reconstitution of Greek drama. In the eighteenth century Gluck used Aristotle's theories as a basis for his opera reforms; in the nineteenth century Richard Wagner borrowed from the Greek aesthetic for his approach to opera. And our musical vocabulary still contains words of Greek origin, including "rhythm," "melody," "harmony," and "symphony."

Ill. 7:2. *Girl playing the aulos. From Greek altar (the "Ludovisi Throne"), 5th century* B.C. *Courtesy of Alinari-Art Reference Bureau.*

The Hellenistic Period

The two centuries between the death of Alexander the Great (323 B.C.) and the Roman conquest of Greece (146 B.C.) are commonly referred to as the Hellenistic era. During this time, music remained an integral part of education: children received musical instruction and sang in festive processions and on patriotic occasions. But the attitude toward music began to change in the Hellenistic era. In an earlier Athens, both music and gymnastics had been performed by free citizens as a public duty and privilege as well as for pleasure. Now athletics, some dances, and other entertainment were done by professionals. Associations called Dionysian *technites*—like guilds or unions—arose with stage managers, actors, mimes, dancers, and musicians included in their membership.

At Tralles in Phrygia, archeologists have unearthed a tombstone, dating from the second century B.C., incised with four lines of poetry with accompanying musical notation. It is an epitaph offered by a certain Seikolos for his wife Euterpe (Ex. 7:1).

Ex. 7:1. ***Song of Seikolos***

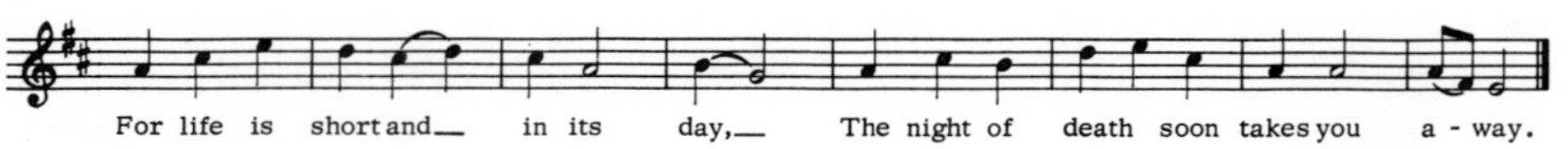

The song is a type known as a *skolion,* or drinking song, a kind of ditty sung in turn by banquet guests during toasts or libations. Seikolos' *skolion* is in Phrygian mode: its range spans the octave *E* to *E,* and the tonal center is *A*.

A few other examples of Hellenistic music exist, notably two attractive Delphic Hymns to Apollo dating from around 138 B.C. But these few fragments cannot furnish us with even a vague idea of the music that must have been played and sung in Greece and elsewhere in the ancient world.

THE MUSIC OF ANCIENT ROME

Others will mould their bronzes to breathe
with a tenderer grace,
Draw, I doubt not, from marble a vivid life
to the face,
Plead at the bar more deftly, with sapient
words of the wise,
Trace heaven's courses and changes, predict
us stars to arise.
Thine, O Roman, remember, to reign over
every race!
These be thine arts, thy glories, the ways of
peace to proclaim,
Mercy to show to the fallen, the proud with
battle to tame.[4]

[4] *Virgil in English Verse,* translated by Sir Charles Bowen (London: J. Murray, 1887), lines 847–853.

With these lines Virgil (70--19 B.C.) summed up the Roman's inborn talent to conquer and rule, but the great poet underestimated the effect Roman civilization was to produce on later cultures. It is true that from its inception as a small settlement on the banks of the Tiber, Rome expanded brilliantly until, as Virgil ordained, she did reign over nearly every race. But when the mighty Empire crumbled, the Roman way of life endured. The practical, disciplined, order-loving Romans bequeathed to the Western world a rich, lasting heritage created not only by what they adopted from the Greeks but by their own nobility.

If any one trait applies to the Romans in all that they thought and did, it is that of *organization.* Organization accounts for Rome's success in conquest and her ability to maintain order and well-being within the subjugated countries. The result was a unified civilization. A religion focused on emperor worship served to alleviate temporarily man's natural craving for spiritual sustenance. A unified body of laws assured a higher degree of justice to a greater number of individuals. Organized public work projects—roads, ports, aqueducts—increased the efficiency and strengthened the potential of the Empire. To accommodate large crowds, the Romans constructed huge public buildings. This same desire to accommodate the masses led to a broader, and frequently less lofty, interpretation of the arts. As a result, art deteriorated into showy entertainment.

The Roman's inborn genius for organization received strong support from his pronounced tendency toward *utilitarianism.* Maintaining the Empire at its highest capacity gave the greatest good to the most people. Thus building an aqueduct was more important than building a luxurious palace. Sculpture, an impractical art, served the state by recording in solid form the virtues and heroic deeds of the emperor. Virgil's masterpiece the *Aeneid* performed a similar role in literature.

Roman utilitarianism permitted a wide range of taste in art, a practical step to entertain the masses, and it brought about a general artistic decline. Athenaeus, a Greek writing in Rome about 200 A.D., reminisces that "in olden times the feeling for nobility was always maintained in the art of music, and all its elements skillfully retained the orderly beauty appropriate to them." But he regretfully admits, "Today, however, people take up music in a haphazard and irrational manner . . . The musicians of our day set as the goal of their art success with their audiences."[5]

Music thus had a popular place in daily life during the Roman Empire. Guests at extravagant banquets were entertained with music, pantomime, and Atellan farces (Ill. 7:3) ; at funerals, choruses of weepers joined the sound of oboe and brass in songs of lamentation; at sacrificial ceremonies, oboes accompanied the ritual. Latin literature contains references to popular songs as well as evidence that the Romans were somewhat familiar with music and considered it part of education, at least for the upper classes.

Liking instrumental music, the Romans adopted Greek instruments. The Greek aulos became the *tibia* in Rome. The kithara, the Greek national instrument, was treated less respectfully by the Romans: the kitharist maintained rhythm by beating out time loudly with his foot. Romans also had brass instruments (trumpet and horn types, such as their *tuba*—Ill. 7:4) , which were used for military purposes, but these did not resemble our modern brass instruments.

[5] Athenaeus, *The Deipnosophists,* translated by C. B. Gulick (Cambridge: Harvard University Press, 1937) . Loeb Classical Library, Vol. 6, p. 409. Reprinted by permission.

Ill. 7:3. *Comic scene. Mosaic from Pompeii. Museo Nazionale, Napoli. Courtesy of Alinari-Art Reference Bureau.*

Ill. 7:4. *Boy playing a tuba. Piazza Armerina.*

Despite this popular musical activity, Rome did not produce any serious musical texts or documented source materials. We have a few phrases gleaned from writers like Seneca, Petronius, Silius Italicus, and Quintilianus, but that is all, and the reasons for this lack are quite obvious. As with most of the arts and luxuries brought over from Greece, the Romans accepted Greek music and were little inclined to develop it further.

Music, which had been an integral part of early Greek drama, degenerated in the Roman theater. An overture on the tibia preceded the play, and there were usually instrumental interludes during the course of the performance; however, by the second century B.C., Roman authors no longer bothered to compose music, and the actors, too lazy to sing their songs, merely gesticulated while an extra singer sang the part.

The Romans deserve credit for having had music in their lives and for passing along the musical advances made by the Greeks, but they did not contribute any particular developments on their own. Perhaps one reason for this fact is that Roman musicians, especially during the Republic, were drawn from the lower classes, even from among slaves. In sharp contrast to the practice of the Greeks, who acknowledged music as an indispensable part of education and honored their musicians, the Romans treated their musicians indifferently.

With the advent of the Empire under Augustus (27 B.C.), Roman aristocracy paid more attention to music, perhaps because it became an imperial pastime. Nero (37–68 A.D.) was a musician, the depraved emperor Caligula (12–41 A.D.) showered honors upon his favorite singer, and Vitellius (15–69 A.D.) and Domitian (51–96 A.D.) both encouraged musicians. Even with the patronage of the emperors, the music heard at public performances in imperial Rome must have been notable for its quantity rather than quality. Seneca (*c.*54 B.C.–39 A.D.) describes what must have been a usual—but to us extraordinary—performance.

"In our present-day exhibitions we have a larger number of singers than there used to be spectators in the theatres of old. All the aisles are filled with rows of singers; brass instruments surround the auditorium; the stage resounds with tibiae and instruments of every description."[6]

The Romans were satisfied with this superficiality in their music and either could not or would not acknowledge, as the Greeks had done, the full value of music in both education and pleasure. They overlooked music's spiritual potentialities and produced nothing concrete—at least nothing that has been discovered—to advance this art. It was left to the Middle Ages to rediscover and nurture the musical aesthetic.

FOR DISCUSSION AND ASSIGNMENT

1. Listen to Debussy's piano prelude *Danseuses de Delphes* (Delphic Dancers). What aspects of ancient Greece does he succeed in evoking, if any?
2. Poetry, dance, and music were closely allied in the Greek theater. Are any vestiges of this discernible on today's stage?
3. Read the sections on music in Plato's *Republic.* Write a short essay outlining his views on the essence of music and its purposes.

[6] Seneca, *Epistulae Morales,* translated by R. Gummere (London: William Heinemann, 1917), Vol. II, letter 84, p. 283.

FOR FURTHER READING

Barnes, Harry Elmer. *An Intellectual and Cultural History of the Western World,* Vol. I. New York: Dover Publications, Inc., 1965. PB. This 30-year-old standard reference work has been updated and made available again. Chapter IV deals with "Hellenic Thought and Culture," and Chapter V is titled "Roman Culture and Intellectual Life."

Butterfield, Roger. *Ancient Rome.* New York: The Odyssey Press, 1964. This small, inexpensive book offers a wealth of information about the subject and is filled with delightful illustrations.

Hamilton, Edith. *The Greek Way.* New York: W. W. Norton & Co., Inc., 1958. PB. Miss Hamilton's penetrating survey of Greek life, thought, literature, and philosophy has become a classic.

———. *The Roman Way.* New York: W. W. Norton & Co., Inc., 1960. PB. A fitting companion to *The Greek Way.*

Horizon Book of Ancient Greece. New York: American Heritage Publishing Co., Inc., 1965. A glorious anthology of essays and pictures; a book that should be in everyone's library.

Horizon Book of Ancient Rome. New York: American Heritage Publishing Co., Inc., 1966. Equally as authoritative and informative as the volume on Greece.

The Middle Ages 8

How greatly did I weep in Thy hymns and canticles, deeply moved by the voices of Thy sweet-speaking church! The voices flowed into mine ears, and the truth was poured forth into my heart, whence the agitation of my piety overflowed, and my tears ran over, and blessed was I therein.

ST. AUGUSTINE
Confessions

The Roman Empire attained its peak during the first and second centuries of the Christian era but, during the next two centuries, disintegrated under the strain of barbarian infiltration and inner corruption. By the fifth century it could no longer assimilate and control the new Germanic races settling within its borders; as the great Roman civilization faltered, small uncivilized nations arose, crude beginnings of national states in Gaul, Britain, Spain, even parts of Italy. Rome had been able to enforce law and order among her conquered barbarians, but after the Empire gave way these primitive tribes had neither the desire nor the ability to maintain that law and order. The Western world descended into a shadowy era, often referred to as the Dark Ages, when for about six centuries the new Germanic peoples were learning the rudiments of culture and government and fighting off neighboring tribes as well as invaders from across the seas.

However, the once accepted theory of a desolate, unfruitful Middle Ages followed by an instantaneous, glorious Renaissance is false. It must be agreed that at times progress seemed to stand still, blocked by rigid conservatism, fear, ignorance, or wars, but that was not true for ten whole centuries. The term "Middle Ages," with its deprecating implication, was the somewhat ungracious idea of the Renaissance humanists, who grandly decided to dismiss all that went on in the Western world between the decline of classical antiquity and their own fervent efforts to recapture classic ideals and revitalize the arts. We use the term Middle Ages here because it is familiar to most readers as pertaining to certain dates, not because of what it has unfortunately come to imply.

The Middle Ages, spanning many hundreds of years, had no single idea or set of ideas to provide unifying themes throughout those centuries. Each age had its own problems and settled them accordingly. Each age felt differently about intellectual and spiritual matters.

The early Middle Ages were stamped with a stern but necessary *authoritarianism.* In order to preserve her doctrines and spread the gospel effectively, the Church developed a hierarchy—Pope, Council, Patriarch, Metropolitan, Bishop —that bore more than a passing resemblance to Rome's ruling hierarchy of Emperor, Senate, Imperial Governor, Provincial Governor, and Civitas. Emperors struggling to revitalize the crumbling Empire ruled with the authoritarianism (and frequently the outward trappings) of oriental potentates.

As the age progressed, the strong hand of *feudalism* touched every aspect of medieval life. Literary works—like the *Song of Roland*—glorified war and the chivalric moral code. Troubadours and trouvères extolled the feudal themes of love, honor, and valor in their songs. Great art works retold history in a manner so pictorial that all could understand—as, for example, in the Bayeux tapestry, which narrates in color and thread the Norman conquest of England.

During the eleventh and early twelfth centuries—the age of the Romanesque cathedral—an increase in monasteries and abbeys brought about *asceticism.* Religious art became significantly symbolic. As symbols of spiritual intangibles, Romanesque sculptured figures are not humanly realistic; they appear to be consumed by some inner holy fire. Symbolic figures enliven medieval painting: legendary beasts dot highly imaginative landscapes as saints undergo unbelievable temptations and tortures.

Symbolism found a congenial medium in music. Highly ornate, florid lines of wordless ecstatic chant carried the believer beyond the confines of spoken prayer.

In the twelfth and thirteenth centuries, *dualism* of thought and action eventually activated a powerful Gothic synthesis. This dualism, vividly predicting the future Renaissance, exhibited its polarity in many ways. In politics a struggle persisted between Church and state. In social life aristocrats and clergy faced a formidable adversary, the rising bourgeoisie. In literature Latin fought to survive amid the growing vernacular tongues. Sculpture became the bible of the unlettered as well as a highly developed artistic medium.

Music created its own dualism, for the later Middle Ages produced a good quantity of secular music along with its church music. With the troubadours and trouvères, music for entertainment and pleasure stood on its own merits. From then on sacred and secular music each led a comparatively distinctive intrinsic existence.

THE MASS

Christianity dominated thought and disciplined art during the Middle Ages, and it was also the watchful guardian of music. As might be expected, musical influences from the Hellenistic-Oriental societies around the eastern Mediterranean had been incorporated into early Christian music. In particular, "the Church received from its Jewish ancestry a heritage that was to affect strongly the basic approach to its own liturgy . . . On the purely musical side, it is evident that many of the formulae and melodies used by the Jews were preserved as a basis for Christian practice; in many cases, the oldest chants of the Church have been matched against Jewish melodies, making clear the close connection of the two."[1]

[1] Albert Seay, *Music in the Medieval World* (Englewood Cliffs, N.J.: Prentice-Hall, Inc., 1965), p. 11.

To eliminate any association with the pagan past, early Church fathers banned all music connected with public spectacles and convivial celebrations, and even frowned on instrumental music. Yet while the Church rejected music purely for enjoyment or as an essential to education, it recognized music's beneficial adornment at the services offered medieval man for the comfort and salvation of his soul. The most important of these services is the Mass, which re-enacts the events of the last supper, when Jesus presented to His disciples the elements of bread and wine as part of Himself and as memorials of His impending crucifixion.

Prayers, petitions, and other texts composing a Mass are distributed into two basic categories: the *Ordinary,* referring to unchanging texts—Kyrie, Gloria, Credo, Sanctus-Benedictus, Agnus Dei; and the *Proper*—Introit, Gradual, Offertory, and other prayers—those texts that vary according to the religious emphasis of a particular day or feast.

Until recently the Mass has been celebrated in Latin except for the first text of the Ordinary, the Greek *Kyrie eleison.* To conform with the Roman Catholic program of liturgical reform, much of the Mass is now recited or sung in the vernacular.

A brief outline of the Ordinary of the Latin Mass, with an English translation, may be helpful. (The complete Mass was formulated over a period of many centuries; the date given for each section indicates its approximate appearance in the Western Mass) .

1. *Kyrie* (*c.*500 A.D.)

Kyrie eleison.	Lord, have mercy.
Kyrie eleison.	Lord, have mercy.
Kyrie eleison.	Lord, have mercy.
Christe eleison.	Christ, have mercy.
Christe eleison.	Christ, have mercy.
Christe eleison.	Christ, have mercy.
Kyrie eleison.	Lord, have mercy.
Kyrie eleison.	Lord, have mercy.
Kyrie eleison.	Lord, have mercy.

The Kyrie eleison consists of short petitions; the first to God, the second to Christ, then a return to the first. Such a threefold pattern emphasizes the Trinity—Father, Son, and Holy Spirit. Moreover, each petition is repeated three times. The text's ninefold structure *aaa bbb aaa* encourages equally logical musical settings based on repetition and variation of musical phrases.

2. *Gloria* (*c.*500 A.D.)

Gloria in excelsis Deo. Et in terra pax hominibus bonae voluntatis. Laudamus te. Benedicimus te. Adoramus te. Glorificamus te. Gratias agimus tibi propter magnam gloriam tuam. Domine Deus, Rex coelestis, Deus Pater omnipotens. Domine Fili unigenite Jesu Christe. Domine Deus, Agnus Dei, Filius Patris. Qui tollis peccata mundi, miserere nobis. Qui tollis peccata mundi, suscipe deprecationem nostram. Qui sedes ad dexteram Patris, miserere nobis. Quoniam tu solus Sanc-

Glory to God in the highest. And on earth peace to men of good will. We praise Thee. We bless Thee. We adore Thee. We glorify Thee. We give Thee thanks for Thy great glory. O Lord God, heavenly King, God the Father Almighty. O Lord Jesus Christ, the Only-begotten Son. O Lord God, Lamb of God, Son of the Father Who takest away the sins of the world, have mercy on us. Who takest away the sins of the world, receive our prayer. Who sittest at the right hand of the Father, tus. Tu solus Dominus. Tu solus Altissimus, Jesu Christe. Cum Sancto Spiritu in gloria Dei Patris. Amen.

have mercy on us. For Thou alone art holy. Thou alone art the Lord. Thou alone, O Jesus Christ, art most high. Together with the Holy Ghost in the glory of God the Father. Amen.

A song of praise is encountered in the *Gloria.* In setting this vast prose poem, composers achieved unity by using repeated and juxtaposed motives.

3. *Credo* (1014 A.D.)

Credo in unum Deum, Patrem omnipotentem, factorem coeli et terrae, visibilium omnium et invisibilium. Et in unum Dominum Jesum Christum, Filium Dei unigenitum. Et ex Patre natum ante omnia saecula. Deum de Deo, lumen de lumine, Deum verum de Deo vero. Genitum, non factum, consubstantialem Patri: per quem omnia facta sunt. Qui propter nos homines, et propter nostram salutem descendit de coelis. Et incarnatus est de Spiritu Sancto ex Maria Virgine: et homo factus est. Crucifixus etiam pro nobis; sub Pontio Pilato passus, et sepultus est. Et resurrexit tertia die, secundum Scripturas. Et ascendit in coelum: sedet ad dexteram Patris. Et iterum venturus est cum gloria judicare vivos, et mortuos: cujus regni non erit finis. Et in Spiritum Sanctum, Dominum et vivificantem: qui ex Patre Filioque procedit. Qui cum Patre, et Filio simul adoratur, et conglorificatur: qui locutus est per Prophetas. Et unam, sanctam, catholicam et apostolicam Ecclesiam. Confiteor unum baptisma in remissionem peccatorum. Et expecto resurrectionem mortuorum. Et vitam venturi saeculi. Amen.

I believe in one God, the Father Almighty, Maker of heaven and earth, and of all things visible and invisible. And in one Lord Jesus Christ, the Only-begotten Son of God. Born of the Father before all ages. God of God; Light of Light; true God of true God. Begotten not made; of one being with the Father; by Whom all things were made. Who for us men, and for our salvation, came down from heaven. And was made Flesh by the Holy Ghost of the Virgin Mary: and was made man. He was also crucified for us, suffered under Pontius Pilate and was buried. And on the third day He rose again according to the Scriptures. And ascending into Heaven, He sitteth at the right hand of the Father. And He shall come again in glory to judge the living and the dead; and of His kingdom there shall be no end. And I believe in the Holy Ghost, Lord and Giver of life, Who proceeds from the Father and the Son. Who together with the Father and the Son is no less adored, and glorified: Who spoke by the Prophets. And I believe in One, Holy, Catholic and Apostolic Church. I confess one Baptism for the remission of sins. And I look for the resurrection of the dead. And the life of the world to come. Amen.

The *Credo* is a statement of belief. In prose style like the Gloria, the Credo received similar musical treatment from composers.

4. *Sanctus-Benedictus* (*c.*120 A.D.)

Sanctus, Sanctus, Sanctus, Dominus Deus Sabaoth. Pleni sunt coeli et terra gloria tua. Hosanna in excelsis. Benedictus qui venit in nomine Domini. Hosanna in excelsis.

Holy, Holy, Holy, Lord God of Hosts. Heaven and earth are filled with Thy glory. Hosanna in the highest. Blessed is He Who comes in the name of the Lord. Hosanna in the highest.

The fourth part of the Ordinary has two sections. The first, *Sanctus,* is a song of adoration to God. The same ardor is shown the Son of God in the second section, the *Benedictus.* The threefold Sanctus of the first section and the refrain "Hosanna in the highest"—which closes both sections—make this text especially congenial for a musical setting.

5. *Agnus Dei* (*c.*700 A.D.)

Agnus Dei, qui tollis peccata mundi, miserere nobis.	Lamb of God, Who takest away the sins of the world, have mercy on us.
Agnus Dei, qui tollis peccata mundi, miserere nobis.	Lamb of God, Who takest away the sins of the world, have mercy on us.
Agnus Dei, qui tollis peccata mundi, dona nobis pacem.	Lamb of God, Who takest away the sins of the world, grant us peace.

The *Agnus Dei* is simplicity itself: a supplication is stated three times. The poignant mood and clear three-part structure offer the composer satisfying emotional material for ending his musical setting of the Ordinary of the Mass.

THE DIVINE OFFICES

The Mass is not the only important worship service of the Roman Catholic Church. In addition, there are the Divine Offices (also called Canonical Hours)—eight devotional services held throughout the day from before dawn until after sunset. The principal musical features of the Divine Offices are hymns and psalms. In the Middle Ages the Offices were of paramount importance both spiritually and musically, but today they are observed in their entirety only in monasteries.

GREGORIAN CHANT

The music that accompanied the medieval Mass and the Divine Offices is called *plainsong* or *plainchant,* but it is more commonly known as *Gregorian chant,* in honor of Gregory I, Pope from 590 to 604, who supposedly supervised its codification into the unified, homogenous corpus that now exists (Ill. 8:1); actually a great deal of chant was composed after Gregory. This chant as it emerges in modern scholarly restoration has the following characteristics:

1. The music is monophonic; that is, one line of melody is sung by all participants without accompaniment.

2. The chant has the same rhythm as speech; in other words, it is rhythmically free and the beats fall irregularly, not metrically as in poetry.

3. In contrast to later Western music, which generally uses only two modes—major and minor—there are eight modes or melodic patterns used as structural bases for Gregorian melodies. They can best be understood as scales using the white keys of the piano, each mode starting on a different key. Melodies constructed in any of the four *authentic* modes remain within the octave of the final (tonic). The corresponding *plagal* modes use the same white keys but have a compass that puts the final in the middle of the octave (Ex. 8:1). These modes (they were employed until the seventeenth century and still survive in folk song) explain the archaic sound of some of the music. While features of both major and

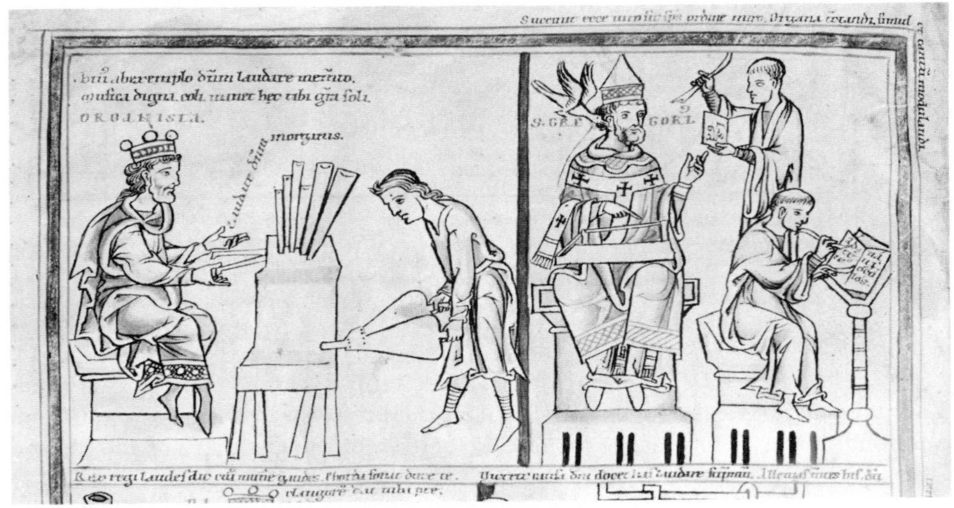

Ill. 8:1. ***Right: Pope Gregory writing chant. Left: King David playing the Organ. Cod. lat. 17403 (1424), Staatsbibliothek, Munich.***

minor tonalities appear in some modes, modal music has its own vitality and character.

Ex. 8:1. ***Authentic and plagal modes***

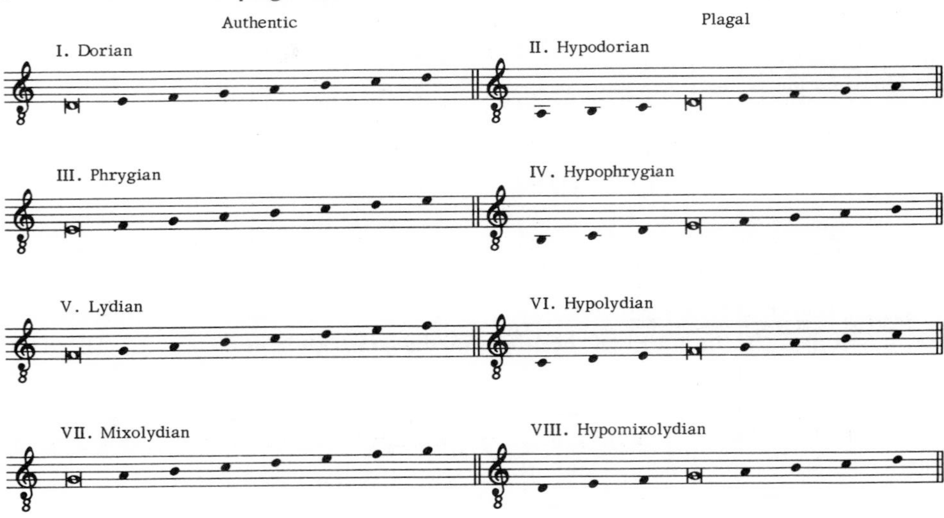

4. The melodic style varies according to the written text. *Syllabic* style sets one melody tone to one syllable of text. The texts with more words—Credo, Gloria—usually have an appropriately simple musical setting in *neumatic* style, with one or a small group of notes sung to each syllable. *Psalmodic* style, used in singing the psalms, is the simplest of all. With the exception of a short introduction, a half-verse ending, and verse ending, all verses of a given psalm are chanted on a single musical pitch. Sometimes numerous tones are sung to a single syllable, a style called *melismatic*. Exuberant passages having few words—Alleluia, Kyrie eleison—are often very ornate. The melody forms an uninterrupted flow of soaring flight and repose.

ODIE·NOBIS
CELORUM REX
de uirgine nasci dig
natus est: ut hominem per
ditum ad regna celesti
a reuocaret. gau
det exercitus angelorum. quia salus eterna hu
mano generi apparuit. Gloria in excelsis
deo et in terra pax hominibus bone uoluntatis. Gaude.
Hodie nobis de celo pax uera descendit.
hodie per totum mundum melliflui facti sunt celi.

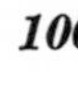

Ex. 8:3. *Kyrie "Altissime"*

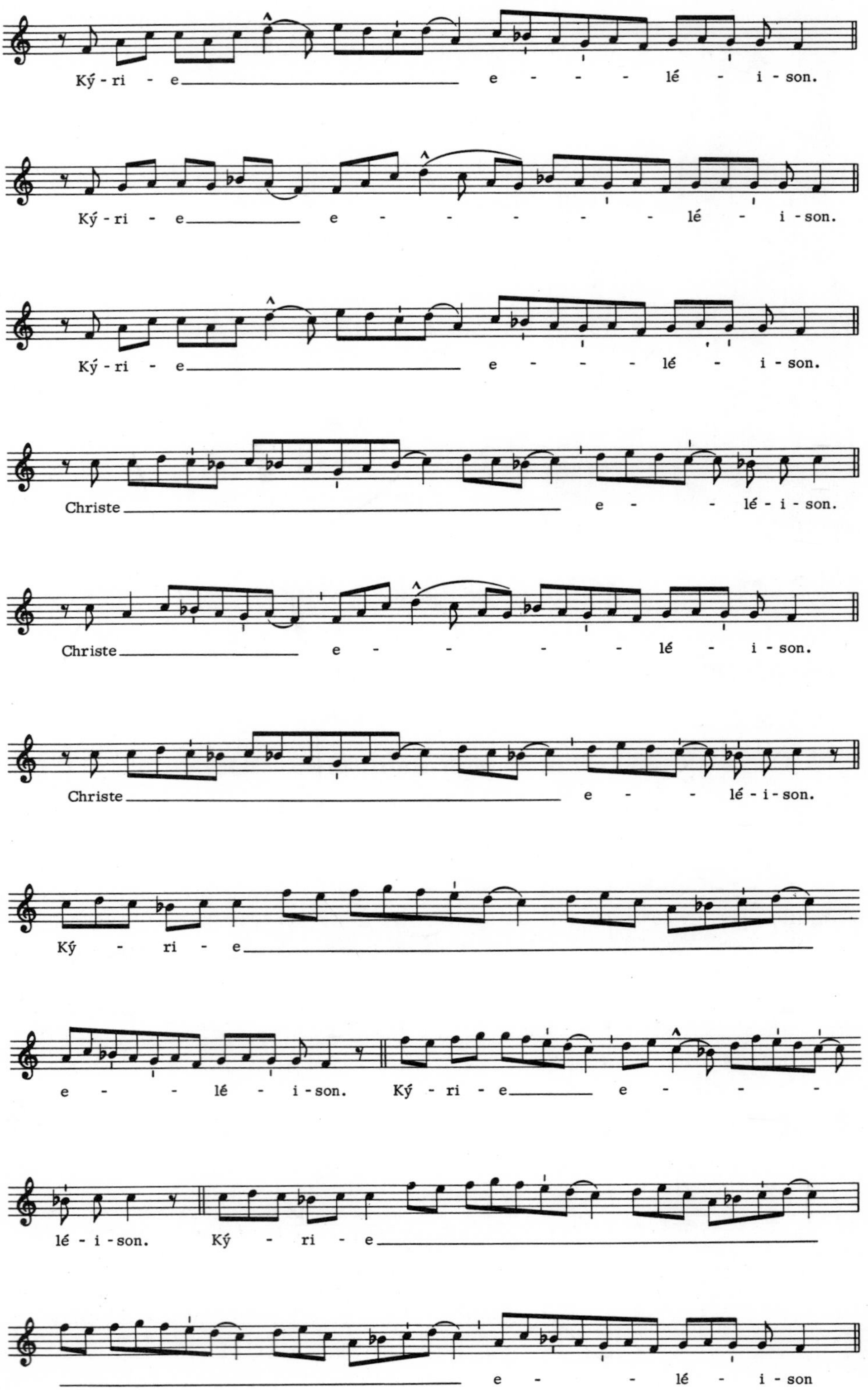

Ký - ri - e ____ e - - - lé - i - son.

Ký - ri - e ____ e - - - - - - lé - i - son.

Ký - ri - e ____ e - - - lé - i - son.

Christe ____ e - - lé - i - son.

Christe ____ e - - - - lé - i - son.

Christe ____ e - - lé - i - son.

Ký - ri - e ____

e - - lé - i - son. Ký - ri - e ____ e - - -

lé - i - son. Ký - ri - e ____

____ e - - lé - i - son

5. There are various ways of singing Gregorian chant. The early Church placed great emphasis on psalm singing, following traditions established by Hebrew synagogue liturgy. Thus it was only natural that the performance of all early Christian chant should have continued the traditions prevalent in psalmody. Based on performance practice, there are three categories of chants:

a. Direct performance: the chant is sung straight through by either a soloist or a choir.
b. Antiphonal performance: the choir is divided into two groups singing alternately.
c. Responsorial performance: the soloist sings a portion of the chant followed by a succeeding portion from the entire choir.

6. Gregorian chant is actually sung prayer and sung praises; therefore, the music's true meaning lies in its relation to the text.

One problem confronting the growing Church was how to notate (write down) its musical repertoire. The notation system used by the ancient Greeks had fallen into disuse by the time of the early Christian era, and for several centuries plainsong survived only by oral tradition. By the ninth century the Church had worked out a system of *neumes*—signs intended merely to remind the singer of a melody that he already knew. By the thirteenth century the neumes had been grafted to a staff, thus indicating relative pitch more precisely. Gradually the signs—which indicated only pitch, not rhythm or meter—were replaced by notes. The new method eventually permitted an indication of time values. Example 8:2 shows a chant in neumes and its modern transcription.

The eleventh-century *Kyrie "Altissime,"* which is available on records,[2] is a magnificent example of pure melodic composition. In it the simple request "Lord, have mercy, Christ, have mercy" is transformed into an ecstatic symbol of eternal supplication (Ex. 8:3).

(1) In the first petition, the first and third Kyries are identical. The melody rises in thirds to the peak (*E*), then descends smoothly and gradually. The middle Kyrie in this group gives the impression of several smaller phrases, yet the ending is similar to that of the first and third Kyries. (2) The first and third Christes of the second petition provide interesting contrast. Starting higher, each curves gracefully downward, then soars even more before coming to rest. The middle Christe starts out independently but soon reveals that it is derived from the Kyrie melody. (3) The three Kyries of the final petition are the most dramatic. The first starts on a *C* and shortly rises to a *G;* then it begins a florid, devious descent to its lower octave. The second is quite short, containing fragments of the first. The final Kyrie begins like the first but is longer; more than half of the initial melodic line is repeated.

EARLY POLYPHONY

By a process of extension, the monophonic chant of the Roman Catholic Church provided a basis for two significant musical developments that have influenced Western culture ever since. One is polyphonic music. To us music containing several simultaneous melodic lines is taken for granted today; to

[2] *The History of Music in Sound,* Vol. 2 (RCA Victor).

medieval church congregations, the idea of *adding* one melody to another must have seemed revolutionary indeed. We have documentation that polyphony existed as early as the ninth century: in a "Handbook of Music" (*Musica enchiriadis*), in which the word *organum* is used to describe the two different ways of "singing together." Both types are generally referred to as *parallel organum.* In one style the first voice part (*vox principalis*) sings a plainsong melody while a second voice part (*vox organalis*) duplicates this melody a fifth or fourth lower. Both voice parts were often doubled at the octave (Ex. 8:4). In the other style

Ex. 8:4. *Musica enchiriadis: Parallel organum*

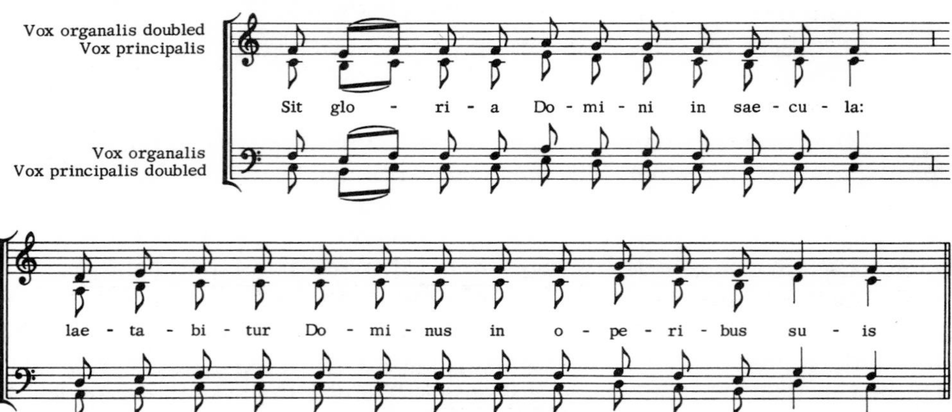

of organum, the two voices start in unison, the *vox principalis* ascends until it makes the interval of a fourth with the *vox organalis,* then both continue in parallel motion and finally return to the unison (Ex. 8:5).

Ex. 8:5. *Musica enchiriadis: Parallel organum*

From Parrish and Ohl, editors, *Masterpieces of Music before 1750* (New York: W. W. Norton & Co., Inc., 1951), p. 17. Reprinted by permission. There is also an accompanying record album released by the Haydn Society.

We have no further reference to organum until the first half of the eleventh century, but obviously experiments in two simultaneous voice parts continued. At first the two melodic lines were strictly parallel; that is, the basic chant and the new melody were written note against note—a technique described by the term *punctus contra punctum* or *counterpoint.* By the twelfth century the original plainsong no longer played its role of "first" melody in the polyphonic texture. Instead this voice was used as a rigid framework—called a *tenor* (from the Latin *tenere*—to hold) or *cantus firmus* (fixed song)—around which the composer embroidered melodies having supple lines and elegant flourishes (Ex. 8:6).

Ex. 8:6. *Organum: Benedicamus Domino*

From Parrish and Ohl, editors, *Masterpieces of Music before 1750* (New York: W. W. Norton & Co., Inc., 1951), p. 21. Reprinted by permission.

> It is important to remember that composers of the early Middle Ages were not permitted to write counterpoint to any plainsong they chose. The Church gave careful instructions as to what sections of the Mass and Office might be elaborated by additional voice-parts. Generally speaking, the greater the feast [day], the greater the amount of elaboration allowed; though an additional factor of considerable significance was the nature of the plainsong itself. Certain kinds of responsorial chant, whose various sections are allocated to chorus and soloist (s) in alternation, might have only the solo portions set.[3]

Each age added its own distinctive ideas. During the twelfth and thirteenth centuries, a flurry of musical activity occurred at the cathedral of Notre Dame in Paris. A composer known as Leoninus wrote a huge compendium of two-part organum, and his disciple Perotinus enriched Notre Dame's choirbooks with compositions containing three and four melodic voices. With increasingly complex writing techniques came a need for rhythmic organization. One of the noteworthy innovations of the Notre Dame school was the introduction of strictly measured rhythm in one of the *rhythmic modes*—rhythmic patterns using arrangements of long and short note values. For example, Mode III uses the pattern ♩. ♪ ♩ . A single mode would be used more or less consistently in each part of a polyphonic composition (Ex. 8:7).

New types of polyphonic music came with experimentation. The most popular type during the twelfth and thirteenth centuries was the *motet*. For the lowest voice—the tenor or cantus firmus—the composer borrowed from liturgical chant and set his material in one of the rhythmic modes. The tenor—based on a short, wordless *melisma* or flourish of a chant (for example, the extended melody on the final "a" of alleluia)—had no written text and was probably played by an

[3] Denis Stevens and Alec Robertson, editors, *The Pelican History of Music* (Baltimore, Md.: Penguin Books, 1960), Vol. 1, p. 213. Reprinted by permission.

Ex. 8:7. Perotinus: *Organum, Alleluya*

From Parrish and Ohl, editors, *Masterpieces of Music before 1750* (New York: W. W. Norton & Co., Inc., 1951), p. 24. Reprinted by permission.

Ex. 8:8. Motet: *En non Diu.' Quant voi. Eius in Oriente*

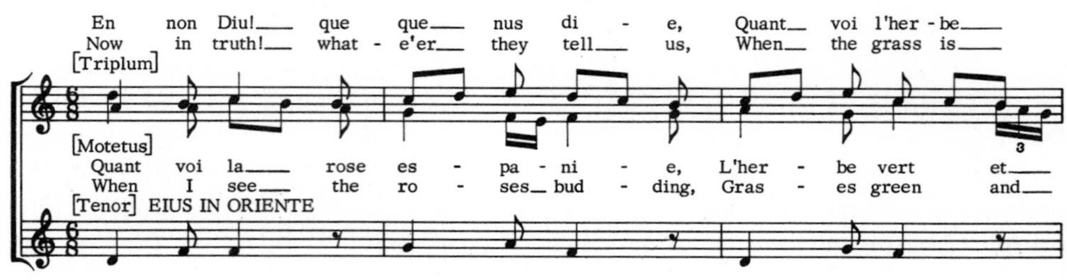

From Parrish and Ohl, editors, *Masterpieces of Music before 1750* (New York: W. W. Norton & Co., Inc., 1951), p. 29. Reprinted by permission.

instrument or instruments. Then the composer fitted a second voice—called *duplum* or *motetus* (having words) —above the tenor so that consonants (unison, fourth, fifth, octave) were formed at accented points. Composers frequently added a third voice—*triplum*—but, since this voice heeded only the tenor part, frequent discords occurred between duplum and triplum. Sometimes Latin texts were used, sometimes vernacular; often both appeared side by side. Sacred and secular sentiments mingled surprisingly well (Ex. 8:8).

In the *canon,* a favorite contrapuntal type in England, a melody is presented by one voice or one instrument and repeated by one or more different voices (or instruments), each entering before the previous voice has finished, so that overlapping results.

The organum settings, including the motet compositions, were drawn from the Mass Proper, but the fourteenth century witnessed a move to polyphonic settings of the Ordinary texts. Several such polyphonic Masses are extant, but the first Mass signed by a known composer is the famous *Messe de Notre Dame* (Mass of Our Lady). Written by Guillaume de Machaut (*c.*1300–1377)—a poet, courtier, composer, and man of the church—this Mass blends the five sections of the Ordinary into one beautiful, convincing musical unit. It is written for a men's choir and contains rhythmic vitality and rich melodic invention.

CHURCH DRAMA

The second significant offshoot of monophonic chant also developed from simple origins and had far-reaching results. In the same way that Greek tragedy originated in the dithyrambic choral hymn, Western drama began in Christian liturgy. Since the ritual forms of Christian worship lend themselves eminently to dramatic expression, simple liturgical dramas were soon being enacted. At quite an early period, possibly before the eighth century, official liturgy was supplemented with extra texts and music, for either explanation or expansion. These additions were called *tropes.* Elaboration of the liturgy led naturally to dramatic representation: the vignette of the three women at the sepulchre, the colorful Christmas stories, and stories based on the lives of the saints became very popular in musical settings resembling plainsong.

One of the most delightful medieval liturgical dramas is *The Play of Daniel,*[4] written sometime around the twelfth century by students at the cathedral of Beauvais, France. Daniel's prophecy concerning the coming of the Son of Man had brought him honor as the great announcer of the Messiah's birth; therefore the play was intended for the Christmas season. It comprises songs, laments, dancelike pieces, processionals, and narrative. An early example of free theater, this drama was still connected with the liturgy but was a step toward independence. In the fully developed liturgical dramas of the later twelfth and thirteenth centuries, sacred and secular elements were so interwoven that they became indistinguishable. When these dramatic performances were finally removed from the church and performed in a secular atmosphere, drama arrived at complete independence. The ensuing mystery plays and the later morality plays gradually dispensed with music, but by then drama had become an art form.

[4] *The Play of Daniel* has been published in a modern edition. A recording by the New York Pro Musica (Decca) is also available.

SECULAR MUSIC

Because it was not preserved throughout the Middle Ages as carefully as was religious music, we have less information about medieval secular music. But although only a few secular music manuscripts survived, enough documented nonmusical evidence is available to determine what kind of "popular" music was accessible to medieval man.

Before the Christian era, Caesar had written about Celtic singers and harpists in Gaul and Briton, and Anglo-Saxon poetry, especially after the sixth century, refers again and again to bards, gleemen, and minstrels who "cultivated the art of music." The references indicate that these musicians were honored minstrels like the ancient Greek bards, ready at call to perform spontaneously in the service of religion, patriotism, or merely entertainment. Farther north more complete collections have preserved the heroic poems and eulogies of the Scandinavian *skalds* (polishers or smoothers of language), who were renowned Norse warriors as well as poet-singers. Throughout Europe and as far north as Iceland, minstrels kept alive the tradition of popular music.

The earliest secular music manuscripts we have are satirical and often coarse songs from the eleventh, twelfth, and thirteenth centuries. They were composed and sung in Latin by singer-jesters called *goliards*—students and young ecclesiastics in England, France, and Germany, who wandered from school to school in the days before university centers were established. Unlike the respected minstrels of earlier centuries, these amateur performers were social outcasts because of their irresponsible wanderings, loose living, and rioting. Some historians feel that their unconventional behavior and protest riots indicate a revolt against medieval asceticism and rigidity.

France had another group of itinerant musicians, professional *jongleurs* who not only sang and played instruments but performed acrobatic tricks and exhibited animals. Unacceptable to society, they lived by their wits. Although not creative musicians but merely performers who sang and danced what others had composed, the jongleurs' ability to entertain people as they wandered from village to village must be recognized as a sustaining link in the development of secular music in Western Europe. In the eleventh century they organized into brotherhoods, which later became musicians' guilds.

France also produced an exceptional class of aristocratic poet-musicians during the twelfth and thirteenth centuries: known as *troubadours* in southern France and *trouvères* in northern France, they were far removed from goliards and jongleurs. Many were gentlemen, frequently noblemen, gifted in versification and music. Troubadours wrote in Provençal, the dialect of southern France; trouvères used the vernacular dialect of medieval France, which ultimately became modern French. Several collections of troubadour and trouvère poems and melodies have been preserved. They usually tell about love and nature, God and faith, chivalry and the purity of woman. Bernart de Ventadour, a twelfth-century troubadour, eloquently describes the joys of nature (Ex. 8:9).

The melody is measured—it fits into a $\frac{3}{4}$ meter—but otherwise this music bears a strong resemblance to plainchant, in which troubadour and trouvère music undoubtedly had its beginnings. Although the music is monophonic, most likely there was some kind of accompaniment—lute or viol—but how this was done we cannot be sure.

An early type of vernacular song and one especially appropriate for the talents of troubadours and trouvères was the *chanson de geste* (literally "song of

Ex. 8:9. Bernart de Ventadour: ***Quan vei l'aloete***[5]

(*Translation:* When I see the lark in joy rise on its wings in the rays of the sun and then, oblivious, let itself fall, because of the gladness that fills its heart, such great envy comes upon me to see it so joyful, I wonder then that I do not rave and that my heart does not melt with desire.)

great deeds"), dealing with heroic and often legendary exploits belonging, roughly, to the age of Charlemagne. *The Song of Roland,* thought to have been composed about the twelfth century, is one of the most beautiful—and most historically inaccurate—of these classic French lyric poems. It recounts the last battle and death of Roland, Charlemagne's nephew, during the great emperor's campaign in Spain in 778 A.D.

In Germany the *Minnesingers* (*Minne* meaning love), inspired by the art of the troubadours, produced refined poems about love and nature. The lyrical poems of these knightly poet-musicians have great charm and vitality.

By the end of the thirteenth century, French troubadours were coming from a cultivated middle class rather than predominantly from the aristocracy, as in earlier times; in Germany the Minnesingers eventually gave way to the *Meistersingers,* phlegmatic burghers whose rigid rules made their music stiff and inexpressive in comparison with that of the Minnesingers. Meistersinger guilds lasted into the eighteenth century.

In thirteenth-century Spain, king Alfonso the Wise supervised the compi-

[5] Example 8:9 and the translation are from *The History of Music in Sound,* Vol. 2 (New York: Oxford University Press and RCA Victor). Reprinted by permission of Oxford University Press.

Ill. 8:2. *Musicians playing instruments.* Cantigas de Santa María, *El Escorial, Spain. Courtesy of Mas-Art Reference Bureau.*

lation of the *Cantigas de Santa María* (Songs of the Virgin), a series of quasi-popular songs based on Marian legends. These *cantigas* reveal a troubadour influence, but their general mood is unmistakably Spanish. Although the music of the *cantigas* is always monophonic, various miniature paintings found in the original manuscript show musicians with a variety of instruments (Ill. 8:2).

Independent instrumental repertoires were nonexistent in the Middle Ages. There were numerous instruments—harp, hurdy-gurdy, viols, flutes, trumpets, oboes, cymbals, drums, castanets, tambourines—but they served mostly as support for singers and as dance accompaniment.

Sometimes instruments were added to strengthen the vocal parts in a motet, or one vocal part in a polyphonic ensemble was replaced by one instrument. The instruments most frequently participating in performances of polyphonic music were the flute, harp, organ, and bowed strings. When *all* vocal parts were transcribed (arranged) for instrumental groups, composers used certain figurations—ornaments that anticipated a future instrumental style and repertoire.

During this era, people were not particular about instrumental tone color. For dance accompaniments, they merely gathered together two or three different instruments. Thus a dance tune like the thirteenth-century *estampie*[6] might have been played by flute, tambourine, oboe, or any other combination of melody and rhythm instruments (Ex. 8:10).

Ex. 8:10. *Estampie*

From Davison and Apel, *Historical Anthology of Music,* Vol. 1 (Cambridge, Mass.: Harvard University Press, 1949). Reprinted by permission.

The thorough work done by the medieval Church to encourage, guide, and preserve sacred music is of course the most valuable contribution made to music during the Middle Ages. It must be remembered, however, that through successive centuries and without any official sponsor, European minstrels kept alive a popular music tradition and a love and appreciation for that music. All medieval secular music shows sincere emotion and enjoyment of life beneath its conservative cover of chivalrous mysticism.

SUMMARY

The Middle Ages, through a long period of assimilation, experimentation, and invention, provided music with durable and practical working materials for future development. The Mass established a structural and inspirational framework that has been indispensable to composers to the present day. The first musical settings of the Mass were based on Gregorian chant. This chant—

[6] The *estampie* was an instrumental form of the thirteenth and fourteenth centuries. It consisted of from four to seven sections, each provided with a half cadence and a full cadence.

monophonic, rhythmically free, and modal in character—was composed in one of four styles, then sung in various ways by soloists and choir or congregation. A primitive notation in neumes helped singers to retain the numerous melodies used during the different church services.

Other medieval musical developments had far-reaching results. The narration and enactment of extraliturgical texts (lives of saints and the birth and passion of Christ) in musical settings led to church drama, a medium that eventually—without its musical accompaniment—became Western secular drama.

Church music did not remain exclusively monophonic. Organum provided the impetus for polyphonic music, and gradually well-developed motets and canons revealed the potential of contrapuntal music.

Although the Middle Ages made its greatest musical contribution with the preservation and development of church music, it also fostered secular music. Itinerant goliards and jongleurs and sensitive troubadours and trouvères produced a large repertoire of secular songs and dances that faithfully mirror the thoughts, hopes, and ideals of medieval man.

FOR DISCUSSION AND ASSIGNMENT

1. Listen to a recording of sections from a Gregorian Mass. Why do you think music became so important to the Church in the Middle Ages? Services were almost invariably sung or chanted. Why? Why did the Church adopt Gregorian chant as the "official" music for its rituals?
2. Gregorian chant, troubadour and trouvère songs, and Spanish *cantigas* are all monophonic. Many people find it difficult to appreciate this type of music. What are the obstacles to appreciation and what might be done to overcome them?
3. Sing some of the examples of organum, or listen to a recording. Does the music sound "archaic"? Why?
4. The motet, sung in church, was often in two languages and used two or three different texts simultaneously. Does this strike you as being effective devotional music?

FOR FURTHER READING

Ainaud, Juan. *Romanesque Painting,* translated by J. Stewart. New York: The Viking Press, 1963. A Compass PB. This book provides a good introduction to the unique concept of art during this highly important period.

Barnes, Harry Elmer. *An Intellectual and Cultural History of the Western World,* Vol. I. New York: Dover Publications, Inc., 1965. PB. Part Three of Dr. Barnes' notable publication is titled "The Medieval Synthesis." Covering over 200 pages, it traces all aspects of medieval history, Christianity, thought, and culture.

Jones, Charles W., ed. *Medieval Literature in Translation.* New York: David McKay Co., Inc., 1950. This is the best anthology of medieval literature available. It is comprehensive and the selections are well chosen.

Mâle, Emile. *Gothic Image: Religious Art in France in the Thirteenth Century,* translated by D. Nussey. New York: Harper & Row, Publishers, 1958. A Torchbook PB. An excellent book dealing with one of the great periods of medieval art.

Seay, Albert. *Music in the Medieval World.* Englewood Cliffs, N.J.: Prentice-Hall, Inc., 1965. Prentice-Hall History of Music Series. PB. There is obviously no such thing as a "popular" history of medieval music, but this book, written by a talented specialist, is extremely readable and can be interesting and valuable to the inquisitive musical amateur.

9 The Renaissance

> . . . just as Josquin has still to be surpassed in his compositions, so Michelangelo stands alone and without a peer among all who have practiced his arts; and the one and the other have opened the eyes of all who delight in these arts, now and in the future.
>
> COSIMO BARTOLI
>
> *Accademic Discussions* (1567)

Like the Middle Ages, the Renaissance cannot be confined within exact dates; medieval attitudes and thought yielded to change at different times in different countries and in many different ways—politically, artistically, intellectually, and socially. There was no abrupt revolt, for thinking men in the late Middle Ages had already protested against ecclesiastical and feudal despotism and founded universities to satisfy their enthusiasm for learning. In fact there never has been a complete break with medieval institutions or thought, for the best features of the Middle Ages were retained, broadened, and passed on by the Renaissance.

Of the various ideas or themes that pervaded the Renaissance—humanism, scientific inquiry, individualism—humanism was perhaps the most powerful, the most outwardly pervasive. This thought movement devoted itself to the rediscovery, direct study, and revival of the literature and philosophy of ancient Greece and Rome. In a larger sense humanism represented man's dedication to creative worldly and personal affairs. As the power of the two medieval strongholds—Church and feudalism—weakened, nations assumed dignity and national pride. Intellectual as well as geographical exploration transformed the indecisive fears of the Middle Ages into constructive thought and action. Man began to think less about a divine life hereafter and more about himself as a free being with an earthly life to enjoy.

Fourteenth-century Italy was a natural seedbed for the intellectual and moral attitudes adopted by the Renaissance. The classic tradition had never been wholly blotted out in Italy; almost everywhere the Italian looked he saw some reminder of the glories created by his illustrious ancestors. In the fragments of ancient classicism he found inspiration for a new culture—a culture that gradually spread throughout all of Europe.

The arts blossomed during the Renaissance because they were generously patronized by wealthy business men, ruling families, and popes. The powerful Medici family, for instance, controlled Florence throughout the fifteenth century and enthusiastically fostered the arts. Cosimo, who guided the family from 1429 to 1464, not only ably managed the affairs of Florence but gave painting commissions to the artists Fra Angelico (Ill. 9:1) and Fra Filippo Lippi, collected

Ill. 9:1. ***Fra Angelico*** **(*1387–1455*), Christ Glorified in the Court of Heaven,** ***central panel. Courtesy of the National Gallery, London.***

manuscripts, and created the Platonic Academy to stimulate interest in Plato and the Neoplatonic philosophers. Cosimo's ambitious grandson, Lorenzo de' Medici (the "Magnificent"), used his power and wealth to beautify Florence with art and to immortalize his name as the most universal and splendid of all the Medici.

Renaissance social and cultural reforms grew logically and deliberately from the legacies of the Middle Ages, but within the Renaissance era the sixteenth century gave birth to a genuine religious revolution—the Reformation—which ultimately divided Western Christendom into Catholic and Protestant. For several centuries European rulers had been complaining about losing royal revenue to the church and papal interference in political and economic affairs. At the same time sincerely devout Christians felt misgivings about contemporary church practices.

An Augustinian monk and university professor at Wittenberg brought about the irrevocable break with the established church. Martin Luther (1483–1546) believed that man could be saved solely by faith in God's grace and mercy; that the Scriptures, rather than a pope or a council, constituted the ultimate authority in all religious matters; that marriage for priests was the only remedy for clerical concubinage. Excommunicated from the Roman church, Luther proceeded to formulate his ideas into a persuasive theology. Lutheranism spread through parts of Germany and northward to Sweden, Norway, and Denmark.

A second major branch of Protestantism developed in Switzerland under John Calvin (1509–1564). Calvinism traveled into France, the Netherlands, Germany, and Bohemia. The English Reformation was largely political and social, based on Henry VIII's revolt against papal interference in England, but even the king still considered himself a Catholic despite the rupture with Rome.

Protestantism developed its own church music, for most Protestant sects allowed music in their services. The Lutherans in particular encouraged the composition and use of Protestant-oriented music; their most distinctive musical form, the *chorale,* later reached perfection in the music of Johann Sebastian Bach.

The humanistic, cultural Renaissance looked upon music as one of life's necessities. Besides carrying on the fine religious music tradition of the Middle Ages, Renaissance society wanted secular music for its leisure enjoyment. As a result, Renaissance secular music equaled church music in both quantity and quality. Unlike medieval composers, who had modestly refrained from signing their works, Renaissance composers won recognition through their music. Princes and prelates competed to obtain the finest composers and musicians for their private chapels, and a well-trained choir conducted by a famous composer represented not only piety but the cultural refinement sought by every Renaissance prince.

SACRED VOCAL POLYPHONY

The art of combining melodies began in the ninth century. For 500 years composers experimented, refined, and discarded, until by the fifteenth century they had arrived at a mature polyphonic style. That is why the musical Renaissance is often called the "golden age of polyphony."

Almost all Renaissance music is based on polyphonic (contrapuntal) practice. Renaissance polyphony has a characteristic quality stemming from the use of old ecclesiastical modes, but its rhythm is based on a regular beat, not the free movement of plainsong; that is, the rhythm is measured even though the arbitrary bar line was not then generally used for vocal music. Clarity, symmetry, balance, restraint—all apply to Renaissance polyphony.

In *imitative polyphony* one or more voice parts restate a melodic idea or figure already presented by another voice part (Ex. 9:1); if the restatement is exact, it is *strict* imitation; if merely similar, it is *free* imitation.

Sometimes the complete melody is imitated by one or several different voice parts, each imitation entering in such a way that the successive melodic statements overlap. The result is a *canon.* The familiar "Row, Row, Row Your Boat" is a simple canon.

A distinctive factor in polyphonic writing is the vertical tonal relationship brought about when tones in different voices sound simultaneously. As we saw in Chapter 3, the resulting intervals are known as consonances if they are agreeable and restful to the ear, dissonances if they sound harsh or incomplete. Both definitions are entirely subjective; interpretation actually depends on the listener. During the Renaissance the traditional consonances (unisons, thirds, fifths, sixths, and octaves) could be used with freedom, but dissonances (seconds, fourths, and sevenths) were restricted by certain contrapuntal rules designed to render them unobtrusive.

To most early Renaissance composers, harmony existed much more as the result of linear effects than for its own sake, but by the middle of the sixteenth century harmony became an actual vertical function (first at cadence points) and pointed the way to harmonic dominance in the Baroque era.

Renaissance melodies have a basically vocal character, usually confined within a small range and free of wide skips. In vocal music the text determines the melodic contour. Long phrases are common.

Ex. 9:1. Josquin des Prez: *Motet, Ave Maria*

From Parrish and Ohl, editors, *Masterpieces of Music before 1750* (New York: W. W. Norton & Co., Inc., 1951), p. 60. Reprinted by permission.

The Renaissance tradition of vocal polyphony did not originate in Italy, where so many artistic innovations had taken root; it developed farther north, in Burgundy and Flanders—the modern regions of Holland, Belgium, Luxembourg, and a good part of northeastern and central France. Early polyphonic experiments took place at the sumptuous court of Philip the Good, the duke who reigned over the duchy of Burgundy from 1419 to 1467. Because of his generous patronage of musical composition and performance, the style developed at that time is known as *Burgundian*.

The leaders of the Burgundian group were Gilles Binchois (*c.*1400–1460) and Guillaume Dufay (*c.*1400–1474). Binchois composed some church music, but he is best known for his excellent chansons—polyphonic settings of courtly French poetry. Dufay worked with both sacred and secular forms. His skillful counterpoint and limpid melodic lines reveal his association with Italy, where he had worked for nine years as a singer in the papal chapel.

The Burgundians introduced a new musical style for settings of the Mass. Before their time the Kyrie, Gloria, Credo, Sanctus, and Agnus Dei had been conceived as separate compositions (although Machaut's Mass—see page 105—is an exception). Burgundian composers supplied unity to these five sections of the Ordinary by often using the same thematic material in each section.

Most compositions from this period have only three voice parts. The medieval *tenor* (*cantus firmus*—the lowest part) is retained. Added to it are the melodic *cantus* or *discantus* (the highest part) and a *contratenor* or *contra* (the middle part). During the second half of the fifteenth century, composers expanded three-part polyphony into four-part by splitting the contratenor into two separate melodic lines: *contra altus* (between cantus and tenor) and *contra bassus* (the lowest part).

Four-part writing improved with Flemish composers such as Johannes Ockeghem (*c.*1425–1495) and Jacob Obrecht (*c.*1450–1505), who helped to stabilize the principles of imitative counterpoint, and Josquin des Prez (*c.*1440–1521), who made polyphonic music a truly expressive art. One of the great composers of all time, Josquin was celebrated as the "prince of music" by his contemporaries.

Of the dozens of renowned composers writing inspired and serviceable music for the Church during the late sixteenth century, two of the most outstanding are the Italian Giovanni Pierluigi da Palestrina (*c.*1525–1594) and the Netherlander Roland de Lassus (1532–1594). No other composer before Bach is as well known as Palestrina, just as no composer before Bach was as universally talented as Lassus.

The main body of Palestrina's writing is for the Church: Masses and motets. He raised pure *a cappella* (chapel or unaccompanied) singing to a lofty status not only by adopting themes from Gregorian chant (as Renaissance composers often did) but by weaving true plainsong spirit and technique into his polyphonic fabric. His flowing melodies impart serenity to his music, which is dignified, restrained, and wholly appropriate for church performance.

Lassus, on the other hand, is more typical of his era in that he composed almost every type of music, religious and secular. His compositions reflect his versatility and cosmopolitanism; he traveled widely, knew many languages, and received honors at home and abroad.

While Palestrina was master of the musical Mass, Lassus preferred to use the motet for his church music. The Renaissance motet—based on Latin texts usually taken from the Scriptures—ordinarily contains from four to six voice parts. Imitation of one voice part in another is one of its prominent characteristics. The motet was used as part of the Proper of the Mass and in some nonliturgical performances.

Lassus' motet *Tristis est anima mea* is based on a sad, expressive text for Holy Week.

> My soul is exceeding sorrowful, even unto death: tarry ye here, and watch with me: now ye will see the multitude that will surround me: ye will take flight, and I shall go to be sacrificed for you.[1]

As a musical complement for this text, Lassus chose a polyphonic setting of five voices moving in slow, solemn cadence (Ex. 9:2). Even without understanding the Latin words, the listener can feel the sadness through Lassus' handling of the musical framework; he always followed his texts carefully, conveying the drama in every phrase by means of his musical technique. In this talent for dramatic expression, Lassus predicts the age of the Baroque.

From 1400 to 1600 many musical Masses were based on motets and madrigals as well as Gregorian chant. Palestrina's Mass *Veni sponsa Christi* (Come, Bride of Christ), for example, is known as a "parody" Mass. He had already written a motet based on a Gregorian refrain; for his Mass he borrowed

[1] The musical score can be found in Parrish and Ohl, editors, *Masterpieces of Music before 1750* (New York: W. W. Norton & Co., 1951).

Ex. 9:2. Lassus: *Tristis est anima mea*

From Parrish and Ohl, editors, *Masterpieces of Music before 1750* (New York: W. W. Norton & Co., Inc., 1951), p. 80. Reprinted by permission.

freely from the motet, including some musical sections almost in their original form, and he treated other sections somewhat in the manner of a series of variations. In the *Agnus Dei,* Palestrina has transformed the motet theme into a series of plastic melodic curves, each preserving its characteristic outlines and at the same time adhering to the contrapuntal web with unity and dignity (Ex. 9:3).

There were many other fine Renaissance composers. The Spanish mystic Tomás Luis de Victoria (*c.*1549–1611) composed a Requiem Mass (funeral Mass) revealing unusual dramatic intensity and spiritual fervor. In Venice composers such as Adrian Willaert (*c.*1490–1562) and Giovanni Gabrieli (*c.*1551–1612) experimented with sonorous tonal effects. Willaert developed polychoral compositions, to which technique Gabrieli added instrumental color. These innovations matured during the Baroque era.

The Lutheran Reformation in Germany in the early sixteenth century inspired a new type of religious music: the *chorale* (hymn tune). It was introduced to encourage congregational participation in the new Protestant Church. Hymn texts were in the vernacular, and the melodies either were borrowed from the Roman Catholic Church or from folk repertoire or else were newly composed. As an example of direct borrowing, the Catholic hymn *Veni redemptor gentium* became *Nun komm der Heiden Heiland* (Come Now, Savior of Men).

As early as 1524 hymns (chorales) began to appear in three, four, five,

Ex. 9:3. Palestrina: ***Agnus Dei from the Mass Veni sponsa Christi***

From Parrish and Ohl, editors, *Masterpieces of Music before 1750* (New York: W. W. Norton & Co., Inc., 1951), p. 88. Reprinted by permission.

and even six polyphonic voice parts, similar to the Latin motet. The Lutheran hymn thus established itself as a staple fixture in religious life and embarked on a long, splendid musical history.

SECULAR RENAISSANCE MUSIC

Continental Music

While Europe's cathedrals resounded to polyphonic Masses and motets by masters like Palestrina and Lassus, secular music also enhanced Renaissance life. In Italy the favorite musical recreation was singing *madrigals.* The madrigal can be traced back to the late-fifteenth-century *frottola,* a popular but sophisticated song in four voices with the melody in the top voice.

The sixteenth-century Italian madrigal uses a framework of four or five melodic lines. Despite this basically contrapuntal writing, harmony is very much in evidence. Madrigal texts are poetic, frequently sad, and often nostalgic and sentimental. The madrigal was first cultivated by masters of the Flemish and Burgundian schools working in Italy. Toward the latter part of the sixteenth century composers, striving to imbue the madrigal with dramatic expression, indulged in exaggerated effects, experimented in chromaticism, and attempted descriptive passages and coloristic devices. After these embellishments it was only a short step to Baroque music.

Secular-music composers enjoyed international reputations. Luca Marenzio (1553–1599), highly esteemed at Rome and at the Polish court, exemplifies the ideal love poet with his refined yet impassioned writing. Don Carlo Gesualdo, Prince of Venosa (*c.*1560–1613), was a romantic, adventuresome composer. His concept of chromaticism and his preference for dissonance created madrigals that even now have a convincingly "modern" ring to them.

The greatest sixteenth-century Italian madrigal composer and the greatest seventeenth-century Italian opera composer are one and the same—Claudio Monteverdi (1567–1643). His eight sets of madrigals for five voices are masterpieces in this genre: they are overwhelmingly beautiful in their sensitive tone color, and they amaze by the manner in which the music translates the slightest textual nuances. An often-heard example is Monteverdi's *Ecco mormorar l'onde* (Hear the Waves Murmur). The composer starts with a minimum of melodic material. Then, as the text expands into a warmly colorful nature picture ("And the east is brightly smiling . . . the peaks of the mountain turn gold. O! Beautiful and lovely is the dawn!"), Monteverdi matches the poem with an increasingly expansive musical framework, convincingly transforming word painting into tone painting.

The nearest French counterpart to the Italian madrigal is the *chanson*. Its style resembles that of the imitative sacred motet, although—like the madrigal—a strong harmonic feeling often prevails. One outstanding feature of the chanson is its pungent, spontaneous rhythm. The chanson covers a wide range of subjects and sentiments: it may express the collective passions of a crowd or one individual's personal meditation; it may glorify love or extol patriotism; it may revel in satire, allusions, or moral lessons. Like the late-sixteenth-century madrigal, the chanson suggests the latent possibilities in descriptive music.

Many composers wrote effective chansons—for example Clément Jannequin (*c.*1475–*c.*1560), Claude de Sermisy (*c.*1490–1562), Claude le Jeune (1528–1600), and the prodigious Roland de Lassus, who composed 148 chansons. Jannequin was one of the best in this field, and his descriptive chansons have gone through many editions. In *La bataille de Marignan* (The Battle of Marignan) he literally paints a fresco of a battle that occurred in 1515 by imitating battle sounds and cries; here is action and here also is superb vocal writing. Among his other descriptive works are *Le chant des oyseaux* (The Song of the Birds), *Le caquet des femmes* (The Prattle of Women), *Les cris de Paris* (The Cries of Paris), and *Le siège de Metz* (The Siege of Metz).

Instruments were popular during the Renaissance, although their musical repertoire was not so extensive nor mature as the vocal repertoire. Frequently instruments and voices were combined, thereby strengthening the vocal line. Sometimes they even substituted for a voice part.

When instrumentalists started looking for a repertoire of their own, they often made instrumental transcriptions—for organ, harpsichord, lute, guitar, viol ensemble, and so on—of vocal pieces. In time composers began to write original compositions inspired by contemporary vocal forms.

The instrumental *ricercar* derived from the motet. It consists of several sections, each section being worked out in counterpoint and imitation. The *canzona* drew inspiration from the French chanson; it is similar to the ricercar but livelier.

Not all instrumental music derived from vocal forms. Dances like the *pavane, galliard, passamezzo,* and *saltarello* provided Renaissance society with a bright array of suitable ballroom and salon music. Composers also experimented with sonorities. The enterprising Giovanni Gabrieli wrote sonatas, using the term *sonata* to designate a "sounded" composition in contrast to a "sung" one. His *Sonata pian' e forte* (actually a canzona) is famous for its precise instrumentation. Gabrieli was also the first composer to prescribe in a score the degree of loudness and softness desired in performance.

Music in England

During the transition from the Roman Catholic Church to the Church of England, Tudor composers showed surprising flexibility by writing both Latin Masses and *anthems.* The anthem was essentially an Anglican motet. It differed from the Catholic motet because of its English text, syllabic diction, square rhythm, and style that was more chordal than polyphonic. Composers like Thomas Tallis (*c.*1505–1585) and William Byrd (1543–1623) wrote superb church music at this time, easily changing from Latin Masses and motets to English anthems.

Keyboard instruments were very popular among English Renaissance society. In 1477 William Horwood, master of choristers at Lincoln Cathedral, received an appointment to teach the boys "playing on the clavychordes." In his satirical poem "Against a Comely Coistrown," England's poet laureate John Skelton (*c.*1460–1529) exclaims:

> Comely he clappeth a pair of clavichordes;
> He whistleth so sweetly, he maketh me to sweat;
> His descant is dashed full of discordes;
> A red angry man, but easy to entreat.

The virginal (small spinet) became a great favorite of the English monarchs. Henry VIII, Elizabeth of York, Catherine of Aragon, Mary Tudor, and Queen Elizabeth all performed on the instrument, and Mary Stuart was said to play "reasonably for a queen."

What music did such clavier-minded monarchs play? All types were available: fantasies, motets, preludes, airs, contrapuntal inventions, masquerades, liturgical plainsong, and dances (the solemn pavan, spritely galliard, or energetic jig).

Along with virginal music and an organ repertoire, composers produced numerous fantasias for viols and other instruments. The title *fantasia* applies to a wide variety of compositions supposedly characterized by their improvisatory nature, although actually they were carefully and skillfully worked out—free versions of the contrapuntal and learned ricercar. Composers like William Byrd and Orlando Gibbons (1583–1625) wrote excellent fantasias for viol consort.

Although English composers wrote sacred music for both Roman and Anglican churches, they still found time to compose secular music. Despite royal interest in instrumental music, the finest secular music of the English Renaissance is the vocal polyphonic repertoire, which developed quite late in the era.

Elizabethans enjoyed social group singing to an amazing degree. Thomas Morley (1557–1602), "Bachelor of Musicke and Gentleman of Her Majesty's Chapel Royal," in his famous book on music and music teaching, *A Plaine and*

Easie Introduction to Practicall Musicke (1597), relates a fictitious conversation at a supper party.

> Among the rest of the guests, by chance master Aphron came thither also, who, falling to discourse of music, was in an argument so quickly taken up and hotly pursued by Eudoxus and Calergus . . . as in his own art he was overthrown; but he still sticking in his opinion, the two gentlemen requested me to examine his reasons and confute them; but I refusing and pretending ignorance, the whole company condemned me of discourtesy, being fully persuaded that I had been as skilful in that art as they took me to be learned in others. But supper being ended and music books (according to the custom) being brought to the table, the mistress of the house presented me with a part earnestly requesting me to sing; but when, after many excuses, I protested unfeinedly that I could not, every one began to wonder; yea, some whispered to others demanding how I was brought up.[2]

According to this literary fancy, an educated man had to be able to take his part in a madrigal and understand the niceties of musical theory.

From the 1580s into the second decade of the seventeenth century, England enthusiastically developed the madrigal. The English madrigal borrowed some features from the Italian form. Basically it was still a vocal *a cappella* composition written for from three to six voice parts. For its structure it often borrowed techniques from sacred music: the text is divided into various sections; each section begins with its own musical motive, which is subsequently treated polyphonically. Occasionally some sections are in chordal style. English madrigal composers paid special attention to details of the text and tried to give variety to their compositions.

The contrapuntal style of the continental madrigal appealed to the English taste; however, instead of adopting the frequently artificial, sophisticated style of the earlier madrigal, English composers approached the form with so much enthusiasm that it almost became a new form. They preferred popular, amorous, pastoral, or even humorous poetry rather than the serious texts of the Italian madrigals, and their use of nonsense syllables like fa-la-la is a decided innovation. Titles often betray their typically English contents: "Come Away, Sweet Love"; "Clorinda False"; "This Sweet and Merry Month of May"; "About the Maypole."

Successful vocal music depended upon each composer's skill in interpreting the words of his text. Also in *A Plaine and Easie Introduction to Practicall Musicke,* Thomas Morley advises composers on setting words to music:

> . . . you must have a care that when your matter signifieth ascending, high heaven and such like, you make your musick ascend: and by the contrarie where your dittie speaks of descending, lowness, depth, hell and others such, you must make your musick descend. For as it will bee thought a great absurditie to talke of heaven and point downward to the earth: so it will be counted great incongruity if a musician upon the words he ascended into heaven should cause his musick to descend.[3]

The best-known English madrigal composers are William Byrd, Thomas Morley, Orlando Gibbons, John Wilbye (1574–1638), and John Bennet (*c.*1575–*c.*1625). Bennet, who ranks high among skilled madrigalists, published a

[2] Thomas Morley, *A Plain and Easy Introduction to Practical Music,* edited by R. Alec Harman (New York: W. W. Norton & Co., Inc., 1952), p. 9.

[3] Morley, p. 291.

set of 17 *Madrigalls to Foure Voyces* in 1599. Although designed on a small scale, they reveal excellent workmanship and a rare instinct for beauty. Number eight, "Thyrsis, Sleepest Thou?,"[4] is a good example of Bennet's ability to produce a finished work on a diminutive canvas. It has a pastoral text, for which Bennet employs a technique sometimes referred to as "madrigalism": a type of tone painting achieved by such musical devices as overlapping triple rhythms accompanying the words "sleepest thou," and quaint but charming settings of words such as "cuckoo" and "sighed." By changing from lively polyphonic to strictly chordal texture, Bennet creates interest and diversity.

The *ayre* (also called *canzonet*) was a simpler type of vocal composition: the music was set for a single voice accompanied by one or several instruments or by other voices. The ayre's uncomplicated musical structure made it easy for singers to go through many verses without difficulty. When this form reached its high point during the early seventeenth century, it began to replace the madrigal in popularity; once the ayre became established, there were not many books of madrigals printed.

John Dowland (1562–1626), a celebrated singer and lutenist, is also famous as a composer of ayres. The love song "My Thoughts Are Wing'd with Hopes"[5] is an especially fine example of Dowland's sensitive, lyrical talent.

> My thoughts are wing'd with hopes, my hopes with love,
> Mount, Love, unto the moon in clearest night
> And say, as she doth in the heavens move,
> In earth so wanes and waxeth my delight.
> And whisper this but softly in her ears:
> Hope oft doth hang the Head and Trust shed tears.

This stroph and two others are set to an enchanting melody based on a static rhythmic pattern.

Ensemble chamber music generated an even more "popular" atmosphere. Composers such as Thomas Weelkes (*c.*1575–1623) and Orlando Gibbons made musical arrangements of some of the sounds from daily English life—as for instance Gibbons' *London Street Cries,* set for voices and viols. The singsong cries of the different itinerant vendors on London's streets are blended into a fantasy that offers the listener such inconsistent fare as hot mutton pies, new mackerel, and ripe "cowcumbers."

Music had been part of English drama before the Elizabethan era, but by the late sixteenth century it had become more important to dramatics. Shakespeare, for example, incorporated music in many of his plays (*As You Like It* and *Twelfth Night* have six songs each), and he seems to have been familiar with musical terminology.

"It must be stressed that all of these songs were not what we now might call incidental music, but that the playwrights used music as a deliberate device to suggest moods, provide atmosphere, prepare the spectators for coming action, and emphasize dramatic situations. Of course, it supplied extraneous entertainment as well."[6]

[4] See Parrish and Ohl, pp. 110–114.

[5] The musical score can be found in C. Parrish, editor, *A Treasury of Early Music* (New York: W. W. Norton & Co., Inc., 1958), pp. 192–193.

[6] Dorothy E. Mason, *Music in Elizabethan England* (Washington: The Folger Shakespeare Library, 1958), p. 12. Reprinted by permission.

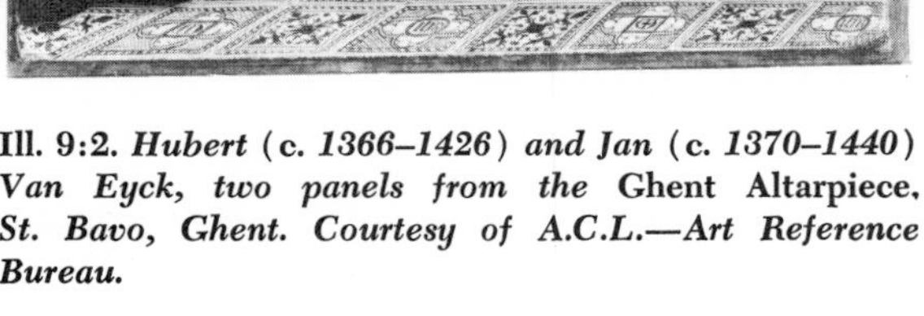

Ill. 9:2. *Hubert* (c. *1366–1426*) *and Jan* (c. *1370–1440*) *Van Eyck, two panels from the* Ghent Altarpiece, *St. Bavo, Ghent. Courtesy of A.C.L.—Art Reference Bureau.*

SUMMARY

Three basic themes dominated the Renaissance—*humanism, individualism,* and *scientific inquiry*. They permeated the arts and unified the era.

Classical humanism implies a deliberate revival of ancient traditions, styles, and philosophies. This return to the past was more easily accomplished in Italy, where Roman remains were everywhere in evidence: the Italians studied Greek, replaced medieval Latin with Ciceronian Latin, and read Plato.

Musicians reinterpreted Greek musical theory. Josquin des Prez was hailed as a modern Orpheus who had revitalized the dormant art of the ancients. With few exceptions, composers happily turned to secular composition and created innumerable madrigals and chansons.

Renaissance individualism was an integral part of the whole humanistic attitude. Each artist, whether writer, painter, sculptor, or musician, was a potential virtuoso whose "performance" was applauded or derided by both his aristocratic patron and the bourgeois public. When the painters and sculptors realized that they were no longer bound by convention or tradition, they made their human figures more lifelike and expressed themselves more intimately (Ill. 9:2).

Scientific inquiry led to curiosity and investigation (Ill. 9:3), both encouraged in the humanistic Renaissance. This scientific spirit also affected music.

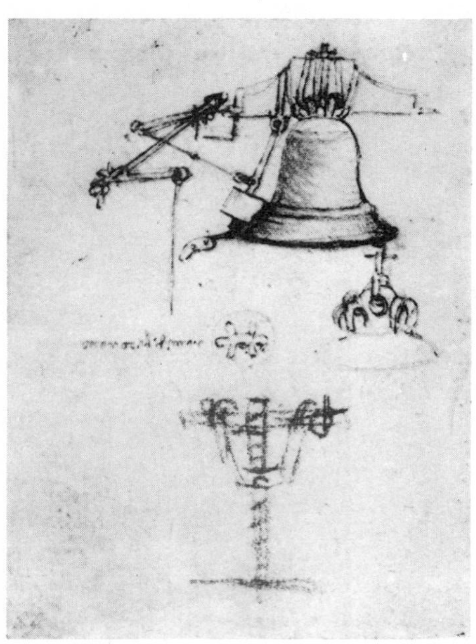

Ill. 9:3. ***Leonardo da Vinci (1452–1519), drawing of a mechanical hammer for ringing bells. Cod. Forst. II, fol. 10v. Courtesy of Art Reference Bureau.***

The art of counterpoint—writing polyphonic music—became so highly developed and refined during the sixteenth century that the rules then established for writing this music are studied by twentieth-century composers.

The efforts of medieval church music composers to create a contrapuntal language reached fruition in the Renaissance. Music written during this "Golden Age of Polyphony" still retained its modal character but relied on imitation, rhythmic symmetry, clarity, and suavely expressive melodic lines to create compositions of lasting quality. Although Renaissance musical history discloses many skilled and sensitive composers, Palestrina, Lassus, and Victoria perhaps represent the epitome of mastery in the polyphonic idiom.

Contrapuntal style was not limited to sacred music. The Italian madrigal, French chanson, and English madrigal used the same basic approach, but in these secular forms polyphony's classic severity was tempered as the occasion demanded.

The Renaissance produced magnificent vocal music, and at the same time created a significant instrumental repertoire. Dance music, keyboard music, and viol consort music were written by some of the era's finest composers and enjoyed with obvious relish by Renaissance society.

FOR DISCUSSION AND ASSIGNMENT

1. Renaissance madrigals do not please us as much as they did sixteenth-century society. Why?
2. Listen to a Kyrie by William Byrd, one by Palestrina, and one by Victoria. Does one actually sound any more Spanish, more English, or more Italian than another?
3. Do you think that Renaissance sacred music was performed by large or small choral ensembles? Why?
4. Shakespeare makes frequent allusions to music throughout his plays and sonnets. Find some of these and draw your own conclusions about the playwright's familiarity with music.
5. Listen to some Renaissance music played by an ensemble of viols. Then listen to a similar group of strings from the violin family play chamber music—Renaissance music if possible. How would you describe the difference in sound and effect?

FOR FURTHER READING

Blume, Friedrich, *Renaissance and Baroque Music,* translated by M. D. Herter Norton. New York: W. W. Norton & Co., Inc., 1967. PB. This book is a translation of two articles written by Prof. Blume for a German encyclopedia of music. The articles, both interesting and informative, provide a good introduction to the music of these two eras.

Burckhardt, Jacob. *The Civilization of the Renaissance in Italy*. New York: Harper & Row, Publishers, 1958. 2 Vols. A Torchbook PB. For many decades this book, first published in 1860, was the undisputed authority. It still has much to offer. Burckhardt vividly re-creates the past with a dedication that few volumes project.

Greenberg, Noah, W. H. Auden, and Chester Kallman, eds. *An Elizabethan Song Book*. Garden City, N.Y.: Doubleday & Co., Inc., 1955. PB. This is a delightful anthology of Renaissance secular music from England. It contains songs with lute accompaniment (transcribed for piano), madrigals, and rounds.

Horizon Book of the Renaissance. New York: American Heritage Publishing Co., Inc., 1961. An inspired volume of essays in word and picture reanimating the colorful, multifaceted Renaissance life.

Mason, Dorothy E. *Music in Elizabethan England*. Washington: The Folger Shakespeare Library, 1958. PB. This slender booklet (15 pages of text, 20 pages of illustrations) emphasizes the importance of music in English society.

Roeder, Ralph. *The Man of the Renaissance*. Cleveland: World Publishing Co., 1933. A Meridian PB. Mr. Roeder has written penetrating studies of four outstanding Renaissance personalities: Savonarola, Machiavelli, Castiglione, and Aretino.

Sellery, George Clarke. *The Renaissance: Its Nature and Origins*. Madison, Wisconsin: The University of Wisconsin Press, 1950. PB. An excellent guide to this era. In his readable style, the author comments on politics, economics, literature, fine arts, inventions, and works of philosophy, criticism, and history.

The Baroque Period 10

There's sure no passion in the human soul,
But finds its food in music.

GEORGE LILLO
Fatal Curiosity

The Renaissance occurred because men rebelled against the intellectual sluggishness of the Middle Ages. Yet the time arrived when the newer attitudes toward perfection, beauty, learning, and purity could not fully compensate for man's loss of spiritual disciplines. In the sixteenth century doubt and disillusionment rankled men's minds as Europe divided and subdivided, politically and religiously; the peoples of Europe, no longer subservient to one crown, royal or papal, learned to pay allegiance to the nation intellectually and physically strong enough to win it.

Under the pressures of religious conflicts and power struggles all over Europe, the glowing artistic movement of the High Renaissance gradually lost momentum. All the Western world seemed to be agitating—politically, religiously, economically, scientifically, philosophically, socially—propelled by an urgency that left in its wake tension, paradox, intensity, and a restlessness that often pushed men to extreme limits. Amidst their striving, men and nations awoke to a sense of power and the realization that in addition to having rights and dignity they could mold their own destinies. This awareness of power affected every endeavor and set the tone for the new age. Closely associated with it and possibly created by it, the modern state assumed definite form during the period.

In arts and letters the term *Baroque* applies especially to the elaborate and often bizarre style prevailing from about 1550 until late in the eighteenth century. This artistic movement was not national, although, as with all styles, each nation contributed to its development. For many years, art connoisseurs derided Baroque art for its ornamental distortions and lack of restraint, but as analyzed by the art historian Heinrich Wölfflin and other perceptive critics, the era has been redeemed as an essential phase in man's development. After all, an age that produced a Milton, a Corneille, a Descartes, and a Rembrandt can hardly be dismissed as having no value. According to Wölfflin:

> The baroque uses the same system of forms [as the Renaissance], but in place of the perfect, the completed, gives the restless . . . in place of the limited,

the conceivable, gives the limitless, the colossal. The ideal of beautiful proportion vanishes, interest concentrates not on being, but on happening [Ill. 10:1]. The masses, heavy and thickset, come into movement. . . .

This analysis is certainly not exhaustive, but it will serve to show in what way styles express their epoch. It is obviously a new ideal of life which speaks to us. . . . The relationship of the individual to the world has changed, a new domain of feeling has opened, the soul aspires to dissolution in the sublimity of the huge, the infinite [Ill. 10:2].[1]

Ill. 10:1. ***Jan Vermeer (1632–1675)*****, The Concert.** ***Courtesy of Isabella Stewart Gardner Museum.***

BAROQUE MUSICAL STYLE

Although music from one period rarely represents the antithesis of the music from the preceding era, Baroque music might well be considered the antithesis of Renaissance style. Many Baroque techniques derived from the Renaissance, of course, but in most instances Baroque treatment caused a complete change in musical character.

Baroque music is charged with exuberance, drama, flamboyancy, and that

[1] Heinrich Wölfflin, *Principles of Art History,* translated by M. D. Hottinger (New York: Dover Publications, Inc., n.d.), p. 10.

Ill. 10:2. ***Gianlorenzo Bernini (1598–1680),*** **St. Theresa in Ecstasy.** ***Church of Sta. Maria della Vittoria, Rome. Courtesy of Alinari-Art Reference Bureau.***

sense of urgency associated with the whole period. Polyphonic style, which Renaissance composers had adopted for all composition, both sacred and secular, succumbed to new style concepts as Baroque composers began to differentiate between secular and church music, between chamber and opera music. Because Renaissance composers wrote all their compositions in one style, we find little variety in Renaissance music. For example, Renaissance musical settings for Masses and motets were deliberately restrained because such music served as an adjunct to meditation; therefore secular music, conceived in the same style, also sounds restrained. Baroque composers tried to interpret their texts as vividly as possible, with the result that their textual settings are far more emotional than those of their Renaissance predecessors.

Other changes occurred in the early seventeenth century. Whereas all polyphonic compositions from the fifteenth and sixteenth centuries could be performed by voices or instruments or a combination of the two, Baroque composers created vocal music specifically for voice and instrumental music to exploit the potential of one instrument or an instrumental ensemble.

During the seventeenth century, modal scales were gradually superseded by major and minor scales, and the science of harmony established itself well enough to compete with polyphony and eventually overtake it. Chords—the result, in the Renaissance, of cross-sectional cuts through polyphonic voices at accent points—became independent agents governed by tonality. Modulation (see page 40) was another outgrowth of this tonal stabilization. Dissonance, customarily treated with respect and some timidity by Renaissance composers, found a natural place in the expressive language of Baroque writers.

As part of this expressive language, Baroque composers subscribed to what is commonly called the "doctrine of the affections." In attempting to interpret a wide range of emotions and ideas by musical means, they devised an elaborate system of musical figures. Thus different affections—contemplation, sadness, excitement, heroism—could (theoretically) be transmitted by a consistent use of the appropriate figures.

> It must be strongly emphasized that the musical figures were in themselves necessarily ambiguous, and took on a definite meaning only in a musical context and by means of a text or title. Since they did not "express" but merely "presented" or "signified" the affections, musically identical figures lent themselves to numerous and often highly divergent meanings.[2]

In his organ chorale prelude *When Adam Fell, The Human Race,* Bach presents the Fall by the "fall" of a seventh (Ex. 10:1), yet another composer might use this same device to suggest a different affection. Consistent elaboration of a chosen figure established the significance of the desired affection.

Ex. 10:1. Bach: *When Adam Fell, The Human Race*

Baroque composers paid strict attention to the outer voices in a composition; that is, they highlighted the bass line and what amounted to a soprano or treble line and assigned accompanimental duties to the other parts. A keyboard instrument was indispensable to the Baroque musical ensemble (although in early Baroque music the lute usually performed this function). As harmony instruments, the harpsichord or organ furnished chords to give cohesion to the music—whether operatic aria, trio sonata, or concerto. Used in this fashion and not as a solo instrument, the harpsichord or organ was known as the *continuo.* The continuo's part consisted of a bass line that was often reinforced by a cello,

[2] Manfred F. Bukofzer, *Music in the Baroque Era* (New York: W. W. Norton & Co., Inc., 1947), p. 389. Reprinted by permission.

Ill. 10:3. ***Church Concert. Frontispiece from the*** **Musikalischer Lexicon** ***(Leipzig, 1732) by Johann Gottfried Walther (1684–1748).***

viola da gamba, or similar sustaining instrument. Sets of numbers placed beneath the bass line showed the keyboard performer which chords to play; this line is called a *figured bass* (as shown in Ex. 10:4, page 135). A skillful clavierist not only played the correct chords but from them he improvised a keyboard style in keeping with the other parts being played.

The keyboard not only dominated musical fabric (Ill. 10:3) but to a large extent influenced some expressive techniques. Since the harpsichord and organ are incapable of crescendo or diminuendo and their dynamic levels are static, the only way to achieve gradation and variety is to shift from one dynamic level to another—that is, from one keyboard to another. The ensembles, dependent upon a keyboard, adopted a similar dynamic approach. Composers, particularly in instrumental compositions, would frequently insert sections of repeated phrases or motives that called for a loud-to-soft or soft-to-loud dynamic treatment. This technique was described as an echo effect or as *terraced dynamics*.

Baroque melodies are long and expansive. When in slow tempo, these melodies are abundantly supplied with ornamentation; in rapid sections, they move in flowing cascades. Composers lengthened their melodies by using repeated phrases, sequential patterns, implied modulation, characteristic motives, false cadences, and other devices (Ex. 10:2). Often they broke up a melody and distributed it among several parts of an ensemble.

Ex. 10:2. Bach: *Brandenburg Concerto No. 2*

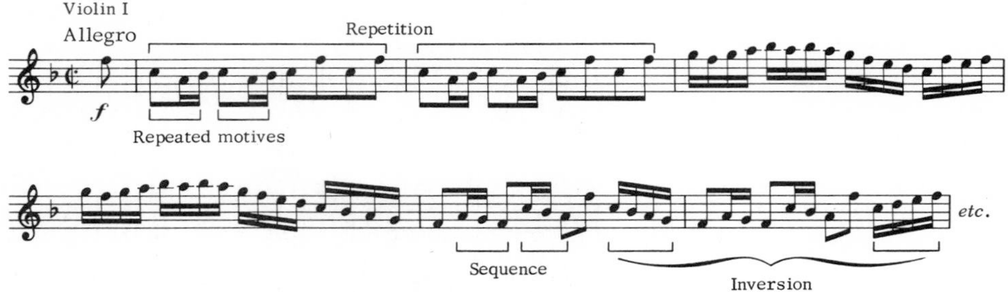

Baroque rhythm is spirited. Since accent per se was impossible on keyboard instruments and ensemble music followed keyboard patterns, rhythm came to depend largely on phrasing, note values, harmony, and ornamentation. Ornamentation is very important in Baroque music. Each composer maneuvered the assorted embellishments—trills, mordents, appoggiaturas, turns—to his personal liking. Ornaments (indicated in the score by means of signs rather than notes) were effective in maintaining a rhythmic accent; they were deemed necessary for indicating a slow, lyrical phrase line; they were suitable for introducing dissonances. Ornaments were not mere decorations; they had a definite expressive function that endowed Baroque music with elegance and flair (Ex. 10:3).

Ex. 10:3. Bach: *Goldberg Variations: Aria*

One important characteristic of much Baroque music was the *concertato* style (*stilo concertato*). Here the composer used various combinations of musical ensembles—both instrumental and vocal—employing them separately and together to achieve a particular type of contrast. One possibility was color contrast: choirs dialogued with each other, or contrasting instrumental groups played against one another, or voices alternated with instruments. Another possibility explored dynamic contrasts—perhaps a small group of soloists (vocal or instrumental) against a larger ensemble. Frequently compositions employing concertato style were called *concertos,* although by the late Baroque the term "concerto" was more often used for exclusively instrumental compositions.

Musical texture changed substantially during the Baroque era. In the early seventeenth century, composers concentrated on a purely homophonic style—basically one melody with chordal accompaniment. Gradually, beginning in the mid-seventeenth century, composers judiciously combined this homophonic approach with elements of polyphonic texture. This synthesis achieved its most perfect expression in the music of Bach.

The late Manfred Bukofzer, an authority on Baroque music, divided the era into three periods.[3] Beginning about 1580 and extending to 1630, the first phase is notable for its planned opposition to polyphony. Textual settings were very extravagant; harmony, still in its infancy, was experimental; and the typical forms (ricercar, solo song, variation, dances, etc.) of this early phase were not only brief but frequently sectionalized into even shorter fragments.

During the second phase (1630–1680) two significant factors in future opera development came into being: the aria and recitative. At the same time, instrumental music gained in stature and activity. *Bel canto* style—a manner of singing that emphasizes beauty of sound and virtuosity—began to enhance cantata and opera works. And the major and minor modes (scales) developed from the church modes at this same time.

Although most arts reached their Baroque peak during the late seventeenth century, music attained its high point somewhat later. During the final Baroque phase (1680–1730) and even later, composers worked confidently with fully established tonality and a firm concept of tonal harmony. They specialized in large forms like the concerto, pleasing both performer and listener. Composers' emphasis on persistent rhythmic patterns imparted a peculiarly agitated quality to their music.

Many changes occurred during the final Baroque phase. Composers explored some existing forms, such as the Mass and the variation, and carried them along to new expressive and dramatic depths, but for the most part the Baroque was a completely new age with new musical creations. In the vocal field, opera, oratorio, and cantata were developed; in instrumental music, the solo sonata and trio sonata were added to the chamber-music repertoire; in keyboard music, the prelude and fugue, the chorale prelude, and the chorale fantasy took form. The appearance of the concerto grosso (see page 141) and solo concerto proved without question that music was coming of age.

The term *Rococo* applies to certain composers and compositions of the late Baroque and pre-Classic eras. Rococo music is characterized by profuse ornamentation, light texture, and occasional superficiality. It was used primarily by French and Italian composers and is known also as the *style galant*.

Several historically important musical advances transpired during the seventeenth and eighteenth centuries. Opera matured through the works of Alessandro Scarlatti and Handel; the concerto reached its first zenith with the masterful works of Vivaldi and Bach; the oratorio found its first master in Handel. And Bach, writing glorious music for the Protestant church, created the greatest organ repertoire of all time.

VOCAL FORMS

Opera

The idea of using music and drama together is as old as man; but true *opera*—a sung theatrical production—began at the end of the sixteenth century. The Merriam-Webster Dictionary defines opera as "a drama in which music is the essential factor comprising songs with orchestral accompaniment (as recitative, aria, chorus) and orchestral preludes and interludes." This definition must be

[3] Bukofzer, pp. 16–18.

modified, for some comic operas and even a few grand operas (Mozart's *The Magic Flute,* Beethoven's *Fidelio*) include spoken dialogue.

An opera audience experiences a total effect—music and story blended into one form; however, numerous separate parts go into the making of an opera. First of all there is the vocal cast: soloists, who individually sing recitatives and arias and jointly perform duets, trios, quartets, and the like; and a chorus, which either participates in the dramatic action or merely comments on it. These vocalists are guided and supported by the orchestra and conductor, who also set the scene musically (overture, prelude) and provide various purely instrumental passages during the action. In addition to the singers and orchestra, some operas incorporate a ballet into the operatic fabric. A librettist is the writer who supplies the text, either an original work or an adaptation from another literary source. The composer creates an appropriate musical setting for this text. Some composers double as librettists and even supervise the mechanics of production. Stage sets and costumes are designed and executed by special artists, and a stage director resolves any problems of dramatic interpretation.

Opera is not typically realistic. Unlike opera characters, people do not sing their way through life, nor do they habitually converse in blank verse. Possibly opera has survived not only because of its beautiful music and heightened drama but because it provides an enjoyable escape from reality. Operas purporting to be realistic are only partly so and usually are only moderately successful.

As musical drama, opera follows certain conventions that give it its character. Chief among these is the fact that the text is in song rather than speech. Also, the dramatic action in opera must be forcibly prolonged or exaggerated to suit the musical treatment, for sung dialogue absorbs more time than spoken dialogue.

Although opera is a complex musical medium involving many combined talents and artistic forms, it can also be one of the most exciting musical experiences available to the discerning listener.

Opera was born during the last years of the sixteenth century through the efforts of a small cultural group in Florence, Italy: poets, musicians, and scholars of antiquity who met at the home of Count Giovanni Bardi to try to re-create the music and drama of ancient Greece. The lutenist-composer Vincenzo Galilei (*c.*1520–1591)—father of the famous astronomer—the poet Ottavio Rinuccini, and the musician and singer Jacopo Peri (1561–1633) collaborated to create a musical drama along the lines of the ancient Greek tragedies, which they believed had been sung throughout, not spoken. Their efforts produced the first opera, *Dafne,* performed at Florence in 1597. Only a few fragments of their music survive. In 1600, on the occasion of the marriage of Henry IV of France and Maria de' Medici, another new work in this vein was also presented in Florence. It was *Euridice,* with libretto by Rinuccini and music mostly by Peri. Then in 1602 the singer-composer Giulio Caccini (*c.*1550–1618), another member of Count Bardi's circle, published his *Nuove musiche* (New Music), a collection of musical settings illustrating the characteristics of the new melodic style.

Caccini claimed that he had originated a new vocal style—*stile rappresentativo* or *stile recitativo*—designed to eliminate all devices that might interfere with the emotional content of the text. He discarded polyphonic texture and contrapuntal development in favor of accompanied monody, in which a single expressive vocal line is projected against a harmonic background (Ex. 10:4). This recitative (*stile recitativo*) was closely related to speech. Its rhythm and accentuation—frequently even the melody—depended on the text. Using a keyboard instrument or lute, the accompanist improvised the background above a single line of bass notes, guided by figures above or below the notes—hence the "figured bass." This innovation—called variously *basso continuo, general bass,* or *thorough bass* by reason of its constant presence throughout the composition—soon became an indispensable foundation for all Baroque ensemble music, instrumental as well as vocal.

Opera production spread from Florence to Mantua and then to Rome, where it became a grand spectacle with splendid scenery and magnificent décor.

Ex. 10:4. Caccini: *Sfogava con le stelle*

From Davison and Apel, *Historical Anthology of Music,* Vol. 2 (Cambridge, Mass.: Harvard University Press, 1950). Reprinted by permission.

Claudio Monteverdi (1567–1643) was the genius who assured opera's lasting success. While chapelmaster at the court of Mantua, he composed in 1607 the opera *Orfeo,* a landmark in opera history because of its versatile use of music for dramatic representation. From 1613 until his death he was chapelmaster at the cathedral of St. Mark in Venice, where in 1641 he wrote a mature masterpiece, *Il ritorno d'Ulisse,* and in 1642 *L'incoronazione di Poppea.*

Although only three of his twelve operas survive in complete form, Monteverdi is an imposing figure in operatic history because of his wonderful gift for expressing emotions in music. He enriched the declamatory recitative, which he used lavishly, by giving it vigor and meaning. With his instinctive sense of drama and action, he also knew how to employ the songlike *arioso,* derived from the recitative but decidedly more lyrical. He took full advantage of instruments such as viols, gambas, lutes, and organs for color effects, and even at this early period he created a truly theatrical atmosphere for musical productions.

Other early opera composers active in Venice were Pietro Francesco Cavalli (1602–1676), who wrote more than 40 operas and was probably a pupil of Monteverdi, and Marc'Antonio Cesti (1623–1669), who helped to develop the aria in musical drama. The *aria* constitutes the lyrical passages in opera, oratorio, and cantata. Unlike the recitative, the aria has little relation to speech: whereas recitative is used to unfold the plot, the aria permits the composer to show his musical talent and the singer to exhibit his vocal skill.

At the end of the seventeenth century, Naples rather than Venice became the center of opera. The most illustrious representative of this school is Alessandro Scarlatti (1660–1725), whose operas contain rich musical color. He wrote 115 operas, 700 cantatas and oratorios, and numerous intermezzos, madrigals, and instrumental works. Neapolitan operas depended on the aria; indeed, each opera was built around a series of arias linked together by recitative. The aria form was strictly organized into three parts according to the scheme A B A, and it was known as a *da capo* ("back to the beginning") aria.

Dramatic opera was obviously too exciting to be confined within one country. As soon as operatic principles and techniques were successfully established in Italy, other countries began to cultivate the new medium. In France opera met strong competition from the ballet, a favorite French entertainment, and any composer hoping to make his mark in French opera had to include elements of the court ballet in his works. Jean Baptiste Lully (1632–1687) proved to be eminently successful in this endeavor. A favorite of Louis XIV, Lully virtually ruled over French opera until his death. He gave the French public what it craved. He incorporated ballet into his operas and often added a chorus as a decorative element. He insisted on fine librettos, he studied speech accent, and he employed a large, colorful orchestra. In fact, Lully formulated the basic model for what was to become the traditional French opera. In addition, he established the basic form for the French overture (slow-fast-slow) and set the standard for this type of writing.

In the late Baroque another interesting but entirely different composer dominated French opera—Jean Philippe Rameau (1683–1764). During the early part of his career, Rameau gained fame as organist, theorist, and composer of miniature harpsichord pieces. As theorist, he laid the foundations for the science of modern harmony with his book *Treatise of Harmony Reduced to Its Natural Principles* (1722). Rameau's harpsichord collections reveal charming examples of realism: a clucking hen is convincingly etched in *La poule;* in *Les trois mains* he gives the illusion of three hands at the keyboard instead of two.

Rameau did not attempt opera until he was past 40, but he did so with great éclat. In 1733 his opera *Hippolyte et Aricie* made him famous overnight. A great musico-dramatist, Rameau recognized opera as a requisite in contemporary French intellectual and social life. To make music drama even more attractive, he conceived his operas for the eyes as well as the ears of his public. His superb ballet music, powerful musical characterizations, subtle dialogue settings, and rich, varied harmony brought Rameau well-deserved recognition. It is a pity that we neglect his operas today.

When opera moved into England it faced another kind of competition—not ballet but the English *masque,* a public favorite since Elizabethan times. The masque, a type of musical play, employed many of the adornments of opera: costumes, scenery, actors, dancers, singers. It had become a conventional feature of festive celebrations, such as weddings, and it served as preliminary entertainment at court galas. Masque texts were often written by well-known men of letters such as Ben Jonson (*c.*1573–1637) and Francis Beaumont (1584–1616).

The only opera composer of stature in seventeenth-century England was Henry Purcell (*c.*1659–1695), highly respected by his contemporaries and often described as the British Orpheus. His repertoire comprises music for stage plays, religious music (anthems, cantatas, services), songs, odes for choir and orchestra, harpsichord pieces, and the opera *Dido and Aeneas* (1689). This opera is generally conceded to be his masterpiece, yet when completed it received only one stage performance and not another until 1895; it had, however, been heard in numerous concert performances. Its miniature proportions—it lasts for about an hour—do not in any way detract from the total effect: Purcell presents compactly the story of the tragic Queen Dido of Carthage with all the emotion, fervor, and drama of a nineteenth-century Romanticist.

England had conspicuously neglected opera during the seventeenth century, but with the arrival of Handel and his competitors in the eighteenth century the English public became almost possessed by Italian opera.

Italian operatic form also found its way into Germany and Austria. The works performed were usually imports from Italy, although a few German and Austrian composers wrote operas following the Italian models. This admiration for Italian opera and Italian vocal style continued into the late eighteenth century, for both Haydn and Mozart set most of their operas to Italian librettos.

Oratorio

The *oratorio*—a musical setting for a religious, contemplative, or sometimes heroic text—closely parallels opera in both form and development. Seventeenth-century oratorio, like opera, included recitatives, arias, a chorus, and an orchestral ensemble (plus a narrator or *testo*). Unlike opera, the oratorio assigns important parts to the chorus, and it is usually performed in a church or concert hall without scenery, costumes, or dramatic action. Also, the rapid dialogue often necessary to indicate action in opera is not common with the oratorio.

One of the great masters of the seventeenth-century sacred oratorio, the German Heinrich Schütz (1585–1672) is the most important link between the Italian monodists and the German church composers preceding Bach. Bach himself wrote a *Christmas Oratorio,* but it was Handel who, in his 19 oratorios, gave oratorio form its definitive character and stamp of nobility. (Handel's oratorios are discussed in Chapter 12.)

There are other works for chorus, soloists, and orchestra similar to the oratorio—Mass, Requiem, and Passion—but they are based on strictly Biblical or liturgical texts.

Cantata

The precise definition of the *cantata,* as given by the Merriam-Webster Dictionary, is "a sacred or secular composition comprising choruses, solos, recitatives, interludes, usually accompanied by organ, piano, or orchestra, and arranged in a somewhat dramatic manner but not intended to be acted."

In early-seventeenth-century Italy the term "cantata" designated somewhat extended settings of secular verse for one or two voices with accompaniment. This *cantata da camera* or chamber cantata derived its style from contemporary opera. Early cantatas used recitative almost exclusively, but as the operatic aria developed, the new form was incorporated into cantata compositions. Soon chamber cantatas were being written by English, German, and French composers.

During the course of the seventeenth century the cantata concept was extended to include settings of religious texts. The *cantata da chiesa* or church cantata became increasingly elaborate. Typical early-eighteenth-century church cantatas were written variously for soloists and chorus and different combinations of instruments, usually an orchestral ensemble of some sort. In Germany the Lutheran chorale (see page 117) became the backbone of the cantata, serving as the basis for extended treatment. The German cantata reached a high point with Bach's numerous sacred compositions.

Suite

The term *suite*—ordinarily for harpsichord or clavichord, sometimes organ or orchestra—usually denotes a cycle (or series) of dance pieces, changing in tempo and meter yet preserving key unity throughout. In the Baroque period, each suite section—excluding optional introductory movements (prelude, overture, toccata)—was constructed in binary form (see page 43). Baroque composers used this structure not only in suite movement but elsewhere, such as in a theme that was to be submitted to variation technique.

The suite (German: *Partie, Partita, Ouverture, Suite;* Italian: *Partita, Sonata da camera;* French: *Ordre, Suite;* English: *Lessons*) can be traced back to the paired dances written for the lute about the fourteenth century in France, Germany, and Italy. Lute composers in these countries preferred a set of two dances, with the second dance treated as a kind of variation of the first.

The stately *pavane,* a sixteenth-century dance in duple meter, came to be coupled with the lively *galliard* in triple meter. Sébastien de Brossard, an early-eighteenth-century writer, defined the *allemande* as a "grave symphony, usually in duple time, often in quadruple: it has two sections, each of which is played twice."[4] The *courante,* a lively dance in triple time, stood to the allemande in the same relation as the galliard to the pavane.

The *minuet,* originally a French rustic dance, became a favorite instrumental ensemble piece during the reign of Louis XIV. It consisted of three sections: Minuet I, Minuet II, and Minuet I. The second minuet is sometimes called a *trio* because composers often used only three instruments: usually two oboes and bassoon. In the eighteenth century the form Minuet I–Trio (whether for three players or not)–Minuet I was adopted as the third movement of a four-movement sonata (see page 169).

The *sarabande* was a dance of noble character, usually written with notes of long value yet displaying considerable ornamentation. Written in ternary meter, it begins on a strong beat, and the second beat is often prolonged. England apparently introduced the *gigue* or *jig,* a piece in ternary meter. A gigue is "an air ordinarily for instruments, almost always in triple time, which is full of dotted syncopated notes, which make the melody gay and, in a manner of speaking, sparkling."[5] The *bourrée,* a gay, rapid dance in duple meter, was discovered in Auvergne, France, at the end of the sixteenth century; it was assimilated into the suite group about the time of Lully.

This abundant fund of dance forms and occasional pieces—gradually formed over a long period—was drawn upon by Baroque keyboard composers. The early English virginal composers had been content with individual dances wherein variations of the several sections took on an important role. Later English harpsichord composers grouped dances into suites (*lessons*), although they paid little heed to the sequence of the dances. Early French *clavecin* composers grouped their *pièces de clavecin* into suites; however, they concentrated more on each separate piece than on group arrangement, so that one suite might contain several allemandes, courantes, gigues, or other dances. When descriptive compositions found favor in France, suite form became even more irregular.

[4] Sébastien de Brossard, *Dictionnaire de Musique* (Paris: Ballard, 1703), p. 5.
[5] Brossard, p. 30.

What is known as the classic suite finally emerged with Johann Froberger (1616–1667), a German who blended continental dance forms with the style characteristics of the French Baroque. In his earlier suites Froberger included only three dances: allemande, courante, sarabande. Soon four basic dances were standard for the suite, and by the eighteenth century, chiefly through the influence of Bach, the German suite had become more or less standardized into (1) an introductory optional movement, such as a *prelude, overture,* or *fantasia;* (2) an *allemande;* (3) a *courante;* (4) a *sarabande;* (5) optional dances: *gavotte, bourrée, passepied,* etc.; and (6) a *gigue.*

Sonata

During the late seventeenth century and through the early eighteenth, many instrumental composers produced individual pieces in binary form; they called these pieces *sonatas.* However, the Italians—and their imitators—also used the term "sonata" to designate groups of pieces, in some instances actual suites. The term "sonata" is an abbreviation of two Italian forms: the *sonata da camera* or chamber sonata (a series of dance movements using a common or nearly related tonality), and the *sonata da chiesa* or church sonata (a group of pieces contrasting in texture and tempo, each piece retaining the binary structure). Sonatas were written for all combinations of instruments, but the most important type was the trio sonata. It was regularly performed on four instruments: two violins, a cello (or viola da gamba), and a harpsichord, which realized (constructed) the harmonic structure from the bass line. Since harpsichord and cello worked from the same bass line, these sonatas were designated *a tre* (for three) rather than for four musical parts.

Variation

The principle of variation is based on simultaneous contrast and repetition. An idea is presented and then reiterated, always accompanied by or enveloped in various alterations or diversions.

There are several types of variation procedures, and they may be used singly or in combination. In the *recurring bass line* a melodic phrase of either four or eight measures is stated, frequently in triple meter and minor tonality. This bass melody remains constant; anything else may change. Compositions utilizing this method bear names such as *ground, basso ostinato, chaconne,* or *passacaglia.*

Since the terms chaconne and passacaglia were used interchangeably during the Baroque era, they both apply to variation based on a *recurring harmonic pattern.* The basic harmony is the constant factor in this method. The composer is free to use his imagination for rhythmic, melodic, and motive changes, but he must preserve the harmonic outline.

In the *recurring binary melody,* a theme from 16 to 32 measures long is presented in binary form, often sustained by a comparatively simple accompaniment. While this accompaniment remains rather stable, the theme is ornamented, changed rhythmically, and otherwise paraphrased. In fact, if the theme happened to be a well-known dance tune or song, the Baroque composer frequently refrained from stating it at all. Instead, he started his composition with the first variation.

Sixteenth-century Spanish music supplies some early examples of keyboard variation. What these amount to are polyphonic settings of a theme (usually a popular song or dance) presented in different contrapuntal voices.

English virginal composers applied variation treatment to individual dances, such as the pavane, and they also created independent sets of variations that display superior skill and imagination.

The Baroque *theme and variations* found its greatest success in Germany and Austria. Some composers, such as Froberger, combined variation technique with the suite, producing a hybrid form called the *variation suite*. In this event, the courante, sarabande, and gigue became variations on the initial material presented in the allemande. In Germany the theme and variations attained its most distinguished development with Bach's *Goldberg Variations*.

Fugue

The *fugue,* which reached its prime in the Baroque era, developed from the Renaissance contrapuntal keyboard forms.

It is also a contrapuntal composition, worked out according to prescribed rules and tenets of counterpoint. It habitually employs three or four voices, occasionally five. The subject—a fairly short melodic phrase—is stated in one voice, unaccompanied. Then the second voice (or answer) enters with the same melody—this time at another pitch level, generally up a fifth or down a fourth—while the first voice either begins the countersubject (a new melody) or continues in counterpoint. When the second voice has completed the subject, it may begin the countersubject, and so on. The exposition of a fugue takes place when the subject has been stated in all voices.

After this, the fugue proceeds to alternate "episodes" and "entries." An episode occurs when a section of a fugue does not have a voice part stating the subject in full, whereas an entry occurs when there is a return of the complete subject in one of the voice parts. Toward the end, at the climax of the fugue, all voice parts may enter with the subject in close succession (*stretto*). Here the original theme may be presented in one voice and simultaneously offered by another voice in either stretched or contracted form. The fugue, generally speaking, consists of an exposition followed by alternating episodes and entries; it terminates with a closing section containing statements of the subject.

A composition in contrasting style usually preceded the fugue, and for this the Baroque composer could select from several quasi-improvisatory types, such as the *prelude, toccata,* or *fantasy*. The prelude consisted of a principal motive that was expanded by repetition and modulation. The toccata, fundamentally a work in rapid tempo, had alternating passages of different textures. The fantasy included elements from both prelude and toccata. The three types actually had many characteristics in common, especially in relation to harpsichord composition. The desired objective was music in free style, or noncontrapuntal style, to contrast with the fugue's polyphonic character.

Chorale Settings for Organ

The organ *chorale*—a general term for an organ composition based on a hymn tune—took form in German Lutheran churches during the seventeenth century, when it was customary for the organist to play an introduction to the hymn (chorale) to be sung by the congregation. In time this keyboard setting for the hymn became a distinctive and highly refined compositional art, particularly among German Protestant composers, and out of this practice of playing organ preludes and interludes (organ passages between verses of hymn tunes) grew four characteristic forms of organ chorale music: chorale prelude, chorale fantasy, chorale partita or chorale variation, and chorale fugue.

For the chorale prelude, the hymn melody is often borrowed line by line, enriched by other melodic parts, and then woven into elaborate keyboard polyphony. Sometimes the melody remains intact, and sometimes it is ornamented so much that it becomes unrecognizable.

In the chorale fantasy, the hymn tune is not reproduced completely. Fragments of the chorale melody emerge in skillful contrapuntal elaboration and decoration, then disappear to make way for other fragments.

The chorale partita or variation uses variation technique to transform the hymn tune. Sometimes a true variation suite results.

In the chorale fugue the initial phrases of the chorale serve as the fugue subject. Sometimes the rest of the melody is presented phrase by phrase in a series of little fugues.

Although many composers before and after Bach wrote prolifically in this field, no one has equaled the emotional depth and endless variety of his chorale settings.

Concerto

The most expressive orchestral form of the late Baroque is the *concerto grosso.* One of the most exciting Baroque musical types, the concerto grosso explores contrasts in sonority (tone color) and volume (dynamics). In the Baroque era it was performed by two contrasting tonal media. The *concertino* (*principale*), a small group of instruments playing together or as soloists, usually consisted of two violins, cello, and harpsichord. This concertino alternated with the full orchestra, called variously *tutti, concerto,* or *ripieno,* which at first included only a small number of strings but later expanded to include such instruments as trumpets, oboes, flutes, and horns.

The seventeenth-century concerto grosso originally consisted of a series of short movements, often styled like the various dances found in the suite; later a four-movement sequence like that of the sonata da chiesa became common. Antonio Vivaldi (1678–1741) began a new trend using three movements—allegro-adagio-allegro—showing little evidence of counterpoint. In the quick (allegro) movements Vivaldi established schematic principles for future composers: the tutti (which was also called a *ritornello* because it "returns") alternates with different episodes played by the concertino. Bach followed this pattern in his *Brandenburg Concertos.*

The Baroque solo concerto, introduced in the eighteenth century, reached perfection in the works of Vivaldi and Bach. Initially this form had three or four movements written in ample homophonic style, with increasing emphasis on the melodic elements present in solo passages. Vivaldi reduced the form to three movements, stressing virtuoso passages for the soloist. He wrote numerous violin concertos—perhaps one reason why the solo concerto remained a favorite in Italy throughout the eighteenth century.

FOR DISCUSSION AND ASSIGNMENT

1. Listen to the first movement of a typical Baroque concerto or concerto grosso by Vivaldi, Corelli, or Bach. Does the "Baroque" sound conform to the musical characteristics discussed in this chapter? Can you now hear the difference between Baroque and Renaissance music?
2. Listen to a solo passage ("Tu se' morta," for example) from Monteverdi's opera *Orfeo.* Then listen to an aria from an opera of Alessandro Scarlatti. Describe the development that occurred within a hundred years.
3. Is it possible to create tension and emotion in music by using strict technical devices? Listen to "Dido's Lament," from Purcell's opera *Dido and Aeneas*—an aria built on a ground bass or basso ostinato. What do you think?
4. Listen to a harpsichord suite by Bach, Handel, or Rameau. Most of the pieces will be dances. Do you think they are suitable for dancing? Do you find them attractive just for listening?

FOR FURTHER READING

Barnes, Harry Elmer. *An Intellectual and Cultural History of the Western World.* Vol. 2. New York: Dover Publications, Inc., 1965. PB. Dr. Barnes devotes almost the entire volume to a survey of the seventeenth and eighteenth centuries. The narrative is nontechnical, informative, and interestingly written.

Dent, Edward J. *Opera.* Baltimore, Md.: Penguin Books, 1965. A Pelican PB. Obviously written by an Englishman for his countrymen, this little pocket book is a good condensed history of opera. The history of English opera is saved for the climax.

Friedrich, Carl J. *The Age of the Baroque: 1610–1660.* New York: Harper & Row, Publishers, 1952. A Torchbook PB. This excellent book explores all phases of a fifty-year segment within the Baroque.

———. "The Baroque Age," article in *Horizon.* New York: American Horizon, Inc., July, 1960. Dr. Friedrich presents the finest introduction to the Baroque to be found anywhere.

Tapié, Victor-L. *The Age of Grandeur,* translated by A. R. Williamson. New York: Frederick A. Praeger, 1961. PB. A large book devoted exclusively to a discussion of Baroque art and architecture. Lavishly illustrated, it gives a vivid picture of the era.

Johann Sebastian Bach

11

Departed Bach! Long since thy splendid organ playing
Alone brought thee the noble cognomen "the Great,"
And what thy pen had writ, the highest art displaying,
Did some with joy and some with envy contemplate.

GEORG PHILIPP TELEMANN
Poem in Praise of Bach (1751)[1]

The name Bach commands a respect unsurpassed in the musical world. This remarkable family produced several generations of creative musicians, the most important being Johann Sebastian Bach (1685–1750), who was born in the Thuringian town of Eisenach, Germany, where his father, Johann Ambrosius Bach (1645–1695), worked as a court musician. Johann Sebastian's mother died when he was nine, his father's death followed within a year, and the youngster's rearing became the responsibility of his eldest brother Johann Christoph, organist at the small town of Ohrdruf. This brother taught him the clavichord and in all probability other instruments and composition.

Young Bach was precocious and avid for learning; he did exceptionally well in his school studies, helped his brother with household expenses by earning money as a singer, and received a sound training in Lutheran orthodoxy. When he was almost fifteen he left his brother's house to become a choir member—on a scholarship with free board and tuition—at St. Michael's Church in Lüneburg, 200 miles away from Ohrdruf. As usual, he did brilliantly at the *Michaelisschule,* the Latin school that scholarship boys had to attend, and advanced in his keyboard and violin studies. During this period Bach had opportunities to enlarge his musical horizons, and he took advantage of every occasion that arose. The distinguished organist Georg Böhm, then employed at Lüneburg's *Johannes-kirche,* consented to take him as a student. It was due to Böhm's stories about the musical life in Hamburg that young Bach walked 30 miles to hear the great organist J. A. Reinken, then 78 years old, and to drink in all the other musical

[1] From David and Mendel, editors, *The Bach Reader* (W. W. Norton & Co., Inc., 1945). Reprinted by permission.

events in that city. At other times he went over to Celle to become acquainted with the French instrumental music played there at the court.

When he finished his studies at the Lüneburg *Michaelisschule* in 1702, Bach returned to Thuringia to find work. In 1703 he spent several months as servant-violinist to a younger brother of the Duke of Weimar; in August of that year he became organist at a small church in Arnstadt. While at Arnstadt, he obtained a month's leave to go to St. Mary's at Lübeck—230 miles north—where the famous organist Dietrich Buxtehude was presenting his fine choral-instrumental performances. So entranced was Bach by Buxtehude's spectacular music that he remained in Lübeck four months—without permission from his employers—instead of four weeks.

In 1707 Bach left Arnstadt to become organist at St. Blasius' in Mühlhausen. That same year he married his second cousin Maria Barbara Bach, who bore him seven children. In 1708 he was back at Weimar, first as organist, then in a newly created post as concertmaster. At Weimar he reached his full powers both as organist and as creative composer, and he received numerous invitations to perform at other courts and cities. It is an interesting point that Bach's wide-ranging compositional repertoire, a historical monument in musical art, was not much appreciated during his lifetime; it was only his skill as a keyboard virtuoso that spread his fame throughout all Germany. Fortunately for posterity, Bach the composer continued to write prodigiously.

After nine years at Weimar he moved on to become court conductor to Prince Leopold of Anhalt-Cöthen, an entirely different assignment for Bach, for he was expected to concentrate on instrumental music and was not required to play the organ or to compose church music, duties which up to this time had constituted the most important part of his work. Life at Cöthen was full and happy with his family, his work, and his students, until Maria Barbara died suddenly in 1720, leaving her husband with four children—the others had died in infancy—between the ages of five and twelve.

A year and a half later Bach married Anna Magdalena Wilcken, a soprano singer at the Cöthen court. This second marriage was also happy; it lasted 29 years and produced 13 children, seven of whom died young. In 1722 the post of cantor at St. Thomas' Church in Leipzig became vacant when the renowned Johann Kuhnau died. Johann Sebastian was granted the coveted position and in 1723 moved his family from Cöthen to Leipzig, where he remained as the Thomas Cantor until his death 27 years later.

Bach's importance in music history cannot be exaggerated. Almost everything he wrote is a testament to his genius. His music brims over with invention. Bach's inherent inspiration to write such works was no doubt encouraged by the positions he held, since most of his music was written for either particular churches or noble patrons. In Bach's time, German life centered around the church, and music was vital to church services. Nearly all of his some 200 extant sacred cantatas were composed expressly for a feast day of the ecclesiastical year. They include chorales, choruses, recitatives, ariosos, Italianate arias, duets—all revealing melodic richness.

Yet Bach lived in a society where the sacred and the secular formed two equally compelling and complementary forces. Besides composing church music, he experimented with every compositional form of his time except opera. His concerti grossi, suites, and sonatas confirm his reputation as a universally minded composer fascinated with all musical types and styles.

Coming on the scene at a crucial time in musical history—that period when contrapuntal style began to merge with a predominantly harmonic style—Bach and his art reflect the image of that moment. His writings pinpoint a crossroad at which influences from the north, south, and west were gathered. Although he masterfully assimilated these historical and geographical influences, his own originality is ever present, even in his youthful works. Almost everything Bach wrote displays his talent for melodic and rhythmic invention and harmonic audacity.

CHORAL MUSIC

Cantatas

Bach is said to have composed five complete sets of church cantatas for Sundays and holy days—which add up to 295 works—but less than 200 now exist. These works mirror Bach's Christian character, expressing his spirituality, symbolism, and intense emotions.

Serving as a musical commentary on the gospel for each holy day, the Bach cantata lasted from 20 to 30 minutes. It was sung after the Creed and before the sermon; if constructed in two parts, the second followed the sermon. Cantata texts were either original or borrowed from chorale stanzas, in which case they were often paraphrased. Some cantatas are for solo voice, but Bach's typical cantatas require soloists, chorus, and orchestral accompaniment (Ill. 10:3).

The style varies in these cantatas. Bach sometimes enjoyed using texts written by contemporary poets, whose "librettos" usually contained six or seven stanzas in free poetry based on the gospel of the day. Bach set these stanzas variously for chorus, da capo arias, and recitatives, and he de-emphasized the chorale's importance. Examples of cantatas based on poetical texts are No. 21, *Ich hatte viel Bekümmernis* (I Was Sore Distressed), and No. 161, *Komm du süsse Todesstunde* (Come Sweet Death, Thou Blessed Healer), both composed for the Trinity season.

At Leipzig, however, Bach chose the chorale cantata as his favorite vehicle, with texts taken directly from chorale stanzas or free paraphrases thereof. After an instrumental introduction, the opening chorus often expands into a fantasy based on the hymn melody; successive text stanzas are set in recitatives and arias; the ending is usually a simple setting of the chorale melody.

The Easter cantata *Christ lag in Todesbanden* (Christ Lay by Death Enshrouded), No. 4, has seven movements, each based on a stanza from the hymn. The first-movement chorus is a polyphonic setting designed to enhance the chorale melody. *Ein feste Burg ist unser Gott* (A Mighty Fortress Is Our God), No. 80, is based on Luther's Reformation chorale, and four of the eight movements were inspired by the hymn tune. The well-known chorale *Wachet auf* (Sleepers, Wake) received an especially beautiful chorale setting in cantata No. 140. This cantata's fourth movement, for tenors and orchestra, was transcribed by Bach for organ.

Magnificat

Bach created this elaborate cantata to mark his first Christmas season at Leipzig; then in 1730 he revised the work to make it suitable for performance on other occasions. The text is the canticle of Mary when she is told that a miracle is about to be achieved through her. Bach held to the Latin, which had preserved the biblical text for so many centuries, and created a joyous hymn that fits perfectly with the text. It seems as though in composing the choruses—not in his customary four voices but in five, according to seventeenth-century practice—Bach wished to accentuate the work's liturgical character and link it to past traditions. In using the first chorus theme in the concluding section, he followed the Italian idea that a Magnificat should end the way it began.

One noteworthy fact about this imposing work is that Bach holds the listener's attention throughout. He has done so by constructing the *Magnificat* in eleven sections (described below), each section being so brief and concentrated that the whole composition lasts only about 30 minutes. A section for chorus alternates with two sections for solo or duet, thus sustaining the listener's interest.

1. *Magnificat anima mea Dominum.* (My soul doth magnify the Lord.) An exuberant orchestral introduction sets the mood. With a virtuoso polyphonic fanfare, the chorus joins the orchestra.

2. *Et exsultavit spiritus meus in Deo salutari meo.* (And my spirit hath rejoiced in God my Savior.) In this soprano aria the joyfulness continues but is more subdued. An upward flourish initiating each melodic phrase asserts the textual meaning.

3. *Quia respexit humilitatem ancillae suae. Ecce enim ex hoc beatam me dicent omnes generationes.* (For He hath regarded the low estate of His handmaiden: For behold, from henceforth all generations shall call me blessed.) Bach's lyrical setting leads into a dramatic explosion: an oboe d'amore blends with a soprano solo up to the words *omnes generationes,* whereupon the full chorus and orchestra burst into a contrapuntal peroration.

4. *Quia fecit mihi magna qui potens est, et sanctum nomen ejus.* (For He that is mighty hath done to me great things, and holy is His name.) Sonorous bass tones convey the Lord's power and munificence in an aria developed from a single short motive.

5. *Et misericordia ejus a progenie in progenies timentibus eum.* (And His mercy is on them that fear Him from generation to generation.) A contralto and tenor duet in $\frac{12}{8}$ meter is heightened by an obbligato for two flutes, the whole supported by strings and continuo.

6. *Fecit potentiam in brachio suo, dispersit superbos mente cordis sui.* (He hath shewed strength with His arm: He hath scattered the proud in the imagination of their hearts.) Another virtuoso exposition by the chorus, terminating with a brief, moving *Adagio,* contrasts with the reserve in the preceding section.

7. *Deposuit potentes de sede et exaltavit humiles.* (He hath put down the mighty from their seats and exalted them of low degree.) This vigorous aria is set for tenor solo supported by all the violins in unison, with continuo. The melodic line descends on the word *deposuit* and rises by sequence on *exaltavit.*

8. *Esurientes implevit bonis et divites dimisit inanes.* (He hath filled the hungry with good things; and the rich He hath sent empty away.) Against a background duet played by two flutes with continuo, the contralto sings a

rhythmically varied melodic line employing scale passages. At the final statement the word *inanes* (empty) is sung without accompaniment.

9. *Suscepit Israel puerum suum recordatus misericordiae suae.* (He hath holpen His servant Israel, in remembrance of His mercy.) Bach evokes an ethereal atmosphere with a three-part women's chorus in imitative counterpoint, above which two unison oboes intone in held notes the old plainchant Magnificat melody.

10. *Sicut locutus est ad patres nostros Abraham et semini ejus in saecula.* (As He spake to our Father, to Abraham and his seed forever.) This buoyant, five-part fugal chorus brings the *Magnificat* proper to a close.

11. *Gloria Patri, Gloria Filio, Gloria et Spiritui Sancto. Sicut erat in principio, et nunc, et semper, et in saecula saeculorum.* (Glory to the Father, Glory to the Son, Glory also to the Holy Ghost. As it was at the beginning and is now and shall be forever in all eternity.) The coda, formed by the Gloria, begins with the chorus weaving sinuous lines of triplet figures. But at the word *sicut* (as it was in the beginning . . .) Bach literally returns to the beginning, concluding with joyous music from the first section.

Passions

During the Middle Ages it had become traditional at Holy Week services to chant the account of Christ's Passion, dividing the biblical roles among several participants: one intoned the narrative, a second Jesus' words, a third the lines of all other characters involved, and a chorus delivered the crowd's comments. Luther held to this tradition, and both Catholic and Protestant churches evolved three different ways to sing the Passion.

First and simplest, they continued the established practices. A tenor sang the evangelist role, a bass that of Christ, and an alto represented other participants. In order to break up the monotony created by successive declamations, the congregation sang a hymn from time to time or the chorus sang before and after narrative episodes.

In another method, in vogue when purely polyphonic style reached its peak, everything was sung by choruses—in five, six, or eight parts.

The third method combined elements from the other two, and Bach's Passions fall within this category. Solo voices again carry the evangelist and Jesus roles, but the chorus assumes equal importance, presenting portions of the scriptural account as well as free poetic texts reflecting on the unfolding drama. Though Bach supposedly wrote several Passion settings, only two are now known: the Passions according to St. John and St. Matthew. Of the two, the St. Matthew Passion—based on Chapters 26 and 27 in the Gospel—speaks more forcefully to the listener.

Bach employed the full resources at his command: two orchestras, two choirs, and a boy soprano choir to sing the hymn tune "O Lamb of God" in the monumental first chorus. Bach injects a somber feeling into this work by omitting all brass instruments.

Conforming to tradition, Bach assigns St. Matthew's lines to a tenor and the role of Jesus to a bass. All female parts are sung by a soprano. The evangelist is accompanied only by figured-bass chords, but the words of Jesus are supported by strings.

Mass in B Minor

In 1733 Bach composed a Kyrie as a memorial to Augustus the Strong and a Gloria to celebrate the ascension of the new Saxony Elector, Augustus III. He sent both pieces to the new ruler with a petition for a court title, a favor granted three years later.

The Latin Mass had never been totally excluded from the Lutheran service. In Bach's time the Missa (Mass) consisted of the Kyrie and Gloria, and occasionally other sections. By 1738 Bach had added a Credo, Sanctus, and Agnus Dei to his Missa of 1733 (the *Mass in B Minor*), thus completing the Latin Ordinary of the Mass. However, the intricate structure and inordinate length of this Mass renders it unsuitable for either Catholic or Protestant liturgical service.

The *Mass in B Minor* lacks the direct emotional appeal of the St. Matthew Passion because its proportions and intricacies tend to make it sound aloof and impersonal. As the music progresses, however, the listener often discovers that his initial reservations have changed to attachment.

The five parts of the Mass are broken up into subsections; the Gloria and Credo, for example, each have eight separate movements, while the Kyrie appears as a huge vocal fugal exposition. Bach borrowed heavily from his church cantatas for this Mass but usually altered them radically. Gregorian melodies appear in the Credo, and various forms and compositional devices appear throughout—fugues, canons, variations, motets, Italian-style arias, and duets. Yet these are not disparate, dislocated musical sections. The Mass is a cohesive cycle in which Bach combines love, faith, and innate musicality to create a work with universal appeal.

KEYBOARD MUSIC

Organ Chorales

Bach's organ music, with its rich texture, diverse forms, and the incredible variety often found within a single form, excels all organ music written before and after his time. There had been tremendous activity in organ composition before Bach, and organists such as Buxtehude and Böhm naturally influenced him, but no one had ever graced organ music with the special quality that Bach achieved. He was also a virtuoso on the instrument. According to stories told by his contemporaries, Bach could improvise on a theme for two hours or more, using all forms appropriate to the organ yet never changing the thematic material.

Bach left about 140 hymn-tune settings, or organ chorales as they are commonly known. Most of them can be found in four collections arranged by the composer himself: *Orgel-Büchlein* (1739); *Catechism Chorale Preludes* (1739);

Schübler Chorales (1746); and *Grosse Choräle* (Eighteen Chorale Preludes, 1750).

The organ chorales in the *Orgel-Büchlein* (Little Organ Book) are constructed on a slight framework. In each setting the entire melody is present, without interludes, and usually appears in the soprano voice. For accompaniment Bach used small rhythmic and melodic motives that serve to unify and intensify the hymn tune's textual meaning; for example, in "O Lamb of God" a succession of sighs (descending appoggiaturas) in the accompanying parts underscores the poignant sadness.

The Eighteen Chorale Preludes have broad form and invention; their deeply personal mood marks them as forerunners of the great choruses composed for the Leipzig cantatas. The six *Schübler Chorales* are organ arrangements of portions of Bach's own cantatas. One, *Wachet auf, ruft uns die Stimme* (Sleepers, Wake), has a particularly beautiful hymn setting. In the original cantata tenors sing the chorale melody accompanied by strings playing a countermelody over a figured bass; for the organ arrangement Bach fashioned a trio for two manuals and pedals and placed the chorale melody in the left hand.

Organ Fugues

Although the chorale settings offer perhaps the finest examples of Bach's diversified art, his fugues are better known, doubtlessly because their virtuoso character and rhythmic exuberance make them so appealing. About 50 organ fugues are known today, dating from almost every period of Bach's life.

Bach fugues are typically preceded by an introduction—prelude, fantasy, or toccata—sometimes having polyphonic texture and always in improvisatory style. Bach allowed his imagination a freer reign in the introductions than he did in the fugues, which are limited by formal contrapuntal rules; for instance, the *Toccata in F Major* may at first glance appear to be only a tour de force calculated to highlight dexterity in pedal technique, but close examination reveals abundant modulation. In the *Fantasy* preceding the *Fugue in G Minor,* Bach pours out torrents of power and passion with dramatically free movement, and a lengthy, lilting theme predominates throughout.

Two fugal works far outrank all others in popularity. One is the *Toccata in D Minor* (popularly called *Toccata and Fugue in D Minor*), an early work that demands virtuoso technique. This toccata begins and ends with rhapsodic sections seemingly intended to create an improvisatorial impression. In the center Bach introduces a freely designed fugue, where runs and broken-chord episodes separate the theme's various entrances. Though written by a youthful hand, this *Toccata in D Minor* proves that its creator's zestful energy is always tempered with genuine musicianship, good taste, and artistic discrimination.

The second in this duo of popular organ works is the *Passacaglia and Fugue in C Minor,* in which Bach uses variation form for his introduction instead of a prelude, toccata, or fantasy. The simple theme has eight measures, the first four borrowed from a French composer named André Raison. While preserving this theme in its essential outline, Bach tailors 20 paraphrases to it. The fugue following the passacaglia is a double fugue: the first subject evolves from the first four measures of the theme, but the counterpoint accompanying it is important enough to take on the role of a second subject.

The Well-Tempered Clavier

While at Cöthen (1717–1723), Bach had neither a choir nor an adequate organ at his immediate disposal. With ease he turned from choral and organ writing to harpsichord, orchestral, and chamber music.

The *Wohltemperiertes Clavier* (Well-Tempered Clavier) includes two sets of preludes and fugues in all the major and minor keys. The first volume dates from 1722; the second was finished in Leipzig between 1740 and 1744. A lengthy subtitle on the first volume emphasizes that its primary purpose is to instruct, but never before had any work written for instructional purposes achieved such high artistic value. Bach's *Well-Tempered Clavier* raised the harpsichord (and clavichord) to the same heights that he had established for the organ fugue. A word of explanation about the title: "well-tempered" refers to a newly developed method of tuning keyboard instruments; "clavier" in German means any keyboard instrument; therefore, this collection is for keyboard instruments in general. Some preludes and fugues do seem clearly meant for a specific instrument; for example, in the first book the *Prelude and Fugue in C-Sharp Minor* and the *Prelude and Fugue in E-Flat Minor,* with their sustained lyrical quality, are most effective on the clavichord; on the other hand, the *Fugue in A Minor* from the same book sounds best when played on an organ with pedals.

The relationships between the various preludes and fugues in the *Well-Tempered Clavier* vary considerably. Frequently the prelude sparkles rapidly, like a virtuoso piece. Sometimes it is related to the fugue. At other times it is in complete opposition to the fugue, the only similarity being the common key in which both are written. The lilting *Prelude in D Major* contrasts strongly with the *Fugue in D Major,* whose dotted rhythms recall an overture in French style. One of the most beautiful fugues in the first book is the last one (in *b* minor), whose chromatic subject (Ex. 11:1) is subjected to skillful development.

Ex. 11:1. Bach: *Well-Tempered Clavier, Book I: Fugue in B Minor*

When Bach used fugal form he always created a theme having some identifiable characteristic. This might be a subtle emotional quality or a rhythmic principle, either of which could then provide the basic mood or motion for the entire movement. Consequently his fugues portray every sentiment, from melancholy to gaiety.

The Goldberg Variations

Bach's harpsichord masterpiece, the crowning achievement of Baroque keyboard music, is the *Aria with Thirty Variations,* better known as the *Goldberg Variations* (*Clavier-Übung IV*). This work sums up all that the Baroque period could offer in variation technique.

The theme for the *Goldberg Variations* came from a notebook that Bach compiled and presented to his second wife, Anna Magdalena Bach, in 1725. It is a two-part lyrical theme (*Aria*), ornate but sustained by a solid harmonic support

(Ex. 11:2). This support forms the framework on which the variations are based; the only harmonic change is from major to minor.

Ex. 11:2. Bach: *Goldberg Variations: Aria*

The formal plan comprises ten series of three variations each—two characteristic variations plus a canon. (The canons start at the unison and progress through the ninth.) These contrapuntal works are so skillfully conceived that one seldom realizes their technical intricacies. Often the two canonic parts are accompanied by an active bass obbligato, thus creating a three-voice instead of a two-voice variation.

The variations framing the canons are even more remarkable when one considers that they are all within the same harmonic framework: the fifth variation exploits crossing of hands in a light, gay spirit; the seventh variation is a kind of siciliana (a piece in $\frac{6}{8}$ meter with dotted rhythm); the tenth is a fughetta (a short fugue). Variations 13 and 25 are embellished arias, beautifully devised and grandly stated. The sixteenth variation is an overture in French style. The last variation is singular: a potpourri in which Bach adroitly fuses two popular German folk songs.

A work Bach definitely specified for a harpsichord with two keyboards, the *Goldberg Variations* shows an exceptional talent for idiomatic keyboard writing. One must agree with the English writer Sir Donald Tovey:

> Until Beethoven wrote the 'Waldstein' Sonata, the 'Goldberg' Variations were the most brilliant piece of sheer instrumental display extant. No other work by Bach himself, or by Domenico Scarlatti, not even any concerto by Mozart or any earlier work of Beethoven could compare with it for instrumental brilliance.[2]

ORCHESTRAL MUSIC

Brandenburg Concertos

In 1721, while surrounded by the glamour and excitement at the Cöthen court, Bach wrote six concertos dedicated to Christian Ludwig, Margrave of Brandenburg. In essence they form a compendium of orchestral ensemble music as it existed in Bach's time.

Each concerto is scored for a special combination, with traditional German emphasis on wind instruments. Each includes strings and continuo, and all except the first and third have the three-movement sequence of fast-slow-fast.

There is considerable variety in the concertos' formal aspects.

[2] Donald Francis Tovey, *Essays in Musical Analysis: Chamber Music* (London: Oxford University Press, 1944), p. 35. Reprinted by permission.

> In three of them (nos. 1, 3, 6) the orchestra is composed of evenly balanced instrumental choirs which toss the themes to and fro among themselves in charming conversation, only occasionally surrendering the lead to a single instrument out of their midst. Such compositions, based upon the old Venetian *canzona,* with its contrasting instrumental choirs, are known as "orchestra concertos" or "concerto-symphonies."[3]

The other concertos have concerto grosso form: the accompanying orchestra—ripieno or tutti—alternates with the concertino, a group of three or four instruments.

It would be difficult to name any one of these six concertos as the best. *Number 5, in D Major* is vastly interesting. A string orchestra contrasts with a concertino of violin, flute, and harpsichord. However, the harpsichord part dominates to such an extent that the work doubtlessly constitutes the first harpsichord concerto. Bach achieved dramatic effects in the first movement: a lighthearted cuckoo-like motive played by the various solo instruments; a flute and violin duet accompanied by a brilliant harpsichord obbligato; toward the end a dazzling harpsichord solo of 65 measures. The pensive middle movement—*Affetuoso*—requires only the solo instruments. In gigue rhythm, the merry final movement combines fugal style with da capo form, the first 78 measures being literally repeated at the end.

> The Brandenburg Concertos seem to embody the splendor and effervescence of court life at Cöthen, and, moreover, they reveal the composer's delight in writing for a group of highly trained instrumentalists. There is an exuberance and abundance of inspiration in this music which only a genius, aware of his newly achieved full mastery, could call forth. Craftsmanship and richly flowing melodic invention, logic and zest for experimenting, counterpoise each other here to an extent rarely equaled again even by Bach himself.[4]

Orchestral Suites

The keyboard suite as apostrophized by Bach typically offered four dance movements in a prescribed sequence, frequently prefaced by a rather long introduction.

Eighteenth-century orchestral suites were often called Overtures (*Ouvertures*) and were constructed differently from their keyboard counterparts. The opening movement was likely to be a French Overture similar to that standardized by Lully (see page 136) : a slow, solemn introduction, a spritely fugal middle section, and a slow conclusion similar to the beginning. After this opening movement came a series of dance movements, not in prescribed order but freely arranged for variety and contrast.

Bach wrote four *Ouvertures,* now called *Orchestral Suites.* The first two, in *C* major and *b* minor respectively, are scored for woodwinds and strings. For the other two (both in *D* major), he added trumpets and timpani.

After the first movement, called *Ouverture* in each case, Bach selects from a highly diversified group of dance movements: *Bourrée, Gavotte, Minuet, Courante, Forlane, Passepied, Sarabande, Polonaise, Gigue, Rondeau, Badinerie, Air,* and *Réjouissance.*

[3] Karl Geiringer, *Johann Sebastian Bach* (New York: Oxford University Press, 1966), p. 319. Reprinted by permission.

[4] Geiringer, p. 322. Reprinted by permission.

Each suite is a tribute to Bach's ability to express wit and sophistication through sonorous orchestral texture. The Lully-based initial *Ouverture* is so enriched that it loses all resemblance to its model. The fugal middle section often recalls concerto form in its alternation between tutti and solo. And the dances themselves show Bach's talent for handling instrumental form and texture and his gift for organizing musical materials into moments of grandeur.

Two orchestral suites especially are heard today. *Suite No. 2 in B Minor* uses strings, continuo, and a solo flute. Bach followed the opening *Ouverture* with a *Rondeau,* a form he seldom used. Its principal theme (later strikingly inverted) is both effective and unusual. The following *Sarabande* uses flute and cellos in canon. Two *Bourrées* come next, the second featuring a solo flute. The next dance, *Polonaise and Double* (variation), is noticeably original: in the variation the flute plays a virtuoso variant of the theme over the *Polonaise* tune in the continuo. After the *Minuet* comes a swift, playful *Badinerie* (banter) as the flute weaves silver arabesques amid the strings.

Equally appealing is *Suite No. 3 in D Major* for strings and harpsichord, two oboes, three trumpets, and timpani. Its second movement is the famous *Air,* elsewhere known as the *Air for the G String* through its arrangement in C major for violin solo. In its original setting the *Air* is scored for string orchestra: the violins play an expansive, emotion-charged melodic line against a bass accompaniment of curious but convincing octave motives. The following two *Gavottes* call for full orchestra wherein bright trumpets provide a pleasing foil to the preceding *Air.* A *Bourrée* and an elegant, graceful *Gigue* round off one of Bach's most appealing works.

MUSICAL OFFERING AND ART OF THE FUGUE

Toward the end of his life, Bach composed two extended fugal works that affirm his peerless contrapuntal technique. The *Musical Offering* was occasioned by Bach's invitation to Berlin in 1747 to perform for Frederick the Great of Prussia. Greatly impressed by Bach's improvisations, particularly in fugal style, the king offered him a theme that he had composed. Back in Leipzig, Bach set to work and in a couple of months completed the *Musical Offering.* Written for clavier and chamber music combinations, the "offering" contains numerous skillfully wrought fugues and canons built on the royal theme. The work was of course dedicated to Frederick.

Elated by his success with the *Musical Offering,* Bach continued to explore the fugal idiom. His last great composition, *The Art of the Fugue,* demonstrates the art of fugue and counterpoint from its simplest to its most complicated forms. Building on a rather short theme (Ex. 11:3), Bach constructed magnificent fugues, but he never indicated the instruments for which they were intended. The final fugue was unfinished when he died. *The Art of the Fugue* is an impressive last testament from the greatest composer of the Baroque era.

Ex. 11:3. Bach: *The Art of the Fugue: theme*

FOR DISCUSSION AND ASSIGNMENT

1. Listen to a Bach organ fugue or a chorale prelude. Now listen to similar examples by one or two of Bach's lesser contemporaries, such as Vincent Lübeck, Nicolaus Bruhns, or Georg Böhm. Does Bach's work make a better impression? Why?
2. Bach's instrumental works are supposedly paragons of abstract music. See if you agree. While listening to the *Air* from Bach's *Orchestral Suite No. 3,* read a poem that creates a sad mood. Is the music satisfactorily complementary? Continue the music and read an emotional love sonnet. Is not the same music equally effective for this mood?
3. Listen to a Bach organ fugue, and then listen to an orchestral transcription of the same fugue. How does it compare with the original version?
4. Based on your reactions to the foregoing questions, write a short essay explaining why Bach is considered the greatest composer of the eighteenth-century Baroque period.

FOR FURTHER READING

David, Hans, and Arthur Mendel, eds., *The Bach Reader,* revised edition. New York: W. W. Norton & Co., Inc., 1966. PB. A life of J. S. Bach in letters and documents. The unusual approach makes for interesting reading and also supplies valuable and pertinent information.

Geiringer, Karl. *Johann Sebastian Bach.* New York: Oxford University Press, 1966. The latest—and finest—of the one-volume studies of Bach, his life, and his music.

Grew, Eva Mary, and Sydney Grew. *Bach.* New York: Collier Books, 1962. PB. A short, readable account of Bach the composer and organist. It also contains a biographical calendar and a catalog of his works.

Gurlitt, Wilibald. *Johann Sebastian Bach,* translated by O. C. Rupprecht. St. Louis, Mo.: Concordia Publishing House, 1957. PB. This book is unusual in that it discusses Bach in the light of the religious and social aspects of his times.

Pirro, André. *J. S. Bach,* translated by M. Savill. New York: Crown Publishers, 1957. A Bonanza PB. Pirro's book concentrates on Bach's life and choral compositions.

Terry, Charles Sanford. *The Music of Bach: An Introduction.* New York: Dover Publications, Inc., 1963. A Dover PB. This nontechnical guide is so brief as to be almost an outline, but it is an excellent elementary introduction to Bach's music.

Other Baroque Composers 12

Strong in new Arms, lo! Giant Handel stands,
Like bold Briareus, with a hundred hands;
To stir, to rouse, to shake the Soul he comes,
And Jove's own Thunders follow Mars's Drums.

ALEXANDER POPE
The Dunciad (1743)

GEORGE FREDERICK HANDEL

George Frederick Handel (1685–1759) was born in Halle, Germany, to Georg Händel, an elderly barber-surgeon, and his second wife, Dorothea Taust, daughter of a Bohemian Lutheran pastor. When he was about seven his father took him to visit the court at Weissenfels, where the duke, recognizing the boy's musical talent, urged his father to get him a music teacher. For three or four years thereafter Friedrich Wilhelm Zachau, organist at the Halle cathedral, took Handel as a pupil and worked conscientiously to develop his talent for composing and playing. Although sacred music was not Handel's first choice, Zachau made him compose a church cantata each week. For his general education, he attended the Lutheran Gymnasium, a grammar school in Halle.

On a visit to Berlin in 1696 Handel so impressed the court that the Elector of Brandenburg (one of the princes entitled to take part in choosing the emperor) offered him further music training in Italy as a preliminary to a court appointment. Handel's realistic father, who felt that a musical career could not provide tangible profits, discouraged the offer and took his son back to Halle.

In 1702 Handel entered Halle university as a law student—in deference to his father, who had died five years earlier—but he continued to study music and soon became organist at the cathedral, a position that required him to compose ecclesiastical music. After giving up his law studies in 1703, he gravitated to Hamburg, where he played second violin in the opera house and absorbed that progressive city's musical life. Handel wrote and produced his first opera, *Almira,* in 1705, proving unquestionably that he had an extraordinary gift for dramatic music. This success brought him fame and also aroused jealousy in a fellow composer, Reinhard Keiser (1674–1739). Because of the unpleasant rivalry that ensued, Handel decided to leave Hamburg in 1706.

Choosing Italy as having the best atmosphere for an aspiring opera composer, Handel acquired the flowing Italian vocal style with incredible ease and gained quick fame as both composer and performer. Italian audiences adored him, and his three-year stay in Italy added greatly to his knowledge, reputation, and friendships. His immensely successful opera *Agrippina,* produced in Venice in 1709, turned out to be his farewell to Italy, for shortly afterward he accepted an invitation from the Elector of Hanover to return to Germany.

Handel assumed his duties as Kapellmeister at Hanover in the summer of 1710; just a few months later he took leave to go to England. *Rinaldo,* his first opera in England, opened in February of 1711 before a wildly enthusiastic audience. Returning to Hanover at the end of the opera season, Handel waited a year before requesting another leave. Although the court granted permission on the condition that he return in a reasonable time, Handel—except for short visits to Ireland and back to the Continent—remained in England until his death almost fifty years later. By 1715 he had established a great reputation there as master composer and virtuoso performer. Acclaimed as the most brilliant harpsichordist in England, Handel often performed for his former patron the Elector, who became George I of England.

From 1719 until 1728, Handel composed and produced operas for the Royal Academy of Music; *Radamisto, Ottone, Giulio Cesare,* and others belong to this period. Throughout its brief existence—about eight years—the academy wavered between success and failure. Harassed by politics, temperamental singers, composer jealousies, public quarrels, and often poor performances, the academy closed in 1728. Handel formed a new company a year later, producing *Sosarme, Orlando,* and others, but this group ultimately faced the same problems. When a new company hired some of his singers, Handel retired from the opera field to devote his talents to writing oratorios, a form he had cultivated sporadically since 1732.

In 1741 he visited Ireland. After twelve successful concerts in Dublin, where his music was warmly appreciated, Handel in April of 1742 presented the first performance of his oratorio *Messiah.* Its brilliant success restored his confidence, but his health was failing. Later that year he returned to London, where he continued to write and produce more oratorios. By 1745 Handel and his music had again won the respect and affection of the English people. Despite his ill health, his final works reflect mature genius. Among the principal oratorios are *Esther, Deborah, Saul, Israel in Egypt, Messiah, Judas Maccabaeus, Joshua, Solomon,* and *Jephtha.* His sight failed while composing *Jephtha* in 1751 and, although blind after 1753, he spent his last years in contentment, knowing that his music was still successful, still being heard. This music, in fact, remained the strongest influence in English musical life for nearly a century. When Handel died in 1759, he was buried in the Poets' Corner at Westminster Abbey, honored and mourned by all England.

Born in the same year as Handel, Bach found inspirational sources in Pachelbel, Buxtehude, Corelli, Vivaldi, and Dieupart. Handel looked to Zachau, Buxtehude, the Scarlattis, Lully, and Purcell for his inspiration. Handel was a practical composer. He wrote neither to enlighten the soul nor to lay bare his innermost feelings, but rather to move his audience. His music belongs to the category of arts intended for the masses: architecture, decorative painting, tragedy. Its dramatic, robust character reflects the composer's own nature.

Handel's latest biographers agree that his personality and character represent the mood of his era. He was a vigorous, generous, sociable man with practical good sense, a love for food and drink, and a flair for the dramatic. His appearance has been described as majestic and leonine, and numerous stories attest to his impetuous temperament. Whereas Bach had composed music to glorify God and express his faith, Handel composed more for man and the world.

Handel's music has complete clarity, but it is less profound than Bach's music. It is decorative, and meant to be enjoyed for its vitality and frank rhythm. Symmetrical formulas—clichés, if one were to be unkind—are prominent. However, as a composer he was full of inspirations that he developed not only with vigor but often with grace and tenderness.

Another Handel characteristic is universality. Rather than confine himself to being strictly a German musician—though with his genius this could have had its own greatness—he became a European musician, and his teacher Zachau had prepared him well for that role. Handel's personal curiosity and travels expanded this knowledge. His greatest strength lies in his innate Saxon robustness, steadily enriched and modified by foreign influences. However, more predominant is the Italian influence, which shows particularly in his compositional procedures and lofty, noble approach to style. He also enjoyed and absorbed French music—*clavecin* music and the *chansons*. Finally, the English composer Henry Purcell exerted a very positive influence on him, providing just the right leavening between German vigor and Italian virtuosity.

Handel's massive repertoire includes operas, oratorios, passions, anthems and other church music, vocal chamber music, instrumental chamber music, three harpsichord collections, numerous concerti grossi in a highly lyrical and decorative style, a ballet, incidental music, and twelve concertos for organ and orchestra—masterpieces whose sovereign logic and sparkling writing have never been equaled in this form.

Opera

Handel wrote more than 40 operas, but few are performed today except when some enterprising college workshop or music society revives *Julius Caesar* or *Xerxes* as a matter of historical curiosity. From our viewpoint it is difficult to understand eighteenth-century England's obsession with Italian opera and its adulation for the composers who wrote such opera. At one point the rivalry between Handel and the Italian composer Giovanni Buononcini (1670–1747) reached such a high emotional pitch that the English poet John Byrom (1692–1763) wrote the following doggerel verse:

Some say, compared to Buononcini
That Mynheer Handel's but a ninny;
Others aver that he to Handel
Is scarcely fit to hold a candle.
Strange all this difference should be
'Twixt Tweedle-dum and Tweedle-dee.

Italian opera in Handel's day amounted to a succession of flamboyant da capo arias linked together by recitative. Bravura singing by prima donnas and castrati was much more important than the libretto, usually a piece of extravagant, high-flown nonsense. Handel adhered to the style that pleased contemporary taste, yet some of his operas contain very attractive music and should be heard more often. *Rinaldo*, for example, has two fine arias: "Cara sposa," which Handel thought was his best aria, and the well-known "Lascia ch'io pianga," which he lifted note for note out of his earlier opera *Agrippina.* While the opera *Serse* (*Xerxes*) is unfamiliar to most listeners, one aria from it has become widely known as an instrumental composition: during Queen Victoria's time, "Ombra mai fù" changed to Handel's *Largo.* Had Handel conceived opera as a dramatic entity, we might still be hearing his operatic repertoire.

Oratorio

In 1741 Handel produced his last opera, *Deidamia,* a disastrous failure that collapsed after three performances. With sturdy Saxon spirit he set about to readjust his thinking, ultimately concentrating on a musical form destined for perennial acceptance by the English public—the oratorio. Just a few months after the *Deidamia* catastrophe he was hard at work on *Messiah* (1742), now the most popular oratorio among English-speaking peoples. He had previously written several oratorios, including *Esther* and *Israel in Egypt.* As he continued to create one fine oratorio after another—*Samson* and *Judas Maccabaeus* among them—Handel proved that he was a choral composer in the grand style.

The *Messiah* text, supplied by Charles Jennens and most likely supervised by Handel, deals with the prophecy, birth, crucifixion, and teachings of Christ, but beyond that this text reflects the humanistic spirit of Handel's era: a universal spirit that transcends theological doctrines.

As an oratorio, *Messiah* is carefully written and carefully reverent. While one cannot say that the music springs from deep religious faith—it was meant for the concert hall, not the church—it reveals thorough unity and skill. Handel instinctively reacted dramatically to the religious text for *Messiah,* always keeping in mind the audience's emotional response. In bold outlines, he composed an epic of hope, suffering, and faith. At times he obtains his effects very simply; if occasionally he gives the impression that he is walking with temporal kings rather than biblical saints, this grandiose atmosphere merely expresses the attitude of his age.

A complete *Messiah* performance requires more than two hours, and today we often hear only those parts that pertain to Christmas (Part I) and Easter (Part II). Since the Christmas music is most frequently heard, we shall consider that part briefly.

Messiah opens with an expert overture in French style. In the oratorio proper, recitatives and airs—really arias—alternate with chorus singing. The opening tenor recitative, "Comfort ye," moves above a serene, flowing accompaniment and is followed by the air "Every valley shall be exalted," which allows the tenor to display his virtuosity in undulating scale passages and bold leaps. The chorus climaxes this prophecy with the lightly contrapuntal "And the glory of the Lord."

Convincing pictorial realism stands out in the bass recitative "Thus saith the Lord," for at the words "I will shake the heavens and the earth," the bass soloist sings cascades of operatic-like roulades. Although the following bass air, "But who may abide," begins lyrically, it has dazzling pyrotechnics accompanying the words "For He is like a refiner's fire."

Handel adopts a magnificently ornate fugal style for the chorus "And He shall purify," introducing technical intricacies on the word "purify." The prophecy narrative then continues with the recitative "Behold a Virgin shall conceive," which Handel designed for traditional male alto instead of contralto. "O Thou that tellest good tidings," an alto air, maintains a serene pace until it ends vigorously with an entrance by the chorus. The bass soloist takes his second turn with a recitative ("For behold, darkness shall cover the earth") and an air ("The people that walked in darkness"), both employing dark tone colors, minor mode, chromatics, and sinuous melodic patterns.

When the text approaches the nativity, the joyful chorus sings "For unto us a Child is born." The thunderous bursts on the words "wonderful" and "counselor" show Handel's instinctive dramatic genius. After a brief "Pastoral Symphony" orchestral interlude, the nativity scene in shepherds' field is described in four well-constructed recitatives. In the succeeding chorus "Glory to God"—here Handel uses trumpets in *Messiah* for the first time—the heavenly host comes musically nearer and nearer (from mezzo piano to fortissimo).

A brilliant soprano air, "Rejoice greatly," and a pastoral alto aria, "He shall feed His flock," provide first a spontaneous and then a meditative comment on the nativity. To the latter Handel has grafted yet another soprano air, the lovely "Come unto Him."

The Christmas section of *Messiah* concludes with the chorus singing "His yoke is easy," which has strange flourishes on "easy." However, tradition decrees that the "Hallelujah" chorus is the proper finale for the Christmas music from *Messiah,* even though it rightfully belongs toward the end of the oratorio in the section dealing with spreading the gospel. And another tradition, said to have been started in 1743 by George II, is that the audience stands when the "Hallelujah" chorus is sung. Most likely Handel would approve.

Concerti Grossi

Handel's instrumental music represents only a small portion of his total repertoire, yet some orchestral works compete favorably with his most expertly designed choral compositions. Several organ concertos—Handel used to play them between sections of his oratorios—are magnificent examples of music for that rare combination of organ and orchestra, and some of the oboe concertos are especially fine. The works that consistently substantiate Handel's reputation in the field of instrumental music are the twelve *Concerti Grossi, Opus 6,* which he composed in 1739 in only 32 days. This tremendous accomplishment must have been easy for Handel: he had written his opera *Rinaldo* in 14 days and completed *Messiah* in less than a month.

The twelve concerti grossi show ingenious variety, no two being quite alike. This musical form—each concerto comprising from four to six principal movements—belongs somewhere between the suite and the sonata and occasionally resembles the symphonic overture. As pure sound, the concertos are Italianate: a sweetness reminiscent of Corelli, and rhythmic passages hinting strongly of Vivaldi. Granted that the music is in some respects derivative, in its total presentation it shows Handel at the peak of his inventive powers.

Many movements use Italian terms as titles—*Allegro, Andante, Larghetto*—not only to indicate tempo but to suggest mood; that is, allegro indicates both a fast tempo and a gay atmosphere. Many allegro movements turn out to be skillfully organized fugal fantasies. Other movements use dance titles: *Minuet, Polonaise, Musette, Hornpipe, Siciliana, Gigue.*

Although these concertos are uniformly mature and unquestionably effective, they are not all equally important. Quite short—from 12 to 20 minutes—they range emotionally from the spontaneity of the second through the geniality of the fifth to the melancholy of the sixth.

Water Music

For many years Handel's *Water Music* remained enveloped in the legend that King George I, supposedly angry with Handel because he had abandoned his post as Kappellmeister at Hanover, forgave the composer when he heard this enchanting music played in England. The story is not true, but the original *Water Music* performance must have been charming, to judge by the following eyewitness description:

> Some weeks ago the King expressed a wish to Baron von Kilmanseck to have a concert on the river, by subscription, like the masquerades this winter which the King attended assiduously on each occasion. . . . Baron Kilmanseck . . . resolved to give the concert on the river at his own expense, and so the concert took place the day before yesterday. The King entered his barge about eight o'clock. . . . By the side of the Royal barge was that of the musicians to the number of fifty, who played all kinds of instruments, viz., trumpets, hunting horns, oboes, bassoons, German flutes, French flutes *à bec,* violins and basses, but without voices. This concert was composed expressly for the occasion by the famous Handel, native of Halle, and first composer of the King's music. It was so strongly approved by His Majesty that he commanded it to be repeated, once before and once after supper, although it took an hour for each performance.[1]

The *Water Music* includes 22 compositions distributed among three groups (suites)—in *F, D,* and *G* major. Six movements were formed into a suite by Sir Hamilton Harty, who also supplemented the orchestration. While Harty's arrangement suggests the music's character, a hearing of the complete collection gives a much better idea of the exciting atmosphere of that first performance.

Suite in F Major needs an orchestra composed of strings, continuo, two oboes, two horns, and bassoon; in addition, there are parts for two solo violins. A French *Ouverture* serves as the introduction; it has an adagio section featuring oboe and strings and a brisk allegro section in triple meter. A plaintive *Adagio e staccato* for oboe and strings suddenly interrupts this overture. The third movement is the familiar *Allegro,* with horn fanfares and oboe roulades. *Andante,* a dialogue between woodwinds and strings, fades into a repeat of the *Allegro*. An untitled scherzo with aristocratic overtones follows; its trio is designed for strings alone. The leisurely rhythmic beat, suave melodic line, and self-assured harmony of the famous *Air* account for its popularity. More horn fanfares usher in a bright *Minuet,* which sounds tailored for dancing; even its trio is dancelike, although it has subdued minor tonality. A breathless *Bourrée* and rhythmically interesting *Hornpipe* come next in succession, and the suite concludes with a dialogue—again Handel provides no title—in which phrases travel back and forth between woodwinds and strings.

Suite in D Major adds two trumpets to the orchestration. The score guides along a fourfold interplay among trumpets, horns, oboes, and strings. An aura of medieval pageantry colors the first movement (no title) when instruments

[1] Otto Zoff, editor, *Great Composers* (New York: E. P. Dutton & Co., Inc., 1951), pp. 49–50. Reprinted by permission. This description is from a report made by Frederic Bonnet, the Brandenburg envoy to the English court.

dialogue in fanfare. An *Alla Hornpipe* with its majestic trumpets and horns, a regal *Minuet,* and a gigue-like movement marked *Lentement* precede the conclusion, a *Bourrée.*

Suite in G Major is lightly scored: strings, flute, piccolo, and two oboes. This collection opens with a rococo sarabande (no title) for flute and strings. Then a rambunctious *Rigaudon* precedes and follows after an untitled contrasting section. The graceful upward melodic sweep in the *Minuet* makes it one of the loveliest movements in this suite. Handel's brisk conclusion presents three short dances.

Bach and Handel represent the ultimate in Baroque music, for they created the most musically interesting and aesthetically satisfying examples of eighteenth-century tonal art. But many other composers attained fine reputations in the Baroque era, and their music can still be heard today.

ARCANGELO CORELLI

Throughout the whole Baroque era, Italy's musical scene sparkled with such busy operatic activity that the immense instrumental production is sometimes forgotten. One of the greatest violinists ever known, Arcangelo Corelli (1653–1713) spent most of his mature life in Rome. His fame as performer and composer brought him pupils from all over Europe and invitations to perform at royal courts. His music was played everywhere, and his eventual contribution to music history has been twofold: as a master violinist he established a playing style that strongly affected subsequent developments in violin technique; as a composer of large-scale compositions, such as concerti grossi and sonatas, he greatly enriched both the concerto and solo repertoires. His works include five books of sonatas (twelve in each) and one book of concerti grossi. Corelli's sonatas have become classic prototypes. He chose a trio setting: two violins and harpsichord, with the bass line supported by a viola da gamba. The *sonata da chiesa,* Corelli's most felicitous form, usually has four movements. The opening movement, typically slow and majestic, is in duple or quadruple meter. Frequently the second movement has rapid fugal style and the third, often in triple meter, is lyrical. The final movement—in binary form like movements in a dance suite (*sonata da camera*) —contrasts with these other movements because it has a dancelike character.

ANTONIO VIVALDI

Antonio Vivaldi (*c.*1678–1741) also contributed generously to the stringed-instrument repertoire. His works include about 50 concerti grossi and 450 other concertos. He wrote 200 concertos for solo violin and orchestra, the others for oboe, flute, or bassoon. During his lifetime Vivaldi was known as the Red Priest (*il prete rosso*) —he was a priest and he was redheaded—although soon after being ordained in 1703 he had ceased to say Mass, reportedly on account of poor health. From then until 1740, a year before his death, he served as teacher, composer, and musical director at the conservatory attached to the *Ospedàle della Pietà* in Venice, an orphanage for young girls. According to contemporary accounts, the conservatory had an excellent orchestra, which very likely inspired Vivaldi to devote his talent to music for strings. The solo concertos, which he seemed to prefer, typically have three movements: fast-slow-fast. Like concerto grosso form, the basic formal plan in his concertos revolves around alternation between tutti and solo. He often extracted material for solo passages from the tutti, although occasionally the solo instrument possesses its own melodic themes. Vivaldi influenced many of his contemporaries and successors. Bach admired him greatly and arranged several Vivaldi works in keyboard score for study and performance.

DOMENICO SCARLATTI

Domenico Scarlatti (1685–1757), the son of Alessandro Scarlatti (see Chapter 10), worked almost exclusively with miniature forms, creating exquisite examples that have continually enchanted keyboard connoisseurs. More than any of his contemporaries, Scarlatti prepared the way for a future school of piano composition. Although born in Naples, most of his harpsichord works were composed in Madrid or other Spanish cities where the royal court stayed, for during the latter part of his life Scarlatti lived in Spain under the patronage of Queen María Bárbara.

Although Scarlatti did not avail himself of the suite framework per se, he did adopt individual dances from the suite. The little one-movement compositions he fashioned bear the title "sonata." He conceived these small sonatas not as mere technical exercises but as études similar in purpose and intent to those later works by Chopin—short, concise essays in which the composer exploits one particular technical device or figuration. Today many Scarlatti sonatas appear as piano solos, extremely pleasant works for both pianist and listener, but Scarlatti actually wrote the sonatas for harpsichord. His coloristic effects, tonalities, harmony, and audacious modulations find their perfect fulfillment in the different registers of the harpsichord.

Generally speaking, each Scarlatti sonata has one movement divided into two sections, each marked to be repeated if the performer so desires. Most Scarlatti sonatas are based on a single theme, but sometimes two or even three themes appear. Many betray a Spanish influence, for he frequently infuses into this music a spirit recalling Spanish popular dance forms, such as the *zapateado* or *polo*. Beyond a lively dance spirit, Scarlatti provided Spanish flavor by using note repetition; repeating one note is characteristic in Spanish guitar music, especially music for *flamenco* singing and dancing.

Scarlatti's music may not strive for profundity, but it is always elegant. A relentless searcher for brilliant, new effects, Scarlatti avoided triviality and aimed for an expressive, sometimes dramatic line. He was, in effect, anticipating Romanticism.

FRANÇOIS COUPERIN

In Baroque France, harpsichord (*clavecin*) music reached mature style and technique through the magnificent creations of François Couperin

(1668–1733), surnamed the Great. From mid-seventeenth century to 1826, seven Couperins successively filled the organ post at the church of Saint-Gervais in Paris—indeed a musical dynasty. Several Couperins were extremely talented, but François Couperin was a genius. Instead of gathering his pieces into suites according to common practice, Couperin arranged his compositions into larger groups called *ordres* (orders): in each group the first and last compositions have the same tonality. The other compositions either have this same tonality or are in closely related keys. The *ordre* was Couperin's personalized version of the keyboard suite.

Couperin's art was objective; his purpose was to describe exactly what he saw in nature rather than to express his inner sentiments. He used every facet of his technique and inspiration—melodic contour, ornaments, harmonic color, rhythms—to achieve this goal, and his objectivism can be recognized in many characteristic traits: his use of what might be described as arpeggiated harmony, his preciseness in matters of phrase balance, his frequent use of dotted rhythms coupled with fantasy and imagination.

Not only did Couperin have a firm command of harpsichord style—he composed for this instrument as no one previously had done—he also possessed a truly creative talent. His melodic imagination seems wonderfully fresh, his harmonic sense appropriately delicate. His themes reveal an impassioned musician: they are perfectly created, firm in line, vivid and enduring in color. Couperin's art never wavers; it consistently exhibits magnificent technique.

GEORG PHILIPP TELEMANN

In Baroque Germany, Georg Philipp Telemann (1681–1767) occupied a position comparable to that of his contemporary Johann Sebastian Bach. As a matter of fact, the important organist post at St. Thomas Church in Leipzig had been offered first to Telemann, who refused it because he was content at Hamburg, where he was musical director of the city's five principal churches from 1721 until his death. Telemann and Bach were good friends, the former standing as godfather to one of Bach's sons, Carl Philipp Emanuel.

Telemann, one of history's most prolific composers, earned an excellent reputation during his lifetime, but now his music is seldom heard except on phonograph recordings. He composed 40 Passion settings, 40 operas, more than 600 overtures, and numerous other works. Handel—also a close friend—once remarked that Telemann could write a strict vocal motet in eight parts as easily as anyone else could write a letter. This fertile inventiveness received ample support from his skillful contrapuntal writing and technical control of all contemporary compositional forms. Telemann's works offer a fine example of gracious, entertaining Baroque music.

SUMMARY OF THE BAROQUE PERIOD

The period from about 1600 to 1750 proved to be one of the most productive in music history. Experimentation and innovation continued throughout. A new homophonic writing style combined with elements of contrapuntal technique to produce the science of harmony.

As they put the newly developed style to practical use, Baroque composers created many new forms that in turn fostered vast instrumental and vocal repertoires. These versatile composers continued the tradition of writing Masses and motets and in addition developed new vocal forms: opera, cantata, and oratorio. They also produced numerous instrumental works, creating a lasting and important corpus of fugues, chorale settings, variations, and suites. When writing chamber music, they highlighted the trio sonata. With the solo concerto and concerto grosso, they often achieved a dazzling interplay between soloist and orchestra.

Thus almost every musical form commonly used today was either developed or created during the Baroque era. Only sonata form in its various manifestations—string quartet, piano sonata, symphony, and so on—was lacking. This form was to be provided by the ensuing Classic period.

Bach and Handel—the ultimate Baroque spokesmen—raised both choral and instrumental music to a point where no further enrichment was possible without a new aesthetic and a new expressive language. The oncoming Classic period supplied them both.

FOR DISCUSSION AND ASSIGNMENT

1. Listen to an aria from a Handel opera—for example, "Cara sposa" from *Rinaldo* or "Ombra mai fù" from *Serse*. Follow this with an air from an oratorio—for example, "Rejoice greatly" from *Messiah* or "Arm, arm, ye brave" from *Judas Maccabaeus*. Does one seem more "sacred" or "secular" than another? Could you tell the difference if the texts were omitted?
2. Compare a chorus and an air from Handel's *Messiah* with a cantata chorus and air by Bach. What similarities and differences do you find? What problems did the texts present to each composer and how did each solve them? One wrote for the Lutheran Church, the other for the general public. Is this evident in the music?
3. Listen to some short harpsichord pieces by Couperin. Do the titles serve any function? If so, what do they express?

FOR FURTHER READING

Bukofzer, Manfred. *Music in the Baroque Era*. New York: W. W. Norton & Co., Inc., 1947. This is the standard work on Baroque music in general. Although oriented to the musically informed reader, much of it can be assimilated by the inquiring amateur.

Mellers, Wilfrid. *François Couperin and the French Classical Tradition*. New York: Dover Publications, Inc., 1950. Besides concentrating on Couperin's life and music, this authoritative book devotes three chapters to French culture in general during Couperin's era.

Pincherle, Marc. *Vivaldi*, translated by C. Hatch. New York: W. W. Norton & Co., 1957. PB. A readable and reliably informative study of this composer.

Young, Percy. *Handel*. New York: Collier Books, 1962. PB. Dr. Young's sympathetic synthesis of biography and musicology draws a portrait of Handel that substantiates his fame and reputation.

The Age of Reason 13

When Nature her great masterpiece design'd,
And fram'd her last, best work, the human mind,
Her eye intent on all the wondrous plan,
She form'd of various stuff the various Man.

ROBERT BURNS
To Robert Graham

The eighteenth century is an excellent illustration of the inconsistency found in almost any art epoch. During the preceding century John Donne and Andrew Marvell had reached the high point in Baroque literature and Rembrandt the peak of Baroque painting. Music lagged behind at that time, for the most significant Baroque musical works—from Bach and Handel—did not appear until the first half of the eighteenth century. By that time literature had progressed to Classicism and most fine arts were not far behind her. Yet music did not reach its golden age of Classicism until the latter part of the century.

The "Age of Reason" and the "Enlightenment" are two descriptive titles applied to eighteenth-century intellect and culture. The term "Classicism" is often used in connection with the arts of the period, and in many respects it is the most graphic term, for eighteenth-century thought and action revived Renaissance ideals and the Renaissance dependence on ancient classics. Eighteenth-century literature and art returned to classical models emphasizing pure taste, proportion, and restraint. Even Renaissance scepticism and distrust of religious dogmatism reappeared in an eighteenth-century equivalent—Deism.

But the two eras show sharp differences as well: Renaissance exhilaration, impatience, and drama were replaced by convention, sobriety, and authoritarianism during the Age of Reason. Throughout Europe the middle class increased in numbers, power, and social status as their prosperity grew with more industry, exploration, and trade. This rising class found absolute monarchs to be just as oppressive and confining as the old feudal nobility; it therefore rebelled against its rulers and the decadent society spawned by court life.

Reason, the eighteenth-century key to utopia, whether in economics, science, religion, politics, art, or even manners, was interpreted as being a disciplined compound of common sense, emotion, taste, and universality amounting to conformity. What came to be considered classic concepts of taste, order, and symmetry developed quite naturally as men organized their intellect and actions to conform to this kind of reason and attempted to pattern their creative arts on ancient classical principles.

Eventually this complete reliance on reason led to freedom in all pursuits—intellectual, political, economic, spiritual, artistic—a human advancement that produced splendid achievement on one hand and on the other spawned the cataclysmic French Revolution (1789–1795), the apotheosis of freedom in its most abject state.

THE PRE-CLASSIC YEARS

Late-eighteenth-century music had no model to imitate, no ancient classic forms from which to draw inspiration. An entirely new aesthetic developed, based on *abstract* ideals of symmetry, balance, and clarity. However, musical Classicism never produced a wholly new product, because composers retained some Rococo stylistic elements—profuse ornamentation, facile harmonies—and fused them, particularly during the Pre-Classic period, with a sentimentality described by the Germans as *Empfindsamkeit.*

The term "Pre-Classic" commonly refers to the years between the era of Johann Sebastian Bach and the mature stages of Joseph Haydn and Wolfgang Mozart—that is, roughly from 1740 to 1775. During these some 35 years a strikingly different musical style emerged, a basically German-Austrian style that contrarily displayed many characteristics directly traceable to Italy and France.

Even before Bach's death, popular taste had turned from Baroque to Rococo style. The emotional doctrine of the affections gave way to more delicate musical expression. Couperin's sensitive clavecin miniatures and Scarlatti's playful sonatas are rococo in essence and spirit. Wit, lightness, and sentimentality characterize the Rococo style, which rose almost simultaneously with the Baroque decline. Rococo music stresses grace and elegance; it pleases rather than excites. To heighten this essentially delicate character, Rococo composers had freely used embellishments and ornaments.

In sculpture and painting, Classicism represented a distinct reaction against Rococo style, but this was not true in music, where Rococo style flowed unhampered into Classic style. By 1780 a new, more serious attitude toward music had asserted itself, as Rococo influences were absorbed into Classicism.

Many musical developments occurred in the Pre-Classic period: the foundation for symphony form, the beginnings of the string quartet, the development of the piano sonata, and the emergence of sonata form as the eighteenth century's most important construction principle. In addition, composers constantly experimented with new expressive patterns and thematic construction.

So many varied sources contributed to musical Classicism that the music generates an international atmosphere despite Austrian orientation. France provided the old Rococo flair and the Germanic composers tempered it with restraint and seriousness. Italy formulated the symphony's basic outline through the *opera overture.* During the years from Monteverdi to the final phase of the seventeenth century, the overture had progressed from an unimportant curtain raiser to a substantial composition meriting several contrasting sections. By 1700 the Italian overture, which thematically had little or no connection with the opera that followed it, contained three sections: a fast opening section, often a separate movement in binary form; a section in slow tempo; and finally another fast section. By natural expansion, this three-section overture became (before 1750) a three-movement *sinfonia* (symphony) and received frequent performances outside the opera theater.

Classicism also gained impetus from the music created at Mannheim, Germany, where the Elector Karl Theodor's court orchestra was acknowledged as the finest in all Europe. It was also one of the largest, boasting twenty violins, four cellos, two basses, and winds that included four horns. Under such directors as the violinist-composer Johann Stamitz (1717–1757), orchestral crescendo and diminuendo gradually replaced the terraced dynamics of the Baroque concerto grosso, the minuet appeared as a symphony movement, and the symphony's first movement began to take on its "classic" design. The harpsichord eventually dropped out as the support in instrumental ensembles. In fact, early in this period the piano began to compete with the harpsichord, finally forcing it into temporary retirement except for accompanying opera recitatives.

In North Germany, Bach's sons are the outstanding musical personalities of this Pre-Classic era, especially Carl Philipp Emanuel Bach (1714–1788), who helped to develop the modern clavier sonata and the symphony. As court clavierist to Frederick the Great in Berlin and later as church music director in Hamburg, Emanuel propounded a theory of musical embellishments. He also wrote a superb book on the art of playing keyboard instruments. He was an outspoken advocate of the *Empfindsamer Stil* (expressive style), which emphasized subtle nuances and broad sentiment, frequently in rapid succession within one movement. Musical phrases were short and rhythmic patterns changed often. Emanuel's own keyboard sonatas reveal expressive melodic lines and a serious intent, two important factors in the oncoming Classicism. All this represents a considerable change in style from the consistently maintained "affection" of a Baroque movement.

In addition to the Mannheim and North German "schools," composers based in Vienna experimented with symphony form and chamber music. Being partial to woodwinds, this school exploited their characteristic sonorities whenever possible. Composers active in Vienna included Georg Christoph Wagenseil (1715–1777), piano teacher to the Empress Maria Theresa, and Leopold Mozart (1719–1787), father of Wolfgang Amadeus Mozart.

THE CLASSIC STYLE

Perhaps an outline will provide the clearest description of the characteristics of Classic style and language as they appeared during the last 30 years of the eighteenth century.

A. Melody
1. Lyrical melodic lines predominated, often assuming a folklike character, as a result of German *Empfindsamkeit.*
2. A typical Classic melody was composed of a double phrase. Thus Classic melodies are comparatively shorter than the long melodic lines of the Baroque period.
3. Characteristic ornaments from Rococo and *Empfindsamer* styles were incorporated into the new melodic language.
4. Melodic contour frequently derived from its accompanying chordal harmony.

B. Rhythm
1. Classic composers preferred uncomplicated rhythmic structures. In chamber music and symphonic music, they employed the same rhythmic patterns in all parts.
2. Tempo remained constant throughout a movement or a section, while frequent changes of rhythm accentuated the changing themes.
3. Silence was important in rhythm. Rests were often inserted to set off contrasting themes or melodies.

C. Harmony
1. Harmony in the Classic period is remarkable for its simplicity, with diatonic triads and sevenths occasionally relieved by chromatic harmonies.
2. Harmony's most significant role in Classic music lies in the key relationships between themes and between movements in various forms.

D. Texture
1. Although Classic music uses counterpoint, particularly in thematic development, counterpoint is not a prime factor. Contrapuntal forms appear only infrequently.
2. Homophonic texture predominates, with special emphasis on melodies and themes, yet composers were careful in relating the harmonic background to the melody.
3. A musical device associated with the Classic period was the *Alberti bass.* It consists of an accompaniment figure in which a triad is separated into a broken-chord figure having a repeated rhythmic pattern (Ex. 13:1).

Ex. 13:1. ***Alberti bass***

E. Dynamics
1. Composers sought expression by means of dynamic nuance. Instead of changing the musical texture and using terraced dynamics as Baroque composers had done, Classic composers employed subtle dynamic shading, using crescendo and diminuendo as well as sudden changes from fortissimo to pianissimo.

In vocal music the opera, oratorio, and cantata forms adjusted to the new Classical style and continued to develop. In instrumental music the suite form gradually disappeared, the toccata was lost for some time to come, and the fugue was employed only sporadically. Variation form, however, has to this day kept its place among active musical forms.

THE SONATA

Classicism created a finished, refined musical style in which objectivity and emotional restraint fitted into an elegant, original formal structure: the sonata. During the Baroque period this term "sonata" had been rather indiscriminately applied to several musical types. The binary, one-movement piece of the Scarlatti school was called a sonata; series of dances were described as sonatas, although they were actually suites; and the so-called church sonata—a series of movements in which sections were contrasted by different textures and tempos—was a common Baroque form.

During the Pre-Classic and Classic periods, the sonata crystallized into a specific musical form: a composition having three or four movements designed according to certain predetermined rules for one instrument or an instrumental combination. Its exact origins are uncertain, because the final form incorporates ideas borrowed from many sources. Most likely the three movements in fast-slow-fast sequence can be traced to the Italian overture. Both Scarlatti and Rameau—in whose one-movement works several themes and their development can be detected in embryo—predicted the idea of developing more than one theme within a single composition.

Each sonata movement is constructed on formal principles, and from the composer's viewpoint the first movement is the most significant. For analysis purposes the form for the first movement is now called *sonata-allegro* (the allegro here has nothing to do with tempo). This movement may be preceded by a slow introduction, something that occurs more often in chamber music and symphonies than in keyboard music. The first movement proper is divided into three sections: (1) exposition, (2) development, and (3) recapitulation.

The *exposition section* "exposes" or states the themes; there are at least two themes—one vigorous, the other contrastingly lyrical. If the first theme is in a major key, a modulation to the dominant (the key built on the fifth note above the principal key) ushers in the second theme; but if the first theme is in a minor key, the second theme appears in the relative major key (located a minor third above the principal key). After these themes have been stated, the exposition section terminates with a *codetta,* a little ending usually based on the first theme. In most sonatas of this era, the exposition section was marked to be repeated, thus impressing the listener's mind with the themes used for the entire movement. The *development section* allows the composer to exercise his imagination and ingenuity by manipulating the two themes. Pre-Classic and Classic composers sometimes employed the old contrapuntal devices for stretching or shortening themes, but a composer could use any device at his disposal (and discretion) to display the inherent flexibility of his themes. After this development there is a modulation back to the original key. Finally, the *recapitulation section* restates the themes (this time the second theme remains in the original key), and the first movement may close with the addition of a *coda* (tailpiece).

The second sonata movement—a slow movement—may be constructed in any one of several forms. Once again the composer may choose sonata-allegro; or simple song form A B A; or a theme and variations; or possibly a type of rondo. It is essential to establish and maintain the spirit of the slow movement, to create lyricism, and to build melodies with sustained, expressive outlines.

The third and last movement of a three-movement sonata may also be written in sonata-allegro form, but Pre-Classic and Classic composers customarily chose a rondo derived from the French rondeau favored by François Couperin and his contemporaries. In the rondo a basic theme alternates with new material (couplets or episodes) and always comes back for a final statement. There are several rondo types. The simplest form has a basic theme (A) alternating with different episodes: it could be outlined as A B A C A D A, etc. In another frequently encountered type—the symmetrical rondo—the first episode returns later, creating a form such as A B A C A B A.

If a sonata has four movements, the extra movement follows immediately after the slow movement. During the late eighteenth century the extra was usually a minuet, the only dance form preserved from the old suite. Like the Baroque minuet, it had three parts: minuet proper, a trio or contrasting section, and a repeat of the initial minuet.

It must be stressed that the sonata form is a loose framework on which the composer builds. Almost every sonata has some deviation from the typical pattern that we have been discussing.

Composers used sonata form for many different instrumental combinations, although the nomenclature changes slightly. The word "sonata" becomes part of the title in music conceived for piano or for two instruments: a piano sonata or a sonata for violin and piano. Otherwise a work in sonata form is named by the number of instruments: a trio is a sonata for three instruments; a quartet is a sonata for four instruments. The final projection is the symphony, which is a sonata written for symphony orchestra.

OPERA IN THE CLASSIC ERA

By logical extension of Baroque and Rococo music, several opera types existed by the mid-eighteenth century, and each maintained its individuality despite borrowing from other opera forms. *Opera seria* (Italian grand opera) tried to carry on the great traditions begun by Handel and Alessandro Scarlatti. At its height this opera form relied on grandiose décor and florid splendor for its total effect. A typical opera seria libretto involved a long parade of heroic characters, and a typical score contained numerous virtuoso—and possibly irrelevant—arias to show off the leading voices. Such operas are frequently called "number" operas because they were built on a succession of arias punctuated by recitatives. Opera seria gradually declined during the period from about 1750 to 1800, due partly to various attempts at reform and partly to the growing popularity of other kinds of opera.

Opera buffa (Italian comic opera) originated early in the eighteenth century from the brief comic scenes inserted between acts in opera seria. In time composers conceived these interludes as independent operas having simple plots, a few plain characters, and short, tuneful arias. Opera buffa's primary purpose was to amuse the audience. The solo bass voice, seldom encountered in opera seria, found an important role as a comic star in opera buffa. Another operatic development—the *ensemble finale*—became a characteristic feature of opera buffa: composers traditionally ended each act by bringing all the principal singers onstage to complicate or resolve the plot. One of the earliest comic operas, *La serva padrona* (The Servant as Mistress) by Giovanni Battista Pergolesi (1710–1736), still receives an occasional performance.

Opera buffa also flourished in France, where the public eventually divided into two camps hotly debating the merits of Italian opera versus French opera. An Italian opera buffa company that had performed for two seasons in Paris with sensational success set off the spark between the two factions, and verbal war erupted in 1752. Defending Italian-style comic opera, Jean Jacques Rousseau (1712–1778) argued that comic opera portrayed real life. Carried away with his fervor, Rousseau wrote a French opera in Italian style; *Le devin du village* (The Village Soothsayer), written in 1752, became so popular that it remained in the Paris repertory for 75 years.

Opéra comique, a French light-opera form, was introduced in France around 1710. It was a popular entertainment using familiar tunes. By the mid-eighteenth century, a typical opéra comique had spoken dialogue and simple songs called *ariettes* rather than the former well-known tunes.

England produced the *ballad opera,* also a popular entertainment consisting of spoken dialogue and popular tunes of the day. (Until the mid-nineteenth century, all comic operas with the exception of opera buffa used spoken rather than sung dialogue.) *The Beggar's Opera* (1728), by John Gay and John Pepusch, was the most successful ballad opera.

A similar operatic form, known as the *Singspiel,* appeared in various Germanic countries, as German composers created nationalistic, melodic new material from translations or arrangements of English ballad-opera material.

A cosmopolitan composer named Christoph Willibald Gluck (1714–1787) mediated the French argument about opera. After Rousseau so convincingly defended Italian opera, the traditional French opera developed by Lully and Rameau lost standing, and until Gluck's reforms there was nothing to replace them except the improved opéra comique. Gluck wanted to abolish the distinction between national styles and to create music with a beautiful simplicity that would suit all countries. His operas are rarely heard now, but his reputation as an opera reformer, particularly for opera seria, holds firm today.

Gluck wanted to get away from the hollow virtuosity, superficial plots, and artificial libretto settings in Italian opera. He maintained that the librettist was an extremely important factor in the creation of an opera, and he expected the librettist to produce straightforward plots, unburdened with side intrigues. Musically he introduced great changes. He replaced virtuoso aria passages with expressive songs; made the chorus and ballet pertinent to the opera action; changed the recitative to make it more subjective; and gave the opera orchestra more responsibility by allowing it to contribute to the musical characterization and to present the overture as a meaningful introduction to the opera.

The only Gluck opera regularly revived is *Orpheus and Eurydice* (1762), but he carried out his reforms in other successful operas, such as *Alceste* (1767); *Iphigenia in Aulis* (1774); and *Iphigenia in Tauris* (1779). He hoped that his reforms would accomplish a balance between drama and music by using all operatic resources; that is, to use soloists, choruses, orchestra, and ballet to create a total Classical effect of proportion, nobility, and symmetry. Many later composers referred to Gluck's ideas and scores for guidance.

MUSICAL PATRONAGE

The rich middle class arising in prosperous cities during the eighteenth century eventually produced music sponsors and patrons. While formerly the Church or royalty or the aristocracy had hired private musicians as permanent employees, the new bourgeois patron was more likely to commission single works from his favorite composer and have them performed in his home by musicians hired just for that occasion.

An even more important change occurred as the general public became music's most demanding, influential patron. During the eighteenth century the public concert with paid admission became the vogue. As more public concert halls were built, the musically informed population grew until ultimately many listeners became enthusiastic amateur performers, making music for their own pleasure in their homes. Chamber music formed the backbone of their repertoire as the family string quartet bowed and plucked its way through a large quantity of new, well-written, and intrinsically interesting music. This lively activity in music-making developed with ever increasing fervor during the eighteenth century and continued unabated into the Romantic period.

FOR DISCUSSION AND ASSIGNMENT

1. Listen to a movement from a symphony by a Pre-Classic composer such as C. P. E. Bach or Johann Stamitz. Compare it with a movement from a mature Haydn symphony. Do the styles sound identical? If not, why not?
2. Listen to a piano sonata by C. P. E. Bach or another of J. S. Bach's sons. Why are these works not heard more frequently?
3. In less than 40 years a momentous change took place in musical style. Contrast the first movement of J. S. Bach's *Brandenburg Concerto No. 6* with the first movement of Mozart's *Symphony No. 40, K. 550.* Consider the following: length of melodies or themes; types of melodies or themes; use of dynamics; type of orchestra and orchestration; rhythm; and concept of form.

FOR FURTHER READING

Dr. Burney's Musical Tours in Europe, Percy A. Scholes, ed. London: Oxford University Press, 1959. 2 Vols. Dr. Charles Burney's highly diverting volumes take the reader on an extended trip to the great European music centers. Apart from being a mine of information on eighteenth-century music, the books provide fascinating reading.

Durant, Will, and Ariel Durant. *The Story of Civilization.* New York: Simon and Schuster. Vol. 7, *The Age of Reason Begins* (1961), Vol. 8, *The Age of Louis XIV* (1963), and Vol. 9, *The Age of Voltaire* (1965), constitute a complete, authoritative compendium of the late-seventeenth and eighteenth centuries.

Hodeir, André. *The Forms of Music,* translated by Nöel Burch. New York: Walker & Co., 1966. This compact dictionary of musical forms is typical of M. Hodeir's writing: clear, to the point, concise.

Pauly, Reinhard G. *Music in the Classic Period.* Englewood Cliffs, N.J.: Prentice-Hall, Inc., 1965. PB. To date, this is the only book in English dealing specifically with Classic music. It offers a well-planned, well-written survey of the period.

Franz Joseph Haydn 14

There is a general cheerfulness and good humour in Haydn's allegros, which exhilarate every hearer.

CHARLES BURNEY
History of Music (1789)

Franz Joseph Haydn (1732–1809) was born in Rohrau, Austria. He lived with music from early childhood, and the native folk melodies he absorbed influenced his composing career significantly. From the age of eight until his voice broke at seventeen he served as a choirboy at the Vienna cathedral. When he left the choir, he earned his livelihood by giving lessons and playing at odd jobs, all the while following a rigid program of self-instruction. He met some musically influential people in Vienna, had a few lessons in composition with the famous Italian composer Nicola Porpora, and in 1755 wrote his first string quartet at the request of a musical amateur, J. von Fürnberg.

After two years' employment as music director for Count von Morzin, a Bohemian nobleman, Haydn in 1761 had the good fortune to become orchestral conductor and composer for the Esterházy family at Eisenstadt. For more than 30 years his creative talents and his music belonged to this noble family. After his retirement in 1790, Haydn officially resided in Vienna, although he spent two successful seasons as a conductor-composer in London (1791–1792 and 1794–1795).

When Haydn died, he left an immense repertory of fine works, although the exact number is unknown because no one compiled an accurate catalog in his lifetime and a complete edition has not yet been issued. There are approximately 83 quartets, several dozen compositions for wind and string ensembles, more than 50 concertos, almost 70 instrumental trios, more than 50 sonatas for violin and piano, three oratorios, 200 songs, airs, and canons, some 30 works for stage, more than a dozen Masses, about 200 pieces for baryton (a now obsolete stringed instrument played by Haydn's patron Prince Esterházy), and at least 104 symphonies.

Joseph Haydn occupies a unique niche in musical history, if for no other reason than his long life span. Born in 1732, he was a child of the Baroque, but he lived to be 77 and so passed through the later eighteenth-century Classic era into the early Romantic period. Thus he included Handel, Mozart, and Beethoven among his contemporaries!

Haydn's numerous instrumental works affected the course of musical development, for he raised instrumental music to the same status as vocal music. Although Bach and Handel had composed instrumental music, it was not equal to their vocal-music output. Inversely, Haydn contributed many operas and Masses to the vocal field, but his symphonies, string quartets, and piano sonatas represent the best Haydn to modern audiences.

His success in these media lies in the fact that he realized the latent possibilities—both formal and dramatic—in sonata form, whether piano sonata or quartet or symphony. Musical form apparently interested him keenly, and being an active observer and artful assimilator, he was able to dissect existing forms and then reassemble the parts in an entirely new guise. For models he was indebted to his immediate predecessors, particularly Carl Philipp Emanuel Bach. It is also possible that Viennese composers like Georg Christoph Wagenseil (1715–1777) and Georg Matthias Monn (1717–1750) supplied Haydn with helpful examples.

Classic music by its very nature would seem to be governed by rather stringent rules. Yet Haydn frequently remarked that freedom was an indispensable factor in composing. "Art is free and will be limited by no pedestrian rules. . . . The ear, assuming that it is trained, must decide, and I consider myself as competent as any to legislate here."

On the other hand, he admitted that there should be some inherent rules governing artistic creation. Speaking in retrospect about his own composing method, the aging composer said:

> I sat down [at the piano], began to improvise, sad or happy according to my mood, serious or trifling. Once I had seized upon an idea, my whole endeavor was to develop and sustain it in keeping with the rules of art. . . . I was never a fast writer, and always composed with deliberation and industry.[1]

Haydn's ultimate creative style strikes us now as a truly advanced concept—for his time—of instrumental writing, especially in sonata form. Comparison between his early and late works shows that he was the first important innovator in thematic manipulation. While his predecessors had used themes in abundance, they had not been overly concerned with organic development. Haydn fashioned his themes carefully and then diffused them into a tonal mosaic. This inborn talent for creating and developing themes foreshadows Beethoven. Haydn's melodies are not always original; he borrowed freely from Hungarian and Croatian folk melodies, often incorporating them with naturalness and freshness.

Haydn's music proves his innate musicianship. His straightforward harmonies, daring modulations, and thorough knowledge of what each instrument could accomplish indicate a sophisticated musical skill, yet his melodies always appealed to the widest audience. At the time he reached youthful maturity, polyphonic texture and contrapuntal techniques were restricted mostly to Masses, motets, and other church music. Haydn rescued counterpoint from these media by appropriating certain contrapuntal features for use in his personal musical language.

[1] These remarks are taken from a biographical sketch of Haydn by his good friend Georg August Griesinger in *Biographische Notizen über Joseph Haydn* (1809). Reprinted with permission of the copyright owners, The Regents of the University of Wisconsin, from Vernon Gotwals, editor and translator, *Joseph Haydn: Eighteenth-Century Gentleman and Genius,* The University of Wisconsin Press, 1963.

SYMPHONIES

Haydn's lifelong attention to symphonic form helped the orchestra assume definite proportions. Thanks in large part to Haydn's music and reputation, instrumentation became standardized so that by the end of the Classic period an average orchestra would have included eight to ten first violins, eight to ten second violins, four violas, four cellos, four basses, and two each of flutes, oboes, clarinets, bassoons, horns, trumpets, and timpani.

When Haydn began using symphonic form it was still in the Pre-Classic experimental stage that had developed from the Italian operatic overture—a three-movement structure having an initial allegro, a central slow movement, and a final allegro. He also had some examples from the Mannheim school, where composers had broadened the symphonic concept by adding a minuet, and he himself freely acknowledged that Emanuel Bach had exerted an important influence on him.

Haydn's early symphonies show variety in form and in instrumentation. He experimented with the number and the sequence of movements, frequently designing them in contrapuntal style. In the 1770s his personal reaction to the artistic emotional crisis known as "Storm and Stress" (see page 217) resulted in a propensity for minor keys and intense, dark moods. At the same time he kept experimenting, such as introducing new themes in the development section.

By 1780 Haydn's style was mature and controlled. This style shows particularly in the first movements of almost all the late symphonies. His themes are concise, simple, and pliable, and his orchestral color becomes more vivid as he allows different instruments to develop the thematic material. And, of course, Haydn's polished techniques for thematic development are in evidence throughout. A slow introduction, frequently very Romantic in feeling, precedes the movement proper.

Haydn often created three themes for the first movement of his sonatas, but they are not always strongly contrasted. Many Haydn themes are built in irregular periods of three, five, or seven measures, and he reveals a tendency to suppress the importance of the second subject (theme). By contrast, in passages where Mozart would automatically introduce a new (second) theme, Haydn frequently presents his first theme in a different manner, thus reserving new themes for less obvious occasions. With his personal predilection for clarity, he often neatly separates the first movement's three sections by a retard, a silence, a measure or two of chords, or an organ point. A favorite Haydn device occurs in the development section; he constructs the first part of this section around the second theme and then goes on to develop the first theme, leading to the recapitulation. His developmental section is usually short, although at times it may contain the emotional climax of the entire first movement.

Haydn also employed new tactics in his symphony slow movements by preferring a theme and variations to the two-part (binary) form then in favor. The finales offer enduring testimony to his musicality; the listener always knows that this *is* the finale because each Haydn symphony leaves the listener emotionally satisfied. In many instances he uses the indications *presto* and *prestissimo,* setting in motion an exhilarating finish.

Historians agree that Haydn wrote at least 104 symphonies. The earliest reflect his dependence on contemporary models, a crutch he soon discarded. Even the early *Symphonies Nos. 6, 7,* and *8* are designed on a scale larger than customary at the time, they are more richly scored than his predecessors' symphonies, and they are definitely intended to exploit the orchestral instruments' virtuoso capabilities. These early symphonies also contain extensive solo writing, a distinctive feature of the earlier concerto grosso.

The titles now applied to many Haydn symphonies and other compositions seldom originated with the composer; added later, they reflect the popularity of these particular works.

The best known among the earlier symphonies is *No. 45 in F-Sharp Minor* (1772), commonly known as the "Farewell" symphony. It is extremely interesting, due perhaps to the story surrounding its composition. According to this story, Prince Nicholas had been spending more and more time with his court at a new estate named *Esterháza,* though he insisted his entourage's families remain at Eisenstadt, some distance away. Intent on bettering morale among his musicians, Haydn decided on a subtle musical hint. When the *Symphony in F-Sharp Minor* was played for the prince, it seemingly contained the ordinary movements—allegro, adagio, minuet, presto—but suddenly the last movement broke off, changing to another adagio. From this point on, each performer arose one by one, snuffed out the candle on his music stand, and left the room, so that when the adagio ended only two violins remained as orchestra. The story says that the prince got the point and the following day packed up to return to Eisenstadt.

From this time on Haydn turned out one superb symphony after another, and many now appear in the standard concert repertoire. The 12 symphonies (93–104) that Haydn composed and conducted in London during 1791–1792 and 1794–1795 confirm his genius as a symphonist. Known as the Salomon set, these twelve works offer examples of his freedom and variety with form, and each is unique.

Symphony No. 101 in D Major (1794) takes its title, the "Clock," from the *Andante,* where a Haydnesque melody rises above an accompaniment produced by pizzicato strings and bassoons. Other features include a lusty *Minuet* displaying a flute solo in the trio and a vigorous finale notable for its contrapuntal character.

A pianissimo drum roll in the opening *Adagio* of *Symphony No. 103 in E-Flat Major* (1795) explains why it is called the "Drum Roll" symphony. This adagio is important, for Haydn introduces it again shortly before the end of the first movement. The entire symphony has a noble cast and its grandeur suggests Beethoven.

The perennial Haydn favorite is *Symphony No. 94 in G Major* (1792), known as the "Surprise" symphony because an unexpected fortissimo chord appears at the end of a soft passage in the second movement. Legend insists that Haydn, noticing drowsy people at his London concerts, contrived this orchestral effect to rouse the audience. Whether or not this story is true, Haydn offers many delightful and more enduring surprises throughout this symphony. For example, the slow introduction to the first movement includes an almost romantic dialogue between strings and winds, and the first movement proper, *Vivace assai,* reveals another surprise: its exposition section contains not two distinct themes but three. The first begins outside the main key of G major (Ex. 14:1). After three colorful

Ex. 14:1. Haydn: *Symphony No. 94 in G Major: Vivace assai*

Ex. 14:2. Haydn: *Symphony No. 94 in G Major: Vivace assai*

Ex. 14:3. Haydn: *Symphony No. 94 in G Major: Vivace assai*

versions of this theme, the second subject starts with vigorous syncopated dance rhythms (Ex. 14:2) and then melts into a pastoral third melody, a melodic type decidedly characteristic of Haydn (Ex. 14:3). Although the development section begins rather meekly, it rises to an opulent operatic-type climax before the thematic recapitulation. Another surprise occurs in the recapitulation, where Haydn interpolates what amounts to a false (and long) coda between the dance tune and the pastoral melody.

The second movement, *Andante,* contains variations on a theme that seems familiar enough to be a folk song. (Some years later Haydn gave it a different character in his oratorio *The Seasons* when he enlivened the tempo and gave it to a piccolo to represent the whistling ploughman as he "tunes his wonted lay.") The *Andante's* first eight measures are played softly by strings and repeated even more softly. Following this repetition, when it seems as though the sound will disappear, the full orchestra, including drums, explodes into a sudden fortissimo chord (the surprise). The theme continues with its second part, performed mostly by strings and woodwinds. Then the two-part theme is treated to several imaginative variations. In the first variation the lower strings play the theme while a violin countermelody soars above. The dramatic second variation, in minor, discloses the latent possibilities in Haydn's folklike theme. The return to the major tonality, initiated by a variation of the theme in repeated notes, constitutes one of the most captivating passages in all of Haydn's music. In the coda the theme and its accompanying harmony take on a romantic character, a prediction of things to come.

The aristocratic, courtly minuet finds no place in this symphony (even though the composer labeled the third movement *Menuetto*); instead Haydn substitutes a robust, heavy-footed Austrian *ländler* with bourgeois rhythms. The contrasting trio is delicately scored, with a lyric violin melody reinforced by various solo wind instruments.

The concluding movement, *Allegro di molto,* gives further evidence of Haydn's originality and love of surprises. It starts out as a typical Haydn rondo with a busy, bustling theme (Ex. 14:4) and gradually changes into a kind of

Ex. 14:4. Haydn: *Symphony No. 94 in G Major: Allegro di molto*

sonata-allegro form having a contrasted second subject. "The returns of these themes show the height of Haydn's power in the unexpected-inevitable."[2]

STRING QUARTETS

Although Haydn was the first to grasp the expressive and formalistic possibilities inherent in the string quartet, he did not "invent" it. Before Haydn's time, four-part music for strings had been written by lyrically minded Italian composers such as Tartini and Pugnani and progressive composers such as Stamitz and Richter in Mannheim, Germany.

While there were also some early attempts at chamber music—one instrument to each part—most eighteenth-century string compositions written in four parts must be classified as orchestral music. Several players performed each part and a supporting continuo was always present to bind the parts into a unified tonal mass.

True chamber music in the mid-eighteenth century existed primarily in the trio sonata (three strings with continuo). Haydn used this form in his earlier years and, more significantly, he wrote music destined for open-air performances: serenades and divertimenti without continuo. With the keyboard thus removed, individual parts were able to develop on their own.

Although Haydn worked consistently with chamber music in general, the string quartet proved to be the best vehicle for his genius. Almost entirely unaided by earlier models and drawing inspiration mainly from his own inexhaustible resources, he evolved model after model and masterpiece after masterpiece for the string-quartet repertoire.

Haydn set out his dramatic ideas in a surprisingly simple harmonic form. The melodic phrases sung by violin or viola (or frequently the cello) result from his ability to balance variety and repetition. His musicianship is especially evident in the way he handles form; that is, he can work within a constraining framework and simultaneously transform quite prosaic phrases into variegated moods.

Many Haydn string quartets have been given titles to emphasize some distinguishing feature. Thus *Opus 64, No. 5* is called the "Lark" quartet because of the soaring, cantabile melody designed for the first violin in the initial movement. The finale to this quartet is fascinating: a real *perpetuum mobile* (perpetual motion), it cavorts in sixteenth notes running headlong into a fugato section and then out again.

Opus 76 contains two typical Haydn quartets. *No. 2 in D Minor* has come to be known by three different titles, but the most justifiable is *Quinten* (Fifths), since the entire first movement is governed by a motive of a descending fifth. This movement's emotional impact derives from the tension caused by the musical fabric escaping from the governing motive and then returning to it (Ex. 14:5). A very pleasing *Andante* second movement balances the theatrical first movement, but even here a modified version of the drooping fifth occurs in a transitional passage, not as a main theme. The *Menuetto* movement is responsible for another title given to this quartet: *Hexenmenuett* (Witches' Minuet). Haydn releases

[2] Donald Francis Tovey, *Essays in Musical Analysis: Vol. 1, Symphonies* (London: Oxford University Press, 1935), p. 148.

Ex. 14:5. Haydn: *Quartet in D Minor, Opus 76, No. 2: Allegro*

some earthy humor in which octave-doubling and counterpoint meet, and he effectively uses a canon between the upper and lower strings. The witches seem to enter during the trio. A bright peasant dance provides a Hungarian-type finale, wherein an upward-leaping fifth has given rise to still another title, the "Donkey."

The *Quartet No. 3 in C Major,* also *Opus 76,* is often called the "Emperor" quartet because the slow-movement theme comes from the Austrian national anthem, *Gott erhalte Franz den Kaiser* (God Save Our Emperor Franz). Haydn had every right to borrow this melody. While in England he had been impressed by the public's emotion whenever "God Save The King" was played or sung. Feeling that Austria had a similar need, he wrote the anthem in 1797; on February 12, the emperor's birthday, it was introduced to the Austrian people. It was an instant success and always remained close to Haydn's heart; in fact it was reputedly the last music he played before his death.

This quartet is a symphonic jewel. Haydn's propensity for octaves and double-stopping, as well as for using the cello's low register, all find fulfillment here. In the first movement, *Allegro,* he presents a master theme that keeps reappearing in different forms. In the second movement, *Poco adagio cantabile,* he submits his anthem melody to four variations, each in its noble simplicity an excellent example of Classic style. The actual tune is not noticeably varied; in each variation Haydn assigns the melody to one quartet member while the others weave arabesques and countermelodies about it. The succeeding *Menuetto* is vigorous in outline but forcibly romantic. A serious, powerful finale, *Presto,* caps the work.

PIANO SONATAS

It seems curious that Haydn, who was not a pianist, should have composed more than 50 piano sonatas and several short piano pieces. Far more logical is the fact that he progressively lost interest in keyboard composition and devoted his talents to the string quartet and symphony. Haydn wrote only three piano sonatas during the last 20 years of his life.

He experimented with the piano sonata much more than did Mozart. With only three exceptions, Mozart's sonatas adhere to a three-movement structure: a fast opening movement in sonata-allegro form, a slow movement in song form or rondo form, and a finale in rondo or sonata-allegro form. Haydn followed this same pattern in many compositions, but in addition he composed nine sonatas having just two movements and two sonatas having four movements. Haydn's first movement is sometimes a theme and variations, and frequently his final movement is cast in minuet form.

Other interesting comparisons can be made between Haydn and Mozart keyboard music. Haydn seldom used a virtuoso approach to the sonata. In contrast to Mozart's allegro markings, Haydn often chose allegro moderato or even moderato. However, the two composers show an affinity in choosing tonality. It is quite remarkable that only five of Haydn's 52 sonatas are in a minor key (in some sonatas all movements remain in the same key),,and only two of Mozart's 17 sonatas are in a minor key.

From 1774 to 1784 Haydn produced about ten sonatas emphasizing lyricism and ornamentation. One of the most popular sonatas in this group is *No. 37 in D Major,* which shows Haydn in full command of his style. It is an excellent example of the Classic sonata. The first movement's brilliancy is indicated in its title, *Allegro con brio.* The first theme (in *D* major) is stated (Ex. 14:6),

Ex. 14:6. Haydn: *Sonata No. 37 in D Major: Allegro con brio*

extended, and then separated from the second theme by a rest. There is a real codetta, which is later expanded into the concluding coda. The development section is skillful though short. The second movement, *Largo e sostenuto,* is little more than a four-line interlude ending on an *A*-major chord that presupposes an immediate entry of the *Finale.* In the *Finale* a lively two-part theme is stated three times, the statements being separated by highly contrasting interludes—a fitting climax for this invigorating sonata.

Although a composer's last works are not necessarily his best, in Haydn's case all the experience and skill acquired through the years culminate in his later keyboard compositions. *Sonata No. 52 in E-Flat Major,* one of his last piano sonatas, is a masterwork embodying his lifetime efforts at keyboard composing.

The impact of the first movement, *Allegro,* is established right from the opening bars (Ex. 14:7). Haydn stresses the significance of this theme, and even

Ex. 14:7. Haydn: *Sonata No. 52 in E-Flat Major: Allegro*

extends it, as though trying to delay the entrance of the second idea, a theme (in *B*-flat) that lightens the prevailing mood and leads to bare, mysterious octaves in the codetta. Excellent modulations take place in the development, with passages in *C* major, *A*-flat major, and *E* major. The recapitulation is abbreviated.

Haydn's *Adagio* for this sonata is more effective than usual, although it is still not so convincing as similar examples by Mozart. It is written in ample song form (A B A), and the initial rhythmic motive dominates the entire movement. The strong rhythmic pattern, little cadenza figures, and light ornamentation add luster to this movement.

The *Presto* finale uses a form mixing elements from both sonata-allegro and rondo—a hybrid, really, but with its own logic and forceful expression. Haydn employs the rest and the pause here with impressive results.

SACRED MUSIC

To the twentieth-century listener, opera is the most representative vocal music from the late eighteenth century. Even during the Classic period, operatic style permeated other areas. Most sacred works of the time depended on other forms for their musical vocabulary, and opera offered an especially attractive language.

Haydn's sacred-music repertoire, mostly Masses, contains more than a touch of opera style. Perhaps operatic arias clothed in the essentially buoyant spirit of the eighteenth century do seem incongruous as a setting for the Mass, but in fact the listener responds to this music according to its surroundings; when heard in a typically rococo Austrian church, a Haydn or Mozart Mass complements the religious atmosphere.

Haydn's last six Masses (1796–1802) owe their existence to Prince Nicholas Esterházy's fondness for sacred music. Haydn's weighty choruses and the prominent orchestral woodwinds stem from his visits to London, where he heard Handel's oratorios.

Two late Haydn works, *The Creation* (1798) and *The Seasons* (1801), are partly responsible for the oratorio's popularity in the nineteenth century. Besides that, these two expansive oratorios, full of imagery, lyrical arias, and rousing choruses, assert that Haydn is indeed the logical successor to Handel.

> The artistic message of the humble Austrian musician was eagerly accepted by some of the greatest composers of the nineteenth and twentieth centuries; in their instrumental compositions they followed his lead. Beethoven, while refusing to be Haydn's pupil in counterpoint, nevertheless found in the older composer's skillful part-writing, his developments full of dramatic tension, his economy and concentration sufficient reasons for imitation. Schubert was influenced in his piano works as well as his chamber music by Haydn and Brahms was one of the most faithful students of the old master's works. Even the chamber music of a contemporary composer like Hindemith is in some respects dependent on the quartets of the composer of Esterháza.[3]

FOR DISCUSSION AND ASSIGNMENT

1. During his many years with the Esterházy family, Haydn had full charge of the court orchestra. In what ways could this responsibility have influenced his career as a composer?
2. How do you account for the fact that Haydn's music became well known all over Europe and England within a rather brief period?
3. Listen to different selections from Haydn's music. See if you notice passages reminiscent of folk music. Do you notice any dancelike rhythms?
4. Listen to three symphonic movements—the second movement of the "Surprise" (No. 94), the second movement of "Le Matin" (No. 6), and the

[3] Karl Geiringer, *Haydn: A Creative Life in Music* (New York: W. W. Norton & Co., Inc., 1946), p. 324. Reprinted by permission.

finale of the "Farewell" (No. 45). Can one portray humor in music? How would you characterize Haydn's humor?

FOR FURTHER READING

Geiringer, Karl. *Haydn: A Creative Life in Music,* Revised Second Edition. Garden City, N.Y.: Doubleday and Co., Inc., 1963. An Anchor PB. Dr. Geiringer's study, originally published in 1946, is the definitive critical biography of Haydn in English.

Hughes, Rosemary. *Haydn.* New York: Collier Books, 1963. PB. For its size, this handbook offers much that is valuable and interesting. The author first presents a biography of the composer, then discusses his compositions by category. The yearly calendar of Haydn's life is very helpful.

Pauly, Reinhard G. *Music in the Classic Period.* Englewood Cliffs, N.J.: Prentice-Hall, Inc., 1965. PB. For a discussion of Haydn in his cultural, social, and religious milieu, Dr. Pauly's book is excellent.

Wolfgang Amadeus Mozart 15

> Mozart is modern too, that is, he is not afraid
> to touch on the melancholy side of things, but, like
> the men of his time. . . . Mozart combines just enough of
> this touch of pleasurable sadness with the easy
> cheerfulness and elegance of a mind lucky enough to
> take in what is agreeable.
>
> EUGÈNE DELACROIX
> *Journal* (1853–1856)

Wolfgang Amadeus Mozart (1756–1791) was born in Salzburg, Austria. His father, Leopold (1719–1787), a composer-violinist employed by the Archbishop of Salzburg, put aside personal ambition to educate—and exhibit—his two talented children: Wolfgang and his older sister Marianne, nicknamed "Nannerl." By publicizing Mozart's precocious talents—composing, playing, sight-reading, improvising—the father hoped to secure a good appointment for his son's adult career. From his sixth until his fifteenth year, Mozart was largely on tour with his family, performing in London and many major European cities: Paris, Munich, Vienna, Milan, Rome, Naples, Mannheim, Dresden, Leipzig, Potsdam, Augsburg. All the while his ambitious though devoted and conscientious father carefully developed his children's remarkable musical talents.

Mozart composed his first minuets before he was six, a symphony before he was nine, an oratorio at eleven, and his first opera when he was twelve—this in addition to being an acclaimed virtuoso clavier performer and a fine organist and violinist. His talents were unquestionably prodigious and his childhood concerts must have been amazing. Throughout his short life he wrote continuously, a prolific composer who left more than 600 numbered works. His most important compositions include 20 operas and stage works; 15 Masses, including the famous *Requiem;* more than 100 songs, airs, choruses, etc.; almost 50 symphonies; divertimenti, serenades, and other works for various orchestral groups; about 50 concertos, of which more than half are for piano; 17 piano sonatas; 42 sonatas for violin and piano; 26 string quartets; and many other chamber-music compositions.

Leopold Mozart's hopes for his son never materialized. A new Archbishop of Salzburg appointed Mozart as concertmaster and court organist, but the pay was small and his status in the archbishop's household was more servant than court official. When his father's attempt to get him a court position at Vienna failed, Mozart stayed on in Salzburg, composing effortlessly and abundantly while living in straitened financial circumstances. From the time the archbishop dismissed him in 1781 until his death, Mozart lived in Vienna, earning a meager living by giving lessons and appearing as composer-soloist at concerts he arranged for himself. His marriage to Constanze Weber in 1782 only increased his financial difficulties, and anxiety together with a general breakdown caused his early death at the age of 35. He was buried in a pauper's grave.

For Mozart the term genius seems rightfully appropriate. One has merely to compare a minuet written by the six-year-old Wolfgang with one composed by his father to realize that the son had a God-given gift for music. Even as a child he displayed an enormous capacity for assimilation, and everything that impressed him he could store away in his memory. All through his life he felt the influence of other composers—Johann Christian Bach, Carl Philipp Emanuel Bach, Handel, Haydn, Gluck—but never at any time did their various styles become his. Mozart's talent for assimilation was controlled by sure technique, unfailing design, and an intuitive dramatic sense that made his style unique.

In the late eighteenth century, Germany and Italy possessed the two most distinctive national musical idioms. The sturdy, scholarly Germans sought expression in their music; the emotional Italians wanted tasteful musical entertainment. (This is an interesting paradox of the Classic period and in each case represents a reaction to the previous era and style.) With unerring instinct, Mozart combined these two idioms in every area of music, for he had been endowed with the taste, knowledge, and technique to blend the two styles into a new "Mozart" style typifying the ideal of Classical music. An instinctive musician, he could create exactly the right stylistic approach for each instrument or voice.

Probably the most passionate of all Classical composers, Mozart had definite ideas about displaying emotion in music. ". . . Passions, whether violent or not, must never be expressed in such a way as to excite disgust, and as music, even in the most terrible situations, must never offend the ear, but please the hearer, or in other words must never cease to be music . . ."[1]

Both trained and untrained listeners will find that Mozart's melody is the most accessible factor in his music. This conforms with the composer's ideas, for he wrote: "Melody is the essence of music. I compare a good melodist to a fine racer, and counterpointists to hack post-horses."[2] Because of his masterful technique, his melodic lines have clarity, facility, and lightness. Structurally he fitted his melodies to a simple eight-bar period, a design that of course he often altered. Guided by his inherent feeling for design, his melody generally first occurs with a simple harmonic accompaniment; that is, he advocated clarity before complexity.

It has often been claimed that Mozart's music preserves perfect balance between form and content and between the objective and the subjective. Just as it is easy to accept these facts as true, it is equally difficult to explain how he accomplished them. Perhaps the best thing we can do is to remember that he had a natural and perfect musicality; musical compositions apparently flowed effortlessly and steadily from his imagination, and no matter what occurred in his daily life, good fortune or bad, his musical genius never failed to produce that perfect balance indicating taste and knowledge. His lifelong habit of observing and

[1] Letter dated Sept. 26, 1781. In Emily Anderson, editor, *Letters of Mozart and his Family* (London: Macmillan and Co., 1938), Vol. 3, p. 1144. Reprinted by permission.

[2] This remark was addressed to the English tenor Michael Kelly, about 1786, in answer to Kelly's question whether or not he should take up the study of counterpoint.

absorbing other composers' music awakened him to the different emotional qualities in national music; his acute dramatic sensibility blended these emotions into a universal musical language.

PIANO CONCERTOS

Far more important than his solo piano music are Mozart's concertos for piano and orchestra, composed largely for his own performances. These works are important both in the history of concerto form and in the history of music.

Being a concert pianist throughout most of his life, Mozart always needed new music. In his era just performing was hardly sufficient; a concert artist was expected to be able to compose music for his concerts. A clavierist was further expected to be skilled at improvisation, so that he could take a given theme or melody and construct a sonata or fugue on the spot—instant music, so to speak. Mozart naturally possessed all these abilities, and doubtlessly many of his extant keyboard works were first improvised and later written down. Since he frequently gave piano concerts in Vienna to augment his small income, many concertos were composed for these occasions. Besides his 30 piano concertos, which include arrangements of music by other composers, he wrote concertos for violin, bassoon, flute, oboe, clarinet, and French horn.

Mozart's piano concertos dominate the present-day concerto repertoire in quantity and quality. Within his personal repertoire the finest piano concertos equal the finest symphonies, and there are more of the former than the latter. He spent so much of his creative talent on the concerto for piano and orchestra that it appears to have been his favorite writing form. A survey of his piano concertos would provide an excellent outline of his general artistic development, for he produced these concertos from early boyhood until the last year of his life.

In the Baroque era, Bach and Handel had preferred either the harpsichord or organ concerto to the violin concertos so popular with Italian composers, and in the Pre-Classic period Bach's sons had adhered to their father's preference for keyboard works. Mozart not only continued this tradition; his piano concerto writing established a basic compositional pattern for this form—one that was to be used for many years. Whereas composers like Beethoven, Chopin, and Schumann indulged in personal variations and techniques, the indefinable grandeur and elegance that *is* the concerto came only from Mozart.

Before analyzing any individual concerto, we must understand the general concerto form that Mozart used. His first movements do not follow the Baroque practice of constant alternation between solo theme and orchestral ritornello (refrain): he preferred sonata-allegro form. His concerto structure is that of a three-movement symphony having a fast-slow-fast tempo pattern. Unlike a symphony, the principal stylistic trait in the concerto is the contrast between dissimilar media; for example, between piano and orchestra in the piano concerto, between violin and orchestra in the violin concerto. To point up the differences in these unlike media, the solo parts are deliberately composed to allow the soloist to exhibit brilliant technique; still the soloist never dominates the performance, for in a Mozart concerto the orchestra and the soloist participate as equal partners.

Mozart's first movements offer infinite variety. The movement proper opens with a double exposition of the themes (the sonata and symphony used a repeated exposition; see page 169). The first exposition, stated by the orchestra alone, is typically compact and direct; for the second exposition the piano joins the orchestra and adds at least one new theme. Mozart's dramatic instinct here is similar to that found in his operas. Another dramatic element arises toward the end of the recapitulation: after a closing section assigned to the orchestra, a seemingly final cadential movement is abruptly halted; then the soloist executes a *cadenza,* a spectacular unaccompanied passage designed to show off both instrument and performer. The conclusion of the cadenza is signaled by the soloist, and the orchestra enters and terminates the movement with a brief coda. In Mozart's day performers were expected to improvise cadenzas on the spot, and he must have done this countless times. He also wrote out 36 cadenzas, including some for the second and third movements of his concertos. Since Mozart looked upon the cadenza as an embellishment, his cadenzas are only slightly thematic.

What Classic composers like Mozart actually did in their first movements was to modify the Baroque concerto form to fit the sonata-allegro form. The comparison is too striking to be accidental (in the following diagram, T means "tutti" or all together; S means "soli" or soloists):

Baroque:	T	S	T S T S	T S	S	T
Classic:	Orchestral Exposition	Orchestral and Solo Exposition	Development	Recapitulation	Cadenza	Coda

The second movement of a Mozart concerto is typically slower and more introspective than the first movement. He often chose an extended keyboard aria in ternary form, or a theme and variations, or simplified sonata-allegro form. A prominent characteristic of the Mozart slow movement is his emphasis on woodwind instruments. The last movement is usually a lively, elaborate rondo (often approaching sonata-allegro form) or a theme and variations.

Since the early nineteenth century, Mozart's most consistently popular piano concerto has been the *Concerto in D Minor, K. 466,*[3] a somber and passionate work. It was a prime favorite during the nineteenth century—Beethoven composed two cadenzas for it—and it remains a standard repertoire item today. Mozart played the premier performance on February 11, 1785, and according to history he not only had no rehearsal but supposedly did not even have a chance to play through the last movement.

The initial measures of the opening *Allegro* expose an ominous atmosphere rather than a well-defined theme. The first exposition uncovers at least three principal ideas, and the piano adds two more in the re-exposition—one in *d* minor having the style of a lament, and one in *F* major that is expanded and sent back and forth between keyboard and orchestra. The development adroitly fuses the first orchestral idea and the first piano theme; however, the latter never appears in the recapitulation.

Mozart used ternary form for the second movement of *K. 466.* Entitled *Romanze,* it contains beautiful moments as the piano, supported by strings, expresses an extended lyrical passage through a single melodic line. The violent middle section of *Romanze* reasserts the somber aura pervading the entire concerto.

[3] The letter K. refers to a chronological catalog of Mozart's works made by Ludwig Koechel. He was sometimes incorrect in his assumptions and Alfred Einstein issued a revised catalog in 1937 (new edition 1964). However, the Koechel numbers are still used as a means of identification.

A rocket-like principal theme that still manages to emanate pathos overshadows all other material in the *Rondo* finale. Mozart reserved a surprise for this movement: toward the middle he inserted an *F*-major melody that might almost be described as frivolous. The somber mood assumes control again until the conclusion, when the bright melody reappears and Mozart gives it free rein, terminating the entire concerto in the key of *D* major.

ORCHESTRAL MUSIC

Mozart composed his first symphonies for the London concerts he gave when he was only eight and his final symphonies when he was thirty-two. In the course of his short, prolific career he produced more than 50 symphonic compositions. At that time the title "symphony" or *sinfonia* was another term for an overture having three movements, frequently connected. In the skillful hands of Haydn and Mozart, symphonic form broadened structurally and emotionally. By the late 1780s this form had graduated from divertissement status to the Classic symphony. As Haydn and Mozart developed the form, each profited from the other's knowledge and experience.

By the time Mozart reached the period of his last symphonies, he was writing with increasing freedom, expressing what he felt rather than what might be expected of him. His ability to handle contrapuntal style shows up particularly in these later orchestral works, where he seems to favor this type of writing in his development sections, perhaps as a relief from homophony.

Mozart supposedly wrote his last three symphonies within six weeks—*K. 543 in E-Flat Major* (composed in Vienna, June 1788), *K. 550 in G Minor* (July 1788), *K. 551 in C Major* (August 1788). There is no evidence that they were commissioned and no explanation for his writing them in such quick succession; it is even quite possible that Mozart never conducted any of them or even heard them performed.

He prefaces the first movement of *Symphony No. 39 in E-Flat Major, K. 543* with a slow, *Grave* introduction. The themes in the succeeding *Allegro* seem to demand different tempo shadings, and they are so worked over in the exposition that only a brief development is needed. The *Andante* in the rarely used key of *A* major is chiefly notable for its far-reaching modulations and skillful contrapuntal designs. In the festive *Minuet* the trio imitates a barrel organ. The spirited *Finale* offers nothing but cheerful entertainment and is as near to Haydn as Mozart ever got.

Symphony No. 40 in G Minor, K. 550 was completed in Vienna on July 25, 1788. It is a supremely Classic work: three of its four movements are in the key of *g* minor, and three movements are written in sonata-allegro form, a feat that only Mozart could have carried off so convincingly. This is essentially a work for small orchestra; there are no trumpet or drum parts, and, although the original score included two oboes, Mozart later replaced them with two clarinets and assigned the oboes to lesser roles.

In the first movement, *Molto allegro,* the exposition is decidedly tinged with melancholy. There is no introduction; the listener is at once face to face with a rhythmic theme sung by the strings (Ex. 15:1). This first theme, dynamically exciting with a basic descending motion punctuated by upward leaps, adds to the restlessness created by an agitated accompaniment. It is interesting to notice how

Ex. 15:1. Mozart: *Symphony No. 40 in G Minor, K. 550: Allegro molto*

the first three tones of the theme later become melodically and rhythmically important, especially in the development section. The second theme (Ex. 15:2) is separated from the first by a rest and is in the related key of *B*-flat major. Its smoothly chromatic and diatonic character, shared by winds and strings, provides a distinctive contrast to the first theme's fitful mood. The exposition closes with a passage for full orchestra in typical Mozartean style. The polyphonic development section contains complicated modulations, while the recapitulation is regular with a short coda.

Ex. 15:2. Mozart: *Symphony No. 40 in G Minor, K. 550: Allegro molto*

The second movement, *Andante,* also has sonata-allegro form. Beginning in *E*-flat major, it molds its principal theme (Ex. 15:3) into an intricate texture woven from imitative entries. Detached thirty-second-note figures in measure seven occur throughout the movement, adding solidity to the structural unity. The lyrical second theme—first in *B* flat and later in *E* flat—is flecked with the same thirty-second-note figure, and this theme assumes unexpected eloquence.

Ex.·15:3. Mozart: *Symphony No. 40 in G Minor, K. 550: Andante*

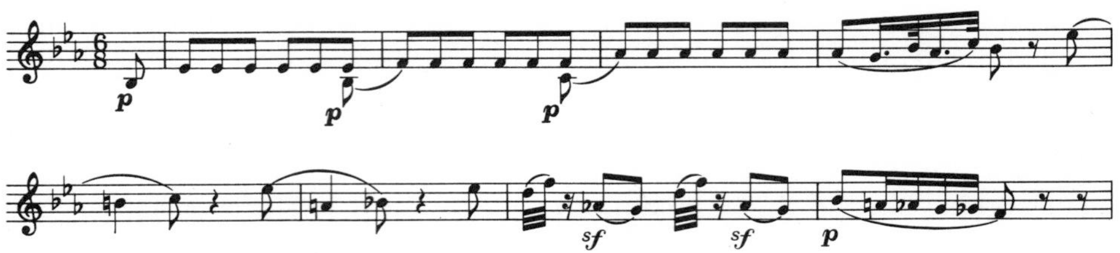

Although called *Minuet,* the third movement is just as far removed from that sophisticated dance form as Haydn's minuet in the "Surprise" symphony. Mozart spurns elegance for passion and agitation. The vigorous opening subject soon changes into a more workable contrapuntal subject, which Mozart manipulates polyphonically. An entirely different mood governs the pastoral trio, where prominent passages are allocated to the horns.

With equal success Mozart used sonata-allegro form again in his *Allegro assai* finale, and he also used the home key of *g* minor for the third time. Here the first theme begins with a soft *g*-minor broken-chord figure, which is answered by a raucous chattering motive (Ex. 15:4). This expands to broad proportions before giving way to the serenely lyrical second theme, which suggests pathos without ever

Ex. 15:4. Mozart: *Symphony No. 40 in G Minor, K. 550: Allegro assai*

stating it. The development is lively with bold counterpoint and harmony and intricate rhythmic distortions. A standard recapitulation ends this unorthodox work.

Symphony in C Major, K. 551 is Mozart's last symphony. For some reason it became known after his death as the "Jupiter" symphony. Its first movement, *Allegro vivace,* dwells on contrasts, displaying aloof grandeur and simple tenderness. The distinctive *Andante cantabile* forms a chain of happy melodies against muted strings, while simultaneously it introduces strange syncopations that seem to imply that the $\frac{3}{4}$ meter has changed to $\frac{2}{4}$. Like the first movement, the subdued *Allegretto* alternates softness and strength. In the *Allegro molto,* built in classic sonata-allegro form, the exposition, development, and coda all contain expertly designed fugato passages.

In addition to his symphonies, Mozart wrote works for different orchestral combinations: cassations, divertimenti, serenades. Of these three instrumental types, the most familiar is the *serenade.* The eighteenth-century serenade comprised a set of movements for chamber orchestra or wind instruments. The first movement was in sonata-allegro form, and at least one of the others was a minuet. Mozart wrote over a dozen serenades, but by far the most popular is *Serenade in G Major, K. 525,* subtitled *Eine kleine Nachtmusik* (A Little Night Music). Mozart composed this work in Vienna in 1787, the same year he produced his opera *Don Giovanni.*

Although the score indicates only four-part music for strings, *Serenade, K. 525* is not a string quartet. In his catalog, Mozart used the plural *bassi* when describing the lowest part, thus indicating several bass instruments. Also, this *Serenade* bears no resemblance to Mozart's complex quartet writing of that time. It is a slight but totally charming divertissement for string orchestra and may well be a composition that he wrote for his personal pleasure. Singularly perfect in its cosmopolitan sophistication, *Eine kleine Nachtmusik* deserves its popularity; in length and content this is a remarkably compact, faultlessly balanced work. Each of the four movements speaks briefly and flawlessly.

The opening *Allegro* has clear-cut first-movement form: an energetic principal theme in *G* major opposes the second subject, softly stated in *D* major. A miniature development modulates the first subject before the uneventful recapitulation. *Romanze* extends a simple theme through repetition and variation; a new subject introduced in the middle section evokes a mysterious atmosphere: flutterings occur in the second violins and violas while violins and basses engage in dialogue. The brief *Minuet* has three-part form: the first and third sound like a formal court dance, while the central trio presents a pleasing, weaving melody. Mozart concludes his enchanting *Serenade* with a typical Viennese *Rondo:* its sparkling theme is repeated five times, and its second subject acts as a foil to this vivacity.

Wolfgang Amadeus Mozart

CHAMBER MUSIC

Mozart composed about 60 chamber works. Since to our knowledge he was not commissioned to write most of these chamber-music compositions, we can only assume that he enjoyed writing in this form.

Most of this repertoire consists of string quartets, although there are some string quintets, a justly famous clarinet quintet, piano trios, piano quartets, and works for other instrumental combinations.

Of the 26 Mozart string quartets, only the last ten are regularly played now. The first six in this group date from 1782–1785 and carry an affectionate dedication to Joseph Haydn describing the quartets as "the fruit of a long and laborious work." The musical results are certainly not "laborious." On the contrary, they stand as perfect models for this form as well as superlative examples of Mozart's genius. In these works Mozart acknowledged his debt to the older composer, for he once said, "It was a duty that I owed to Haydn to dedicate my quartets to him; for it was from him that I learned how to write quartets."[4]

The most popular among these six "Haydn" quartets is *K. 465,* the last and most unusual. It is frequently called the "Dissonant" quartet because of the introduction: eight measures of unorthodox harmonic progressions that broaden into sonorous, expressive, chromatic harmony.

Mozart's last three quartets (*K. 575, 589, 590*) were probably intended for King Friedrich Wilhelm in Berlin, who played the violoncello. Nearly every movement in each quartet features the violoncello.

Mozart's enthusiasm for chamber music went beyond the string quartet. His string quintets are exceptional in that the majority use two violas, creating rare warmth and eloquence. And the *Clarinet Quintet, K. 581* is one of the few outstanding works for clarinet and string quartet. It should be heard more frequently.

OPERAS

Literally hundreds of operas were written and produced from about 1600 to 1780, but only a few of these are performed today. Our present-day operatic repertoire begins with Mozart's stage works, although not every Mozart opera is now performed. Mozart loved opera form, but when he began writing operas he had to prove himself to public and critics by conforming to conventional operatic patterns.

In his youth, opera seria represented important opera, so he composed opera-seria works and won an excellent reputation at the time; however, these early operas—*Mitridate* (1770) and *Lucio Silla* (1772)—are rarely presented today. Perhaps to solidify his reputation in this field, he later wrote *Idomeneo* (1781) and *La clemenza di Tito* (1791), his last operas in this form.

Fortunately for succeeding generations of opera lovers, Mozart's sure instinct led him to opera buffa. Within five years he had turned out three comic masterpieces in the Italian style: *The Marriage of Figaro* in 1786; *Don Giovanni*

[4] Reported by Georg Nissen, Mozart's early biographer. In *Mozart: The Man and the Artist Revealed in His Own Words,* compiled by Friedrich Kerst, translated by Henry Krehbiel (New York: Dover Publications, Inc., 1965), p. 42.

in 1787; and *Così fan tutte, ossía la scuola degli amanti* (So Do They All, or The School for Lovers) in 1790. All three librettos were written by a talented libertine named Lorenzo da Ponte.

Mozart felt strongly about the relationship between operatic text and music.

> Why do Italian comic operas please everywhere—in spite of their miserable libretti—even in Paris, where I myself witnessed their success? Just because there the music reigns supreme and when one listens to it all else is forgotten. Why, an opera is sure of success when the plot is well worked out, the words written solely for the music and not shoved in here and there to suit some miserable rhythm (which, God knows, never enhances the value of any theatrical performance, be it what it may, but rather detracts from it) —I mean, words or even entire verses which ruin the composer's whole idea. Verses are indeed the most indispensable element for music—but rhymes—solely for the sake of rhyming—the most detrimental. Those high and mighty people who set to work in this pedantic fashion will always come to grief, both they and their music. The best thing of all is when a good composer, who understands the stage and is talented enough to make sound suggestions, meets an able poet, that true phoenix; in that case no fears need be entertained as to the applause even of the ignorant.[5]

Mozart's scampering, contriving comic opera characters—timid servant, wise chambermaid, crafty old doctor, and the like—are neither his creations nor those of the librettist, for long before their time such characters were stock figures in Italian *commedia dell' arte*. Nor are Mozart's plots realistic. The complicated, ludicrous situations often border on absurdity, yet—and herein lies the secret of Mozart's success—in each opera the audience quickly senses what might be called Mozart's realism. An even better word would be humanism, for every Mozart character is alive. He always seemed to be aware of human emotions and behavior; the marvelous thing is that he was able to give such convincing musical expression to these realities.

Mozart's basic expressive tools are not outwardly impressive. Apparently he never shared Gluck's anxiety about contemporary opera's excesses. Mozart's recitatives adhere rather closely to old practices, employing rapid-fire *secco* dialogue supported by chords from the harpsichord (even though the piano was already in common use). His choruses never become important except in his last opera, *The Magic Flute*. He ignored Gluck's suggestion that an opera's melodies should be previewed in a full-blown programmatic overture, although sometimes he introduces an important theme in the overture in order to call attention to it. He retained the da capo aria (see page 136) in spite of its natural resistance to realistic treatment, and he created virtuoso vocal passages whenever he felt them to be musically appropriate. His ensemble numbers, particularly those used as act finales, contribute significantly to the action because they contain dramatic developments pertinent to the opera's plot. These ensembles owe their superb musical texture to Mozart's brilliant contrapuntal skill and masterful part writing. In them—as well as in some arias—he maintains a close relationship between stage and orchestra, preserving a general unity that is rare for his time.

Thus Mozart continued the practices of his predecessors and contemporaries; nevertheless, his inherent genius changed opera form. In every Mozart opera the music is tailor-made: he never borrows material from his earlier works;

[5] A letter from Mozart to his father dated October 13, 1781. In Anderson, pp. 1150–1151. Reprinted by permission.

each aria is written for a certain character in a certain role and that is the only purpose of that music. Handel and his contemporaries wrote operas with noticeably sparse action, so much so that when a Handel opera is occasionally revived, it can be performed equally well in concert version without costumes, décor, or action. Although this sterility also exists in Mozart's opera-seria works, his comic operas represent a conspicuous dramatic change in opera form. Sensing that opera buffa demands action—frequently a lot of it—and that this kind of opera depends on good acting and timing on the part of the singers, Mozart styled his opera-buffa works to suit the medium's theatrical potentialities. The only way to experience the full impact of a Mozart opera buffa is to attend a staged performance.

The plot of *The Marriage of Figaro* can be traced to the second play in the Almaviva Trilogy (Count Almaviva plays an important role in each), three plays written by Pierre Augustin Caron de Beaumarchais (1732–1799). *The Barber of Seville* (1775)—later set to music by Rossini—and *The Marriage of Figaro* (1784) are comedies based on humorous intrigue; *The Guilty Mother* (1792) is a commonplace sentimental drama.

Figaro is a perfect situation comedy, and Mozart's score interprets it with sparkling wit. Count Almaviva's valet, Figaro, plans to marry Susanna, the Countess's maid. The plot follows Figaro as he successfully thwarts the philandering Count's attempts to seduce Susanna. The Countess also has problems; she is weary of her husband's infidelities and annoyed by the attentions of Cherubino, an amorous young page.

The opera's bustling overture sets exactly the right mood for the high-spirited action, and there are several excellent arias, one reason for *Figaro's* steady popularity. Figaro sings two. As he works out a plan to cure the Count's unfaithfulness, he sings the witty "Se vuol ballare" (If you wish to go dancing, my little Count, go ahead, but I'll play the tune); and when the Count attempts to dispense with Cherubino by sending him off to the army, Figaro congratulates the unhappy page in the tongue-in-cheek aria "Non più andrai." Of course there are love songs—"Porgi amor," sung by the Countess; "Voi che sapete," by Cherubino; "Deh vieni, non tardar," by Susanna—and ensemble numbers, such as the Act II finale, a spectacular writing achievement in which everyone comments simultaneously on the complicated state of affairs.

Così fan tutte has never been as popular as *Figaro* or *Don Giovanni,* although critics agree that Mozart's score is a rare example of concentrated writing. Two engaged young men pretend to leave for war service in order to test their fiancées. They return disguised and prove the young ladies' unfaithfulness by seducing each other's betrothed. The amusing plot implies disrespect for womanhood, and Mozart's intense, polished score keeps pace with the plot. Perhaps one reason for this opera's lesser popularity is that Mozart complicates the plot by switching from musical parody to sincerity, and one is never quite sure of his intent. Another reason is that the opera lacks exciting arias.

In many respects *Don Giovanni* is Mozart's finest opera. His powerful character delineations in this work have seldom been equaled; the skillful intermingling of comic and tragic elements is pure Mozart at his mature best; and some of the most delectable arias and scenes in all operatic history belong to *Don Giovanni*. The opera is called a *dramma giocoso* (comic drama)—perhaps suggesting that the story must not be taken too seriously. It remains an opera buffa until the last scene, so the whole opera might be described as a tragicomedy.

The original story of *Don Giovanni* (Don Juan) goes back at least to the seventeenth century. The French dramatist Molière wrote one called *Le festin de pierre* in 1665; Thomas Shadwell's version, *The Libertine* (1676), was furnished with incidental music by Henry Purcell; in Italy, Carlo Goldoni brought out *Don Giovanni Tenorio ossía Il dissoluto* in 1736; and many operatic versions of the tale were composed before and after Mozart. It is the familiar story of a pleasure-bent gentleman and his comic manservant. As Da Ponte planned it, the libretto is an amusing comedy with a touch of social satire and a great deal of impossible fantasy. The main character is not the Don but his servant Leporello, who represents reality and holds the action together. He endures extraordinary situations for his master's sake, never questioning the latter's authority and always ready to face new problems caused by the Don's amorous machinations.

The story is laid in seventeenth-century Spain. Following an unsuccessful attempt to win Donna Anna, young daughter of the Commandant of Seville, the licentious Don meets the girl's irate father and slays him. Because the Don is disguised, Anna does not know his identity.

Arriving at a lonely inn, the Don is confronted by the beautiful Donna Elvira, whom he had recently cast aside. She berates him, but while Leporello holds her attention the deceiver slips away. Leporello tells her to be comforted —an ironic comfort—as he sings the famous "Catalog" aria. "Look," he tells her, "you haven't been the first to receive such treatment and you won't be the last." Then from an enormous scroll he reads a list of his master's conquests: 640 in Italy, 231 in Germany, 100 in France, 91 in Turkey, and in Spain the staggering total of 1003. This blatant summary of the Don's immorality is accompanied by some of Mozart's most effervescent music. The accompaniment in the first section actually sounds like irrepressible laughter (Ex. 15:5). The list of

Ex. 15:5. Mozart: *Don Giovanni:* "Catalog" *aria*

conquests is as indiscriminate as the Don: countesses, servants, marchionesses, peasants. As for the most desirable type, it is slender and plump, light and dark, young and not-so-young!

Don Giovanni then returns to his estate, where he soon tries to capture a pretty peasant girl named Zerlina. Giovanni's courtly grace and the girl's hesitant yielding are beautifully expressed in the duet "La ci darem la mano" (Your hand in mine, my dearest). The conquest is spoiled when Anna appears with Ottavio (her finance) and Elvira, all three seeking revenge. Anna recognizes the Don and he is forced to flee. Undaunted, he sings the celebrated "Champagne" aria, "Finch' han dal vino," and orders a party for the peasants. Zerlina appears (a separate scene) with her betrothed Masetto, who scolds her for encouraging the Don. She replies with the bewitching "Batti batti, o bel Masetto" (Scold me, dear Masetto), a plea so tender and flirtatious that no man could resist it (Ex. 15:6).

At the ball in the Don's palace an orchestra plays the incomparable *Minuet,* an illustration of Mozart's genius for instrumental writing. At a typical eighteenth-century Viennese ball, orchestras played different dances in different rooms to provide something pleasing for everyone. Mozart duplicates this atmos-

Ex. 15:6. Mozart: *Don Giovanni:* "Batti batti"

phere by having three instrumental groups play three dances—at the same time. One group plays the minuet. At the repetition, another group adds a contradance (a kind of square dance), while the third superimposes an old-fashioned German waltz (Ex. 15:7).

Ex. 15:7. Mozart: *Don Giovanni: Minuet*

The three dances separate the dancers according to social status: Donna Anna and Don Ottavio dance the aristocratic minuet; peasants enjoy the accented waltz strains; Don Giovanni and Zerlina join in the middle-class contradance (Ill. 15:1).

During the festivities the Don tries again to seduce Zerlina. To escape the crowd's anger, he flees from his palace. A few weeks later he tries a third time, after Zerlina has become a maid in Donna Elvira's house. Leporello, disguised as the Don, lures Elvira into the garden while the Don serenades Zerlina with the charming "Deh! vieni alla finestra" (Appear, love, at thy window). Masetto and Zerlina are finally reunited; Leporello runs away after he is forced to reveal his identity to Don Ottavio and Elvira. Ottavio swears vengeance, then sings "Il mio tesoro" (Fly then, my love, entreating), one of the loveliest and most difficult tenor arias ever written.

Meanwhile Don Giovanni passes by a newly erected statue of the slain Commandant and jeeringly invites it to dinner. During the sumptuous banquet that follows, the Don forgets his jest until a heavy tread sounds on the stairs: the marble statue has responded to the invitation. It enters the room and seizes the unrepentant Don Giovanni; flames leap up and demons drag him down through the banquet-hall floor.

Mozart re-establishes the *buffa* character of the opera in a little epilogue where the surviving sextet moralizes on the fact that Don Giovanni has received his just reward.

Ill. 15:1. *Mozart,* Don Giovanni, Minuet *from Act I, Scene V. Royal Opera House, Covent Garden. Courtesy of Houston Rogers.*

Mozart also composed German operas. As early as 1768 he wrote a German comic opera (*Singspiel*) called *Bastien und Bastienne.* The original plot was not German: it was based on a French libretto which in turn derived from Rousseau's *Village Soothsayer. Bastien* is slight but pleasing. There are only three characters, much of the dialogue is spoken, and the simple airs can be sung easily by amateurs.

Mozart's later concept of the *Singspiel* broke with earlier tradition. The Austrian Emperor Joseph II liked German opera but he wanted it to be of higher caliber. Mozart fulfilled this wish by writing *Die Entführung aus dem Serail* (The Abduction from the Harem) in 1782. The action still takes place through spoken dialogue, but the musical score is difficult and consequently the opera is not too often heard. Mozart employs ornate vocal lines and simple songs in this opera. It concludes with a finale called *vaudeville,* a kind of rondo in which each participant sings a stanza and everyone joins in the refrain.

Mozart wrote his last stage work, a German opera called *Die Zauberflöte* (The Magic Flute), in 1791 for a popular theater on the outskirts of Vienna. Initially designed as a fairy tale, the ultimate story is an allegory on Freemasonry. Both Mozart and his librettist Schikaneder belonged to a Masonic lodge, a secret order not condoned in Catholic Austria although its ideals and principles attracted many men in the eighteenth century, including Voltaire, Goethe, and Frederick the Great.

At first *The Magic Flute* seems to be a curious hodgepodge. The libretto is complicated and incongruous, there are 13 scene changes, and the characters wear strange bird costumes and other costumes suggesting ancient Egyptian priests. Nevertheless, the opera makes complete sense and some critics think it is Mozart's most superior stage work. It might be interpreted as a musical morality play, for it deals fundamentally with man's eternal search for spiritual truth and moral goodness. The stern ordeals facing those who aspire to these high standards are intended to remind the listener of the degrees of Masonic initiation. Mozart's characters are exquisitely drawn. Sarastro (a word play on the Persian deity Zoroaster?), high priest of an Egyptian Isis-cult, represents truth and virtue. He is a basso and his arias "O Isis and Osiris" and "Within These Sacred Halls" are solemn and stately. In contrast, the Queen of the Night embodies all evil. She is a coloratura soprano whose famous aria "The Revenge of Hell Is Seething in My Heart" is a virtuoso masterpiece (Ill. 15:2). The less abstract roles of Prince

Ill. 15:2. ***Mozart,* The Magic Flute, *"Vengeance" aria of the Queen of the Night. Royal Opera House, Covent Garden. Courtesy of Reg Wilson.***

Tamino and Princess Pamina represent those who strive for the high ideals to which Sarastro holds the key.

Obviously *The Magic Flute* is no mere *Singspiel,* although Mozart provides a humorous element with Papageno, a bird-catcher. When Papageno is permitted a glimpse of Papagena, his future mate, Mozart unveils one of the best comedy scenes in all opera. It is impossible to say what *The Magic Flute* was really meant to be—comedy or serious drama. Whatever his purpose, Mozart created one of man's most sublime musical experiences.

THE REQUIEM

Despite the fact that Mozart wrote many Masses, including the dramatic, impressive *Coronation Mass, K. 317* (1779), his best-known sacred work is one that he did not live to complete. The *Requiem Mass, K. 626,* on which he worked to the last day of his life, had to be completed by his pupil Franz Süssmayer.

Far removed from the placid, stylized, highly contemplative Renaissance Masses and the Baroque's agitated virtuoso sacred works, Mozart's *Requiem* is utterly personal. Except for a few solos, he devotes himself to substantial choral movements, which range from the double fugue of the *Kyrie* to the massive chordal structure of the *Dies Irae.* He never exploits virtuosity for its own sake. Simplicity and spiritual awareness give his *Requiem* integrity and create a final testament of haunting beauty and sadness.

SUMMARY OF THE CLASSIC PERIOD

The attitudes prevailing during the eighteenth-century "Enlightenment" incited action and reaction, frivolity and seriousness, emotionalism and restraint—all seemingly antipathetic contrasts. Yet somehow the mood of the time brought them into balance.

Musical Classicism covered about 60 years and produced many competent composers whose works were widely performed in their own day. Domenico Cimarosa (1749–1801) won fame with his operas, particularly *The Secret Marriage* (1792). Another Italian, Luigi Cherubini (1760–1842), wrote church music and operas that Haydn and Beethoven admired. Jean Jacques Rousseau, spokesman for the Enlightenment and prophet of the French Revolution, defended comic opera as typifying daily life and even composed one, *The Village Soothsayer* (1772), which sustained his view. The Viennese Karl von Dittersdorf (1739–1799) wrote successful Classical symphonies, church music, and opera.

Today we rarely hear the music of these composers, while Haydn and Mozart enjoy undiminished popularity. It is easy to see why. These two composers offer the most eloquent testimonial to eighteenth-century Classicism. They complement each other, literally and figuratively: they admired each other greatly, learned from each other, and unhesitatingly incorporated this knowledge into their respective works. Between them they created the repertoires for the most typical forms of musical Classicism—symphony, string quartet, concerto, Mass, oratorio, opera—each repertoire distinguished by quality, originality, and universality.

Haydn's melodic inspiration had been nourished by folk music; Mozart intuitively mastered the elegant, aristocratic cantabile melody. Haydn ensured a future for the string quartet; Mozart strengthened Haydn's foundation, freely acknowledging his artistic debt to his friend.

Haydn experimented constantly—a desire fostered by his musical isolation at Esterházy—and created new dimensions for the symphony; Mozart lent his skill in instrumental counterpoint to symphonic writing and also created the Classic solo concerto. Haydn's language tends to be uncomplicated, but he reveals great imagination in exposing and developing thematic material. Mozart's symphonies, chamber music, and operas combine all the eighteenth-century characteristics. His brilliant mind absorbed all his epoch had to offer, sifted it through his creative consciousness, and refined it into pure musicality.

FOR DISCUSSION AND ASSIGNMENT

1. Considering the fact that Mozart wrote so many concertos, why are most of them rarely heard today?
2. Listen to a mature Haydn composition. Follow this with a similar work by Mozart. Can you tell who wrote which? If so, how can you tell? What conclusions do you draw from your observations?
3. How do you account for the fact that Mozart led a comparatively penurious life and was buried in a pauper's grave?
4. The Classic period should stand as the high point of abstract music. Do you find Mozart's music exclusively intellectual or does it contain emotional value? If the latter, can you suggest reasons for its still being considered the essence of Classicism?

FOR FURTHER READING

Biancolli, Louis, editor. *The Mozart Handbook.* New York: Grosset & Dunlap, 1954. A Universal Library PB. Consisting of essays by many contributors, this self-sufficient handbook explores Mozart's life through biography, letters, and contemporary documents; it discusses every important category of Mozart's composition, with backgrounds and analyses; and it provides, through appendices, a classified list of Mozart's works and a chronology.

Blom, Eric. *Mozart.* New York: Collier Books, 1962. PB. This biography and critical study is excellent from many points of view. The biographical material is well written; Mozart's compositions are analyzed as fully as space permits; a calendar and list of works supply handy reference data. Mr. Blom is rather dogmatic at times, doubtlessly due to his enthusiasm for his subject.

Pauly, Reinhard G. *Music in the Classic Period.* Englewood Cliffs, N.J.: Prentice-Hall, Inc., 1965. PB. This book contains a competent, meaningful discussion of Mozart and his cultural, social, and religious milieu.

Turner, W. J. *Mozart: The Man and His Works,* Revised Edition by C. Raeburn. New York: Barnes & Noble, Inc., 1966. A University PB. Turner's critical biography, originally published in 1938, still retains its popularity as one of the finest studies of the Austrian master.

Ludwig van Beethoven 16

"What's that?" he cried, pointing to the music on the wall.

"What?" said the other. "Oh, that! It's music; it's a phrase of Beethoven's I was writing up. It means destiny knocking at the door."

ROBERT LOUIS STEVENSON
The Ebb Tide

Ludwig van Beethoven (1770–1827) was born in Bonn into a middle-class German family. His father, employed as a chapel singer by the Archbishop-Elector of Bonn, seems to have been a dour man who determined to develop his musically talented child to be a second Mozart. Although Beethoven's musical gift had manifested itself early, unlike Mozart he was not a child prodigy. His general education was more or less neglected while his father forced him to excessive practice and discipline to further his music. He experienced the first sympathetic influence in his life when he became a student of the kindly, educated court organist Christian Gottlob Neefe (1748–1798), who not only broadened his musical knowledge but introduced him to classical literature.

During a brief stay in Vienna in the spring of 1787, Beethoven played the piano for Mozart, who predicted a fine musical career for him, and he might have stayed on in Vienna except that his mother's illness recalled him to Bonn. After her death he remained five years at Bonn as a viola player in the court opera orchestra, where he was able to observe firsthand how an orchestra functioned and to learn the important operas of that time. During this period he met Count Ferdinand von Waldstein, who became his lifelong friend and benefactor, and the cultured Stephan Breuning.

In 1792 the Archbishop-Elector sent Beethoven to Vienna for further study and the composer settled there for the rest of his life. He began lessons with Haydn but they were not too successful; he was happier in his counterpoint studies with Johann Albrechtsberger (1736–1809) and dramatic composition training under Antonio Salieri (1750–1825). Beethoven's astonishing piano technique soon attracted attention among the Viennese aristocracy. To the end of his life this generous aristocratic class treated him with genuine affection and respect, bearing his arrogance and irascibility with patience and understanding.

For a time his phenomenal piano performances overshadowed his composing, and critics complained that some of his works were too exaggerated and difficult; however, once the Viennese public realized his creative genius, hostility changed to acclaim.

Beethoven first noticed his deafness—a cruel affliction for a musician—in 1798. Always brusque and isolated, even as a child, he grew lonelier as this deafness increased. When his attempts at courtship and marriage failed, he retreated deeper into his isolation, becoming more uncouth, abrupt, even offensive. By 1824 he was so completely deaf that he had to be turned around on the concert stage in order to *see* the audience wildly applauding his ninth symphony.

At the beginning of 1827, Beethoven had plans under way for a tenth symphony, a project to set Goethe's *Faust* to music, and numerous sketches for choral pieces, but his health failed. Nevertheless, a week before his death he was still planning future works. A visit from Schubert, whose music had aroused his interest, was arranged, but Beethoven was unable to speak to his Viennese admirer. He finally succumbed on March 26, 1827.

Beethoven's will constitutes one of the most touching documents in musical history. Written in 1802 as a letter to his brothers, it has come to be known as the Heiligenstadt testament since he wrote it from Heiligenstadt, now a suburb of Vienna. In despair and fear because of his oncoming deafness, Beethoven tells his brothers that he has a natural love for society but that he dreads facing it in his present and future condition. He reproaches those who judge him to be pugnacious and obstinate without suspecting that he might be incurably ill, and he admits that he dreads letting people know he is deaf. He reveals his anguish when others near him hear a flute and a singing shepherd and he hears nothing. He concludes by saying that only his art prevents him from suicide, for it seems impossible to him that he should leave the world before producing all he feels capable of creating.

This lonely, tortured man composed a musical repertoire that must be described as monumental rather than vast. His 32 large-scale piano sonatas, often called "the pianist's bible," include many—such as "Pathétique," "Appassionata," "Moonlight," "Les Adieux," "Waldstein"—that have never lost their emotional appeal. He also wrote five concertos for piano and orchestra; the last two of these—in *G* major and *E*-flat major (the "Emperor" concerto)—revealed new expressive possibilities in the piano. Apart from the piano concertos, he wrote one violin concerto and a triple concerto for pianoforte, violin, and violoncello. His large chamber-music repertoire includes sixteen string quartets, ten violin sonatas, five violoncello sonatas, one septet, one octet, and numerous trios, quintets, and sextets. He also composed overtures, lieder, choral works—including the grandiose *Missa Solemnis*—and one opera, *Fidelio*. His nine symphonies are so important in musical history and to humanity that they belong in a class by themselves.

Ludwig van Beethoven's greatness has gone beyond the limits of musical sound. This incredible, talented man constructed magnificent tonal edifices which, through the impact of his personal nature, touched deep into the inner core of his fellow man. He possessed an indomitable will tempered with a rare capacity for love and tenderness, and he had the gift to translate his emotions into music that continually enriches mankind's spiritual treasures. His music reaches us today as passionate and powerful; for him it was painfully personal.

The inherent vitality in Beethoven's music can be partially accounted for by the frenzied, significant times in which he lived. His era rebelled against traditional ideas and institutions. The middle class fought against princely autocracy and advanced rapidly as it freed itself from aristocratic domination. Beethoven participated in this turbulent period, and perhaps the era's fighting spirit helped him to overcome the frustrations of deafness and poor health.

In the eighteenth century, music was designed to assist at ceremonial and social functions: at religious services, at royal diversions, or simply as public entertainment. A composer's emotional temperament naturally affected his music, but intimate feelings had to be suppressed and appeared only discreetly or not at all. Before Beethoven, music's primary purpose was to please the audience, which meant nothing could be too serious, nothing too difficult—an attitude that tended to produce an impersonal kind of music. Beethoven changed this approach. The more freedom he allowed his genius, the more personal he made his art. The public could enjoy his music, too, but along with their listening pleasure they could share the composer's intense emotions.

It would take an entire book to describe with full justice Beethoven's contributions to musical art, and indeed many books have been written on this subject. The Bonn master was a direct precursor of the Romantic period. Before Beethoven, musical composition was usually formalized and impersonal—though often inspired—and composers generally adapted to public tastes. With Beethoven, music became absolutely personal. To him it was a dramatic art capable of interpreting every human emotion, and he poured his deepest feelings into it.

He was a slow, methodical composer, arriving at a finished melody only after numerous sketches and reworkings. Each composition seems to have been thoroughly polished and revised. Every note seems artistically logical; anything added or omitted would detract from his music's basic character and impact. He was well aware of his disciplined "routine," and once explained it:

> I carry my thoughts about me for a long time, often a very long time, before I write them down; meanwhile my memory is so faithful that I am sure never to forget, not even in years, a theme that has once occurred to me. I change many things, discard, and try again until I am satisfied. Then, however, there begins in my head the development in every direction, and, inasmuch as I know exactly what I want, the fundamental idea never deserts me,—it arises before me, grows,—I see and hear the picture in all its extent and dimensions stand before my mind like a cast, and there remains for me nothing but the labor of writing it down, which is quickly accomplished when I have the time, for I sometimes take up other work, but never to the confusion of one with the other. You will ask me where I get my ideas. That I can not tell you with certainty; they come unsummoned, directly, indirectly,—I could seize them with my hands,—out in the open air; in the woods; while walking; in the silence of the nights; early in the morning; incited by moods, which are translated by the poet into words, by me into tones that sound, and roar and storm about me until I have set them down in notes.[1]

Beethoven's personal and professional behavior bettered the social status of musicians. Traditionally musicians depended on patronage from nobility or the Church, and consequently they were expected to compose on command. Beethoven changed this situation. By deciding for himself what he would write and when he would write it, he encouraged later musicians to be independent.

[1] Said to Louis Schlösser, a young musician whom Beethoven accepted as a friend in 1822. In *Beethoven: The Man and the Artist, as Revealed in His Own Words,* compiled by Friedrich Kerst, translated by Henry Krehbiel (New York: Dover Publications, Inc., 1964), p. 29.

His often rough social manners are well illustrated in an anecdote concerning a performance he gave in Vienna. A Count Palffy and other nobles talked so loudly that Beethoven rose from the piano with the remark, "For such swine I will not play."

It may be true that Beethoven's deafness prompted the separation between composer and performer. Up to that time performers customarily wrote works for their own concerts; for instance, Bach, Handel, and Mozart all wrote countless compositions for their public performances. Haydn is one notable exception, although he was a performing orchestral conductor.

In matters of musical aesthetics and style, Ludwig van Beethoven is one of history's true innovators. His instrumental works in particular display this gift. For example, he extensively modified the traditional eighteenth-century forms for solo sonata, chamber music, and symphony. He enlarged the first movement's design and dramatized its subject matter: the "Eroica" symphony and "Pathétique" sonata excellently illustrate how he accomplished this change. He decided that the second (slow) movement should be more expressive, thus carrying out an idea that Mozart had previously implied. As for the minuet, Beethoven gradually transformed this essentially light-textured, dancelike movement into an extended, sprightly humorous scherzo. His fourth-movement finale, in either sonata-allegro or rondo form, is often extended to encompass the climax of the preceding movements.

While enlarging the sonata's traditional content and design, Beethoven added new elements. He employed unusually free modulations; he expanded his secondary themes or ideas associated with the principal theme; he discovered rare harmonies that fashioned new musical textures; and he frequently broadened the coda—which before had been merely an ending to a symphonic or sonata movement—by giving it the proportions and function of a second development section.

Beethoven's creative instinct gave particular emphasis to rhythm. He clothed his themes in rhythms that pulsate through an entire work. His developmental skill, another facet of his genius, is always closely related to his unique concept of rhythm. His developments are never mechanical or coldly scholastic; they seem alive, spontaneous, and emotional. His thoughts, never vapid, never mediocre, are translated into music perpetuating his intense emotions.

BEETHOVEN'S STYLES

In a book called *Beethoven and His Three Styles* (1855), Wilhelm von Lenz divides Beethoven's works into three consecutive periods, each having special stylistic features. In some ways this classification, later adopted by Fétis, d'Indy, and others, is not entirely acceptable. Beethoven's cumulative technique and progress—traceable in his handling of form and counterpoint—cannot be arbitrarily fragmented and classified. On the other hand, artificial as they may seem, these categories do partially correspond to reality, for an artist expresses himself differently during youth, maturity, and old age.

The principal characteristics of these three periods apply to the sonata in general, whether a piano sonata, a work for string quartet, or a symphony. We should keep these characteristics in mind as we examine some of the outstanding compositions Beethoven created for piano, chamber-music groups, and symphony orchestra.

First Period

The first category is called the "period of imitation or assimilation" and includes youthful works up to 1802, when Beethoven was 31. The sonatas, chamber music, and symphonies written during this time conform to the Classic shape bequeathed by Haydn and Mozart. Yet little by little his growing genius indulged in liberties that foretell the coming metamorphosis. During this first period he began to discard the minuet, the last surviving member of the suite. When he did include a minuet in a four-movement composition, it was a far cry from the elegant, sophisticated Mozartean type. More frequently Beethoven would replace the minuet with a lively scherzo. The ternary form (scherzo–trio–scherzo) is still retained in most examples of this movement, so it is structurally related to the minuet.

In many instances he rearranges the traditional order of movements or else inserts rather unorthodox movements. In the piano sonata *Opus 26*,[2] a funeral march becomes the third movement and the scherzo moves to second position. Instead of having a slow movement in his *String Quartet, Opus 18, No. 4,* he chose a moderately paced, graceful scherzo, which opens with a fugato.

Besides these technical transformations, Beethoven changed the purpose and spirit of sonata form. Where earlier this form had been no more than a divertissement, in a master's hands it quickly assumed a serious intent, surpassing mere grace and sophistication. Each Beethoven work uncovers a personal emotion for the listener according to the composer's musical dictates. Thematic contrasts dominating the design—especially in the first movements—act as dramatic protagonists that forcefully interpret the feelings Beethoven seemed compelled to relay through his music. The eventual change that he produced in the underlying meaning of sonata form was already taking shape in his first published compositions, in which he gives new significance to the traditional formulas used by Haydn and Mozart.

Second Period

The second category is known as the "period of realization." It includes works written between 1802 and about 1816, when Beethoven was 46. During this time he worked resolutely to develop a sonata of vaster dimensions. Since he no longer felt bound to the restricting details of Classic form, he treated the sonata's basic outlines with complete liberty, keeping them subservient to his imagination. He retained only those Classic elements that would not interfere with his ever expanding inspiration.

Beethoven's new attitude began in 1802, the year of the testament of Heiligenstadt. After a time of mental depression, he had determined to struggle on forcefully and intensely, and in this second period he achieved spiritual maturity.

Throughout this period he worked with a new stylistic detail: similarity between themes or rhythmic patterns of different movements in a sonata, chamber

[2] The *opus* (often abbreviated to Op.) number is used by composers to indicate the order in which their works have been composed. Beethoven was the first to use opus numbers with any degree of consistency. Some composers—Schubert, for example—used opus numbers erratically, so that they do not always accurately indicate the chronological order of composition.

work, or symphony. Frequently a basic rhythmic formula dominates his principal themes, yet it does not disturb their inherent character. He also allowed himself to be very liberal with form during this period. Some compositions have only two movements, others the customary three or four; the slow movement is often missing or is minimized.

Third Period

The final category extends from 1816 to 1827 and is referred to as the "period of contemplation." The works in sonata form belonging to this period uphold Beethoven's mature creative genius. His confident spirit and artistic integrity, which had made possible the tumultuous, passionate works of the second period, stayed with him to the end of his life. When his everyday existence turned into disorder, when he shunned his friends, and when his health failed, his inner strength and conviction sustained him. He rose above his unhappy circumstances and went on to create works more impressive than ever before.

During this final period he subjected sonata form to the extraordinary fantasy of his mature musicianship. Works from this period indicate an avid interest in developmental techniques. Individual movements are sometimes interrupted by foreign episodes, resulting in a totally new expressive style; Beethoven often uses the fugue and dramatic recitative for these passages. Contrapuntal writing becomes more frequent and more complex, harmonic concepts more daring. Several of the final sonatas and string quartets challenge performers with tremendous difficulties, the consequence of a creative style that sometimes seems to transcend the limitations of the instruments. At the same time, Beethoven's preoccupation with the relationship of themes persisted, affirming itself with subtle force.

PIANO SONATAS

Beethoven's piano sonatas reveal that he was engrossed with form and with creating a convincing expressive language to fit the form's design. In his early years he seemed to prefer a four-movement structure, which may have been an attempt to lift the piano sonata to trio or quartet status. However, a three-movement sonata soon proved to be the most satisfactory vehicle for his prodigious creative powers: an agitated first movement in which opposing elements are played against each other; an introspective, lyric second movement; and frequently a dramatic finale that resolves the conflicts of the first movement. Whenever Beethoven expanded the slow movement it assumed first importance, interrupting continuity between the first and last movements. At times he reduced the slow movement to a brief episode, but in *Opus 109* and *Opus 111* he moved it to the end to climax the entire sonata.

When Beethoven first began to work in this form, the piano sonata had only recently attained Classic perfection through Haydn and Mozart. Besides knowing their music, Beethoven in his early years must have been influenced by other composers, such as Muzio Clementi (1752–1832), whose sonatas Beethoven had played and admired as a young man. Beethoven perhaps borrowed some of

Clementi's writing procedures for his first sonatas; after that, everything came from his own creativity.

Many Beethoven piano sonatas have acquired international popularity as well as esteem. Among the great favorites is *Sonata in C Minor, Opus 13,* which appeared in 1799 with a dedication to a patron, Prince Karl von Lichnowsky. Beethoven's editors supplied the descriptive title "Pathétique," doubtlessly with his permission. This French adjective (meaning "touching" or "moving") graphically sums up the mood of the sonata, which was composed while Beethoven was experiencing the first signs of the deafness that blighted his mature life. He wrote to a friend several years later:

> In order to give you some idea of this strange deafness, let me tell you that in the theatre I have to place myself quite close to the orchestra in order to understand what the actor is saying, and that at a distance I cannot hear the high notes of instruments or voices. . . . Already I have often cursed my Creator and my existence. Plutarch has shown me the path of resignation. If it is at all possible, I will bid defiance to my fate, though I feel that as long as I live there will be moments when I shall be God's most unhappy creature.[3]

The "Pathétique" sonata has three movements. An initial *Allegro molto e con brio* is preceded by a dramatic slow introduction (Ex. 16:1) whose tragic

Ex. 16:1. Beethoven: *Sonata in C Minor, Opus 13: Grave*

overtones set the mood for the whole sonata. Sadness and futility prevail in the first movement, *Allegro,* which is so closely connected to the introduction that the latter must be partly repeated before the development section begins—and repeated again as part of the coda. The two principal themes in the first movement proper are completely characteristic: the first is an ascending melody that pours out passion; the second theme, in *e*-flat minor, increases the agitation although less dramatically. Beethoven used rondo form for the *Adagio cantabile,* a movement full of grandeur and decidedly lyrical. The final movement has a classic *Rondo* with four refrains and three interludes, followed by a brilliant coda.

Beethoven avoided sonata-allegro form in the first movements of his two sonatas of *Opus 27,* and to accentuate the omission he added *quasi una Fantasia* (in the manner of a fantasy) to each sonata title, proving once more that he was

[3] Emily Anderson, editor, *The Letters of Beethoven* (New York: St. Martin's Press, Inc., 1961), Vol. 1, p. 60. Reprinted by permission of Macmillan & Company, Ltd.

not overly concerned with the sonata's traditional structure. The musical content of the second sonata in *Opus 27* justifies the term "Fantasia." Its subtitle, "Moonlight," came not from Beethoven but from a publisher who had borrowed it from an article by the writer Heinrich Rellstab. Rellstab compared the first movement of *Opus 27, No. 2* with the moonlight scenery of Lake Lucerne.

Beethoven wrote the "Moonlight" sonata (*Opus 27, No. 2*) in 1802. Breaking established tradition, he began it with a quasi-improvisatory slow movement, *Adagio sostenuto* (Ex. 16:2), a lyrical, dramatic composition with rich

Ex. 16:2. Beethoven: ***Sonata in C-Sharp Minor, Opus 27, No. 2: Adagio sostenuto***

harmonic color. It is constructed in eighth-note triplets whose melodic design echoes in the finale. Although the second movement—Liszt called it "a flower between two abysses"—is titled *Allegretto,* it is really a scherzo with an invigorating Classic trio. The *Presto agitato* finale—more extended than in any previous sonata—reverts to the drama of the first movement; but while the first movement expresses calm sadness, the finale is violent and tragic. It is based on sonata-allegro form.

Beethoven isolated himself during 1804 and 1805; he felt friendless and badly treated because the public had received his "Eroica" symphony coldly, and his increasing deafness heightened his solitude. At this time he wrote *Sonata in F Minor, Opus 57*. Begun in 1804 and completed about 1806, this work—known as the "Appassionata"—is the one Beethoven considered his greatest sonata up to that date. His editor Cranz in Hamburg furnished the name "Appassionata." This sonata marks a climax in Beethoven's keyboard writing; he approaches perfect unity in which form and idea fuse to achieve equilibrium between content and expression, between structure and feeling.

Formally speaking, the sonata has three movements: *Allegro assai, Andante con moto,* and *Allegro non troppo*. Both allegros are in sonata-allegro form, but for the first time Beethoven omits repeat marks in the first-movement exposition. This procedure is part of the work's logic since the predominant mood demands that the music keep moving forward—to repeat would disturb the aesthetic effect. The central movement is very short. A 16-measure theme is developed and amplified through three successive variations rising progressively to the upper part of the keyboard. A reference to the original theme follows the last variation and proceeds without pause into the final *Allegro non troppo,* where Beethoven introduces a new theme in the development section and places repeat signs for both development and recapitulation.

These three movements preserve unity through thematic relationships. In the initial *Allegro assai* the principal theme contains two complementary elements (Ex. 16:3). The first element helps to shape the second theme (measures 36 and

Ex. 16:3. Beethoven: ***Sonata in F Minor, Opus 57: Allegro assai***

37) and bears a strong resemblance to the finale's principal theme (measures 20 and 21). The second element is like the *Andante* theme (measures 1 to 4) and has some rhythmic and melodic features in common with the finale's second theme.

Beethoven's genius lives in his piano sonatas. The long list of his keyboard works from *Opus 2* through *Opus 111* reveals a unique transformation in style and musical vocabulary.

SYMPHONIES

Beethoven's nine symphonies also document his progressive development as a musician and composer. He began working on his first symphony around 1800, possibly earlier, and completed his ninth symphony toward the end of 1823.

With this series of symphonic masterpieces, Beethoven brought homophonic instrumental style to a perfection otherwise unknown in the early nineteenth century. Melody was destined to become an important element in the emerging Romantic school, and Beethoven's symphonies supplied models of superb melodies and melodic treatment. Every part of a Beethoven symphonic score has a dominant melody; and because he was such a master, the harmony, accompaniment, and subsidiary voices are inseparably bound to the melody, strengthening its meaning and expression. His melodies are often so broadly constructed that their component parts must be divided among several instrumentalists; these expansive themes contribute much to the grandeur in Beethoven's symphonies. No less remarkable is his gift for thematic development. As he reworks these monumental themes—sectionalizing, combining, transforming, juxtaposing—his uncanny ability to create myriad designs from the most basic material stands out brilliantly.

When compared with the Classic symphonies of Haydn and Mozart, Beethoven's symphonies clearly prove that he had a different understanding of the orchestra's function, formed perhaps during his years as violist in the Bonn court opera company. He assigned new, unconventional roles to some instruments. For example, the double bass had never been given very exciting parts in the Classic orchestra; its sustained bass tones usually served merely as stable support for other instruments. Beethoven created character for the double bass and even wrote some solo passages for it. Two French horns had held the Haydn-Mozart Classic orchestra together through their combined ability to achieve sustained harmony. Beethoven used three French horns instead of two and allowed them to participate freely in the melody. Another striking instrumental innovation in Beethoven's scoring was the three trombones appearing in the fifth, sixth, and ninth symphonies.

Musically his most noticeable departure from tradition is that he permits most orchestral instruments to contribute to the symphony's melodic development. He employs clarinets, oboes, flutes—even timpani—in the traditional manner, but he also lets each one speak as a soloist.

His humor seems to be most vividly realized in the orchestral scherzo. This is *musical* humor, and moreover it is Beethoven's own special brand of humor—lusty, obvious, and abrupt. The lumbering calisthenics maneuvered by the double basses in the third movement of *Symphony No. 5* convincingly illustrate this, and so does the rambunctious scherzo in *Symphony No. 9*.

Symphony No. 1 in C Major, Opus 21 (1800) attests to Beethoven's warm affection for Classic traditions, yet its breadth, implicit seriousness, and growing independence in the woodwind instruments foretell a new spirit. Even the *Menuetto* predicts the future scherzo. *Symphony No. 2 in D Major, Opus 36* (1802) was composed early in Beethoven's second period. Idiomatic writing, formal compactness, and skillful orchestral color make this work more advanced than the first symphony. While Beethoven was applauded for his lyrical writing in the opulently textured slow movement, he was criticized for his daring modulations in the last movement.

Written between 1802 and 1804, *Symphony No. 3 in E-Flat Major, Opus 55* seems to announce a completely new concept in symphonic writing. An ardent champion of human rights—liberty, equality, fraternity—Beethoven respected Napoleon Bonaparte as a social redeemer and had planned to dedicate this symphony to him—hence the subtitle "Eroica" (Heroic). However, when Napoleon crowned himself emperor in Paris in December, 1804, Beethoven destroyed the dedication, retaining only the subtitle. This symphony is one of the most repeated works in the orchestral repertoire; its spiritual, formal, and dramatic elements nearly overwhelm the listener.

The first movement, *Allegro con brio,* proposes thematic groups rather than single themes, and new thematic material arises in the development section. A *Marcia funèbre* (Funeral March) replaces the usual slow movement. The pathos and sorrow instilled here cannot be found in any of Beethoven's earlier works. Some critics thought the *Scherzo* was too harsh, redundant, and long; today we find it magnificent. A scintillating *Allegro molto* provides an ideal climax to the symphony.

The Romantic composer Robert Schumann called *Symphony No. 4 in B-Flat Major, Opus 60* "a slender Greek maiden between two Norse giants." Even if this comparatively modest work suffers by comparison with *Symphonies 3* and *5* it will always be valued for its description of nostalgia and tenderness. Beethoven composed it in 1806 during one of his few really happy periods. The first of the four well-balanced movements has an exceptionally impressive *Adagio* introduction. With superb timing Beethoven changes the introduction's ruling mood from mystery and romance to unchecked merriment as the music proceeds into the first movement, *Allegro vivace.* The sheer beauty of sound and texture in the slow *Adagio* movement is unforgettable, and the other two movements are equally fine: a rhythmic scherzo labeled *Minuet* and an exuberant finale, *Allegro ma non troppo.*

Symphony No. 5 in C Minor, Opus 67 (1808) is said to be the most popular symphony in the orchestral repertoire. Its unequivocal formal logic may partially account for its durability: each musical element fits neatly into place. Beyond this musical logic, the fifth symphony is an emotional tour de force. Its dramatic conflicts and tragic overtones must have germinated deep within Beethoven's intense emotions.

Allegro con brio. The opening four-note "motto" is one of the best-known flourishes in symphonic literature (Ex. 16:4). When an admirer ques-

Ex. 16:4. Beethoven: ***Symphony No. 5 in C Minor: Allegro con brio***

tioned the composer about its significance, Beethoven reportedly answered, "Thus Fate knocks at the door." Whether or not the story is true, that opening rhythm inexorably controls the entire movement. The tragic feeling takes hold as the first theme unfolds, an expansive declamation terminated only by the appearance of the second subject (Ex. 16:5). This second subject begins with the persistent

Ex. 16:5. Beethoven: ***Symphony No. 5 in C Minor: Allegro con brio***

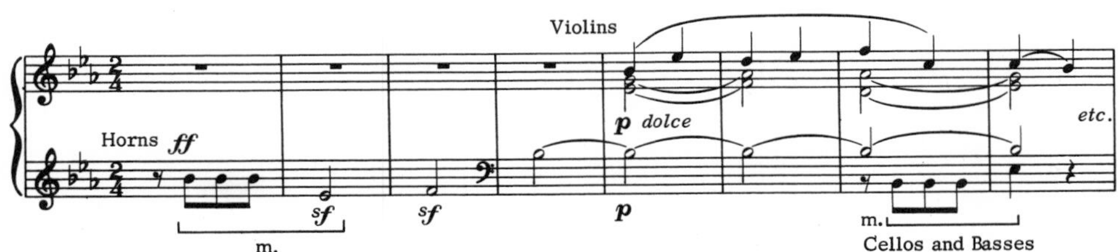

rhythm of the first; as it expands, the same rhythm sounds in the bass. The second and third measures of this new theme are especially significant: they inspire the chordal dialogue between strings and winds in the wonderful diminuendo near the end of the development, and they also provide material for the coda's fanfare opening.

The development is a marvel of concentrated thematic manipulation. The recapitulation proceeds normally except for a solo oboe passage interrupting the first theme. This solo seems irrelevant at first hearing, but closer observation discloses that it grows logically out of a melodic line which has been in process for the preceding 16 measures.

Andante con moto. The second movement emphasizes sound: martial strains, pastoral sections, sinuous weaving lines, and quasi-oriental passages. Beethoven employs a standard form—the variation—to display these manifold musical experiences. More correctly, the form is a set of continuous variations joined by an alternating (second) theme. The lyrical first theme—in *A* flat—is sono-

Ex. 16:6. Beethoven: ***Symphony No. 5 in C Minor: Andante con moto***

rously sung by violas and cellos against a pizzicato bass (Ex. 16:6). Although the second (alternating) theme begins quietly, it soon bursts out jubilantly in the key of *C* major (Ex. 16:7)—the key and mood of the last movement. Beethoven varies

Ex. 16:7. Beethoven: ***Symphony No. 5 in C Minor: Andante con moto***

his melodic line in the first theme by changing note values, a procedure that originated in the Renaissance. Toward the movement's end, the bassoon poignantly intones a lament (in minor tonality) with oboe interjections; then an exultant mood takes over to conclude the *Andante*.

Scherzo. This *Scherzo* might almost be called an adventure into the macabre, and it may be due to Beethoven's shifting mood accents. Two violently opposing themes control the *Scherzo* proper: one is a mysterious motive (Ex. 16:8) rising from the depths of the lower strings; after it is repeated, the second

Ex. 16:8. Beethoven: ***Symphony No. 5 in C Minor: Scherzo***

theme enters, a solemn march whose rhythmic pattern refers back to the first movement (Ex. 16:9). The trio, with its fugal scurrying in the lumbering double

Ex. 16:9. Beethoven: ***Symphony No. 5 in C Minor: Scherzo***

basses, is the epitome of sardonic humor. The *Scherzo* returns, but the strident march is now subdued to a whisper. Instead of an ending, drums beat a steady rhythm while violins play fragments of the *Scherzo*'s initial theme. An overwhelming crescendo leads directly into the finale, a passage that only a musical genius could create.

Allegro. The first movement's tragic emotion, the mood conflicts in the *Andante,* and the mystery in the *Scherzo* are all resolved in the positive brightness of the finale. To accent the festive atmosphere, Beethoven uses trombones for the first time in symphonic music. The first theme actually comprises two great fanfares, both in *C* major. The second theme also has two parts: a section in triplets (Ex. 16:10), whose cello countermelody is later pertinent in the development; and a second, less active melody (Ex. 16:11) that ultimately serves as the basis for the lengthy presto coda. Just before the recapitulation, the *Scherzo*'s brassy theme intervenes briefly, no longer sonorous and foreboding, just a whisper that quickly disappears.

Ex. 16:10. Beethoven: *Symphony No. 5 in C Minor: Allegro*

Ex. 16:11. Beethoven: *Symphony No. 5 in C Minor: Allegro*

Considering the dramatic intensity of *Symphony No. 5,* it is extraordinary that Beethoven was able to create four more memorable symphonies, each one possessing a distinct emotional character. *Symphony No. 6 in F Major, Opus 68*—the "Pastoral" symphony—was first performed in 1808, although Beethoven had been jotting down preliminary sketches for five years. It is sometimes described as a programmatic work, but Beethoven cautioned that it was "more an expression of feeling than painting." Each movement has absolute symphonic logic independent of the accompanying descriptive titles. *Cheerful Impressions on Arriving in the Country,* the first movement, presents sonata-allegro design as convincingly as any of Beethoven's other initial movements. The scene *By the Brook* with its triplet "water" figure and nightingale, quail, and cuckoo birdcalls is also in sonata-allegro form. The scherzo, titled *Peasants' Merrymaking,* realistically portrays a village festival. The following movement, *Storm,* imitates a thunderstorm (musical thunderstorms were to be very popular throughout the nineteenth century), which subsides as the thunder moves away; long-sustained sounds can be heard in the distance, perhaps a hymn of thanksgiving sung by grateful peasants. This is actually the introduction to the fifth-movement rondo finale, a buoyant *Shepherds' Hymn.* The last three movements are musically joined together, as were the last two movements in the *Symphony No. 5.*

Symphony No. 7 in A Major, Opus 92, completed in 1812, was called the "apotheosis of the dance" by Richard Wagner. This symphony's rhythmic drive is persistently conspicuous: each movement has a distinctive rhythmic figure permeating its whole fabric. The introduction to the *Vivace* first movement is more extensive than any other used by Beethoven. The second movement, *Allegretto*—which strongly influenced later Romantic composers—brings to mind a solemn ritual procession, and the brilliant scherzo, entitled *Presto,* has a trio said to be based on an old pilgrims' hymn. The steady rhythmic character of the symphony becomes especially prominent in the rousing finale, *Allegro con brio.*

Symphony No. 8 in F Major, Opus 93 is not performed as frequently as some of the others. Here Beethoven returns to more Classic form. Written the same year (1812) as *Opus 92,* it is sometimes described as humorous, and the music has abundant sparkle and unabashed wit. Occasionally this delightful composition is called the "metronome" symphony because repeated staccato notes in the *Allegretto scherzando* (which replaces the slow movement) remind some listeners of a ticking metronome.

The third movement contains an old-fashioned Classical minuet and trio: the minuet offers some unusual two-part writing for bassoons, while horns and clarinet share the trio. In the humorous *Allegro vivace* finale, the timpani (tuned in octaves) and bassoons engage in what appears to be a little dance.

Symphony No. 9 in D Minor, Opus 125 certified Beethoven's reputation as a symphonic genius; it also revealed many of his composing secrets, an inspirational legacy to countless future composers. He finished this "Choral" symphony, as it is often called, late in 1823, during his most mature period. It has four movements, and in every one Beethoven departed from traditional symphonic concepts. Intense power and liberal musical ideas emanate from the entire work.

The first movement (*Allegro ma non troppo*) opens mysteriously; as it unfolds, several secondary themes seem to germinate from the initial theme. When the second movement is played as indicated—*Molto vivace*—it becomes the mightiest of Beethoven's scherzos. The slow movement, *Adagio molto e cantabile,* moving to third place in this symphony, combines rondo and variation elements in a song of deep pathos.

The finale is unique. Nothing like it existed before Beethoven and none of the imitations can approach it. Basically it is a musical setting—for chorus, four vocal soloists, and orchestra—of Friedrich Schiller's poem *An die Freude,* translated "Ode to Joy." A long introduction recalls themes from the preceding movements and then adds a new theme. The cello and double bass intone an instrumental recitative. Beethoven chose variation form to fit Schiller's verses; there are eight variations, ending with a huge double fugue and monumental coda. A giant symphony thus immortalizes a giant among composers.

CONCERTOS

In contrast to Mozart's some 50 concertos, Beethoven wrote only seven—five for piano, one for violin, and an unusual "Triple Concerto" for piano, violin, and violoncello. Just as he had altered the symphony, string quartet, and piano sonata to accommodate his exciting concepts of monumental form, so in these concertos he molded the sonata for solo instrument and orchestra to his ideal: Classic form and powerful emotion existing interdependently.

His first two piano concertos (1794, 1797) seem to be preliminary studies, for their clear Classic form, old expressive patterns, and folklike tunes look to the past rather than ahead. The last three piano concertos belong to a decidedly different category: not lighthearted, graceful diversions but a poetic synthesis of exquisite orchestral and pianistic art.

Piano Concerto No. 3 in C Minor, Opus 37 (1800) forms a bridge between the first two and last two concertos. It displays the piano's newly acquired stature and sweep, and clearly indicates rapidly growing command of orchestral resources.

Many critics believe that *Concerto No. 4 in G Major, Opus 58* (*c.*1805) is the most poetic piano concerto in the whole repertoire. The soft-spoken initial *Allegro* achieves its effect from Beethoven's lyrical melodic materials. The middle movement, *Andante con moto,* is a deeply moving meditation designed as a dialogue between piano and orchestra. The concerto's only outward brilliance shows in the *Rondo,* which has a peculiarly fascinating ornamented theme.

Piano Concerto No. 5 in E-Flat Major, Opus 73 (1809) usually bears the title "Emperor." It has grand, heroic themes, vigorous rhythms, comparatively few lyrical sections, and a bravura-style solo part in the opening *Allegro*—trills, scales, thundering chords, and passages in thirds and octaves. The slow movement, *Adagio un poco mosso,* is short, just a brief interlude leading into the lengthy, brilliant *Rondo.*

Beethoven's *Concerto for Violin in D Major, Opus 61* (1806) is one of the finest works for violin and orchestra. It creates a jubilant feeling as marchlike rhythms and lyric moods alternate without disturbing the continuity. This is not a virtuoso concerto; the violin part requires a soloist with taste and discrimination. Beethoven must have been pleased with this concerto, for he later arranged it for piano and orchestra.

Concerto for Piano, Violin, and Violoncello with Orchestra, Opus 56 (1804) derives from the earlier concerto-grosso tradition. Despite the competent writing and imaginative ideas, this "Triple Concerto" never attains the sublime heights of Beethoven's works for solo instrument and orchestra.

CHAMBER MUSIC

Beethoven composed chamber music throughout his lifetime: there are three piano trios among his earliest works, and his last work was a string quartet. This lifelong interest effected fundamental changes in the medium, for he developed the trio, quartet, and quintet into warmly personal expressive vehicles.

The *Trio in B-Flat Major, Opus 97* for piano, violin, and cello was written in 1811—although not published until 1816—and is therefore contemporary with *Symphonies 7* and *8*. It is familiarly known as the "Archduke" trio because it is dedicated to Archduke Rudolph, younger brother of the Austrian emperor and an enthusiastic Beethoven supporter. Today we rank it as one of the most important nineteenth-century chamber-music compositions.

> Its true superiority makes itself felt in the powerful, straightforward inevitability of the musical current, while its special skill is evident in the result—in the way the instruments are made to build a sonority suggesting far more than three—the way, too, that the discourse achieves its transitions and its sweeping impulsion. This, in a word, was the heroic Beethoven.[4]

[4] John N. Burk, *The Life and Works of Beethoven* (New York: The Modern Library, 1946), p. 400.

Ex. 16:12. Beethoven: *Trio in B-Flat Major, Opus 97: Allegro moderato*

In the first movement, *Allegro moderato* (marked *dolce*), the piano presents the initial theme (Ex. 16:12). This lyrical theme dominates the whole movement; when the second theme appears, stated by full piano chords, it seems to be merely an interlude. Beethoven's development section here is a testament to his originality and musicianly logic. The principal theme is sectionalized: the first motive travels back and forth among the three instruments, and the second motive shows wonderful imagination. Pizzicato string figures and unusual piano passages in staccato and trills provide not only new textures but emotional contrasts.

Beethoven's masterful treatment of the three instruments in the second movement, a *Scherzo* (allegro), is equally imaginative. The lively principal melody is developed, transformed, and given a new setting, all the while generating other countermelodies. Syncopation, chromaticism, and heavy-footed phrases make the trio sound mysterious and somewhat lugubrious.

For his slow movement, *Andante cantabile,* Beethoven created a hymnlike theme and a series of variations. He progressively changes his original melodic outline and at times submerges it, but eventually he returns to a comparatively simple presentation of the theme. Instead of ending, this movement—via a few chords—leads into the finale, *Allegro moderato.* The listener is unprepared for this last movement, for it is a rondo whose main theme (rondo refrain) is completely frivolous, not a usual Beethoven mood. The principal episode, separating the statements of the rondo refrain, becomes even more casual, and in its last appearance the rondo theme (marked presto) is nothing less than ebullience. This finale is disarmingly rustic but no less artful than Beethoven's more serious last movements.

OTHER WORKS

Although Beethoven's most obvious and significant contributions are in the instrumental field, he by no means ignored vocal music, either secular or sacred. However, his creative powers never proved overly compatible with stage music. It may be that he was too preoccupied with the expressive qualities of abstract instrumental music. He composed incidental music for several plays, including an overture and nine numbers for Goethe's tragedy *Egmont.* This

Overture (1810) to *Egmont* is often heard at orchestral concerts, but another stage work, a ballet entitled *The Creations of Prometheus, Opus 43* (1800), is seldom performed today.

Beethoven's one opera, *Fidelio* (he originally wanted the heroine's name Leonore to be the title), was written in 1805 and underwent two later revisions. Formally speaking, it is a German *Singspiel* in two acts. Ensemble numbers—duets, trios, quartets—alternate with solo arias that allow each of the five principal singers to dominate the stage. There is some spoken dialogue to speed up lighter matters or to facilitate dramatic disclosures; however, Beethoven sometimes sets extremely emotional dialogue in recitative style over a running orchestral commentary.

Fidelio's libretto deals with two subjects cherished by Beethoven: conjugal love and justice for mankind. The opera turned out to be a type of stage melodrama sometimes called a "rescue" opera; in this instance an account of a woman's heroism as she (disguised as a man, Fidelio) rescues her husband from his political enemy. Although individual arias and ensembles have much to recommend them, the opera lacks organic unity. Beethoven was never satisfied with *Fidelio* and felt frustrated as an opera composer.

He wrote four overtures for this opera. For the original version (1805) he composed what is now called *Leonore Overture No. 2. Leonore Overture No. 3,* written for the 1806 revision, now usually appears as an introduction to Act II. *Leonore Overture No. 1* had been intended for a scheduled, then cancelled, performance in Prague. The *Fidelio Overture,* composed for the 1814 revision, currently appears as the regular overture.

Beethoven firmly believed in God and was what we would today call a Deist, yet he wrote comparatively few choral works: a few cantatas, one oratorio (*Christ on the Mount of Olives*), and a *Mass in C Major, Opus 86.* They all possess merit, but none can compare with Beethoven's monumental setting of the Ordinary of the Mass, the *Missa Solemnis in D Major, Opus 123* (1822).

He composed the *Missa Solemnis* (Solemn Mass) to celebrate the enthronement of his friend, sponsor, and pupil, Archduke Rudolph of Austria, as Archbishop of Olmütz, but the ceremony took place in 1820 and Beethoven's Mass was not finished in time. Although this musical Mass was meant to enhance a colorful, elaborate church service, it seems not to be liturgically oriented: the music is so overwhelming that it relegates the liturgy (the text and its meaning) to the background.

If Romanticism were to be defined as an imaginative power, as a lyricism stirred up by vehement passions, then Beethoven could be considered the first, indeed the greatest, Romantic. However, the word Romanticism denotes a break with tradition, and Beethoven was reared in an atmosphere of tradition. One must envisage him, therefore, as a Classic composer with broad scope, one who not only endowed the old forms with greater plasticity but who in his mature years offered a glimpse of future horizons to the coming Romantics.

FOR DISCUSSION AND ASSIGNMENT

1. In what ways does Beethoven's music cling to Classical style and in what ways does it prophesy the emerging Romantic period?

2. Listen to a movement from an early Beethoven string quartet, then one from a late quartet. Do you agree that Beethoven's style changed considerably throughout his life? How is this evident?
3. Do you think Beethoven's eventual deafness affected his late compositions in any way? How?
4. Listen to either *Piano Sonata, Opus 13* or *Piano Sonata, Opus 57* and write a short essay about the dramatic and emotional qualities in evidence. Make a comparison with a Mozart sonata.

FOR FURTHER READING

Burk, John N. *The Life and Works of Beethoven.* New York: The Modern Library, 1943. An extremely useful book. Mr. Burk briefly analyzes almost every Beethoven composition.

Pryce-Jones, Alan. *Beethoven.* New York: Collier Books, 1962. PB. A concise, penetrating biography and a splendid introduction to both the man and the musician.

Rolland, Romain. *Beethoven the Creator: The Great Creative Epochs: Vol. 1: From the Eroica to the Appassionata* (translated by Ernest Newman). New York: Dover Publications, Inc., 1964. PB. This reprint of a standard work first published in 1929 is still usable and valuable. M. Rolland's writing style is markedly romantic.

Schindler, Anton Felix. *Beethoven As I Knew Him,* edited by Donald W. MacArdle, translated by Constance S. Jolly. Chapel Hill: The University of North Carolina Press, 1966. A colorful—if not always completely accurate—biography written by an admirer who knew Beethoven personally.

Sullivan, J. W. N. *Beethoven: His Spiritual Development.* New York: Alfred A. Knopf, Inc., 1960. A Vintage PB. This book, written for the musical amateur, discusses the nature of music and then offers a study of Beethoven based on his spiritual development.

Tovey, Donald Francis. *Beethoven.* London: Oxford University Press, 1944. An Oxford PB. A posthumously published study by an eminent musicologist. The author bases his study solely on the evidence provided by Beethoven's works.

17 The Romantic Era and Its Early Composers

> In a word, what love is to man, music is to the arts and to mankind, for it is actually love itself, the purest, most ethereal language of the emotions, containing all their changing colors in every variety of shading and in thousands of aspects . . .
>
> CARL MARIA VON WEBER
> Essay on the opera *Undine* (1817)

The nineteenth century is usually known as the Romantic era, a reaction—intellectually and artistically—against Classicism. Toward the end of the eighteenth century an incongruous element intruded upon the arts, a forerunner of the Romantic period. Artists decided to express themselves freely and personally, a reactionary development summed up in the term *Sturm und Drang* (Storm and Stress). The name comes from a play (1776) by Friedrich von Klinger, but the movement's ideology had been formulated earlier. Essentially a German inspiration, it found adherents everywhere. A desire to release emotion and achieve freedom in all things prompted the Storm and Stress movement. In France, even the classicist Jacques David displayed almost unrestrained emotion in his turbulent painting *The Battle of the Romans and Sabines,* completed in 1799. In Germany, Goethe was inspired to create *Faust,* an independent man who defied convention. In Austria, Mozart's *Don Giovanni* had as its hero a passionate, immoral, convention-defying rogue who pays for his evil at the finale, a lurid spectacle portraying eternal damnation. Thus Romanticism became practically an accomplished fact—in literature, in drama, in painting, and in music—before the turn of the century.

Basically the Romantics cared more about emotions than cold reason and more about their fellow men than ancient civilizations. For the fine arts—music, painting, sculpture, literature, poetry—Romanticism became a beneficent cult during the first half of the nineteenth century. Of course Romanticism and all that it implies was never confined to any one period. Supremacy of heart over intellect, of emotion over reason, has its advocates in every age. No one who has read a Shakespeare sonnet, observed a Rembrandt painting, or heard a Mozart sonata can deny that, although other factors may predominate, Romantic elements are vitally present.

The nineteenth-century Romantics professed impatience with Classicism's rules and restraints on thought and art. They strove for total originality, avoiding everything related to convention and tradition; they became absorbed with the individual's emotions and desires rather than mankind in general. While the Romantics were acutely aware of the mystery in the universe, they could not agree with the Deists that such a universe was a machine and that every natural phenomenon could be rationally explained. Preferring to meditate on the mystery of creation, and rejecting harsh reality for the gentle world of fantasy, emotion, and religious sentiment, the Romantics felt a spiritual tie with medieval legends and culture, Gothic architecture, and the mysterious Orient. Exoticism was an inevitable by-product of this turning away from reality.

Such strong emphasis on emotion and imagination led to exaggerated sentiments, whether violent, tender, sad, nostalgic, or joyous. In protecting the validity of emotion, Romantics went to extremes: intuition became the only avenue to spiritual truth, and imagination became almost synonymous with intuition. Sentiment produced an intense appreciation of nature's beauties. Artists scrupulously attempted to describe the picturesque in nature: poets elaborated on the forest foliage; painters meticulously duplicated wildflower colors; composers—like Berlioz in the third movement of his *Fantastic Symphony*—reproduced pastoral visions in music.

Romanticism provided a splendid environment for music. A distinguished writer on music has this to say: "Musical Romanticism may be characterized as an art which emphasizes the subjective and the emotional possibilities of music and neglects the formal and structural point of view."[1]

This is a good beginning. We already know that inspiration was essential to the Romantics. To find inspiration they searched into nature's beauties and explored her phenomena; they delved into history's stirring events and pageantry. However, the statement that Romanticism in music "neglects the formal and structural point of view" must be somewhat qualified because the best, most representative Romantic composers conscientiously observed formal and structural principles.

Every age has its distinguishing manner or mood, but it is always accompanied by elements from other styles. Although composers in the nineteenth century emphasized the subjective and the personal, the natural and the fantastic, they intended that their inspiration should be governed by universal rules of form and structure. Composers who selected their working materials wisely have survived; the others dwindle down through mediocrity to oblivion.

Romanticism's conspicuous characteristics affected musical composition; for example, the Romantics' obsession with drama and mystery stands out sharply in the flamboyant operas of the period, and it obviously influenced Franz Liszt's dashing musical style. That Romantic composers felt a close bond with literature is evident in the numerous descriptive titles—*Tasso, Mazeppa, Harold in Italy*—given to Romantic music. Program music advanced more than in any other period, and the symphonic poem, symphonic suite, and program symphony enjoyed their greatest popularity.

Romantic composers favored the piano piece and the art song. Equally at

[1] Willi Apel, *Harvard Dictionary of Music* (Cambridge: Harvard University Press, 1944), p. 650. Reprinted by permission.

home in a salon or on the concert stage, the piano could convey a composer's innermost feelings as well as his vivid, sometimes theatrical emotions. Although composers still wrote piano sonatas, they preferred stylized dances like the waltz and mazurka, the étude (study piece), and other free forms such as the fantasy, arabesque, and nocturne. These free forms relied on contrasting themes, but frequently composers neglected formal thematic development.

The so-called "character piece," therefore, was the favorite keyboard form during the nineteenth century. It was most often in ternary form (A B A) whether two pages or twelve pages long. Beyond this basic formal outline, the composer could release his imagination and inspiration to embellish the framework.

The *art song* (solo song) is the vocal counterpart to the idiomatic, epigrammatic piano piece. When composers combined Romantic poetry with voice and piano, they produced highly subjective musical expression. German composers such as Schubert and Schumann set poems by such masters as Heine, Schiller, and Goethe, creating the Romantic *lied* (German art song). Liszt and Berlioz selected from a vast repertoire created by French poets such as Victor Hugo and Théophile Gautier.

Romanticism's exaggerated emotional emphasis brought into music the seemingly contradictory qualities of virtuosity and intimacy, yet the subjective piano piece and solo song fared just as well as flamboyant extravaganzas such as the orchestral symphonic poem. Chopin captured his audiences with his delicate, introspective nocturnes, while his contemporary Hector Berlioz thrilled his listeners with programmatic symphonies.

Romantic music developed over a period of almost a hundred years. Its salient characteristics might be outlined as follows:

A. Melody
   1. Romantic melodies have a warm, intense personal feeling.
   2. Many melodies are fully effective only when heard with their supporting harmonies.

B. Rhythm
   1. By the middle of the nineteenth century, composers consistently employed cross-rhythms (the simultaneous use of contrasting rhythmic patterns) and syncopations as part of their rhythmic vocabulary.
   2. Numerous complex and rhapsodic rhythmic designs greatly enhanced the subjective character of Romantic music.
   3. Composers frequently changed tempo and used rhythmic subtleties like *rubato* (see page 32).

C. Harmony
   1. Harmonic concepts broadened in the nineteenth century and furnished the means to create tone color and subjective expression. New chords—altered, seventh, and ninth—and imaginative chord progressions appeared.
   2. Romantic composers used modulation for its own effect rather than as a means to an end.
   3. Chromaticism fostered an increasingly obscure tonality that gradually resulted in a disintegration of the major-minor system.

D. Texture
   1. Generally, contrapuntal and harmonic tendencies combined to form a vibrant, stimulating texture. Counterpoint was seldom strict, for it was used more as a device than as an actual style.

Beethoven's positive influence lasted through the whole nineteenth century: his idea of tonal drama and his concept of motive construction had revealed myriad developmental possibilities. Some early Romantic composers were directly influenced by him; others drew on their own resources. Thus the music written during approximately the first forty years of the nineteenth century has great variety, a matchless diversity created almost within the shadow of Classic restraint.

FRANZ SCHUBERT

Franz Peter Schubert (1797–1828) was born into a modest family at Lichtenthal, near Vienna. His schoolteacher father and other members of his musical family instructed him in violin, piano, and organ, and he received a formal musical education at the imperial chapel in Vienna, where he served five years as a choirboy under Antonio Salieri.

Ill. 17:1. *Moritz von Schwind (1804–1871)*, A Schubert Evening at Josef von Spaun's (*Schubert is playing the piano). Schubert Museum, Vienna. Courtesy of The Bettmann Archive.*

Schubert's brief mature life was uneventful. He taught school unsuccessfully for four years, never managed to obtain a permanent music position, and of necessity lived penuriously. In 1818 and 1824 he worked in the summer as music teacher to the Esterházy family in Hungary, but he lived most of his life in Vienna among admiring, faithful friends: the poets Schober, Mayrhofer, and Grillparzer; singers such as Vogl and Baron von Schönstein; the painter von Schwind; and of course many musicians, including Hüttenbrenner (Ill. 17:1). He died in Vienna, having contracted typhus at the age of 31.

Where Beethoven, whom he knew only slightly, had been a genius with symphonic form, Schubert found his perfect medium in the *lied* (art song). Although within 17 years he composed nearly a thousand works—603 songs, nine symphonies, overtures, sacred and secular choral music, operas, incidental music, 35 chamber works, piano sonatas, music for piano duet—it is his lieder that assure him a place among the master composers.

Schubert is the acknowledged creator of the Romantic art song, yet he was spiritually bound to the Classic eighteenth century and used Haydn, Mozart, and to some extent Beethoven for his models. A Classic tendency notable in his music is the fine instrumental equilibrium he achieved in orchestral works and in the art songs, where voice and piano maintain perfect balance.

The essence of Schubert's style derived not from technical form but from his own genius, for he was born with a superior melodic gift. His predecessors had employed melody as only one component of musical expression; for Schubert melody was an end in itself. Melodies came to him easily and abundantly, a perfect talent for the songwriter but sometimes a problem for the instrumental composer. Adopting sonata form for piano, string quartet, and symphonic forms, he produced an extraordinary quantity of fine themes. Because his development sections do not always show Schubert's interest or imagination in transforming these themes, in manipulating them as Haydn, Mozart, and Beethoven would have done, these sections often lack tension and energy. However, this deficiency is more than counterbalanced by the many attractive qualities in his music.

The Romantic aspect is of course the most prominent feature of Schubert's style. His musical Romanticism stems chiefly from the new sonorities he created and from his faith in pure sound. His treatment of wind instruments imparts a lush, vibrant quality to the orchestra, and his rich harmonies and alternating major and minor tonalities produce an emotional, emphatic musical language. Schubert is also a Romantic in his widely varied repertoire. He never followed a set pattern; each work represents another unique product of the driving musical force that compelled him to write.

Lieder

A German word meaning "song," *lied* (plural *lieder*) now applies specifically to the German art song, as opposed to the folk song. As used now, the lied is a musical setting of a poem, written usually for one solo voice and piano. The composer tries to translate the poem musically or to enhance its mood. Either way the result is a highly subjective musical composition that singer and pianist attempt to interpret convincingly. The lied embraces a gamut ranging from rather simple folklike settings to highly sophisticated works.

Since the lied requires subjective music, intimate poetry, and an emotion-charged blend of verse and melody, this form naturally appealed to Romantic composers. Just as the nineteenth-century Romantic lied was dominated by Schubert, so was Schubert dominated by the lied. He was not the first to compose lieder. Haydn, Mozart, and Beethoven had done so before him. But considering the prodigious number of songs that he produced and his intuitive mastery of this idiom, he must be recognized as the creator of the Romantic lied.

From a formal viewpoint, Schubert's songs divide into three categories. The most straightforward type is the *strophic* song, in which every stanza of the poem is sung to the same melody. Of all lied types, strophic has the simplest melodic lines and the most basic rhythms and harmonies.

The *varied-strophic* or *modified-strophic* type is similar to strophic in that most stanzas have identical settings; exceptions occur when the text demands a different setting in order to emphasize a special mood or idea. Schubert developed the modified-strophic song and used it increasingly throughout his lifetime, thus avoiding the rigid framework of strophic song.

In the *through-composed* type (a literal translation of the German term *durchkomponiert*) there is no formal melodic design; the musical setting changes to match the poem. This dramatic type is especially suited to narrative poems such as the ballad, and many song masterpieces belong to this category.

The sung melody in Schubert's lieder seems so fresh and spontaneous that his songs are instantly appealing to the listener. Many songs have a Viennese flavor, but for the most part their inspiration and creation are pure Schubert: a vocal melody that is plastic, ample, simple, and vigorous.

Schubert's piano part is usually not a mere accompaniment, for he makes voice and piano equal partners. In some strophic songs the piano provides just a solid, unobtrusive support for the voice, but more often it participates actively. In *Der Leiermann* (The Hurdy-Gurdy Man) the pianist's left hand imitates the drone characteristic of a hurdy-gurdy (Ex. 17:1). And in *Gretchen am Spinnrade* (Gretchen at the Spinning Wheel), a setting of a poem from Goethe's *Faust,* Schubert gives the piano a repeated motive that mimics the monotonous turning of a spinning wheel (Ex. 17:2). There are hundreds of examples like these, yet Schubert's musicality was so ingenious that he never seemed to repeat himself; each setting is a new experience. That he loved nature is obvious in his choice of poems: *Der Lindenbaum* (The Lime Tree); *An die Nachtigall* (To the Nightingale); *Frühlingstraum* (Dream of Spring). His favorite nature poems seem to speak about water: *Auf dem Wasser zu singen* (To be Sung on the Water); *Am Meer* (By the Sea); *Der Müller und der Bach* (The Miller and the Brook). And of course his huge repertoire contains songs about love, sadness, and just about every other mood and sentiment.

Ex. 17:1. Schubert: *Der Leiermann*

Ex. 17:2. Schubert: *Gretchen am Spinnrade*

Schubert's lieder repertoire includes two song cycles—that is, songs based on texts conceived as a unified group of poems. One cycle is *Die schöne Müllerin* (The Fair Maid of the Mill), set to poems by Wilhelm Müller; the other is *Die Winterreise* (The Winter Journey), also to texts by Müller. A third group, called *Schwanengesang* (Swan Song), was compiled after Schubert's death and contains his last 14 songs. Except for these three collections, he composed his songs as independent works with individual settings.

It would be difficult to single out any of Schubert's songs as being finer or more typical than others, but it is possible to select from his better-known songs one representative of each structural type.

Strophic: Heidenröslein (*Hedge Rose*)

Sah ein Knab ein Röslein stehn, Röslein auf der Heiden, War so jung und morgenschön, Lief er schnell, es nah zu sehn, Sah's mit vielen Freuden. Röslein, Röslein, Röslein rot, Röslein auf der Heiden.	Once a boy a rose espied, Growing in a hedge row. It was so fresh and morning-sweet That when he saw it His heart overflowed with joy. Rosebud, rosebud, rosebud red, Rosebud in the hedge row.
Knabe sprach: "Ich breche dich, Röslein auf der Heiden!" Röslein sprach: "Ich steche dich, Dass du ewig denkst an mich, Und ich will's nicht leiden." Röslein, Röslein, Röslein rot, Röslein auf der Heiden.	Said the boy, "I'll just pick you, Rosebud in the hedge row!" Said the rose, "Then I'll stick you, So that you will never forget me. And then I won't care at all." Rosebud, rosebud, rosebud red, Rosebud in the hedge row.
Und der wilde Knabe brach 's Röslein auf der Heiden; Röslein wehrte sich und stach, Half ihm doch kein Weh und Ach, Musst es eben leiden. Röslein, Röslein, Röslein rot, Röslein auf der Heiden.	Then the brash boy pulled The rosebud from the hedge. The rose assembled her thorns And pricked him mercilessly But to no avail, alas. Rosebud, rosebud, rosebud red, Rosebud in the hedge row.

Schubert produced the simplest setting for this poem by Goethe. Without any keyboard prelude to set the scene or mood, voice and piano begin simultaneously. The vocal line weaves an unpretentious, charming melody above a piano framework of unadorned chords. By combining the rustic poem with a straightforward musical setting, Schubert has almost *created* a folk song.

Modified Strophic: Die Forelle (*The Trout*)

In einem Bächlein helle, Da schoss in froher Eil Die launische Forelle Vorüber wie ein Pfeil. Ich stand an dem Gestade Und sah in süsser Ruh Des muntern Fischleins Bade Im klaren Bächlein zu.	In a sparkling stream, Swimming merrily along, A playful trout Went past like an arrow. I stood on the bank Watching contentedly This lively little fellow There in the clear stream.
Ein Fischer mit der Rute Wohl an dem Ufer stand, Und sah's mit kaltem Blute, Wie sich das Fischlein wand. So lang dem Wasser Helle, So dacht ich, nicht gebricht, So fängt er die Forelle Mit seiner Angel nicht.	A fisherman with his rod Stood also on the bank, And coldly watched The fish's playfulness. As long as the water Stays so clear, I thought, He will never catch the trout With his line.
Doch endlich ward dem Diebe Die Zeit zu lang. Er macht'	But at last the thief Had waited long enough.

Das Bächlein tückisch trübe,	He muddied up the water
Und eh ich es gedacht,	And before I knew what was happening
So zuckte seine Rute,	He pulled up his rod
Das Fischlein zappelt' dran,	And the fish hung from it.
Und ich mit regem Blute	I felt the blood stir within me
Sah die Betrogne an.	As I witnessed this betrayal.

This is one of Schubert's famous nature songs about water, and he chose an unceasing flow of rippling sixteenth notes by the piano to construct the "water" music (Ex. 17:3). A sophisticated melody accompanies the text by C. F.

Ex. 17:3. Schubert: *Die Forelle*

D. Schubart. The song remains strophic for the first two stanzas, until the "thief" muddies the water; then it becomes more dramatic as it describes the "betrayal." Schubert's piano figures are terse and his vocal line declamatory as he sustains the somber mood for a time, but he concludes the song with the rippling music from the beginning.

Through-Composed: Erlkönig (The Erl King)

Wer reitet so spät durch Nacht und Wind?	Who rides so late through night and wind?
Es ist der Vater mit seinem Kind;	It is a father with his child;
Er hat den Knaben wohl in dem Arm,	He holds the boy safe in his arms,
Er fasst ihn sicher, er hält ihn warm.	He holds him fast, he holds him warm.
"Mein Sohn, was birgst du so bang dein Gesicht?"	"My son, why do you hide your face?"
"Siehst, Vater, du den Erlkönig nicht?	"Father, do you not see the Erl-King?
Den Erlenkönig mit Kron und Schweif?"	The Erl-King with his crown and cape?"
"Mein Sohn, es ist ein Nebelstreif."	"My son, it is only a streak of mist."
"Du liebes Kind, komm, geh mit mir!	"Sweet child, come away with me!
Gar schöne Spiele spiel ich mit dir;	I will play such fine games with you.
Manch bunte Blumen sind an dem Strand,	Many gay flowers grow by the shore;
Meine Mutter hat manch gülden Gewand."	And my mother has many golden robes."
"Mein Vater, mein Vater, und hörest du nicht,	"Father, father, do you not hear
Was Erlenkönig mir leise verspricht?"	What the Erl-King is whispering to me?"
"Sei ruhig, bleibe ruhig, mein Kind:	"Be calm, stay calm, dear child:
In dürren Blättern säuselt der Wind."	It is only the wind rustling the leaves."

"Willst, feiner Knabe, du mit mir gehn?	"My fine lad, will you come with me?
Meine Töchter sollen dich warten schön;	My daughters will wait upon you.
Meine Töchter führen den nächtlichen Reihn	My daughters lead the nightly dance,
Und wiegen und tanzen und singen dich ein."	They will rock you and dance with you and sing you to sleep."
"Mein Vater, mein Vater, und siehst du nicht dort	"Father, father, do you not see
Erlkönigs Töchter am düstern Ort?"	The Erl-King's daughters just over there?"
"Mein Sohn, mein Sohn, ich seh es genau:	"My son, my son, I see it clearly:
Es scheinen die alten Weiden so grau."	It is the gray gleam of the old willow-trees."
"Ich liebe dich, mich reizt deine schöne Gestalt;	"I love you, your beauty allures me,
Und bist du nicht willig, so brauch ich Gewalt."	And if you do not come willingly, I will force you."
"Mein Vater, mein Vater, jetzt fasst er mich an!	"Father, father, he has taken hold of me,
Erlkönig hat mir ein Leid's getan!"—	The Erl-King has hurt me!"
Dem Vater grauset's, er reitet geschwind	The father shudders, he rides swiftly,
Er hält in den Armen das ächzende Kind,	Holding the moaning child in his arms;
Erreicht den Hof mit Müh und Not;	With effort and toil he reaches the house;—
In seinen Armen das Kind war tot.	In his arms the child lies dead.

The text is a famous ballad by Goethe, but there is a wide gulf between the German poet's childlike *Heidenröslein* and his tragic *Erlkönig*. Schubert's setting of the latter is as macabre as his treatment of the former is unpretentious.

The *Erl King* is one of the most difficult art songs in the entire repertoire. Merciless right-hand triplet figures (octaves and chords) require a virtuoso pianist, and the vocalist faces problems that are equally as difficult. Through voice inflection and interpretation he must effectively portray four roles: the commentator, who sets the opening scene and ends the song; the father, who races through the night with his sick child; the delirious son; and the insidious Erl King, who personifies death. This stands as one of the greatest dramatic songs ever written.

Schubert's lieder are usually sung in German. The listener may encounter a language barrier when listening to his and other composers' art songs. We would improve our understanding if all songs were sung in English, regardless of the original text, but German, French, and other poetry does not always translate well. Besides that, the sonorous experience of, say, a German poem set to music cannot be duplicated in a translation.

Chamber Music

Although Schubert wrote a quantity of chamber music, the quality is uneven. Twelve of his fifteen string quartets are experiments, or perhaps one should say they are essays in *Hausmusik*—chamber music written for an amateur quartet. These twelve quartets adhere to the Haydn-Mozart traditions and display Classic characteristics. The last three quartets are fine, mature works. They appear not to be influenced by Beethoven, although Schubert would have had ample opportunity to hear that master's chamber music.

"Trout" Quintet

Schubert's outstanding chamber-music composition remains the superb *Quintet in A Major, Opus 114* (1819), known as the "Trout" quintet. In 1819 Schubert and the singer Michael Vogl went on a walking tour in the mountains of upper Austria. During a stop at the town of Steyr, Sylvester Paumgartner, assistant manager of mines and an amateur cellist, asked Schubert for a composition. Paumgartner and some musician friends had formed a chamber group that included violin, viola, cello, double bass, and piano. They wanted Schubert to write a quintet for their unusual group and to include variations on his song *Die Forelle* (The Trout). Schubert's compliance produced one of the masterworks in chamber music, a work of inordinate beauty and warmth. The structure of the five movements, including a theme and variations, suggests an eighteenth-century divertimento, but Schubert's quintet is Romantic and emotional.

> Schubert's ceaseless preoccupation with color is again in evidence; now, in addition to colorful harmonies and textures, he employs characteristic instrumental ranges. And the experiment is successful. Hardly any work of Schubert's, or of many another composer, is as brilliant, as sparkling, and as alive as the *Forellen Quintet*.[2]

Allegro vivace. The first movement starts buoyantly with ascending piano arpeggios and chords. A theme emerges slowly, not reaching completion until measure 27. In this movement Schubert often gives the impression that he is developing his themes from the very beginning and that actual development is only another episode along the way. Form is not important: so much happens melodically—there seems to be a chain of melodies—that there simply is not time to think about structure.

Andante. This gracious movement has three sections; one is predominantly lyric, one has a melancholy cast, the third is restrained. After their first appearance these three sections are merely restated in other keys. This movement's rich tone color and harmonic contrast provide an excellent illustration of Schubert's Romantic sound.

Scherzo (Presto). The third movement is a lusty dance with energetic rhythms and a touch of Austrian folk song in the trio.

Andantino. This movement encompasses the promised variations based on the song *Die Forelle,* and throughout the six variations all the instruments—even the double bass—assume a dominant role at one time or another. The strings state the theme, which is easy to hear during the first three variations,

[2] Homer Ulrich, *Chamber Music* (New York: Columbia University Press, 1948), p. 291. Reprinted by permission.

where it is only slightly transformed; but in the next two variations Schubert has deliberately disguised the basic shape of the original song: the fourth variation is dramatic, the fifth is tender. The sixth variation is marked *allegretto* and uses the piano accompaniment from the original song.

Allegro giusto. This Hungarian-style finale needs a virtuoso pianist. A fragmentary melody emerging from an instrumental dialogue gradually assumes a definitive form played by the violin and viola, with support from the piano in dotted rhythms and triplets. There is only a brief development section because the finale proceeds quickly to the recapitulation.

Symphonies

Schubert learned the art of orchestration by playing in an orchestra. He knew how to blend woodwinds and strings into enchanting fabrics, and he learned to associate certain moods with specific instruments. Above all, he viewed the orchestra as one multifaceted instrument that could be played as one plays the piano.

Although the Schubert catalog lists nine symphonies, there may have been ten: references exist indicating that he composed a symphony at Gastein, but the work has never been found. His symphonies mostly follow the eighteenth-century tradition of Haydn and Mozart; however, the last two are masterpieces displaying wonderful tone color and Romantic emotionalism. *Symphony No. 9 in C Major* (1828), known as the "Great C-major" symphony because of its length, was discovered by Schumann in 1838 and conducted in performance by Mendelssohn. The other symphonic masterpiece, *Symphony No. 8 in B Minor,* was written in 1825 and premiered in Vienna in 1865—40 years later!

"Unfinished" Symphony

This, the most perfect of Schubert's orchestral works, relies absolutely on sound. It is called the "Unfinished" symphony since there are only two movements. Schubert sketched a few measures for a third movement, then put the score away and never got around to doing anything more with it. No matter, the two completed movements constitute a symphonic masterpiece rarely equalled by any Romantic composer.

Allegro moderato. The compelling poetic mood of this first movement is immensely attractive. What appears to be the principal theme—a tune by oboe and clarinet—is actually not very significant; it serves only to introduce the

Ex. 17:4. Schubert: *Symphony No. 8 in B Minor: Allegro moderato*

exposition and recapitulation. The important theme—an ominous phrase in the bass (Ex. 17:4)—sounds in the first eight measures. Then fluttering strings initiate an accompaniment figure while oboe and clarinet sing a plaintive melody (the one mentioned above). With skillful modulation Schubert carries his listeners into the secondary theme (Ex. 17:5) before they realize it. This lyrical melody

Ex. 17:5. Schubert: ***Symphony No. 8 in B Minor: Allegro moderato***

is sung by the cellos, and Schubert borrows figures from it to devise what appears to be a development within the exposition. The genuine development depends heavily on the opening phrase (Ex. 17:4). One intriguing section here uses the accompaniment for the secondary theme but not the melody itself. In the recapitulation Schubert omits the initial ominous phrase and leads off with the plaintive oboe and clarinet theme. The rather short coda begins like the development section.

Andante con moto. The radiance of this movement (in *E* major) contrasts beautifully with the prevailing *pathétique* mood in the first movement. The design—called sonatina form—is one that Schubert liked to use: an exposition section and a recapitulation but no development section. The first theme (Ex.

Ex. 17:6. Schubert: ***Symphony No. 8 in B Minor: Andante con moto***

17:6) has a serene pastoral nature, and the contrasting theme (Ex. 17:7) is unusually expansive.

Ex. 17:7. Schubert: ***Symphony No. 8 in B Minor: Andante con moto***

The clarinet initiates this contrasting theme, oboe and flute take it up, and strings supply syncopated accompanimental chords. This theme alone is beautiful, but the four long notes leading to it are also important even though at the time they do not seem so. In the coda Schubert combines these four notes with the first theme (Ex. 17:8), a stroke of genius that must be attributed to his innate musicianship.

Ex. 17:8. Schubert: *Symphony No. 8 in B Minor: Andante con moto*

FELIX MENDELSSOHN

Abraham and Leah Mendelssohn were strangely prophetic in naming their son Felix, meaning happy, for his life was to be one of the happiest and most satisfying in musical history. Felix Mendelssohn (1809–1847) was born in Hamburg with a family background that almost predestined success. Moses Mendelssohn, his grandfather, was a famous Jewish philosopher whose book *Phädon,* on the immortality of the soul, won him fame as the German Plato. Moses was also the first great champion of Jewish emancipation in the eighteenth century, yet his son Abraham, Felix's father, embraced the Lutheran faith and added the name Bartholdy to his own.

When Felix was three, his cultured, prosperous parents moved the family to Berlin, where his schooling began: private tutors in all subjects assured a fine education for the Mendelssohn children. After 1818, when he first performed in public, Felix gradually acquired a reputation as pianist, composer, and conductor, and as a practicing musician he formed valuable friendships with Weber, Goethe, Rossini, and Meyerbeer. A happy marriage brought him five children. In true Romantic fashion, Mendelssohn was a man of the world: musician, linguist, athlete, watercolorist, conversationalist. Besides composing successfully, he revived interest in Johann Sebastian Bach's music: in 1829 he conducted the *St. Matthew Passion* in its first performance since Bach's death.

Mendelssohn lived in a professional and social whirl. He traveled extensively through England, Scotland, and the Continent. From 1833 to 1835 he was music director at Düsseldorf and after 1835 he served as director of the Leipzig Gewandhaus orchestra, which his untiring efforts promoted and improved until it was the finest orchestra in Europe. In 1843 he assembled a group of teachers and founded the Leipzig Conservatory, which rapidly became the most renowned music school on the Continent. But this demanding musical life, public appearances, and official duties taxed his constitution severely; he literally wore himself out and died of apoplexy in 1847.

The prolific Mendelssohn worked in almost every medium except opera. Many of his works are no longer heard, yet enough remain in the standard repertoire to ensure him permanent recognition. Two symphonies—"Scottish" (1842) and "Italian" (1833)—are enjoyable; two other orchestral compositions—*Incidental Music to A Midsummer Night's Dream* (1826, 1843) and the *Hebrides Overture* (1830)—rank as masterpieces of their kind. Other significant compositions are the *Violin Concerto in E Minor* (1844); the oratorios *St. Paul* (1836) and *Elijah* (1846); the dramatic *Piano Trio in D Minor* (1839); and several attractive piano works such as the *Rondo Capriccioso, Serious Variations,* and *Prelude and Fugue in E Minor.*

In the nineteenth century Mendelssohn's music was widely performed and warmly acclaimed, but contemporary musicians have reservations about him, and his music now receives only sporadic hearings. Perhaps there is still time for a twentieth-century reappraisal, for Mendelssohn is far from being an inconsequential composer. Although his range of musical ideas is limited and his thematic material frequently repeats familiar melodic patterns, his music is worthwhile for its immediate accessibility. It charms instantly and persuasively. He was a Romantic composer, but his music has eighteenth-century Classic polish and clear design. The smoothly flowing symmetrical melodies, contrapuntal dexterity, and suave musical texture account in part for his singular style. Our musical experience should not be confined to intense, involved masterworks; it should also embrace satisfying, pleasant music like Mendelssohn's.

Orchestral Music

Incidental Music to A Midsummer Night's Dream

The Mendelssohns were avid readers, and Felix and his beloved sister Fanny particularly enjoyed Shakespeare, which may explain the *Overture to A Midsummer Night's Dream,* a masterpiece written when he was only 17. In 1843—seventeen years later—when Wilhelm IV of Prussia asked him to supply incidental music for Shakespeare's comedy, he obligingly wrote 12 new pieces perfectly matching the style and mood of the overture. When performed as a concert suite, only four of Mendelssohn's original compositions are customarily presented—*Overture, Scherzo, Nocturne,* and *Wedding March*—but these are enough to prove his magic touch for re-creating the fairyland atmosphere of Shakespeare's fantasy.

Overture. Mendelssohn's themes convey dissimilar ideas, yet they blend into a diaphanous web. Shakespeare most likely would have loved this music, for it evokes a magical atmosphere and translates the play's laughter and enchantment into multihued tonal patterns.

Four chords set the scene: flutes sound the first; two clarinets join the flutes for the second; horns and bassoons enter for the third; and oboes complete the woodwind choir for the fourth.

Four themes constitute the melodic material. The first is a fairylike theme in *e* minor played by violins and punctuated by occasional pizzicato notes from the violas. The next theme is a pompous outburst recalling Theseus's court. After more whisperings of the fairyland theme, a lovers' theme emerges, to be succeeded by rollicking buffoon music in which the brass section imitates a braying donkey, recalling the play's Bottom and his ass's head.

A long, imaginative development displays superb writing for the woodwinds. Starting off animatedly, it loses momentum before it reaches a climax with a repeat of the court theme. Mendelssohn reintroduces all his melodies in the recapitulation. In the coda the fairies have the final word; as quiet comes, the four original chords peacefully conclude the overture.

Scherzo. Originally designed as a prelude to the second act of the play, this is the most extended scherzo that Mendelssohn wrote. Upon close listening we find that the clattering main theme is an exaggerated pixie transformation of the overture's buffoon theme. Fluttering motives by the flute subside to a quiet, dreamy ending.

Nocturne. Mendelssohn intended this composition for the end of the third act, when sleep overtakes all the characters. The horn resounds sweetly in the opening passage—such music was not to be heard again until Richard Wagner—and the "night" music continues as strings contrast with the horn, first in the lower ranges and then on a sustained high note. A countertheme by woodwinds and strings later accentuates the night atmosphere.

Wedding March. This flamboyant transformation of the court theme, garnished by bright fanfares, has acquired undeserved popularity as *the* recessional music at weddings; if only it could be left in its make-believe setting, where it is far more appropriate!

Hebrides Overture

A masterpiece in symphonic literature, Mendelssohn's concert overture *The Hebrides* (or *Fingal's Cave*) resulted from his visit to this cave, situated on a small island in the Hebrides group off the west coast of Scotland.

Touring Scotland in 1829 (the "Scottish" symphony also resulted from this trip), Mendelssohn and his friend Carl Klingemann, Secretary to the Prussian Legation in London, were fascinated by Fingal's Cave, a popular tourist attraction. Klingemann wrote, "A greener roar of waves surely never rushed into a stranger cavern—its many pillars making it look like the inside of an immense organ, black and resounding, and absolutely without purpose, and quite alone, the wide gray sea within and without."[3] Mendelssohn reported that he wrote down the first 21 bars of his overture's basic theme as he sat in a tossing skiff within the cave, but he did not complete the work until the following year, while in Rome.

The nineteenth-century concert overture is an independent orchestral composition. Generally such a work uses a form similar either to the first movement of a Classical symphony or to a symphonic poem. At any rate, the concert overture usually bears a descriptive title. Mendelssohn's short overture has the general outline of first-movement sonata form, but one becomes so engrossed in the dramatic tone colors and rhythmic transformations that strictly formal elements are almost forgotten. The entire work is dominated by variations of the lapping motive with which it begins (Ex. 17:9). This motive, which suggests an

Ex. 17:9. Mendelssohn: *The Hebrides*

advancing and retreating sea, eventually appears in all sections of the orchestra, accompanied by bold crescendos. A new melody, somewhat derivative, rises above the lapping motive to accompany it. A broadly lyrical melody intrudes, yet the

[3] Letter dated August 10, 1829. In Sebastian Hensel, *The Mendelssohn Family,* translated by Carl Klingemann (New York: Harper and Brothers, 1882), Vol. 1, p. 204.

initial motive persists and later receives an original rhythmic treatment, almost martial in its sound. Toward the end of the overture, the clarinet sings the lyrical melody and the lapping motive is developed into a dramatic coda.

Violin Concerto

Mendelssohn contributed one uncontested masterpiece to concerto repertoire. If his *Concerto in E Minor, Opus 64* for violin and orchestra is not the greatest of its kind, it is surely the most popular. Completed in 1844, three years before his death, this concerto is the result of cooperative effort. He wrote it for his longtime friend Ferdinand David, his concertmaster at the Gewandhaus, and David helped immeasurably with technical problems in the concerto.

Allegro molto appassionato. Mendelssohn dispenses with a separate orchestral exposition: soloist and orchestra share honors from the start. The sonata-allegro form is crystal clear. With less than two measures of preparation, the first theme—a high-pitched violin solo—enters (Ex. 17:10). A bridge theme

Ex. 17:10. Mendelssohn: ***Concerto in E Minor: Allegro molto appassionato***

(frequently called a transition) leads orchestra and soloist to the second theme, in *G* major (Ex. 17:11). Here, in a very unusual turn, the solo violin sustains a low *G* while clarinets and flute etch the thematic material.

Ex. 17:11. Mendelssohn: ***Concerto in E Minor: Allegro molto appassionato***

Trills in the orchestra announce the development section, which emphasizes the bridge theme and the opening figure of the first theme. A cadenza terminates this development. As the cadenza approaches its conclusion in quiet arpeggios, the orchestra breaks in with the first theme to announce the recapitulation.

Andante. There is no break between movements. The bassoon dextrously links the *Allegro* to the *Andante* (Ex. 17:12). This central movement is

Ex. 17:12. Mendelssohn: ***Concerto in E Minor: Andante***

simply a lyric violin solo with orchestral accompaniment. Mendelssohn uses ternary form (A B A) and shortens the reprise, simultaneously changing and enriching it. The first section offers a restful theme in graceful phrases; the excited mood of the B section contrasts with this A section.

Allegretto non troppo: Allegro molto vivace. The violin is accompanied by other strings for 14 measures (allegretto), one of the most original passages in the concerto. Then a fanfare by trumpets, horns, bassoons, and drums is answered by arpeggios on the solo violin. A rondo—the effusive *Allegro molto vivace,* whose principal theme recalls the composer's earlier elfin music—precedes the sparkling conclusion.

ROBERT SCHUMANN

An unfortunate heredity molded the tragic life of Robert Schumann (1810–1856). His father suffered from a nervous disorder and his mother was afflicted with melancholy; his sister Emilie drowned herself when she was 20 and his three brothers all died young. Schumann began to show signs of his future aberrations when he was only 23.

He was born in Zwickau, about 40 miles from Leipzig. His father, who died when Schumann was 16, had encouraged his son's musical and literary interests, and the boy's hero during his teen years was Jean Paul Richter, an extravagantly romantic writer who signed his works Jean Paul. Schumann's mother persuaded him to enroll as a law student in Leipzig, but by 1830 he had abandoned that career to study piano and harmony with Friedrich Wieck, not a wholly satisfactory arrangement because of Schumann's erratic practice and study habits. He might eventually have settled down to a career as a concert pianist except that in 1832 he damaged his right hand permanently by using a contrivance designed to strengthen the fingers. From then on he devoted his energies to composing.

In 1833 Schumann helped to found the magazine *Neue Zeitschrift für Musik,* and as its editor (1833–1844) he became Europe's most famous music critic through his numerous excellent articles. During the early decades of the 1800s music criticism had sunk to a very low level, and the existing musical periodicals were unimaginative and conventional. Schumann, concerned about this state, invented the League of David, which he described as "a spiritual and romantic league." The organization included Schumann and those friends whose sympathies were with him in his war against the "Philistines" (for the composer, the term "philistine" stood for everything shallow, merely pleasant, or mediocre). In other words the League of David advocated a progressive, refined musical culture—not the old conservative traditions and yet not the capricious, superficial music so frequently produced in the Romantic period. Schumann's own criticisms were signed "Eusebius," "Florestan," or occasionally "Raro." Eusebius would be filled with gentle enthusiasm over some new composition, while Florestan would ruthlessly reveal the faults that Eusebius had overlooked. Raro was the most level-headed and objective of the three.

Schumann married Clara Wieck in 1840 after some stormy sessions with Friedrich Wieck, who opposed the marriage as an obstacle to his daughter's career. Clara nonetheless became one of the foremost women pianists of all time, and after Schumann's death she established her own reputation as a virtuoso pianist and interpreter, especially of her husband's music.

When Felix Mendelssohn founded the famous Leipzig Conservatory in 1843, Schumann received an appointment to teach piano and composition, but his peculiar temperament was not suited to teaching and he remained on the staff just a little more than a year. Periodic crises of mental exhaustion were already interfering with his work at that time. After Leipzig he went to Dresden for several years, and then in 1850 he unwisely accepted the position of municipal music director at Düsseldorf. Unable to fulfill the expectations that his fame as a composer had created, he resigned his directorship under unpleasant conditions in 1853.

The next year he attempted suicide by throwing himself into the Rhine, and from then until his death on July 29, 1856, he was confined to a sanatorium at Endenich, near Bonn.

For some, Robert Schumann personifies the Romantic artist of the early nineteenth century, the untiring prophet of the Romantic ideal in music. His hectic courtship and ultimate marriage, his progressive mental illness and final breakdown, have all been stressed too much—often more than his contributions as a composer.

An absolute Romantic, Schumann had a special gift for composing art songs and short piano works. His notable keyboard compositions are finely wrought miniatures—tonal paintings, mood pictures, psychological delineations—and this music preserves his name. Although he ventured into larger keyboard forms, he was more at home with short piano pieces or lieder, and his beautiful examples in both idioms have helped to sustain their tradition. He was most explicit about their value.

> Scorn not the short piece. A certain broad basis, a leisurely development and conclusion may be the ornament of many a work. But there are tone-poets who know how to express in minutes what for others requires hours. The interpretation and reception of such concentrated compositions, however, are exacting matters for the performer and for the listener, and they call for a special effort and for a favorable hour and time. Beautiful, broad form may be enjoyed at all times, but profundity of meaning is not communicable at every moment.[4]

In other media, Schumann's oratorios, the piano quintet, and various chamber-music works reaffirm his inexhaustible fantasy. Although he wrote four symphonies—*B-Flat Major* (Spring), 1841; *C Major,* 1846; *E-Flat Major* (Rhenish), 1850; and *D Minor,* 1841–1851—he never became a genuine orchestral composer, either in handling the instruments or in symphonic inspiration and technique.

Piano Music

Schumann habitually grouped his piano pieces in series. Sometimes the series is a narration, with each separate composition bearing a descriptive title; however, these narratives are usually disjointed, making the order of the pieces unimportant, as in such suites as the *Albumblätter* (Album Leaves, 1845), *Album for the Young* (1848), and the *Fantasy Pieces* (1837). In other instances the group of pieces presents a logical succession of psychological portraits, as in the collections *Carnaval* (1835), *Kinderscenen* (1838), and *Waldscenen* (1849). And finally, some series of piano pieces bear only a general title—*Kreisleriana* (1838), *Papillons* (1832), *Davidsbündlertänze* (1837), and *Noveletten* (1838)—but each

[4] From *On Music and Musicians,* p. 73, by Robert Schumann, translated by Paul Rosenfeld and edited by Konrad Wolff. Copyright 1946 by Pantheon Books, Inc. Reprinted by permission of Pantheon Books, a Division of Random House, Inc.

piece illustrates or comments upon that main title. For some of the piano collections, Schumann supposedly took inspiration from literary sources; the *Papillons* (Butterflies) were purported to be inspired by Jean Paul's *Flegeljahre* (Years of Indiscretion), and the *Kreisleriana* was drawn from E. T. A. Hoffmann's *Phantasiestücke in Callot's Manier* (Fantasy Pieces in Callot's Style, 1815). On the other hand, the literary association can be misleading, for as Schumann himself confessed, "The titles of all my compositions never occur to me until I have finished composing."[5]

Despite this confession, the composer defended using titles.

> Titles for pieces of music, since they again have come into favor in our day, have been censured here and there, and it has been said that "good music needs no sign-post." Certainly not, but neither does a title rob it of its value; and the composer in adding one at least prevents a complete misunderstanding of the character of his music. If the poet is licensed to explain the whole meaning of his poem by its title, why may not the composer do likewise? What is important is that such a verbal heading should be significant and apt. It may be considered the test of the general level of the composer's education.[6]

An overall look at Schumann's pianoforte works shows typical characteristics of his keyboard compositions. Unlike Beethoven, Schumann did not markedly change his style. Apart from the *Gesänge der Frühe, Opus 133* (Morning Songs, 1853) and the *Introduction and Allegro, Opus 134* (1853), both of which betray his advancing insanity, the late works differ little from his youthful writings except in technical matters.

Schumann's piano works, mainly written between 1829 and 1839, breathe intimacy, sentimentality, and subjectivity. Extremely acute to everything around him, he was sentimental in a positive sense. A dreamer and idealist whose inner life became his real life, Schumann in his music exalts passion to a degree seldom surpassed in the nineteenth century. His compositions do not relate exclusively to musical or literary sources, for he was also interested in psychological matters, a preoccupation—evidenced by musical complexities, enigmas, and obscure descriptive titles—that imbues his music with fantasy.

Concerto in A Minor

Schumann's *Concerto in A Minor, Opus 54* for piano and orchestra continues to be an unqualified success: pianists find it stimulating to play; audiences and listeners delight in its opulent melodies.

When Clara asked him for a composition to play with orchestra, Schumann obliged with a *Phantasie* in *a* minor, completed in the summer of 1841. Later he decided to use this *Phantasie* for the first movement in a concerto. He finished two more movements by 1845, and although *Phantasie* creates more interest than these later movements, the concerto as a whole is excellent.

Allegro affettuoso. Still preserving its character as a fantasy, the opening movement contains a skillful formal structure. Schumann enlivens his abundant thematic material by meter and key changes, and his orchestration here is excep-

[5] Letter to Simonin de Sire, March 15, 1839. In Schumann, p. 259. Reprinted by permission.

[6] Schumann, pp. 72–73. Reprinted by permission.

Ex. 17:13. Schumann: *Concerto in A Minor: Allegro affettuoso*

tionally adept. The *Allegro* begins with a brisk piano flourish before the orchestra states the plaintive *a*-minor theme (Ex. 17:13)—a theme that inspires much of this first movement and also the last. When the time is right for a second theme in *C* major, Schumann merely transposes his principal theme, changing its general character slightly. With solo woodwinds presiding, the development section suggests a variation of the exposition. Schumann's splendid cadenza to this movement carefully sustains the mood of the foregoing material.

Intermezzo: Andantino grazioso. This restrained second movement is a true *romanza* in its lyricism. Built in *F* major, the simple ternary form outlines two contrasting themes: the first rises from a dialogue between piano and orchestra; the cellos introduce the second theme, a broadly lyrical melody. At the very end of the *Intermezzo* the orchestra recalls the first movement's principal theme. This leads into the finale and generates its principal theme in the key of *A* major.

Allegro vivace. A wealth of thematic material overruns the finale. The second subject, with its rhythmic dislocation, is the most ingenious feature of the movement. There is an elaborate development—unusual for a concerto finale—and a very lengthy coda. Unrestrained joy permeates the entire finale.

Lieder

Schumann continued the grand Romantic lied tradition that Schubert created through his song masterpieces. Before 1840, Schumann had composed primarily for piano, but during his first year of marriage he enthusiastically began to write lieder and composed nearly a hundred songs within that one year.

This "song year" includes *Liederkreis, Opus 24* (poems by Heine); *Myrthen, Opus 25* (poems by Rückert, Goethe, Heine, Byron, etc.); and another *Liederkreis, Opus 39* (poems by Eichendorff). The most famous collections from 1840 are the two cycles *Frauenliebe und Leben, Opus 42* (Chamisso) and *Dichterliebe, Opus 48* (Heine). For many listeners and critics, *Opus 48* contains the essence of Robert Schumann's vocal writing.

In his famous poetry collection *Buch der Lieder* (Song Book, 1827),

Heinrich Heine (1797–1856) "unquestionably struck a new lyric note, not merely for Germany but for Europe. No singer before him had been so daring in the use of nature-symbolism as he, none had given such concrete expression to the spiritual forces of heart and soul. At times, it is true, his imagery is exaggerated to the degree of absurdity, but it exercised, none the less, a fascination over his generation."[7]

Schumann apparently liked Heine's poetry very much. Franz Schubert preferred texts by eighteenth-century poets (Goethe, Schiller), but Schumann's Romanticism found sympathy in nineteenth-century subjective poetry. For his *Dichterliebe* (A Poet's Love) he selected 16 poems from Heine's *Buch der Lieder;* the poems create unity in that they generally describe elusive love, despair, nostalgia, bitterness, and frustration. Schumann's songs based on the poems are emotional musical experiences that compare favorably with his most exquisite piano pieces.

Whereas Schubert's song cycles are dramatic (*Die schöne Müllerin*), Schumann's are inclined to be lyrical. Schumann was never restricted by form when setting his chosen poems. Sometimes he tried strophic form, but more frequently he varied the stroph. If he felt that some textual words needed repeating, he did so. Both Schumann and Schubert often employed the through-composed idea.

One prominent characteristic of Schumann's lieder is the skillfully designed piano part, due possibly to his long experience in writing piano music. The piano is essential in his lieder, never a mere support or accompaniment. For example, the piano frequently plays most of the notes found in the vocal line. Sometimes the piano continues or finishes off a musical thought introduced by the voice part. Elsewhere, piano and voice dialogue in a kind of recitative. Schumann employs introductory piano passages to set a mood, and he often adds an unexpected postlude; for instance, after the final song in the *Dichterliebe,* the piano continues alone for more than a page.

SUMMARY

Each of these early-nineteenth-century composers—Schubert, Mendelssohn, and Schumann—contributed substantially toward the establishment of a stable Romantic tradition, and their combined influence has endured, for elements of that tradition are discernible in twentieth-century music.

Schubert repeatedly stressed the impact of simplicity in his music, and his melodic versatility has been the admiration of many who would, if they could, learn his lyric secrets.

Mendelssohn proved an effective bridge leading to the height of the Romantic period. He demonstrated that Baroque and Classic techniques could be successfully merged with the new ideals, giving them a necessary solidity.

Schumann, with his extramusical preoccupations and his sometimes obscure experiments in musical description, is perhaps the most typical Romantic composer. His achievement in transferring pure emotion into pure sound was unique in his time and remains so today.

[7] *Encyclopaedia Britannica* (Chicago: Encyclopaedia Britannica, Inc., 1948), article entitled "Heinrich Heine," Vol. 11, p. 389. Reprinted by permission.

FOR DISCUSSION AND ASSIGNMENT

1. What "Romantic" traits do you find present in Baroque music and in the Classic music of Haydn and Mozart?
2. The nineteenth-century composer no longer depended on aristocratic or clerical patronage. Do you think there is any connection between the composer's new status and the music he produced?
3. Baroque and Classic compositions are easy to identify and to distinguish one from the other. Listen to some Schumann, Mendelssohn, Schubert. Is there an equally distinctive "Romantic" sound? Is it easily identifiable?
4. What accounts for the romantic "color" in Schubert's orchestral music?
5. Schubert was poor, Mendelssohn was well-to-do. Does this play any role whatsoever in the type of music each produced?
6. Why did lieder composers sometimes choose poems by great poets and at other times choose mediocre poems? Did they have no discrimination?
7. Write an essay explaining each of the three composers' contributions to the early-nineteenth-century musical scene.

FOR FURTHER READING

Barnes, Harry Elmer. *An Intellectual and Cultural History of the Western World:* Vol. 3. New York: Dover Publications, Inc., 1965. PB. A splendid survey of the nineteenth-century intellectual revolution and Romanticism in the arts and literature.

Chissell, Joan. *Schumann.* New York: Collier Books, 1962. PB. Like most of the Collier Great Composers Series, this study begins with a biography of the composer, then proceeds to analyze the music by category. A good biographical calendar, a catalog of works, and a bibliography further enhance this book.

Einstein, Alfred. *Music in the Romantic Era.* New York: W. W. Norton & Co., Inc., 1947. Although first published 20 years ago, the late Dr. Einstein's book is still the only comprehensive study of Romantic music in the English language.

———. *Schubert: A Musical Portrait.* New York: Oxford University Press, 1951. This is one of the best studies of Schubert as man and musician.

Flower, Newman. *Franz Schubert.* Chester Springs, Pa.: Dufour Editions, 1949. Originally published in 1928, this book presents Schubert's life with so much color and excitement that it almost reads like a novel. Yet it is a fine biography.

Hugo, Howard E., ed. *The Portable Romantic Reader.* New York: The Viking Press, 1957. PB. This is, of course, an anthology and suffers from the incompleteness of most anthologies. However, for a picture of the extravagances, inconsistencies, flamboyance, and the attractiveness of the nineteenth century, no other volume can compare with it.

Janson, H. W. *History of Art.* Englewood Cliffs, N.J.: Prentice-Hall, Inc., 1962. Dr. Janson's impressive volume contains a fine account of Romanticism as seen through painting and sculpture. The illustrations are well chosen and beautifully produced.

Radcliffe, Philip. *Mendelssohn.* New York: Collier Books, 1963. PB. A brief but penetrating study, this book places Mendelssohn in his proper perspective through a balanced evaluation of the music.

Schumann, Robert. *On Music and Musicians,* edited by Konrad Wolff, translated by Paul Rosenfeld. New York: McGraw-Hill Book Co., 1946. PB. Schumann's writings on music are indispensable reading for anyone attempting to fathom the composer's nature and music.

The Romantic Pianists: Chopin and Liszt

18

The difference between Liszt and Chopin lies in this, that the basis of the former's art is universality, that of the latter's, individuality.

JAMES HUNEKER
Franz Liszt (1911)

FRÉDÉRIC CHOPIN

Of all the composers who have created piano music, Frédéric François Chopin (1810–1849), universally idolized in his own century and in ours, holds the enviable position of being the one whose music is most frequently performed. His contemporaries, perhaps from jealousy, were sometimes slighting. "A sick room talent," said John Field. "He was dying all his life," remarked Hector Berlioz. Even in distant Russia, Mily Balakirev compared him to "a nervous society lady." Despite these disparaging epithets, the fact remains that Chopin invented a keyboard style ideally suited to nineteenth-century Romanticism. His music is subjective and tinged with melancholy; it suggests a never ending search for the unattainable, yet invariably the mood is clothed with an impeccable technical apparatus.

Born in Poland of a Polish mother and a French father, Chopin gave his first public piano recital at nine and began concertizing at an early age. Performing in Austria and Bohemia in 1829, he was acclaimed as a pianist and as the composer of extremely original piano music. But he found his musical home in Paris, for Poland was torn by revolution, and Paris—at that time Europe's liveliest music center—befriended many exiled Polish aristocrats. While there, Chopin formed congenial friendships with Franz Liszt, Vincenzo Bellini, Honoré de Balzac, Eugène Delacroix (Ill. 18:1), and Heinrich Heine, and began his highly publicized relationship with the French writer George Sand (Mme. Aurore Dudevant). What started as maternal affection turned into a *grande affaire,* and for seven years Chopin remained under her care and influence—in Paris, at her country home in Nohant, and in Majorca for one season. They quarreled and

Ill. 18:1. ***Eugène Delacroix (1798–1863).*** **Chopin.** ***Louvre, Paris. Courtesy of Bulloz-Art Reference Bureau.***

separated in 1847, and from then on Chopin's health failed rapidly as the consumption that had long plagued him worsened. Although ill and weak, he performed in England and Scotland in 1848 to earn money. Returning to his beloved Paris, he died there the following year.

Chopin's music is exceptionally individualistic; it can be as readily identified as an El Greco painting or a Baudelaire poem. It is also easily understood, and one reason for this easy access to his works is their ready charm. Chopin's melodic structure is a prominent and very engaging feature of his music. His melodies are basically vocal rather than instrumental, and his music may therefore be said to derive more from Schubert than anyone else. Unlike Beethoven he seldom uses symphonic-type melodies that lend themselves to ample development and to motive construction. Chopin's melodies are capable of elaboration, but it is a kind of self-development relying on harmonic change, modulation, rhythmic transformation, and—above all—ornamentation.

Most Chopin melodies can be traced to the dance or to song. The melodies for the mazurkas, polonaises, and waltzes are clearly dance-inspired, while melodies in other types, such as the *Étude, Opus 25, No. 9* (Ex. 18:1), are

Ex. 18:1. Chopin: ***Étude, Opus 25, No. 9***

disguised dances. Almost all of his slow themes come from vocal models—for example, the theme in *Étude, Opus 10, No. 3* (Ex. 18:2). Chopin liked Italian

Ex. 18:2. Chopin: *Étude, Opus 10, No. 3*

opera, particularly Bellini operas, and many of his melodies reveal a touch of Bellinian bel canto—always, however, molded into his personal manner of expression.

Chopin's melodies often seem deliberately designed for the voice because they are lyric (usually diatonic) and fashioned into regular eight-bar periods. Frequently he repeats a melodic idea several times, such as in the *Nocturne, Opus 9, No. 2,* the *Prélude, Opus 28, No. 6,* and the *Polonaise, Opus 53.* With Chopin this repetition intensifies the original idea and can give rise to thrilling consequences.

Chromaticism, which he uses to vary or to develop themes, is an important factor in Chopin's melody. Compare the three different statements of one melody in the *Nocturne, Opus 27, No. 2, in D-Flat Major* (Ex. 18:3). Notice that

Ex. 18:3. Chopin: *Nocturne, Opus 27, No. 2*

the entire melodic spirit changes through the chromatic variances. Sometimes this procedure produces a favorite Chopin device: the melodic line is interrupted by a cadenza-like chromatic figure that eventually comes to repose, allowing the melody to continue.

Chopin's concept of harmony adds another distinguishing characteristic to his music. His writing shows no inclination toward strict polyphony and counterpoint, yet his unique harmonic practices were so ahead of his time that they puzzled even Schumann. Chopin's ideas about harmony were extraordinary for the early nineteenth century, and they influenced many later composers. His harmonic idiom is complicated, as the following points indicate. (1) The modulation—remarkably free for the period—is accomplished in two ways: by moving freely back and forth between major and minor and by assuming a key without actually establishing it cadentially. (2) Dissonance is also liberally treated. Sometimes there are so many passing and nonharmonic tones that the harmony is veiled, as though the composer were trying to disguise it. The boldness in some series of dissonances completely perplexed Chopin's contemporaries, but these dissonances create harmonic color not encountered again until Debussy. (3) Frequently the harmony engenders the melody. For example, in *Étude, Opus 25, No. 1, in A-Flat Major* (Ex. 18:4), the melody emerges as the result of

Ex. 18:4. Chopin: *Étude, Opus 25, No. 1*

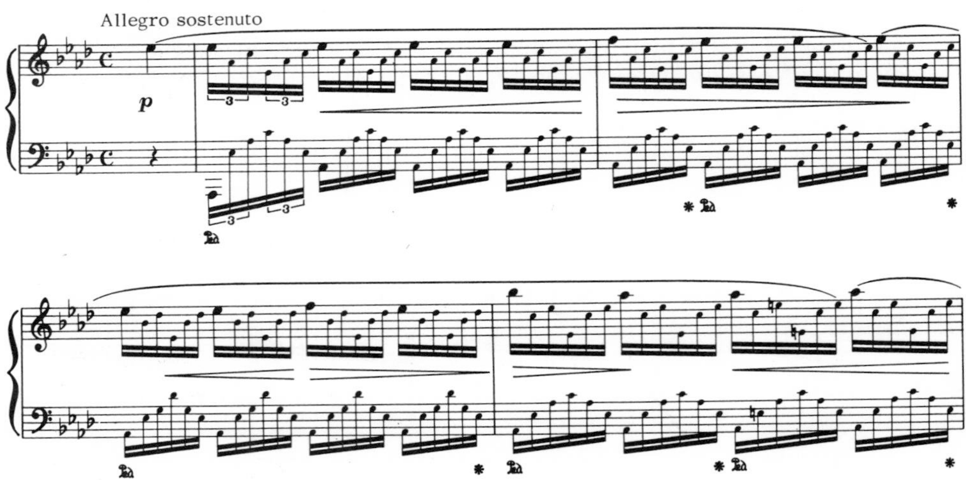

shimmering arpeggios; it retains its vigor only when considered in its harmonic framework.

His dramatic rhythmic control regardless of the prevailing mood is well displayed in the *Prélude, Opus 28, No. 24, in D Minor* and the opening movement of *Sonata, Opus 35*. By the same token, the lyric effect in pieces like *Étude, Opus 10, No. 6* depends principally on the inherent rhythmic concept. But the mazurkas best illustrate Chopin's deftness with rhythm because there the basic impression is created by rhythm—the rhythm *is* the mazurka. Although the waltzes and mazurkas are both written in triple meter and have similar texture, they are rarely confused, thanks to the characteristic rhythm each one possesses.

Another distinctive characteristic of Chopin's pianistic style—and the one most abused—is his use of *tempo rubato* (literally, "stolen time"), which calls for a loosening of strict tempo. Without rubato his music loses some of its charm and emotional impact. On the other hand, undisciplined use of this expressive device results in sugary sentimentality, a complete distortion of his original intent. He gave the clue to correct usage when he said that the hand supplying the accompaniment should keep strict rhythm while the melodic line is played in tempo rubato.

Still another conspicuous feature of Chopin's music stems from his preoccupation with the *sostenuto* (damper) pedal, which either curtails sounds or permits them to vibrate through the air. Chopin's genius lies primarily in lyrical music—a cantabile art—and he uses the sostenuto pedal to achieve his sustained melodic lines and to coordinate his characteristic widely spaced accompaniment figures.

Préludes

Chopin composed his 24 *Préludes* over a considerable period of time. He made the final additions to the set in Majorca in 1838 and 1839, and they were published in the latter year. George Sand, who accompanied Chopin to Majorca, described the composer and the music he produced while there.

> It was there that he composed the most beautiful of those short pages he modestly entitled *Préludes.* They are masterpieces. Several bring to mind visions of deceased monks and the sound of the funeral chants which haunted him; others are melancholy and sweet; the inspiration for them came to him in the hours of sunshine and of health, from the noise of the children's laughter under the window, from the distant sound of guitars, from the warbling of the birds among the humid foliage and the sight of pale little full-blown roses on the snow.[1]

With all due regard to the novelist's description, Chopin's preludes do not need flowery romanticization; they stand firmly on their beauty and artistic merit. Schumann found them amazing, a pure enchantment; Liszt felt that, although brief, they had magnificent spiritual proportions.

There are two singular points about these works. First, they are very like Bach's preludes, not in technical style but in attitude and basic concept. Like Bach, Chopin wrote 24 preludes (plus a later single one), one in each major and minor key. Often his prelude is based on a single idea, sometimes only a motive. The first one is built on a series of simple modulating figures (Ex. 18:5).

Ex. 18:5. Chopin: *Prélude, Opus 28, No. 1*

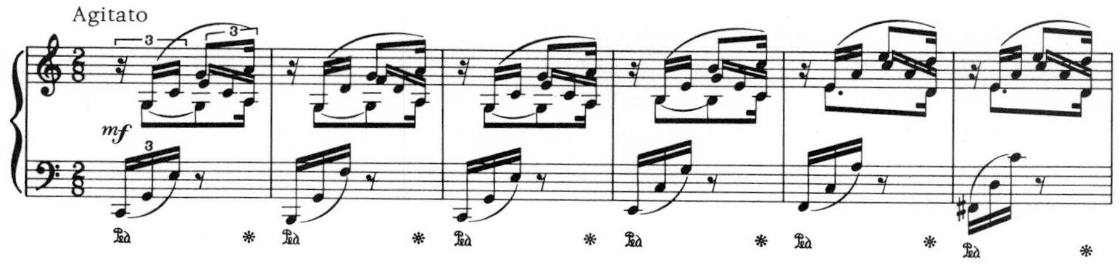

[1] George Sand (Mme. Aurore Dudevant), *Histoire de ma vie* (Paris: Calmann-Lévy, 1928), Vol. 4, p. 439. English translation by the author.

Second, Chopin's preludes are complete in themselves. Before his time the prelude had been coupled with the fugue or had been used as an introduction to a suite of dances. Chopin's works are preludes to nothing in particular, except perhaps a mood or a fleeting impression. Played as a set, they provide a tonal mosaic; heard singly, each emerges as a delectable musical experience inspired by personal emotion.

Études

Chopin's *Études* contain the essence of his special traits: the harmonic fluidity, melodic voluptuousness, and inner spirit that characterize his whole piano repertoire. All the more remarkable is the fact that they were written when he was a young man. The *Études, Opus 10* were composed between the ages of 18 and 23—a masterpiece for such an early work. Although the second set was published later (1837), the *Études, Opus 25* are almost contemporary with the first set.

The golden age of the étude (study piece) began in 1817 with the *Gradus ad Parnassum* of Muzio Clementi (1752–1832). In succession came the études by Clementi's disciple J. B. Cramer (1771–1858) and the prodigious collections of Karl Czerny (1791–1857), some of which appeared at the time Chopin started to compose. The early études were usually based on classical late-eighteenth-century techniques—exploitation of scales and arpeggios—so they do not explore many problems perceivable in the final Beethoven sonatas. Excellent as they are, they remain studies in technique. Chopin's études go beyond this, for they include the expected studies in various technical matters and also studies pertaining to musicianship.

Each étude exploits one particular pianistic problem. *Opus 10, No. 1* consists of a series of brilliant right-hand arpeggios; *No. 5,* the so-called "Black Key Étude," is played chiefly on black notes; *No. 11* is based on a series of widely spaced harplike chords. The last étude of *Opus 10,* the "Revolutionary Étude," develops a spectacular succession of left-hand scalar passages. *Opus 25, No. 6* emphasizes parallel thirds, particularly hard for pianists.

Technique is only one aspect of piano music and piano playing, in some ways merely a means to an end. Realizing this, Chopin designed many études to call attention to subtler problems of musicianship—phrasing, legato, and the like. Occasionally he combines such refinements with virtuoso passages, as in *Opus 10, No. 3:* a lyric melodic line in the first and last sections opposes the dramatic middle section, where sets of augmented and diminished intervals, in both hands, brilliantly compete.

Nocturnes

Of all Chopin's works, the *Nocturnes* are the most introspective, the most genuinely subjective, although he did not originate this form. The Irishman John Field (1782–1837) created the title and content of the nocturne: a short elegy of great lyric intensity. Field's classic model has a simple melody with harmonic accompaniment.

By refining the nocturne's contours and enriching its harmonic texture, Chopin transformed it into a sensitive, personal art form. His nocturnes are like musical readings of nineteenth-century French poetry, recalling Alfred de Musset's line, *"Les plus désespérés sont les chants les plus beaux"* (the most beautiful songs are the saddest songs).

Chopin's 19 nocturnes—scattered from *Opus 9* through *Opus 72*—were composed at different periods. Most have basic ternary form (A B A); however, the original theme's restatement varies according to his unique ornamentation. Melancholy permeates most of them, and many melodies have an initial downward sweep, increasing the pensive atmosphere (Ex. 18:6).

Ex. 18:6. Chopin: *Nocturne, Opus 37, No. 1*

The texture in the nocturnes generally comes from an elaborate melody supported by undulating broken figures in the bass. At times extremely florid, these melodies often show instances of Chopin's little cadenza-like fioriture. By the time he reached *Opus 27,* he was using the nocturne to give his deepest emotions their most appealing expression. *Opus 27, No. 2, in D-Flat Major* (1835) is one of the loveliest; the melody dips downward, then rises successively higher while parallel thirds heighten the emotional effect. Such progressions in thirds, in company with sixths and other intervals, also produce wonderful results in *Opus 37, No. 2* (1839).

For the most part these nocturnes are not dramatic. *Opus 48, No. 1, in C Minor* (1841) is an exception. Like the others, its first section is meditative, but the middle section grows to a lavish climax—massive harplike chords are interrupted by octave passages in both hands. Then the third section, instead of returning to the calm spirit of the initial section, continues the turbulence and is even marked *doppio movimento* (double the speed of the preceding).

As a collection Chopin's nocturnes are unequal in quality, yet separately they present moments of pure lyricism, and several achieve perfect mood painting. Above all, they disclose the emotions of their creator.

Polonaises

J. S. Bach, J. Christian Bach, Weber, and other composers had used the title polonaise, meaning a dance of noble allure and moderately fast tempo. Liszt remarked of Chopin's polonaises:

> Characterized by an energetic rhythm, [they] galvanize and electrify the torpor of indifference. The most noble traditional feelings of ancient Poland are embodied in them. . . . They bring vividly before the imagination the ancient Poles, as we find them described in their chronicles; gifted with powerful organizations, subtle intellects, indomitable courage and earnest piety, mingled with high-born courtesy and a gallantry which never deserted them, whether on

> the eve of battle, during its exciting course, in the triumph of victory, or amidst the gloom of defeat.[2]

These dances should, therefore, be played with a certain majesty—often emphasized by Chopin through the tempo marking *allegro maestoso.*

Chopin's typical polonaise has tripartite form somewhat resembling a scherzo, with contrasting textures in the center section. The rhythm is ternary. Although he kept the title and used the basic ideas as a foundation, Chopin revitalized the spirit of the polonaise, designing a keyboard poem to praise his native land—its struggles, eternal hope, and sorrows. Of his 18 polonaises, the early ones were not wholly conceived in this frame of mind and consequently are less impressive than the others.

Chopin reached full maturity in this form with *Opus 26, No. 2, in E-Flat Minor* (1835), which arouses feelings of foreboding. Sometimes subtitled "Revolt," this troubled work suggests a struggle against relentless fate. The "Military Polonaise," *Opus 40, No. 1, in A Major* (1838), is much brighter—a brisk march in triple meter, expansively melodic in the middle section. Number two of the same opus (in *c* minor) admirably fits its sometime title "Pathétique." A broad left-hand melody in octaves receives support from solemn full chords in the right hand; the middle section, largely chromatic, uses motive repetition for emphasis.

Opus 44 in F-Sharp Minor (1841) is Chopin's first *Grande Polonaise,* and its spirit is like that of his more profound scherzos. He generously uses his mature technical devices for this work. Melodic lines are variously created: singly, in thirds and sixths, and in octaves. Frequent trills accentuate the dramatic content. In the center a *Mazurka, doppio movimento* provides unexpected contrast.

Opus 53 in A-Flat Major (1842) remains the grand example of all polonaises (familiar to many through the popular adaptation as the song "Till the End of Time"). It is still a superb epic even though it has been played nearly to death, often very badly. The primary theme, with its surprisingly bare accompaniment, is an aristocratic march without any pretension. In the trio—after a fanfare of arpeggiated chords—an equally rhythmic melodic motive appears accompanied by a formidable series of descending octaves. A lyric passage follows, and then the initial noble theme returns.

Chopin's last work in this form, the *Polonaise-Fantaisie, Opus 61* (1846) is a proper climax to his compositions in this particular style. It combines the poetic qualities of his ballades with the rhythmic drive and lofty disposition that distinguish his polonaises.

The *Préludes, Études, Nocturnes,* and *Polonaises,* plus the *Mazurkas, Ballades, Impromptus, Waltzes, Scherzos,* and *Concertos*—all show Chopin to be a true poet of the piano. He realized that his talents were best suited to solo piano music; he remained almost exclusively a keyboard composer, and in that field he was a genius.

FRANZ LISZT

The Hungarian Franz Liszt (1811–1886) remains an enigmatic musical celebrity. Was he a genius, a daringly original composer who created new musical

[2] Franz Liszt, *Life of Chopin,* translated by M. Cook (Boston: Oliver Ditson & Co., n.d.), p. 31.

forms and eloquence? Or was he a charlatan, a facile performer who designed his compositions to pamper the artificial taste of the public? To be accurate, one must concede that there is some truth in both propositions.

Liszt was a true son of the nineteenth century, a typical product of the Romantic age. His music can prompt the listener's scorn as well as admiration, but no one can ignore the extraordinary personality of this "Mephistopheles disguised as an abbé," as he was once described. In the fashion of the inconsistent Romantics, he was spiritual yet worldly, religious yet skeptical. He produced more than 700 works, including many that are either uneven in quality, superficially constructed, or downright dull. Nevertheless, Franz Liszt has strongly influenced late-nineteenth- and twentieth-century composers.

Liszt's personal life affected his music. In his youth (until about 1838) he was a piano wizard, a flamboyant Romantic defying convention by his liaison with the Comtesse Marie d'Agoult, who bore him three illegitimate children. Virtuoso pieces predominate in his works from these years: the first version of the *Transcendental Études;* the *Études* based on Paganini violin pieces; the bravura *Grand galop chromatique;* and numerous fantasias and transcriptions. Still, all was not fire and brilliance, for at this time he also wrote the first two books of the *Années de pèlerinage* (Years of Pilgrimage), in which he often attains moments of absolute lyrical beauty.

For eight years (1839–1847) before the so-called Weimar period, Liszt concertized extensively in England, Poland, Russia, and Portugal. Considering the unsettled, difficult life facing a traveling concert artist, one is surprised that he composed as much as he did then. These works are mainly fantasias based on operas (*Sonnambula, Norma, Lucrezia Borgia, Don Giovanni*), most of which have been forgotten. The *Hungarian Rhapsodies,* although not completed in these years, were sketched and reworked as he became increasingly interested in Hungarian popular music.

Liszt's most fruitful writing years occurred between 1848 and 1861, while he lived at Weimar when not conducting or playing elsewhere. Many mature masterworks took shape at Weimar, and at the same time he was extremely generous in promoting music by other composers. He also began a new love affair, this time with the Princess Sayn-Wittgenstein.

In 1861 Liszt—who had waited vainly in Rome to see whether the Princess might obtain a divorce so that they could be married—took minor orders and became Abbé Liszt. Thereafter, until his death in 1886, he divided his time between Rome, Budapest, and Weimar, composing some of his most convincing religious works.

Liszt did more to develop piano technique than any of his predecessors or contemporaries, with the possible exception of his teacher Karl Czerny. Liszt's compositions abound in obvious technical devices, such as octave passages. Sometimes he uses these devices to reinforce a melodic line, sometimes as accompaniment figures, and sometimes simply to add bravura. Chromatic progressions by octaves (occasionally tenths!) and massive chords figure prominently along with trills, double trills, and all kinds of ornamentation.

The recitative-cadenza, handled with restraint and caution by Chopin, received lavish treatment from Liszt. His cadenzas varied from short fragments to lengthy, glittering, and often diffuse scalar designs to showy sequential passages.

Liszt's piano transcriptions of orchestral works, such as Berlioz' *Symphonie fantastique* or Beethoven's symphonies, prove that he had an uncanny ability for re-creating orchestral fabric at the keyboard. However, technical aspects far outshine the musical substance in much of his music. Liszt, king of pianists in his day, wrote to display his own phenomenal technique and he was very successful, but the music produced for that purpose falls short in musical value and in many cases exhibits what is today called bad taste.

Frequently Liszt is not to blame. When transcribing certain operas, he could do little to improve upon the stilted quality and artificial content of the original vehicle, especially with operas like *Niobe* by Pacini, Raff's *King Alfred,* and *La Fiancée* by Auber.

Beyond technique there are many worthwhile features in his music. Although he was born a Hungarian and resided for many years in Germany, Liszt was at heart a French Romantic. His music shows this and so does his temperament, which was typical of the *mal du siècle.* Early in life he recognized his cultural deficiencies and read avidly to improve himself, becoming especially fond of the French literati of his day. As a result, most Liszt compositions have French titles. Lamartine and Victor Hugo exerted significant extramusical influences on his composing. Following the precedent set by Berlioz, Liszt's music is preponderantly programmatic or, at the least, dependent on ideas and concepts outside the music field.

In some respects Liszt anticipated Impressionism much more than any of his contemporaries. He was not so interested in successions of sounds as in the simultaneous blending of sounds or tone clusters—that is, in music for the sake of sound. A natural showman and exhibitionist, he delighted in sounding together as much of the keyboard as physically possible.

In his large-scale orchestral and piano works Liszt used a procedure that he called *transformation of theme.* He states a series of themes or motives, then submits each one to various transformations. In other words, development in itself became a form for Liszt. Such an approach was more suitable for works of broad scope; yet his works, pianistic and otherwise, indicate that he avoided direct repetition of sections and even phrases. He preferred his own developmental method, using constant variation and transformation of thematic material.

Piano Music

Liszt's most consistently well-written piano compositions reside in three volumes entitled *Années de pèlerinage* (the last book came out several years after the composer's death). On the whole the pieces are brief, but they possess uncommonly compact texture and formal structure.

The second volume, *Années de pèlerinage: Deuxième année: Italie* (published in 1858), is superior to the others. Most of the seven pieces maintain a tighter framework, the musical ideas are broader, and the expression clearer. Each was inspired by a work of art: a painting, sculpture, poem, or song.

Sposalizio (Wedding), first in this series, was inspired by a Raphael painting (Ill. 18:2) at the Milan Brera Gallery; *Il Penseroso* (The Thoughtful One) recalls Michelangelo's imposing statue of Lorenzo de Medici (Ill. 18:3) in the New Sacristy at Florence. These two dignified tonal portraits are drawn carefully and imaginatively. The latter's bold chromatic progressions anticipate what later proved to be a powerful tool in the hands of Richard Wagner (Ex. 18:7).

Ex. 18:7. Liszt: *Il Penseroso*

Canzonetta del Salvator Rosa seems to be a keyboard setting of a text by that fabulous painter-poet-musician. Liszt's straightforward harmonic design and simple melodic line make a charming setting.

Liszt wrote three songs in 1838–1839 using the Petrarca sonnets numbers 47, 104, and 123 as texts. Later on he changed these songs into piano compositions for this Italian album.

The final portrait in the second volume, *Après une lecture du Dante*

Ill. 18:2. *Raphael Sanzio (1483–1520)*, The Marriage of the Virgin. *Brera Gallery, Milan. Courtesy of Alinari-Art Reference Bureau.*

Ill. 18:3. *Michelangelo Buonarroti (1475–1564)*, Tomb of Lorenzo de' Medici. *New Sacristy, San Lorenzo, Florence, Italy. Courtesy of Alinari-Art Reference Bureau.*

(After Reading Dante), was inspired by a Victor Hugo poem, and Liszt added the subtitle *Fantasia quasi sonata.* A veritable tour de force, it bristles with technical difficulties.

In 1854 Liszt published the *Sonata in B Minor,* on one hand acclaimed as a unique masterpiece and on the other rejected as an awkward attempt at expanded pianistic writing. Yet between Beethoven's late works and Brahms's *Sonata, Opus 5, in F Minor* few really fine sonatas appeared, and certainly none as original as this one by Liszt. For a work written *en plein romanticisme,* it is incredibly disciplined, molded with meticulous attention to detail. Some critics find the melodic ideas insipid and the various bridge passages careless and inconsistent, but it is safe to assume that these critics do not care for Liszt in any form. In this sonata Liszt adheres steadily and creatively to his basic construction principle—transformation of theme.

Three sections divide the sonata: *Lento assai-Allegro energico, Andante sostenuto,* and *Allegro energico.* The first opens with the immediate statement of three motives (Ex. 18:8), which are followed some four pages later by the passage

Ex. 18:8. Liszt: *Sonata in B Minor*

shown in Ex. 18:9. Each motive is subjected to different transformations or guises;

Ex. 18:9. Liszt: *Sonata in B Minor*

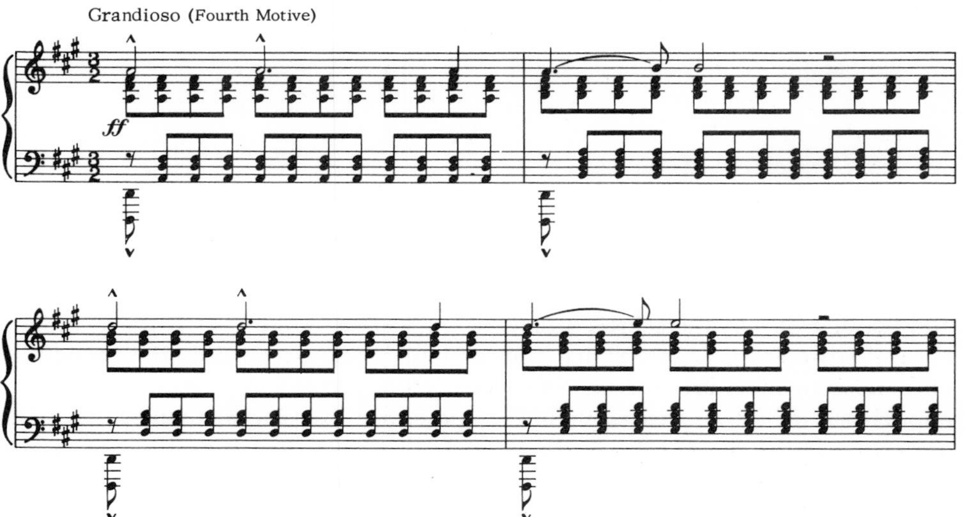

for example, the second motive appears in Ex. 18:10 with a completely changed

Ex. 18:10. Liszt: *Sonata in B Minor*

character. The original third motive, a vigorous one, becomes lyrical (Ex. 18:11).

Ex. 18:11. Liszt: *Sonata in B Minor*

The final *Allegro energico* begins with a fugato section whose subject derives from motives two and three. Recapitulation of a great deal of material from the first movement leads to a jubilant stretto passage based on the second motive; then the *Sonata* ends quietly. This sonata creates a dramatic poem of heroic proportions.

The *Hungarian Rhapsodies* have been more widely played—and over-played—than anything else Liszt wrote. The second *Rhapsody,* especially, has been subjected to every conceivable transcription from harmonica to jazz band. He composed 20 of these works, but only the first 15 are generally performed. These 15 were published between 1851 and 1854. Although not equal to his finest works, the *Rhapsodies* are convincing in their coloristic effects. In many passages Liszt successfully creates impressions of other instruments, such as the violin and cimbalom.

Orchestral Music

Classic symphonic form had matured grandly in the works of Haydn, Mozart, and Beethoven. Romantic composers, seeking new forms of orchestral expression, evolved the *symphonic poem,* a type destined to become important and popular in the nineteenth century.

Since Franz Liszt was first and foremost a pianist, possibly the greatest of all pianists, it is natural that as a composer his superior works are for piano. He approached orchestral writing with some hesitancy. Lacking firsthand knowledge of the orchestra ensemble, he used a collaborator for his orchestrations; that is, he would write out his compositions on three or four staffs, indicating what he wanted orchestrally, and then a friend would make a full score from this. Liszt would revise the score, and often the process would be repeated until he was wholly satisfied. In spite of this assistance, Liszt's final versions of his orchestral works represent his ideas, not those of any collaborator.

During the Romantic period, two especially significant developments occurred in the field of instrumental music. One was the method of linking movements by using some musical material common to all of them. Another was the musical exploitation of extramusical ideas. Liszt pioneered in both procedures. Attracted by the Romantic movement of his day, Liszt brought literary, dramatic, and pictorial elements into his music; in other words, he wrote "program music." He realized that in a continuous one-movement work having more or less free form he would be less restricted by formal considerations and could, in fact, let form mold itself to thought; for this protean form he invented the name "symphonic poem."

Les Préludes

Liszt wrote 12 symphonic poems during his Weimar period, the most popular being *Les Préludes.* The music was originally the prelude to his unpublished choral work *Les quatre éléments.* When he later decided to publish the prelude as an independent symphonic poem (final revision around 1854), he needed a "program" to fit the music. He chose *Les Préludes* from Alphonse de Lamartine's *Meditations poétiques.*

Les Préludes has four contrasted sections preceded by a short introduction (there is a marked similarity here to cyclic sonata form). Liszt weaves his musical fabric from two basic motives, varying and disguising them in imaginative ways. The first theme is simply a three-note motive that expands into an ample lyric flourish (Ex. 18:12), and the second is a conjunctively designed

Ex. 18:12. Liszt: *Les Préludes*

songlike theme (Ex. 18:13). In the introduction to the four sections, the first

Ex. 18:13. Liszt: *Les Préludes*

theme appears as in Ex. 18:12, but in the first section, *Andante maestoso,* this three-note motive enlarges into an elaborate paraphrase (Ex. 18:14). The second

Ex. 18:14. Liszt: *Les Préludes*

theme also appears in the first section, which means that in the succeeding three sections Liszt has complete freedom to apply his transformation technique.

The second section, *Allegro tempestoso,* which has been likened to a storm, reveals Liszt's theatrical nature as he manipulates the first theme into an ominous frenzy. In the following section, *Allegretto pastorale,* he dramatically presents one of the loveliest passages he ever created for orchestra. It opens with a horn call and presents the second theme in a delightfully lyric setting. The *Allegro marziale animato* ushers in a flamboyant finale typical of Liszt: both themes participate (Ex. 18:15), now redesigned into a sturdy, thrilling sound.

Ex. 18:15. Liszt: *Les Préludes*

Mephisto Waltz

Another attractive orchestral work is the *Mephisto Waltz No. 1,* or perhaps more correctly *The Dance in the Village Inn.* Liszt made two versions of this composition, one for piano solo and another for orchestra. They date from approximately the same period (*c.*1860) and are based on a long dramatic poem entitled *Faust* (1836) by the Austrian poet Nikolaus Lenau (1802–1850).

In the passage that inspired the music, Faust and Mephistopheles enter an inn in search of pleasure; Mephisto seizes a violin and hypnotizes the dancers with his playing. Two by two the revelers slip out into the starlit night, Faust with the landlord's daughter; a singing nightingale is heard through the open doors; at the end, enveloping the lovers and the nightingale, Mephisto's diabolical laughter rings out.

The *Mephisto Waltz* is highly effective in both the orchestral and the piano versions. Liszt's adroit showmanship and competent command of structural principles are always in control. The first of the two themes is rambunctious, so much so that it almost loses its waltz character. Liszt begins by using this theme singly, presenting it in different styles before proceeding to the second theme, whose unusual syncopation and sinister implication form a sharp contrast to the first theme. He then exploits this second theme: in what amounts to a third section, the pianist-composer combines his two themes, using the greatest imagination and ingenuity to create a finale that is exciting—and exhausting.

It is true that one must search diligently through Liszt's repertoire to find the works having quality and substance. He composed many piano pieces for himself or for special occasions or circumstances, and they were perhaps played only by him. But his best works prove his talent. They bear the mark of a dedicated, original composer who endowed his music with moments of nobility, beauty, and daring expressionistic power.

FOR DISCUSSION AND ASSIGNMENT

1. Would you call Chopin's music programmatic or abstract? Or perhaps both? Why?
2. Listen to several interpretations of one Chopin composition. Which impresses you the most? Why?
3. Listen to several works by Chopin. Do they sound like those of any other composers? Can you differentiate the various types—that is, distinguish a polonaise from a nocturne?
4. Listen to a work (by another composer) that Liszt transcribed—for example, a violin caprice by Paganini or a Bach organ fugue. Then listen to a Liszt piano transcription of the same composition. Is the Liszt version as effective? Does it adequately convey the character and essence of the original?
5. Listening to *Les Préludes* and the *Sonata,* do you find Liszt's transformation-of-theme principle easy to follow? How does it compare with standard sonata-allegro form?
6. What do you think accounts for the popularity of *Les Préludes?*

FOR FURTHER READING

Beckett, Walter. *Liszt.* New York: Farrar, Straus and Cudahy, Inc., 1963. A good, compact study of Liszt's life and music. Some criticisms seem dogmatic, but in general the composer is placed in proper perspective.

Fay, Amy. *Music-Study in Germany.* New York: Dover Publications, Inc., 1965. PB. Miss Fay, a young pianist, lived in Germany from 1869 to 1875. Her letters to her family, collected in this volume, provide a delightful insight into the musical life of that era. Miss Fay's personal recollections of Liszt are quite enjoyable.

Friedheim, Arthur. *Life and Liszt,* edited by Theodore L. Bullock. New York: Taplinger Publishing Co., Inc., 1961. Arthur Friedheim was associated with Liszt from 1880 to 1886 as friend, secretary, and pupil. His intimate, colorful recollections make interesting reading and help in evaluating the Hungarian composer.

Hedley, Arthur. *Chopin.* New York: Collier Books, 1962. PB. A good, brief study of the man and his music. Like other Collier books in this series, it contains a biography, brief surveys of the music by types, a calendar, catalog, and bibliography.

Huneker, James. *Chopin.* New York: Dover Publications, Inc., 1966. PB. Huneker's classic of 1900, in a new reprint, is still a fascinating, informative book. It brings the composer to life as no other book has done.

Searle, Humphrey. *The Music of Liszt.* New York: Dover Publications, Inc., 1967. PB. As the title states, this book deals strictly with Liszt's music and does so very competently. The sympathetic musical analysis is followed by a calendar and a useful catalog of the composer's works.

Sitwell, Sacheverell. *Liszt.* New York: Dover Publications, Inc., 1967. PB. This book, first published in 1934, is an intriguing biography of the pianist-composer.

Weinstock, Herbert. *Chopin.* New York: Alfred A. Knopf, 1949. The outstanding feature of this book is the analysis of Chopin's compositions.

19 Nineteenth-Century Opera

> An *opera* is a poetical tale or fiction, represented by vocal and instrumental musick, adorned with scenes, machines, and dancing.
>
> JOHN DRYDEN
> Preface to *Albion and Albanius* (1685)

Early-nineteenth-century composers could choose from abundant source material if they wanted to write operas, for by that time an operatic tradition had been firmly established. Handel and Mozart had advanced opera seria, whose heroic plots and dazzling da capo arias made realism not only undesirable but impossible. Mozart had also polished opera-buffa form to sophisticated perfection when he created the entertaining characters cavorting through *Le nozze di Figaro* and *Così fan tutte.* In *Die Zauberflöte* he mixed serious and comic elements with plausible, invigorating results.

Gluck had attempted opera reforms based on his belief that librettos and musical settings could be credible and still be dramatic. Although many of his contemporaries and successors ignored Gluck's ideas, his operas embodying these reformatory precepts were available to early-nineteenth-century musicians for observation and study.

Romantic composers appropriated elements from all previous styles and traditions. Many grand operas written in the early nineteenth century retained the grandeur and artificiality typical of opera seria. Rossini and others continued Mozart's humorous approach but not on the same high level. Some composers followed Gluck's advice that the da capo aria did not make for good theater and inserted flamboyant through-composed arias into their operas as showpieces.

The best way to learn about opera is to attend live performances. However, most standard operas are available on recordings, either in complete performance (sometimes on as many as five discs) or on a single record containing highlights from a given opera. In addition, many books provide summaries of opera plots and analyses of the music; some of these are listed at the end of the chapter. This chapter will introduce you to nineteenth-century opera and will provide a general outline of its history and development. Because many operas are famous for specific sections—overtures, arias, choruses—these passages have been singled out.

During the early part of the nineteenth century, Italian composers increasingly commercialized opera. Since they no longer depended on royal subsidy or aristocratic patronage, they wrote to please a larger, bourgeois audience, which preferred melodramatic plots, ribald comedy, and exciting music. One Italian composer knew how to please this public to perfection: Gioacchino Rossini.

Gioacchino Rossini

Gioacchino Antonio Rossini (1792–1868) was born into a musical family in Pesaro, but he lived and worked mostly in Bologna. He spent some years in Florence before 1855, when he moved to Paris, his home until his death.

Rossini's sure theatrical sense is largely responsible for his success in opera. His inborn dramatic flair and native instinct for comedy account for the steady popularity of many of his operas. He was able to give the public what it wanted without compromising his reputation as a serious musician.

One of the most striking characteristics of a Rossini opera is his masterful handling of voice and orchestra: he controls each medium separately, and he skillfully balances one against the other, combining taste and elegance with power and delicacy. Having learned to sing as a youth, he understood the human voice as few composers have done. His vocal lines are decidedly singable, even those demanding virtuosity from the singer, and the lasting success of some of his operas rests chiefly on their melodic arias. He should not be compared with melodists like Schubert, however, for Rossini composed expressly for stage performance, and his vocal line is more florid, more expansive than Schubert's.

Rossini bluntly stated his opinion that the composer is the rightful prima donna in opera.

> I maintain that in order to perform his part well, the good singer should be nothing but an able *interpreter* of the ideas of the master, the composer, and he should try to express them with great skill and all the brilliance of which they are susceptible. Therefore the performers should be nothing but accurate *executants* of what is written down. In short, the composer and the poet are the only true *creators*. Sometimes a clever singer will burst into additional ornamentation and would like to call this his creation, but it often happens that this creation is false, and even more often that it ruins the composer's ideas, robbing them of the simplicity of expression they should have.[1]

Critics have pointed out frequent carelessness in the way Rossini sets his texts—squeezing words together or distorting accent—and this is true to some extent, because his inspiration came to him in purely musical language. He reportedly once said, "Give me a laundry list and I will set it to music." Such instinctive musicality overcomes any textual deficiencies. Although he regarded himself as a craftsman, posterity has judged him to be a genuinely gifted composer. He provided nineteenth-century Italy with an opera form especially tailored to the Romantic temperament—colorful plots, dramatic persuasiveness, ear-titillating arias, exciting orchestral scores—and this opera type served as a fine model for future composers.

[1] Letter to Ferdinando Giudicini, dated February 12, 1851.

Rossini, his Italian contemporaries, and his disciples liked the kind of singing called *bel canto,* literally the art of beautiful singing. More specifically, bel canto indicates virtuoso singing, the *stile fiorito* (flowery style) in which the melodic line is embellished with myriad ornaments: arpeggios, mordents, appoggiaturas, trills.

Rossini ventured into opera form in 1810 with a one-act comic opera, and he produced his last opera (*William Tell*) in 1829. During 19 years of opera writing he composed 38 operas. Not all of these were wholly original, for he often resorted to *pasticcio* (patchwork) opera—that is, an opera containing some original music along with successful arias and ensembles from earlier operas. If one of Rossini's arias, overtures, or other selections proved especially successful, he would use it again in another opera, and sometimes even a third time.

Currently the Rossini repertoire is known primarily by certain popular overtures or arias (except in Italy, where many Rossini operas are still presented). Although it is an excellent example of early-nineteenth-century grand opera, Rossini's *Guillaume Tell* (William Tell), written in 1829 to a French libretto, is rarely performed outside of Italy; yet its overture has become a standard orchestral composition. This overture offers wide contrasts in its different sections, and it contains a good example of the so-called Rossini crescendo—a passage repeated several times, usually with increasing tempo, higher pitch, and fuller orchestration. Rossini's treatment of the orchestra was unusual for his time. He kept it properly in the background when accompanying solos and then used it freely to unify dramatic action and sustain excitement. This orchestral skill has upheld the popularity of many overtures and ensembles even though the operas themselves have not endured.

Two operas written in 1817 are represented today principally through their overtures: *La Cenerentola* (Cinderella), a rather realistic setting of the fairy story, and *La gazza ladra* (The Thieving Magpie), a tragedy caused by the thieving practices of a magpie. The overtures to these operas and the one written for *La scala di seta* (The Silken Ladder, 1812) are exceptionally charming.

Premiered in 1816, *Il barbiere di Siviglia* (The Barber of Seville) continues to be Rossini's outstanding opera. Its libretto derives from the first play in Beaumarchais' dramatic trilogy (Mozart had already set the second play, *The Marriage of Figaro*). Rossini's *Il Barbiere* is an opera-buffa masterpiece; its rapid-fire action and witty inventiveness hold the listener's interest. The overture is very pleasing but hardly original, for Rossini had used it twice before in serious operas: *Aureliano in Palmira* (1813) and *Elisabetta, regina d'Inghilterra* (1815).

The plot centers on Count Almaviva's love for Rosina, a ward of Dr. Bartolo, an old scoundrel who wants her for himself. Figaro brings the lovers together after many hilarious, ludicrous situations. Some of the opera's best-known excerpts are found in the first act. "Ecco ridente in cielo" (Lo, smiling in the eastern sky), is a serenade sung to Rosina by the count. "Largo al factotum" (Make way for the factotum), Figaro's famous patter aria, is the whirlwind lament of an overworked jack-of-all-trades. "Una voce poco fà" (A little voice I heard just now) is primarily a florid display piece for soprano (Rosina); it is followed by "Io sono docile" (With mild and docile air). "La calunnia" (Calumny) is a flawless buffa aria in which Rosina's music teacher tries to help Bartolo thwart the lovers; he advocates slander in a solo remarkable for its descriptive crescendo.

Vincenzo Bellini

Two of Rossini's contemporaries, Bellini and Donizetti, enjoyed their share of fame in nineteenth-century Italy, but their operas are heard only occasionally now, particularly outside the Italian peninsula.

Vincenzo Bellini (1801–1835) was born in Sicily. He became a successful opera composer while still a student at the Naples Conservatory, but he died before realizing his full potential. Bellini never achieved Rossini's mature workmanship, and he neglected orchestration in his operas. Despite his inadequacies, Bellini is remembered as one of the greatest exponents of bel canto style. He had a gift for graceful melody and a talent for dramatic projection. His suave, expressive melodic line (Ex. 19:1) greatly influenced composers such as Chopin and Liszt.

Ex. 19:1. Bellini: ***Melody from I Puritani***

Bellini's most popular operas among the ten he wrote are *La Sonnambula* (The Sleepwalker, 1831), a masterpiece of florid style; *Norma* (1831), which contains one of the great bel canto arias of all time—the "Casta diva" (Chaste Goddess); and *I Puritani* (The Puritans, 1835), which is Bellini's most dramatic, mature opera and shows Rossini's influence.

Gaetano Donizetti

Gaetano Donizetti (1797–1848) wrote almost 70 operas within about 26 years. His prodigious melodic gifts compared with Bellini's, but his harmonies were less monotonous and his orchestration more meticulously worked out. He supplied grateful roles to a golden age of singers. At the same time his music shows dreary accompaniments and more than one example of stilted, feeble passage work. Although in his era Italian comic opera was disappearing from the stage, he wrote three fine works in this form: *L'elisir d'amore* (The Elixir of Love, 1832); *La fille du régiment* (The Daughter of the Regiment, 1840); and *Don Pasquale* (1843). These are occasionally staged today.

Donizetti's *Lucia di Lammermoor* (1835), however, is still presented regularly. The libretto, based on Sir Walter Scott's novel *The Bride of Lammermoor,* tells of two lovers tragically separated. This opera belongs to the prima donna, a coloratura soprano who must cope with the rippling scales and arpeggios of typical bel canto style, sometimes accompanied by flute obbligato.

Lucia has two celebrated excerpts. The sextet "Chi mi frena in tal momento" (Who dares to stop me at such a moment?) is sung by the six principal characters as the tragic heroine signs an undesirable marriage contract because she thinks her lover Edgardo has deserted her. His sudden appearance is the signal for the sextet, one of the most spectacular ensemble numbers in operatic history. Lucia's lover exclaims "Who dares to stop me at such a moment?" while

Lucia's brother Enrico retorts "Who dares to restrain my fury?" Lucia enters with "I had hoped that terror would end my life," while Raimondo, the chaplain, comments "What a terrible moment!" The objectionable suitor Arturo declares "I cannot even speak," and Lucia's companion Alisa bemoans "Like a faded rose, she seems more dead than alive." This is an extraordinary example of effective ensemble writing.

In the third act, after Lucia has lost her reason and killed her unwanted husband, she enacts her famous mad scene, fifteen minutes of coloratura virtuosity. The unhappy bride sings an elaborate *scéna,* a tour de force demanding the full resources of even the finest soprano.

Giuseppe Verdi

Opera could survive on meager plots and sparkling virtuoso arias for just so long. Giuseppe Verdi (1813–1901) introduced a sorely needed naturalism and simplicity to the medium. Working painstakingly, he needed nine years and twelve operas to create his first unqualified success.

Verdi was more than a great opera composer. He was an ardent patriot who participated in the events leading to Italy's unification under Victor Emmanuel, King of Piedmont. As a matter of fact, Verdi's name was used as a rallying cry: *Evivva Verdi* actually signified *Evivva V*ittorio *E*mmanuele *R*e *D'I*talia (Long live Victor Emmanuel, King of Italy).

Verdi sought to base his music on genuine human feelings, creating melodies to convey these emotions, not merely to entertain. His style emphasizes human passions expressed in song, and everything else—melodies, orchestration, fantasy—is subordinated to that end. He asserts authority through simplicity. The naturalness and vigor in his melodic lines create sensuous, powerful music that is universally appealing.

Verdi was explicit in his approach to composition. He declared:

> I believe in inspiration . . . I look for Art in all its manifestations.[2]
>
> I wish that every young man when he begins to write music would not concern himself with being a melodist, a harmonist, a realist, an idealist or a futurist or any other such devilish pedantic things. Melody and harmony should be simply tools in the hands of the artist, with which he writes music.[3]

Verdi's early operas retain the recitative and aria tradition, but gradually he adopted the practice of using through-composed sections. He placed lyrical arias in dramatically strategic positions and in general followed a rather standardized plan: a prayer (sometimes with chorus) frequently opens the fourth act; a duet occurs in the middle of the third act; acts two and three usually have extended finales. In his last works, however, Verdi produced an almost continual flow of music, an approach similar to that found in Richard Wagner's mature operas.

The vocal lines always dominate Verdi's operas, for his remarkable melodic talent created superb arias, some veritably exploding with exuberance or passion and others quietly attaining sublime expression (Ex. 19:2).

[2] Letter to Camille du Locle, dated December 7, 1869.

[3] Letter to Count Opprandino Arrivabene, dated July 14, 1875.

Ill. 19:3. ***Puccini,*** **La Bohème,** ***Musetta's "Waltz." Royal Opera House, Covent Garden. Courtesy of Donald Southern.***

depends on his Italianate vocal line and novel harmonies, the latter being so distinctive and personal that they can be instantly associated with Puccini. He had an instinct for the theater, he knew how to write especially well for voice, and he possessed a poetic imagination—all attributes that ensured his success as a theatrical composer. Frequently he sustains excitement by using motives or short melodic flourishes as identification themes that keep reappearing throughout an opera without any noticeable change in character.

Puccini's highly successful *La Bohème* (1896) is somewhat like Verdi's *La Traviata* in that it is a chamber-opera type. Puccini makes each character in this credible love story a real person. Events move rapidly; a first-act love scene offers opportunity for three of the most popular portions in the whole work: the tenor aria "Che gelida manina" (Your little hand is frozen) ; the tender soprano aria "Mi chiamano Mimi" (They call me Mimi) ; and the exquisite love duet "O soave fanciulla" (O gentle maiden) . Act II contains an outstanding example of verismo in Musetta's "Waltz" (Ill. 19:3) , where Musetta sings her solo while her friends engage in lively conversation.

Puccini's next opera, *La Tosca* (1900) , is a chilling mixture of murder, torture, and vindictiveness. Here the composer proves that he was aware of contemporary music; he experimented with whole-tone scales and created unorthodox harmonic relationships. Throughout the opera he paints a series of climaxes with such beloved excerpts as "Recondita armonia" (Hidden harmonies) , "Vissi d'arte" (I live for art and love) , and "E lucevan le stelle" (And the stars were shining) .

Puccini's *Madame Butterfly* (1904) also remains a great favorite. These three—*Bohème, Tosca,* and *Butterfly*—preserve his name and fame. Based on John Luther Long's story and David Belasco's play, *Butterfly* is more romantic than realistic, possibly due to its exotic oriental atmosphere. Although it oddly combines an American-Japanese story with an Italian score, the music is beautiful, and passages like Cio-Cio-San's paean of hope "Un bel dì, vedremo" (One fine day he'll return) reveal melodic genius.

FRANCE

During the last part of the eighteenth century none of the opera composers working in France could equal Austria's Mozart. French operas from this period are scarcely remembered, and although many composers achieved fame in their time, their reputations have not held up. The operas produced in France from around 1800 to 1850 have also been neglected, even in France, because they are difficult to stage. So-called French grand opera typically suggests a scenic spectacle and a musical extravaganza; its heroic subject matter, usually drawn from history, necessitates elaborate stage effects, and the action often needs large casts to carry out the dramatic effect, especially vast choruses in important roles. It was not until the second half of the nineteenth century that France produced operas that have survived.

Apart from grand opera, the terms defining French musical stage works are confusing. *Opéra comique* originated in the mid-eighteenth century and relied on spoken dialogue, tuneful songs, and comic or moral plots. Gradually this type changed countenance, and by the mid-nineteenth century it differed from *opéra lyrique* only in the fact that it contained some spoken dialogue rather than continuous music with recitatives. Often even the spoken dialogue was converted into sung recitative. Lyric opera, a typical late-nineteenth-century French product, falls between operetta and grand opera. Constructed on a smaller scale, lyric opera is more emotionally introspective and more unified.

French operetta, a frivolous form of *opéra comique,* became extremely popular in France and for a long period set the tone for light opera everywhere. Jacques Offenbach (1819–1880), who controlled the French stage during the Second Empire, is the most celebrated composer in this field. He wrote more than 90 operettas within 25 years, most of which are now forgotten; and the rest—such as *Orphée aux enfers* (1858) and *La belle Hélène* (1864)—survive solely through their delightful orchestral overtures.

After so many successful light operas, Offenbach wanted to write a serious opera. In 1880 he began *Les contes d'Hoffmann* (The Tales of Hoffmann), his only opera sung throughout, but he died before it was produced in February 1881. This opera is based on three autobiographical tales by E. T. A. Hoffmann; it is a series of contrasting episodes. Among its high points are Olympia's "Doll Song," a tour de force for coloratura soprano, and the "Barcarolle," a duet sung to the gentle swaying of a gondola.

Charles Gounod

The master of French Romantic opera is Charles Gounod (1818–1893), an imaginative composer with a talent for interesting harmonies and suave melodies. He composed the first of his 12 operas when he was 33; his fourth opera—*Faust* (1859)—is his best.

The legend about an old German scientist-philosopher who sells his soul in return for youth has long intrigued dramatists and composers. Gounod's

Ill. 19:4. ***Gounod,* Faust, *"Jewel" scene. Sadler's Wells Opera. Courtesy of Reg Wilson.***

operatic setting is by far the most prevalent musical version and in many ways the best. The opera is based on the first part of Goethe's drama, although Gounod's French librettists sentimentalized the text. Even with a weak libretto, this opera is a masterpiece. Gounod's orchestration is superb and his special gift for emotionally involved melody is always in evidence. Almost every aria has something special about it: the "Waltz" has an appealing, easily remembered tune; Marguerite's "Jewel Song" (Ill. 19:4) is a virtuoso study; Mephistopheles' "Serenade" is artfully demoniac; and Faust's "Salut! demeure chaste et pure" (All hail, thou dwelling pure and holy) is a purely lyric soliloquy.

Georges Bizet

The only serious rival to *Faust* appeared in 1875 when Georges Bizet (1838–1875) presented *Carmen,* his one unquestionable operatic masterwork and a more plausible opera than *Faust.* Because Prosper Mérimée's original novel about a promiscuous gypsy girl was considered too bold for public performance, the characters had to be softened, but the libretto is exceptionally well done.

This opera musically follows the progressive humiliation and degradation that the gypsy Carmen inflicts on one of the victims of her passion, the soldier Don José. Carmen is still Mérimée's dissolute, seductive girl of the streets when she sings her enchanting "Habanera" and "Seguidilla" (Act I), and a violent gypsy as she leads the frenetic "Chanson Bohème" (Act II). Don José, whose weak character she destroys, engenders sympathy as he sings his lyrical "Flower Song" (Act II—see Ill. 19:5). Offsetting the character of Don José, the bullfighter is a braggadocio whose swaggering has been immortalized in the "Toreador Song" (Ill. 19:6) from Act II. Bizet deftly creates musical characteriza-

Ill. 19:5. *Bizet,* Carmen, *"Flower Song." Royal Opera House, Covent Garden. Courtesy of Anthony Crickmay.*

tions from the libretto and furthermore makes his listeners believe that this is authentic Spanish music.

> Fundamental, however, is the firm, concise, and exact musical expression of every situation in terms of which only a French composer would be capable: the typical Gallic union of economy of material, perfect grasp of means, vivid

Ill. 19:6. *Bizet,* Carmen, *"Toreador Song." Royal Opera House, Covent Garden. Courtesy of Roger Wood.*

orchestral color, and an electric vitality and rhythmic verve, together with an objective, cool, yet passionate sensualism.[5]

RUSSIA

Native Russian opera began before the end of the eighteenth century. Previously most operas performed in Russia had been written by Italians, many of whom lived there. Russian nationalist opera achieved importance in the early nineteenth century through such works as Mikhail Glinka's (1804–1857) *A Life for the Tsar* (1836). Peter Ilich Tchaikovsky's (1840–1893) operas include two that have occasional performances outside Russia: *Eugen Onegin* (1879) and *The Queen of Spades* (1890). And among Nikolai Rimsky-Korsakov's (1844–1908) several operas, *The Golden Cockerel* (1907) contains some delightful passages, such as the "Hymn to the Sun." Alexander Borodin's (1834–1887) *Prince Igor* (completed by his friends and first performed in 1890) will endure if only for the colorful, barbaric "Polovtsian Dances."

Modest Mussorgsky

To date the greatest opera composed by a Russian is Modest Mussorgsky's (1839–1881) *Boris Godounov* (1874). The composer also wrote the libretto, using Pushkin's drama of the same title. Boris Godounov was a real historical figure, but of course artistic license permits the libretto to depart from history, at times rather noticeably. Whether fantasy or fact, the operatic character of the half-mad Boris, a basso role, is one of the most colorful in all the repertoire.

Mussorgsky uses a type of dramatic recitative that melts almost imperceptibly into more lyrical, songlike sections. His melodies show unusual intervals, irregular phrase structure, and an archaic modal vocabulary. He frequently repeats short melodic patterns to construct a more expansive melodic line. He also uses unusual chord combinations, whose harmonies derive from modal scales. His choice of harmonic progressions often creates an impressionistic effect.

Boris Godounov displays splendid orchestral color, particularly in the great "Coronation Scene" from the Prologue: Boris, about to be crowned czar, is greeted by great tolling bells, the people sing a magnificent folk chorus, and the procession moves into the cathedral.

At the end Boris, apparently insane and paralyzed by fear and remorse, realizes that he is dying. This death scene marks one of opera's most thrilling episodes, unsurpassed in emotional intensity and dramatic impact.

GERMANY

Beethoven's opera *Fidelio* did not establish an operatic tradition in Germany. The intense composer, lacking a sense of the theater, apparently found little challenge in the details requisite for good opera. His arias are not memora-

[5] Donald J. Grout, *A Short History of Opera,* Second Edition (New York: Columbia University Press, 1965), p. 427. Reprinted by permission.

ble, and the listener rarely feels emotionally transported by inherent dramatic persuasion. The only music preserving *Fidelio* for the average listener is that which Beethoven discarded, the *Leonore Overtures No. 2* and *No. 3*.

Carl Maria von Weber (1786–1826) made a beginning for German Romantic opera. Weber was vastly talented. He knew how to set melodrama to music, how to evoke atmosphere, how to emphasize orchestral color; in short, he knew how to write for the stage. In three of his operas—*Der Freischütz* (1821), *Euryanthe* (1823), and *Oberon* (1826)—he created an operatic vocabulary that might have carried Germany into first place among her foreign competitors. Yet of the three only *Der Freischütz* is occasionally performed today.

Richard Wagner

The composer who alone dominated German opera during the nineteenth century was Richard Wagner (1813–1883). From 1836 until 1882 Wagner molded this musical form to his personal concept, stamping it with a persuasive, revolutionary aesthetic that gradually influenced opera all over the world.

Wagner's haphazard education in Leipzig awakened in him a deep interest in drama—especially Shakespeare, Schiller, and the Greek classics—and a devotion to Beethoven's music. At 20 he was appointed chorus master at the Würzburg opera house and in 1834 opera conductor at Magdeburg; from there he moved on to Königsberg (1836) and Riga (1837). His mature life is a story of frequent moves, love affairs, and financial and political troubles. In Paris for four years (1839–1842) he supported himself with journalism and musical hack work and did some composing. In Dresden between 1842 and 1849 he produced two operas: *Der fliegende Holländer* (The Flying Dutchman), an initial failure, and *Tannhäuser,* which was successful. *Lohengrin* was premiered in Weimar in 1850. Exiled from Germany for a decade because of his political activities, Wagner returned in 1864 to settle in Munich under the patronage of the new King of Bavaria, Ludwig II. Gradually Wagner became the greatest name in German music. In 1872 in Bayreuth he laid the cornerstone for a theater especially designed to stage his operas; the theater opened in 1876 with performances of the four operas of *Der Ring des Nibelungen* (The Ring of the Nibelungs).

Wagner's ideas about opera composition took years to formulate; he experimented with them in fragmentary form in several operas before achieving their ultimate expression in the *Ring.* He decided that traditional opera used the wrong subject matter, for he believed that legend offered the finest dramatic material. He was also convinced that opera had slighted drama in favor of music; in his view the music should enhance the textual poetry, and to emphasize this theory he called his later operas *music dramas.*

Since the poetry had to be emotional just as the music was emotional, Wagner turned poet-composer in order to create librettos to suit his purposes. Early in his career he wrote:

> I really lay no claim to a poet's reputation and assure you I at first took to writing for myself of necessity, since no good librettos were offered me. I could not now, however, compose on another's operatic text for the following reasons. It is not my way to choose some story or other at pleasure, get it versified, and then begin to consider how to make suitable music for it. For this mode of procedure I should need to be twice inspired, which is impossible. The way I set to work is quite different. In the first place I am only attracted to matter the

poetic and musical significance of which strike me simultaneously. Before I go on to write a verse or plot or scene I am already intoxicated by the musical aroma of my subject. I have every note, every characteristic motif in my head, so that when the versification is complete and the scenes arranged, the opera is practically finished for me; the detailed musical treatment is just a peaceful meditative after-labour, the real moment of creation having long preceded it.[6]

Although Wagner sometimes used the traditional operatic ensemble of aria, duet, and chorus, he wanted to discard this general form. To preserve what he considered to be essential continuity, he evolved a type of declamatory melody, a vocal counterpoint to the orchestra. At the same time he assigned the orchestra a more active role in the drama.

With his early operas—*Flying Dutchman* and *Tannhäuser*—Wagner provided a climax to nineteenth-century German Romantic opera. Then he proceeded to incorporate his many advanced ideas into his succeeding works, thus transforming the whole approach to opera composition.

The text for *Lohengrin* (1850) comes from a medieval legend about a knight of the Holy Grail who champions Elsa, noblewoman of Brabant, when she is accused of murdering her brother. Wagner emphasizes philosophical theories; the knight perhaps symbolizes divine love, longing for reciprocation; Elsa represents the human element, incapable of unquestioning trust.

Wagner enlarged the system of motives he had already used in *Tannhäuser;* for instance, he reintroduces a melodic phrase whenever he needs its symbolic meaning in the action. A declamatory style predominates, except for a few separable items such as "Elsa's Dream" and the "Wedding March." Wagner's orchestration predicts his ultimate aesthetic; he divides the orchestra into its constituent choirs of sound, but as yet the harmonies are basically diatonic.

The "Prelude" to Act I and the "Introduction" to Act III are beautiful examples of his orchestral style during this period.

Very likely the original story of *Tristan und Isolde* (1865) has roots in Celtic legend. Wagner adapted his version from a thirteenth-century epic poem by Gottfried von Strassburg. As drama *Tristan* is disturbingly static. Nothing happens on the stage for long intervals and what action does occur is short and terse. External events are simplified, the real action is almost entirely subjective and is expressed by the music. Words often melt into music.

Wagner's musical language in *Tristan* is more complex than that in the earlier operas. This advance is noticeable in the opening "Prelude," where a series of highly emotional passages is expressed through consistent chromaticism. A few motives serve as accent points, but generally the continuously flowing melodic textures form a design of three large movements or acts, each developing its own dominant idea. In Act I the magic potion represents love. Isolde's extinguishing the torch in Act II symbolizes night. Act III is partially a tragic recapitulation of the first act. Isolde's poignant "Liebestod" proclaims the triumph of love over grief and death.

Wagner reverted to an earlier style in composing *Die Meistersinger von Nürnberg* (The Mastersingers of Nuremberg, 1868). It is his only comic opera and it is good comedy. The story takes place in the sixteenth century, when tradesmen of the Mastersinger guilds wrote verses and staged singing contests. Wagner used at least one real person as a character: the cobbler-poet-composer Hans Sachs (1494–1576). *Die Meistersinger* is Wagner's most human opera and

[6] Letter to Karl Gaillard, dated January 30, 1844.

the easiest to understand. Musical motives exist, but the harmony reverts to diatonic quality. There are several arias, ensemble numbers, and choruses. The most distinctive melody in this comedy is Walter's "Prize Song," which is hinted at in the delightful "Overture," rehearsed in Act III as an aria and as a quintet, and heard again when the opera comes to its felicitous end.

During his long exile in Switzerland, Wagner took time to clarify his new ideas on music and the theater, and he wrote a series of essays, the most significant being *Oper und Drama* (*Opera and Drama,* published in 1851). These new ideas show up very clearly in *Der Ring des Nibelungen* (1869). To assemble his story, Wagner combined elements from two Germanic myths: the Siegfried story and the downfall of the Teutonic gods. His first dramatic text was called *Siegfried's Death* (which later became *Die Götterdämmerung*). This finished, he felt the need for another to explain the background of the first. Eventually he created four: a prelude called *Das Rheingold* (The Rhinegold); *Die Walküre* (The Valkyries); *Siegfried;* and *Die Götterdämmerung* (The Twilight of the Gods). He finished the text of the tetralogy in 1852, and the first complete performance of the operas took place in Bayreuth in 1876.

For this his greatest operatic venture, Wagner employed myth as subject matter. To give these mythical texts as much force as possible, he created symbols: sometimes they are objects, such as "Gold," "Valhalla," and the "Sword"; elsewhere they are people: Brünnhilde, Siegfried, Wotan.

Wagner believed that poetry and music should be mutually interdependent within a dramatic setting. For him music was a vitally subjective experience, and he felt that it was drama's function to give outward expression to this inner emotion. Since music interpreted the inner action—a continuous process—the music should be continuous; hence the consistent declamatory or "open" style of his mature operas.

To achieve this endless stream of melody, Wagner employed constant modulation and chromaticism and avoided cadences. To delineate his symbols, he stretched his *leitmotiv* (leading motive) theory to its ultimate extremes. Each motive is short—from one to four measures—and contains both melodic and harmonic elements. Each motive is associated with either a basic dramatic idea or an individual. Whenever the action needs the idea or when the individual faces some crisis, the pertinent motive reappears, usually in altered form, for each motive is susceptible to change and symphonic development.

For example, in the first *Ring* opera, *Das Rheingold,* a motive (Ex. 19:3)

Ex. 19:3. Wagner: ***Das Rheingold: Valhalla motive***

appears in connection with Valhalla, the newly built castle of the gods. When, in the second act of *Die Götterdämmerung,* the gods' destruction is prophesied, the Valhalla motive is transformed (Ex. 19:4).

The leitmotivs are rarely sung. They appear in the orchestra, for the gravitational center of thematic material is there rather than on the stage. Vocal lines form a counterpoint to the instrumental parts.

Wagner's orchestration in the *Ring* is amazing. He takes advantage of all the orchestra's resources, at times calling for as many as six harps, three flutes,

Ex. 19:4. Wagner: *Die Götterdämmerung*

three oboes, three bassoons, eight horns, four drums, and so on. Minutely marked dynamics indicate his fastidious approach.

To hear the complete *Ring* requires four consecutive evenings with a minimum of four hours each time. The operas are almost never performed as a unit outside Bayreuth. In fact, only the largest opera houses attempt even one Wagnerian opera in a season, so great are the performing demands. Episodes are performed out of context, however, sometimes with the original vocal lines, sometimes in an orchestral synthesis. The "Prelude" from *Das Rheingold* is often programmed. The second opera is more popular because the "Ride of the Valkyries" is gloriously barbaric and its finale, the "Magic Fire Scene," is impressively magical. In Act II of *Siegfried* the orchestral interlude called "Forest Murmurs" creates the sensation of woodland sounds. The last opera, in which Valhalla and the gods are consumed, is known especially for the orchestral interlude "Siegfried's Rhine Journey."

After the *Ring,* Wagner wrote just one more opera: *Parsifal* (1882). Taken from the legend of the Holy Grail, it contains some of Wagner's most beautiful music—for example, the "Prelude" and the "Good Friday Spell"—but as drama it is less compelling than the *Ring.*

Why have Wagner's operas persisted? They are verbose; the music practically obliterates any textual comprehension, even if one understands German; and there are few arias to delight the ear.

In Germany they have retained their lofty position because they appeal to national pride. And they are attractive to foreigners as magnificent stage spectacles with dramatic dignity. Musically, no other composer has endowed his art with such frank sensuality. Wagner's music is descriptive and distinctive; it is unique in its approach and unique in its impact on the human spirit.

SUMMARY

Opera was a favorite musical form of the nineteenth century, for through this medium Romantic composers could synthesize various musical and nonmusical elements into one stimulating artistic experience. In general, Romantic operas were extravaganzas dealing with heroic, melodramatic, or sometimes supernatural subjects.

Early Italian opera emphasized bel canto style in its virtuoso arias and flamboyant ensembles. Later in the century Verdi's works added dramatic unity and musical profundity to Italian opera. And in the last decade of the nineteenth century, Realism (verismo) exercised a strong influence on opera form.

The golden age of French opera arrived with the second half of the century. *Opéra lyrique, opéra comique,* and operetta were all popular, and

French composers responded to public interest by creating a generous repertoire of stage works, many of which are still performed today.

German opera began to develop when composers wrote Romantic operas early in the century. Then the music dramas of Richard Wagner—in essence a musical revolution—produced a lasting effect on opera form.

Nationalism provided stimulus for opera composition, especially in Russia, where composers like Mussorgsky created original, important works.

FOR DISCUSSION AND ASSIGNMENT

1. Listen to several of Rossini's opera overtures. Do you think they were meant to have any connection with the operas they introduce? If not, what was their function?
2. Do you think that operas should be sung in English translation? What are the advantages and disadvantages?
3. Do you think that Wagner successfully carried out his principles of operatic composition?
4. Choose a nineteenth-century opera. Listen to it (or at least a recording of highlights) and discuss it as a musical work of art: treatment of the orchestra; types of arias; effectiveness of musical characterization; dramatic impact; use of chorus or ballet, if any; and other characteristics that may exist in it.

FOR FURTHER READING

Dean, Winton. *Bizet.* New York: Collier Books, 1962. PB. For anyone interested in an intelligent analysis of *Carmen* and a general discussion of Bizet's other significant works, this book is important and useful.

Dent, Edward J. *Opera.* Baltimore, Md.: Penguin Books, 1949. A Pelican PB. This is the best short history of opera available.

Goldman, Albert, and Evert Sprinchorn, editors. *Wagner on Music and Drama.* New York: E. P. Dutton & Co., Inc., 1964. PB. The editors have prepared a compendium of Richard Wagner's prose works. The style and content make for rather heavy reading but this book is indispensable for understanding the composer.

Hussey, Dyneley. *Verdi.* New York: Collier Books, 1962. PB. This brief volume in the Collier Great Composers Series gives an adequate and interesting picture of Verdi the man, the musician, and the patriot.

Jacobs, Robert L. *Wagner.* New York: Collier Books, 1962. PB. The literature on Richard Wagner is of course voluminous, and Mr. Jacobs' small book only scratches the surface. Nonetheless, it is an intriguing introduction to a very complex personality.

Toye, Francis. *Rossini: A Study in Tragi-Comedy.* New York: W. W. Norton & Co., Inc., 1963. PB. Originally published in 1934, this book remains the definitive study of Rossini and his music.

Opera Handbooks

Numerous handbooks relating the stories, principal arias, and other details of the better-known operas are available. Here are a few:

Cross, Milton. *Stories of the Great Operas.* New York: Washington Square Press, Inc., 1955. PB.

Fellner, Rudolph. *Opera Themes and Plots.* New York: Simon & Schuster, 1958. An Essandess PB.

McSpadden, J. Walker. *Grand Opera in Digest Form.* New York: Thomas Y. Crowell Co., 1954. An Apollo PB.

Peltz, Mary Ellis, ed. *Introduction to Opera,* 2nd Edition. New York: Barnes & Noble, Inc., 1963. PB.

Simon, Henry W. *100 Great Operas and Their Stories.* New York: Doubleday and Co., Inc., 1960. A Dolphin PB.

Simon, Henry W., and Abraham Veinus. *The Pocket Book of Great Operas.* New York: Pocket Books, Inc., 1949. PB.

20 Romantic Music in Austria and Germany

During the winter of 1880 I went . . . to Hamburg, and we chanced by good luck on a concert at which Brahms played his Second Concerto in B flat, then a novelty. The reception given to the composer by his native town was as enthusiastic as we anticipated. His pianoforte playing was not so much that of a finished pianist, as of a composer who despised virtuosity.

SIR CHARLES VILLIERS STANFORD
Pages from an Unwritten Diary (1914)

JOHANNES BRAHMS AND THE CLASSIC IDEAL

Years have passed—almost as many as I once devoted to the editing of these pages—ten indeed, since I have made myself heard in this place so rich in memories. Despite intense productive work I often felt impelled to continue. Many new and significant talents have arisen; a new power in music seems to announce itself; the intimation has been proved true by many aspiring artists of the last years, even though their work may be known only in comparatively limited circles. To me, who followed the progress of these chosen ones with the greatest sympathy, it seemed that under these circumstances there inevitably must appear a musician called to give expression to his times in ideal fashion; a musician who would reveal his mastery not in a gradual evolution, but like Athene would spring fully armed from Zeus's head. And such a one *has* appeared; a young man over whose cradle Graces and Heroes have stood watch. His name is *Johannes Brahms,* and he comes from Hamburg, where he has been working in quiet obscurity, though instructed in the most difficult statutes of his art by an excellent and enthusiastically devoted teacher. A well-known and honored master recently recommended him to me. Even outwardly he bore the marks proclaiming: "This is a chosen one." Sitting at the piano he began to disclose wonderful regions to us. We were drawn into even more enchanting spheres. Besides, he is a player of genius who can make of the piano an orchestra of lamenting and loudly jubilant voices. There were sonatas, veiled symphonies rather; songs the poetry of which would be understood even without words, although a profound vocal melody runs through them all; single piano pieces, some of them turbulent in spirit while graceful in form; again sonatas for violin

> and piano, string quartets, every work so different from the others that it seemed to stream from its own individual source. And then it was as though, rushing like a torrent, they were all united by him into a single waterfall the cascades of which were overarched by a peaceful rainbow, while butterflies played about its borders and the voices of nightingales obliged.
>
> Should he direct his magic wand where the powers of the masses in chorus and orchestra may lend him their forces, we can look forward to even more wondrous glimpses of the secret world of spirits. May the highest genius strengthen him to this end. Since he possesses yet another facet of genius—that of modesty—we may surmise that it will come to pass. His fellow musicians hail him on his first step through a world where wounds perhaps await him, but also palms and laurels. We welcome a strong champion in him.
>
> There exists a secret bond between kindred spirits in every period. You who belong together, close your ranks ever more tightly, that the Truth of Art may shine more clearly, diffusing joy and blessings over all things.[1]

Thus Robert Schumann, in his last and most famous article ("New Paths") for the *Neue Zeitschrift für Musik* (Oct. 23, 1853), prophesied the future of the young Johannes Brahms (1833–1897), who became one of the two foremost composers in nineteenth-century Germany. Richard Wagner was the other.

Brahms is Schumann's rightful artistic and spiritual successor in the music world. A "Romantic Classicist," he was a consummate musical craftsman who fortunately happened to be born in the "Romantic" nineteenth century; hence, under his able touch seemingly contradictory attributes of Romantic and Classic merge successfully in his music—a happy fusion of poetry and sound workmanship, a delightful mixture of Classical form wrapped in the multicolored hues of German Romanticism.

Brahms's life seems prosaic and colorless. He was born in Hamburg and while quite young revealed that seriousness and tenacity which typically characterize the North German. His father, a moderately successful orchestral musician, had married a woman 17 years his senior and also his intellectual superior.

Brahms received lessons in piano and composition and quickly acquired skill in playing; he also composed a good deal, but later in life he destroyed these immature works. As a young man he learned much about stringed instruments through professional associations with the violinists Reményi, with whom he briefly toured North Germany, and Joachim, who became his close friend. His affectionate ties with the Schumann family continued after Robert Schumann's death; Brahms remained a dear friend to Clara Schumann until she died 40 years later, and she exercised a profound influence on his life.

Brahms's reputation grew rapidly. From 1857 to 1859 he directed the seasonal court concerts and the choral society of the Prince of Lippe-Detmold; he spent the year 1863 as conductor of the Vienna *Singakademie;* his final appointment lasted from 1872 to 1875, when he served as conductor of the *Gesellschaft der Musikfreunde*. Despite other tempting positions offered after 1875, Brahms stayed in Vienna for the rest of his life, living on the income from his compositions and making occasional tours as pianist and conductor.

He had many loyal friends even though his gruffness and gaucherie often caused brief estrangements. Under his rough exterior he was a kindly, sentimental, and modest man who gave freely of his money and affection to many who crossed his path. Although on several occasions he seemed to be on the verge of marriage, he remained a bachelor all his life.

[1] From *On Music and Musicians,* pp. 252–254, by Robert Schumann, translated by Paul Rosenfeld and edited by Konrad Wolff. Copyright 1946 by Pantheon Books, Inc. Reprinted by permission of Pantheon Books, a Division of Random House, Inc.

Brahms attempted almost every media except opera; the Brahms catalog lists 122 opus numbers and many other works (chiefly arrangements) without numbers. His most ambitious choral work is the *German Requiem* (1868) for soloists, chorus, and orchestra, a selection of Biblical passages set to music. Another very distinguished work is the *Alto Rhapsody* (1869) for contralto solo, men's chorus, and orchestra. And one of his most charming compositions is a collection of waltzes—the *Liebeslieder Waltzer* (1869)—for piano duet with optional mixed vocal quartet. In the smaller vocal idioms Brahms composed more than 200 fine lieder, of which the lasting favorite is the lovely *Wiegenlied* (1868).

Brahms produced four symphonies—each a masterwork—and several shorter orchestral works, such as his two overtures and the *Haydn Variations.* He also makes full use of the orchestra in his four concertos—two for piano, one for violin, and a double concerto for violin and cello. An expert musical craftsman, he composed many fine chamber works and exquisitely wrought piano compositions.

In his music he shunned bravura and brilliance for their own sake, seeking instead to create a durable foundation from which he fashioned tonal compositions distinguished for craftsmanship, vitality, and above all an innate musical coherence.

Brahms's music is often difficult to play and frequently difficult to listen to because his musical language stemmed from a universal concept of music and craftsmanship. As a result, his music at times transcends any confining performance medium. Like Chopin and Schumann, Brahms wrote highly personalized music. His works, with passages in thirds, sixths, and octaves, and doublings of these intervals, often show a thick texture. Many chamber-music compositions have an orchestral quality, but whether this quality was achieved deliberately is hard to say. He had the advantage of possessing a superior rhythmic sense, and his music abounds in syncopations, polyrhythms, and other similar devices of rhythmic transformation. One prominent feature of his style is its contrapuntal character, which should be expected when we know that Brahms enjoyed playing Bach's fugues, often transposing them from one key to another at sight.

Piano Music

The solo piano works span 40 years. Brahms began in 1853 with *Sonata, Opus 1, in C Major* and continued intermittently until 1893, when he completed his final piano composition, the *Klavierstücke, Opus 119* (Piano Pieces).

Some interesting observations can be gleaned from the Brahms music catalog. Among the first five works he published there are three sonatas—*Opuses 1, 2,* and *5*—but after that he never again attempted a piano sonata. The catalog also reveals that his piano works fall chronologically into three rather distinct groups. The first group includes the three sonatas and the *Scherzo, Opus 4,* which—structurally at least—qualifies as a sonata movement. A second group comprising four opus numbers (*Opus 9, Opus 21, Nos. 1* and *2, Opus 24,* and *Opus 35*) consists of variations on themes by Schumann, Paganini, Handel, and Brahms himself, and one based on a Hungarian song. The third group, covering works scattered from *Opus 76* through *Opus 119,* lists mostly short character pieces clustered into collections under such titles as *Fantasien* or *Klavierstücke.*

Thus Brahms in his creative career passed from the complexity of sonata form to the flexibility of the variation, finally arriving at the point where his inner feelings could find expression only in the introspective, epigrammatic piano piece.

He evidently felt—and correctly so—that variation form was his best expressive vehicle, for only theme and variations allows great freedom within a limited harmonic and melodic framework, permitting the composer to indicate several different moods within one self-contained composition. Brahms had used this general framework in two of his sonatas. He continued to apply it in five sets of variations for piano solo, one for piano duet, and another (*Variations on a Theme by Haydn*) for two pianos. There are also examples of variation in other media.

His final venture in solo-keyboard variation form is the two-volume *Variations on a Theme by Paganini, Opus 35* (1863), each volume supplied with a finale. In concert these are often played as one continuous work by omitting the last section (finale) of the first set. This work is one of the rare exceptions to Brahms's habit of avoiding technique for its own sake. The variations (studies) are fiendishly difficult, abounding in complicated passages of sixths and thirds, glissando octaves, prolonged trills, prodigious leaps, and rhythmic complexities; yet beneath the frankly bravura surface of the variations in general, the music discloses sound musicality and logical construction.

Liszt used this same Paganini theme in the last of his *Grandes Études de Paganini*. It is a rhythmically interesting melody enveloped in extremely simple harmonies, and Brahms takes advantage of every possibility it offers, at one time accentuating its harmonic outline and at another time borrowing its motives and rhythm. Because their emotional elements have a secure musical background, Brahms's variations have escaped being labeled pretentious studies.

Excluding comparatively large-scale works, most of Brahms's piano music lies within seven opus numbers: the *Ballades, Opus 10;* three books of *Klavierstücke, Opuses 76, 118, 119;* one book of *Fantasien, Opus 116;* three *Intermezzi, Opus 117;* and two *Rhapsodies, Opus 79* (another rhapsody is included in *Opus 119*).

These works (excepting the *Ballades*) date from the last 20 years of the composer's life. They were created by a mature mind aided by a musical finesse that strips away external effects and rejects any display of superficial strength. Instead of being dazzling, many are brief, introspective pieces in which lyricism, conciseness, and emotional experience merge for short, even fleeting moments. Here speaks the Brahms of the lied, for these keyboard compositions are truly songs.

The same techniques and expressive modes that evolved in the larger keyboard works are here applied by Brahms in abbreviated, concentrated form. For structure he prefers song form (A B A), but the harmonic details develop from his ever evolving musical style. He approaches the primary melodic interest diversely. Sometimes the melody is concealed in an inner voice (*Opus 119, No. 3*); or the opening melodic idea may be based on a chord outline (*Opus 116, No. 3*). Individual titles only hint at a composition's content. Most are entitled either *Capriccio* or *Intermezzo*—three *Rhapsodies*, a *Romance,* and a *Ballade* are exceptions—with the *Capriccios* typically being more outgoing, direct, and vigorous than the *Intermezzi.* Naturally the three *Rhapsodies,* broader in scope and content, belong to a different category. They are "rhapsodic" even though restricted to a fairly severe framework. Fervent, impetuous outbursts stamp the character of the first two *Rhapsodies, Opus 79,* while the final one, *Rhapsody, Opus 119, No. 4,* is stately and heroic.

Thus far we have accounted for the major portion of Brahms's solo keyboard works. Besides the five studies based on pieces by other composers, he wrote 16 light, attractive *Waltzes* (*Opus 39*). One of these—in *A*-flat—is unique in its simplicity and personality.

Orchestral Music

Brahms's four symphonies, reflecting spiritual fervor and intellectual craftsmanship, are orchestral masterworks, sometimes almost formidably logical and coherent yet always subtly Romantic. In addition to the symphonies, he completed two rather ordinary serenades, two overtures, and the excellent *Variations on a Theme by Haydn.*

Brahms's respect for the eighteenth-century masters and for Beethoven influenced his style. As director of the Society of Friends of Music in Vienna, he regularly presented Bach's cantatas, and he was overjoyed to receive a supposed gift of the first five volumes of Bach's complete works (44 volumes in all) issued by the Bach Society. (He eventually had to pay for the five volumes and the remaining ones as well.) The contrapuntal mastery evidenced in the passacaglia finale of Brahms's fourth symphony can be traced to Bach's influence.

While Brahms revered these past composers, he had very little sympathy for many of his contemporaries. Program music did not interest him, and he had only meager praise for Liszt's symphonic poems. His cool attitude toward Richard Wagner was usually concealed beneath an exchange of polite courtesies.

In his formal structure, Brahms was a classicist. He chose sonata form for his most ambitious works, and Schumann even claimed that Brahms's first two sonatas were veiled symphonies. His two serenades are Haydnesque; they are really small symphonies, differing from actual symphonic form only in their more informal style.

Brahms's orchestral coloring is completely unique, and some critics have complained about his preference for gray tones. His music does not, it is true, exploit the upper reaches of the strings like that of, say, the more flamboyant Berlioz or Tchaikovsky. Yet Brahms was severely self-critical and is known to have destroyed compositions that he considered unsatisfactory; it must be assumed that he was satisfied with the orchestral music that survives.

Variations on a Theme by Haydn

Although the symphonies represent the essence of Brahms's orchestral style, the uninitiated listener may find it difficult to understand the sometimes dense musical texture and intricate developmental processes. But the listener will find no problems in the *Variations on a Theme by Haydn, Opus 56A* (1873), which in many respects is Brahms's finest orchestral piece. He wrote two versions of this joyous, frankly sensual composition: *Opus 56A* for orchestra and *Opus 56B* for two pianos. Both clearly demonstrate his expert workmanship and his ability to create unity in variation form.

There is no proof that the theme is by Haydn. Brahms discovered it in a *Feldpartita* composed by Haydn for Prince Esterházy's military band. In the second movement of the *Feldpartita* this theme is identified as the "St. Anthony Chorale," which in turn was probably based on a long-forgotten pilgrims' chant.

Haydn's suite is scored for two oboes, two horns, three bassoons, and one serpent (a now obsolete bass wind instrument).

In Brahms's adaptation, the two-part theme begins with two five-measure phrases. A dotted rhythm in the first measure dominates the theme, which ends on a *B*-flat stated five times. Brahms gathers a chorus of oboes, bassoons, contrabassoons, horns, and pizzicato double basses to announce this bright theme. The eight variations that follow strictly observe the theme's basic rhythmic structure and harmony; the thematic notes are often surrounded or even buried by tonal masses, but they are always there. Motives and themes rove from one instrument to another, enriching the already variegated orchestral framework.

Variation I: Poco più animato. This first variation concentrates on the theme's concluding notes. Basses and high woodwinds alternately repeat the *B*-flat while strings construct a network of delicate figurations in triplets.

Variation II: Più vivace. Here the dotted rhythm prevails, prolonged in passages of sixths by clarinets and bassoons. The strings supply ornamental figures.

Variation III: Con moto. Oboes and bassoons, then violins, play a lyric melody derived from the theme, and then all three combine.

Variation IV: Andante con moto. Brahms's combination of horn and oboe (in a minor key) accompanied by strings introduces an unusual tone quality. Later the strings take over the wind variation.

Variation V: Vivace. This variation is scherzando in character, humorous and flippant in mood. The original theme, now distorted, is enlivened by scurrying figures in the woodwind and given brilliance by the piccolo.

Variation VI: Vivace. In this second scherzando variation, pizzicato strings sharply etch the theme.

Variation VII: Grazioso. Flute with viola and clarinet with violin engage in graceful descending figures set to a rocking $\frac{6}{8}$ meter.

Variation VIII: Presto non troppo. Pianissimo throughout with the theme inverted, this ghostly dance uses muted strings supported by bassoon, clarinet, and piccolo.

Finale. This is a type of passacaglia having its bass line (five measures) modeled on the theme. The five-measure pattern is repeated 17 times with 17 short variations above it; then Haydn's theme returns in the glorious conclusion.

Hungarian Dances

Brahms was always intrigued by the wild, passionate music of Hungary. At the Prater in Vienna he would have the Hungarian gypsy fiddlers play for him, and on a tour with the Hungarian violinist Reményi he heard more of the native repertoire. Hungarian music unquestionably influenced his compositions—as, for example, in the finale of the violin concerto, the finale of the *Piano Quartet, Opus 25,* the *Variations on a Hungarian Song* for piano, and the *Zigeunerlieder.*

When he sent the first set of his *Hungarian Dances* to the publishers, Brahms included this note: "I offer them as genuine gypsy children which I did not beget, but merely brought up with bread and milk." The *Hungarian Dances* originally appeared as a group of four-hand piano *arrangements*—three dances (numbers 11, 14, and 16) are original with Brahms. The first two books (ten dances) appeared in 1869, and in 1880 two more sets (eleven dances) were published.

Brahms's publisher made a great deal of money from these *Hungarian Dances,* for they became immediately popular. Brahms arranged the first book for piano solo; the violinist-conductor Joachim transcribed them for violin and piano; and two were arranged for two voices and piano by the singer Pauline Viardot. As for the orchestral version frequently heard now, Brahms himself arranged only numbers one and three from the first book and number ten from the second book. The rest were orchestrated by Dvořák and others.

When she first heard the *Hungarian Dances,* Brahms's good friend Elisabeth von Herzogenberg exclaimed, "You have said the last word about these melodies! You have taken material which concealed beauty within itself and raised it to a level of the purest art, without sacrificing any of its wildness and elemental power." Her description is perfect, for this is why the *Hungarian Dances* maintain their undiminished popularity.

Academic Festival Overture

There is an interesting story about one of Brahms's most engaging orchestral compositions. In March of 1879 the university at Breslau offered the composer an honorary doctorate. After accepting, he learned that he was expected to compose something for the university as a token of acknowledgment. He read the honorary diploma that described him as *"viro illustrissimo . . . artis musicae severioris in Germania nunc principi."* Doubtlessly amused at finding himself the greatest German composer of "serious" music, he may have decided to show another side of his nature. In 1880 he produced the *Academic Festival Overture, Opus 80,* which had an overwhelming success when performed on January 4, 1881, at Breslau. Brahms had based his composition on four well-known student songs, thus equipping it with a built-in popularity.

The work begins with a stately theme played pianissimo and developed briefly. A long drum roll launches the brass choir into the first student song, *Wir hatten gebauet ein stattliches Haus* (We had built a stately house, Ex. 20:1). After some transitional passages, a reference to the opening theme leads to the second student song, *Der Landesvater* (The Country's Father), played by the

Ex. 20:1. Brahms: *Academic Festival Overture*

violins (Ex. 20:2). The mood changes for a jovial freshman hazing song called *Fuchslied* (Fox Song), beginning *Was kommt dort von der Höh'* (What comes there from on high). It tells about a poor student who is asked impertinent

Ex. 20:2. Brahms: *Academic Festival Overture*

questions about his family and given a pipe too strong for a freshman's lungs. In Brahms's score this song is "sung" by laughing bassoons (Ex. 20:3) to a viola and cello accompaniment.

Ex. 20:3. Brahms: *Academic Festival Overture*

In the last section all the student songs return to be developed; the full orchestra proclaims the fourth and most famous song, *Gaudeamus igitur* (Wherefore let us rejoice, Ex. 20:4), and the overture ends in a burst of color.

Ex. 20:4. Brahms: *Academic Festival Overture*

This somewhat slight although thoroughly enjoyable work required the largest orchestra of any of Brahms's writings. His score calls for two flutes, piccolo, two oboes, two clarinets, two bassoons, double bassoon, four horns, three trumpets, three trombones, bass tuba, a set of three kettledrums, bass drum, cymbals, triangle, and strings.

Chamber Music

Brahms's *Quintet for Clarinet and String Quartet in B Minor, Opus 115* is one of his finest, most beautiful chamber works. It is a late composition and shows to good advantage that happy synthesis of emotion and structural clarity typical of the composer.

As he reached his fifty-eighth year, Brahms planned to retire. He worked on his will and busied himself with projects demanding less creative effort, revising earlier works, completing others. However, in 1891 he was so deeply impressed by the wonderful playing of the well-known Meiningen clarinetist Richard Mühlfeld that he experienced a new surge of energy and was inspired to compose the clarinet quintet.

In this work Brahms achieves a restrained, nostalgic atmosphere through imaginative details, multiple textures, inspired developments, and exquisite melodic beauty. He displays the clarinet's most distinctive qualities by commanding it to exhibit its complete range. He assigns it delicate passage work, rhapsodic and dramatic phrases, and lyrical melodic lines to show its sensuous beauty. Nevertheless the quintet is not an overt showpiece for clarinet; rather it is an exquisite example of perfectly conceived chamber music. In the first movement, *Allegro,* Brahms seems to revel in exploiting the full instrumental ensemble.

> The clarinet may soar over the strings, as at the opening; it may contribute to the dark, rich quality of its lowest register, as at the beginning of the development; most characteristic of all, it may wander in the middle of the harmony, hardly discernible as an individual voice yet tinting the whole texture.[2]

[2] Peter Latham, *Brahms* (New York: Collier Books, 1962), p. 133.

The succeeding *Adagio* is built on a motive extracted from the first movement's principal theme. The basic lyricism is interrupted by a middle section providing a definite Hungarian gypsy atmosphere: rhapsodic flourishes sound against rich tremolos and harmonies. The third movement opens quietly and has two related parts, a melodious *Andantino* and a *Presto* having scherzo rhythm.

For the *Vivace* finale Brahms chose his favorite writing form—variations. In this instance the variations take on a rondo character, since the third and fifth highlight the theme more forcefully than do the others. The coda reveals a master stroke in the art of variation: Brahms combines the variation theme with the first-movement theme in a passage unsurpassed in its beauty and tragic import.

OTHER COMPOSERS

Brahms immediately comes to mind at the mention of music in Germany and Austria during the late nineteenth century. Yet there were other serious composers of that epoch, especially three significant orchestral composers: Bruckner, Mahler, and Strauss.

Anton Bruckner

Anton Bruckner (1824–1896), Brahms's contemporary, wrote nine monumental symphonies that have caused countless discussions about their artistic and aesthetic qualities. Some critics find the symphonies meandering, musically inconsistent, and tedious because of their uncontrolled digressions.

On the positive side, the unassuming simplicity of many Bruckner melodies is charming, and he frequently attains moments of breathtaking grandeur. His magnificent *Te Deum,* a choral work often used as a finale for his incomplete ninth symphony, is an excellent illustration of Bruckner's heroic music.

Gustav Mahler

Gustav Mahler (1860–1911) almost wrote himself out of the performance field: by the time the first movement of his *Symphony No. 3* is over, 45 minutes have elapsed and five more movements are still to be heard! His nine symphonies cover a wide range of musical materials; there is sublime beauty in some passages, but others contain only commonplace musical ideas.

Mahler was a complex person who wrote involved, uncompromising music. An emotional man, he endowed some musical phrases with sensuous beauty or subjective sentimentality. In attempting to transfer his own experiences and moods into corresponding sound patterns, he produced program music, but he was a professed intellectual, a well-read, well-rounded musician who meticulously heeded form and stylistic details in his musical scores.

Richard Strauss

During the last half of the nineteenth century, two leading musical camps existed in Germany and Austria: the Wagnerites and the Brahmsites. A composer could scarcely avoid the influence of one or the other. Bruckner and Mahler followed Wagner more closely than Brahms in their approach to musical composition.

Wagner's style also provided Richard Strauss (1864–1949) with the basic ingredients for his highly personal musical language, and Strauss has proved to be Wagner's most vital and successful admirer. His operas *Salome* (1905), *Elektra* (1908), and *Der Rosenkavalier* (1910) powerfully emphasize the orchestral apparatus and let the drama serve as a picturesque commentary.

Strauss's symphonic poems belong to the repertoire of every major symphony orchestra. His orchestral music is flamboyantly programmatic because of his masterful orchestration. He can literally describe or at the least suggest almost anything—windmills, a carnival, clattering pots and pans, death—with his imaginative orchestral instinct.

The structure in each symphonic poem reflects the literary subject matter that inspired it, and the poem's thematic contour and descriptive passages relate to the literary plot. Strauss had an astonishing talent for choosing the perfect musical form to accommodate the plots for these symphonic poems.

Don Quixote (1897) has variation form, and each adventure of Cervantes' hapless hero becomes another variant of the principal theme. *Tod und Verklärung* (Death and Transfiguration, 1889) is in recognizable sonata-allegro form. *Don Juan* (1888) and *Till Eulenspiegel* (1895) are both rondos: in the first the principal subject, Don Juan, returns after each amorous episode; in the latter a prologue and an epilogue serve as the main theme, while different episodes enact the various escapades of the mischievous legendary joker.

Till Eulenspiegel's lustige Streiche (Till Eulenspiegel's Merry Pranks) allowed Strauss ample opportunity to display his descriptive ingenuity. Till Eulenspiegel is a practical joker who indulges his malicious compulsions in a series of catastrophic mishaps. Each can be clearly recognized in the musical score; an outline may help to show the composer's skill and intent.

I. The introduction presents two principal themes. The violins play the first theme, which we can call the Till theme (Ex. 20:5), a reflective, lyrically

Ex. 20:5. R. Strauss: *Till Eulenspiegel*

oriented motive. An exceptionally difficult French horn solo introduces the second theme (Ex. 20:6). Strauss's clever syncopation suggests the rogue's tricky character. According to the composer, these two themes "pervade the whole in the most manifold disguises, moods and situations."

II. Till sets about his "business" in a variant of the lyric theme (Ex. 20:7). He insolently tramples down the market stalls, spurring his horse through a crowd of frightened women (woodwinds) and upsetting pots and pans in a noisy clatter.

Ex. 20:6. R. Strauss: *Till Eulenspiegel*

Ex. 20:7. R. Strauss: *Till Eulenspiegel*

III. When Till masquerades as a priest, Strauss gives the orchestra a hymnlike tune in popular style. Even in the religious sequence, Strauss makes us "see" the scoundrel by recalling the Till theme on the clarinet.

IV. This is a love scene musically initiated by a descending glissando on a solo violin. The music takes on Italianate coloring with a serenade derived from the original horn melody. Till's rejection by the lady (or ladies?) calls for a violently loud orchestral passage.

V. Now our hero meets a group of dull, pompous professors (bassoons and contrabassoon) and proposes an impossible problem in the form of a canon. While they all talk at once Till departs, accompanied by a merry street tune from the clarinet and violin.

VI. Tragedy replaces comedy: the French horn theme sounds in canon with strange harmonies when Till is carried off to court. He is still impudent, however, in his theme played by the clarinet. Eight horns and six trumpets pronounce his death sentence. A "fall" of a major seventh indicates that the hangman's duty is finished, and Till dies to the sound of trilling flutes.

VII. In the epilogue the composer gently reminds us—in a simple folk-like orchestral statement—to think kindly of the rascal by remembering his better side.

Till Eulenspiegel is a masterpiece of thematic transformation; despite the amusing narrative, its musical strength lies in this thematic treatment rather than in the "story."

After Brahms, Bruckner, Mahler, and Strauss, music in Germany and Austria bid a lingering farewell to Romanticism. It was a tradition not easily broken or relinquished, for these countries had nourished that emotional aesthetic for a hundred years.

In some ways the late nineteenth century might be labeled Post-Romantic. Johannes Brahms had felt the need to fit Romantic musical language to classic forms. Strauss, Bruckner, and Mahler were not attracted by the subjective and intimate elements so prevalent in the music of their immediate predecessors. They envisioned musical portrayals in monumental terms and they helped Wagner to break down the major-minor system. Twentieth-century music was just a short step away.

FOR DISCUSSION AND ASSIGNMENT

1. Listen carefully to the first movement of Brahms's *Symphony No. 1.* Do you find it difficult to understand? If so, why?
2. Listen to several of Brahms's short piano pieces. Are they as introspective as similar ones by Chopin? Are they as emotional as those Schumann wrote? Do they verify Brahms's reputation as a Romantic Classicist?

3. In works such as the *Variations on a Theme by Haydn,* do you think one should listen intently for fragments of the theme or enjoy each variation merely as an attractive piece of music?
4. Do you find Strauss's *Till Eulenspiegel* effective as a symphonic poem? Is the "program" necessary in appreciating the work?

FOR FURTHER READING

Brockway, Wallace, and Herbert Weinstock. *Men of Music.* New York: Simon and Schuster, 1958. PB. This collection of musical biographies contains essays on Brahms and Strauss.

Geiringer, Karl. *Brahms: His Life and Work.* New York: Doubleday and Co., 1947. An Anchor PB. To date this is the best Brahms biography in English. Dr. Geiringer draws extensively upon more than a thousand letters written by Brahms or addressed to him.

Latham, Peter. *Brahms.* New York: Collier Books, 1962. PB. Prof. Latham's study of Brahms's life and works is informative and useful. A good book for the musical amateur.

21 Romantic Music in France

> Music is so powerful that in given instances it can conquer alone, and it has a thousand times earned the right to say with Medea: "Myself, which is enough."
>
> HECTOR BERLIOZ
> Letter of August 12, 1856

By the mid-nineteenth century, France had produced only one composer equal to Schubert, Mendelssohn, or Schumann. Its music was largely dominated by foreigners. For the last few decades of the eighteenth century and about 40 years of the nineteenth, Frenchmen preferred opera above any other music, but this medium was cultivated in their country by Rossini, Meyerbeer, and Cherubini, who were by nature unequipped to further French musical culture.

From 1840 to 1860 the French public showed increasing interest in music written by French composers, and by 1860 this public was wholly receptive to such music. For approximately 50 years thereafter, French music production was as intense as it was creative—so outstanding that historians record this era as a golden age in French musical history. The Franco-Prussian war (1871) stimulated the movement, for after that war France turned to nationalism in an attempt to recoup her spiritual and moral forces; works by French composers quickly multiplied, and instrumental music assumed its rightful place beside opera.

HECTOR BERLIOZ

Perhaps the most representative composer of the French Romantic movement is Hector Berlioz (1803–1869), who had enrolled at the Paris medical school in 1821 but left soon afterward to study music. Nine years later he won the *Prix de Rome*. It took almost ten more years before his reputation as composer and conductor was sufficiently established to assure him a livelihood. From then on his history describes moderately successful tours and composing projects until the last six years of his life, when illness kept him from writing.

Of Berlioz' four symphonies, the first two—*Symphonie fantastique*

(1830) and *Harold in Italy* (1834)—are more likely to be heard today. In these he shows extraordinary descriptive power. His dramatic *Romeo and Juliet* (1839) symphony with choruses is currently neglected, although it contains some exquisite sections, and his final symphony, the *Funereal and Triumphal Symphony* (1840), is often condemned for being banal. Berlioz' most important stage work and his last composition is *The Trojans* (1859), a grand opera in two parts. His works require huge orchestras and complex staging—requirements that preclude regular performance. His repertoire consists mostly of some 50 large-scale instrumental, operatic, and choral works.

Berlioz' admirers claimed that he was Beethoven's rightful successor, a statement with a certain amount of truth in it. Beethoven had shown that something new could be tried with Classic symphony form, thus preparing the way for innumerable experiments. In following Beethoven, whom he admired, Berlioz created a new symphonic apparatus; he cannot, however, be ranked with Beethoven, for while he had a lively imagination, he lacked Beethoven's creative genius. Berlioz' unique imagination produced intensely personal music, but imagination alone could not substitute for genuine inspiration. His particular imagination often produced strange, beautiful music; it also at times led to absurdity. One of the most pertinent remarks about Berlioz came from the great German poet Heinrich Heine, who pronounced that "Berlioz had not sufficient talent for his genius."

Since Berlioz wrote with words as fluently as he did with musical notes, he had no difficulty in analyzing his own musical style.

> Generally speaking, my style is very bold, but it has not the slightest tendency to subvert any of the constituent elements of art. On the contrary, it is my endeavour to add to their number. . . . The prevailing characteristics of my music are passionate expression, intense ardour, rhythmical animation, and unexpected turns. When I say passionate expression, I mean an expression determined on enforcing the inner meaning of its subject, even when that subject is the contrary of passion, and when the feeling to be expressed is gentle and tender, or even profoundly calm.[1]

Berlioz is justly described as an innovator in the field of orchestral composition. Symphonic form had always been susceptible to exploration and change: Joseph Haydn's Classic treatment of the symphony was just one of numerous possibilities for growth in this form, and Berlioz' programmatic symphonies mark another important symphonic development. Besides his contributions to the symphony, Berlioz' experiments in orchestral sonority corroborate his reputation. He was one of the finest orchestrators of the nineteenth century, with a talent rivaling that of Rimsky-Korsakov and Ravel.

Symphonie fantastique

This symphony fully illustrates Berlioz' belief that within limits music is capable of expressing anything. It is described as an "episode in the life of an artist," the artist being Berlioz. The fact that he had been reading Thomas DeQuincy's *Confessions of an English Opium Eater* accounts for the symphony's "story." Disappointed in love, the young artist takes an overdose of opium; his

[1] *Memoirs of Hector Berlioz,* edited by Ernest Newman (New York: Tudor Publishing Co., 1935), pp. 487–488.

nightmarish dreams center on his beloved, musically represented by a leading theme (*idée fixe*) that reoccurs in different forms throughout the movements.

There are five movements: the slow movement functions as pivot, with a scherzo and an allegro before and after. Although this symphony sounds convincing, it is really a patchwork product: the fourth movement and much of the slow movement came from Berlioz' unfinished opera *Les Francs-Juges;* the finale and very probably the second movement go back to a Faust ballet he had begun but abandoned; the opening movement belongs to an early work; and even the *idée fixe* had been used before in *Herminie,* a cantata Berlioz had composed for a *Prix de Rome* competition.

Reveries and Passions: Largo leading to an *Allegro agitato.* An eloquent introduction starts this first movement. Quiet woodwinds and horns give way to strings. The *Allegro* is classic in its broad outlines if not in its details. As it begins, violins play the *idée fixe* (Ex. 21:1), an undistinguished melody later appearing

Ex. 21:1. Berlioz: *Symphonie fantastique: idée fixe*

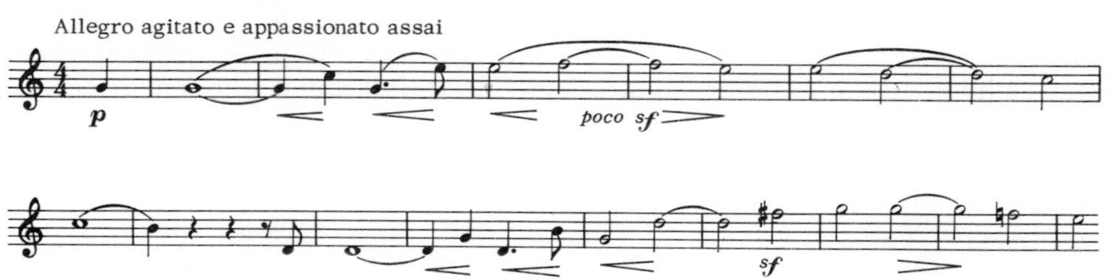

in various guises. Busy scale passages and meandering strings lead one to question the innate musical substance of this movement.

A Ball: Valse allegro non troppo. Bustling strings with harp commentary create pleasant excitement until the music settles down to the waltz proper with its romantically lush theme. Flute and oboe sing a portion of the *idée fixe* above the waltz rhythm. The "beloved," carried away in a cloud of dancers, is seen again briefly in a clarinet passage just before the boisterous conclusion.

In the Fields: Adagio. This rare, original symphonic movement revolves around a pastoral dialogue between oboe and English horn. It is a long, nostalgic movement only briefly interrupted by brighter passages. Near its end, ominous rolls on the kettledrums announce distant thunder, perhaps foretelling events in the fourth movement. Strings and one horn quietly conclude this third movement.

March to the Scaffold. The title sounds terrifying but the music is not at all grim. Although the first theme is somber, the secondary melody is so outgoing that it seems totally out of character with the rest of the movement. In the final measures the clarinet recalls part of the *idée fixe* but is abruptly cut off by the crash of the guillotine knife. The noisy conclusion cheers the listener, and he anticipates the next movement with renewed interest.

A Witches' Sabbath. This highly original final movement is bizarre and at times harsh. Brilliant orchestration carries the listener by degrees to the peak of the witches' orgy. Strings imitate their screaming; the clarinet grossly paraphrases the *idée fixe;* the weird sounds continue in full orchestral shrieks and wails; the *idée fixe* returns, this time with vulgar ornamentation. The noble *Dies Irae* (a plainchant from the Catholic Requiem) emerges, but its melody is deformed in the orgy. Then the listener hears the witches' rondo, ending with a frenzied fugal treatment. Here again the process of thematic transformation is at work; unlike thematic development, transformation tends to retain the melodic contour while changing the mood of the thematic material.

CÉSAR FRANCK

César Franck (1822–1890), one of France's most impressive musicians, was Belgian by birth and German by blood, but he chose to live as a Frenchman and became a naturalized French citizen in 1870. He held the organist post at various Parisian churches: Notre Dame de Lorette, Saint-Jean-Saint-François au Marais, and finally Sainte-Clotilde. In 1872 he was appointed to teach organ at the Paris Conservatory; however, his class soon developed into a composition study group that produced many distinguished composers.

Franck has been compared musically to Bach, spiritually to the painter Fra Angelico. There is, to be sure, some similarity between Bach and César Franck: both spent their lives in rather lowly positions, both preferred contrapuntal forms, and both conceived music as a means to an end—the glorification of God. The comparison with Fra Angelico is another matter. It might be said that each man's art reflects an essentially pure soul and that Franck's splendid musical works and Fra Angelico's lofty frescos at the monastery of St. Mark were inspired by the same spiritual source—but there the likeness ends. Techniques separate the two artists, the musician's approach being more complex, more scholarly.

César Franck's German roots enabled him to nourish French music with a sorely needed solidity and technical firmness, which later bore fruit not only in his compositions but in his disciples' works. In the first place, his music suggests an architect at work erecting solid tonal structures capable of flexibility and mutation. Secondly, he is a contrapuntist; it is evident in his writing that he preferred the canon and fugue forms and, of course, their respective substructures. Franck achieved unity in his works by using cyclic structure with several dominant themes that reappear in different sections (spiritually, if not technically, similar to Berlioz and Liszt).

Franck was more than a craftsman, for besides his sound background he possessed emotional capacities. His intensely expressive melodies, often diatonic, are quite dependent on the harmonic framework, and this is where he reveals great originality: unexpected resolutions, series of seventh and ninth chords, parallel fifths, and much chromaticism. This entirely new harmonic concept and Franck's eloquent melodic lines—nearly all having a downward sweep—are enveloped by a strong framework.

Prelude, Chorale and Fugue

Franck's reputation depends on comparatively few works, all written after 1870 and affected by two factors: the psychological aftermath of the Franco-

Prussian war and the composer's stimulating experience as a teacher at the Paris Conservatory. The only two significant solo piano works in this group—*Prelude, Chorale and Fugue* (1884) and *Prelude, Aria and Finale* (1887)—are both masterpieces. The more often played *Prelude, Chorale and Fugue* is somewhat similar to Bach's *Toccata and Fugue in C Major* for organ. Bach has an expansive adagio separating his fugue from the toccata. Franck separates his with a chorale whose melodic pattern governs the entire composition.

With striking originality the *Prelude's* initial theme appears as a syncopation; this theme's quizzical mood persists throughout the work. Fragmentary sections (*a capriccioso*) interspersed between statements of the initial theme contain seeds of a subject that later appears in the fugue. By means of a suspension and assumption of key, the *Prelude* merges into the *Chorale,* initially in *E*-flat but soon moving to *c* minor. The opening of the *Chorale* shows how closely Franck interwove melody and harmony in his music (Ex. 21:2).

Ex. 21:2. Franck: *Chorale*

This opening theme (Ex. 21:2) is calm yet inquisitive; the second theme—the chorale, properly speaking—replies with a melody consisting of the top notes from a series of widely spaced arpeggiated chords. An intensifying chain of these questions and answers leads to a *poco allegro* section, a transitional passage to the *Fugue.* The fugal subject in *b* minor enters fragmentarily several times before it is finally stated completely. This fugal theme is chromatic, in a descending direction, and the four-voice fugal exposition is exactly what one would expect from Franck's classic approach.

A short digression precedes three successive statements in major mode and a short episode in which the fugal theme is inverted. Then a triplet motive in *f*-sharp minor predominates; it is an undulating motive that accompanies further thematic entries. A great crescendo occurs when the theme returns in octaves. Without warning a series of modulating arpeggios recalling the *Prelude* appears, followed by a return of the *Chorale* theme. As the music swells to its climax, the *Fugue* subject can be heard underneath and simultaneously with the *Chorale* theme; it makes one last entrance, and then the work closes in a peal of chords.

Sonata in A Major

Franck's *Sonata in A Major* for violin and piano (1886) marks a high point in his career. In it he creates a rare fusion of poetical and dramatic elements.

The first movement, *Allegretto ben moderato,* is musically poetic from its inquisitive introductory bars to its wistful epilogue. There are two main themes, one designated for each instrument, and they are seldom interchanged. The second movement, *Allegro,* is dramatic and passionate. Although tempo changes occur, one theme controls the mood. The title *Recitativo-Fantasia* nicely suits the third movement, a growing improvisatory structure that discloses poetic lyricism as well as one especially impassioned theme (Ex. 21:3). The famous *Allegretto*

Ex. 21:3. Franck: *Sonata in A Major: Recitativo-Fantasia*

poco mosso finale presents its principal melody in canon. This theme is joined by a second subject derived from lyrical material heard in the third movement. Even Example 21:3 reappears in a burst of glory.

Symphony in D Minor

Franck's one symphony, finished in 1888, only two years before his death, is the only nonprogrammatic symphony by a French composer to be accorded a place in standard orchestral repertoire. *Symphony in D Minor* is built on a cyclic structure similar to that in the *Prelude, Chorale and Fugue,* and it has only three movements. Franck's improvisatory skills and organ talents stand out sharply in this symphony.

Although the first movement contains several sections (*Lento—Allegro non troppo—Lento—Allegro non troppo—Lento—Allegro—Lento*), Franck unifies them with an initial theme based on a three-note motive (Ex. 21:4). This theme

Ex. 21:4. Franck: *Symphony in D Minor: Lento*

is answered by a countertheme, a falling chromatic motive in Franck's characteristic style (Ex. 21:5). The first *Allegro* states the principal theme more vigorously. Two new themes enter, the last a blatant melody stressing one tone (*A*). Franck makes a gesture toward development, then assertively restates the opening theme. This movement might be described as the development of a basic idea: an introduction and allegro repeated three times.

The second movement, *Allegretto,* combines elements of a slow movement with a scherzo divided into two contrasting sections. Chords on plucked

Ex. 21:5. Franck: *Symphony in D Minor: Lento*

strings and harp set the opening mood. Then the English horn presents a pensive melody (based on *F*) that begins with a note pattern like that of the initial theme in the first movement. This melody is later sung by clarinet, horn, and flute. A new, songlike theme enters on the violin with a countertheme in cellos and basses. Then a fluttering theme in the violins introduces the scherzo middle section, while clarinets provide contrast with a countertheme in the lower strings. The fluttering theme and the earlier pensive melody ultimately combine.

In the final movement, *Allegro non troppo,* the first theme's buoyant sound is cut off by the brasses introducing a morbid theme. Strings and woodwinds provide a dialogue; the brass subject is heard again; the movement's main theme reappears; and the principal theme from the first movement returns. A repeat of the finale's buoyant opening theme brings in the conclusion.

CAMILLE SAINT-SAËNS

Rarely has one individual been so generously endowed as Camille Saint-Saëns (1835–1921), one of the first composers to promote French music. An exceptionally gifted pianist, he was praised by his contemporaries for his keyboard agility and grand style, disciplined by a certain dryness in touch. Highly intelligent, his interests ranged beyond music and he could converse authoritatively on many subjects. A true neo-Classicist, he had been reared in Bach-Mozart traditions; his works display logical construction and pure style. And as a progenitor of French nationalism, Saint-Saëns founded—with Romain Bussine—the National Music Society for the explicit purpose of propagating and exploiting French music.

With so many positive attributes to his credit, why is this composer not honored with Beethoven or even Liszt? What is missing from his music? Saint-Saëns himself has unwittingly supplied an answer that is well documented in his music. To him emotion and sensitivity were synonymous with sentimentality, and he believed such elements could lead to decadence in musical art. He described his attitude to his friend Camille Bellaigue:

> The search for expression, truthful and legitimate though it may be, is the germ of decadence, which begins the moment the search for expression precedes that of formal perfection. . . . Art is made to express beauty and character; sensitivity comes only afterward and art can perfectly well do without it. It is even better for it when it does without it. . . . I have said and I will never cease to repeat, because it is the truth, that music like painting and sculpture exists by itself outside of all emotion. . . . The more that sensitivity develops, the more music and the other arts are estranged from pure art.[2]

This regrettable attitude helps to explain why Saint-Saëns' music so often lacks conviction. His attitude especially affected his melodies, which, although correct in detail and constructed upon perfectly acceptable tenets of tension and climax, seem lifeless and unsatisfying. Just how wrong he was in his basic thinking is evident from the fact that nowhere in his music can one find a cantabile melody to compare with any of the slow movements in Mozart's sonatas.

[2] Camille Bellaigue, *Paroles et Musique* (Paris: Perrin et Cie., 1925), p. 152. English translation by the author.

In general Saint-Saëns' harmony offers nothing new, no innovations of any kind. On the positive side, he created original, imaginative rhythms that stem from his acquaintance with French musical traditions.

Saint-Saëns tried nearly all types of musical composition. Though his technical ability, orchestrational skill, and formal ideas were exceptionally fine, only a few of his many compositions survive. Among these are *Carnival of the Animals* and *Danse Macabre,* for orchestra, *Introduction and Rondo Capriccioso,* for violin and orchestra, and the opera *Samson and Delilah.*

Danse Macabre

Many Romantic composers elaborated musically on the subject of death. Berlioz created a horrifying spectacle in his *Witches' Sabbath,* and Franz Liszt paraphrased the *Dies Irae* in his *Dance of Death* for piano and orchestra. Saint-Saëns adopted a more lighthearted approach in his *Danse Macabre,* which first appeared as a song with words by Henri Cazalis:

> Zig, zig, zig, Death is striking a tomb with his heel in cadence. Death is playing a dance tune on his violin at midnight. The winter wind blows, and the night is dark. From the linden-trees come moans. White skeletons move across the shadows, running and leaping in their shrouds. Zig, zig, zig, each one gives a tremor, and the dancers' bones rattle. Hush! They suddenly leave off dancing, they jostle one another, they flee—the cock has crowed.

After publishing the song, the composer declared that it was unsingable (it is not a bad song at all), and he reworked the song's musical material into a symphonic poem that has had lasting success.

Danse Macabre begins with the harp striking the midnight hour. Seated on a tombstone, Death tunes his fiddle and the weird dance begins. A sinister waltz alternates with a more genial melody. The xylophone simulates rattling bones, and when the *Dies Irae* is introduced it is so rhythmically transformed and grotesque that it is barely recognizable. The movement quickens with intensity and excitement. Suddenly horns announce dawn, the cock crows (an oboe motive), and the gruesome procession slowly disappears to the sounds of Death's ever-present cadence.

Introduction and Rondo Capriccioso

This brief concert piece for violin and orchestra has been applauded the world over. Written in 1863 when the composer was 28, it was first performed by the famous violinist Sarasate, to whom it was dedicated. Saint-Saëns composed this work to please the taste of his day, coldly calculating how to make it a popular success, yet his score is so appealing that it still attracts even the very discerning listener.

The *Introduction* bears the performance indication *Andante malinconico.* The violin sings a plaintive, drooping melody accompanied by pizzicato strings. When the *Rondo Capriccioso* enters, Saint-Saëns marks it *Allegretto ma non troppo.* The violin states the principal theme, a beautifully wrought, self-contained melody. A contrasting theme intrudes to converse musically with the main theme. There is a new theme in the orchestra, which the solo violin reiterates. A well-calculated climax brings in the principal theme, and the coda permits the soloist a few choice virtuoso passages.

PAUL DUKAS

Paul Dukas (1865–1935) was a music critic and distinguished teacher as well as a composer respected by his contemporaries. As a composer he was partly self-taught. He approached music like a logician, building on a vast scale, but he softened this intellectualism with disciplined sensitivity, a virile rhythmic concept, and a feeling for color. Dukas influenced the styles of many twentieth-century composers.

The Sorcerer's Apprentice

In contrast to the macabre, sinister, and sardonic moods exploited by Liszt, Berlioz, and Saint-Saëns, Dukas interprets demoniac subjects with humor and sarcasm. His delightful orchestral "scherzo" (or symphonic poem) *The Sorcerer's Apprentice* (1897) was inspired directly by Goethe's descriptive ballad *Der Zauberlehrling* and more remotely by Lucian's centuries-old tale called *The Lie Fancier.*

In both versions the chief figures are a magician—who could change brooms and pestles into animate beings capable of performing domestic chores—and his apprentice. Unknown to the sorcerer, the apprentice discovers the magic words and calls a broom to life. He commands it to draw water, but unfortunately he has not learned the words necessary to de-activate the broom. Water quickly fills the room and only the sorcerer's timely intervention prevents the entire *dramatis personae* from being swept away. With both tragic and comic elements present, comedy outweighs tragedy.

Dukas' slow introduction sets the stage as the eager apprentice ponders his course of action. Timidly he speaks the magic words (muted horns and trumpets) and the orchestra swells to a climax. Then silence. Gradually low woodwinds and timpani articulate the rhythm as the bassoon outlines what might be called the "broom theme" (Ex. 21:6). The charm works, the broom begins to

Ex. 21:6. Dukas: *The Sorcerer's Apprentice*

carry water, and the tempo increases; little subthemes intensify the excitement. Horns and cornets assume the theme as the apprentice tries vainly to stop the buckets of water. Resorting to violence, he splits the broom, but gradually the two parts (bassoon and clarinet) rise to activity in a rambunctious fugato. The tempo again quickens, the orchestra builds to another climax, and at the height of impending disaster the magician appears. The brass section declares the counterspell, and the broom theme appears timidly for a moment before the little drama comes to an abrupt end.

With Paul Dukas, French music almost imperceptibly reaches the path of contemporary music. He was extremely adroit in fusing techniques of the past with the devices of his time, thus creating a musical framework that pointed to the future.

FOR DISCUSSION AND ASSIGNMENT

1. Do you think Berlioz was a good melodist? What about his harmonic language? What do you think was Berlioz' best talent?
2. Is César Franck's skill as an organist visible in the *Prelude, Chorale and Fugue* and the *Symphony in D Minor?* Does Franck's attempt at unity through reiterated motives or themes (cyclic treatment) appear to accomplish its purpose?
3. If Saint-Saëns believed that sensitivity was not necessary to composing and that musical craftsmanship was the important requirement, how does one account for the sinister atmosphere of *Danse Macabre,* the delightful humor and sophistication of the *Carnival of the Animals,* and the voluptuous passion of *Samson and Delilah?*
4. Paul Dukas felt that humor could be expressed through musical means. Do you think his *Sorcerer's Apprentice* proves this?

FOR FURTHER READING

Barzun, Jacques. *Berlioz and His Century*. Cleveland, Ohio: The World Publishing Co., 1956. A Meridian PB. Besides being the finest Berlioz biography in print, Jacques Barzun's book offers a fascinating view of the nineteenth-century musical scene.

Berlioz, Hector. *Memoirs,* edited by Ernest Newman. New York: Dover Publications, Inc., 1966. PB. In this reprint of a 1932 publication, the French composer describes himself and his music as no biographer could ever do.

Cooper, Martin. *French Music from the Death of Berlioz to the Death of Fauré.* London: Oxford University Press, 1951. PB. In tracing French music from 1869 to 1924, Mr. Cooper places each composer in his proper historical and musical niche.

d'Indy, Vincent. *César Franck,* translated by Rosa Newmarch. New York: Dover Publications, Inc., 1965. PB. First published in 1910, d'Indy's penetrating, sympathetic study of César Franck still provides good source material and interesting reading.

22 *Nationalism*

> I am passionately fond of the national element in all its varied expressions. In a word, I am a Russian in the fullest sense of the word.
>
> PETER ILICH TCHAIKOVSKY
> Letter to Mme. von Meck, 1878

Nationalism—a word increasingly encountered in the twentieth century—refers to a state of mind that pledges an individual's loyalty to national interests and unity; generally speaking, it identifies a nation with its people. Nationalism first appeared at the beginning of the eighteenth century in western Europe and North America, its early historical manifestations being the French and American revolutions, and it continues to be a powerful factor in history.

Nationalism became a major tenet of nineteenth-century social order, and it quite logically affected literature and the fine arts. Music seemed the best medium for expressing nationalistic sentiments. While remaining within the bounds of Romanticism, music followed the patriotic movement in many countries; often the result was not so much a change in style and content as a change in spirit. For example, after the Franco-Prussian War (1870–1871) French musical activities increased, possibly an instinctive move to recoup the nation's spiritual forces. Before that war most nineteenth-century musicians working in France had been foreigners (Rossini, Cherubini, Meyerbeer), but in 1871 the French founded a National Music Society to encourage compositions and performances by French artists. This was the goal of the French nationalist movement; it did not attempt to preserve the folk element in French culture.

In some instances composers from this period betray patriotic feeling in their compositions even though they were not ardent nationalists. Brahms, for instance, was very fond of German folk songs and arranged many of them for young people, but Brahms was not a nationalist composer. Wagner shows pronounced nationalist tendencies in his subject matter based on traditional myth and legend, yet there is little evidence of the folk element in his approach to musical composition. However, there can be little doubt that these composers represent the German spirit of their time.

Before music could serve any nationalist cause, composers had to be free of foreign influences; their inspiration and techniques had to come from within their own culture. As nationalistic music gained a foothold, folklore invaded serious music in some countries; that is, folk melodies either were absorbed into a serious musical composition or inspired the composer to create a similar musical fabric.

Some musical styles and types are definitely more nationalistic than others. Nationalism grew strongest in countries that were politically and culturally dominated by foreign powers and in those that were semi-isolated. Russia, Bohemia, Spain, and Norway developed their classical music late, chiefly because for many generations their musical audiences favored the forms and styles of Italy, France, or Germany and preferred imported compositions and composers. Spain admired Haydn and Boccherini, and Russia enthusiastically cultivated Italian music. Once these countries caught the patriotic spirit, each made unique contributions to late-nineteenth-century music.

RUSSIA

Up to the end of the seventeenth century, Russia had produced only a small amount of secular classical music but an unusual variety of folk music. This abundant folk-music repertoire characteristically showed a strong modal quality, oriental inflections, irregular rhythmic patterns, and a Slavic mood. During the reign of Peter the Great (1682–1725) Russia opened her doors to musical influences from the West, and for about a hundred years Russian concerts and operas offered music largely created by non-Russians residing in Russia. Composers like Baldassare Galuppi (1706–1785) supplied the Russian aristocracy with the Latin-inspired music later rejected by many native Russian composers.

Mikhail Glinka (1804–1857), called the father of Russian classical music, was at least Russia's busiest native-born composer during the first half of the nineteenth century. Glinka and his contemporary Alexander Dargomyzhsky (1813–1869) used a dramatic form of opera heavily dependent on folk art.

The Five: Cui, Balakirev, Borodin, Mussorgsky, Rimsky-Korsakov

The composers who came to be known as the *Russian Five* became the passionate standard-bearers of native Russian music, for they recognized the originality and richness flowing through the vast corpus of Slavic folklore. Some Russian folk songs are ancient epics retelling time-honored Russian legends; others narrate happenings in daily family life—songs about love, marriage, work, or death. The rhythms are quite free and the melodies are modal rather than tonal. From this plentiful source the Russian Five—the first notable group of Slavic composers—gathered their prime inspirational material.

Around 1857 Cui introduced Balakirev, whom he had recently met, to Mussorgsky. In 1862 Mussorgsky introduced Borodin to Balakirev. Rimsky-Korsakov joined the group last. These musicians, nearly all of them at one time or another dependent on a nonmusical profession for a livelihood, nevertheless shared a common dream of writing music inspired by Russian folk elements. Since Russian classical music furnished scant technical models, these composers were forced to turn to the West, to the works of Beethoven, Schumann, Liszt, and

Berlioz. Thus equipped with the semblance of a technique (in some cases rather inadequate), they sought inspiration from their native folk music in an attempt to create a national Russian music school.

César Cui (1835–1918), whose French father had settled in Russia, rose to the rank of lieutenant-general in his career as an army engineer. Although he may have been the most prolific composer of the group, his music has proved to be the least enduring. The only Cui works currently heard are a few piano pieces that can be described only as not very good salon music.

Mily Balakirev (1837–1910) has met a similar fate. He headed the group, and it was he who urged the others to attempt musical composition. Besides adding oriental-flavored music to the national repertoire, Balakirev compiled into accessible form some of the immense treasures contained in Russian folk song and dance.

Alexander Borodin (1833–1887), although by vocation a professor of organic chemistry, was a cellist, pianist, and skilled composer. In this last capacity he is best represented by his symphonic music and the remarkable opera *Prince Igor*. One of Borodin's letters contains his views about successful operatic composition.

> In opera, as in decorative art, details and minutiae are out of place. Bold outlines only are necessary; all should be clear and straight-forward and fit for practical performance from the vocal and instrumental standpoint. The voices should occupy the first place, the orchestra the second.[1]

Borodin never completed *Prince Igor,* although he had spent years developing it. His friend Rimsky-Korsakov finished the work, aided by a colleague, Alexander Glazounov (1865–1936). While there are few performances of the opera outside Russia, a concert version of the *Polovtsian Dances* from the second act has carried Borodin's fame well beyond his native land. It is paradoxical that these wild, intoxicating dances sprang from the logical, scientific mind that conceived the standard work on *The Solidification of Aldehydes.*

Interspersed among the dances are choral parts for women's voices, but these choral sections are frequently omitted in concert performance. In the opera the dances celebrate a festival devised by Konchak Khan, chief of the Polovtsi, as entertainment for his prisoner Prince Igor, whom Khan respects as a mighty warrior and a great man.

Borodin's rhythm is marvelously developed and his themes have genuine Russian spirit. There are dances (Ex. 22:1) featuring wild men, young girls and boys, slave girls, and prisoners; dances praising the great Khan; and a turbulent

Ex. 22:1. Borodin: *Prince Igor: Polovtsian Dances*

[1] Letter to Mme. Ivanova Karmalina, dated June 10, 1876.

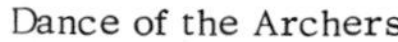

general dance with vigorous, captivating rhythms. Borodin plays off his themes one against the other before combining them. The exciting climax occurs in the middle section with the passionate syncopations of a barbaric dance in triple meter.

Modest Mussorgsky (1839–1881), the most talented of the Russian Five, had only five or six years of piano lessons for his early musical training. He was a junior officer of the Guards when he met Balakirev and caught the spirit of Russian nationalism. Around 1858 he resigned his commission to try musical composition, a career that led him to difficulties, poverty, and alcohol. At 42 he died of acute alcoholism.

Mussorgsky possessed a fine creative mind. Although his nervous temperament made it difficult for him to finish a composition, his creative instincts were wholly original and profound. He was outspoken in his views on artistic creation and its ramifications.

> Creation itself bears within itself its own laws of refinement. Their verification is inner criticism; their application is the artist's instinct. If there is neither one nor the other, there is no creative artist; if there is a creative artist, there must be one as well as the other, and the artist is a law unto himself.[2]

In the field of program music, Mussorgsky's *Pictures at an Exhibition* (1874) equals the finest pages of Schumann or Liszt. This piano collection was occasioned by the tragic death in 1873 of Mussorgsky's close friend Victor Hartmann, an artist and noted architect. At a memorial exhibition of Hartmann's works in 1874, Mussorgsky, strolling among the watercolors and drawings hung on the walls, hit on the idea of composing short pieces to describe Hartmann's various scenes. He became so engrossed in his project that the writing took only a few weeks. Although the composer was pleased with the result, the public paid little attention and the work remained unpublished until five years after his death. In 1923 Maurice Ravel arranged it for orchestra in a magnificent version that is presented more frequently than the original piano score.

The *Pictures*—ten tonal portraits joined together by an interlude (*Prom-*

[2] Letter to N. Rimsky-Korsakov, dated August 15, 1868.

enade) that is varied four times—could well have been modeled after any of Schumann's cyclic suites, such as *Carnaval.* Mussorgsky's typical works clearly indicate that he needed an extramusical stimulus; in this instance his inspiration came from Hartmann's pictures, many of which have long ago disappeared. The only clue to their pictorial content lies in a few notes made by Mussorgsky's friend Vladimir Stassov for the first edition of the piano score.

Serving as a link between pictures and as a musical accompaniment for the observer as he wanders from picture to picture, the opening *Promenade,* in alternating measures of $\frac{5}{4}$ and $\frac{6}{4}$ meter, is reduced and altered in subsequent appearances. The first picture—"a little *Gnome* walking awkwardly on deformed legs"—comes pathetically to life in this musical portrait. *The Old Castle* with a minstrel singing beneath its ancient walls seems less impressive than the other musical portrayals. The mood brightens with the next sketch, *Tuileries: Children at Play,* based on Hartmann's scene of children and their nurses in the Tuileries gardens in Paris. This picture prompted Mussorgsky to write a happy, noisy piece echoing the children's playful cries.

In the musical version of *Bydlo* (a Polish oxcart), the cart rumbles up from afar on two immense wheels, passes by, and fades into the distance. A costume designed by Hartmann for the ballet *Trilby* (based on the tale by Charles Nodier) furnished inspiration for *The Ballet of Unhatched Chicks,* an entrancing scherzino. Mussorgsky achieved some really effective program music with *Samuel Goldenberg and Schmuyle,* an amusing caricature of a rich merchant and a poor merchant wrangling. After the bold, pompous rich man has his say, the poor merchant answers in high-pitched tones, and then they argue simultaneously in a clever sequence of polymelody.

A clattering, bustling market square plainly emerges from the music of *The Market Place at Limoges,* a toccata-like piece that proceeds without interruption to *The Catacombs.* Hartmann's picture showed himself and some friends exploring the Roman catacombs in Paris. In the musical version the atmospheric introduction is intensified by two verbal notations: the Latin *"Con mortuis in lingua mortua"* (With the dead in a dead language) and then (in Russian) "Hartmann's creative departed spirit leads me to the place of skulls, and calls to them—a light glows faintly from the interior of the skulls." *The Hut on Chicken Feet* depicts the mythical hut of Russia's famous witch Baba Yaga. Mussorgsky describes the witch and her weird dwelling in a feverish dance leading directly into the thrilling finale, called *The Great Gate at Kiev;* with the sounds of monks chanting against a background of great, glad bells, the *Pictures at an Exhibition* comes to a close.

Mussorgsky composed an exciting symphonic poem that at times borders on hysteria: *A Night on Bald Mountain.* In 1867 he wrote a piece called *St. John's Night on Bald Mountain,* which his friends rejected. Then in the winter of 1871–1872 the director of the Imperial Theater invited Cui, Borodin, Rimsky-Korsakov, and Mussorgsky to cooperate in producing a score for a fairy-tale opera called *Mlada.* Among the sections assigned to Mussorgsky was a fantastic scene entitled "The Sacrifice to the Black Goat on Bald Mountain." He went back to his discarded *St. John's Night* score and revamped it for the new opera. *Mlada* never materialized, although Mussorgsky made several unsuccessful attempts to build his scene into a larger work. After his death Rimsky-Korsakov undertook to revise the music, retaining Mussorgsky's intended description of it:

> Subterranean din of supernatural voices. Appearance of Spirits of Darkness, followed by that of the god Tchernobog. Glorification of the Black God, The

Black Mass. Witches' Sabbath, interrupted at its height by the sounds of the far-off bell of the little church in a village. It disperses the Spirits of Darkness. Daybreak.

The Bald Mountain of the title refers to Mt. Triglav, near Kiev, Russia, where according to legend a witches' sabbath is held on every June 24, the Feast of St. John the Baptist. The Black God, Tchernobog, in the form of a black goat, presides at this peculiar rite of witchcraft and religion.

Mussorgsky's score follows its program quite clearly: there are rustling and whistling sounds, abrupt changes from pianissimo to fortissimo, some shrill high notes from the piccolo, and then an uncanny silence. A monotonous theme by oboes and bassoon announces the arrival of the spirits and rises to a noisy climax to introduce the Black God. His appearance prompts a reckless dance urged on by impulsive rhythms in the strings and increasing chromaticism in the winds. When the themes combine, the climax occurs with heavy strokes from the orchestra: homage to the Black God. The witches' sabbath continues in the reprise, where it suddenly breaks off in the middle of a frenzied passage. In the unexpected silence, faraway bells toll; violins echo the insistent chromatic motive; harp tones and a pastoral clarinet melody herald the dawn.

Mussorgsky's songs provide an excellent illustration of his imagination and descriptive powers ("The Song of the Flea," "Songs and Dances of Death"). And his opera *Boris Godounov,* a nationalistic work rich in historical color, ranks as one of the finest operas from the nineteenth century (see page 269).

Nikolai Rimsky-Korsakov (1844–1908) was born into an aristocratic family that had him trained for the navy, and he began a service career even though he possessed musical talent. When he resigned from the navy in 1873, he had already been teaching composition at St. Petersburg Conservatory for two years.

This composer seemed to spend as much time correcting and revising his friends' sometimes haphazard works as he did creating his own small repertoire, which includes Russian fairy-tale operas, such as *Sadko* and *The Golden Cockerel,* chamber works, choral pieces, and numerous piano compositions.

Because he was a master of orchestral color equalled only by Berlioz and Ravel, his orchestral music is what upholds his reputation. In his book *Principles of Orchestration* he wrote:

> Orchestration is *part of the very soul of the work.* A work is thought out in terms of the orchestra, certain tone colours being inseparable from it in the mind of its creator and native to it from the hour of its birth. . . .
>
> The power of subtle orchestration is a secret impossible to transmit, and the composer who possesses this secret should value it highly, and never debase it to the level of a mere collection of formulae learned by heart.[3]

An outstanding example of his orchestrational skill is *Scheherazade, Opus 35* (1888). He originally planned a programmatic symphony having a story for each of its four movements, but he later decided to omit the stories. Lacking even movement titles, the listener will appreciate this symphonic suite better if he knows something about the composer's original intention. The plot, taken from the *Thousand and One Nights,* tells of Sultan Schahriar, who, having lost faith in women, vows to execute every wife after spending one night with her. However, Sultana Scheherazade, the latest wife, beguiles her husband with won-

[3] Nikolai Rimsky-Korsakov, *Principles of Orchestration,* translated by Edward Agate (New York: Dover Publications, Inc., 1964), p. 2.

derful stories, spinning 1,001 tales for as many nights. Impressed with his wife's ability—and agility—the sultan recalls his vow.

For his symphonic synthesis of this story Rimsky-Korsakov chose two principal themes. At the very beginning an assertive, stentorian phrase sounds in unison from the trombone, tuba, horn, woodwinds, and strings. This phrase is sometimes known as the sultan's theme (Ex. 22:2). After a short interlude the

Ex. 22:2. Rimsky-Korsakov: *Scheherazade*

second theme enters, a playful cadenza-like figure played by the violin with support from chords on the harp (Ex. 22:3). This theme may refer to the clever storyteller. Both themes appear early in the first movement, originally titled *The Sea and the Vessel of Sinbad.* The sultan's theme is the stronger, now threatening, now passionate, now quiet. As it gets livelier and more rhythmic, episodes break into it to permit Scheherazade to tell her tales.

Ex. 22:3. Rimsky-Korsakov: *Scheherazade*

A lustrous oriental atmosphere surrounds *The Tale of the Prince Kalender,* the second movement. Scheherazade narrates the tale through a solo violin, with several interruptions by the sultan's theme. In the third movement, *The Young Prince and the Young Princess,* Scheherazade relates a tender love story while the sultan listens in silence. The fourth, *Festival at Bagdad,* begins with a harsh outburst from the sultan. Then Scheherazade tells of a wonderful festival. At the climax, powerful trombones state the sultan's theme, the solo violin answers, and the two unite as the story ends.

Whereas the Russian Five searched their native culture for inspiration, other Russian composers—while remaining within the nationalist framework—preferred to work from predominantly German models and some French models. Tchaikovsky belongs to this category.

Peter Ilich Tchaikovsky

Peter Ilich Tchaikovsky's (1840–1893) early love of music received small encouragement from his parents. He began his working career as a clerk in the Ministry of Justice, relinquished that position in 1863 to study music at the conservatory in St. Petersburg, and in 1866 joined the faculty of the music conservatory in Moscow, where he taught sporadically for 12 years. For the rest of his life he lived quietly in the country when not touring as a conductor. He had ample leisure for composition because of the generous patronage of Nadezhda von Meck, a wealthy widow who guaranteed him an income for 13 years. Tchaikovsky died of cholera nine days after he had conducted the first performance of his sixth symphony.

Although recognized primarily for his orchestral works, Tchaikovsky was not a symphonist by nature. He found it difficult to express himself in abstract sonata form and needed programmatic elements to inspire him. He has been accused of excessive sentimentality, and it must be conceded that his neurotic, emotional nature compelled him to express himself with deep feeling. Thus his symphonies lack strong symphonic character; they make an immediate pleasing impression on the uncritical ear, but they do not wear too well, for emotion needs to be tempered with restraint. Yet his music is inordinately beautiful. His melodies, unlike those of Beethoven and Brahms, came to him not as seeds but as full-blown blossoms.

Tchaikovsky acknowledged his subjective approach to music in a letter to his patroness:

> At the moment of composing, when I am aglow with emotion, it flashes across my mind that all who will hear my music will experience some reflection of what I am feeling myself.[4]

And in describing his general attitude about composing, he wrote:

> I never compose in the abstract; that is to say, the musical thought never appears otherwise than in a suitable external form. In this way I invent the musical idea and the instrumentation simultaneously. . . . As regards the Russian element in my works, I may tell you that not infrequently I begin a composition with the intention of introducing some folk melody into it. Sometimes it comes of its own accord, unbidden. As to this national element in my work, its affinity with the folk songs in some of my melodies and harmonies comes from my having spent my childhood in the country, and, from my earliest years, having been impregnated with the characteristic beauty of our Russian folk music.[5]

Tchaikovsky's phenomenal success is due primarily to the exotic qualities in his music. Two improbable mixtures—a shy nature blended with a passionate temperament, and an Asiatic primitivism with Western culture—produce sensuous, beautiful music that attracts by sheer magnetism.

In *Symphony No. 5 in E Minor, Opus 64* (1888), Tchaikovsky's most popular symphonic work, an introspective melancholy overshadows each movement, creating atmosphere and unity. He places special significance on the theme for the slow introduction: a somber melody (Ex. 22:4) intoned in the low clarinet register and repeated several times. This melody appears in all four movements, thus providing another unifying factor.

Ex. 22:4. Tchaikovsky: *Symphony No. 5 in E Minor*

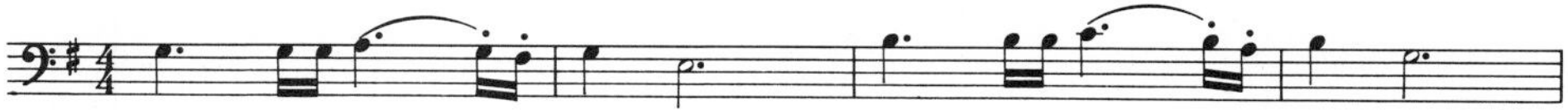

[4] Letter to Mme. von Meck, dated May 3, 1883.

[5] Letter to Mme. von Meck, dated March 5, 1878.

Allegro. In this first movement, the principal theme rises in a pianissimo melody by clarinets, flutes, and then strings, while the orchestra mounts to a march-like climax. The syncopated second theme is equally lyrical and outgoing; after an extended development it combines with the first theme. The development proper emphasizes a little wind motive that was introduced between the two themes. In the recapitulation all climaxes are sharper and stronger, and the long coda fades away into quiet.

Andante cantabile. In this movement the thematic material depends on two melodies, one nostalgic and the other brighter. The movement opens with a horn solo, the clarinet joins in, and then we hear the oboe with horn counterpoint. Before the second section begins, a highly emotional passage sweeps through the orchestra. It begins as a dialogue between clarinet and bassoon, but suddenly the gloomy introductory theme appears. The violins reintroduce the nostalgic first theme and the orchestra again builds to a mighty climax, also capped by the introductory theme. In movements like this, Tchaikovsky's unabashed emotionalism leaves the listener fairly exhausted.

Waltz. This is one of Tchaikovsky's most elegant waltzes. He passes the waltz melody around among the various instruments, using the beautiful ornamented writing typical of his style. In the contrasting middle section a spiccato (played with bouncing bow) figure runs through the violins, breaks up, and later ornaments the reappearing waltz theme. In the coda the clarinets and bassoons recall the ominous theme of the introduction.

Andante maestoso, Allegro vivace. The *Andante* begins with the principal motive of the first movement now stated in a major mode, and the mood changes from gloom to triumph. The ensuing *Allegro vivace* leads the listener through wild dance melodies and stirring rhythms to a lyrical flowing melody. Once again the somber motto theme makes an entrance, heightened by forceful rhythms. The opening maestoso theme is heard again, and a final presto exhibits all the themes.

Of Tchaikovsky's six symphonies,[6] the first three are seldom performed. The fourth, *Opus 36 in F Minor,* confirmed his skill with large orchestral forms. Written in 1877, it is dedicated to Mme. von Meck. His sixth symphony, *Opus 74 in B Minor* (1893), bears the appropriate title *Pathétique,* a symphony of passion and resignation. Tchaikovsky thought this was his best work and referred to it as his most honest, upright creation. It is a masterpiece in Russian music.

Tchaikovsky wrote some of his most engaging music for the ballet: *Swan Lake* (1876), *Sleeping Beauty* (1889), and *The Nutcracker* (1892). With this form he gave free rein to his natural inclination for broad, expansive themes, emotional outbursts, and dramatic fantasy. Of course the ballet music was originally written to be danced to, but Tchaikovsky reworked the ballets into concert suites. For example, the *Swan Lake* ballet suite opens with the first appearance of the swan, from Act I of the ballet. Then follows the celebrated *Waltz* from Act III, with its fine rhythmic details. Next comes the *Dance of the Swan* from Act II

[6] There are, in addition to *Symphonies 1–6,* two unnumbered works: *"Manfred" Symphony in B Minor* (1885) and the recently reconstructed *Symphony in E-Flat Major* (1892).

and the beautiful *Andante non troppo* for violin solo and harp, also from Act II. The suite's fifth movement is the *Hungarian Dance,* a czardas from the last act. And the suite ends with an agitato scene from Act II, displaying a lyrical interlude and resplendent coda.

The Nutcracker ballet suite seems to be a universal favorite. Its bright, happy music shows not a trace of Tchaikovsky's characteristic pessimistic attitude. The story, based on a French version (by Dumas *père*) of E. T. A. Hoffmann's fairy tale "The Nutcracker and the Mouse King," is essentially a Christmas fantasy about a little girl named Clara and her favorite gift, a nutcracker in the form of a man (his jaw cracks the nuts). When her brothers break the precious gift, Clara tenderly treats it as an invalid. Unable to sleep, she creeps downstairs to check on it and finds a great battle in progress between an army of mice and toy soldiers. She hurls her slipper, killing the mouse king, whereupon the nutcracker changes into a Prince Charming who takes Clara to his Kingdom of Sweets and holds a great festival in her honor. This colorful festival forms the material for Act II of the ballet and for Tchaikovsky's concert suite.

I. *Miniature Overture.* Lacking cellos and basses, this music has a light, airy quality. Two contrasting themes seem designed to make the listener smile.

II. *March.* This lovely little march starts softly with trumpets, clarinets, and horns and is graciously taken over by the strings.

III. *Dance of the Sugarplum Fairy.* Here a charming celesta melody sounds above a pizzicato string accompaniment.

IV. *Russian Dance: Trepak.* Wild and coarse, this entire movement is based on a rhythmic figure initiated in the opening measure.

V. *Arabian Dance.* Open fifths in the bass help to create the languid atmosphere of this dance. The oriental-style melody is given first to the clarinet but is soon transferred to the violins.

VI. *Chinese Dance.* In this quaint sketch Tchaikovsky combines the shrill register of the flute with delicate pizzicato figures in bassoons and double basses.

VII. *Dance of the Mirlitons.* A mirliton is similar to a kazoo—a toy instrument into which the player hums. Flutes, replacing the mirlitons in the concert version, present the main subject, a delicate graceful tune, and trumpets provide a contrasting middle section.

VIII. *Waltz of the Flowers.* An introductory passage employs woodwinds and horn with harp cadenza; the principal theme enters first in the horns, then the clarinet. Other melodic passages feature flute, oboe, and strings. A brilliant coda ends the waltz and the ballet suite.

BOHEMIA

Although Bohemia (now part of Czechoslovakia) has been musically active since the sixteenth century, during that century and through the seventeenth most professional musicians working there were foreigners. In the eighteenth century, Bohemia produced her own native performers and composers. One of these, Jan Ladislav Dussek (1760–1812), gained an international reputation in his day, but most of his compositions are now undeservedly neglected.

Bedřich Smetana

The Bohemian composer Bedřich Smetana (1824–1884) has fared considerably better than his predecessors. As a child he revealed a conspicuous talent and became a piano virtuoso. After a term as conductor of the Philharmonic Society of Gothenburg (Sweden) he returned to Bohemia as chief conductor of the National Theater at Prague. Sudden deafness in later life and disappointment from the failure of some of his works impaired his physical and mental health. He died in an asylum for the insane.

Smetana wrote several operas on national subjects, the most important being *The Bartered Bride* (1866), an exceptionally charming comic opera. Its crisp, sparkling *Overture* is a stable item in symphonic repertoire.

Like the opera, the *Overture* is characterized by fresh, Bohemian folk-tune elements. A lively fugato develops from the first theme, which is stated by strings and woodwinds against sonorous brass and accented kettledrums; the swiftly paced fugal treatment leads to a rustic dance. The lyrical secondary theme in the oboe cannot resist the general excitement, and the music rushes on to a frenzied end. This music's entrancing quality springs from Smetana's melodic talent and his lively, forceful thematic treatment.

Toward the end of his life Smetana preferred instrumental composition. In 1874 he wrote two symphonic poems, *Vyšehrad* and *The Moldau.* Later he produced four additional poems and grouped the six into a large cycle (1874–1879) called *Má Vlast* (My Fatherland).

Antonin Dvořák

Whereas Smetana is usually associated with the tone poem, Antonin Dvořák (1841–1904) belongs among the outstanding nineteenth-century symphonists. Dvořák's parents were sympathetic with his musical ambitions. Born in Nelahozeves, near Prague, he studied voice, violin, organ, and viola, and ultimately came under the influence of Smetana, a contact which confirmed his natural penchant for a nationalistic style.

He taught composition at the Prague Conservatory for a brief period and in 1892 was invited to be director of the National Conservatory of Music in New York, a post he held for three years. For a time he lived in the predominantly Bohemian town of Spillville, Iowa, where he worked on his famous *Symphony in E Minor, Opus 95* ("From the New World"), and the *Quartet No. 6 in F, Opus 96* ("American," 1893).

The *Symphony in E Minor* (1893) always pleases audiences with its melodic richness and poetic content. Dvořák uses a few melodic ideas derived from Indian and Negro folk elements, but melodies and rhythms from his homeland constitute the lifeblood of the symphony. The whole work reveals his superb sense of orchestration; his use of woodwinds and horns is particularly adept. Orchestras enjoy playing Dvořák symphonies, for every instrument takes a prominent role at some time during the course of action. He learned his orchestration firsthand when he served as violist in the Czech National Theater orchestra.

Adagio: Allegro molto. The slow introduction gradually introduces a mysterious atmosphere as lower strings outline a phrase answered by flutes and oboes. A preliminary hearing of the principal theme's first section leads to a brief orchestral outburst. Shortly thereafter the *Allegro molto* ushers in the entire first theme (Ex. 22:5). There are two phrases: the first is a straightforward ascending and descending arpeggio motive on the horns; the second phrase, in thirds, is played by the woodwinds (clarinets and bassoons).

Ex. 22:5. Dvořák: *Symphony in E Minor: Allegro molto*

This movement contains two more themes. The second, in *g* minor, has a peasant-dance character. The flute plays this melody and oboe and clarinet present a countertheme, while shimmering strings form a supporting background. Sung by the flute, the third theme, in *G* major, reminds some listeners of the spiritual "Swing Low, Sweet Chariot." The development of all these melodies is artful, if uneventful: themes one and three are combined and juxtaposed in colorful sequences of skillful orchestration.

Largo. In this musical landscape one almost "hears" the silence of nature. Hushed chords in the brasses and low woodwinds carry the tonality from *e* minor to *D*-flat major in four measures of modulation. Then muted strings support the English horn as it presents one of the most famous melodies in orchestral literature (Ex. 22:6). An episode on the oboe over a sustained note by cellos is, according to Dvořák, meant to suggest the awakening of animal life on the prairie. Retaining the listener's interest, the trombone states the first movement's principal theme. Then the lovely horn theme enters, bringing the *Largo* to an exquisite conclusion.

Ex. 22:6. Dvořák: *Symphony in E Minor: Largo*

Scherzo: Molto vivace. In customary symphonic fashion Dvořák's turbulent, elemental scherzo sweeps away all traces of the nostalgic slow movement. Strumming strings intone a repeated chord that is actually an unresolved discord. High flutes and oboes chirp out the principal melody. Later a passage marked *poco sostenuto* intrudes as Dvořák sets up an idyllic, graceful dance played first by flutes and oboes, then by bassoons and cellos.

After a repeat of the first theme the trio emerges. It seems as though the composer determined to make this a flute and oboe scherzo, for here again these two woodwinds play a kind of rustic dance. As in the slow movement, there is a flash of the first movement's arpeggio theme before the scherzo concludes.

Allegro con fuoco. This vibrant finale contains three highly contrasted themes. The leading theme blares from horns and trumpets against a fortissimo orchestral accompaniment. A solo clarinet provides a lyric passage as it sings the expansive second theme to an accompaniment of tremolo strings. The vigorous closing theme ends in an unintentional tribute to "Three Blind Mice."

Themes from the three previous movements appear in the colorful coda, as though making a final bow, but after an intriguing recall of the finale's main theme the listener is startled to hear the arpeggio theme from the first movement—in *E* major. With this fitting surprise Dvořák ends his symphony.

THE NORTH COUNTRIES

During the nineteenth century Scandinavia and Finland, like Russia, lagged behind in producing serious music. Scandinavian composers usually received their educations in Germany—frequently at the Leipzig Conservatory—so their musical development in some respects parallels that of the German composers. But there the similarity ends; in sharp contrast with Germany, the Scandinavian countries have produced only a small amount of music by major composers.

Norway: Edvard Grieg

One name immediately comes to mind when the subject of Norwegian music arises: Edvard Grieg (1843–1907), who was born in Bergen and reached maturity along with Norway's renowned literary figures Björnson and Ibsen. Following the custom of the times, he was educated in Germany, but early in life he knew he wanted to write music that would reproduce Norway's vigorous spirit. His good friend Richard Nordraak—a promising composer who died at 22—encouraged him in this desire and aroused his interest in folk material.

Opinions differ about Grieg's real value as a composer: some critics dismiss him as mediocre; others consider him a master craftsman. The truth lies somewhere between these two extremes. He might be called a "*petit maître*"—a composer excelling in miniature compositions (the song and the short piano piece). But even in this respect he cannot be compared with Schubert and Schumann, for he was an entirely different type of composer. He was a realist who found inspiration in nature: fjords, mountain streams, and Norway's magnificent landscapes. As Norway's balladeer, Grieg sang well.

If Felix Mendelssohn is conceded the honor of having written the most popular violin concerto, Edvard Grieg has earned equal status in the piano field with his *Concerto in A Minor, Opus 16* (1868). Although the formal and structural logic of this piano concerto might be challenged, all arguments vanish before the composition's inimitable charm: the melodies are warm, the rhythms piquant; and the concerto as a whole emanates a picturesque quality that very clearly speaks of Norway.

Finland: Jean Sibelius

Jean Sibelius (1865–1957), Finland's outstanding musical patriot, showed his talent at an early age, but his family decided on a law career and he enrolled at the University of Helsingfors. At the same time he began violin lessons at the conservatory and after a year was allowed to devote himself wholly to music. In 1889 he took advanced studies in Berlin and then Vienna; by 1893 he was back in Finland to stay. In recognition and appreciation of his talents, the

Finnish government granted Sibelius a life pension in 1897, permitting him to give his undivided attention to musical composition. For 30 years he carved out an enviable reputation as Finland's foremost citizen, composing musical works that stirred the hearts and emotions of his countrymen. During the last 30 years of his life he published nothing.

Sibelius' reputation rests on his symphonic music. His concept of symphonic form remains pretty much within a basically nineteenth-century idiom, and his style involves repeated short motives from which themes develop. He later transforms these themes, producing an extremely fluid melodic style. His interesting orchestration reveals that he liked dark woodwind colors. Frequently he highlights individual instrumental choirs: string passages (often pizzicato), woodwind sections, brass phrases.

Despite the artistic merits of the symphonies, the tone poems stand as his most beloved works. Many of them are based on the Finnish national epic *Kalevala*—for example, the early *En Saga* (1892, revised 1901), the *Legends* (including *The Swan of Tuonela,* 1893), and the symphonic fantasy *Pohjola's Daughter* (1906).

Sibelius' most popular single composition is *Finlandia.* For foreigners this is a warmly evocative tone poem; for Sibelius' compatriots this dramatic work was and is a symbol of national pride, their anthem of independence. When he wrote this epic work, his tiny country lay under Russian domination; he finished it in 1899, but it was banned until 1905.

Finlandia's formal scheme is fairly simple. It begins with an introduction *andante sostenuto,* notable for a few powerful brass chords. Trombones proclaim the religious solemnity of the initial theme. The *allegro moderato* section launches spirited rhythmic figures into a dancing tune. When the tempo quickens to *allegro,* a militant trombone theme appears, and the drum and triangle create distinctive orchestral coloring. This mood is interrupted by a contrasting theme, a sad folklike tune played by the woodwinds and echoed by the strings. The vigorous coda is based on the introductory section.

SPAIN

Early-nineteenth-century Spanish composers produced few masterworks, and Spanish music shows only slight progress until late in the century. The Italian music that invaded the Iberian peninsula played a large part in stifling Spanish nationalism for many decades. Fortunately, during the late nineteenth century and the early part of the twentieth, Spain came into her own with a musical renaissance created by three composers: Isaac Albéniz, Enrique Granados, and Manuel de Falla. Although many basic technical elements of this repertoire originated in foreign lands, the spiritual and inspirational qualities definitely stem from the heart of the Iberian peninsula.

Isaac Albéniz

Isaac Albéniz (1860–1909) made the first significant contributions with a repertoire of dazzling, picturesque, and thoroughly refined piano music. As a child prodigy he gave his first piano recital at age four, followed later by the usual routine of concert tours and studies in Paris, Leipzig, and Madrid. He finally settled in Paris as professor of piano at the *Schola Cantorum,* remaining there until his death in 1909.

He composed his finest, most representative music toward the end of his life while he lived in Paris in the ambience of Ernest Chausson, Gabriel Fauré, and Paul Dukas, but his association with this French force did not prevent his own music from reflecting his innate Spanish culture. The masterworks of this most Spanish of Spanish composers clearly reveal the basic characteristics of his art: objectivity and realism.

Albéniz was not a true Romantic in the sense that Chopin and Schumann were Romantics; emotionally he was a more objective composer than even his contemporaries, but like them he received his creative inspirations from the natural beauties in his native country and from the vividly dramatic characteristics of his own people. His musical language and forms set Albéniz apart from his fellow-composers in Spain, for in his works these elements derive from a foreign culture, particularly the French music of his period.

Published in 1906–1909, the suite *Iberia* is Albéniz' masterpiece of pianistic writing. Its twelve pieces—distributed in four volumes—are all based on Spanish scenes and landscapes. Claude Debussy wrote one of the best testimonials to *Iberia:*

> Few works of music equal *El Albaicín* from the third volume of *Iberia,* where one recaptures the atmosphere of those evenings in Spain which exude the odors of flowers and brandy. . . . It is like the muffled sounds of a guitar sighing in the night, with abrupt awakenings, nervous starts. Without exactly using popular themes, this music comes from one who has drunk of them, heard them, up to the point of making them pass into his music so that it is impossible to perceive the line of demarcation.
>
> *Eritaña,* from the fourth volume of *Iberia,* describes the joy of mornings, the propitious encounter of an inn where the wine is cool. An incessantly changing crowd passes by amid gales of laughter punctuated by the tinkles of the tambourine. Never has music attained such diverse, such colored impressions; the eyes close as if dazzled by having seen too many images.
>
> There are many other things in these volumes of *Iberia,* where Albéniz has put the best of himself and carried his scruples of "writing" to exaggeration by this generous need which went to the point of "throwing the music out of the window."[7]

Iberia exhibits in varying degrees all the characteristics of Albéniz' creative art and pianistic ability. This music has a richness and density that make it extremely difficult to play. Just the same, it must not be considered as purely virtuoso music; it is, rather, a set of tone pictures. In many sections Albéniz uses formulas that appear to be closely related to those employed by Scarlatti, whose works Albéniz often performed at concerts. Albéniz' personal concept of contrapuntal writing also adds to his music's effectiveness.

Enrique Granados

Born in Catalonia to a Cuban father and a Galician mother, Enrique Granados (1867–1916) completed his early studies in Spain, then in 1887 went to

[7] Claude Debussy, *"Les Concerts,"* in the *Revue Musicale de la Société Internationale de Musique* (December 1, 1913), p. 43. English translation by the author.

Paris as a private piano student with Charles Bériot. After his first piano recital in Barcelona in 1890, he performed in Spain and France, both as soloist and accompanist, and in 1900 he returned to Barcelona where he founded the Society of Classical Concerts.

Granados has been criticized for being less "Spanish" in his music than Albéniz and others. It may be true that his works do not sound as "authentic" as those of his contemporaries, for his subjective approach carried him beyond the limitations of Hispanicism. With Granados, Hispanicism served only as a basic outline, a means to an end.

The technical problems encountered in Granados' works are less complicated than those in Albéniz' music. Granados favored passages in thirds and contrapuntal figurations, and at times he ignored standard notational practices, but these must be recognized as offshoots of his tonal language and necessary components of his style.

In a letter to a friend Granados wrote:

> I have composed a collection of *"Goyescas"* of great sweep and difficulty. They are the reward of my efforts to arrive. They say I have arrived. I fell in love with Goya's psychology, with his palette. With him and with the Duchess of Alba; with his lady *maja,* with his models, with his quarrels, his loves and his flirtations.[8]

Granados worked for a long time on the *Goyescas,* jotting down ideas and sketches. Their definitive form began to take shape in his mind in 1909, and the six piano pieces, conceived as a suite, appeared in 1911.[9] This his greatest work is a masterpiece in the history of Spanish music. Its musical scenes, inspired by the paintings of Francisco Goya, the eighteenth-century Spanish artist whom Granados passionately admired, invoke the singularly dramatic atmosphere of Spain at the time of Carlos III and Carlos IV. Like the painter, the composer revivifies the aristocratic and popular life that distinguished the age of Goya.

Manuel de Falla

Esteemed as one of Spain's greatest composers, Manuel de Falla (1876–1946) is the spiritual father of Spanish contemporary music. His mother was an excellent pianist who instilled in him his love for music. When he was 20, the family moved to Madrid and there Falla studied piano and composition. In 1907 he realized his dream of a trip to Paris, where he planned to spend just one week listening to music and learning about the works of his contemporaries. His seven-day visit stretched to a seven-year stay, during which he made friends with Debussy, Ravel, Dukas, and even Albéniz, who visited Paris for a time.

Falla's friendship with Debussy and Ravel could account for the impressionistic feeling evident in some of his compositions. Still, he is only partly an Impressionist; the weaker impressionistic elements are missing from his music. Its form and melodic line are sharply defined, and the rhythmic vitality is astonishing and attractive. If any one person influenced Falla's style, it was Paul Dukas, whose music displays the same craftsmanship and refinement.

[8] Antonio Fernández-Cid, *Granados* (Madrid: Samarán Ediciones, 1956), pp. 191–192. English translation by the author.

[9] In 1914 Granados completed an opera, also called *Goyescas,* based mostly on material from his piano suite.

Falla's repertoire is small, but almost all of it is important. His most significant, representative works include two operas, *La vida breve* (Life Is Short, 1905) and *El retablo de Maese Pedro* (Master Peter's Puppet Show, 1923), the latter being an opera for puppet theater; symphonic impressions for piano and orchestra entitled *Nights in the Gardens of Spain* (1909–1915); a *Concerto* for harpsichord and chamber ensemble (1926); and two ballets, *The Three-Cornered Hat* (1919) and *El amor brujo* (1915).

El amor brujo, Falla's most popular work, was first produced in 1915. He had been asked to compose some music for a famous Spanish dancer named Pastora Imperio, whose mother (another dancer) briefed Falla with *soleares, seguiriyas, martinetes,* and other songs and dances typical of Andalucia. Even though the ballet receives only infrequent performances, the music is often played in a concert version.

A literal translation of the title is unsatisfactory (the word *brujo* means male witch); perhaps The Specter's Bride would be the best English equivalent. The plot comes from a folk tale in which the ghost of a dead lover always appears at the moment when a new lover tries to take his place.

In Falla's ballet a beautiful gypsy girl named Candélas fears the ghost of an evil, jealous gypsy who once loved her. Whenever the handsome Carmélo approaches her to press his suit, the ghost appears and the girl runs away. Carmélo persuades Candélas' friend Lucia to allow the ghost to make love to her, so Lucia is present when Carmélo comes next day to see Candélas. When the ghost arrives, he finds Lucia irresistible; Carmélo has opportunity to convince Candélas of his love; the lovers embrace and the ghost is conquered forever.

The ballet music is scored for a small orchestra with piano, and a contralto sings from the orchestra. She sings *Canción del amor dolido* (Song of Sorrowful Love) followed by three sighing chords for strings. A muted trumpet sounds an agitated phrase to announce the ghost, and the orchestra plays a *Dance of Terror.* The clock strikes twelve. Candélas dances the *Ritual Fire Dance* to drive away all evil spirits, but still the ghost returns. A voice (from the orchestra) is heard singing the *Canción del fuego fátuo* (Song of the Jack-o'-lantern).

A *Pantomime* (a slow dance) in $\frac{7}{8}$ meter follows. As Lucia diverts the ghost's attention with the *Danza del juego de amor* (Dance of the Diversion of Love), the mysterious voice is heard again. Finally, after the ghost vanishes, some of the dancers find his clothes and exhibit them. Then bells announce daybreak.

THE WALTZ KING: JOHANN STRAUSS II

It would be grossly unfair to conclude a survey of nationalist music without mentioning the Viennese Waltz. During the latter half of the nineteenth century, the Lanner family and the Strauss family (among others) supplied Viennese society with dozens of scintillating, effervescent orchestral waltzes, which since then have pleased listeners all over the world.

As the most famous composer of these fascinating pieces, Johann Strauss II (1825–1899) was known as the "Waltz King." He literally raised the waltz to the status of an art form. A typical Strauss waltz is actually a series of waltz melodies unified through great imagination and skillful orchestration. Such waltzes as *Acceleration, Artist's Life, The Blue Danube, Tales from the Vienna*

Woods, and *Wine, Women and Song* have been played by the world's greatest orchestras and heard by millions. Strauss also used his melodic gifts to create perennially famous operettas such as *Die Fledermaus* (The Bat, 1874) and *The Gypsy Baron* (1885).

SUMMARY: THE ROMANTIC ERA

If it were possible to reduce the nineteenth century to commonly held ideas, these would doubtlessly contain *freedom, nationalism, love of nature,* and *interest in the past* as key words.

The French Revolution culminated a long period of social and economic dissatisfaction in France, while other European countries kept working to relieve their living conditions, each with varying success. Freedom as an idea and an ideal appeared in the arts first as individualism. The individual artist became a potential unique virtuoso. Victor Hugo's masterful, vivid prose and emotion-charged verse created his personal fame. Delacroix's technique in his dramatic, sensuous paintings earned his particular reputation. Extroverted musical showmen such as Paganini and Liszt astonished audiences with unbelievable virtuoso performances.

As the nineteenth century progressed, nationalism provided the individual artist with a cause to champion, and each promoted it in his own way. Musicians discovered unlimited inspiration for operas and symphonic poems in the rich hoard of historical and folk material available in nearly every country. In Russia, Modest Mussorgsky based his opera *Boris Godounov* on the tragic life of that pseudo-czar. In Bohemia, Antonin Dvořák caught and preserved his nation's essential spirit in his stylized *Slavonic Dances.*

The back-to-nature doctrine originally sponsored by Rousseau in the preceding century stimulated a strong nineteenth-century interest in natural, simple subject matter. Even Beethoven made a rare excursion into the field of descriptive music with his "Pastoral" symphony. Wagner's *Forest Murmurs,* from *Siegfried,* is a musical nature sketch, and Mendelssohn's overture *Fingal's Cave* is a sensational musical seascape.

Romanticism has always symbolized interest in the past. Nineteenth-century artists, writers, and composers all found congenial subject matter by exploring and reviving the past, from antiquity to their own day. Berlioz wrote an opera based on Virgil's *Aeneid.* Liszt was inspired by Petrarca, Dante, and Michelangelo. And Felix Mendelssohn revived the music of Bach almost 80 years after that master's death.

> The period of "nationalism" in music was a short one. Speaking in lexicographic parlance, the various "fathers" of the music of their countries—Glinka in Russia, Smetana in Bohemia, Grieg and Sinding [Norwegian composer, 1850–1941] among the Scandinavians—are all recent figures, the latter within our own memory. The high-water mark was reached at the turn of the nineteenth century, apparently coinciding with the collapse of the so-called postromantic era, as impressionism salvaged and arbitrarily appropriated many of the new and heretofore characteristic means of expression, making out of them a new international style the components of which suited Debussy as well as a Falla, a Respighi, or a Delius.[10]

[10] Paul Henry Lang, *Music in Western Civilization* (New York: W. W. Norton & Co., Inc., 1941), pp. 943–944. Reprinted by permission.

FOR DISCUSSION AND ASSIGNMENT

1. Listen to one of Mussorgsky's short compositions. Does it sound "Russian"? Also listen to one of Grieg's and Dvořák's. Do you think that ethnic characteristics can be expressed musically?
2. Several years ago the popular Broadway musical comedy *Kismet* drew extensively from Borodin's music. Another, the *Song of Norway,* featured Grieg's music. Listen to some selections. Do you think that transformations such as these help or hurt a composer's reputation? Do they spoil the enjoyment of the original musical version?
3. Compare the music of Albéniz, Granados, and Falla. Does one sound more authentically "Spanish" than the others?

FOR FURTHER READING

Abraham, Gerald, editor. *Grieg: A Symposium.* Norman, Oklahoma: University of Oklahoma Press, 1950. A select collection of essays on Grieg and his music by acknowledged authorities.

Calvocoressi, M. D. *Mussorgsky.* New York: Collier Books, 1962. PB. Calvocoressi died before finishing his book; the English musical historian Gerald Abraham completed the text. This excellent book contains among other attractive features an abundantly illustrated analysis of *Boris Godounov.*

Chase, Gilbert. *The Music of Spain.* New York: Dover Publications, 1959. PB. This history of Spanish music provides a superb introduction to the musical culture of the Iberian peninsula.

Einstein, Alfred. *Music in the Romantic Era.* New York: W. W. Norton & Co., Inc., 1947. The author has made an interesting survey of nineteenth-century music. The language is somewhat flowery but then so was the Romantic period.

Evans, Edwin. *Tchaikovsky,* revised by Gerald Abraham. New York: Collier Books, 1963. PB. Edwin Evans based this study on Modest Tchaikovsky's (the composer's brother) *Life and Letters.* Evans' standard work, published in 1906, has been brought up to date by Gerald Abraham.

Leonard, Richard Anthony. *A History of Russian Music.* New York: The Macmillan Co., 1957. This is a succinct, interesting, and informative survey for the general reader.

Robertson, Alec. *Dvořák.* New York: Collier Books, 1962. PB. This popular little book (Collier's Great Composers Series) offers a very readable account of Dvořák's life and musical repertoire.

Impressionism 23

Music must come first:
Choose for this an irregular rhythm,
More indefinite, more soluble in air,
With nothing clumsy or affected.

You must not at all
Choose your words without some contempt:
The finest song is a vague song
Where indecision joins precision.

PAUL VERLAINE
The Art of Poetry (1884)

During the last quarter of the nineteenth century the fine arts adopted a new aesthetic, called Impressionism, which lasted for only a few decades into the twentieth century. Around 1870 a group of young artists rejected the then accepted schools of Romanticism and Realism in favor of a new painting movement dedicated to ideals considered revolutionary by their contemporaries. Searching for an escape from the typical nineteenth-century Romantic approach, they evolved an art premised as a direct, immediate portrayal of the artist's impression of a subject.

In 1874, Claude Monet exhibited a painting called *Impression—Sunrise.*

> At first, *impressionism* was picked up as a term of critical derision. But the word has a certain appropriateness, implying as it does something unfinished, incomplete, an affair of the moment, an act of instantaneous vision, a sensation rather than a cognition.[1]

The Impressionist movement flourished predominantly in France, and its finest products are French. Although the members of this early avant-garde school—Monet, Edouard Manet, Pierre Auguste Renoir (Ill. 23:1), and Edgar Degas (Ill. 23:2) among others—admitted that realistic presentations could also be artistic, they maintained that for their purposes realism played little or no part in achieving an artistic result. Completely indifferent to subject matter,

[1] William Fleming, *Arts and Ideas,* p. 675. Copyright © 1966 by Holt, Rinehart and Winston, Inc., New York. Reprinted by permission.

Ill. 23:1. ***Auguste Renoir (1841–1919),*** **The Lerolle Daughters at the Piano.** ***Louvre, Paris. Photo courtesy of Bulloz-Art Reference Bureau.***

they concentrated on the *manner* in which a picture was painted, and they used dabs or strokes of unmixed primary colors to simulate the natural appearance of their subjects.

In literature, and especially in poetry, Impressionism extended into a movement known as Symbolism. The Symbolists wanted to free verse techniques in order to achieve fluidity. Poetry's new function was to suggest, to evoke, rather than to describe realistically. The prophet for literary Impressionism was Charles Baudelaire, who in his poetry vividly demonstrated his theories about sound and poetic music and the symbolic relations of scent and color. The Symbolist movement attracted such gifted poets as Arthur Rimbaud, Paul Verlaine, and Stéphane Mallarmé. These poets chose to express their immediate reactions to a subject through symbolic images, and they advocated that syntax should be ignored and that words should be arranged for their emotional and aesthetic value. Verlaine illustrated this doctrine in one of his poems when he stated *De la*

Ill. 23:2. *Edgar Degas (1834–1917)*, Degas' Father Listening to the Guitarist Pagans. *Courtesy of Museum of Fine Arts, Boston, bequest of John T. Spaulding.*

musique avant toute chose (music before everything), referring, of course, to the musicality of words and word combinations.

The sonorous art of music proved to be a perfect vehicle for demonstrating Impressionism's basic theories. Since music is essentially an abstract art, it was ideally suited to the projection of Impressionism's vague images. Impressionist composers settled on two favorite mediums: the orchestra, because of its multi-hued tonal palette; and the piano (both as a solo instrument and as a copartner in the French art song), because its damper pedal permitted vibrating harmonies to suspend in mid-air.

CLAUDE DEBUSSY

The ideals and aims of the Impressionists and Symbolists were introduced into music principally by Claude Achille Debussy (1862–1918), one of the most important composers in history. Like Chopin and Liszt before him, Debussy refused to accept the tonal and stylistic restrictions set up by his predecessors and so proceeded to invent new writing techniques and coloristic devices. He also introduced a new approach to musical composition with a theory influenced more by other arts than by purely musical considerations. The music Debussy created through this unique approach has profoundly affected twentieth-century music.

Debussy showed little promise as a student at the Paris Conservatory. He bewildered his professors with his audacious chord progressions and unorthodox attitude toward musical composition. A summer tour through Russia as personal pianist for Mme. von Meck, patroness of Tchaikovsky, broadened his musical horizons; he listened avidly to works by Russian nationalist composers and eagerly sought out the colorful Slavic folk music. After winning the coveted *Prix de Rome,* he spent considerable time in that romantic Italian city, playing through Wagnerian opera scores and suffering from homesickness. His admiration for Wagner waned after he became acquainted with Mussorgsky through *Boris Godounov,* and he found other unusual musical pleasures in the Javanese music he heard at the Paris Exposition of 1889.

No matter what musical influences touched Debussy, they were always relegated to secondary importance. (Where in his music does one find the stark realism of *Boris?*) Although he did use oriental scale types from time to time, his basic art is French. In truth the direct influences stimulating Debussy did not lie within musical bounds, for this original composer found his creative inspiration in Impressionist paintings and Symbolist literature. The painters revealed to him the restless beauty of chiaroscuro (contrasts between light and shadow) and how to record the immediate impression. Symbolist writers—perhaps the stronger inspiration—showed him the art of suggestion through a word or turn of a phrase, the drama of half tones, the beauty of sound for sound's sake. These different influences unquestionably had a major role in shaping Debussy's approach, but his interpretation of these ideas was unique: the style was evolved, molded, and developed by Debussy alone. (Debussy disliked the term Impressionism, as had the painters when it was first applied to them. However, the word has persisted in reference to his style.)

Several of Debussy's stylistic traits are easily perceivable, at least in general outline, because they were so unusual in his day. His harmonies are especially noticeable. When compared with standard nineteenth-century harmony, Debussy's harmonic method appears to have challenged all accepted writing practices; rules meant nothing to him, for he cared only about expressing his inner self.

What are his harmonic concepts? First, Debussy used dissonance freely: sevenths, ninths, and elevenths appear on the dominant or other degrees of the scale, neither prepared nor resolved, often in series used consecutively. He also depended on various altered chords or a sustained chord with superimposed foreign harmonies that suggest polytonality. In many instances he used parallel series of perfect intervals: fifths, fourths, and octaves.

The melodic element in Debussy's music is more difficult to analyze. One attractive characteristic arises from his diversified melodic procedures. Many times he preferred to construct melodies on modal scales. This blending of old and new—fusing a kind of Gregorian chant with a highly original harmonic apparatus—produced ultrasensitive tonal pictures. Modality happened to be only one of several melodic possibilities available to Debussy. When he desired an oriental mood, he based his melodic ideas on the pentatonic scale: a five-note sequence (corresponding to the black notes on the piano keyboard) found in the music of many Eastern cultures. Elsewhere Debussy worked out a completely personalized scale, the whole-tone scale.

He deftly and artistically handled other facets of composition. His works rely heavily on modulation enhanced by the many passing and nonharmonic tones found in his music. His ideas on form and development were considered outlandish by his contemporaries. As he once wrote to his publisher:

> I am more and more convinced that music, by its very nature, is something that cannot be poured into a tight and traditional form. It is made up of colors and rhythms.[2]

With Debussy the music develops somewhat organically: one idea is initiated and expanded; in the process another idea blossoms in a seemingly logical manner, and it in turn receives the same treatment. Naturally Debussy often used a type of A B A ternary form for his short piano pieces, but even then he took great liberties with structure. Finally, he runs a full course in rhythms: from compositions almost intentionally static to sparkling pieces containing the most modern animated rhythms.

Piano Music

As a practicing musician, Debussy was a pianist. He had no command of any other instrument and was only an indifferent conductor; therefore, in composing for the piano he took advantage of the one expressive medium responsive to his personal touch. Since the piano is an instrument of harmonic and tonal blending rather than simple melodic statement, it was a natural experimental medium for his personal art. He provided his piano scores with scrupulous directions for performance, insisting that his music required no personal interpretation by the pianist but that it should be played exactly as he stipulated.

Debussy's first indications of strong individualism appeared in *Suite bergamasque* (1890–1905). Although this suite contains four pieces, there is no

[2] Letter to Jacques Durand, dated September 3, 1907.

attempt at tonal unity as there would be in a classic French suite by Couperin or Rameau. On the whole, the collection barely hints at the masterpieces he would later produce. *Prélude* is clever in the Romantic vein; *Passepied* shows a pavane spirit; the *Menuet* is classic, a style Debussy soon discarded; and the well-known *Clair de lune* is that portion of *Suite bergamasque* anticipating the preludes he composed 20 years later. With its volatile harmonies and diatonic melodic lines it is a pleasing piano work, but the attention given to it could be far better spent on some of Debussy's finer works.

During the last decade of the nineteenth century Debussy wrote little piano music. In this period he discovered his true style and produced more mature works, such as the *String Quartet in G Minor* (1893), the orchestral *Nocturnes* (1893–1899), and the opera *Pelléas et Mélisande* (1892–1902). His second significant collection of piano pieces was his first keyboard masterpiece, the suite *Pour le piano* (For the Piano, 1896–1901). After *Pour le piano* he published a new piano collection almost every year: *Estampes* (1903); *Images* (1905, 1907); *Children's Corner* (1906–1908).

The essence of Debussy's talent for piano writing rests in two volumes of *Préludes* (12 pieces in each). The first book appeared in 1910, the second in 1913. These 24 *Préludes* reveal his genius guided by firm technique and honest, satisfying expressive means.

It seems unnecessary to consider each *Prélude* as it appears in the collections because there is no connection at all between consecutive works. One could invent an arbitrary classification of the basic ideas for the preludes; for instance, some are definitely based on the dance or elements taken from the dance. One of the most impressive of these is *La puerta del vino.* Manuel de Falla had sent Debussy a postcard showing that famous gate in Granada, but whether this prelude is or is not an attempt at music pictorialization is hardly important. More significant is the distinct Spanish mood achieved by means of habanera rhythm, melodic embellishment, and guitar-like chord clusters (Ex. 23:1).

Ex. 23:1. Debussy: *La puerta del vino*

Permission for reprint granted by Durand and Cie, Paris, copyright owners; Elkan-Vogel Co., Inc., Philadelphia, agents.

Of the several *Préludes* drawn from legend and myth, one is heard more than any other Debussy prelude: *La cathédrale engloutie* (The Engulfed Cathedral), very likely inspired by the story of the legendary kingdom of Ys, a tale that another French composer, Edouard Lalo (1823–1892), expanded and transformed into an opera (*Le roi d'Ys*). Debussy introduces a mystical feeling through a series of parallel fifths and octaves. An undulating motive in the piano's lower register suggests swirling waters as the cathedral surges up out of the sea. A fragmentary chantlike melody becomes audible before the cathedral, accompanied by more undulations, slips back into its watery home. Such a graphic account may go beyond Debussy's original intention, but whatever the story this is amazingly descriptive music.

Most of the *Préludes* were designed simply to create atmosphere. For example, the title *Les sons et les parfums tournent dans l'air du soir* (Sounds and Perfumes Are Turning in the Evening Air), from Baudelaire's poem *Harmonie du soir,* is as vague and yet as suggestive as the prelude it accompanies. *Voiles* (Sails) is constructed almost entirely on the whole-tone scale and is a wonderful example of Debussy's singular individuality. And titles like *Bruyères* (Heather), *Brouillards* (Mists), *Feuilles mortes* (Dead Leaves), and *Ce qu'a vu le vent d'ouest* (What the West Wind Has Seen) substantiate the belief that Debussy hoped only to project a mood or a reaction.

The final prelude in the second book contains elements from all the earlier types in the two books. *Feux d'artifice* (Fireworks) creates a decidedly tense atmosphere, but the fireworks explosions are surprisingly pictorial and realistic. A touch of patriotism—a reference to the *Marseillaise*—closes the final prelude.

Debussy's *Préludes*—or even just one—offer a profusion of new sounds. But more than that they supply valid proof that music can be forcefully expressive, that it is capable of illustrating the inexpressible, and that it can suggest the unreal in a quite realistic fashion.

Chamber Music

Claude Debussy wrote comparatively few chamber works, and those were written at the beginning and at the end of his career. One of his first works to be published and performed was the *String Quartet* of 1893. Afflicted with cancer toward the end of his life, he worked feverishly, announcing six forthcoming sonatas for various instrumental combinations. Only three of these appeared: a sonata for violoncello and piano, one for flute, viola, and harp, and one for violin and piano. The next sonata was intended for the unusual combination of oboe, horn, and harpsichord.

Debussy's *String Quartet in G Minor, Opus 10,* written when he was only 31, shows him with one foot in the camp of César Franck and his followers, the other anticipating an entirely new procedure (his next work was to be the *Afternoon of a Faun*). The cyclic form apparent in the quartet is of course inherited from Franck. Debussy employs it in three of his four movements but always with absolute freedom. Contrary to Franck's procedure, Debussy uses only minimal thematic development.

The quartet's cool restraint, its shimmering arpeggios and tremolos, and its refinement and elegance create an expressive subtlety and veiled coloring previously unknown. It contains minute variations pieced together into a mosaic of prismatic harmonies, while the overall impression suggests progressive transformations of a single musical idea.

Animé et très décidé (Animated and very decisive). Bold, sudden mood distinctions mark the clean-cut opening of this movement. The first measure sets up a vigorous germinal theme; a second, more tranquil subject—with violin and viola solos in octaves and ninths—provides suitable contrast. An interesting point occurs in the development when the theme is restated with double stopping for all instruments.

Assez vif et bien rhythmé (Rather lively and rhythmic). In this scherzo in ternary form the germinal theme changes from a $\frac{4}{4}$ to $\frac{6}{8}$ metrical scheme: this theme first appears on the viola with pizzicato accompaniment; the next interpretation is a violin solo in long notes; at the end the theme is freely transformed with a colorfully ornamental accompaniment.

Andantino doucement expressif (Andantino with mild expression). There are three sections. The first begins with passionate strains by muted strings. In the more extended middle section, violin and cello spin a haunting melody whose modal feeling is enhanced by the use of fifths. Then music from the first section reappears.

Très modéré (Very moderately). An impetuous drive that creates tension forms the predominant characteristic of this finale. The basic (germinal) theme is heard everywhere: in the introduction, in a fugato built from the cello upward, in the viola with syncopated long notes in the accompaniment, and in the violin during the emotional climax and conclusion.

Songs

As do the piano pieces, Debussy's songs reflect his personality. He is the most personal of all French song composers, and his new style in setting poetry and poetic prose to music remains unique.

He wrote more than 50 songs, a great many of them to texts by important poets. He used poems by Verlaine, Baudelaire, Mallarmé, Alfred de Musset, and others. Almost half of his songs were composed before 1890. They are songs of fantasy, typically describing a melancholy world more content in shadows and sorrows than in happy sunlight. Debussy expresses futility and desolation with exquisite tenderness tinged with irony. His songs are not dramatic declarations; rather than action they display shimmering fantasy and impeccable taste.

Beau soir, composed in 1878, is taken from a poem by Paul Bourget. The poet speaks of happiness:

Lorsque au soleil couchant les rivières sont roses	When in the setting sun the rivers are rosy,
Et qu'un tiède frisson court sur les champs de blé,	And when a warm ripple flows over the fields of wheat,
Un conseil d'être heureux semble sortir des choses	An advice to be happy seems to go forth from these things,
Et monter vers le coeur troublé.	And rises toward the troubled heart.
Un conseil de goûter le charme d'être au monde	An advice to savor the charm of being in the world
Cependant qu'on est jeune et que le soir est beau . . .	While one is young and while the evening is beautiful

And Debussy initiates a languid eighth-note accompaniment in triplets with an accent on the last in each measure. His vocal line is composed of short undulating phrases.

The poet speaks of death:

Car nous nous en allons, comme s'en va cette onde:	For we depart, even as this wave is departing:
Elle à la mer,—nous au tombeau!	It goes to the sea, we to the grave.

And Debussy reduces the vocal line to a series of repeated notes, almost like a recitative.

Debussy's best-known songs (settings of Paul Verlaine poems) are in the collection entitled *Ariettes oubliées* (Forgotten Airs, 1888). In the highly subjective *C'est l'extase langoureuse* the poet believes that he sees his emotions reflected in forest murmurs and shadows, and his amorous lassitude sets the poetic mood:

C'est l'extase langoureuse,	This is languishing ecstasy,
C'est la fatigue amoureuse,	This is amorous weariness,
C'est tous les frissons des bois	This is all the rustling of forests
Parmi l'étreinte des brises,	Amidst the embrace of breezes;
C'est, vers les ramures grises,	This is, about the gray branches,
Le choeur des petites voix.	The chorus of little voices.

The composer complements the poet's mood with a sensuous voice line and sinuous accompaniment in chromatic harmonies. This is a very typical Debussy song.

Orchestral Works

In his orchestral works Debussy attempted to create a transparency in which basic timbres never lose their individuality. He possessed a natural French preference for woodwinds, writing for them with refined taste and sensibility. He also liked the harp, which he rescued from its category of assisting in sonorous orchestral climaxes and restored to significant participation. Debussy used the orchestra skillfully; he could summon color glints to match his rhythms because his instrumentation technique was fully equal to his imaginative concept.

Although not a miniaturist, he did not attempt large-scale orchestral works. Rather than a broad musical panorama, he communicates to his listener some one aspect of the sea, the sky, the season, or a dream. *Printemps* (Spring), a symphonic suite for orchestra and humming chorus inspired by Botticelli's painting *Primavera,* appeared in 1887. In 1899 he completed a trilogy entitled *Nocturnes,* consisting of three richly imaginative tonal pictures: *Nuages, Fêtes,* and *Sirènes. La Mer* (The Sea, 1905), one of his most popular works, contains three symphonic sketches, three different views of one subject. Four years later he completed his *Images,* another trilogy bearing the titles *Iberia, Gigues,* and *Rondes de printemps.*

Of all Debussy's orchestral writings, the best known is *Prélude à l'après-midi d'un faune* (Prelude to The Afternoon of a Faun), based on a Mallarmé poem. In 1892 Debussy started to compose an orchestral triptych that was to include a prelude, an interlude and paraphrase, and a finale. By 1894, when the work was scheduled for performance, he had completed only the prelude, and he never got around to writing the other two movements.

No other music so deftly and exquisitely captures the heat, silence, and voluptuousness of a golden afternoon. In vague, complex language Mallarmé's poem describes a faun who, upon awakening, is not sure whether he has lived or dreamed the memory of finding two nymphs sleeping in the grasses. His speculations arouse in the reader that hazy ambiguity familiar to everyone who in his waking moments has tried to find his way out of a dream and back to reality.

Debussy's musical translation is delicate and languid, its phrases sung in polished tones by an unaccompanied flute (Ex. 23:2). A woodwind chord,

Ex. 23:2. Debussy: *Prélude à l'après-midi d'un faune*

Permission for reprint granted by Jean Jobert, Paris, copyright owners; Elkan-Vogel Co., Inc., Philadelphia, agents.

horn calls, and harp arpeggios contribute an aura of mystery. The flute theme is repeated by the strings and expanded. A plaintive and rapturous theme from the oboe reveals the same downward and upward sweep as the flute theme. Then a brief motive for horns and woodwinds leads to a climax, followed by a solo-violin soliloquy. When the opening theme returns, it soon passes to flute and cello, then in a disguised version moves to horns and violins. At the end small cymbals sound softly as chords from muted horns and violins evoke a remote and mysterious atmosphere.

MAURICE RAVEL

There has long been a tendency—either spoken or implied—to regard Claude Debussy and Maurice Ravel (1875–1937) as the two truly representative Impressionist composers; this view is only partly correct. Although they were contemporaries and admired each other's works, they had substantially different ideas about musical composition. It is true that Debussy's unorthodox harmonic techniques often appear in Ravel's music; and—vice versa—Ravel's *Jeux d'eau* (1901) disclosed to Debussy a wealth of coloristic sound combinations. But the two composers did not approach musical composition in the same way. Ravel's background, musical education, and keen intellect guided him in creating works as expert in craftsmanship as Debussy's are superior for freedom of form.

Ravel was born at Ciboure, between Saint-Jean-de-Luz and the Spanish frontier. His father was a naturalized Swiss from Savoy; his mother was Basque. At the Paris Conservatory he studied with Bériot and Fauré, as well as others, and while in Paris he met Erik Satie, whose bold experiments in composition interested him. Ravel made several unsuccessful attempts to win the *Prix de Rome,* and one jury's remark ("Mr. Ravel may take us for country bumpkins; but he shouldn't consider us imbeciles") resulted in a *cause célèbre* that made Ravel famous. The rest of his life is the history of his compositions.

Through his mother Ravel had a sympathetic link with the Iberian peninsula, a fact that may account for his preoccupation with Spanish motifs. He used Spanish titles, Spanish rhythms, and imitations of Spanish instruments consistently throughout his career. In addition to this Spanish propensity, Ravel loved the dance more than any other musical form. He drew on both ancient and modern dances, infusing into them his highly personal, expressive technique. Many of his compositions display humor—at times lugubrious, at times sarcastic.

When it comes to examining Ravel's musical texture, a general comparison with Debussy is inevitable. Like Debussy, he worked out an original harmonic concept that was considered quite provocative at the time. Whereas Debussy prefers ninth and eleventh chords built on the dominant, Ravel likes major sevenths and supertonic ninths. Ravel's harmony is generally crisper and more outgoing than Debussy's, and his rhythms are more piquant and sharply punctuated. The two composers are also disparate in form. Ravel adhered more closely to classic rules. He was a musical architect who unfailingly fitted his tonal fabric into a logical, self-analytical framework.

During Ravel's lifetime some critics felt that his painstaking fastidiousness with form detracted from the lyric and emotional content of his music. Ravel once said that it was not necessary for the musician to possess the sensitivity he wished to communicate through his works—a statement not to be taken too seriously when we discover that Ravel's friends claimed that he himself was very emotional and subjective. To confirm this claim, one has only to listen to Ravel's music—the *Oiseaux tristes* from *Miroirs,* or the *Mother Goose Suite.* To communicate in a manner so intimate and expressive, the composer surely must have possessed a deep sensitivity.

Piano Music

Ravel's major works for solo piano are *Pavane pour une Infante défunte* (1899), *Jeux d'eau* (1901), *Miroirs* (1905), *Sonatine* (1905), *Gaspard de la nuit* (1908), *Valses nobles et sentimentales* (1911), and *Le tombeau de Couperin* (1917).

Pavane pour une Infante défunte (Pavane for a Dead Infanta) is now usually heard in the orchestral transcription prepared by Ravel. This has become one of his most beloved works, but in later life he felt dissatisfied with the *Pavane.* "It doesn't bother me to speak of it. It is so old that the composer has become its critic. In retrospect, I no longer see the qualities. But, alas, I easily discern the errors: the too flagrant influence of Chabrier and the rather poor form."[3] Ravel's severe self-criticism is scarcely justified, even though the *Pavane* is not equal to many of his later works. The original version is rather unpianistic—which is surprising because Ravel was a good pianist—and the melodic lines seem quite undistinguished when compared with his later linear concepts. Nonetheless, it offers pleasant music, solemn and earnest; and its harmonic element is given new interest in the two successive restatements of the principal theme.

Ravel's *Jeux d'eau* (Fountains) opened up a new era of sound. The piece is dedicated to Gabriel Fauré and is prefaced by an epigraph from the poet Henri de Régnier: "The river god laughing from the water which is tickling him." Ravel's concentration on form is already evident in this music. He wrote of the work:

[3] From a self-criticism in the *Revue Musicale de la Société Internationale de Musique* (February 1912).

> Inspired by the noise of water, cascades, springs, the *Jeux d'eau* is based on two motives, in the manner of first-movement sonata form without, however, conforming to the classic tonal scheme.[4]

Ravel's technical procedures in the difficult, dazzling *Jeux d'eau* are similar to those in Liszt's *Jeux d'eau à la Villa d'Este*. But not at all like Liszt is the end effect achieved by Ravel: a delicacy emanating from his exploration of the half tones in the pianistic palette; myriad fleeting sensations created by cascades of eleventh chords, dominant ninths, and major sevenths.

The suite *Gaspard de la nuit* is one of the most difficult compositions in the solo-piano repertoire. It poses baffling problems to the pianist, which may be the reason why the work is rarely heard, except on phonograph records. Still, *Gaspard de la nuit* cannot be classified as a virtuoso work because a lot of the problems involved are musical, not technical. The difficulties stem from Ravel's superb craftsmanship and innate "sensitivity"; they never obtrude on their own.

Ravel's three poems—as he called them—in *Gaspard de la nuit* were inspired by three poems by an obscure mid-eighteenth-century poet, Aloysius Bertrand. According to the esoteric Bertrand, his poems were vivid, vivacious watercolors, poetic paintings like the graphic pictures of Jacques Callot.

In the first poem, *Ondine,* the sea sprite has left her lake to sing her song at the poet's window: "Listen! It is I, Ondine, flecking with drops of water the sonorous panes of your window illuminated by the pale rays of the moon." But her avowal of love is for naught because the poet loves a mortal. Hearing this, "she cried several tears, burst into laughter, and disappeared in droplets, which streamed down my blue window panes." A rhythmic-harmonic motive creates a murmuring effect while the melody emerges, rising upon itself in a melancholy wave. This initial melodic invention is heard again and again, but each time it is enveloped in swirls of arpeggiated arabesques.

"It is the bell which sounds from the walls of a town on the horizon and a corpse hanging from a gibbet, reddened as the setting sun." Thus Bertrand describes the subject matter of *Le Gibet,* the second poem of *Gaspard de la nuit*. Ravel maintains this lugubrious feeling by an almost hypnotic insistence on a repeated octave *B*-flat. Seventh and ninth chords, a mournful melody always bordering on despair, and alterations of all kinds make this brief piece (written on three staffs rather than two) a memorable venture into the macabre.

Scarbo, the final piece, depicts a grotesque dwarf who might have come straight from the *Tales of Hoffmann*. Musically speaking, *Scarbo* is a brilliant scherzo—an adventure into the fantastic—in which two themes are subjected to super imagination. The first theme is powerfully rhythmic: "How often have I seen him descend from the ceiling, pirouette on one foot, and roll across the room like the bobbin from a witch's distaff." The second theme, gay and dancelike, describes the apparition of Scarbo dancing by moonlight. "Did I expect him to disappear? The dwarf grew tall between the moon and me like the tower of a Gothic cathedral." This singular scherzo, so glittering and virtuoso, fades away in a whisper of sound.

[4] These remarks of Ravel are taken from an autobiographical sketch that first appeared in print in the *Revue Musicale* (October 1938).

Orchestral Works

One of Ravel's finest talents was his treatment of the orchestra. In addition to his masterful orchestral arrangement of Mussorgsky's *Pictures at an Exhibition,* he created a repertoire of small but significant orchestral works. Some are original works, others are orchestral versions of his piano works.

Ravel's best-known orchestral work is *Boléro* (1928), a fascinating composition written on commission for Ida Rubinstein, a noted mime, dancer, and actress. It was first produced at the Paris Opera as a ballet. After composing it, Ravel wrote the following explanation:

> In 1928, at the request of Mme. Rubinstein, I composed a Boléro for orchestra. It is a dance with a very moderate and constantly uniform movement, as much by the melody as by the harmony and the rhythm, this latter marked incessantly by the drum. The only element of diversity is introduced by the orchestral crescendo.[5]

Within a few weeks *Boléro* brought Ravel more public notice than he had ever achieved previously. As an exercise in orchestration and an experiment in psychology, the music is unsurpassed. One theme is insistently present for nearly 20 minutes. The music, in triple meter, has a strong Spanish flavor. Ravel's theme has two distinct parts: two sixteen-measure phrases, each divided into two sections containing eight bars (Ex. 23:3). Each phrase is repeated. The form thus consists of five statements of this theme and repetitions.

Ex. 23:3. Ravel: *Boléro*

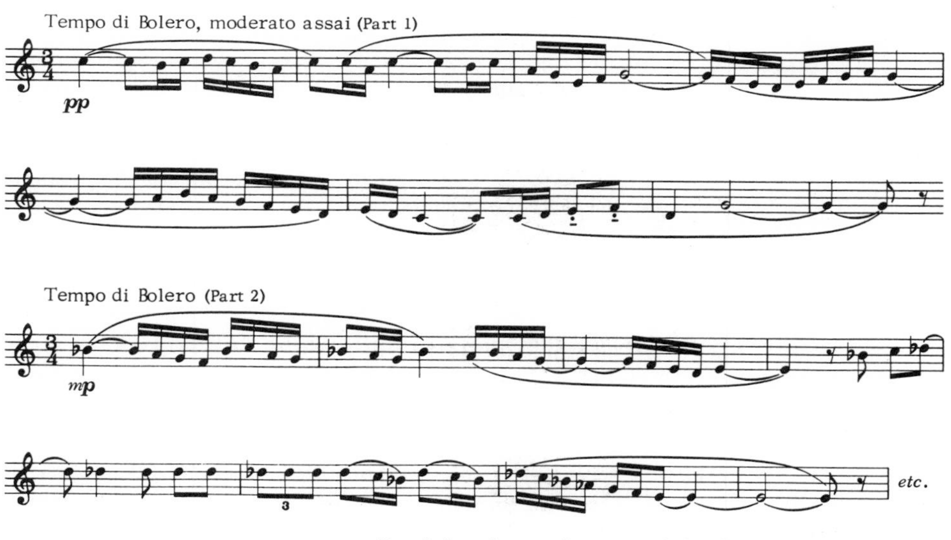

Permission for reprint granted by Durand and Cie, Paris, copyright owners; Elkan-Vogel Co., Inc., Philadelphia, agents.

1. The rhythm is first played alone by soft drums, accompanied by double-bass pizzicato notes. The drums continue this rhythm monotonously

[5] Ravel, in *Revue Musicale.*

throughout while an increasing number of instruments take it up. The theme in its first appearance is shared by flute, clarinet, bassoon, and *E*-flat clarinet.

2. The theme is divided among the oboe d'amore, trumpet, and saxophone, accompanied by an intensified rhythmic complement.

3. Horns play the theme in harmony with celesta and two piccolos. Later entrances feature oboe, clarinet, and trumpet. The dynamic level has now reached a mezzo-forte.

4. The intensity rises to forte as violins spin the theme, rhythmically supported by horns, trumpets, and pizzicato strings.

5. The first part of the theme is heard once. All instruments participate fortissimo as the tonality moves to *E* major. The basses leap back to *C* major, and with a final loud shriek the tonal frenzy collapses.

La Valse follows closely behind *Boléro* in public favor. The idea for writing such a work had come to Ravel as early as 1906; he planned to compose a symphonic poem on the apotheosis of the Viennese waltz, and his first title was *Wien.* In 1920 he again took up the project, fashioning it as a ballet on the suggestion of the Russian impressario Serge Diaghilev, but when it was finished Diaghilev offended Ravel by refusing to produce it. Ravel described his intentions.

> After *Le tombeau de Couperin* the state of my health prevented me from writing for some time. When I started to compose again it was only to write *La Valse,* a choreographic poem the idea of which had come to me before I wrote the *Rapsodie espagnole.* I conceived this work as a kind of apotheosis of the Viennese waltz, with which was associated in my imagination the impression of a fantastic and inevitable whirling dance. . . . This work, which I had intended to be essentially choreographic, has up to now only been staged at the Antwerp theatre and at Mme. Rubinstein's season of ballets.[6]

The musical score has an explanation, most likely meant for stage directions:

> Through whirling clouds can be glimpsed now and again waltzing couples. The mists gradually disperse, and at letter A [in the score] a huge ballroom is revealed filled with a great crowd of whirling dancers. The stage grows gradually lighter. At the fortissimo at letter B the lights in the chandeliers are turned full on. The scene is an imperial palace about 1855.

According to the celebrated composer and pianist Alfredo Casella, Ravel had some thought of a dance production in mind when he wrote *La Valse,* although he never designed a choreographic plan. Casella further explains that the music can be divided into three sections: "The Birth of the Waltz," "The Waltz," and "The Apotheosis of the Waltz." Ravel's untypical work is an essay in full-blown Romanticism; it is very like the Liszt tone poems, but its melodic source comes from Johann Strauss.

Grumbling basses mold a mysterious atmosphere from which waltz fragments gradually emerge. When a fully developed Straussian waltz springs to life, it is soon overcome by discordant, strident chords. The waltz returns but the mood is now menacing. Despair intensifies the atmosphere as the music plunges into a feverish climax.

Ravel's small repertoire includes songs, two concertos, an opera, an

[6] Ravel, in *Revue Musicale.*

operatic musical fantasy (*The Child and the Sorcerers*), and several fine chamber works. He was not a prolific composer, but each of his superbly designed works has intrinsic musical value and always provides an enjoyable listening experience.

SUMMARY

French Impressionism injected new artistic vitality into a musical world surfeited with the emotionalism of an exhausted Romanticism. Musical Impressionism provided fresh ideas, techniques, and theories. Composers became literally scientific experimentors in their search for new harmonic combinations and exciting, sensual tone colors.

An outstanding characteristic of this era is the fact that impressionistic music demands a sympathetic bond between composer and public. The listener almost has to participate in the musical composition to bring about its completion as a work of art.

The Impressionist movement was short-lived. There were other composers, of course—Respighi in Italy, Delius in England, Griffes in the United States—who appropriated certain Impressionist techniques, but pure Impressionism is essentially French, and Debussy and Ravel remain the finest authors of this unique musical language.

FOR DISCUSSION AND ASSIGNMENT

1. Listen to one or two of Debussy's *Préludes* for piano without observing their titles. Can you possibly discern what sensation or impression each is trying to impart? Now look at the titles and listen again. Are the titles necessary or helpful?
2. Listen to *Prelude to The Afternoon of a Faun* or a movement from Debussy's *String Quartet*. In works like these, the composer scandalized some of his contemporaries by his disregard of traditional rules. Do you find the music in any way dissonant, distasteful, clumsy, or lacking in form? If not, why not, since it is not written "correctly"?
3. Listen to Ravel's *Pavane* or *Alborada del gracioso* in the piano version. Then listen to the orchestral version. Are both equally effective? What musical element do you think Ravel considered to be of prime importance in any musical composition?
4. Write a paragraph describing which composer—Debussy or Ravel—you find most interesting and enjoyable. Give your reasons.

FOR FURTHER READING

Demuth, Norman. *Ravel*. New York: Collier Books, 1962. PB. Most of Professor Demuth's book is an analysis and evaluation of Ravel's music. It is an absorbing study.

Lockspeiser, Edward. *Debussy*. New York: Collier Books, 1962. PB. This book, first published in 1936, offers a first-rate study of Debussy's life, his role as an Impressionist, and his importance as a composer.

Myers, Rollo H. *Ravel: Life and Works.* New York: Thomas Yoseloff, 1960. A concise and accurate study by a competent scholar.

Rewald, John. *The History of Impressionism,* Revised Edition. New York: The Museum of Modern Art, 1962. John Rewald's excellent study of Impressionism in art has been and continues to be the most readable, authoritative book available.

Thompson, Oscar. *Debussy: Man and Artist.* New York: Dover Publications, Inc., 1965. PB. First published in 1937, Thompson's pertinent book discusses both the life of Debussy and his musical compositions in lucid, interesting prose.

Three Classics in the Aesthetic of Music. New York: Dover Publications, Inc., 1962. PB. One of the "classics" in this book is the engaging *Monsieur Croche the Dilettante Hater,* a series of articles written by Debussy for several French periodicals of the early twentieth century.

Vallas, Léon. *The Theories of Claude Debussy.* Translated by Maire O'Brien. New York: Dover Publications, Inc., 1967. PB. In this book, first published in 1929, Vallas presents and discusses Debussy's theories on critics and music criticism, as well as on the education of young musicians.

Twentieth-Century Music—I

24

. . . anyone who assumes that there's an essential difference between consonance and dissonance is wrong, because the entire realm of possible sounds is contained within the notes that nature provides—and that's how things have happened. But thc way one looks at it is most important.

ANTON WEBERN

The Path to the New Music (1932) [1]

It is extremely difficult for any age to evaluate its own worth, and this statement applies notably to the twentieth century. So many events and changes affecting almost every area of endeavor have taken place during the last six decades that a just appraisal of this era is as yet impossible.

Two world wars and almost continual localized conflicts have aroused widespread fatalism and futility. Spectacular scientific progress has inevitably led to educational and intellectual emphasis on science; as a result, spiritual and cultural requirements often seem neglected. In this century colonialism has nearly disappeared, replaced by newborn nations now struggling to adjust to their independent status. Communism's influence in world affairs has caused fear, uncertainty, even despair in subjected countries, in small unprotected nations, and at the conference table.

The arts—literature, painting, music—have tried to keep abreast of the times by reflecting the salient features of twentieth-century life. Many artists have attempted to reformulate traditional materials and subjects into contemporary settings (Ill. 24:1); others have ignored the past completely—if this is possible—in a frantic search for new expressive methods (Ill. 24:2).

Twentieth-century artistic developments have struck countless observers as paradoxical. Many contemporary composers have professed a compulsion to communicate to their audience their deeply felt inspirations, which, they have claimed, only a creative artist has previously been able to experience. Such communication is an excellent idea, but frequently the finished art work—picture, sculpture, musical composition—has merely succeeded in baffling or even

[1] German edition copyright 1960 Universal Editions, AG Vienna. English edition copyright Theodore Presser Company; used by permission.

Ill. 24:1. *Fernand Leger (1881–1955),* Three Musicians. *1944 (after a drawing of 1924–25; dated on canvas, 24–44), oil on canvas, 68½ x 57¼". Collection, The Museum of Modern Art, New York. Mrs. Simon Guggenheim Fund.*

Ill. 24:2. ***Georges Braque*** **(*1882–1963*), Man with a Guitar. *1911. Oil on canvas, 23¾ x 19¾". Collection, The Museum of Modern Art, New York.***

enraging the public for which it was intended. In his search for a "different" expressive language, the artist has often failed to consider his public's reaction. The result has been an ever widening gap between creator and viewer or listener. The uninformed public, rooted in tradition, has rejoiced in music and painting that it could comprehend or simply enjoy without being emotionally shattered.

Artistic movements have materialized and then faded away so quickly that the public has developed no criteria for enjoyment and appreciation. All too frequently an audience has felt uncertain that the artist actually knows what he is about. Today's public needs to be educated to the new arts, or at least given time to understand the present contemporary scene before even newer frontiers are contemplated.

Previously we noted that there are certain stylistic similarities in the music of all Baroque composers. While each composer developed his personal expressive language, his technique followed generally accepted rules and concepts. This generality of style can also be applied to the Classic composers and, to some extent, to most composers in the first half of the nineteenth century. Later, Nationalism arose to temper and diffuse pure Romanticism, and Impressionism led musical composition far beyond the limits of tradition. As a result, the twentieth century has no single "contemporary" style, for today's music has many sounds and many styles.

An artist supposedly reflects the cultural progress and stature of his era, but the twentieth century is a mechanistic age, an atomic age, an age of doubt and questioning and reassessment. How can such ideas be mirrored in music? A composer is expected to assist in formulating contemporary musical trends, perhaps to prophesy future ones. But what can be done with the overused nineteenth-century materials and traditional scalar systems that have literally been expended? These are some of the problems facing twentieth-century composers.

Each composer approaches these problems according to his spiritual and psychological characteristics. He may be a twentieth-century nationalist who wants to build a musical aesthetic on a folk tradition. Or he may prefer exotic music and will borrow some elements from an Asian or African musical system. On the other hand, if he is intrigued by the possibilities of jazz, he may attempt to synthesize that language with his own style.

Today's composer may be a sensationalist, a musical iconoclast seeking quick fame by breaking down accepted concepts; or he may be a sincere experimentalist patiently searching for new tonal experiences. Some music written in this century clings to another age, which means that its composers are essentially Romantics. Other composers prefer to blend the past with the present to preserve a semblance of stylistic evolution.

Several musical techniques are available to twentieth-century composers. In one method, the composer starts with existing scales, divides and subdivides their intervals, and thus produces microtonal music. Another approach attempts to restate and rearrange older traditions of harmony, melody, and rhythm. The results show infinite variety. For example, some writers have changed the traditional habit of chords in thirds to chords in fourths—quartal harmony; others superimpose one harmonic progression on top of another—polytonality; still other composers employ atonality. And comparatively new fields, electronic music, musique concrète, and aleatory music, are still in their infancy.

About 1909 Arnold Schoenberg (1874–1951) made a startling impact on the musical world with a new aesthetic—eventually expressed by means of twelve-tone composition—and Schoenberg's followers have generously endowed this century with works either derived from him or partially influenced by his techniques. Schoenberg and his school developed a writing style commonly called *atonal,* but *pantonal* might be more accurate. The presence of atonality did not necessarily constitute a musical revolution; the foundation for it had been well prepared. In the nineteenth century, Richard Wagner had extended chromaticism almost to the point of tonal disintegration. In the early years of the twentieth century, Debussy and the Impressionists staunchly repudiated traditional harmonic concepts of consonance and dissonance. The final step was to reject all rules governing tonality and key relationships. Once tonality was disposed of, there was no difference between the seven diatonic notes within a scale (*C–D–E–F–G–A–B*) and the five auxiliary chromatic notes (*C♯–D♯–F♯–G♯–A♯*): all twelve tones of the octave were equal in every respect and were treated as such.

Atonal composing is frequently based on a tone row (or set), a somewhat synthetic melody made up of all the twelve tones forming the chromatic scale but stated in a particular order. Usually a note appears only once within the set. The sequence of notes (called the tone row) is used to create harmony and melody and to construct all contrapuntal materials. Transformations of the row through inversion (statement of the row upside down), retrograde (backward), and retrograde-inversion (upside down and backward) make further expansion possible. Finally, the tone row—plus each of its transformations—is statable on any degree of the semitonal scale.

Atonal music frequently displays remarkable vitality, the result of imaginative rhythmic treatment, and it is amply supplied with expressive and interpretative markings. The following example by Ernst Krenek (*b.*1900) illustrates the basic approach to *dodecaphony*—twelve-tone technique (Ex. 24:1).

Ex. 24:1. Krenek: *Example from Twelve Short Piano Pieces Written in the Twelve-Tone Technique, Opus 83.*

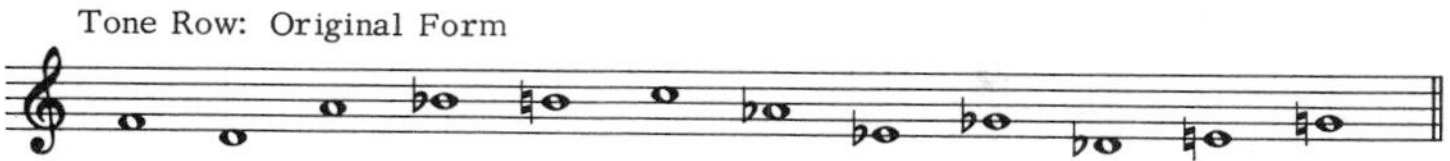

Copyright 1939–1966 by G. Schirmer, Inc. Used by permission.

The use of tone rows (tonal serialization) proved to be only one step in the development of new music. Later composers attempted what they termed "complete serialization." In addition to tone rows, they set up rows of note-value patterns, rows of dynamic intensities, and rows of rhythmic values. Thus, in complete serialization nothing is left to chance: every tone, note value, rhythmic value, and dynamic mark is carefully arrived at and precisely indicated.

The invention of the tape recorder has made it possible to rearrange sounds and create previously unknown sonorities. This process is frequently referred to as *musique concrète*. To produce music in this medium, the composer records both natural and musical sounds on magnetic tape. After these sounds are submitted to various procedures, the results are united to form a piece of *musique concrète*, or "concrete music." Running the sounds through different filters removes certain frequencies. Other procedures involve playing the tape backward or altering the pitch. Experiments in process for almost 20 years have exposed the enormous possibilities for creating *musique concrète*. This music is especially effective in dramatic productions, either for producing unique atmosphere or as incidental music. It has also been used well in ballet and modern dance. One imaginative composer, Edgard Varèse (1883–1965), combined sounds on magnetic tape with those produced by a "normal" orchestra. Otto Luening (*b.*1900) and Vladimir Ussachevsky (*b.*1911) have expended serious effort and talent in developing concrete music.

In 1954 an audience in Cologne, Germany, heard the first recital of electronic music, and since that time some composers have adopted this medium. Electronic computers permit these composers to present their works directly to the listener without having to rely on the fallible talents of a performer. The mechanics of this relatively new medium are complicated:

> . . . One can say briefly that the sounds are produced by an electronic oscillator which can be adjusted to any given frequency, pitch or tone-colour. In addition to single tones it is also possible to produce "fat sounds," caused by the use of several adjacent frequencies, and numerous other effects; also, of course, the traditional division of the octave into twelve semitones no longer applies, and in theory any kind of subdivision is possible. This means that the sonorous possibilities of electronic music are even greater than those of *musique concrète,* with the added advantage that they can be exactly determined in advance and even written down in the form of a score. The preparation of such a score, however, needs a good deal of mathematical and scientific knowledge on the part of the composer, and electronic music is not a medium which can be quickly mastered: in addition, the composition of each piece takes a considerable time.[2]

Still another unusual type of music, called *aleatory* music or *chance* music (from the Latin *aleatorius:* chance), permits the performer to help create a musical composition. For instance, the composer may give the performer a series of musical fragments to be played at random. Or the composer may devise a piano piece having several possible right-hand sections and an equal number for the left hand, and the performer arranges and rearranges the different sections at will. Needless to say, almost every performance of an aleatory composition is different from any other.

Contemporary composers ordinarily pass through several developmental stages before arriving at a mature style; since this style more often than not is a mélange of several basic approaches incorporating elements from the different stages, strict classification of a composer is not always possible—or, for that matter, necessary.

Despite seemingly numberless approaches and disparate techniques, certain characteristics are now typical in twentieth-century music. Dissonance has become an objective—whether achieved by polytonality, quartal harmony, atonality, or electronic machinery. Rhythm has attained great flexibility and an even greater complexity. Counterpoint has become newly important. Paradoxically, however, most contemporary composers will insist that they eschew overabundant details and hazy musical substance. Their alleged goal is that their music will clearly and objectively express their reaction to the twentieth century.

GERMANY AND AUSTRIA

One of the musically momentous events in this century occurred with the birth of the Expressionist school pioneered by Arnold Schoenberg, Alban Berg, and Anton Webern. Their music was the German-Austrian answer to French Impressionism. Like Impressionism, German musical *Expressionism* (the term used to describe the atonal aesthetic) derived principally from painting and literature—from artists like Paul Klee and Wassily Kandinsky, from writers like Stefan George. In place of the languid, misty chiaroscuro typical of the Impressionists, the Expressionists dealt with the macabre, violent, hysterical, and irrational. They changed the concept of beauty to fit their own unique views of subconscious reality.

[2] Humphrey Searle, article titled "Experimental Media: I. Musique Concrète—Electronic Music" in *Twentieth Century Music: A Symposium,* edited by Rollo Myers (London: John Calder, 1960), p. 116. Reprinted by permission.

Arnold Schoenberg's early works reflect late-nineteenth-century German Romanticism and have unmistakable Wagnerian overtones. There is nothing very revolutionary in *Verklärte Nacht, Opus 4* (Transfigured Night), composed in 1899, yet this tone poem is heard more frequently than Schoenberg's atonal music. He originally designed it as a string sextet, but his version for string orchestra is now more often performed.

Schoenberg's inspiration for the work came from a Richard Dehmel (1863–1920) poem about a sinful woman who finally finds love because the man can forgive her past transgressions. This poem appears on the score, but Schoenberg's music stands quite satisfactorily on its own merits; it is lushly chromatic and frequently eloquent. Musical ideas merge gracefully, forming sensuous patterns that may defy strict analysis but are always comprehensible.

Early in this century Schoenberg abandoned this late-Romantic style to experiment with a new aesthetic that he hoped would fulfill his desire for organic unity in his compositions. From these experiments he eventually developed the twelve-tone (dodecaphonic) system of composition, which since then has remained the basic approach in atonal writing. While experimenting with this new aesthetic, Schoenberg also advanced musical Expressionism, for his goals were strangely contradictory: he wanted to express his emotions, an inheritance from the Romantics, yet he insisted that the passionate elements must always be controlled by firm intellectual discipline.

Three Piano Pieces, Opus 11 (1908) are his first compositions in atonal style, and the very first piece (Ex. 24:2) reveals that distinctions between conso-

Ex. 24:2. Schoenberg: *Piano Piece, Opus 11, No. 1*

Reprinted by permission of Belmont Music Publishers, Los Angeles.

nance and dissonance no longer exist. Atonality's essentially contrapuntal character emerges in these three pieces, where Schoenberg emphasizes devices such as canonic imitation.

Written during the same year (1908), his *Five Orchestral Pieces, Opus 16* illustrate the new approach as applied to a large instrumental group. He supplied an explanation for the first performance:

> This music seeks to express all that dwells in us subconsciously like a dream; which is a great fluctuant power, and is built upon none of the lines that are familiar to us; which has a rhythm, as the blood has its pulsating rhythm, as all life in us has its rhythm; which has a tonality, but only as the sea or the storm has its tonality; which has harmonies, though we cannot group or analyze them nor can we trace its themes. All its technical craft is submerged, made one and indivisible with the content of the work.

The pieces are very brief. Although they use full orchestra, they also include many instrumental solo passages. Schoenberg reluctantly furnished titles; he felt that titles were unnecessary but he hoped they would help the music gain public acceptance.

The first piece, *Presentiments,* shows how effectively this aesthetic expresses fear and irrationality: the music is restless and tense; a basic motive is stated and reiterated in many different guises, each time accompanied by adroit rhythmic juxtapositions. The second is a lyrical piece entitled *The Past,* in which Schoenberg achieves unusual tone color by using composite chords and assigning each chord tone to a different type of instrument. At the beginning the music borders on tonality but veers from it in the contrapuntal central section.

The third piece has several titles: *The Changing Chord, Summer Morning by a Lake, Colors.* They all relate to a conversation between Schoenberg and Mahler about a favorite technique of Schoenberg's, which he called *Klangfarbenmelodie* (melody of tone colors) : a melody presenting each succeeding tone in a different instrument. Schoenberg maintained that he could even create the illusion of a melody by applying his technique to a series of repeated notes. This piece successfully supports his claim.

Peripeteia, the Greek title of the fourth orchestral piece, is defined as a sudden reversal of circumstances or situation in a literary work or in dramatic action. Schoenberg accomplishes this reversal musically by preserving a brooding atmosphere while simultaneously building tension. In the last piece, *The Obbligato Recitative,* he molds a mass of intricate counterpoint into a splendid climax.

The once revolutionary *Pierrot Lunaire* (1912) is an equally significant composition from his new atonal period. Its 21 short poems exploiting satire and irony are set for chamber orchestra and one voice. The vocal score is not actually sung but declaimed according to specific rhythmic values and general indications of melodic inflection. Schoenberg called his new vocal technique *Sprechstimme* (a kind of speech-song) . In setting the poems he employed different forms: passacaglias, fugues, canons, and freely composed songs.

As he tried out his materials he realized that a definable method might prove more workable, and gradually he resolved such a method, eventually described variously as dodecaphony, twelve-tone system, or serial composition. *Five Piano Pieces, Opus 23* (1923) illustrate his growing recognition of the potentials in his new system: he handles the atonal technique of his earlier works with greater dexterity and freedom, and his rhythms are more pungent and complex. In 1934 he wrote about these pieces:

> Here I arrived at a technique which I called (for myself) "composing with tones," a very vague term, but it meant something to me. Namely: in contrast to the ordinary way of using a motive, I used it already almost in the manner of a "basic set of twelve tones," I built other motives and themes from it, and also accompaniments and other chords—but the theme did not consist of twelve tones.[3]

The last work in *Opus 23* proves that by then Schoenberg had formulated the basic rules of twelve-tone composition and had full command of his technique and resources. His mature works—*Variations for Orchestra* (1928),

[3] Letter from Arnold Schoenberg to Nicolas Slonimsky, June 3, 1937. In Nicolas Slonimsky, *Music Since 1900,* 3rd Edition, Revised and Enlarged, p. 681. Copyright 1949 by Coleman-Ross Company, Inc., New York. Used by permission.

third and fourth string quartets (1926, 1936), woodwind quintet (1924), violin concerto (1936), and a piano concerto (1942)—confirm his success in expressing himself by means of this new aesthetic.

Alban Berg

One of Schoenberg's most gifted pupils, Alban Berg (1885–1935) accented another aspect of Expressionism—emotionalism—and from its abstract patterns he shaped more lyric designs. Known chiefly for his operas *Wozzeck* (1921) and *Lulu* (unfinished, 1934), a violin concerto (1935), and the *Lyric Suite* (1926) for string quartet, Berg passed from Romanticism to Expressionism along the path laid down by his teacher. As a matter of fact, Berg wrote his basically atonal opera *Wozzeck* before he really began to use a twelve-note tone row. Although *Wozzeck* is obviously premised on atonality, there are numerous tonal passages scattered throughout the opera. In other words Berg used whatever approach seemed most effective and plausible for each dramatic situation.

Berg adapted the libretto for *Wozzeck* from a drama of the same name by Georg Büchner (1813–1837), a Romanticist primarily interested in melancholy subjects. His original text is a bitter commentary on man's inhumanity to man, and the music Berg has fitted to it is intense and suspenseful. It is pure theater. The plot is about a soldier, Wozzeck, who offers himself to a doctor for scientific experiments in a pitiable effort to support his mistress, Maria, and her child. She is nevertheless unfaithful and Wozzeck slashes her throat. He throws the knife into a pond, then in dread of its recovery wades in to retrieve it and is drowned.

Berg's declamatory vocal lines move in a disjunct, angular manner. His imaginative orchestration yields extremely evocative and compelling results; for example, as Wozzeck drowns the music almost makes the listener see the ripples as the waters close over him.

The opera is constructed in the methodical manner typical of the atonalists: each of its three acts contains five scenes; each scene employs a specific formal pattern—passacaglia, suite, fugue, sonata, scherzo, and so on. Although the listener is usually so engrossed in the plot and the emotional music that he does not notice the highly formalized structure, it forms a subtle tribute to Berg's articulate command of his Expressionist technique.

When Berg definitively adopted twelve-tone technique, he created works distinctively different from those by Schoenberg. Berg's melodies are smooth and lyrical; his atmosphere is more romantic; his tone rows are so constructed that traditional harmonies may be used, and he also varies the rows from movement to movement. Berg thus treated dodecaphony more freely than did Schoenberg.

Lyric Suite for string quartet is an outstanding example of Berg's style and is also one of the finest contemporary chamber-music works. In 1926 *Lyric Suite* appeared with six movements; in 1928 Berg set the second, third, and fourth movements for string orchestra. Both versions give the listener an enjoyable, worthwhile experience.

Berg's initial tone row and its inversion are interesting (Ex. 24:3). Notice that the second, third, and fourth notes form an *a* minor triad, then in the inversion an *F*-sharp major triad—F♯–A♯ (B♭)–C♯ (D♭). The ninth, tenth, and eleventh notes give an *e*-flat minor triad, with a *C* major triad in the inversion.

Ex. 24:3. Berg: *Lyric Suite: Tone Row*

Looking at the row in another way, we see a pattern of progressively falling intervals: 2nd, 3rd, 4th, 5th, 6th, and 7th. The rising intervals complete the number of intervallic possibilities within the octave.

The six movements alternate between fast and slow, with the fast movements becoming faster and the slow ones slower:

I. *Allegretto gioviale*
II. *Andante amoroso*
III. *Allegro misterioso . . . Trio estatico*
IV. *Adagio appassionato*
V. *Presto delirando . . . Tenebroso*
VI. *Largo desolato*

Berg uses twelve-tone technique in movements one, three, five, and six and a freer atonal style in the other movements. We could analyze each movement by observing the way Berg imaginatively manipulates his atonal materials; however, this is feasible only with a score and meaningful only to a musician. On the other hand, by listening attentively the average listener can discover for himself the expressive power that characterizes the *Lyric Suite*.

> . . . One can enjoy Berg's contrasting moods and emotions: the violent outbursts of the *Trio estatico,* the broad lyrical climax in the *Adagio appassionato,* the mysterious whispers of the *Tenebroso,* and the inconsolable sadness of the ending. The music, like that of *Wozzeck* or the Violin Concerto, speaks to everyone.[4]

Anton Webern

Compared with Berg's style, the music of Anton Webern (1883–1945) shows lean texture, sparse means, and concentrated energy. Webern stresses contrapuntal devices—retrograde inversions, canons, and the like—and sweeping rhythmic and dynamic contrasts.

The list of Webern's complete works—those whose publication he authorized—shows a considerable variety, for they include works for string quartet, songs, vocal cantatas, orchestral pieces, piano variations. Yet all 31 works have been reproduced on just four long-playing records.

He was a true miniaturist, whether working with full orchestra or a few instruments. Of the three pioneers in atonality, he became the most uncompromising in applying twelve-tone principles after he had firmly established them within his own mind. His unique concept of time, precise placement of each note, and habit of using few repetitions all contribute to the brevity of his compositions. Many require less than a minute for performance.

[4] Alec Robertson, editor, *Chamber Music* (Baltimore, Md.: Penguin Books, 1957), p. 402. Reprinted by permission.

Webern's mature style may be summed up as follows: he adheres rigidly to twelve-tone principles with no concessions to tonality; he believes in note economy and also recognizes the importance of silence; he is preoccupied with tone color; he employs manifold contrapuntal intricacies; he maintains precise rhythmic schemes.

The early *Five Pieces for Orchestra, Opus 10* (1911–1913) show how far he searched for perfect brevity and complete unity. All five pieces can be performed in four and one-half minutes. Written before he became engrossed with serialization, these miniatures are built of tiny motives that combine to create their own logic. They require a chamber orchestra that includes mandolin and guitar.

Webern's music is far from popular. If any one work is heard more than others, it might be the *Symphony for Small Orchestra, Opus 21* (1928). The small orchestra includes clarinet, bass clarinet, two horns, harp, and a small string section (no double bass). Following strict Webernian discipline, the symphony's two movements can be played in about ten minutes. His intellectual approach to music can be seen even in the tone row controlling the symphony (Ex. 24:4). If

Ex. 24:4. Webern: *Symphony, Opus 21: Tone Row*

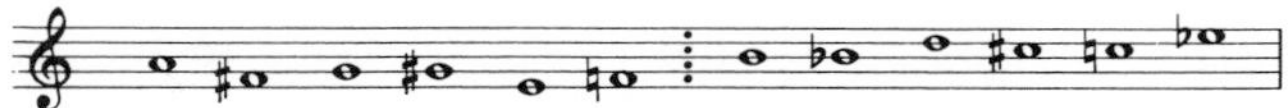

the row is divided into halves, the note intervals in the second half when read backward duplicate those in the first half when read forward. Throughout the symphony the listener can detect the salient features of Webern's strictly dodecaphonic writing: judiciously placed silences, fragmentary melodic phrases only two or three notes long, and specific tone colors allocated to specific notes.

The first movement is a double canon. Two canons, each for two voices, progress simultaneously, each answering voice imitating its leader in contrary motion. The second movement presents a main theme with seven brief variations and a coda. This theme is eleven measures long, with the last half (five and one-half measures) mirroring the rhythmic and melodic structure of the first. Each variation proceeds in the same manner.

Although Schoenberg first developed and elaborated the principles of atonality and dodecaphony, Webern stands as the idol of the younger composers, for to them he is the daring composer who irrevocably broke with tradition to write in a purely twelve-tone idiom. The modern composer's devotion to total serialization is traceable to Webern rather than Schoenberg.

The Avant-Garde

These three Austrians—Schoenberg, Berg, Webern—pledged themselves to twelve-tone writing, and today Germany and Austria still foster a young generation of atonalists and experimentalists. Karlheinz Stockhausen (*b.*1928), perhaps the leading figure in the German avant-garde group, follows Webern in that he strives for wholly abstract expression. Stockhausen's chief interest lies in experimental music that rejects standard concepts of unity, thematic development, and in fact most of the commonly accepted goals in musical composition. The element of chance—where the performer becomes a composer of sorts—is nowhere more prominent than in Stockhausen's *Klavierstück XI* (Piano Piece No. 11, 1956), which comes in several packages. One is a cardboard tube containing a roll of paper (37 × 21 inches) with 19 segments of music. The actual performing of this aleatory piece is complicated, but basically the pianist selects various segments *at random* and plays each according to directions contained in the preceding segment!

Stockhausen's interest in electronic music has produced the provocative *Gesang der Jünglinge* (Song of the Youths, 1956), a composition that harmonizes a human voice with electronically generated tones. To manufacture his "song" Stockhausen recorded the voice of a young boy singing Old Testament verses. Then he superimposed this vocal line upon itself at different pitches (forming at times a one-voice "choir") and blended the result with synthetic sounds. Sometimes vocal sounds and words become intelligible; otherwise they function as pure sound. Stockhausen notes on the score that five loudspeaker systems should be distributed around the audience.

Music written by the German composer Hans Werner Henze (*b.*1926) appeals especially to the younger generation. Originally a dodecaphonist, Henze about 1950 began to enlarge his musical vocabulary by combining old materials with new. As a result his more recent repertoire reveals multiple forms and a variegated language; in these works tonality, polytonality, and atonality coexist with apparent ease. Henze's principal objective seems to be heartfelt musical expressiveness, regardless of the technical means employed. He once remarked:

> Music cannot express a judgment. It cannot describe. It is not active in a sociological sense. But it can carry this message of a human condition: of love, for example, or forgiveness. I am aware that it is a little dangerous to talk like this. Some regard it as foolish and old-fashioned. But I believe it wholeheartedly.[5]

In the United States, Henze's reputation is growing principally on the strength of his instrumental works, such as the five symphonies produced between 1947 and 1962. However, in Europe several of his operas, such as *Elegy for Young Lovers* (1961), are now stable items in operatic repertory. The composer has explained his predilection for opera.

> When I compose instrumental music, I meet with difficulties of form, difficulties in accommodating and distributing the thematic material, difficulties in recognizing the purpose or the meaning of a particular development of abstract motives. Such a situation never occurs in writing for the theater, because here everything is real, tangible, immediately communicable to the senses, and because life itself carries the music with it to such an extent that my senses want to react musically. For me, these facts explain my passionate enthusiasm for "Theatre in Music."[6]

Paul Hindemith

Despite the inroads made by Expressionism, some German and Austrian composers prefer to write music with more conventional outlines. The dean of

[5] Remarks made in an interview for *The New York Times,* June 2, 1963.

[6] From an article entitled "Zur Inszenierung zeitgenössischen Musiktheaters," in *International Congress on Contemporary Music Theatre* (Hamburg: Deutscher Musikrat, 1966), p. 101.

modern German composers was undoubtedly Paul Hindemith (1895–1963). During his early career he experimented with various stylistic formulas—polytonality, atonality, modality, chord systems of unusual intervals—and each experience contributed to his final mode of expression. His ultimate style was rooted in tradition, for Hindemith was not an innovator; he continued to build on the past, and he explains why in his most interesting book, *A Composer's World* (1952).

> A musical structure which due to its extreme novelty does not in the listener's mind summon up any recollections of former experiences . . . will prevent his creative cooperation. He cannot adjust his sense of proportion to the unfolding structure, he loses the feeling for his position in the sounding terrain, he does not recognize the significance of the single structural members in reference to the entity, he even loses the feeling for the coherence of these members.[7]

During his mature phase Hindemith adopted an advanced harmonic concept in which he freely used the twelve tones yet preserved the tradition of tonality. This master musician evolved a personalized, lucid writing style that displays the linear element (dissonant counterpoint) most attractively. At the same time, there is a sameness of sound in his music that can irritate the listener who finds pleasure in variety. Hindemith was a fine craftsman whose serious concern with music's formal elements produced solid, durable tonal canvases. Because of this preoccupation with form he is usually classified as a neo-Classic composer.

Hindemith was a multitalented musician: he played viola in a string quartet, gave recitals on the now rarely heard viola d'amore, and conducted many European and American orchestras. In addition to performing, he proved to be an able administrator and teacher. Yet with all this extra activity, he composed steadily: eight operas; two full symphonies and many smaller orchestral works; more than a dozen concertos; many chamber-music works, including seven string quartets; sonatas for almost every orchestral instrument, even harp; sonatas for piano and for organ; choral works such as oratorios, cantatas, and madrigals. As a neo-Classic composer he preferred traditional forms like the sonata, variation, concerto grosso, passacaglia, and fugue.

Hindemith's opera *Mathis der Maler* (1934) is based on the life and work of the sixteenth-century painter Matthias Grünewald, especially his masterpiece, the Isenheim altarpiece. Like most Hindemith operas, *Mathis der Maler* is seldom performed, but the *Mathis der Maler Symphony* (1934), which the composer extracted from three orchestral excerpts in the opera, is probably his most renowned single work.

The symphony's first movement is also the overture to the opera; named after the most famous panel in the Isenheim altarpiece, it describes a *Concert of Angels* (Ill. 24:3). After solemn introductory chords, three trombones play a modal carol, *Es sungen drei Engel* (Three Angels Were Singing), which is taken up by clarinets, flutes, and glockenspiel. When the movement proper opens, each angel has a theme (Ex. 24:5): the first is quick and bright, the second is more serene, and the third is a flute melody accompanied by high strings.

The concert begins. The first two angel themes combine in a fugal texture, and later the three trombones join in with the carol tune. For a moment

[7] Paul Hindemith, *A Composer's World* (Cambridge: Harvard University Press, 1952), pp. 19–20. Reprinted by permission.

Ill. 24:3. *Matthias Grünewald* (fl.*1500–1530*), **Angelic Concert** *from Isenheim Altar, Colmar. Courtesy of Marburg-Art Reference Bureau.*

the second angel theme predominates but fades away as the third angel theme intrudes to carry the movement to its spirited ending.

Ex. 24:5. Hindemith: ***Mathis der Maler Symphony***

© Copyright 1934 by B. Schott's Soehne, Mainz, Germany. Used by permission of Associated Music Publishers, Inc., sole U.S. agent.

Ill. 24:4. *Matthias Grünewald,* The Entombment. *From Isenheim Altar, Colmar. Courtesy of Marburg-Art Reference Bureau.*

The slow central movement refers to the *Entombment* scene (Ill. 24:4) in the altarpiece and also two scenes at the end of the opera. This moving elegy, sung by flute and oboe solos supported by muted strings, conveys deep compassion.

Hindemith created a dramatic tonal portrait for that panel of the altarpiece depicting the awesome *Temptation of St. Anthony* (Ill. 24:5). This move-

Ill. 24:5. *Matthias Grünewald,* The Temptation of Saint Anthony. *From Isenheim Altar, Colmar. Courtesy of Marburg-Art Reference Bureau.*

ment bears the subtitle *Where wert Thou, good Jesus, wherefore wert Thou not present to heal my wounds?* The music is an orchestral synthesis of the opera scene in which Mathis, like St. Anthony in his painting, faces temptations. A strange recitative-like passage precedes the *Allegro,* a wild section urged on by its strong rhythm. In a lively fugal section, Hindemith symbolizes the saint's triumph by introducing the plainsong hymn *Lauda Sion Salvatorem* and ending the symphony with an exultant *Alleluia.*

Mathis der Maler represents serious treatment of a serious subject. Hindemith's sophisticated and witty *Symphonic Metamorphoses of Themes by Carl Maria von Weber* is just the reverse. It was written during Hindemith's thirteen-year residence in the United States and premiered by the New York Philharmonic orchestra in 1944. The themes for this fine four-movement suite come from virtually forgotten Weber compositions, mostly four-hand piano pieces. Hindemith creates an interesting orchestral work from rather uninteresting themes, for he has indeed metamorphosed them.

The first movement, *Allegro,* is based on a theme (Ex. 24:6) from Weber's *Opus 60, No. 4* entitled *All' Ongarese* (1818). Hindemith at times injects almost oriental harmonies into this theme, and he enlivens it with his customary rhythmical deftness and energetic dynamics. The second movement, *Turandot,* has an interesting history. A dictionary of music published in 1768 by Jean Jacques Rousseau contains a tune, listed as a "Chinese Melody," which Weber used in an overture to some incidental music he wrote for the Schiller translation of *Turandot,* a play by the Italian Carlo Gozzi. Hindemith reworked Weber's "Chinese Melody" into a parody featuring colorful percussion, and he inserted an almost jazz fugato episode in the middle.

Ex. 24:6. Hindemith: *Metamorphoses: Allegro*

Examples 24:6 and 24:7 © copyright 1945 by Associated Music Publishers, Inc. Used by permission.

Andantino, the third movement, comes from the same collection of piano duets as the first movement (Ex. 24:7); Hindemith treats it with restraint. The concluding *March* borrows its melodic material from Weber's *Marcia, Opus 60,*

Ex. 24:7. Hindemith: *Metamorphoses: Andantino*

No. 7. Hindemith sets this one as a grotesque quickstep and later contrasts it with a hunting-horn tune.

Carl Orff

Carl Orff (*b.*1895) might best be described as a latter-day medievalist, for his chantlike vocal parts with strong rhythms and mildly dissonant harmonies revive twelfth- and thirteenth-century polyphonic practice. Coming after the complex styles of Wagner, Strauss, and even Schoenberg, Orff's simple vocabulary, direct expression, and uncomplicated technique create fresh, vital music. Harmony is the least conspicuous element in his musical language; melody, rhythm, and especially sonority are the principal components.

Orff has largely confined his writing to two categories: instructional works and stage works. His five volumes of *Music for Children* (1930–1933) introduce a new approach to music-making and provide young people with a well-rounded experience in contemporary music and music education.

His finest stage works include *Carmina Burana* (1936); two fairy-tale operas, *Der Mond* (The Moon, 1938) and *Die Kluge* (The Clever Woman, 1942); the scenic cantata *Catulli Carmina* (Songs of Catullus, 1943); and two more recent operas, *Antigonae* (1948) and *Oedipus* (1958).

For his stage works (he does not call them operas) Orff nearly always selects old fairy tales and legends. In his view these are not bygone subjects but vital and valid material; for him the time element in these tales and legends disappears, leaving only their spiritual and emotional impact.

> Orff's theatre is elemental and symbolic. Like his music and his teaching, it penetrates through all conventions to reveal the timeless bases. It mirrors not society or illusion, as traditional opera does, but the world. The theatre becomes the symbol of Man, of Life and the World—a true "theatrum mundi." Orff "has in all his works, brought the theatre back to its true role of presenting parable and symbol. Its concern is with an interpretation of life, the inevitability of fate, the powers of the psyche and the spirit."[8]

Although his later works are exceptionally attractive, Orff is still known to the general public chiefly through *Carmina Burana,* his exciting cantata for soloists, chorus, and orchestra. His subtitle is "Secular Songs for Soli and Chorus Accompanied by Instruments and with Magic Pictures."

The song texts are based on poems from a thirteenth-century manuscript found in the monastery of Benediktbeuren in Upper Bavaria. They treat of love, student life, and drinking. Orff's musical settings for 24 of the most typical, colorful poems are instinctively appropriate. He establishes and sustains an atmosphere of medieval pageantry through his forceful, original musical language. He employs ostinato formulas to give form to the musical texture, and he uses percussion and rhythm to heighten the feeling of excitement.

Carl Orff has made a concerted effort to write music that appeals to the general public. He has succeeded.

[8] Andreas Liess, *Carl Orff,* translated by Adelheid and Herbert Parkin (New York: St. Martin's Press, 1966), p. 66. Liess quotes K. H. Ruppel's article "C. Orff und das Theater" (*Musica,* 1948, Nos. 3/4). Reprinted by permission.

Alexander Scriabin

The Romanticism of the two late-nineteenth-century schools—one nationalist, the other more European-oriented—persisted until the 1917 Bolshevik Revolution. Meanwhile, in the early twentieth century Alexander Scriabin (1872–1915) provided a new direction for young composers looking for different, vital expressive methods.

Except for six symphonic works, Scriabin's output is exclusively for piano. He was the least Russian of all the native composers, and his music takes nothing from Slavic folk elements; instead, Liszt, Chopin, and Wagner, whose harmonic patterns he particularly admired, served as his models. Scriabin, who considered himself to be a philosopher as much as a musician, impregnated his writings with the spirit of Nietzsche and oriental philosophy. His personal belief in a free, all-powerful personality that identified itself with the cosmos (I am God, I am the world, I am the center of the universe) affected the style of his nervous, excited works.

He arrived at his mature phase around 1910 when he evolved a harmonic system based on fourths instead of conventional thirds. He built entire compositions on chords, the so-called "mystic" chords, of which Example 24:8 is a classic

Ex. 24:8. Scriabin: *"Mystic" chord*

illustration. Unusual rhythmic groupings, profuse ornamentation, and chromatic harmony make his music extremely difficult to interpret and comprehend.

Scriabin's pseudo-philosophical mysticism influenced the musical poems he composed, some for piano, others for orchestra. Bearing titles such as *Poème tragique* (piano), *Poème satanique* (piano), and *Poème de l'extase* (orchestra), these poems typify Scriabin's highly mystical nature, and they reveal the rich harmonies and complicated rhythms of his later style.

The piano sonata reached fulfillment in Russian music with Scriabin's ten sonatas, in which the musical substance progressively breaks up into a transparent, ethereal framework of sound. The outstanding *Sonata No. 5, Opus 53* (1908) introduced new sensations and sounds. It has a motto, a quatrain emphasizing the composer's ecstatic mood.

> I call you to life, oh mysterious forces!
> Bathed in the obscure depths
> Of the Creator-Spirit, fearful
> Schemes of life, to you I bring audacity.

Scriabin accentuates this mood in the expressive indications for the different sections: *Impetuoso; Languido; Presto con allegrezza; Allegro fantastico;*

Presto tumultuoso esalto. The brief, one-movement work is fragmentary, yet by this very fact Scriabin creates his desired feeling of nervous tension, fervent exaltation, and at times a certain diabolic sarcasm.

Sergei Rachmaninoff

Sergei Rachmaninoff (1873–1943), a spectacular pianist equal to any of the leading twentieth-century virtuosos, also ranks high on the list of composers in his day, not because of his influence on younger artists but because of the inherent beauty in his music. He was not sympathetic with or influenced by the music of his compatriot Scriabin.

> Rachmaninoff's piano style stemmed directly from the romantic masters of the West, especially Chopin and Liszt, with occasional passing reference to Schumann, and even Brahms. It is interesting to note that the Russian composer must have observed, but almost totally disregarded, Debussy's revolutionary treatment of the piano. Instead he concentrated on the Chopin-Liszt framework of singing melodies and rich sonorities, decorated by elaborate technical embellishments. Though the formula was old he yet contrived to use it with individuality.[9]

Being a pianist, Rachmaninoff knew the capabilities of the keyboard, and as a result his compositions are pianistically secure. Endowed with an exceptional melodic talent, he produced some of the most hauntingly beautiful passages to be found in vocal literature. In transferring this talent to the keyboard, he created a characteristically limpid, nostalgic melodic line that is largely responsible for the success of some of his piano works, especially the concertos. Good examples of his melodic skill can be found in the middle section of *Polichinelle, Opus 3, No. 4* and various other pieces in *Opus 3* and *Opus 10*.

Rachmaninoff's finest solo piano works are the preludes. Like Chopin and J. S. Bach before him, he wrote altogether 24 preludes, one in each major and minor key. The famous and exquisitely fashioned *Prelude in C-Sharp Minor, Opus 3, No. 2* (1892) reveals compelling grandeur and impending tragedy. In 1903 Rachmaninoff wrote the 10 preludes of *Opus 23,* and in 1910 the 13 *Preludes, Opus 32* appeared. Each prelude—whether introspective, impassioned, or outwardly virtuoso—is a treasure of pianism, an expertly designed, enchanting tonal picture. The 15 *Études-Tableaux* comprising *Opus 33* (1911) and *Opus 39* (1917) were supposedly inspired by as many paintings, but the composer never clarified the reference. Although they are attractive they cannot match the splendid *Preludes*.

Rachmaninoff's four piano concertos express his melancholy Russian lyricism, and these darkly hued piano and orchestra dialogues, as well as the *Rhapsody on a Theme of Paganini* (1934), have sustained his reputation. His concertos are dramatic and melodious, for he blended a keyboard idiom based on Chopin and Liszt with a Russian lyric style derived partly from Tchaikovsky and Borodin. Although these concertos are not necessarily Rachmaninoff's best works, they are highly characteristic and their emotional impact has gained him indisputable success.

[9] Richard Anthony Leonard, *A History of Russian Music,* p. 238. Copyright © 1957 by The Macmillan Company, New York. Reprinted by permission.

Concerto No. 2 in C Minor, Opus 18 (1901), the most popular, emanates indescribable sadness from start to finish.

Moderato. Powerful piano chords grow in intensity, creating tension that lasts throughout this movement. The long, impassioned first theme (Ex. 24:9) is stated by the strings against swirling pianistic arpeggios. The second

Ex. 24:9. Rachmaninoff: ***Concerto No. 2 in C Minor: Moderato***

Examples 24:9 through 24:13 copyright by Edition Russe de Musique. Copyright assigned to Boosey & Hawkes, Ltd. Reprinted by permission of Boosey & Hawkes, Inc.

theme (Ex. 24:10), played by the soloist, builds to a mighty climax, although it begins and ends in a quiet, lyrical mood. The development section elaborates on

Ex. 24:10. Rachmaninoff: ***Concerto No. 2 in C Minor: Moderato***

the principal subject and a motive (Ex. 24:11) taken from the last measure of the

Ex. 24:11. Rachmaninoff: ***Concerto No. 2 in C Minor: Moderato***

movement's introductory chords. In the recapitulation the horn, not the piano, reintroduces the second theme.

Adagio sostenuto. This second movement contains some of Rachmaninoff's most inspired writing for piano. There are four introductory measures before flute and clarinet sing the principal theme (Ex. 24:12) supported by a

Ex. 24:12. Rachmaninoff: ***Concerto No. 2 in C Minor: Adagio sostenuto***

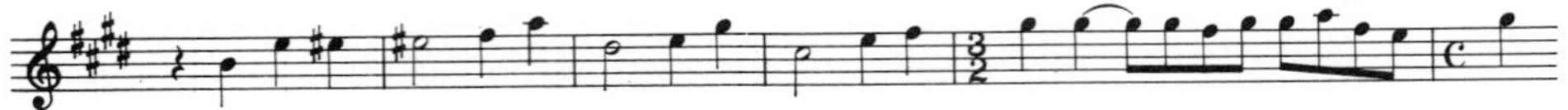

beautiful accompanimental figure on the piano. Shared by orchestra and soloist, this theme is varied and treated developmentally. At this moment most listeners are overwhelmed by the music's poignancy.

Allegro scherzando. The finale contains a rather ordinary first theme and a justly famous, grandiloquent second theme (Ex. 24:13). These two themes

Ex. 24:13. Rachmaninoff: *Concerto No. 2 in C Minor: Allegro scherzando*

alternate. With each new entry the first theme undergoes extensive variation while the second theme remains static, unabashedly displaying its beauty. Soaring emotions control the music right to the last chord.

Rachmaninoff wrote many compositions in other media: sacred and secular choral works; orchestral works such as the macabre symphonic poem *The Isle of the Dead;* and many beautiful songs. But his piano music speaks most forcefully.

After the revolution the Communist government instructed Russian composers to write music that would appeal to the masses, and the Bolshevik party frowned on experimental music. In those years following the revolution, musicians formed various organizations. The "Russian Association of Proletarian Musicians" strove for art forms suitable to the working class; the "Association for Contemporary Music" tried to present advanced types of current European music; in 1932 the "Union of Soviet Composers" was organized to combine the aims and ideals of all the existing groups into harmonious unity, musically and politically. There have been and are many twentieth-century Russian composers who have written attractive, consequential music: Nicolai Miaskovsky, Serge Prokofiev, Igor Stravinsky, Dmitri Kabalevsky, Aram Khachaturian, Dmitri Shostakovich. Several have established international reputations and worldwide audiences.

Serge Prokofiev

In his autobiography, Serge Prokofiev (1891–1953), one of the twentieth-century's finest composers, names five principal factors that have dominated his art in varying degrees at different periods. These are: (1) classicism—an affinity for forms indigenous to the Baroque and Classic periods; (2) innovation—a striving for a new harmonic language and the means for expressing strong emotions; (3) the toccata or motor element, where rhythmic vitality plays an important role; (4) the lyric element; and (5) an element of either grotesqueness, jesting, or mockery (as in the piano composition *Suggestion Diabolique,* 1909).

Prokofiev emigrated to the West after World War I and achieved international fame, but in 1934 he voluntarily returned to Russia. His "Western" period produced some of his most appealing works: *Piano Concerto No. 3* (1921), the *Classical Symphony* (1917), and two operas, of which the satirical *Love for Three Oranges* (1919) has had numerous performances. His Soviet period is notable for the ballets *Romeo and Juliet* (1935) and *Cinderella* (1944), the last four of his nine piano sonatas, and above all the charming *Peter and the Wolf* (1936).

Prokofiev was a neo-Classical composer. His symphonies, sonatas, and concertos all reveal his admiration for the clean-cut logical lines of eighteenth-century formal structures, and his biting sonorities and exciting rhythms go well with this penchant for musical clarity.

His two best-known compositions are the *Classical Symphony* and *Peter and the Wolf.* For the symphony he intended to write a composition in the classical idiom as Mozart or Haydn might have conceived it had either lived in the twentieth century. He obviously approached this work in a spirit of sophisticated humor. It is scored for a Classic orchestra: two each of flutes, oboes, clarinets, bassoons, horns, trumpets, kettledrums, plus strings. There are four movements: the outside movements have sonata-allegro form, the slow movement has ternary structure, and the third is a gavotte. In every movement the formal design is transparently clear, and the harmony and rhythm are mildly contemporary. The symphony is a delight.

In 1936 Prokofiev's *Peter and the Wolf* was introduced at a children's concert in Moscow. The composer also wrote the text to be spoken with the music and supplied the following explanation on the score:

> Each character of this Tale is represented by a corresponding instrument [Ex. 24:14] in the orchestra: the bird by a flute, the duck by an oboe, the cat by a clarinet in a low register, the grandfather by a bassoon, the wolf by three horns, Peter by the string quartet, the shooting of the hunters by the kettledrums and the bass drum. Before an orchestral performance it is desirable to show these instruments to the children and to play on them the corresponding leitmotives. Thereby the children learn to distinguish the sonorities of the instruments during the performance of the Tale.

The music is so piquant and the text so enjoyable and suspenseful that *Peter and the Wolf* appeals to all ages.

Igor Stravinsky

Igor Stravinsky (*b.*1882), undoubtedly the most famous twentieth-century Russian composer, has significantly influenced contemporary music. He is mostly self-taught, except for his studies with Rimsky-Korsakov, who initiated him into the art of orchestration. Stravinsky quickly became the most brilliant composer of his generation, producing three consecutive successful—and notorious—works written for Paris performances of the Ballet Russe. *L'oiseau du feu* (The Firebird) was produced in 1910. The next ballet, *Petrouchka* (1911), shows more advanced writing, and *Le sacre du printemps* (The Rite of Spring, 1913) indicates that he had by then stabilized the highly individual writing style that has become his trademark. These three masterworks caused a furor in their time, for Stravinsky's dissonant, bizarre, and super-rhythmical style shocked audiences accustomed to impressionistic and post-impressionistic music.

Shortly before World War I, Stravinsky moved to Switzerland for a six-year residence; during this time he produced the ballets *L'histoire du soldat* (1918) and *Pulcinella* (1919). During World War I and after, he developed a sparser, classical manner in keeping with his increasing interest in handling raw musical materials: rhythm, form, and tonality. After Switzerland, he spent almost 20 years in France, writing among other things the *Symphonies for Wind Instruments* (1920); *Les Noces* (The Wedding, 1923), a ballet with songs and choruses; the ballet *Apollon Musagète* (1928); the opera-oratorio *Oedipus Rex* (1927), with libretto by Jean Cocteau; and the *Dumbarton Oaks Concerto* (1938) for wind instruments. Stravinsky was in the United States when World War II broke out, and he eventually settled in California, becoming an American citizen in 1945. Among his compositions written since his arrival in the United States are *Danses*

Ex. 24:14. Prokofiev: *Peter and the Wolf*

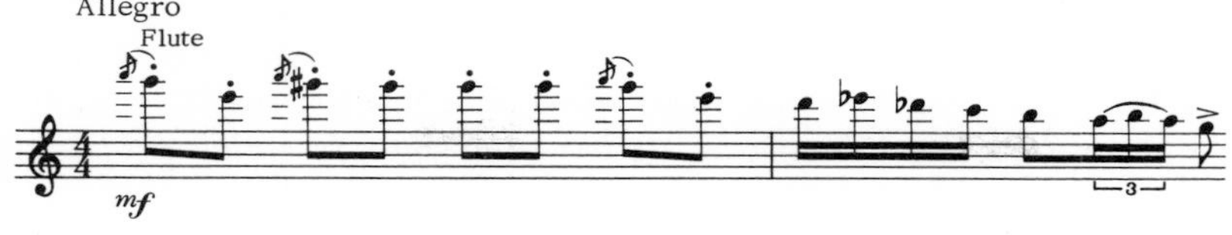

Copyright by Edition Gutheil. English edition copyright 1942 by Hawkes & Son (London) Ltd. Reprinted by permission of Boosey & Hawkes, Inc.

concertantes (1942), for chamber orchestra, the ballet *Orpheus* (1947), *Mass* (1948), and the opera *The Rake's Progress* (1951). The *Cantata on Elizabethan Lyrics* (1952) marks Stravinsky's first use of tone-row technique, a writing style he had previously condemned. Some other works in this style, which he took up at 70, are *Septet* (1953), for piano, strings, and wind instruments; the ballet *Agon* (1957); and the oratorio-like *Threni: id est lamentationes Jeremiae prophetae* (1958).

Rhythm dominates Stravinsky's music. The rhythmic vitality set in motion with Borodin's *Polovtsian Dances* acquires fantastic proportions with Stravinsky. Constantly changing rhythms, uneven rhythmic units of seven, nine, and eleven, and imaginative syncopation account for the astonishing energy embedded in his music.

His harmony sounds dissonant but, until recently, not atonal. He piles harmonies and melodic lines one on top of another to produce various polytonal and polyrhythmic textures. Chordal alterations of all types also contribute to his singular harmonies. While melody is important in Stravinsky's music, it is a personalized, instrumental melody that does not interfere with the mass of tonal sound. He is a master orchestrator, skillfully manipulating exotic tonal combinations and strange, exciting color patterns.

Stravinsky's ideas on the nature of music are as revolutionary as the early musical compositions, which perplexed and outraged his listeners.

> I consider that music is, by its very nature, essentially powerless to *express* anything at all, whether a feeling, an attitude of mind, a psychological mood, a phenomenon of nature, etc. . . . *Expression* has never been an inherent property of music. . . . The phenomenon of music is given to us with the sole purpose of establishing an order in things, including, and particularly, the coordination between *man* and *time*. To be put into practice, its indispensable and single requirement is construction. . . . It is precisely this construction, this achieved order, which produces in us a unique emotion having nothing in common with our ordinary sensations and our responses to the impressions of daily life.[10]

To the average listener, Stravinsky's exciting, barbaric ballets are his most intriguing and enjoyable works. Their popularity continues even though there are few occasions to enjoy them as performed ballets, for their hypnotic rhythms and sensuous sounds give the listener an unforgettable musical experience.

The Firebird

In Russian folklore the Firebird is a mysterious, wonderfully beautiful creature with feathers that shine like gold, eyes that gleam like jewels, and a glowing body that shines like fire in the dark. In Stravinsky's ballet the Firebird brings about the destruction of the evil ogre Kastcheï and unites two royal lovers. The orchestral suite fashioned from the ballet contains an introduction and five movements.

The *Introduction* pulsates with mystery (Ex. 24:15) and anticipation. In *Dance of the Firebird,* vibrating strings, woodwinds, and percussion suggest the bird's graceful motion. *Dance of the Princesses* is more melodic; an introductory flute and horn passage precedes the principal theme (Ex. 24:16), a folklike oboe

[10] Igor Stravinsky, *Chronicle of My Life* (London: Victor Gollancz, 1936), p. 91. Reprinted by permission of the composer.

Ex. 24:15. Stravinsky: *The Firebird: Introduction*

Examples 24:15 through 24:19 © copyright 1946 by MCA Music, a division of MCA Inc., New York. All rights reserved. Used by permission.

melody provided with a mellow harp accompaniment and a delicate countermelody in the violins.

Ex. 24:16. Stravinsky: *The Firebird: Dance of the Princesses*

The following movement is the wild *Dance of Kastcheï.* Typically Stravinsky, its frenetic rhythms, pungent syncopations (Ex. 24:17), clashing dissonances, snarling woodwinds, and shouting brasses create unrelieved intensity.

Ex. 24:17. Stravinsky: *The Firebird: Dance of Kastcheï*

This tension is eased in the serene *Berceuse.* Bassoon and oboe sing lyrical phrases (Ex. 24:18) punctuated by orchestral remarks and harp roulades.

Ex. 24:18. Stravinsky: *The Firebird: Berceuse*

Berceuse flows directly into the *Finale.* An expressive horn solo (Ex. 24:19) with fluttering string accompaniment prefaces the rhythmic conclusion.

Ex. 24:19. Stravinsky: *The Firebird: Finale*

The talent displayed in *The Firebird* shines brilliantly in *Petrouchka:* the score is strikingly original; the technique is more complicated than that of the first ballet; and the bright, flexible language is more personal. The climax of Stravinsky's early revolutionary style appeared with *The Rite of Spring,* a ballet depicting pagan ritual dances. The many uncanny orchestral effects are part of an overall plan of carefully balanced contrasts, which Stravinsky creates through daringly original use of his instruments. Rhythm and melody per se acquire new meaning as he establishes complementary relationships between them. In this highly significant contemporary work, Stravinsky proved his complete control over his powerful, startling tonal language.

Aram Khachaturian

Stravinsky's forceful rhythms create the basic character of his music. With Armenian-born Aram Khachaturian (*b.*1903), melody represents the strongest trait in his music. Drawing inspiration from the folk and popular music of Caucasia and the Middle East, Khachaturian designs melodies that are haunting in their sweetness and warmth yet wholly original. His harmonic instinct and intuitive feeling for local color produce music that immediately attracts the listener.

Khachaturian proudly acknowledges the folk element discernible in his music. He wrote:

> I grew up in an atmosphere rich in folk music: popular festivities; rites, joyous and sad events in the life of the people always accompanied by music, the vivid tunes of Armenian, Azerbaijan and Georgian songs and dances performed by folk bards and musicians—such were the impressions that became deeply engraved in my memory, that determined my musical thinking.

He further explains how he utilizes this folk element:

> It would be wrong to denounce the method of quoting genuine folk melodies for achieving definite artistic aims. We know too well that the Russian classics made extensive use of this method. . . . I for my part prefer another approach to the folk melody, the one when the composer, in pursuance of his ideas and guided by his artistic sense, utilizes it as a seed, as the initial melodic motif to be freely developed, transformed, and musically enriched. . . . But in order not to violate the nature of folk melodies, the composer must have a keen understanding of the national style, he must feel the essence of folk music with all his heart and soul.[11]

Khachaturian's most famous work is the orchestral music from his ballet *Gayne* (1942). Set in an Armenian collective farm, the ballet is about Gayne, the heroine, whose husband is a thief. When his thieving is discovered, he tries to murder Gayne but she is saved by her true love, Kazakov.

The ballet contains many delightful sections. The *Sabre Dance* is a wildly rhythmical tour de force highlighted by staccato woodwinds and brass glissandos. In the contrasting *Lullaby* the flute weaves an arabesque above plucked harp sounds before the entrance of a lively middle section. The gently rocking rhythm in *Dance of the Rose Maidens* recalls a Ukranian folk dance. Like the *Sabre Dance,* the *Dance of Ayshe* includes a saxophone in the orchestration. The shifting rhythms here create extraordinarily spontaneous music. The full orchestra presents the *Dance of the Kurds,* a barbaric frenzy dominated by brass and percussion. The *Dance of the Young Kurds* is more subdued: oboes and clarinets

[11] Grigory Shneerson, *Aram Khachaturyan,* translated by Xenia Danko (Moscow: Foreign Languages Publishing House, 1959), pp. 10–11.

play above pizzicato strings; flute and brass enter later. Beating drums announce *Lezginka,* the tumultuous dance that celebrates Gayne's happiness.

Two Khachaturian concertos are heard with enough regularity to establish them as solid items in concerto repertoire. His flamboyant *Piano Concerto,* first performed in 1936, is a kind of symphony for piano solo and orchestra.

> Its exceedingly varied and original rhythm is the Concerto's mainspring. The numerous episodes of different moods following one another are all active and volitional. The gorgeous beauty of expressive themes rooted deeply in Armenian and Azerbaijan folk music, the overwhelming elemental force of rhythm, the all-conquering temperament, are combined in this work with a broad and significant symphonic conception and brilliant virtuoso texture.[12]

In 1940 the Russian violinist David Oistrakh premiered Khachaturian's *Violin Concerto.* Like the *Piano Concerto* this fiery, festive composition has been immensely successful in Europe and America.

Dmitri Kabalevsky

A critic and musicologist as well as imaginative composer, Dmitri Kabalevsky (*b.*1904) has earned many prizes and honors from the Russian government. Basically a traditionalist, Kabalevsky is an expert craftsman with an inherent gift for lyricism. Among his works are four operas, four symphonies, six concertos, a Requiem, many chamber works, and instrumental works for young people. One of his most delightful works is *The Comedians* (1938), an orchestral suite in ten sections. He made the suite from incidental music he wrote for a children's play about a band of itinerant musicians and their amusing escapades as they traveled from town to town.

Dmitri Shostakovich

Like Prokofiev, Dmitri Shostakovich (*b.*1906) prefers to work within the no-longer restraining confines of sonata form. He is a staunch advocate of music based on the Soviet ideology, and accordingly his writing has been affected by political dogmas. His reputation, too, has been influenced by political situations; he and his music have been denounced on several occasions by the Soviet government, then each time later reinstated to official favor. After his youthful first symphony (1925) won wide acclaim for its vigor and skillful orchestration, he became the favorite composer of the official regime, but some ten years later he slipped temporarily from that high position. In 1936 his opera *Lady Macbeth of Mzensk,* which had already been playing successfully for two years, was denounced by the official government newspaper *Pravda:*

> The author of *Lady Macbeth* was forced to borrow from jazz its nervous, convulsive and spasmodic music in order to lend "passion" to his characters. While our music critics swear by the name of socialist realism, the stage serves us, in Shostakovich's work, the coarsest kind of naturalism. The music quacks, grunts and growls, and suffocates itself in order to express the amorous scenes as naturalistically as possible. And "love" is smeared all over the opera in the most vulgar manner.

[12] Shneerson, p. 41.

The overwhelming success of his fifth symphony, premiered in 1937, restored him to official favor. But in 1946 he received criticism because his ninth symphony failed to "reflect the spirit of the Soviet people," and in 1948 the Central Committee of the Communist Party berated him for "decadent formalism." Shostakovich is nonetheless the foremost musical spokesman now working in Russia. He has written at least 13 symphonies, many chamber works, and numerous piano compositions, including a concerto.

His music is decidedly uneven in quality. Pages of inspired writing are suddenly interrupted by passages laden with contrived effects. But he manipulates the orchestra with knowledgeable assurance and employs symphonic form with natural ease. He likes to explore the extreme registers of the various instruments and to use wide melodic leaps; that is, themes having definite instrumental character. Contrasting sounds and chromatically oriented harmonies add interest to his music.

Although Shostakovich has not written anything as instantly captivating as Khachaturian's *Sabre Dance,* his ballet *The Age of Gold* (1930) contains a sophisticated little *Polka* that comes close to it.

Symphony No. 5

Many critics believe that Shostakovich's *Symphony No. 5, Opus 47* (1937) is not only his finest work in this medium but one of the great symphonies of this century. It is long, but each of the four movements possesses strength and character. Shostakovich looked on the symphony as "The artist's reply to just criticism," the "just criticism" being the reprimand he received because of his opera *Lady Macbeth.* He explained the work in these words:

> The subject of my symphony is an individual in the making. The symphony is conceived in a lyrical vein. The finale of the symphony resolves the tense tragedy of the early movements on an optimistic plane. The question is sometimes raised whether tragedy should have a place in Soviet art, confusing tragedy with gloom and pessimism. I believe that Soviet tragedy as a genre has every right to exist. But its contents must be suffused with a positive idea as in the life-asserting pathos of Shakespeare's tragedies.[13]

Moderato. In bold antiphony, the strings declare the first theme (Ex. 24:20)—one that contains great contrasts within its own confines. A second,

Ex. 24:20. Shostakovich: *Symphony No. 5: Moderato*

Examples 24:20 through 24:23 © copyright 1945 by MCA Music, a division of MCA Inc., New York. All rights reserved. Used by permission.

[13] Gerhart von Westerman, *The Concert Guide,* translated by Cornelius Cardew (New York: Arco Publishing Company, Inc., 1963), p. 407.

milder theme soars in expansive leaps. Thematic transformation and trumpet fanfares enliven the development section before the appearance of the recapitulation.

Allegretto. Satire and impudence pervade this scherzo, which has the spirit of a peasant dance. The principal theme (Ex. 24:21) is in *c* minor but the

Ex. 24:21. Shostakovich: ***Symphony No. 5: Allegretto***

tonality of this movement shifts continually. The ternary form is clear and symmetrical.

Largo. The melody of this romantic movement is first heard in the strings (Ex. 24:22). Shostakovich's skill in handling expansive themes in lyrical

Ex. 24:22. Shostakovich: ***Symphony No. 5: Largo***

surroundings is much in evidence as the melody develops into an emotional poem.

Allegro non troppo. In this march the theme (Ex. 24:23) is presented by

Ex. 24:23. Shostakovich: ***Symphony No. 5: Allegro non troppo***

trumpets, trombones, and tuba laid out against beating timpani. The form is rondo. The initial somber mood builds to an exuberant climax; then a subdued section ends this fine symphony.

FOR DISCUSSION AND ASSIGNMENT

1. Do you think it advisable to omit the performer from the musical experience (as in electronic music)?

2. Concerts of contemporary music are usually not so well attended as those featuring classical music. Is there a solution for this seeming indifference? How may it be brought about?
3. By now you have probably heard several substantial examples of twelve-tone music. Do you think it can be appreciated or enjoyed? Does it permit the same type of appreciation as that inspired by more traditional music? What criteria or approach would you apply to gain an understanding of twelve-tone music?
4. Do you think the influence of folk material is just as strong now in Russia as it was in the nineteenth century? Has this influence been beneficial to Russian music in general?
5. Which of the composers discussed in this chapter do you think will survive the test of time? Give your reasons.

FOR FURTHER READING

Barnes, Harry Elmer. *An Intellectual and Cultural History of the Western World.* Vol. 3. New York: Dover Publications, Inc., 1965. PB. Dr. Barnes's survey of the twentieth century (with the assistance of some specialized experts) is meaningful, penetrating, and interesting.

Collaer, Paul. *A History of Modern Music,* translated by S. Abeles. New York: Grosset & Dunlap, 1961. A Universal Library PB. No one book can claim to be complete and up-to-date on contemporary music, but this one provides a good review of musical developments up to 1950.

Eimert, Herbert, and Karlheinz Stockhausen, editors. *Die Reihe.* Vol. 1: *Electronic Music.* Bryn Mawr, Pennsylvania: Theodore Presser Co., 1965. PB. This first issue of a periodical devoted to developments in contemporary music contains essays on various aspects of electronic music. Much of the writing is highly technical, but the first few essays can be read and understood rather easily.

Hodeir, André. *Since Debussy: A View of Contemporary Music,* translated by Noel Burch. New York: Grove Press, Inc., 1961. An Evergreen PB. M. Hodeir studies the work of the major composers since Debussy and makes some rather illuminating—and opinionated—conclusions on the future of contemporary music. A fascinating book.

Howard, John Tasker, and James Lyons. *Modern Music.* New York: The New American Library, 1957. A Mentor PB. This is a brief, somewhat dated summary of contemporary trends. For the musical amateur, it provides a useful introduction to twentieth-century music.

Leonard, Richard Anthony. *A History of Russian Music.* New York: The Macmillan Co., 1957. This book provides a good look at musical activity in Russia up to the time of publication.

Machlis, Joseph. *Introduction to Contemporary Music.* New York: W. W. Norton & Co., Inc., 1961. A highly competent book written in an easily comprehensible style. Many contemporary works are analyzed.

Sypher, Wylie. *Rococo to Cubism in Art and Literature.* New York: Random House, 1960. PB. The approach—aesthetic and philosophical—of this book is unusual. It is difficult reading but well worth the effort involved.

Webern, Anton. *The Path to the New Music,* translated by L. Black. Bryn Mawr, Pennsylvania: Theodore Presser Co., 1963. PB. A good introduction to twelve-tone composition and how it developed.

Twentieth-Century Music—II 25

No man is complete without a feeling for music and an understanding of what it can do for him.

ZOLTÁN KODÁLY

Newspaper Interview
Santa Barbara News-Press
August 1, 1966

FRANCE

Music in twentieth-century France has been overrun with contradictions, with manifestos and countermanifestos. Some ultraconservative composers prolonged Romanticism far beyond its natural productive life. Debussy and Ravel—each in his own way—exercised a far-reaching influence on others. Foreign influences, particularly Germanic, also directed the course of some French music in this era. As a result of these diverse circumstances and pressures, France has produced some superb music, some very interesting music, and some perplexing music.

Erik Satie

A very important yet enigmatic figure during the early years, Erik Satie (1866–1925) is looked upon by some critics as a direct precursor of Impressionism, while others dismiss him as an eccentric dilettante. Both positions are valid, for many different elements account for Satie's style—or styles. For a time he worked as a cabaret pianist, and he often introduced popular elements into his serious writings. His friendships with Debussy, Jean Cocteau, and Pablo Picasso naturally had some effect on his career, and his belated (at 40) contrapuntal studies with d'Indy and Roussel definitely influenced his later writing.

More than anything else, Satie wanted to simplify music, to free it from what he thought was nineteenth-century emotionalism and pretentiousness, from Impressionism's super-refinement, from the too rich harmonies of Debussy and his admirers. In short, he wanted music to be natural and straightforward. His clean-cut, impersonal works have never earned a secure place in concert repertoire, but his approach to music has significantly influenced twentieth-century composers, especially *Les Six* (see page 365).

There are detectable flaws in Satie's music, yet it is so intimate—most of his writing is for piano solo—that it reveals his strikingly original personality. A vital part of this personality grew (about 1887) out of his preoccupation with the mystical secrets of Rosicrucianism. In that year he wrote three piano *Sarabandes* with suave chromatic harmonies that create a distinctly melancholy mood. In his three *Gymnopédies* (1888) and the three *Gnossiennes* (1890), the harmonies become simpler and a feeling of modality prevails. Unlike Debussy's predominantly harmonic approach, Satie's series of parallel chords—sevenths, ninths, and elevenths—are habitually dependent on delicately designed melodic patterns.

Toward the turn of the century Satie entered a phase in which apparent facetious humor disguises his music's serious intent and originality. His amusing, flippant directions for the performer ("moderately and very bored . . . a little cooked . . . like a nightingale with a toothache") camouflaged the seriousness in his music and may have been meant to protect him from possible criticism.

Satie's best style lies in the ten piano suites that appeared from 1912 to 1915. Diatonic harmony disciplined by strict note economy indicates that with these miniatures—bearing outlandish titles such as *Véritables préludes flasques* (Genuine Flabby Preludes), *Embryons desséchés* (Dessicated Embryos), and the unbelievably original *Sports et divertissements*—Satie reached his goal of simple, nonsentimental, nonrhetorical music.

During the latter part of his life Satie composed two works of extended proportions. The first was *Parade* (1917), a realistic satire composed for Serge Diaghilev's *Ballet Russe*. Pablo Picasso designed the curtain, scenery, and costumes, and Jean Cocteau wrote the story—an "entertainment" about touring players who perform in city streets. Satie explained his approach in this way:

> I composed only a background to throw into relief the noises which the playwright considers indispensable to the surrounding of each character with its own atmosphere. These noises imitate waves, revolvers, typewriters, sirens, airplanes—music belonging to the same category as the bits of newspaper, painted woodgrain, and other everyday objects that the cubist painters frequently employ in their pictures in order to localize objects and masses in nature.[1]

Another more serious work from Satie's late period is the three-part symphonic drama entitled *Socrate* (1918), which is based on the *Dialogues* of Plato (*Symposium, Phaedrus,* and *Phaedo*). The score calls for four soprano soloists and a chamber orchestra. Satie's sparse writing, simple expressive means, and weaving polyphonic lines create a classic austerity consistent with the subject matter.

Jacques Ibert

Jacques Ibert (1890–1962) was not a great composer, but his charming music has won him many admirers. Ibert's style follows the Impressionist school but only in its derivations from Ravel, not Debussy. Clarity, precision, wit, and elegance—all qualities admired by the French—abound in his large repertoire.

[1] David Ewen, *The Complete Book of 20th Century Music* (Englewood Cliffs, N.J.: Prentice-Hall, Inc., 1959), p. 344.

Two of his well-known works, one for piano and one for orchestra, date from 1922. The piano collection called *Histoires*—ten delightfully descriptive pieces—is in turn gay, humorous, brilliant, and meditative. The individual titles provide clues to the often quaint musical content: *Le petit âne blanc* (The Little White Donkey); *A Giddy Girl; Le cage de cristal* (The Crystal Cage); *La marchande d'eau fraîche* (The Fresh-Water Vendor).

His three-movement orchestral suite *Escales* (Ports of Call) recalls the Mediterranean ports he visited while in the navy during World War I. He takes his listeners on an impressionistic musical travelogue, re-creating a seaport atmosphere by using popular-type themes, colorful orchestration, and sensuous harmonies.

In the first movement, *Rome-Palermo,* the flute introduces an Italianate air that sounds very authentic (Ex. 25:1).

Ex. 25:1. Ibert: *Escales: Rome-Palermo*

Copyright by Alphonse Leduc & C° (1925), owners and publishers, 175 rue Saint-Honoré, Paris Ier.

The second movement, *Tunis-Nefta,* transports the listener across the Mediterranean to a different culture. Here the oboe intones a mournful, chromatic theme set against oriental rhythms in the strings, while timpani provide accent. The final section, *Valencia,* is an exotic Spanish rhapsody built from a Hispanic theme.

Les Six

As charming as it sometimes is, Ibert's music and that of many of his contemporaries gives little indication of future trends, for this music is fundamentally an extension of Romantic tendencies coupled with out-of-context procedures appropriated from the Impressionists. Reaction was bound to come, and it did. After World War I, composers rebelled against Wagner's Romanticism, Debussy's Impressionism, and Ravel's dilettantism. The musicologist Henri Collet placed several of the young members of this opposition into a theoretical group called *Les Six* (The Six).

One of *Les Six,* Darius Milhaud (*b.*1892), describes the inception of this group in his autobiography.

> After a concert at the Salle Huyghens [in 1919], at which Bertin sang Louis Durey's *Images à Crusoë* on words by Saint-Léger and the Capelle Quartet played my *Fourth Quartet,* the critic Henri Collet published in *Comoedia* a chronicle entitled "Five Russians and Six Frenchmen." Quite arbitrarily he had chosen six names: Auric, Durey, Honegger, Poulenc, Taillefaire and my own, merely because we knew each other, were good friends, and had figured on the same programs; quite irrespective of our different temperaments and wholly dissimilar characters. Auric and Poulenc were partisans of Cocteau's ideas, Honegger derived from the German Romantics, and I from Mediterranean

> lyricism. I fundamentally disapproved of joint declarations of aesthetic doctrines and felt them to be a drag, an unreasonable limitation on the imagination of the artists who must for each new work find different, often contradictory means of expression. But it was useless to protest. Collet's article excited such worldwide interest that the "Group of Six" was launched, and willy-nilly I formed part of it.[2]

Yet Milhaud confessed that what Collet had done proved beneficial.

> The formation of the Group of Six helped to draw the bonds of friendship closer among us. For two years we met regularly at my place every Saturday evening. . . . We were not all composers, for our number also included performers . . . painters . . . and writers. . . . The poets would read their poems, and we would play our latest compositions. . . . Out of these meetings, in which a spirit of carefree gaiety reigned, many a fruitful collaboration was to be born; they also determined the character of several works strongly marked by the influence of the music hall.[3]

Three of these composers—Milhaud, Poulenc, and Honegger—have become the outstanding representatives of the contemporary French school. Faced with a list of works of Darius Milhaud one cannot help thinking that here is enough material for several composers. This prolific writer, a pupil of Dukas and d'Indy, has written more than 400 works, including 15 operas, 16 ballets, 18 quartets, 35 concertos, 12 symphonies, and 6 chamber symphonies. When asked which of his works he considered most significant, the composer responded with a splendid Gallic witticism, "The next one."[4]

Milhaud has created an amazing number of solidly built and impressively attractive works within this enormous repertoire. In every media he displays extraordinary skill in handling polytonal counterpoint and a capacity for assimilating musical influences essentially foreign to his own Gallic nature. In his orchestral compositions he carefully works out his instrumentation, sustaining interest by interchanging tone colors. His imaginative and subtle use of percussion instruments is especially notable.

In his autobiography, Milhaud elaborates on his affinity for polytonality.

> I had noted—and interpreted for myself—that a little duet by Bach written in canon at the fifth really gave one the impression of two separate keys succeeding one another, and then becoming superimposed and contrasted, though of course the harmonic texture remained tonal. . . . I set to work to examine every possible combination of two keys superimposed and to study the chords thus produced. . . . I grew familiar with some of these chords. They satisfied my ear more than the normal ones, for a polytonal chord is more subtly sweet and more violently potent.[5]

One of Milhaud's early successes, an orchestral potpourri called *Le boeuf sur le toit* (The Bull on the Roof, 1919), belongs to that period during World War I when Milhaud served as secretary to the French Minister to Brazil.

[2] From *Notes without Music,* p. 97, by Darius Milhaud, translated by Donald Evans and edited by Rollo N. Myers. Copyright 1952, 1953 by Alfred A. Knopf, Inc. Reprinted by permission.

[3] Milhaud, pp. 98–99. Reprinted by permission.

[4] Communication to the author, dated October 4, 1966.

[5] From *Notes without Music,* pp. 65–66, by Darius Milhaud, translated by Donald Evans and edited by Rollo N. Myers. Copyright 1952, 1953 by Alfred A. Knopf, Inc. Reprinted by permission.

Profiting from this experience, he appropriated nearly two dozen Brazilian dance tunes and skillfully worked them into an orchestral rondo. After hearing this music, Jean Cocteau persuaded Milhaud to let him write a pantomimic farce to go with it. Cocteau placed the action in an American speakeasy, and his stage adaptation became so popular that a bar in Paris was named for it. Although Cocteau's version is now quite dated, Milhaud's music still delights the ear and stimulates the imagination.

During a visit to the United States in 1922, Milhaud stopped off at New York's Harlem section. Fascinated by the jazz music of Negro bands, he later wrote in his autobiography:

> The music I heard was absolutely different from anything I had ever heard before, and was a revelation to me. Against the beat of the drums the melodic lines crisscrossed in a breathless pattern of broken and twisted rhythms. This authentic music had its roots in the darkest corners of the Negro soul. Its effect on me was so overwhelming that I could not tear myself away. . . . More than ever I was resolved to use jazz for a chamber work.[6]

The result was *La création du monde* (The Creation of the World, 1923), a ballet based on African legends about the creation of the world. Milhaud devised an expanded jazz ensemble and peppered his score with jazz rhythms, passages in blues, saxophone solos, and trombone glissandi. Although this is a very interesting work, most musicians now agree that the best thing to do with jazz is to let jazz musicians and composers handle it. When treated "classically," it loses its spontaneity and impact.

Milhaud can be extremely ingenious. His *String Quartet No. 14* (1948) and the *String Quartet No. 15* (1949) are both fine chamber works. What is astonishing is that the two quartets are so written that they can be played simultaneously, thus *creating* a string octet.

Francis Poulenc (1899–1963) most typically represents *l'esprit français.* His elegant, witty style derives from music of the late nineteenth and early twentieth centuries. His approach stems directly from the clavecinists and from sixteenth-century French polyphony; it frequently reveals unashamedly that its sole purpose is pleasure, often the pleasure of the moment. This attitude is refreshing, all the more so in a composer who had so much inherent compositional talent. Naturally, critical examination uncovers defects in Poulenc's music: a mixture of incongruous elements, basically undistinguished ideas hidden in handsome garb, an overt sentimentality. But these faults may be exactly the reason why his music is immediately accessible—and enjoyable.

His fine talent for choral writing is well documented in his difficult works for unaccompanied (a capella) chorus; for example, the splendid *Mass in G* (1937) and *Quatre motets pour un temps de pénitence* (Four Motets for a Time of Penitence, 1939). He also maintained a lifelong interest in songs and is one of the great art-song composers. He chose contemporary poems for texts and typically arranged his songs in cycles. One of his best song cycles—*Le Bestiare* (The Bestiary, 1919), a setting of poems by Guillaume Apollinaire—shows a Satie influence. This collection is scored for mezzo-soprano, string quartet, flute, clari-

[6] From *Notes without Music,* pp. 136–137, by Darius Milhaud, translated by Donald Evans and edited by Rollo N. Myers. Copyright 1952, 1953 by Alfred A. Knopf, Inc. Reprinted by permission.

net, and bassoon. With customary sophistication and wit, Poulenc describes a dromedary, Tibetan goat, grasshopper, dolphin, crawfish, and carp.

Working mostly in small forms did not deter Poulenc from attempting ballets and operas. His finest stage work, the tragic opera *Dialogues des Carmélites* (Dialogues of the Carmelites, 1955), is in the grand-opera tradition.

Poulenc was an excellent pianist, and his large repertoire includes a quantity of piano music. After the early *Mouvements perpétuels* (1918) established him as a significant keyboard composer, he consistently turned out solo keyboard works substantiating this initial impression.

The *Concert champêtre* (Rustic Concerto, 1928), for harpsichord and orchestra, is a welcome repertoire item for the harpsichordist who enjoys playing twentieth-century music. Poulenc's deft hand is apparent in his intriguing use of the harpsichord in a modern idiom. Although this concerto is scored for full orchestra, it is so cleverly written that the harpsichord is never submerged by the other instruments.

Arthur Honegger (1892–1955) believed that structure was highly important, and he handled it with disciplined imagination. His style is dominated by a contrapuntal texture that often creates harsh, uncompromising polytonality, but his dissonance is always accompanied by strong rhythms and abundant lyricism.

Honegger never felt sympathetic with the twelve-tone school that was creating such excitement.

> I believe that for a composer there is no possibility, no future, for expression there, because its melodic invention is subjected to uncompromising laws which shackle free expression of thought. I am not in the least opposed to discipline freely accepted, even sought out, by sensitive artists. But this discipline must have some justification and not be arbitrarily set up as a decree.[7]

In his book entitled *I Am a Composer* he describes how most composers conceive their music.

> The fact is that, for the average man, the act of composing music remains an incomprehensible thing. "Well then, is it not true that when you compose, you try to find on your piano something that will make a piece; but when it's a piece for an orchestra, you can't play all the instrumental parts at the same time?"
>
> I try to explain that composing sound has to be done first in the mind, and then be consigned to paper in its larger outlines. "But without hearing the notes played?" All the more so because I do not, so to speak, play the piano. "You are obliged then to have someone else play it?" No, because that is a mental operation that takes place in the brain of the composer. I do not mean to say that the checking of certain passages on the piano is not useful, if only to help the logical sequence of the different elements, to be used somewhat as a guide.[8]

Honegger had a natural gift for composing dramatic oratorios. One of these—*Le roi David* (King David)—made a sensational success in 1921 and within a few years earned him an international reputation. He described the work as a symphonic psalm in three parts; its text by René Morax tells the story of David from his shepherd days to his role as king and prophet. The music is

[7] Arthur Honegger, *I Am a Composer,* translated by W. O. Clough (New York: St. Martin's Press, 1966), p. 117. Reprinted by permission of St. Martin's Press, Inc., New York, and Faber and Faber Ltd., London.

[8] Honegger, pp. 64–65. Reprinted by permission.

appealing throughout. The listener remains attentive because the composer uses short musical forms—dances, marches, arias, hymns—that keep the narration moving swiftly, and he creates diversion by alternating childlike solo songs with excitingly colorful choral refrains. Honegger conveys the feeling that a noble dramatic pageant is being enacted even though the oratorio is usually presented without costumes or action. With musicianly instinct and obvious sympathy for his subject, he forces his audience into a participating mood.

He composed several large-scale works for chorus and orchestra, such as *Judith* (1926), *Jeanne d'Arc au bûcher* (1935), and *La danse des morts* (1938). *Jeanne d'Arc au bûcher* (Joan of Arc at the Stake), set to a text by the French mystic poet Paul Claudel, is probably Honegger's foremost composition. This stage oratorio contains a prologue and eleven scenes, and a performance entails a large orchestra, two speaking roles, three principal singing roles, other solo parts, mixed chorus, and a children's chorus.

Honegger's first orchestral work to win recognition was a distinct novelty—*Pacific 231* (1923). It is still heard occasionally, although the novelty has long since worn thin. Around 1923, Pacific, model 231, was the huge engine used for heavy express trains in Europe. Honegger explained the work in his book:

> *Pacific 231* sets forth the objective contemplation; the quiet breathing machine in repose, its effort in starting, then gradual increase in speed, leading from the lyrical to the pathetic condition of a train of three hundred tons hurling itself through the night at a speed of 120 kilometers an hour.[9]

Jeune France

In Paris on June 3, 1936, four young French composers who self-styled themselves *Jeune France* presented a concert to exploit their own works. The composers were Daniel-Lesur, Yves Baudrier, André Jolivet, and Olivier Messiaen, and notes appended to the program announced that their group had dedicated itself to "the dissemination of works youthful, free, as far removed from revolutionary formulas as from academic formulas." The statement added further:

> The tendencies of this group will be diverse; their only unqualified agreement is in the common desire to be satisfied with nothing less than sincerity, generosity, and artistic good faith. Their aim is to create and promote a living music.

André Jolivet (*b.*1905) draws his inspiration from widely disparate sources—among others, Rameau, Berlioz, Debussy, Varèse, Berg, and the "popular music of all the people of the earth." He develops symbolic images based on his belief that music is mystical and magical. Jolivet describes his approach to musical composition as "the utilization of the natural resonances [harmonics], employment of certain serial principles to the interior of modal scales."[10]

One of the most magnetic works to come from the contemporary French school is Jolivet's *Suite delphique* (1943). The work is scored for 12 performers on the following instruments: one flute (doubling on piccolo), one English horn

[9] Honegger, p. 101. Reprinted by permission.

[10] Communication to the author, dated September 12, 1966.

(doubling on oboe), one clarinet, two French horns, one trumpet, one trombone, one timpani, two percussion batteries, *ondes Martenot* (an electronic keyboard instrument), and harp.

Delphic Suite contains eight sections: I. *Prelude* (Magic Dawn); II. *The Dogs of Erebus;* III. *Storm;* IV. *Tranquillity in Nature;* V. *Procession;* VI. *Dionysian Delight;* VII. *Invocation;* VIII. *Cortege.* Jolivet has built this work on Greek modal scales, each section being constructed on a mode chosen for its expressive qualities. Thus *Storm* uses a mode dominated by augmented fourths, a mode that for centuries indicated drama and terror; *Tranquillity in Nature* is written in the Lydian mode used for the first Delphic hymn (one of the existing fragments of Greek music); *Dionysian Delight* takes its materials from the first Pythian hymn of Pindar—that is, the Phrygian mode, which Plato condemned for its dionysian vehemence. Jolivet achieves wonderful results with his small number of instruments. The entire work is one that usually pleases even the strongest opponents of "modern" music.

Olivier Messiaen (*b.*1908), like Jolivet, approaches composition spiritually, but his inspiration is propelled by orthodox Roman Catholicism rather than pagan primitivism. And his musical language is of course different. A highly organized and personal aestheticism (he has written a book on the subject, *The Technique of My Musical Language*) enables him to create ideas that clearly translate his mysticism into comprehensive tonal patterns. His principle of "exact repetition" and "varied repetition"—too complex to be treated here—should be investigated if one is to understand his aims and purposes.

Messiaen's familiarity with Gregorian chant and ecclesiastical modes sometimes injects a colorful medieval atmosphere into his music; his interest in Hindu music, particularly its flexible rhythms, frequently provides an oriental mood; and his writing also reveals traces of Impressionism, the result of his admiration for Debussy's opera *Pelléas et Mélisande.* His latest inspiration comes from nature, and he is currently involved in reproducing bird songs and calls in his music.

Messiaen's complex, fascinating *Chronochromie* (Color of Time, 1960), for large orchestra, illustrates his basic style concepts to good advantage. From his viewpoint all music seems to be associated with colors and color combinations. In *Chronochromie* he manipulates 32 different rhythmic durations, fitting them with appropriate color by means of orchestral timbres.

He has constructed the work as a suite with seven sections, which he likens to choruses of a Greek tragedy: Introduction, Strophe I, Antistrophe I, Strophe II, Antistrophe II, Epode, and Coda. Having created a problem with his intricate rhythmic patterns, Messiaen adds further complexity by using orchestral sonorities and melodic material to imitate birdsongs of France, Japan, and Mexico and waterfalls and mountain streams in the French alps. *Chronochromie* is climaxed by an ear-ringing passage in which 18 solo strings each play a separate birdsong simultaneously.

Pierre Boulez

Pierre Boulez (*b.*1925) is one of Messiaen's outstanding students and one of France's very outspoken avant-garde composers. Combining Webern's severe dodecaphony with the imaginative rhythmic doctrines of Messiaen,

Boulez strives for complete serialization: he frequently works simultaneously with twelve-tone rows, fixed rhythmic patterns, and rows of dynamic values. A slow, methodical composer, his repertoire to date includes among other works three piano sonatas; *Visage nuptial* (1946), *Le soleil des eaux* (1948), *Le marteau sans maître* (1954), and *Poèsie pour pouvoir* (1958)—all for various combinations of voice and orchestra; and *Structures* (1952), for two pianos.

Boulez's three piano sonatas offer nearly insurmountable obstacles for the pianist and a puzzling sonorous experience for the average listener. The second sonata is described by the composer as representing "a total and deliberate break with the universe of classical twelve-tone writing . . . the decisive step towards an integrated serial work, that will be realized when serial structures of tone-colors and dynamics will join serial structures of pitch and rhythm."[11] In his remarks to the performer, Boulez cautions that the performer must carefully observe rhythms and rests; that bar lines are only visual aids; that counterpoint is especially important; and that there are no principal melodic lines.

Le soleil des eaux (River in the Sun) brought Boulez to the attention of the general public. He originally scored this two-movement cantata for soprano, tenor, and bass solos with chamber orchestra, but in 1958 he revised it, enlarging the orchestra and adding a three-part chorus of sopranos, tenors, and basses. The texture is quite simple, with much use of counterpoint, and the work contains numerous string solos supplied with precise directions for mode of attack, a basic characteristic of his technique. *Le soleil des eaux* possesses exceptional delicacy: the orchestral fabric is transparent and the vocal lines are treated like improvisations.

The first part, *La complainte du lézard amoureux* (The Lay of the Amorous Lizard), is sung by the soprano soloist. Its text, by the surrealist French poet René Char, describes the thoughts of this singular lizard as he gazes lovingly at a goldfinch. Mostly unaccompanied, the soprano line moves in free dialogue with short-winded orchestral comments.

Char's text for the second part, *La Sorge* (The River Sorge), is a hymn of praise to the river. Boulez's music begins with a flowing orchestral introduction while the chorus hums like an instrument, and here he employs all kinds of vocal expression—from pure melody to a simple speaking voice to declamation on a definite pitch. The text is not meant to be understood; words are used as starting points but they soon surrender their identity in the maelstrom of sound.

ITALY

Nineteenth-century Italy was so deeply engulfed in opera that composers made little effort to develop instrumental music. After composers such as Vivaldi and Corelli passed from the scene, hardly any writers contributed to the instrumental repertoire. What Italy needed—but did not get—was a dynamic talent to compete against opera. At the end of the century, when Italian verismo was shaping the lyric stage, several composers dedicated themselves almost exclusively to instrumental music. But instead of looking to the magnificent Italian Baroque for models, they chose to copy the German Romantics, chiefly Brahms and Wagner.

[11] Joseph Machlis, *Introduction to Contemporary Music* (New York: W. W. Norton & Co., Inc., 1961), p. 435. Reprinted by permission.

In the early twentieth century an intellectual, skillful musician named Ferruccio Busoni (1866–1924) emerged as a powerful figure in European musical circles. Although his music lacks imagination and sensitivity and is not well known today, his formidable technical skill has influenced succeeding composers, for his contrapuntal works make excellent study scores.

Ottorino Respighi

The only twentieth-century Italian composer whose orchestral works have become a part of standard repertoire is Ottorino Respighi (1879–1936). His superb orchestral technique, based on post-Wagnerian writing procedures, is largely responsible for his success. This orchestral skill evolved naturally and effortlessly, helped along by experience as a concert violinist and ensemble player, by lessons with Rimsky-Korsakov, and through the study of other composers' scores. His easily recognizable themes speak to the listener's heart and imagination, for he had an extraordinary gift for pictorial writing. Although in many ways an Impressionist, he is far more vigorous and outgoing than the French pioneers of that aesthetic.

Respighi's most popular works are three symphonic poems honoring Roman fountains, pines, and festivals. He prepared an introductory note for each score and a programmatic description of each movement. The first set of poems, *Le fontane di Roma* (The Fountains of Rome, 1917), contains four sections that are played without interruption. Respighi explained on the score that ". . . the composer has endeavored to give expression to the sentiments and visions suggested to him by four of Rome's fountains, contemplated at the hour in which their beauty appears most impressive to the observer."

> I. *The Fountain of Valle Giulia at Dawn.* The first part of the poem, inspired by the Fountain of Valle Giulia, depicts a pastoral landscape [Ex. 25:2]; droves of cattle pass and disappear in the fresh, damp mists of a Roman dawn.

Ex. 25:2. Respighi: *The Fountains of Rome*

Examples 25:2 through 25:5 © 1918 by G. Ricordi & C., S.p.A., Milan. By permission of the publisher. All rights reserved.

> II. *The Triton Fountain in the Morning.* A sudden loud and insistent blast of horns above the trills of the whole orchestra introduces the second part, the Triton Fountain. It is like a joyous call [Ex. 25:3], summoning troops of naiads and tritons, who come running up, pursuing each other and mingling in a frenzied dance between the jets of water.

Ex. 25:3. Respighi: *The Fountains of Rome*

III. *The Fountain of Trevi at Midday.* Next there appears a solemn theme [Ex. 25:4], borne on the undulations of the orchestra. It is the Fountain of Trevi at midday. The solemn theme, passing from the wood to the brass instruments, assumes a triumphal character. Trumpets peal; across the radiant surface of the water there passes Neptune's chariot, drawn by seahorses and followed by a train of sirens and tritons. The procession then vanishes, while faint trumpet blasts resound in the distance.

Ex. 25:4. Respighi: *The Fountains of Rome*

IV. *The Villa Medici Fountain at Sunset.* The fourth part . . . is announced by a sad theme [Ex. 25:5], which rises above a subdued warbling. It is the nostalgic hour of sunset. The air is full of the sound of tolling bells, birds twittering, leaves rustling. Then all dies peacefully into the silence of the night.

Ex. 25:5. Respighi: *The Fountains of Rome*

Luigi Dallapiccola

Dodecaphony was introduced to Italian music by Luigi Dallapiccola (*b.*1904). During his youth he had been deeply impressed by Verdi, Wagner, Debussy, and Ravel, but later in his career he adopted the twelve-tone technique of the Viennese composers (Schoenberg, Berg, Webern). However, the Latin Dallapiccola adapted the austere Germanic serialization techniques to suit his warm, passionate nature; even when he uses twelve-tone procedures, his approach is unlike Schoenberg's. Atonality for the Italian is an experience rather than a technique.

One of his important works, *Canti di prigionia* (Songs of Captivity, 1938–1941), is a three-movement composition for chorus and small orchestra consisting of the rare combination of pianos, harps, and percussion instruments. The choral texts are words of three famous prisoners, Mary Stuart, Boethius, and Savonarola, written shortly before their respective deaths. Dallapiccola's unusual sonorities in percussion, bells, and strings blend with the chorus, creating a thrillingly beautiful experience.

In 1952—on commission for the Pittsburgh International Music Festival—Dallapiccola wrote *Quaderno musicale di Annalibera* (Annalibera's Notebook), for piano solo; it is a modest collection of 11 short pieces and is one of the choicest keyboard works written by any European composer of this century. He borrowed from the *Quaderno* in 1954 when he composed *Variazioni per orchestra* on commission from the Louisville Orchestra. His orchestration calls for a fairly large instrumental group including harp, celesta, xylophone, and vibraphone.

In a prefatory note the composer explains:

> *Variazioni per orchestra* are not at all variations in the traditional sense of the word. At the base of the whole composition there is the same twelve-tone row that I am using for my *Songs of Liberation,* a work for chorus and orchestra now in progress, and that I used for *Annalibera's Notebook* for piano. The *Variations* represent the orchestral interpretation of the latter. Annalibera is the name of my little daughter, and her name stems from the same root as liberation. In the notebook I have tried to explain the treatment of the twelve-tone row applied to the different elements of music.

Both the *Quaderno* and the *Variazioni* are based on the tone row shown in Ex. 25:6. Despite the difficulties of the twelve-tone system, the composer bases

Ex. 25:6. Dallapiccola: *Quaderno di Annalibera: Tone Row*

Examples 25:6 and 25:7 reprinted by permission of Edizioni Suvini Zerboni, Milano.

the first piece, *Simbolo* (Ex. 25:7), on the name of B-A-C-H (in German notation

Ex. 25:7. Dallapiccola: *Quaderno di Annalibera: Simbolo*

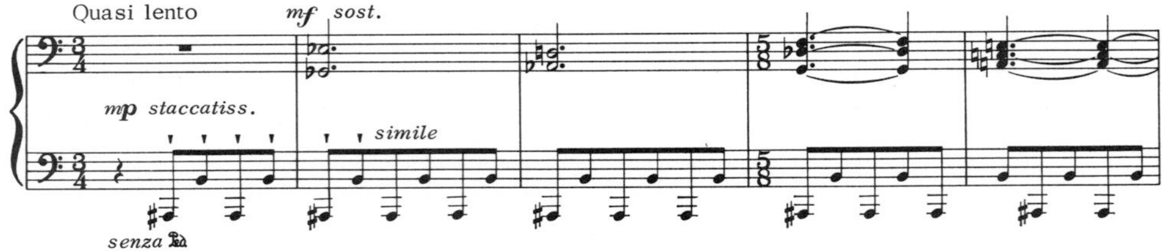

B-flat–A–C–B-natural). This first piece serves as a prelude. For the rest of the work, Dallapiccola's pure style displays subtle rhythms and structural variety as he alternates cerebral canonic works with pieces of fantasy.

The younger generation of Italian composers includes the bright trio of Bruno Maderna (*b.*1920), Luigi Nono (*b.*1924), and Luciano Berio (*b.*1925), each a strong individualist in his own right. Maderna has composed extensively for orchestra, soloists, and electronic media. Nono bases his musical aesthetic on principles expounded by Webern. Berio combines *musique concrète* with "live" instrumental ensembles to construct his carefully computed works. The ultimate evaluation of this highly diversified and intellectually dogmatic music lies with future generations.

HUNGARY

In this century Hungarian music has been dominated by three fine composers—Dohnányi, Kodály, and Bartók.

Ernst von Dohnányi

Ernst von Dohnányi (1877–1960) was an excellent concert pianist, a facility that is usually a great boon to a composer. His style springs from the fount of German Romanticism, notably Johannes Brahms, and this source accounts for his resourceful craftsmanship.

Unlike Bartók and Kodály, Dohnányi never earnestly studied the genuine Hungarian folk idiom, but his personal interpretation of that idiom can be delightful, as he so well proves in *Ruralia Hungarica.* In this colorful suite he treats elements of Hungarian folk music with easy charm. There are three versions, one for solo piano, one for violin and piano, and one for orchestra.

For his *Variations on a Nursery Theme, Opus 25* (1913), for piano and orchestra, Dohnányi borrowed the old French song "Ah, vous dirai-je, maman" (sung in this country to the alphabet) and created from it nine gay, sophisticated, and sometimes satiric variations.

Zoltán Kodály

Zoltán Kodály (1882–1967) began by assimilating Impressionist traits into his compositions. When he later studied Hungarian folk music and collaborated with Bartók to collect native folk songs, this folk element became the strongest influence on his writings. It prevailed for the rest of his life. His characteristic melodic line—which derives principally from Magyar folk music—is the most conspicuous feature of his music.

Unlike Bartók, Kodály was not an innovator. There is nothing really new in his seemingly unconventional approach; it merely grew out of dormant elements in different traditions, which he first absorbed and then logically took for his own.

The late Hungarian composer was cautious but charitable in his attitude toward the music of the so-called avant-garde school. Shortly before his death he explained:

> I have not heard enough of it to say whether it is good or bad. Most of it is "anti-music," so I have not wanted to hear it. But if it has a solid foundation, it will become the conservative music of the future. After all, the music of Bartók and some of the things I wrote—*Psalmus Hungaricus* for one—once were called "far-out."[12]

Among his numerous choral works, the best known is *Psalmus Hungaricus* (1923), for tenor solo, chorus, children's voices, and orchestra. It is at once a sacred composition and a patriotic ode: the sixteenth-century text is an adaptation of Psalm 55 by the poet Michael Veg, who infused so many personal associations into his version that it also became a Hungarian psalm.

After a sixteen-measure orchestral introduction, unaccompanied altos and basses enter in unison chanting "Sad was King David, dismal and downcast." Following this choral offering, the tenor sings a compelling hymn of supplication, "Lord in Thy mercy, hear," a solo interrupted from time to time by the chanting of the unison chorus. In the final section, a beautiful introspective orchestral passage introduces the tenor solo, "Now does fresh courage enter my sad soul."

[12] From an interview in the *Santa Barbara News-Press,* August 1, 1966.

Psalmus Hungaricus rapidly became a "popular" choral work in the same way that Honegger's *King David* had captured the public's enthusiasm. Kodály wrote other fine choral works, such as the *Budavári Te Deum* (1936), and many orchestral works, among which *Marosszék Dances* (1930), *Dances of Galánta* (1933), *Variations on a Hungarian Folksong* (1939), and *Concerto for Orchestra* (1941) are outstanding. Chamber works, piano music, organ works, and songs round out his substantial repertoire.

The one Kodály composition that has won a secure place in the orchestral repertoire is the *Háry János Suite* (1926), based on his opera of the same name. This opera—the plot relates imaginary exploits from an old soldier's past—was immensely successful in Hungary but is known to Americans chiefly through the sparkling orchestral suite that Kodály arranged from his opera score.

The suite is divided into six sections. There is a Hungarian superstition that if anyone sneezes during the telling of a story, the sneeze proves the story to be true. Therefore, *The Tale Begins* with a tremendous, concerted sneeze by the orchestra. A lyrical theme suggests Háry's sentimental mood as he prepares for his storytelling. After a climax by full orchestra, the stage is set.

The piquant, colorful music of *Viennese Musical Clock* takes Háry to Vienna, where he is impressed by the famous musical clock in the imperial palace. All the bells in Vienna seem to chime in the orchestra, filling the air with clanging sonorities. In the following *Song*, Háry and his peasant sweetheart reflect on a peaceful evening in his little village. Kodály uses viola and cimbalom, the characteristic Hungarian gypsy instrument, as solo instruments.

A vivid musical war scene occurs in *The Battle and Defeat of Napoleon*. According to Háry's rose-colored memories, during the struggle between Austrian and French forces he and Napoleon finally met for hand-to-hand combat. Háry won. Vigorous Hungarian music animates the next section, *Intermezzo*. Wayward rhythms and capricious melodic sections are heightened by the cimbalom's distinctive tones, and this section concludes with the three chords that end every typical Hungarian gypsy dance.

At the height of his fantasy, Háry triumphantly appears at the imperial Viennese court. The suite concludes as the full orchestra weaves a brilliant, exciting background for the *Entrance of the Emperor and His Court* (Ex. 25:8).

Ex. 25:8. Kodály: *Háry János: Entrance of the Emperor and His Court*

Used by permission of Universal Editions, copyright owner, and Theodore Presser Company, sole U.S. agent.

Béla Bartók

Next to Stravinsky and Schoenberg, Béla Bartók (1881–1945) has been this century's most influential composer. He has demonstrated to a younger generation that new expressive means within traditional confines are still possible, that musical ideas can be reshaped and restated in countless ways, that nationalism can be energizing, and that rhythmic transformations can be accomplished by infinite variation.

Bartók, who with Kodály collected and analyzed hundreds of genuine

Hungarian folk melodies, gave serious thought to the way this folk element might be used by contemporary composers.

> The question is, what are the ways in which peasant music is taken over and becomes transmuted into modern music? We may, for instance, take over a peasant melody unchanged or only slightly varied, write an accompaniment to it and possibly some opening and concluding phrases. This kind of work would show a certain analogy with Bach's treatment of chorales. . . . Another method by which peasant music becomes transmuted into modern music is the following: The composer does not make use of a real peasant melody but invents his own imitation of such melodies. . . . There is yet a third way in which the influence of peasant music can be traced in a composer's work. Neither peasant melodies nor imitations of peasant melodies can be found in his music, but it is pervaded by the atmosphere of peasant music. In this case we may say, he has completely absorbed the idiom of peasant music which has become his musical mother tongue. He masters it as completely as a poet masters his mother tongue.[13]

Bartók's repertoire shows that he employed all three approaches at one time or another, always with extraordinary skill.

His early music recalls other composers—Brahms, Liszt, Ravel—but his style changed gradually as he realized the need for personal expressive resources, and his exhaustive study of Hungarian folk music caused a decided change in his writing. His ultimate style displays terse musical language and a harmonic framework condensed to bare essentials, resulting in fine transparent textures. But above all, his powerful, vibrant rhythms breathe life and excitement into his music.

Bartók composed in all idioms. To judge from his many keyboard works, he especially enjoyed writing for the piano, perhaps because he was a virtuoso pianist and recognized that it could be simultaneously a melodic, harmonic, and percussive instrument. He made many keyboard settings of folk tunes, giving them exotic dress in his paraphrases. Sometimes his titles belie their debt to folk song. *Sonatina* (1915) is a short three-movement suite based on Romanian folk dances. In 1931 he transcribed this work for orchestra, calling it *Transylvanian Dances.*

In the 1920s he began the mighty task of composing the *Mikrokosmos,* which he originally intended as piano studies for his son Peter. For eleven years (1926–1937) he worked diligently to produce the 153 pieces in the sets. They include every element pertinent to his keyboard style, and the entire work is the essence of Bartók—ranging from his easiest writing to the most complex, from elementary harmonic structures to bitonality (Ex. 25:9). The *Mikrokosmos* al-

Ex. 25:9. Bartók: *Mikrokosmos, Vol. III: Melody against Double Notes*

Copyright 1940 by Hawkes & Son (London) Ltd. Renewed 1967. Reprinted by permission of Boosey & Hawkes, Inc.

[13] From an article entitled "The Influence of Peasant Music on Modern Music," which appeared in *Tempo,* Winter 1949–50, No. 14, pp. 20–22.

most provides a textbook of twentieth-century devices used in musical composition. There are excellent examples of the whole-tone scale (*No. 136*), of chords built in fourths (*No. 131*), of major and minor seconds (*Nos. 140, 142, 144*), of tone clusters (*No. 107*), and of bitonality (*Nos. 70, 105, 142*). Contrapuntal devices are also evident, such as canon (*No. 91*), inversion (*No. 34*), and mirror (*No. 121*). The delightful *Six Dances in Bulgarian Rhythm* (*Nos. 148–153*) are exercises in rhythm. The *Mikrokosmos* is a remarkable collection, a keyboard epic so fine that it alone could perpetuate the composer's name.

Most of Bartók's significant works were written from about 1928 to 1943. The last four of his six masterful string quartets rank among the finest chamber works of this century. Their rhythmic strength and melodic ingenuity reflect his mature style, and they disclose some fascinating experiments in string techniques and sonorities.

His second piano concerto, third piano concerto, and the violin concerto, all from this late period, have also become modern classics. The two prime achievements during this period are *Music for Strings, Percussion and Celesta* (1935) and *Concerto for Orchestra* (1943). With the former work he introduces a new realm of sonorities, indicated by the creative resourcefulness in the scoring: two string quintets, harp, piano, celesta, and a large percussion group. Bartók's rich, expressive style is in command throughout the four movements of this impressive essay.

The *Concerto for Orchestra* is one of this century's genuine symphonic masterpieces. Reviving the spirit of the Baroque concerto grosso, Bartók allows each instrumental group an opportunity to be heard. Single instruments or groups often solo, as in the old concerto grosso. For example, brass instruments are highlighted in the fugato passage of the first movement's development section; pairs of instruments are featured in the second movement; and dazzling string passages enliven the last movement.

The first movement, *Introduzione,* opens *andante non troppo* with rising fourths in the cellos and double basses against tremolos in upper strings and flute. Then the rather irregular sonata-allegro form begins *allegro vivace* with a robust syncopated theme.

The humorous second movement, *Giuoco delle coppie* (Game of Pairs), provides a light touch in this grave work. Independent short sections in the jaunty *allegretto scherzando* accent pairs of wind instruments: bassoons, oboes, clarinets, flutes, and muted trumpets. Brass and drum sound a chorale-like trio, followed by an elaborate recapitulation of the instrumental pairs.

In the following *Elegia,* marked *andante non troppo,* an oboe wails a lament against flecks of sound by clarinet, flute, and harp. This movement is based on material taken from the introduction to the first movement, and its three successive themes become enveloped in a misty texture of motives. The fourth movement, *Intermezzo interrotto,* has a formal scheme: A B A —Interruption—B A. An *allegretto* principal tune in folk-song style played by the oboe is continued by the flute. The "interruption" is a delightful and unexpected parody of the song "Da geh' ich zu Maxim" (I'm Going to Maxim's) from Franz Lehár's (1870–1948) popular operetta *The Merry Widow.*

The *Finale* (*Presto*) has sonata-allegro form with an extended exposition section. Violently agitated string passages suggest perpetual motion. Development takes the form of a fugue built on the last theme of the exposition, the fugue subject being initially stated by the trumpet.

ENGLAND

Few substantial creative works appeared in England in the 150 years following the Purcell era. There was of course an interest in music—the oratorios and operas of Handel's time, the distinguished teaching and playing of composer-virtuosos like Muzio Clementi and John Cramer, the influence of John Field and his *Nocturnes*—but the British tradition of excellence in composition was at a standstill.

One explanation is the fact that the Industrial Revolution lasted longer in England than on the Continent, and the English were happily dedicated to material prosperity. Although the novelist at this time could find abundant material in everyday life to comment on, the poet and musician found little inspiration in such a prosperous, materialistic era.

Music, by nature a relatively abstract art, depends on a continuous active tradition, which England lacked. The liveliest musical note in nineteenth-century England was the satirical Gilbert and Sullivan operetta, a form that literally created its own tradition.

From 1875 intermittently to 1896, Sir Arthur Sullivan (1842–1900) and his librettist Sir William Schwenck Gilbert (1836–1911) turned out 14 captivating operettas, of which *H. M. S. Pinafore* (1878), *The Pirates of Penzance* (1880), and *The Mikado* (1885) remain the perennial favorites.

The Gilbert-Sullivan combination met with an incredible success (Sullivan's other music is seldom heard today), which has continued unabated. Gilbert's verse was whimsical, humorous, and good-naturedly satirical. His endless experiments with poetic meters caused Sullivan to create metrical refinements in his music. In addition, Sullivan brought to the music a sense of fun (including unabashed parody), a rhythmic and melodic talent, an unadventurous yet apt harmony, and a knowing command of orchestration.

Within the space of 17 years, four composers were born who were destined to rejuvenate English musical life. Beginning in 1857 with Edward Elgar, the list continues through Frederick Delius and Gustav Holst to Ralph Vaughan Williams. Early-twentieth-century activity in England thus parallels in quantity and quality that of France, Germany, and other countries.

Edward Elgar

Edward Elgar (1857–1934) loved England and—perfect Victorian gentleman that he was—enjoyed mixing with that well-bred society, which genuinely appreciated his music. He was knighted by Edward VII, for whom he composed a *Coronation Ode*.

Elgar was a natural musician whose music had great vogue during his lifetime. Today he remains a British institution but receives only infrequent hearings outside the British Isles. It is difficult to explain why, for there is nothing basically wrong with his writing. He derived inspiration from Wagner, Strauss, and Brahms; viewing his orchestral scores, one would say that the writing technique is pure Wagner, yet listening to them one realizes that the musical sound is convincingly English.

Elgar took a long while to discover just how he wanted to express himself. He was over 40 when he produced the *"Enigma" Variations* (1899), his first completely characteristic composition. This work and *The Dream of Gerontius* (1900) established him as a serious, talented composer. The latter, based on a poem by Cardinal Newman, is set for three soloists, chorus, and orchestra. Elgar's reputation was further enhanced by two symphonies (1908, 1911), a violin concerto (1910), and a cello concerto (1919).

No discussion of Elgar would be complete without a reference to the five orchestral marches of *Pomp and Circumstance, Opus 39* (1901). Despite his humorous attitude in some compositions, Elgar always approached his art seriously. He was inordinately proud of this work, and justly so, for the first march (in *D* major) ranks second only to "God Save the Queen" in popularity. Some may now disdain *Pomp and Circumstance,* but the fact remains that the music has endured and will likely continue to endure as long as there are commencement exercises. Besides, the music is not unattractive; it has a stately, noble melody and a rhythmic grandeur.

Frederick Delius

Frederick Delius (1862–1934) still commands an audience in England, but he is not a familiar composer elsewhere. His music has never been well received in the United States, possibly because as an Impressionist he cannot keep up with Debussy and Ravel.

Delius' unorthodox approach to life and music tended to estrange him from society. He once wrote:

> This is an age of anarchy in art; there is no authority, no standard, no sense of proportion. Anybody can do anything and call it "art" in the certain expectation of making a crowd of idiots stand and stare at him in gaping astonishment and admiration.[14]

A supreme egoist, he ignored music by other composers except that of Richard Wagner, whom he admired extravagantly. Like Wagner, he was primarily a harmonist whose rich, chromatic chordal sequences give his music a luxurious, sensuous quality; also like Wagner, he based his musical form on short motives, their repetition, and occasional metamorphosis. But unlike Wagner, he had a limited expressive talent and could not successfully produce expansive musical scores.

Various impressionistic techniques show through Delius' music. Like Debussy he often relied on modal scales and used numerous parallel chords. However, his virile orchestration and outward emotionalism bear no resemblance to Debussy's style.

Delius liked to use words with music, yet he was only moderately successful in vocal writing. His talent was better suited to orchestral tone poems; among the many he composed, the most famous and loveliest is the languid *On Hearing the First Cuckoo in Spring* (1912). For his initial theme he composed a typical English melody in which echoed phrases suggest cuckoo calls (Ex. 25:10). He habitually spent summer vacations in Norway, so for his second theme he borrowed the Norwegian folk song "In Ola Valley." This whole poem contains a subtle blend of sound and sentiment that is most appealing.

[14] From an article entitled "At the Crossroads," which appeared in *The Sackbut,* 1920.

Ex. 25:10. Delius: *On Hearing the First Cuckoo in Spring*

Reprinted by permission of Oxford University Press.

Gustav Holst

Gustav Holst (1874–1934), of Swedish descent, was composer, conductor, and choir instructor. Like Delius, early in his career he admired Wagner, but he gradually eliminated Wagnerian characteristics from his music. Like Vaughan Williams, his effective melodic talents developed from preoccupation with folk song. From about 1918 his easygoing, moderately contemporary style became more austere.

Holst's repertoire includes several very effective compositions, such as the *Hymn of Jesus* (1917), for chorus and orchestra, and the delightful *St. Paul's Suite* (1913), for string orchestra; the latter work skillfully relates directly to English folk song. America knows Gustav Holst largely because of his seven-movement orchestral suite *The Planets* (1916).

Holst described this suite as follows:

> These pieces were suggested by the astrological significance of the planets; there is no program music in them, neither have they any connection with the deities of classical mythology bearing the same names. If any guide to the music is required, the subtitle to each piece will be found sufficient, especially if it be used in a broad sense.[15]

Mars—The Bringer of War is a battle scene enacted principally by bassoons, brass, and organ. A violin solo highlights the peaceful and slow second section, *Venus—The Bringer of Peace.* Next appears *Mercury—The Winged Messenger,* a busy scherzo. Brass and woodwinds inaugurate the theme in *Jupiter—The Bringer of Jollity,* a passage of orchestral humor. But solemnity returns with the deep-voiced *Saturn—The Bringer of Old Age.* Incantation and witchcraft create the mood of *Uranus—The Magician,* where basses, tubas, and bassoons play important roles. Holst concludes with the atmospheric *Neptune—The Mystic,* which requires a female chorus. *The Planets* is highly imaginative and its design appeals to most audiences.

Ralph Vaughan Williams

One indication of England's twentieth-century musical awakening has been its revival of folk music, an interest that sent composers out into the countryside to record traditional songs and dances. In time, they naturally incorporated this folk element into their serious works. Simultaneously, British composers rediscovered Tudor church music, the polyphonic style of writing that characterized one of England's great musical eras.

In his enthusiasm for cultivating England's hoard of forgotten music,

[15] From Program Notes of the Boston Symphony Orchestra, January 22, 1932.

Ralph Vaughan Williams (1872–1958) emerges as a great twentieth-century nationalist composer. More than just seeking out folk songs, he absorbed the folk tradition into his own musical aesthetic and urged other composers to foster national music. He accomplished his objective so thoroughly that his music sounds national whether or not he directly appropriates folk song.

Vaughan Williams' music is melody saturated. He uses good melodies, strong in outline, varied in structure, rhythmically vital; in fact, his rhythmic flexibility is second only to his melodic talent. The harmonic schemes are best described as being consistent with his musical orientation; that is, he was determined to reach the common people and he knew he could not do so with highly dissonant textures and intricate rhythmic patterns. Because of his innate musical propriety, he has been able to contribute to our era a substantial number of fine works written in a twentieth-century language yet glowingly and firmly upholding the past.

He composed operas, numerous sacred works, symphonies, and unusual and effective works such as the song cycle *On Wenlock Edge* (1909), which is a setting (for tenor, string quartet, and piano) of poems taken from E. A. Housman's *A Shropshire Lad.*

Of his nine symphonies the second is most frequently performed. He did not intend any programmatic implications with the title *London Symphony* (1914, revised in 1920); as he explained:

> [The title] may suggest to some hearers a descriptive piece, but this is not the intention of the composer. A better title would perhaps be *Symphony by a Londoner,* that is to say the life of London (including its various sights and sounds) has suggested to the composer an attempt at musical expression; but it would be no help to the hearer to describe these in words. The music is intended to be self-impressive, and must stand or fall as "absolute" music. Therefore, if listeners recognize suggestions of such things as the Westminster chimes or the *Lavender Cry,* they are asked to consider these as accidents, not essentials of the music.[16]

Eventually he must have realized that this symphony was entirely too pictorial to pass as abstract music, and he made no comment when his friend the conductor Albert Coates supplied a complete programmatic description for the revised version presented in 1920.

William Walton

Success came early to Sir William Walton (*b.*1902). A friend of the celebrated, eccentric Sitwell family, Walton at the age of 20 created *Façade* (1922, revised in 1926 and 1942)—a musical "entertainment" offering Dame Edith Sitwell's often unfathomable verses recited against an accompaniment furnished by six instrumentalists. Partly due to the music and partly to Dame Edith, *Façade* was an instant success.

Walton outgrew his clever period and ultimately embraced a style best described as contemporary Romanticism. His music is tonal but unswervingly dissonant. He makes free use of the octave's twelve tones pulling toward a center,

[16] From Program Notes of the British Music Society, May 4, 1920.

which recalls Hindemith's approach. His music is very chromatic and he seems to enjoy the ambiguity of major-minor syntheses. But the listener finds warmth and emotion enveloping these contemporary materials.

He has written surprisingly little. Among his noteworthy large-scale works are a viola concerto, a violin concerto, and *Belshazzar's Feast*. He has also provided colorful musical scores for some excellent films, including George Bernard Shaw's *Major Barbara* (1941) and Laurence Olivier's productions of *Henry V* (1944) and *Hamlet* (1947).

If any work has ever succeeded in recapturing the grandeur of the Handelian oratorio, it is *Belshazzar's Feast* (1931), written for baritone solo, chorus, and orchestra. Sir Osbert Sitwell adapted the text from the Psalms and the Book of Daniel. Walton's score demands a large instrumental complement: full orchestra, piano, organ, and two brass choirs. Despite this overwhelming symphonic ensemble, emphasis centers around the massed chorus which changes its identity to suit each dramatic event. The oratorio contains three large sections, and the baritone narrates the story in flowery recitative passages. With sure musicianly insight, Walton swiftly carries the action to the handwriting on the wall and the later destruction of Babylon. His oratorio is extremely effective, for his music unfolds the biblical story with telling directness and power.

Benjamin Britten

Perhaps the most famous among contemporary British composers, Benjamin Britten (*b.*1913) earned international recognition within a very short space of time. He is a lyricist who derives almost all his inspiration from the human voice; thus his finest compositions are those in which several short forms combine to create a large-scale work: suite, song cycle, and opera.

An expert craftsman, Britten chooses to be eclectic in style. He varies his tonal language from one composition to another, yet his finished product is usually impressively original. He is unquestionably the most important English composer of his generation.

Britten has written excellent operas: *Peter Grimes* (1945), *The Rape of Lucretia* (1946), *Albert Herring* (1947), *Billy Budd* (1952), *The Turn of the Screw* (1954), *A Midsummer Night's Dream* (1960). As operas written in contemporary style for contemporary audiences, these are excellent works. Britten is a born theatrical composer; he senses the dramatic implication in each situation and exploits it with uncanny instinct.

He has also composed many collections of beautiful songs: *Les Illuminations* (1939), a song cycle for high voice and orchestra; *Serenade* (1943) for tenor solo, horn, and string orchestra; settings of Michelangelo sonnets; new harmonizations of Purcell songs; and settings of British folk songs. *A Ceremony of Carols* (1942) sets medieval carols for treble voices and harp obbligato.

Among his orchestral works, the *Young Person's Guide to the Orchestra* (Variations and Fugue on a Theme by Henry Purcell)—composed in 1945 on commission from the British Ministry of Education—is widely known and enjoyed. Because it was conceived for an educational film, an explanatory narration accompanies the music (although it is sometimes omitted in concert performance and on recordings).

Ex. 25:11. Britten: *Young Person's Guide to the Orchestra: Theme*

Copyright 1947 by Hawkes & Son (London) Ltd. Reprinted by permission of Boosey & Hawkes, Inc.

Britten designed this work to accentuate the prominent characteristics of the principal orchestral groups. To do so he selected a robust tune (Ex. 25:11) from the incidental music to *Abdelazar, or The Moor's Revenge,* written by the seventeenth-century English composer Henry Purcell. Through 13 variations of this theme Britten designs solo passages for each principal member of the woodwind, string, brass, and percussion groups. A fugue serves as a colorful finale.

A dedicated Englishman and a dedicated composer, Benjamin Britten is admirably articulate about the artist and his role in society.

> I believe that an artist should be part of his community, should work for it, with it, and be used by it. Over the last hundred years this has become rarer and rarer and the artist and the community have both suffered as a result. The artist has suffered in many cases because without an audience, or with only a highbrow one—without, therefore, a direct contact with his public—his work tends to become "ivory tower," without focus. This has made a great deal of modern work obscure and impractical: only useable by highly skilled performers and only understandable by the most erudite. Don't please think that I am against all new and strange ideas. Far from it; new ideas have a way of seeming odd and surprising when heard for the first time. But I am against experiment for experiment's sake, originality at all costs.[17]

Other British Composers

Among the older generation of living British composers, Gordon Jacob (*b.*1895) is outstanding. A pupil of Vaughan Williams, Jacob has written numerous works, but he considers his *Quartet for Oboe and Strings* (1938), *Clarinet Quintet* (1942), *Piano Sonata,* and *Piano Concerto No. 2* to be his most significant compositions. He says of his writing style:

> [It is] based on tonality with free use of dissonance. Classical forms are preferred as a rule. . . . Melody and rhythm are important to me. I do not use avant-garde techniques but do not disapprove of them.[18]

Lennox Berkeley's (*b.*1903) style is rooted in Mozart and the Classic school, but he also admires Stravinsky and Britten. His two most often heard works are the orchestral *Serenade* (1939) for strings, and *Four Poems of St. Teresa* (1947) for voice and orchestra.

[17] From *Britten* by Imogen Holst. Copyright © 1965 by Imogen Holst. Thomas Y. Crowell Company, New York, publishers, p. 70. Reprinted by permission.

[18] Communication to the author, dated September 6, 1966.

Commenting on his own style, he stated:

> My music has always been, and still is, basically tonal but my later works are somewhat freer in this respect. . . . I have used some of the technical devices of serial music, but without adhering to its fundamental ideas.[19]

Sir Michael Tippett's (*b.*1905) output is impressive for its high quality and broad compass, ranging from the *Piano Sonata No. 2* (1962) and *String Quartet No. 3* (1946) to the oratorio *A Child of Our Time* (1941) and *Fantasia Concertante on a Theme by Corelli* (1953) for string orchestra.

> Michael Tippett's music contrasts sharply with that of the majority of contemporary composers. . . . It bears allegiance to no school, trend, or fashion, yet it is in no sense conservative. . . . It is the work of a composer who habitually thinks in large designs and broad spans, avoiding the avant-garde pre-occupation with miniscule methods of composition.[20]

One of England's prominent younger composers, Peter Racine Fricker (*b.*1920) has devoted much time and thought to analyzing scores by Schoenberg, Webern, and Stravinsky. His own musical language is serious, at times uncompromising, and it creates novel and ravishing instrumental sonorities. From his numerous works—including four symphonies, two violin concertos, a piano concerto, chamber music, and choral music—the composer chooses *Symphony No. 2* (1951), *Symphony No. 3* (1960), *Violin Concerto No. 2* (1954), and *Octet* (1958) as being most representative of his musical thinking and inspiration.

OTHER EUROPEAN COMPOSERS

Many other twentieth-century European composers have and are contributing to contemporary repertoire. Spain's finest contemporary composer, Joaquín Rodrigo (*b.*1902), has produced eight concertos, around 50 songs, works for choir, orchestral works, an opera, two ballets, and music for stage and film. In tracing the origins of his style, the composer relates:

> When I was studying in Paris with Paul Dukas, I was influenced by Ravel and maybe some other French composers. But since I composed my *Cantico de la esposa* (1934) and some years later my guitar concerto *Concierto de Aranjuez* my style is very personal. I have created the Neo-Casticismo [a return to a simple and pure musical language].[21]

Although he was born the same year as Jean Sibelius, Carl Nielsen (1865–1931) of Denmark definitely belongs to the contemporary age, not to the past. In contrast to Sibelius, Nielsen was not a Romantic composer. His repertoire—six symphonies (of which *No. 4* is perhaps the most popular), choral works, chamber music, keyboard music, songs—shows that his musical language is

[19] Communication to the author, dated September 18, 1966.

[20] From *Michael Tippett: A Symposium on his Sixtieth Birthday,* edited by Ian Kemp, © Faber & Faber, London, 1965, p. 211. Reprinted by permission.

[21] Communication to the author, dated September 8, 1966.

based on a twentieth-century vocabulary. He was wholly original and adventurous in his writing, and his dynamic treatment of tonalities constitutes one of the subtlest phenomena in music today.

> Nielsen did not set out to be a "difficult" composer, though he did not mind being a controversial one. Even when he presented his hearers with a tough polytonal problem, he did his best to help the ear by making the clash of opposed melodic strains clear by sharply differentiating their tone-colour. But he also wrote music he took care to make immediately accessible to the receptive but untrained ear.[22]

Klaus Egge (*b.*1906) is one of the most prominent personalities in Norwegian music today. Besides being a composer and music critic, he is an ardent promoter of other contemporary Norwegian composers. His own music is unmistakably northern in mood and character. Egge's melodic approach is particularly interesting, for he frequently bases his themes on rhythmic structures inherent in Norwegian folk tunes. From these he sometimes constructs a richly intertwined contrapuntal movement. *Concerto No. 2 for Piano and Strings, Opus 21* (1944) is one of Egge's finest works. Actually this concerto consists of seven variations and fugue *Finale* on a Norwegian folk song. *Symphony No. 3, Opus 28* (1957) is equally representative of Egge's style.

The present dean of Swedish composers, Hilding Rosenberg (*b.*1892) has had a guiding influence on most Swedish composers since the 1920s. He is a prolific writer whose talents perhaps find their most congenial outlet in the string quartet, although his oratorios and dramatic musical works are also impressive. In a typical work such as the *Louisville Concerto* (1955), Rosenberg's style suggests Romanticism that has been generously exposed to standard contemporary trends.

Georges Enesco (1881–1955) of Romania uses folk rhythms and gypsy melodies from his native country in his popular, colorful *Roumanian Rhapsodies, Nos. 1* (1901) and *2, Opus 11* (1902).

Czechoslovakia's Leoš Janáček's (1854–1928) unique approach to composition—a personal concept of harmony and modulation, the use and reuse of similar melodic material, a consistent use of extended variation—makes him a genuine contributor to twentieth-century music (the three-movement orchestral rhapsody *Taras Bulba,* 1918, is typical).

The Polish Karol Szymanowski (1882–1937) liked classical forms, but he tempered this inclination with a natural talent for harmonic subtlety and rhythmic elasticity (*Symphonie concertante, Opus 60* for piano and orchestra, 1932; *Concerto for Violin and Orchestra, Opus 61,* 1933).

The strongest force in contemporary Dutch music has been Willem Pijper (1894–1947). He formed his writing principles from the polyphony of the old Dutch masters, and he believed polytonality to be the logical extension of traditional monotonality. He is best known in America for his *Symphony No. 3* (1926).

This list could be greatly extended; however, even this brief survey proves the strength and durability of European music in the first half of the twentieth century.

[22] Article on Carl Nielsen in *Grove's Dictionary of Music and Musicians,* Fifth Edition (London: Macmillan & Co., Ltd., 1954), Vol. VI, p. 86. Reprinted by permission of St. Martin's Press, Inc.

LATIN AMERICA

Latin America can boast of a long musical tradition, for music played an important role in the three great pre-Columbian cultures: Inca, Maya, and Aztec. Like most highly intelligent primitive peoples, they used music to enhance their religious rituals and various feasts and celebrations, and frequently they accompanied their daily tasks with some kind of music.

In the sixteenth century a new musical influence appeared in Latin America: the European music brought by the Spanish colonials. At first this new element was limited to the sacred chants that the Roman Catholic missionaries taught the Indians as a means of gaining converts, but soon the works of Spanish masters such as Victoria and Morales found their way to the New World. As other Europeans and their descendants settled in Latin America, they introduced secular music from the various countries of Europe.

Slaves imported from Africa also produced a lasting effect on Latin-American music. In those countries where the Negro population remained small and where the Europeans were accepted readily, Portuguese and Spanish elements are still discernible in much of the indigenous music. Some countries clung tenaciously to their own heritage, refusing to succumb to either the "civilizing" influence of Europe or the highly colorful music of Africa. However, in Cuba, Brazil, and Haiti, where the Negro element flourished, the music still reflects a strong African influence.

In the nineteenth century the Italianism that swept over Spain also left its mark in Latin America. Rossini's music became immensely popular, and when Latin-American composers wished to write operas, they modeled them along Italian lines. At this same time the concert-hall tradition began with the emergence of philharmonic societies and the formation of symphony orchestras, and European and American artists toured Latin America with great success.

With the coming of the twentieth century, Latin-American classical music began to demonstrate its own merits. In addition to Romanticism's more attractive aspects, four other trends arose as native composers seriously attempted to make a place for themselves in contemporary music. The nationalists preferred to use native folk arts—song and dance—as basic components in their musical language. Another group favored a more or less international style, using standard techniques—quartal harmony, polytonality—within rather traditional frameworks. The atonalist composers leaned to the precepts laid down by Arnold Schoenberg, the spiritual father of Expressionism. And, finally, experimentalists such as Julián Carrillo (1875–1965) used microtones.

It is impossible to place each composer neatly into one of these four categories. He may, for instance, have begun as a Romanticist, then later changed his style by incorporating melodic folk elements into a contemporary musical texture. Musically speaking, Latin America is young and her energetic composers are receptive to diverse musical currents and cultural trends. In general, three Latin-American nations stand out for their intense, superior musical activity: Mexico, Brazil, and Argentina. In these countries the writing quality matches that of the finest European or American repertoire.

Mexico

Carlos Chávez (*b.*1899), Mexico's outstanding living composer, inaugurated the era of contemporary music in Mexico. His music is vigorous and resourceful, reflecting the age that engendered it; and he has made a deep, durable impression on younger composers. Being a composer who shuns sensationalism and "snobbism" in art, he is able to show his pupils music that gets its vitality from its own Mexican heritage. His music is often difficult to fathom at first hearing because the harmonic outlines are harsh and acrid, the tone color percussive; in short, it seems to be as austere as some Mexican landscapes. But the persevering listener will be rewarded, and repeated hearings will disclose the music's logic. As it unfolds it reveals the composer's single-minded purpose in choosing his materials and techniques. Chávez has literally dedicated his talent to Mexico, her land, her people, and her cultural heritage. He found his inspiration in the traditional music of the Indian mestizo, and that inspiration prompted the rebirth of Mexican music.

Although he has written in almost every field, Chávez is best known for his orchestral works, especially the *Sinfonía India,* composed in New York during the winter of 1935–1936. Besides the usual orchestral ensemble, the score calls for Indian drums, a water gourd, cymbals, rattles, and various rasps (percussion instruments that are scraped). The symphony has one movement and its structure represents Chávez's personal concept of sonata form. The work is unusual because this is the only time Chávez uses actual Indian melodies as musical materials for a major composition. These melodies stress single repeated notes and repeated fragments; Chávez augments them with persistent rhythms and clearly outlined textures, all premised on modal patterns sometimes employing a pentatonic scale.

Sinfonía India opens *Vivo* and has basically a $\frac{5}{8}$ meter. After a brief introduction, oboes and violins play a rhythmical tune of the Huichole Indians from Nayarit (Ex. 25:12). Following a short but spirited elaboration of this tune, the

Ex. 25:12. Chávez: *Sinfonía India*

Examples 25:12 and 25:13 copyright 1950 by G. Schirmer, Inc. Used by permission.

clarinet (*Allegretto cantabile*) intones a beautiful Yaqui melody from Sonora (Ex. 25:13). Slight development follows as the Yaqui melody is heard in various

Ex. 25:13. Chávez: *Sinfonía India*

forms before it combines with a countermelody to the accompaniment of syncopated rhythms, an action leading to a climax. A horn call sounds, and from it arises the adagio theme, another Sonora Indian melody, sung by flutes and horn, then strings. The recapitulation treats the allegro's livelier melodic material. The finale presents a complexly accented theme of the Seri Indians against an orchestral background that increases in tension until the final climax.

Attempting something different, Chávez succeeded admirably with *Toc-*

cata for Percussion Instruments (1942). Eleven types of percussion instruments —including some native Indian instruments—are played by six performers. Each of the three movements calls attention to certain percussion instruments. In the opening movement, *Allegro sempre giusto,* high and low drums predominate; the *Largo* highlights xylophone, chimes, cymbal, and gongs; the finale, *Allegro un poco marziale,* favors rattles, hardwood sound sticks, and a small Indian drum.

Silvestre Revueltas (1899–1940) studied music while very young and gave many violin recitals in Mexico, but not until 1931, urged on by Carlos Chávez, did he try composing. He had no interest in folk melodies ("Why should I put on boots and climb mountains for Mexican folklore if I have the spirit of Mexico deep within me?"), nor did he attempt to re-create ancient musical culture. His music reflects modern Mexico. It catches the contrasting moods of the sophisticated Mexican city and the plain pueblo; it is often witty, always delightful. His style frequently displays primitive elements: sharp rhythms, angular melodies, bold color, and imaginative orchestration.

In a program note for *Planos* (1934), a "geometric dance" for orchestra, the composer summed up his attitude toward musical composition:

> My music is functional architecture, which does not exclude sentiment. Melodic fragments derive from the same impulse, the same emotion as in my other works; they sing in persistent rhythms, ever in motion; they produce sonorities that may seem reminiscent of other rhythms and sonorities, just as building material in architecture is identical with any building material, but it serves for constructions that are different in meaning, form, and expression.[23]

The articulate Revueltas enjoyed explaining his compositions by means of witty comments. In the preface to his orchestral piece *Cuauhnahuac* (ancient Indian name of the Mexican resort Cuernavaca), written in 1930, he wrote:

> This is a music without tourism. In the orchestra, the *huehuetl* [Indian drum] is used as a means of nationalist propaganda. Other instruments in the score are even more nationalistic, but no attention should be paid to them; it is all just anticapitalist agitation.[24]

And in a note for his orchestral *Janitzio* (1933, revised 1936), Revueltas commented:

> Janitzio is a fishermen's island in Lake Pátzcuaro. Lake Pátzcuaro is filthy. The romantic travelers have embellished it with verses and music of the picture postcard type. Not to be outdone, I too add my grain to the sandpile. Posterity will undoubtedly reward my contribution to national tourism.[25]

Revueltas' wit and humor infected his music. His amusing *Ocho por radio* (1933) describes eight ill-equipped but well-intentioned musicians playing for a radio program, and the ear-shattering results are immensely diverting. This talented composer was of course capable of deeper emotions: *Homenaje a Federico García Lorca* (1935), for small orchestra, is a musical memorial to the Spanish poet executed during Spain's Civil War.

[23] In Nicolas Slonimsky, *Music of Latin America* (New York: Thomas Y. Crowell Company, 1945), p. 248.

[24] Slonimsky, pp. 248–249.

[25] Slonimsky, p. 249.

Brazil

Brazilian composers have been equally as distinguished as their Mexican colleagues. For many years the personality of Heitor Villa-Lobos (1887–1959) dominated Brazilian music. His death deprived Brazil of one of her most dedicated sons and Latin America of one of its most vital composers. Although Villa-Lobos' musical vocabulary was inborn, he took some inspiration from Darius Milhaud and, as a matter of fact, from French music in general, for he spent several years in France.

As a composer Villa-Lobos was an ardent nationalist and folklorist. Realizing that rich material lay in his country's indigenous music, he determined to use this treasure in his own compositions. His writing style passed through several phases; he began as a Romanticist; later he changed and turned toward Impressionism; then his passion for Bach led him into a kind of classicism; eventually he assimilated all his earlier styles into a mature—and decidedly complex—personal idiom. This final style depends heavily on chromaticism, polyrhythm, and polytonality, all frequently applied with forcefulness and authority. One must stress the word "frequently," for Villa-Lobos was neither a cautious nor a critical composer. He saved everything he wrote and there is little evidence that he did much revising; as a result, banality and triteness often appear.

Villa-Lobos' large output (some 2,000 works) includes many piano compositions, and of these his piano collections pertaining to children are exceptionally fine. There are three of these collections jointly called *Prole do bebê* (Baby's Playthings): the first set (1918) describes dolls—porcelain, paper, clay, rubber, wooden, rag, Punch, and a little witch doll; the second collection (1921) deals with toy animals—cardboard cat, toy mouse, rubber dog, wooden horse, tin ox, cloth bird, cotton bear, and glass wolf. The third collection (1926) contains musical descriptions of various children's games. These are not pieces children can play; although they vary, most demand an exceptional pianist. Another attractive piano suite, *As três Marias* (The Three Marys, 1939), was freely inspired by a Brazilian children's tale about three little girls who wander through life together. All three pieces are written in the treble clef.

Villa-Lobos composed two series for instrument and voice combinations under the general titles *Chôros* and *Bachianas Brasileiras*. In explaining the *Chôros* (he wrote 15 of them) the composer stated that it "represents a new form of musical composition in which a synthesis is made of different types of Brazilian music, Indian and popular, reflecting in its fundamental elements the rhythm and characteristic melodies of the people." As he employs this form, Villa-Lobos produces an imaginative assortment of instrumental combinations: *No. 1* is for guitar solo; *No. 2* is for flute and clarinet; *No. 4* is scored for three horns and trombones; *No. 13* needs two orchestras and a band; *No. 14* requires an orchestra, band, and chorus. *Chôros No. 10* (1925), for chorus and orchestra, is one of Villa-Lobos' finest compositions, displaying magnificent orchestration and hypnotic rhythms.

The nine *Bachianas Brasileiras* present still another side of this gifted Latin-American composer. To describe them he wrote:

> The *Bachianas Brasileiras,* comprising nine suites, were written in homage to the great genius of J. S. Bach. They were inspired by the musical atmosphere of Bach in respect to harmony and counterpoint and by the melodic atmosphere

of the folk music of Brazil's northeastern region. All the melodies are original, but written in the style of Brazilian folklore.

All nine works have attractive features, but two are particularly interesting. *Bachianas Brasileiras No. 2* (1930) is scored for orchestra and contains four contrasting movements. In the following description the quoted remarks are by Villa-Lobos. "*Prelude* (The Song of the *Capadócio*) is a reflection on a type of Brazilian 'smarty,' the *Capadócio,* who ambles about in Adagio fashion." Melodic interest begins when the saxophone plays a suave but facile tune, a melody taken up by other instruments. This mood is broken by an interlude having almost dancelike rhythm. "*Aria* (The Song of Our Country) and *Dansa* have the sonorous atmosphere of Brazilian witchcraft." *Aria* opens with a cello soliloquy, continues with an impassioned incantation, and concludes by using material from the opening section. *Dansa* combines the sensuous and the sensible with quite charming results. "*Toccata* (The Little Train of the Caipira) represents the impression of a trip in a little train in the interior of Brazil." In this graphic little masterpiece a diminutive narrow-gauge train huffs and puffs to get started, churns its way through fields and valleys, and finally grinds to an asthmatic stop.

Bachianas Brasileiras No. 5, written for soprano and eight cellos, is the most popular of this series. The first movement, *Aria* (1938), contains a setting of a poetic text by Ruth V. Corrêa. *Aria* has three sections: in the first the soprano sings the syllable *ah* to a melodic line obviously inspired by the *Aria* in Bach's *Orchestral Suite No. 3,* while cellos lend a serenade-like pizzicato accompaniment; the middle section sets the poem to a rhapsodic melody stressing repeated notes while descending chromatic harmonies provide the accompaniment; the final section is a hummed version of the first section.

"*Dansa* [the second movement, 1945] represents a persistent and characteristic rhythm much like the *emboladas,* those strange melodies of the Brazilian hinterland. The melody suggests the birds of Brazil." Villa-Lobos creates a lively melodic line here to interpret a poem by the great Brazilian poet Manuel Bandeira.

Camargo Guarnieri (*b.*1907) is one of the ranking modern Brazilian composers. His father was Sicilian, and Guarnieri himself studied for two years in Europe; in addition, he has conducted in the United States. This acquaintance with other musical cultures has served to strengthen his musical vocabulary, though it has barely influenced his ultimate style, which is markedly contrapuntal. Nationalism is the driving spirit behind his writing, a desire to preserve the spirit of Brazilian folk songs and dances within his own music.

Guarnieri has added his contribution to the favorite Latin-American idiom, the dance. Samba rhythms vibrate throughout his colorfully orchestrated *Dansa Brasileira* (1931), accompanied by sudden shifts of tonal intensity. Also for orchestra, the passionate, primitive *Dansa selvagem* (1931), with its series of bare fifths and seventh chords, substantiates Guarnieri's belief that Brazilian music ought to be treated polyphonically.

His attachment for folk subjects is again apparent in his important *Symphony No. 1* (1944). The three movements—*Rude, Profondo, Radioso*—adhere to classic form. The first and third movements have sonata-allegro form and the middle movement is constructed in ternary form. At the same time, Guarnieri adorns these traditional patterns with inspirations born of Brazilian folk music: his modal themes and complex rhythmic patterns are authentic; he blends art forms and folk elements with musicianly virtuosity.

Argentina

The man known as the father of twentieth-century Argentine music really had several careers: composer, author, teacher, lecturer, and musical organizer. Alberto Williams (1862–1952) studied with César Franck, and his style exhibits more than one Franckian trait. Important as Williams was in fostering an Argentine national school of composers, his own music—faded echoes of other eras—is rarely heard.

Talented as many contemporary Argentine composers are, performances of their works are as yet largely confined to Latin America. The one exception is Alberto Ginastera (*b.*1916), one of the best contemporary composers of our century. Blessed with superior musical intelligence, Ginastera is able to employ whatever techniques seem momentarily appropriate, transforming them into personal tools to carry out his musical dictates. Although he borrows occasionally from native melodies, he typically uses them thematically, surrounding them with his highly refined harmonic and rhythmic framework.

> Ginastera's musical language was associated in the past with images of his native land; it has developed since his first works, reaching now a more international and personal outlook. It started with an objective nationalism, as in *Estancia* [ballet, 1941] and *Five Argentine Popular Songs* [voice and piano, 1943] with all the rhythmic strength and wild kineticism of the music of Argentina. . . . It turns then, in works like *Piano Sonata* [1952], *Variaciones concertantes* [orchestra, 1953] or *Pampeana No. 3* [orchestra, 1954] towards a subjective nationalism. . . . It finally reaches a transcendent sublimation, an original neo-expressionist style based, no longer in the external phenomena, or in its symbolic representation, but in a personal view of a fantastic and hallucinating world which belongs substantially to his inner self. This appears in works like *Cantata para América mágica* [soprano and percussion, 1960], *Violin Concerto* [1963], opera *Don Rodrigo* [1964] or cantata *Bomarzo* [1964].[26]

One of Ginastera's finest works is the extremely difficult *Sonata for Piano,* commissioned by the Carnegie Institute and Pennsylvania College for Women. The first performance took place at the 1952 Pittsburgh International Contemporary Music Festival. Although it makes no concessions to the listener, it is one of the most genuinely interesting contemporary works written by any Latin-American composer. The first of the four movements, *Allegro marcato,* is fashioned on multiple meters. Its alternating sections in different textures remind one of the classic toccata, and its opening motive is forcefully dramatic

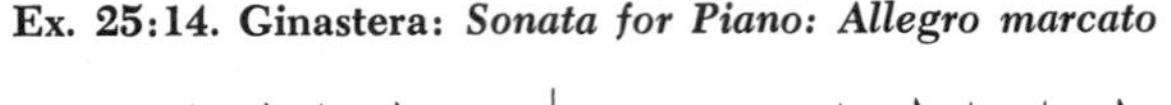

Ex. 25:14. Ginastera: *Sonata for Piano: Allegro marcato*

Copyright 1954 by Barry and Cia. Reprinted by permission of Boosey & Hawkes, Inc., sole agents.

[26] *Alberto Ginastera,* catalog published by Barry Editorial Com. Ind. S.R.L., Buenos Aires, Argentina, 1966.

(Ex. 25:14). In the *Presto misterioso,* passages three octaves apart, in double octaves, and in single melodic lines succeed each other in relentless $\frac{6}{8}$ meter. The third movement, *Adagio molto appassionato,* contains three sections: the first and third are dominated by an ascending seven-note figure alternated with cadenza-like figures; the more harmonic middle section displays pungent, acrid chords. Ginastera concludes this work, which is so characteristic of his art, with a movement marked *Rudivo ed ostinato.* Here he alternates his rhythmic accents; what emerges is a brilliant finale in hemiola rhythm—that is, the first measure ***1***–2–3–***4***–5–6, the next ***1***–2–***3***–4–***5***–6.

This discussion of Latin-American music can serve merely as a starting point for further investigation. Even such a brief outline, however, points out several facts. First, Latin America in general is keeping pace with the United States and continental Europe in musical activity. Second, the Latin-American musical scene presents mixed styles and approaches: some music is based on European traditions, some is nationalistic, and some falls into an international, abstract category. Finally and most important, we can conclude that Latin America's many gifted composers have made lasting contributions to contemporary music.

CANADA

During the nineteenth century, Canadian music existed at about the same level as music in the United States. With her people spread over a vast country, Canada had more urgent problems than that of creating a substantial music repertoire. Also, any good music written in Canada at that time was inevitably rooted in European tradition and did not reflect Canadian culture. Most nineteenth-century Canadian composers wrote oratorios, Masses, or else practical secular music such as operas. Canadian music thus lacked a repertoire of symphonies, chamber works, and songs.

By the time World War I began, however, Canada had produced a number of competent composers, and three of them established international reputations.

Healy Willan (1880–1968), a fine organist as well as composer, wrote several important works, notably *Coronation Suite* (1953), for chorus and orchestra, but his greatest musical contribution was the more than 500 anthems, motets, services, and organ pieces that earned him the gratitude of choirmasters and church organists in Canada, the United States, and England.

Claude Champagne (1891–1965) studied in Montreal and Paris. His catholic outlook—he was a composer, pianist, violinist, violist, teacher, and conductor—and his knowledge of his country's musical heritage made him an influential figure in Canadian musical circles. A nationalist composer, Champagne reveals his style in *Suite Canadienne* (1928)—settings of folk songs for chorus and orchestra—and in *Images du Canada Français* (1943), for orchestra.

Sir Ernest MacMillan (*b.*1893), a composer, writer, conductor, organist, and pianist, was knighted in 1935 by King George V in recognition of his services to music in Canada. MacMillan's romantically oriented, vibrant style is well displayed in his setting of Swinburne's ode *England* (1918), for soprano, baritone, chorus, and orchestra, and in the exuberant *Song of Deliverance* (1945), which he composed to celebrate the end of World War II.

> The remarkable growth of Canadian composition towards the end of the 1930's was encouraged by the more mature cultural setting and the advances made in musical education and performance. The main driving force, however, was the dissatisfaction of younger musicians (especially the generation 1908–18) with the conservative outlook of the professors who taught them conventional harmony and counterpoint and with the restrictions placed by box-office considerations on the performance of music later than that of Debussy and Sibelius. They were determined to extend the range of Canadian composition beyond the utilitarian and academic spheres and sought inspiration in the music and teachings of the world's leading contemporary composers from the neo-classicists to the atonalists. Composers such as Louis Applebaum, Violet Archer, Alexander Brott, Jean Coulthard, Jean Papineau-Couture, Barbara Pentland, Godfrey Ridout, Jean Vallerand and John Weinzweig have succeeded in their aims of introducing an idiom that is genuinely contemporary, promoting the performance of new compositions, and providing leadership to younger Canadian composers.[27]

The pianist-composer Jean Coulthard (*b.*1908) took advanced studies at the London Royal College of Music as well as training in Paris and Canada. Miss Coulthard has concertized widely and won many honors and prizes for her compositions. Her published works maintain high standards of musicianship. They are contemporary—she likes to use dissonance, linear counterpoint, polytonality, and intricate rhythmic patterns—and yet they show that she is aware of past musical traditions.

Barbara Pentland (*b.*1912) graduated from the Julliard Graduate School of Music in New York and studied privately with Aaron Copland. Like Miss Coulthard, she has won several prizes and commissions and has concertized in America and Europe. Miss Pentland's original, tastefully designed music is mostly instrumental: four symphonies (1948, 1950, 1957, 1959), concertos, many chamber works—sonatas, quartets, a duo for viola and piano, a wind octet—and piano music, including the unique *Studies in Line* (1941).

Besides his active career as a composer, Alexander Brott (*b.*1915) is a skilled violinist, teacher, and chamber-music player, and he has served as concertmaster and assistant conductor of the Montreal Symphony Orchestra. One interesting work from his significant repertoire is *Spheres in Orbit* (1960), commissioned by the Montreal Symphony Orchestra.

Jean Papineau-Couture (*b.*1916) received his musical education almost exclusively in the United States: under Nadia Boulanger at the Longy School in Boston and Quincy Porter at the New England Conservatory. His style might be described as neo-Romantic spiced with contemporary dissonance. Among his best instrumental compositions are *Aria* (1946) and *Suite* (1956), both for solo (unaccompanied) violin, and several works for soloists and orchestra, which he calls *Pièces concertantes*.

Harry Somers (*b.*1925) studied piano in San Francisco and worked for a year in Paris with Darius Milhaud. Like Milhaud, he writes prolifically, especially works involving orchestra—two piano concertos (1947, 1956), an unusual *Suite* (1949) for harp and chamber orchestra, and a *Passacaglia and Fugue* (1954) for orchestra.

[27] Helmut Kallmann, *A History of Music in Canada: 1534–1914* (Toronto: University of Toronto Press, 1960), pp. 267–268.

FOR DISCUSSION AND ASSIGNMENT

1. Listening to Bartók's music, can you discern why he is considered one of the great composers of the twentieth century? Does the *Concerto for Orchestra* or *Music for Strings, Percussion and Celesta* seem to reflect any influence of folk song or peasant music?
2. How do you account for the great activity in English music after so many decades of comparative silence?
3. Do you think that Milhaud's works, written with such facility, lack musical substance when compared with the works of more deliberate composers like Honegger? If not, how do you account for this facility?
4. Which of the European countries has up to now contributed the most to twentieth-century music? Give reasons for your choice.
5. In view of the tremendous musical activity in Latin America, how do you account for the fact that we hear so little of the music it has engendered?
6. Compare Villa-Lobos or Ginastera (or both) with some of the prominent composers in present-day Europe. How do they stand?
7. Listen to any of Respighi's orchestral works. Do you detect any elements of Impressionism? Is this style out of place in Italian music? Do you find this music anachronistic and overdone, or has it value as a work of merit?

FOR FURTHER READING

Collaer, Paul. *A History of Modern Music,* translated by S. Abeles. New York: Grosset & Dunlap, 1961. A Universal Library PB. See comments on page 362.

Composers of the Americas. Washington, D.C.: Pan American Union, 1955–1965. 11 Volumes to date. PB. At present the only collection of monographs and catalogs for representative composers from Latin America, the United States, and Canada.

Hartog, Howard, editor. *European Music in the Twentieth Century.* New York: F. A. Praeger, 1957. PB. A collection of essays on different aspects of contemporary music. Appropriate for the reader who has some basic knowledge of music.

Machlis, Joseph. *Introduction to Contemporary Music.* New York: W. W. Norton & Co., Inc., 1961. See comments on page 362.

Music of Latin America. Washington, D.C.: Pan American Union, 1953. PB. A very brief history of Latin-American music from colonial days to the present.

Myers, Rollo, editor. *Twentieth Century Music: A Symposium.* London: Calder, 1960. PB. This "symposium," similar in intent and scope to the Hartog book listed above, contains more recent information. Both books are extremely informative.

Stevenson, Robert. *Music in Mexico.* New York: Thomas Y. Crowell Co., 1952. Out of print and available in libraries only.

Slonimsky, Nicolas. *Music of Latin America.* New York: Thomas Y. Crowell Co., 1945. Available in libraries only.

———. *Music Since 1900,* 3rd Edition, Revised and Enlarged. New York: Coleman-Ross Co., Inc., 1949.

26 Music in the United States

The key to the understanding of contemporary music lies in repeated hearing; one must hear it till it sounds familiar, until one begins to notice false notes if they are played. One must make the effort to retain it in one's ear, and one will always find that the accurate memory of sounds heard coincides with the understanding of them.

ROGER SESSIONS

*The Musical Experience of Composer, Performer and Listener**

One has only to read Gilbert Chase's excellent book *America's Music* (1966) to become aware of America's colorful musical heritage. Musical circles flourished in eighteenth-century America, even though most of the music was supplied by foreign-born musicians.

One of the earliest serious musical projects came from the Moravian Church, a German Protestant sect that began emigrating to America in 1735. They established a settlement in Bethlehem, Pennsylvania in 1741 and a later one in Salem (now Winston-Salem), North Carolina. The Moravians saw to it that their churches had organs, they established trombone choirs, they encouraged instrumental chamber music, and their composers wrote anthems for soloists, chorus, and orchestra. They lived in separate communities and rarely intermingled with other colonies. "Unfortunately for the history of American music, very little of this enormous quantity of music ever entered the stream of musical life in the United States."[1]

During the past decade the Moravian Music Foundation (chartered in 1956) has made available—in modern editions—a considerable amount of this neglected music. Performances and recordings are helping twentieth-century critics to evaluate this unique eighteenth-century musical society.

As with most early musicians in the United States, little is known about James Bremner (*d.*1780). In 1763 he arrived in Philadelphia and opened a school to teach harpsichord, flute, and guitar. He is mentioned as being the

* (Princeton University Press, 1950). Reprinted by permission.

[1] Donald M. McCorkle, *The Moravian Contribution to American Music* (Bethlehem, Pa.: Moravian Music Foundation Publication, No. 1, 1958), p. 9. Reprinted by permission.

organist at Christ Church in 1767, but his chief claim to fame is that he taught Francis Hopkinson (1737–1791), the American author who was one of the signers of the Declaration of Independence and a proficient amateur musician. Hopkinson composed and published a collection of *Seven Songs for the Harpsichord or Forte Piano* (1788), which he dedicated to his friend George Washington.

William Billings (1746–1800) was mostly self-taught. His passion for music—composition, performance, and promotion—and his innate if undeveloped talent earned him a fine reputation during his lifetime. A pioneer composer of American church music, he wrote and published six collections, which included psalm tunes, anthems, "fuguing tunes" (music in imitative style), and canons. Several of his anthems remain usable and attractive today; their rugged vitality, originality, and genuine spirituality preserve them as sturdy musical endeavors in a newly emerging nation.

A really distinguished musician during this early colonial period was Alexander Reinagle (1756–1809), who was born in Portsmouth, England. As a youth he fell under the spell of Johann Christian Bach and also became acquainted with Emanuel Bach in Hamburg. After 1786 he lived in America, making his home in Philadelphia, where we can assume he won a solid reputation, since George Washington engaged him as music teacher to his stepdaughter Nellie Custis.

This brief review of eighteenth-century musical activity reveals few significant composers, but it proves that at least the United States showed interest in music at that time. If we take into consideration the fact that American colonists had more vital things to do than write or listen to music, we can be surprised at finding even this limited cultural atmosphere.

For the first composer of stature we must skip almost half a century to Louis Moreau Gottschalk (1829–1869), who was born in New Orleans of English-Jewish and titled French-Creole parentage. In 1842 he began advanced music studies in France, made a successful piano debut, and eventually concertized; he spent his last seven years touring throughout the United States, Canada, Central America, and South America, where he died in Rio de Janeiro.

Gottschalk wrote well over 100 piano compositions (his operas and orchestral works are long forgotten) in an extremely eclectic, composite style that seems to reflect his cosmopolitan existence. His European training doubtlessly influenced his music, but the exotic ambience and excitement of New Orleans were directly responsible for the authenticity and success of pieces such as *La Bamboula, Ojos criollos* and *Le Banjo. La Bamboula,* one of his most popular piano pieces, introduces elements from the habanera and cakewalk, yet at the same time it has a certain finesse that can be traced only to France. Among his interesting and amusing virtuoso pieces, *L'Union* is a distinct paraphrase of three American patriotic airs: "The Star-Spangled Banner," "Hail Columbia," and "Yankee Doodle."

Although perhaps not classified as a serious musician, Stephen Collins Foster (1826–1864) carved himself an immortal niche in American musical history with his simple, heartfelt songs about the people and the country. Foster, a first-class melodist with a natural talent like Schubert's, had slight formal musical training, but his songs are better than many written by well-trained composers.

Foster confined himself almost exclusively to vocal composition, writing more than 200 songs. The so-called "Ethiopian" (blackface minstrel) category includes nonsense songs—"Oh! Susanna," "Camptown Races," "Ring de Banjo"—and homesick plantation songs—"Old Folks at Home," "My Old Kentucky

Home," "Old Black Joe," "Massa's in de Cold Cold Ground." "Jeanie with the Light Brown Hair" and "Come Where My Love Lies Dreaming" are typical of Foster's sentimental ballad-type works. Stephen Foster was an American troubadour whose songs will be remembered because they are warm, authentic reminders of this country's living tradition.

America's outstanding nineteenth-century musical figure was Edward MacDowell (1861–1908), the first American composer to gain international recognition.

> When Edward MacDowell appeared on the scene, many Americans felt that here at last was "the great American composer" awaited by the nation. But MacDowell was not a great composer. At his best he was a gifted miniaturist with an individual manner. Creatively, he looked toward the past, not toward the future. He does not mark the beginning of a new epoch in American music, but the closing of a fading era, the *fin de siècle* decline of the genteel tradition which had dominated American art since the days of Hopkinson.[2]

With this statement, Gilbert Chase accurately evaluates MacDowell, whose music was based on German Romanticism stemming from his long years in Germany. As a gifted miniaturist, his creative talents developed to their fullest expression in short, epigrammatic tone portraits. His place in time, succinctly stated by Mr. Chase, accounts for his decreasing popularity; he does not belong with the great Romantics Schumann and Brahms, but neither can he be regarded as a genuine precursor of twentieth-century American music.

Due to his admiration for German Romanticism, MacDowell wrote many piano works, and his piano suites became tremendously popular in their day. The most popular set also has the finest quality: the ten *Woodland Sketches* (1896) reveal his typical style at its best, and some are quite charming; the little sketch *To a Wild Rose* impresses through its simplicity and directness.

MacDowell's two orchestral suites have been quite successful. *Suite No. 2 in E Minor, Opus 48* (1892), his last orchestral work, is usually called the "Indian" suite. According to MacDowell's pupil Henry Gilbert, the suite originated as follows:

> MacDowell now became somewhat interested in Indian lore and curious to see some real Indian music. He asked me to look up some for him, so I brought him Theodore Baker's book *Die Musik der Nordamerikanischen Wilden*. "Oh, yes," he said, "I knew of this book, but had forgotten about it." From Baker's book the main themes of his Indian Suite are taken. . . . Although all [the themes] have been changed, more or less, the changes have always been in the direction of musical beauty, and enough of the original tune has been retained to leave no doubt as to its barbaric flavor.[3]

The suite has five movements.

1. *Legend.* Based on an Iroquois and a Chippewa theme, this movement allegedly was inspired by Thomas Bailey Aldrich's Indian legend *Miantowona*.

2. *Love Song.* Woodwinds announce the plaintive principal theme, a love song of the Iowa Indians; it is developed in company with two secondary motives.

[2] From *America's Music* by Gilbert Chase, p. 364. Copyright © 1966 by Gilbert Chase. Used by permission of McGraw-Hill Book Company.

[3] Henry F. B. Gilbert, "Personal Recollections of Edward MacDowell," *New Music Review* (November 1912, Vol. 11, No. 132), pp. 496–497.

3. *In War-Time.* The main theme here is a savage melody found among Indian tribes along the Eastern seaboard. Two unaccompanied flutes introduce the song, which then alternates with a subsidiary theme in a kind of rondo.

4. *Dirge.* Tolling bells precede a women's mourning lament native to the Kiowa Indians. It is sung by muted unison violins.

5. *Village Festival.* This bright music employs two Iroquois themes: a women's dance, played by plucked strings, and a war song, heard in flute and piccolo with string and woodwind accompaniment.

No more need be said about American music of the late nineteenth and early twentieth centuries. Basically this was the era of salon-music composers such as Arthur Foote (1853–1937) and Ethelbert Nevin (1862–1901), author of such saccharine works as *Narcissus.* The United States sorely needed the musical awakening that was to come in the early decades of the twentieth century.

In this century, musical composition in the United States has become so vigorous that it very nearly equals European production. Such a trend is remarkable in view of the fact that, comparatively speaking, this is still a young nation, one that is still choosing from the old and the new as it establishes the foundations of its artistic tradition. Although prospects are bright, tradition takes time.

Early-twentieth-century American composers faced the difficult task of reconciling Romanticism's last embers with the oncoming modern expressive techniques. For the last 40 years musical composition has advanced steadily. Today's styles and methods are too varied to be grouped together categorically, but on the whole modern composers have identical goals: clarity and succinctness uncluttered by extraneous details, the use of dissonant counterpoint, and experiments with untried rhythmic formulas.

Some present-day composers are basically Romanticists even though they usually adjust their attitude to fit a contemporary idiom. There also exists a fairly large nationalist group that tries—with varying degrees of enthusiasm—to write "American" music. Other composers, especially during the earlier years, have been strongly influenced by Impressionism. In direct contrast to them stand the atonalists, or at least the writers who appropriate elements of twelve-tone or serial technique. But the largest group of United States composers—native-born or otherwise—are eclectics or neo-Classicists. Their language is definitely in tune with the times but the scaffold on which it relies usually derives from some Baroque or Classic form: sonata, suite, prelude and fugue, toccata.

Since this century has already produced countless composers, we can deal only with those who have established important reputations. Although each composer is placed in a particular category—which could not be done in previous chapters because of the numerous countries involved—such classification is certainly not immutable. Each composer is grouped according to what seems to be his conspicuous trait or quality, in some cases merely his attitude toward musical art.

IMPRESSIONISTS

Charles Griffes

Charles Tomlinson Griffes (1884–1920), an American Impressionist, was also somewhat of an eclectic: his preoccupation with Far Eastern culture and his admiration for many of his European contemporaries—Debussy, Ravel, Mussorgsky, Stravinsky, Schoenberg—inevitably influenced his own repertoire.

Some of Griffes' typically impressionistic compositions appear in *Four Roman Sketches, Opus 7* (1915–1916): *The White Peacock, Nightfall, The Fountain of Acqua Paola,* and *Clouds.* These piano pieces indicate an extraordinary feeling for tone color and atmospheric re-creation. The first is very well known, and Griffes also arranged it for orchestra. A few years later Griffes wrote a symphonic poem destined to become equally as famous as *The White Peacock.* When he published the score of *The Pleasure Dome of Kubla Khan* (1916), he prefaced it with the opening lines from the famous poem by Samuel Taylor Coleridge. When the Boston Symphony Orchestra premiered the symphonic poem on November 28, 1919, the composer supplied the following program notes:

> I have taken as a basis for my work those lines of Coleridge's poem describing the "stately pleasure dome," the "sunny pleasure dome with caves of ice," the "miracle of rare device." Therefore I call the work *The Pleasure Dome of Kubla Khan* rather than *Kubla Khan.* These lines include 1 to 11 and lines 32 to 38.
>
> As to argument, I have given my imagination free rein in the description of this strange palace as well as of purely imaginary revelry which might take place there. The vague, foggy beginning suggests the sacred river, running "through caverns measureless to man down to a sunless sea." Then gradually rise the outlines of the palace, "with walls and towers girdled round." The gardens with fountains and "sunny spots of greenery" are next suggested. From inside come sounds of dancing and revelry which increase to a wild climax and then suddenly break off. There is a return to the original mood suggesting the sacred river and the "caves of ice."

Griffes' highly attenuated Impressionism stands out sharply in his *Poem for Flute and Orchestra* (1918). In this work he skillfully creates an oriental atmosphere and variegated moods ranging from the opening dark tones to bright, intoxicating excitement.

In 1918 Griffes finished a piano *Sonata* (revised in 1919) that announced a new attitude on his part. Its diversified elements—oriental-type scale patterns, Scriabinesque chromaticisms, deliberate experimentation in new harmonies—certify that this is one of the earliest works written in what is now known as contemporary style. It has three movements: *Feroce-Allegretto con moto, Molto tranquillo,* and *Allegro vivace.*

There are other American composers whose works depend heavily on French Impressionist models, particularly John Alden Carpenter (1876–1951), Arthur Shepherd (1880–1958), and Deems Taylor (1885–1966).

NATIONALISTS

There is more than one definition for "nationalist composer." It may mean that a composer enjoys appropriating genuine folk tunes and using them openly. Or it may mean he uses melodic material that sounds authentic even though he has created it himself. Finally, it may apply to a composer who builds his music around characteristic folk-song rhythms and folk-dance types. And since jazz is considered to be a typically American tradition, some composers have found it interesting to use this idiom in their music. American history supplies a rich lode of source material for the nationally oriented composer: Indian themes, Negro spirituals, white spirituals, songs of the early West, and New Orleans jazz.

George Gershwin

In many parts of the world, jazz is the symbol of modern American music. The term "jazz" in connection with "composed" music suggests the name of George Gershwin (1898–1937), the composer who managed to combine the stable elements of jazz with a romantic, quasi-contemporary style. The premiere of his *Rhapsody in Blue* (1924) marks a high point in the history of American music.

Gershwin had a fair amount of musical training and became a facile pianist. Having an inborn instinct for melody, he quickly assimilated the tin pan alley idiom and from 1919 until 1933 turned out an incomparable series of musical comedies (*Lady Be Good, Strike Up the Band*), each filled with memorable tunes.

When Paul Whiteman, the popular orchestra conductor then publicized as the "king of jazz," decided to explore the possibilities of jazz in serious music, he planned a New York concert for February, 1924, to be called "Experiment in Modern Music." Knowing that Gershwin had recently expressed a desire to write serious music, Whiteman requested a concert piece from him. In ten days Gershwin finished *Rhapsody in Blue,* a work for piano and orchestra.

Whiteman turned the piano score (Gershwin did not attempt an orchestration) over to his arranger Ferde Grofé (*b.*1892), the man almost solely responsible for the sweet-jazz characteristic of the Whiteman orchestra. *Rhapsody in Blue* was as much a triumph for Grofé as it was for Gershwin and Whiteman. Grofé went on to become a composer of light orchestral music, of which the colorful *Grand Canyon Suite* (1931) is the most widely known.

The *Rhapsody* brought Gershwin fame, respect, and wealth. It is as genuine a piece of Americana as a Sandburg poem. This work carries American jazz elements into symphonic form, especially the snappy rhythms and sophisticated musical-comedy tunes identified with Gershwin's jazz. His style leans substantially on Liszt, with some Tchaikovsky effects in the slow section, but he was well equipped to fit these disparate elements together. The *Rhapsody* is a sparkling testament to his personal technique.

When the New York Symphony Society commissioned Gershwin to write a serious piano concerto, he responded with the *Concerto in F* (1925). While some thought it a work of genius, others felt it to be too derivative in style (Debussy, mostly), and both appraisals are partly right. The introspective elements of jazz are not far removed from Impressionism, and it is to Gershwin's credit that he could adapt his hit-tune background to a serious symphonic work.

Another major Gershwin composition, the symphonic poem *An American in Paris,* received its first performance with the New York Symphony in 1928. This piece captures all the exhilarating excitement that endeared Paris to many American tourists in the twenties. The colorful orchestration creates gaiety and realism—it even calls for four taxi horns. And the inevitable nostalgia for America is beautifully implied by one of Gershwin's famous blues themes.

Gershwin finished his only large-scale work just two years before his death. *Porgy and Bess* (1935) had wonderful tunes—"I Got Plenty of Nuthin'," "Bess, You Is My Woman Now," "Summertime"—but some critics felt that the recitatives and the opera in general were not typical of Gershwin's best writing, and others felt that it was neither opera nor musical comedy but some type of in-between hybrid. Its true worth was eventually appreciated. In 1938 it ran successfully in Los Angeles and San Francisco; in 1942 it was revived in New York and became one of the great hits of the season; between 1952 and 1956 a company performed it with even greater success in Europe, the Middle East, the Soviet Union, and Latin America, as well as the United States.

Charles Ives

Charles Ives (1874–1954) has finally been recognized as the foremost pioneer in American contemporary music. His superior compositions are not easy from any viewpoint; for example, the printed page confronts the performer with endless—and seemingly aimless—notes, chromatics, and just about every configuration imaginable. But Ives was able to write as he pleased, without anxiety about public acceptance, because he had a successful insurance business to support him. At first his works were privately printed, but now many are issued by professional publishing houses. They are harshly dissonant and rhythmically complex. Ives was indeed a pioneer. Even before Schoenberg and Stravinsky evolved their respective idioms, he was working with polytonality, atonality, polyrhythms, and other techniques that later became so essential to modern musical language. Yet, paradoxically, he was devoted to simple folklike music, and to this end he depended heavily on hymn tunes for source material. He composed numerous songs, four choral works, two piano sonatas, six compositions for violin and piano (five sonatas and one *Allegro*), one string quartet, and eight works for orchestra (including four symphonies).

Ives's second piano sonata—the *Concord Sonata* (1915)—is a fine example of his fully ripened style. In an attempt to clarify, or justify, this iconoclastic keyboard symphony, he wrote a set of *Essays before a Sonata*[4] to accompany the musical score.

> These prefatory essays were written by the composer for those who can't stand his music—and the music for those who can't stand his essays; to those who can't stand either, the whole is respectfully dedicated. [He describes his piano work as] a group of four pieces called sonata for want of a more exact name. The whole is an attempt to present one person's impression of the spirit of transcendentalism that is associated in the minds of many with Concord, Mass., of over a half century ago . . . impressionistic pictures of Emerson and Thoreau, a sketch of the Alcotts, and a scherzo supposed to reflect a lighter quality which is often found in the fantastic side of Hawthorne.

In addition to the explanatory essays, Ives provided his music with performance and interpretative suggestions. Thematically the entire sonata is based on two motives: one a descending five-note figure stated in octaves; the other is the same four-note motive that opens Beethoven's *Symphony No. 5.*

Some musical passages from the first movement, *Emerson,* are associated with unspecified poetical and prose writings of that transcendentalist. In the second movement, *Hawthorne,* Ives clearly recalls his childhood memories: the gospel hymn, circus parade, and camp meeting; each nostalgic mood rather

[4] These are found in *Three Classics in the Aesthetics of Music* (New York: Dover Publications, Inc., 1962).

brazenly interrupts the composer's ultradissonant language. In the *Essays* he gives a slight clue to the third movement, *The Alcotts:* "And there sits the little old spinet-piano Sophia Thoreau gave to the Alcott children, on which Beth played the old Scotch airs, and played at the *Fifth Symphony.*" Here Charles Ives does indeed play at Beethoven's symphony. *Thoreau,* the concluding part of the *Concord Sonata,* has no key signatures, no time signatures, and no bar lines; in this movement the composer returns to the quasi-impressionistic sketching introduced in *Emerson.*

Many critics consider Ives's *Symphony No. 3* his best. It was written in 1904, revised in 1911, but never had a public performance until 1946. In 1947 it won the Pulitzer Prize in music. Inspired by the many camp meetings Ives witnessed in his hometown of Danbury, Connecticut, this symphony is filled with American accents. It is scored for a small orchestra with bells ad libitum, except for the last two measures, where the bells are specified "as distant church bells."

The first and third movements show religious spirit; the second is more secular. The first movement, *Andante maestoso,* has a section marked *Adagio cantabile* that muses briefly on the hymn "What a Friend We Have in Jesus." The old gospel song "There Is a Fountain Filled with Blood" is also referred to in the first movement. Ives used binary form for his second movement, *Allegro,* employing a folklike principal theme for the opening section and a marchlike refrain for the middle part. Concluding a symphony with a *Largo* is ordinarily considered unusual, but not for an unusually original composer like Ives. For his main theme he borrows the hymn "Just As I Am without One Plea" and treats it contrapuntally with a theme derived from the first movement.

Ives's curious but ingratiating orchestral triptych *Three Places in New England* (1903–1914), sometimes referred to as the *New England Symphony,* consists of three orchestral sketches reminiscent of the past, particularly the past in New England.

1. *The "St. Gaudens" in Boston Common: Col. Shaw and his Colored Regiment. Very Slowly.* Ives wrote a poem for the score, the opening lines of which are:

> Moving,—Marching—Faces of Souls!
> Marked with generations of pain,
> Part-freers of a Destiny,
> Slowly, restlessly—swaying us on with you
> Towards other Freedom! . . .

2. *Putnam's Camp, Redding, Connecticut. Allegro.* To help his listeners place the locale of this second movement, Ives wrote: "Near Redding Center is a small park preserved as a Revolutionary Memorial; for here General Israel Putnam's soldiers had their winter quarters in 1778–9. Long rows of stone camp fire-places still remain to stir a child's imagination." Musically Ives describes a Fourth of July picnic held under the auspices of the First Church and the village cornet band. His music rings with holiday spirit as it recalls the gay festivities. During the inevitable parade two different bands get a little too close to each other and their clashing polyrhythms create a boisterous, dissonant conclusion.

3. *The Housatonic at Stockbridge. Adagio molto.* Typically Ives, this final movement is a serene soliloquy based on a Robert Underwood Johnson poem, which the composer quotes in the score:

Contented river! in thy dreamy realm—
The cloudy willow and the plumy elm. . . .
Thou has grown human laboring with men
At wheel and spindle; sorrow thou dost ken. . . .

. . . Wouldst thou away!
I also of much resting have a fear;
Let me thy companion be
By fall and shallow to the adventurous sea!

Roy Harris

Roy Harris (*b.*1898) stands out among today's American composers. He is respected by his fellow musicians and appreciated by a public that has frequent opportunities to hear his music through concerts and recordings. A deft craftsman, Harris maneuvers twentieth-century techniques with enough moderation to render his music readily accessible. His rhythms are varied and at times involved, but they are never obscure; his harmonies—built by preference in fourths—are dissonant and sometimes polytonal but remain logical. His long, flowing melodies never become commonplace or trite. Harris is a nationalist not so much because he uses folk melodies (although he has done so occasionally) but because his virile, crisp rhythms and sophisticated harmonies are significantly related to contemporary American life.

Harris has written consistently since his late twenties. He is most adept in large-scale instrumental works—for instance, the seven symphonies of which the third and fourth are particularly attractive. The fourth, the *Folksong Symphony* (1939), is not a true symphony; written for chorus and orchestra, it is a fantasy on American folk tunes. His other orchestral works are the overture *When Johnny Comes Marching Home* (1934), *Chorale* (1944), a *Concerto for Two Pianos and Orchestra* (1946), a *Violin Concerto* (1950), and *Elegy and Dance* (1958). His chamber works include three string quartets and a *Quintet for Piano and Strings* (1936). He has also produced choral works, piano music, and songs.

His finest single composition is the *Symphony No. 3* (1938), a one-movement work lasting approximately 17 minutes. This symphony had an immediate impact on both professionals and public, and it ranks now as one of the outstanding symphonic works composed by an American in this century. Harris has skillfully integrated his musical materials. The five sections create continually evolving texture, but with musicianly logic the composer combines these various sections into one splendid whole. He has provided a brief analysis of the symphony's structure:

I. Tragic—low string sonorities
II. Lyric—strings, horns, woodwinds
III. Pastoral—emphasizing woodwind color
IV. Fugue—dramatic
  A. Brass-percussion predominating
  B. Canonic development of Section II materials constituting background for further development of Fugue
  C. Brass climax. Rhythmic motif derived from Fugue subject
V. Dramatic—tragic
  A. Restatement of violin theme of Section I. Tutti strings in canon with tutti woodwinds. Brass and percussion develop rhythmic motif from climax of Section IV.

B. Coda—development of materials from Sections I and II over pedal tympani.[5]

Aaron Copland

Aaron Copland (*b.*1900), one of America's most celebrated composers, has used his multifaceted style in several different types of composition. His works range from quasi-Romantic French music to strident, uncompromising tones, and he keeps alert to all currents in musical vocabulary. During his early career he explored the jazz idiom in *Music for the Theatre* (1925) and *Four Piano Blues* (1926–1948). A modernist by nature, Copland has created works that epitomize the abstract: *Piano Variations* (1930), an excellent example of his seasoned, disciplined, and discerning writing; the austere *Sonata* (1939–1941); and *Piano Fantasy* (1957), a long, through-composed work in one movement with contrasting sections alternating between acidity, sensuous tone colors, and brilliantly fashioned rhythmic designs. In a lighter vein, the highly gifted Copland has turned out expert film scores: *Of Mice and Men, Our Town, The Red Pony,* and *The Heiress.* He extended his popular style into the concert field with such diverting scores as *El Salón México* (1936), and he enhanced the ballet-music repertoire with such works as *Billy the Kid* (1938), *Rodeo* (1942), and *Appalachian Spring* (1944).

An articulate writer as well as talented composer, Copland has written four very worthwhile books: *What to Listen for in Music* (1939), *Our New Music* (1941), *Copland on Music* (1944), and *Music and Imagination* (1952). His ideas about composing are of course best explained in his own words.

> If forced to explain the creative musician's basic objective in elementary terms, I would say that a composer writes music to express and communicate and put down in permanent form certain thoughts, emotions and states of being. These thoughts and emotions are gradually formed by the contact of the composer's personality with the world in which he lives. He expresses these thoughts (musical thoughts, which are not to be confused with literary ones) in the musical language of his own time. The resultant work of art should speak to the men and women of the artist's own time with a directness and immediacy of communicative power that no previous art expression can give.[6]

Copland's early *Music for the Theatre* (1925) drew favorable criticism because of his adroit handling of a jazz idiom in serious music. The work has five sections and is scored for chamber orchestra.

I. *Prologue.* The trumpet ushers in the first theme, the oboe sings the second subject, and then an imaginative development leads to the exhilarating climax.

II. *Dance.* This section emphasizes rhythmic force.

III. *Interlude.* A lyric passage, it serves as a welcome respite between *Dance* and the following section.

IV. *Burlesque* conforms to the pattern A B A B.

V. *Epilogue.* Copland uses material from the first and third sections.

Captivated by Mexico during a visit in the fall of 1932, Copland pre-

[5] Program Notes for the Boston Symphony premiere, February 24, 1939.

[6] From an article "A Modernist Defends Modern Music," in *The New York Times,* December 25, 1949.

served his impressions in the orchestral poem *El Salón México* (1936). He later wrote:

> Any composer who goes outside his native land wants to return bearing musical souvenirs. In this case my musical souvenirs must have been very memorable, since it wasn't until 1933 that I began to assemble them into the form of an orchestral work.

His direct inspiration came from a unique Mexico City dance hall containing three dance areas: in one the atmosphere was formal, in another the dancers could remove their coats, and in the third they danced barefoot. Copland explained:

> All that I could hope to do was to reflect the Mexico of the tourists, and that is why I thought of the *Salón México*. Because in that "hot spot," one felt, in a very natural and unaffected way, a close contact with the Mexican people. It wasn't the music I heard, but the spirit I felt there, which attracted me. Something of that spirit is what I hope to have put into my music.[7]

Copland's orchestration and folk-music rhythms suggest a typical *mariachi* band; he even uses some native tunes, notably *El Mosco,* played lazily by the trumpet after the introduction.

Other nationalist composers working in the United States are Leo Sowerby (*b.*1895), Ernst Bacon (*b.*1898), Randall Thompson (*b.*1899), Elie Siegmeister (*b.*1909), Morton Gould (*b.*1913), Carlos Surinach (*b.*1915), and Gunther Schuller (*b.*1925). Schuller combines jazz sonorities with contemporary writing techniques in his successful opera *The Visitation* (1966), based on Franz Kafka's *The Trial.*

NEO-ROMANTICS

The term neo-Romantic does not indicate a revival of nineteenth-century techniques of harmony, melody, and the like. It usually represents a reaction against the cerebral music favored by some modern composers. Most neo-Romantic composers use contemporary language while emphasizing emotional factors.

Howard Hanson

Howard Hanson (*b.*1896) is one of the founding fathers of twentieth-century neo-Romanticism and was the first American to win the coveted *Prix de Rome.* During a three-year stay in Rome he tried a strictly neo-Classic approach to composition but rejected it in favor of unabashed romanticism. Of his four symphonies, the first and second are most popular. He titled his first symphony "Nordic" (1922) and it is clear that he found inspiration in Sibelius; his most celebrated work is the *Second Symphony* (1930), called "Romantic."

Hanson has been faithful to his professed aesthetic. A subjective atmos-

[7] Quoted in Program Notes of the Boston Symphony Orchestra, October 14, 1938.

phere permeates the textures of his works, in which somber moods, lyric melancholy, and modal harmony blend into an appealing language. Besides the five symphonies, Hanson has written five symphonic poems, various concertos, two excellent choral works (*The Lament for Beowulf,* 1925, and *Three Poems from Walt Whitman,* 1935), and the opera *Merry Mount* (1933).

At the time of his "Romantic" symphony's premiere, Hanson made an explanatory statement which became his credo for future works.

> This symphony represents for me my escape from the rather bitter type of modern musical realism which occupies so large a place in contemporary thought. Much contemporary music seems to me to be showing a tendency to become entirely too cerebral. I do not believe that music is primarily a matter of intellect, but rather a manifestation of the emotions. I have, therefore, aimed in this symphony to create a work that was young in spirit, lyrical and romantic in temperament, and simple and direct in expression.

The "Romantic" symphony is overtly emotional. It concentrates on sheer sound: velvet-toned violin passages in the upper register, pompous trumpet and horn fanfares, spectacular climaxes. Hanson analyzed it as follows:

> The first movement [*Adagio*] begins with an atmospheric introduction in the woodwinds, joined first by the horns, then the strings, and finally the brass choir, and then subsiding. The principal theme [*Allegro moderato*] is announced by four horns with an accompaniment of strings and woodwinds, and is imitated in turn by the trumpets, woodwinds, and strings. An episodic theme appears quietly in the oboe and then in the solo horn. A transition leads into a subordinate theme, with the theme itself in the strings and a countersubject in the solo horn. The development section now follows. . . . The climax of the development section leads directly to the return of the principal theme in the original key by the trumpets. . . . The movement concludes quietly in a short coda.
>
> The second movement [*Andante con tenerezza*] begins with its principal theme announced by the woodwinds with a sustained string accompaniment. An interlude in the brass, taken from the introduction of the first movement and interrupted by florid passages in the woodwinds, develops into a subordinate theme, which is taken from the horn solo of the first movement.
>
> The third movement [*Allegro con brio*] begins with a vigorous accompaniment figure in strings and woodwinds, the principal theme of the movement—reminiscent of the first movement—entering in the four horns and later in the basses. The subordinate theme [*Molto meno mosso*] is announced first by the cellos and then taken up by the English horn; its development leads into the middle section. A brief coda . . . leads to a final fanfare and the end of the symphony.[8]

Samuel Barber

During the last 30 years Samuel Barber (*b.*1910) has built up an enviable reputation as one of today's most elegant craftsmen. His basically tonal works—characterized by alternating major and minor tonalities—display a wonderful lyric talent. His interesting counterpoint reflects his refined taste. Even when Barber attempts atonal writing, his warm personality and humanism still dominate the music.

Barber's compositions for orchestra include the overture to *The School*

[8] Program Notes for the Boston Symphony premiere, November 28, 1930.

for *Scandal* (1932), two *Essays* (1937, 1942), *Music for a Scene from Shelley* (1933), the *Capricorn Concerto* (1944), and several concertos for solo instrument and orchestra, including the excellent *Piano Concerto, Opus 38* (1962). The chamber-music repertoire includes *Dover Beach* (1931), for voice and string quartet, two string quartets, and a cello and piano sonata. There are also many songs and choral works, and two operas: *Vanessa* (1957) and *Antony and Cleopatra* (1966).

Barber's *Adagio for Strings* was composed in 1936 in Rome as the slow movement for his *String Quartet in B Minor.* The first performance of the string-orchestra version took place on November 5, 1938, when Toscanini played it with the NBC Symphony. The score is marked *Molto adagio espr. cantando.* The work is based on a single lyric subject, announced immediately by the first violins (Ex. 26:1) and then taken up by the violas in canonic treatment. This theme continues to enter in the other voices until a rising fortissimo climaxes in the high strings. A pause precedes the tranquil ending.

Ex. 26:1. Barber: *Adagio for Strings*

Copyright 1939–1964 by G. Schirmer, Inc. Used by permission.

Barber's overture (composed in 1932) to Sheridan's eighteenth-century comedy *The School for Scandal* perfectly matches the play's wit, sophistication, and vigor. It has become a classic in this type of writing. Most of the orchestra participates in the energetic opening, and then the first violins present the principal melodic material (Ex. 26:2), a spritely theme later elaborated by other orchestral instruments. A more restrained secondary theme, presented by the solo oboe (Ex. 26:3), is followed by a third melody, played by the clarinet with string accompaniment. These three themes constitute the material for the overture. It concludes boisterously.

Ex. 26:2. Barber: *Overture: The School for Scandal*

Examples 26:2 and 26:3 copyright 1941 by G. Schirmer, Inc. Used by permission.

Ex. 26:3. Barber: *Overture: The School for Scandal*

Barber's *Piano Sonata, Opus 26* (1949) may well be the prime American sonata written in the last three decades. A very difficult work in four movements, it has an affinity with similar Beethoven works in its dramatic impact and skillful motivic development. Barber uses twelve-tone technique here, but his treatment is highly personal.

In the first movement, *Allegro energico,* Barber extracts his motives from a series of twelve-note melodies; however, this is not a slavish attempt at strict dodecaphonic writing, for he dexterously infuses other expressive means. Marked *Allegro vivace e leggero,* the second movement is a short, whimsical scherzo. The third movement, *Adagio mesto,* is based on two twelve-tone rows employed somewhat like a passacaglia but parceled into three sections, A B A. The finale is a *Fuga* in toccata style.

Gian-Carlo Menotti

Few modern composers have attempted a career in opera, but Gian-Carlo Menotti (*b.*1911) has done so with striking success. Although Menotti has lived in the United States since 1928, he is Italian born and his skill with opera stems from that background. When he writes comic opera, he can rely on a long buffa tradition; when he turns to tragedy and serious opera, he can draw from Puccini. This does not in any way imply that he imitates these Italian traditions; it merely emphasizes the fact that his kinship with a country nourished on the lyric theater has been partly responsible for his great success.

As a professional man of the theater, Menotti writes his own librettos and thereby assures a close relationship between text and music. Writing in English, he sets his words so adroitly that they emerge clearly when sung. He creates credible characters and develops his dramatic situations through tightly knit musical textures enclosed in a tense atmosphere.

Some critics object to Menotti's "popular" style. The objection seems ridiculous, for Menotti has done more to popularize opera than anyone in the last 40 years. His opera *The Consul* played on Broadway for almost seven months—a total of 269 performances. (Most operas get only a few performances a year in repertory.)

His first success was *Amelia Goes to the Ball* (1934), a delightful comic opera. *The Old Maid and the Thief* (1938) offers a felicitous combination of romantic comedy and lyricism. *The Medium* (1946), an opera of suspense and terror, has had at least 2,000 performances and in 1951 was made into a film directed by the composer himself. The delightful farce *The Telephone* (1947), subtitled *L'amour à trois,* is a love triangle about a boy, a girl, and her telephone.

The Consul (1950), a contemporary tragedy, received a Pulitzer Prize in 1950. And the first television opera, Menotti's *Amahl and the Night Visitors* (1951), is now a classic favorite for the Christmas season. The later operas *The Saint of Bleeker Street* (1954) and *Maria Golovin* (1958) further substantiate Menotti's talent in his chosen field. Menotti also wrote the libretto for Samuel Barber's opera *Vanessa* (1957).

A "Madrigal Fable" is the subtitle that Menotti gave his most unusual work, *The Unicorn, The Gorgon, and The Manticore or Three Sundays of a Poet* (1956). Inspired by Italian madrigalists of the late sixteenth century, the composer tells his "fable" by means of a series of twelve *a cappella* madrigals. He alternates the chorus with interludes for ten dancers supported by an ensemble of nine instrumentalists.

Gail Kubik

Gail Kubik (*b.*1914), a student of Walter Piston and Nadia Boulanger, has worked with various media during his active career. In addition to abstract concert music and opera, he has written music for films, radio, and television. An articulate spokesman for music, he has lectured widely on many subjects pertinent to contemporary music.

Kubik is a much-honored composer: he has earned two Guggenheim fellowships, a *Prix de Rome,* a Pulitzer Prize, and several other awards.

How does he describe himself and his style?

> Perhaps Neo-Romantic is the best over-all description. I do not subscribe to atonality of the 12-tone variety nor do I hold with the dismissal of the vertical, harmonic factor implicit in the dodecaphonic methodology. My sounds are "conservative" in that though they try to *extend* the language of the past they are not concerned to *break* with it. Life is not, and cannot be, like that; and music is but a reflection of life. My music strives for economy of means and directness of melodic expression. The expressiveness of music is contained most essentially in its melodic element. If this element is combined with musical architecture—which is to say, with a successful dramatic and theatrical instinct—then melody takes on a depth and human significance which can make it a moving, communicative experience. Other compositional techniques can contribute to the expressiveness of music. But unless those techniques succeed in "showing off" melody as the jewel in a (beautiful, one hopes) setting, they fail in helping achieve lasting musical expression.[9]

A sampling from Kubik's substantial catalog discloses great variety in formal structures and diversity in musical content and function: three symphonies; *Violin Concerto* (1942); *Symphony Concertante* (1953), for viola, trumpet, piano and orchestra; *Piano Sonata* (1947); *Celebrations and Epilogue* (1950) for piano; chamber music, band music, and choral music. This clear-thinking composer links some of his important works to significant changes in his style.

> *Symphony No. 1* [1949] and *Sonata for Piano:* these works represent a crystallization of my style, a certain modest mastery of a large architectural form; *Symphony No. 2* [1956]: an effort to pour my "style" into a severe classical form—similar to the Mendelssohn "Italian" or the Roussel "Third"; *Symphony Concertante, Violin Concerto:* though separated by ten years, each work represents an effort to reconcile exhibitionism with large-scaled expressiveness. *Two Divertimenti* [1959], *Sonatina for Clarinet and Piano* [1959], *Gerald McBoing-Boing* [1950]: these are the best of my scores which try, consciously, to achieve humor, lightness, transparency without sacrificing depth or "seriousness" of communication.[10]

Robert Ward

In 1961 the New York City Opera Company gave the first performance of *The Crucible,* an opera based on the play by Arthur Miller with music written by Robert Ward (*b.*1917). Audiences and critics alike found much to praise in Ward's stage work.

[9] Communication to the author, dated March 8, 1967.

[10] Communication to the author.

The sense of life Mr. Ward can inject into even static situations is often remarkable, the result being highly charged, efficient, and absorbing musical theater driving relentlessly to a climax.[11]

If a finer opera has been written since the days of Strauss and Puccini, I have not heard it.[12]

Robert Ward writes music that people enjoy hearing. In 1963, Sioux City honored him with an entire weekend of festivities, lectures, and concerts featuring his works. One event presented his *Symphony No. 2* (1947), a work that has been heard frequently in the past few years. When this symphony was completed, Ward commented:

The typically American qualities that have been so frequently mentioned in my work of more recent years . . . stem directly from an interest in American folk song and jazz. But the more basic penchants for austere contrapuntal writing, simple slow melodic writing with elaborate obbligato, and fast and rhythmic dance tunes are all present in the various movements of my First Symphony [1941].[13]

This composer speaks about his music with ease and naturalness.

I suppose my music is generally considered middle-of-the-road and, by those who think that tonality is dead, extremely old-hat. It is gratifying to me that performers and listeners remember the tunes from my scores. Actually my only concern has been with the expressive content and the abstract musical substance in my music. Those who know my music well are most deeply impressed by the lyric melodic qualities. Since my musical roots are vocal this is perhaps not surprising. I am generally considered to be a capable and thorough craftsman, of which fact I am proud. Though I admire the great musical trail-blazers I realize that my own talents and temperament go in other directions. The quotation from the program notes for my "Second Symphony," written almost twenty years ago, states my feelings fairly well. All this could change, I suppose, since at 49 there is a good possibility that my creative life is only half over. Time will tell. So far the growth in my style has been gradual and there are no dramatic changes. Actually my *Euphony* [1954], *First Sonata for Violin and Piano* [1950], *Third Symphony* [1950] and *First String Quartet* all explore ways of developing musical ideas which if not original are new to me.[14]

William Bergsma

A composer, educator, and administrator (since 1963 he has been Director of the School of Music at the University of Washington), William Bergsma (*b.*1921) consistently writes music of high caliber. His studies with Howard Hanson have left their mark in a musical style that is uncomplicated but solid and imaginative. Following the premiere of Bergsma's opera *The Wife of Martin Guerre* (1956), Richard Franko Goldman reported:

Bergsma possesses what is possibly the rarest thing in American music: a genuine lyrical gift of the utmost refinement. The sensitiveness of his line is extraordinary, as is the delicacy and clarity of his contrapuntal texture.[15]

[11] Paul Henry Lang in the *New York Herald Tribune,* October 27, 1961.

[12] Winthrop Sargent in *The New Yorker,* April 7, 1962.

[13] From a brochure on the composer, his life and works (New York: Broadcast Music, Inc., 1965). Reprinted by permission.

[14] Communication to the author, dated September 27, 1966.

[15] *Musical Quarterly,* July 1956.

Bergsma, who has written in most idioms, lists the following as his most significant works:

> The *String Quartets* [1942, 1944, 1953], of which the fourth is in the writing stage, which are important stylistic landmarks of changes over the years; *The Wife of Martin Guerre,* which, with the recent *Violin Concerto* [1966], represent a combination of drama and lyricism which is, I think, characteristic of most of my work; *Confrontation from the Book of Job* [1963] and *Fantastic Variations* [1961] for Viola and Piano, which represent a more complex, assertive and cryptic side of my work.[16]

These works substantiate Bergsma's fine reputation and stand as realizations of his well-defined artistic credo:

> I want my music to be classic in that it is clear, romantic in that it communicates directly, and experimental in that each work brings out something new. These ideas are, of course, contradictory; but the tension of contradiction is one of the vital forces in art.[17]

Ned Rorem

> I've never consciously worked in any "style" or jumped on any band-wagon. I write the music I myself need to hear. I've been told it's "listenable." I've been told also that I excel in vocal mediums, particularly the Song; and though this may be true—indeed, I'm most at home in such mediums—I dislike being pigeon-holed.[18]

Despite his alarm at being "pigeonholed," Ned Rorem (*b.*1923) is one of the twentieth-century's truly talented composers of vocal music. He spent five years in France and many of his more than 200 songs bear out his contention that his music is influenced by "nearly all of the French, and certainly none of the Germans." Such epigrammatic miniatures as "Lullaby of the Mountain Woman," "The Nightingale," "Alleluia," and "Philomel" confirm Rorem's growing reputation in this field.

His choral music includes unaccompanied anthems and madrigals, anthems with organ, and large-scale works such as *The Poets' Requiem* (1955) for six-part chorus, soprano solo, and full orchestra. He has also written a quantity of music for piano (for example, two concertos, three sonatas), chamber ensembles (*Lovers,* 1964, for harpsichord, oboe, cello, and percussion), orchestra (*Design,* 1955), and the theater (opera, puppet shows, incidental music, ballet music).

Other composers inclined to neo-Romantic writing are Ernest Bloch (1880–1959), Hunter Johnson (*b.*1906), Paul Nordoff (*b.*1909), Peggy Glanville-Hicks (*b.*1912), Peter Mennin (*b.*1923), and William Flanagan (*b.*1926).

THE ECLECTICS

The word "eclectic" implies choosing what seems best from various sources. Eclectic composers do just that, drawing from Romanticism, nationalism,

[16] Communication to the author, dated September 6, 1966.

[17] Communication to the author.

[18] Communication to the author, dated September 13, 1966.

dodecaphony, and polytonality whatever they find attractive or relevant. Most of these composers also belong in the neo-Classic category, for they often prefer to fit their individualized, multitextured language into a traditional framework: suite, sonata, fugue, variations, or the like.

Walter Piston

In his music, Walter Piston (*b.*1894) almost invariably displays fine workmanship, an especially fortunate quality in a musician whose textbooks on music theory are widely used in American colleges and universities. Yet his compositions are not pedantic; far from that, their solidity and usefulness make them durable. Piston is a genuine eclectic; his music ranges from extreme complexity to disarming simplicity, from works conceived with pure logic to compositions built primarily from emotion. Whatever the approach, the result is always rewarding.

These results, understandably enough, stem from Piston's philosophy about composing.

> The major problem for the composer must be to preserve and develop his individuality. He must resist the constant pressures and temptations to follow this or that fashion. He must find what it is he wishes to say in music and how best to say it, subjecting his work to the severest self-criticism.
>
> It is not suggested that this is easy. Strength of will and faith in one's creative gift are essential.
>
> Performances of one's music are a necessary experience for the composer, but failure to obtain such is not by any means proof that the music is unworthy. On the other hand, success achieved through the powerful publicity of contemporary mass media is often devastatingly self-deceiving.[19]

Piston's repertoire includes mostly instrumental works: seven symphonies (1937–1960); a scintillating *Concertino* (1937), for piano and chamber orchestra; four string quartets (1933, 1935, 1947, 1951); two violin concertos (1939, 1960); a solidly constructed viola concerto (1958); and a vibrant piano quintet (1949).

One of his early successes was music for a ballet or dance play called *The Incredible Flutist,* performed in 1938 and again in 1939. The merry plot and the vivacious music were so successful that Piston extracted from the musical score a suite (1940) which has since become a standard item for orchestral concerts.

Roger Sessions

Roger Sessions (*b.*1896) writes distinctive music dominated by intellectualism and firm technical control. Endowed with an ability to absorb foreign elements and then convert them to his own approach, Sessions composes in a style distilled from Bloch, Stravinsky, and Schoenberg influences. To understand his sometimes abstract architectural language, the listener must listen to his works often and intensively. In 1927, speaking of his own generation, he expressed his artistic creed:

[19] From an article titled "Composers Must Stay Individual" in *The Christian Science Monitor,* October 18, 1958.

> Younger men are dreaming of an entirely different kind of music—a music which derives its power from forms beautiful and significant by virtue of inherent musical weight rather than intensity of utterance; a music whose impersonality and self-sufficiency preclude the exotic; which takes its impulse from the realities of a passionate logic; which, in the authentic freshness of its moods, is the reverse of ironic and, in its very aloofness from the concrete preoccupations of life, strives rather to contribute form, design, a vision of order and harmony.[20]

Sessions has composed five symphonies (1927–1964), a very difficult violin concerto (1935), a piano concerto (1956), an *Anglican Mass* (1958), and works in other media. His best-known single work is the orchestral suite *The Black Maskers* (1928) which he extracted from his incidental music for the symbolist drama of the same title by L. N. Andreyev (1871–1919). A later, more characteristic work is *Idyll of Theocritus* (1954), an expressionist tone poem for soprano and orchestra.

Virgil Thomson

Virgil Thomson (*b.*1896), one of many Americans to study with Nadia Boulanger in France, lived for 15 years (1925–1940) in Paris, where he found his true stylistic approach via Satie and *Les Six*. This contact with French music and French musicians explains some of the qualities that are now an integral part of his music: lucid expression and impeccable taste in treating musical materials. Thomson's irreverent façade, his attitude of self-spoofing, is merely part of his witty, sophisticated nature. In his many works he avoids excessive dissonance. He obtains variety through abrupt key changes, short forms, and rhythmic imaginativeness. He is not ashamed to be frankly sentimental; that is one reason why his music is instantly appealing.

An unusual yet congenial collaboration between Thomson and Gertrude Stein produced two unique operas that the composer regards as his most significant works: *Four Saints in Three Acts* (1928) and *The Mother of Us All* (1947). He has also produced some outstanding orchestral works: *Symphony on a Hymn Tune* (1928), *Second Symphony* (1931), and *Concerto for Violoncello and Orchestra* (1949). For the piano he has written sonatas, inventions, études, and "portraits." There are two string quartets among his chamber works. The *Missa Pro Defunctus* (Requiem Mass, 1960) is an important recent work.

Thomson's stature as a serious composer is supported by the orchestral suites that he extracted from his film music: *The Plough that Broke the Plains, The River,* and *Louisiana Story*. Robert Flaherty's documentary film *Louisiana Story* describes—through the eyes of a fourteen-year-old boy—the effect of an oil-development project in Louisiana on a French-speaking family. Thomson's film score won the Pulitzer Prize for music in 1949.

Thomson researched the songs and dances of the Acadian region to create background music for the film, then re-created their collective spirit. He made two orchestral suites (1948) from this score. Here is how he describes the first suite:

> The orchestral suite . . . consists of four movements: the Pastoral, describing bayous, the boy in his rowboat, and the maneuvers of the "marsh buggy,"

[20] From *Our New Music* by Aaron Copland, pp. 107–108. Copyright © 1941 by McGraw-Hill Book Company. Used by permission.

an amphibious bulldozer which is part of the oil-prospecting machinery [an English horn solo sets the mood for this section]; a Chorale, which represents the boy playing in a tree with his pet racoon and his view from there of the drill barge's majestic approach [the composer bases his Chorale on a twelve-tone row in deference to the mechanistic drill barge]; a Passacaglia, which recounts the boy's adventure in robbing an alligator's nest of its eggs, ending with the approach of the mother reptile [the composer creates an atmosphere of facetious suspense]; and a chromatic Fugue in four sections, which is used in the film to accompany the boy's fight to land an alligator that he has hooked with bait.[21]

The second suite, called *Acadian Songs and Dances,* contains seven movements strongly influenced by the waltz and polka rhythms of Cajun folk tunes and dances.

Quincy Porter

In a letter written less than a month before his death, Quincy Porter (1897–1966) analyzed his musical style in typical New England conversational prose:

> I feel that I have been leading toward my present style for quite a long time. I believe in melody (even lyric), and I believe that the rhythmic management of material is one of the most important things in music, too often forgotten about by the so-called avant gardists. To quote T. S. Eliot, "You gotta use words when you talk to me." That sort of fits in with my opinion as to what you have to do when you write music for other people to listen to. And the words can't be used just the same way that someone else used them, or you're not contributing very much to the musical scene. So I guess that what I've been doing, and still am, is to try to build a new vocabulary, and I hope it will turn out to be individual and yet comprehensible.[22]

Porter's down-to-earth philosophy about music stood him in good stead. His list of works is substantial, and—even more important—the mortality rate of his individual pieces has been remarkably low. His mature works show a good performance record, many of his compositions appear on recordings, and his music in general is well liked, all of which should guarantee Quincy Porter a firm place in the history of American music.

When asked which were his most important works, the composer hesitated. "I hate to say. The works written long ago appeal to me for their evident signs of youth, but I would not write that way any more. Four representative recent works are *Concerto Concertante for Two Pianos and Orchestra* [1953]; *Concerto for Harpsichord and Orchestra* [1959]; *Quintet for Oboe and Strings* [1966]; and *Variations for Violin and Piano* [1963]."

The first of these won the Pulitzer Prize in 1954. It was composed in Florence, Italy, while Porter was on sabbatical leave from Yale in 1952–1953. In some respects this concerto is magnified chamber music (Porter wrote nine string quartets and was an excellent violist himself), yet the orchestral writing has imposing moments. Porter gives the two pianists some striking passages, but in general he integrates the piano texture into the orchestral fabric. The work is remarkable in its depth of expression and unusual in that it contains imitative

[21] Program Notes for the Philadelphia Orchestra, November 26, 1948.

[22] Communication to the author, dated October 17, 1966.

writing—from short canons to whole fugal sections—which is a technique not too often apparent in Porter's music.

Paul Creston

Completely self-taught in harmony, counterpoint, orchestration, and composition, Paul Creston (*b.*1906) has composed more than 80 major works. His admiration for Bach, Scarlatti, Chopin, and the Impressionists has influenced his writing style.

> I have always been eclectic in my composition. There are and always have been in my music elements of classicism and romanticism, homophonic and contrapuntal treatments, tonality and pantonality, abstract and programmatic approaches—and *always* emphasis on the rhythmic basis of melody, harmony, counterpoint and form.[23]

Creston considers his five symphonies (1940–1955) to be his most significant works. Of these, the second and third are most frequently heard. *Symphony No. 2, Opus 35,* in two movements—Introduction and Song, Interlude and Dance—was completed in June, 1944, and premiered by the New York Philharmonic-Symphony Orchestra on February 15, 1945. Creston wrote the following explanatory notes for this first performance.

> In the opening of the Introduction are presented four themes as a cumulative ground bass, i.e., successively superimposed. Theme 1, played by cellos, and Theme 2, played by violas, are the main basis of the entire symphony. Whatever new thematic material emerges is either a ramification or a development of these two themes.
>
> The Song is largely built on a variation of Theme 1, tender and simple in character, presented first by the flute and then by the horn. . . .
>
> The Interlude opens with a completely transformed Theme 1, quite aggressive and defiant, leading to a rather quiet section, but soon returning to the aggressive character. This last merges into the Dance without pause, which after a rhythmic introduction begins with another variation of Theme 1 (muted trumpet). Each appearance of this variation of Theme 1 alters further the rhythm and contour of the melody. As the excitement mounts, Theme 2 soars above the ever-recurrent rhythmic pulses, developing to a climax and into the next section of the Dance. In the second section, based on a variation of Theme 1 inverted, the rhythmic pattern has changed and there is a greater sense of driving forward. This theme variant goes through several metamorphoses as the section builds to the major climax and then subsides to an altered version of the original cumulative ground bass. Above three concurrent rhythms which were presented separately earlier in the Dance, the flute theme of the song (now played by violins) becoming more and more intense, brings the composition to a close.

Elliott Carter

When the eminent English musicologist Wilfrid Mellers devotes an entire chapter of his book on music in the United States[24] to one American

[23] Communication to the author, dated September 12, 1966.

[24] Wilfrid Mellers, *Music in a New Found Land* (New York: Alfred A. Knopf, 1964), Part 1, Chapter 5.

composer—Elliott Carter (*b.*1908)—he obviously has a high opinion of that composer. Mr. Mellers views Carter as historically important because Carter's music represents a compromise—an attempt to synthesize the "pioneer heroism" of a Charles Ives with the disciplined order of an Aaron Copland.

Carter's works indicate that he has absorbed a number of influences, particularly from Copland, Piston, Stravinsky, and Hindemith. Nonetheless, he continues to be a notably original composer. Clashing tonalities (approaching atonality), fugal writing, intricate harmonic patterns, and a highly original rhythmic concept, which the composer calls "metric modulation," make his music difficult to assimilate at first hearing, but it is well worth closer examination.

A slow, deliberate composer, Carter has produced a comparatively small repertoire. His typical style formed around 1944 with the exuberant *Holiday Overture. Sonata* (1946), for piano, is a work of large proportions written while the composer held a Guggenheim Fellowship. He has a distinct talent for chamber music. His *Woodwind Quintet* (1948) is an example of meticulous neo-Classic workmanship; *Sonata for Violoncello and Piano* (1948) is an expressive work based on Carter's principle of metric modulation; *String Quartet No. 2* (1959) won him a Pulitzer Prize and two other awards. Among his later instrumental works, the *Variations for Orchestra* (1955) offers the listener a new experience in sonority. And in the *Double Concerto for Harpsichord and Piano with Two Chamber Orchestras* (1961), called a masterpiece by Stravinsky, Carter skillfully employs the challenging combination of plucked and struck strings.

William Schuman

William Schuman (*b.*1910) is primarily a symphonic composer. A former student of Roy Harris, he is a flexible musician even though at times he resembles Roger Sessions in his uncompromising approach. Critics admire Schuman's music for its bold, expansive melody, its intensity and rhythmic drive, its expressive counterpoint and bright sonority. His natural propensity for large-scale instrumental writing has resulted in eight symphonies (1935–1962), a *Concerto for Piano and Small Orchestra* (1942), and the *Concerto for Violin and Orchestra* (1959). His *Fourth String Quartet* (1950) is a fine chamber work.

Schuman describes the *American Festival Overture* (1939), his first notable success, in these words:

> The first three notes of this piece will be recognized by some listeners as the "call to play" of boyhood days. In New York City it is yelled on the syllables "Wee-Awk-Eee" to get the gang together for a game or a festive occasion of some sort. This call very naturally suggested itself for a piece of music being composed for a very festive occasion. From this it should not be inferred that the Overture is program music. In fact, the idea for the music came to my mind before the origin in the theme was recalled. The development of this bit of "folk material," then, is along purely musical lines.
>
> The first section of the work is concerned with the material discussed above and the ideas growing out of it. This music leads to a transition section and the subsequent announcement by the violas of a fugue subject. The entire middle section is given over to this fugue. The orchestration is at first for strings alone, later for woodwinds alone and finally, as the fugue is brought to fruition, by the strings and woodwinds in combination. This climax leads to the final section of the work, which consists of opening materials paraphrased and the introduction of new subsidiary ideas. The tempo of the work, save the last measures, is fast.[25]

[25] Program Notes for the Boston Symphony Orchestra, October 6, 1939.

Among Schuman's early symphonies, *No. 3* (1941) was his first major symphonic success, and it is still widely performed. In two movements—I, *Passacaglia and Fugue;* II, *Chorale and Toccata*—this symphony is constructed on a seventeenth-century framework but the language is definitely contemporary. *Symphony No. 4* (1941) has a neo-Classic cast and contrapuntal texture. In the three-movement *Symphony No. 5* (1943), for string orchestra, Schuman contrasts a highly rhythmic opening movement with a slow, sober central movement, and caps the structure with a brisk finale.

The one-movement *Symphony No. 6* (1948) consists of six differing sections, which Schuman molds into a compatible, uninterrupted unit. *Symphony No. 7* (1960) creates striking sonorities via an extraordinarily complex structure. Reviewing the world premiere of Schuman's *Symphony No. 8,* music critic Louis Biancolli reported in the *New York World-Telegram and Sun* of October 5, 1962:

> Commissioned and performed by the Philharmonic under Leonard Bernstein, the latest score by the versatile president of Lincoln Center is by far the most cogent and gripping he has written to date. . . . From start to finish, it is a wholly consistent work. Idiom, melodic shape, rhythmic drive, all head towards one inevitable goal. There is fresh creative pulse here; also a welcome subjective note far removed from the barren and the abstract.

Norman Dello Joio

Contrasting textures and a taste for the very old and the very new—these elements identify the music of Norman Dello Joio (*b.*1913). Quite often he weaves Gregorian themes into a clear, precise contemporary fabric. Although Dello Joio admittedly writes in a modern spirit, his music frequently shows a need for emotional expression that is decidedly Romantic and reflects his Italian background. His writing can be easy and relaxed or it can overflow with dissonant harmony and exuberance.

He has written in various media. *Ricercari* (1946), for piano and orchestra, is based on an old contrapuntal form that grew into the fugue. Dello Joio develops his basic idea in three ways—harmonically, melodically, and rhythmically—and each treatment is displayed in a separate movement: *Allegretto giocoso, Adagio,* and *Allegro vivo*. Equally unusual and ingratiating, the *Concerto for Harp and Orchestra* (1944) recalls old music in its first movement, *Introduction and Passacaglia;* and in the second movement, *Scherzo—March,* the composer allows the harpist a wonderful opportunity for a virtuoso performance.

Written for orchestra, the *Variations, Chaconne and Finale* (1947) won the New York Music Critics Circle award for 1949. All the movements are based on the Kyrie of the Gregorian *Missa de Angelis* (a theme the composer also used in his *Third Piano Sonata,* 1948). The first movement consists of a prologue and six character variations. The *Chaconne* is built on the first four notes of the Gregorian theme and is very Baroque in its architectural polish. The dynamic *Finale* introduces a fastidious dance element that never conflicts with the religious background of the basic theme; this movement stresses melodic repetition and ends with a vivacious outburst.

Two more Dello Joio orchestral works are *New York Profiles* (1949) and *Meditations on Ecclesiastes* (Pulitzer Prize, 1957).

David Diamond

The composer-painter David Diamond (*b.*1915) studied composition with both Roger Sessions and Nadia Boulanger. This prolific composer, recipient of three Guggenheim Fellowships and other awards and honors, has written to date eleven string quartets, nine symphonies, and 75 songs, all of which he believes are representative works. There are, however, many other compositions: works for piano, music for various chamber ensembles, and film scores.

Diamond's early works—*Concerto for Chamber Orchestra* (1940), *Concerto for Two Pianos* (1941), and *Rounds for String Orchestra* (1944)—brought him well-deserved acclaim, for in them he deftly clothed neo-Romantic and neo-Classic elements in compact, dissonant language. His later works—*Eighth Symphony* (1962), *Sinfonia Concertante* (1955), and *String Quartet No. 4* (1951)—are more complex and present an uncompromising listening experience. The composer himself describes this change in style as "from a severe diatonic (harmonic and thematic) apparatus to a tempered chromatic-polyphonic technique (quartets 7, 10 and symphonies 5 and 8 best examples)."[26]

The round, customarily associated with vocal music, shows greater potentialities in Diamond's *Rounds for String Orchestra.* He had this to say in a program note for his work, which was premiered by the Minneapolis Symphony on November 24, 1944:

> The different string choirs enter in strict canonic fashion as an introduction to the main subject, which is played by the violas and soon restated by the cellos and basses. The Adagio is an expressive lyric movement, acting as a resting point between the two fast movements. The last movement again makes use of characteristic canonic devices, though it may more specifically be analyzed as a kind of fugal countersubject for the principal thematic ideas, so helping to "round" out the entire work and unify the entire formal structure.

Vincent Persichetti

Although he has written in other media—seven symphonies, at least thirteen serenades, much chamber music—Vincent Persichetti (*b.*1915) prefers to write keyboard compositions: eleven piano sonatas, six sonatinas, and a sonata for harpsichord. His music is a joy for pianists because he writes in a supremely pianistic idiom. His *Third Piano Sonata* (published 1945) has three rather unusual movements: *Declaration,* which keeps changing tempo and involves the entire keyboard; *Episode,* where two broad melodic lines alternate in an essentially homophonic texture; and a *Hymn* whose organlike sonorities introduce deceiving simplicity: a rapidly moving section forms the coda to this last movement.

At his best in large instrumental forms, Persichetti chooses as his most significant works the *Symphony for Strings* (1954), *Quintet for Piano and Strings* (1950), *Eleventh Piano Sonata,* and *Concerto for Piano, Four Hands* (1952) "because of their large architectural form created by the 'in one movement' concept and their amalgamation of the various materials and techniques of the 20th century." Further proof of the composer's eclecticism lies within this statement:

[26] Communication to the author, dated September 9, 1966.

> I am not a member of any one camp of composers. I use the available material, tonal and non-tonal, serial and non-serial, etc. to express my musical ideas. I do not specialize in any one segment of 20th century resources but synthesize and amalgamate the wide gamut of material of our time.[27]

Other composers who may feasibly be considered eclectic or perhaps neo-Classic are Louise Talma (*b.*1906) and Halsey Stevens (*b.*1908), a composer-scholar who has written the definitive study of Bartók (*The Life and Music of Béla Bartók*).

COMPOSERS USING SERIAL TECHNIQUES

Wallingford Riegger

Wallingford Riegger (1885–1961) began experimenting with atonality in 1927. In the thirties he theoretically adopted the principle of tone rows but applied it in a completely personal manner. Even in his mature works he does not bind himself stringently to serial procedures but reverts to tonality whenever he feels impelled to do so. Basically, Riegger creates key motives from the tone row and then develops these motives traditionally. His music is original, clear-textured, and enriched with natural integrity.

Riegger composed generously for the modern dance, for dancers such as Martha Graham, Charles Weidman, and Doris Humphrey. One work written for Doris Humphrey was *New Dance* (1935), for piano duet and drums. He later rewrote it for two pianos, for piano solo, and finally for orchestra (1942). The *Finale* from *New Dance,* with its Latin-American rhythms, has been especially well received in concert performances.

Riegger's atonal experiments influenced his orchestral work *Dichotomy* (1932), where he uses two different tone rows, one with eleven tones, the other with thirteen. He employed a strict twelve-tone idiom for *First String Quartet* (1938), a work that adheres precisely to the Schoenberg school. Proof of Riegger's complete mastery of serialization and his musicianly handling of dodecaphony is apparent in a later work: *Symphony No. 3, Opus 24* (1948; revised in 1957 as *Opus 42*).

Ernst Krenek

The Vienna-born Ernst Krenek (*b.*1900) developed his style from several sources: stark rhythms from primitive music, elements from jazz music, and patterns based on abstract expression. He bases his mature style on the "aggressive idiom of atonality, whose main organizing agency was elemental rhythmic force." This is only part of the picture, for he also states that "since the early 50's I have occupied myself very extensively with serial methods of composition but not at all exclusively."[28]

Krenek's music—intensely and successfully abstract—is too severely intellectual to be universally popular, but he seems unwilling to sacrifice his musical ideals for any reason. His large catalog lists 18 stage works, ballet music, inciden-

[27] Communication to the author, dated September 15, 1966.

[28] Communication to the author, dated September 9, 1966.

tal music, film music, orchestral music, electronic music, vocal and choral music, and chamber music. Despite the difficulties they create for the listener, many of his compositions have been recorded.

Other composers who use twelve-tone techniques are Ross Lee Finney (*b.*1906), Ingolf Dahl (*b.*1912), George Perle (*b.*1915), Ellis Kohs (*b.*1916), and George Rochberg (*b.* 1918).

THE AVANT-GARDE

While searching for new expressive means and fresh musical language, some composers have tried unorthodox techniques. Thus they are here classified as members of the avant-garde even though they may have written some music adhering to traditional patterns.

George Antheil

One of the pioneer iconoclasts, George Antheil (1900–1959) ardently advocated "an anti-expressive, anti-romantic, coldly mechanistic aesthetic," which led him to create his notorious *Ballet méchanique* (1924). His original score specified eight pianos, player piano, and airplane propeller, but he later revised the score to include more pianos as well as anvils, bells, automobile horns, and buzz saws. Antheil leaped to fame as "the bad boy of music."

Edgard Varèse

Other composers were more serious in their search for new music. Paris-born Edgard Varèse (1885–1965), who came to the United States in 1915, made dissonance the fundamental element in his music. He subtly contrasted tone colors and rhythms, and he built his polyphony by adding one layer of sound to another, creating strange works that are perplexing and often exotic. Even the titles hint that new sensations await the listener: *Offrandes* (1922), *Octandre* (1923), *Hyperprism* (1923), *Intégrales* (1925), *Ionisation* (1931), *Density 21.5* (1936). With the advent of electronic media, Varèse took advantage of the new discoveries and wrote a *Poème électronique* (1958). He had predicted electronic music 30 years ago.

His most publicized work, *Ionisation,* requires 13 performers who must play a large variety of hissing, banging, and scraping instruments—plus two sirens. Each section of the composition is identified by a special instrumental combination or sound range. Once accustomed to the dissonant language, the listener can discern the superior architecture and masterful sonority in these unusual essays.

Henry Cowell

Henry Cowell (1897–1965) tried to create new sounds with the piano, and from about 1912 to 1925 he composed several piano pieces that have expanded that instrument's potential. For example, in *The Tides of Manaunaun* (1912) the pianist must play tone clusters of over two octaves with his left forearm; in *The Banshee* (1925) the performer is instructed to reach inside the piano lid to strum the strings.

These pieces show one side of Henry Cowell. Besides his unorthodox works he composed the fine series of *Hymns and Fuguing Tunes* (1944–1950), for various combinations of instruments; he also wrote 15 symphonies, Irish reels, ballads, and other compositions.

Luening and Ussachevsky

Musique concrète has advanced rapidly in the United States, largely because of the efforts of two pioneers in this field: Otto Luening (*b.*1900) and Vladimir Ussachevsky (*b.*1911). By manipulating sound tapes through splicing and speed variation, they create a musical dimension that reaches the listener without benefit of "live" interpretation. Their combined imagination and ingenuity have produced such works as *Rhapsodic Variations for Tape Recorder and Orchestra* (1954) and *A Poem in Cycles and Bells* (1954).

John Cage

John Cage (*b.*1912) is the experimenter par excellence in that he is continually looking for new sounds, new techniques, and new ways to compose. Cage describes his development as a composer according to the type of works produced during each writing phase:

> Chromatic composition dealing with the problem of keeping repetitions of individual tones as far apart as possible (1933–34); composition with fixed rhythmic patterns or tone-row fragments (1935–38); composition for the dance, film and theatre (1935–); composition within rhythmic structures (the whole having as many parts as each unit has small parts, and these, large and small, in the same proportion (1939–56); intentionally expressive composition (1938–51); composition using charts and moves thereon (1951); composition using chance operations (1951–); composition using templates made or found (1952–); composition using observation of imperfections in the paper upon which it is written (1952–); composition without a fixed relation of parts to score (1954–); composition indeterminate of its performance (1958–).[29]

Whereas Henry Cowell introduced new methods for vibrating piano strings, John Cage inserted pieces of felt, rubber, wood, and even screws, nuts, and bolts between the strings to gain his desired effects. In his music for "prepared piano"—16 sonatas, four interludes, *Amores* (for prepared piano and percussion, 1943)—these muffled, transformed piano sonorities create a wide variety of intricate rhythms. One of his most characteristic percussion pieces, *Third Construction* (1941), calls for four percussionists. "Instruments" used include wooden sticks, tin cans, rattles, drums, cowbells, lion's roar, cymbal, ratchet, cricket caller, conch shell, and others.

John Cage's most famous single composition is *Fontana Mix* (1958) for magnetic tape. The "score" includes "parts to be prepared from the score for the

[29] Foreword to the *Catalogue* of Cage's works (New York: Henmar Press, Inc., 1962).

production of any number of tracks of magnetic tape, or for any number of players, any kind and number of instruments."

Henry Brant

> Henry Brant is the world's foremost experimenter in the field of antiphonal music—that is, music in which separate groups of performers are placed at some distance from each other so that the sounds come to the listener from several different directions. It is a concept that is currently becoming more familiar to the general public with the increased interest in stereophonic recordings.[30]

Having studied with three composers who possess sharply differing styles—George Antheil, Aaron Copland, and Wallingford Riegger—Henry Brant (*b.*1913) naturally developed a liberal attitude toward composing. During the 1930s he broadened his musical education even further, working as orchestrator and arranger for André Kostelanetz, Benny Goodman, and others. One of the early works created by this composer's fertile imagination was *Angels and Devils* (1932), a concerto for eleven flutes—solo flute, three piccolos, five flutes, and two alto flutes. Since then he has produced several concertos for different solo instruments—clarinet, saxophone, viola, violin—and ensembles. Brant's *Violin Concerto with Lights* (1961) requires a solo violin, orchestra, and projected light patterns notated musically and performed by five musicians working push buttons. Besides these concertos he has written considerable antiphonal orchestral and chamber music.

Brant recently explained his unique approach in composing.

> Charles Ives began the exploration of musical space and was the first to venture into territory where amalgams of sound may proceed simultaneously without rhythmic coordination. No one, subsequently, has interested himself in the systematic codification of a musical spatial grammar, or in the definition of the boundaries at which controlled rhythmic freedom ends and accident begins.
>
> My music, since 1950, has concentrated on these areas, and I have noted my conclusions on the theoretical bases which underlie them in my prose writing[31] on spatial orchestration and the effects of distance and position on harmony, rhythm and counterpoint.[32]

Milton Babbitt

A trained mathematician, Milton Babbitt (*b.*1916) brought his disciplined thinking and scientific spirit with him when he decided on a composing career. After World War II, Babbitt started working with the twelve-tone system; later he became a director of the Electronic Music Center operated jointly by Columbia and Princeton Universities. In both fields—serial music and electronic music—he has achieved some unexpectedly interesting results.

Babbitt lists his most significant instrumental works as being *Partitions* (1957), for piano, *Composition for Four Instruments* (1948), *Composition for Twelve Instruments* (1948), *All Set* (1957), for jazz ensemble, and *Relata*

[30] Howard Shanet in the New York Philharmonic Program Notes, March 31, 1960.

[31] See *Bennington Review,* Vol. 1, No. 1 (published by Bennington College, Bennington, Vermont).

[32] Communication to the author, dated September 1966.

(1965). Among his works with electronic synthesizer, he favors *Vision and Prayer* (1961), for soprano and synthesized accompaniment, *Ensembles for Synthesizer* (1964), and *Philomel* (1964), for soprano, recorded soprano, and synthesized accompaniment.

Larry Austin

Larry Austin (*b.*1930), one of the most imaginative and creative of the younger composers, has given much time and thought to what he calls "total art improvisations." This preoccupation with improvisation is closely allied with his genuine interest in jazz and its potential in contemporary music. One concrete result of Austin's explorations in these areas is *Improvisations for Symphony Orchestra and Jazz Soloists* (1961).

Austin uses the term "open style" to describe his works based on the relative motion of sounds in time. *Open Style for Orchestra with Piano Soloist* (1965) and *The Maze: A Theatre Piece in Open Style for Three Percussionists, Tape, Projections, and Conductor* (1965) illustrate his novel approach to musical creativity. The latter piece lasts 16 minutes, corresponding to the length of the tape used.

Austin's fertile imagination also challenges the listener with aleatory music. Austin describes one of these compositions, *Accidents* (Ex. 26:4—see two-page color example following Ill. 26:1) in the following notes written especially for this book:

> *Accidents* is an open form. The piece ends when the performer successfully completes every gesture in the piece. Sound is produced through accidental rather than deliberate action; i.e., all notes are depressed silently, and sound occurs only when a hammer accidentally strikes a string. *Accidents* occur, depending on the key action, the pressure applied to the keys (i.e., the speed), and the preparation of the strings. The music is read in the conventional way from left to right through the six systems in order. When an *accident* occurs, the player immediately stops playing that gesture and proceeds immediately to the next. Arriving at the last gesture and trying to complete it, the player returns to each of the gestures in which an *accident* occurred, always trying to complete them without an *accident*. With each new try the gesture is begun anew, and each time the uncompleted gestures are read in left-to-right, numbered order.
>
> There are 10 gestures: 3 in the first system, described by the three largest horizontal cross-bars; 2 in the second system, the first ending midway in the system; 1 in the third (the entire system); 2 in the fourth system, the first ending almost halfway through; 1 in the fifth (the entire system); and 1 in the sixth (the entire system). Notes are played according to their relative spatial relationship; *time* is proportionately equal to *space*. The piece should always be played as fast as possible—at the most hazardous pace, making *accidents* highly probable. With successive performances it is possible that the player may develop techniques to avoid *accidents;* this happening, the performer should counter such gradually acquired technique by playing faster and with more abandon.
>
> Five types of notation are used: (1) a black, square notehead, ▪, represents a black key; (2) a white rectangle, ▯, a white key; (3) the end of a headless stem, is either a black or white key; (4) clouds of dashes, , indicate random "wiggling" of the fingers over a random selection of black and white keys; and (5) a long, black and white rectangle, , represents a cluster of black and white keys played with the flat of the hand(s) or the forearm(s), the range depending on the size. Though the general area of the selection of keys is indicated by their position relative to the keyboard at the beginning of each system, specific selection of the keys to be depressed is left to chance.
>
> The piano is prepared as follows:

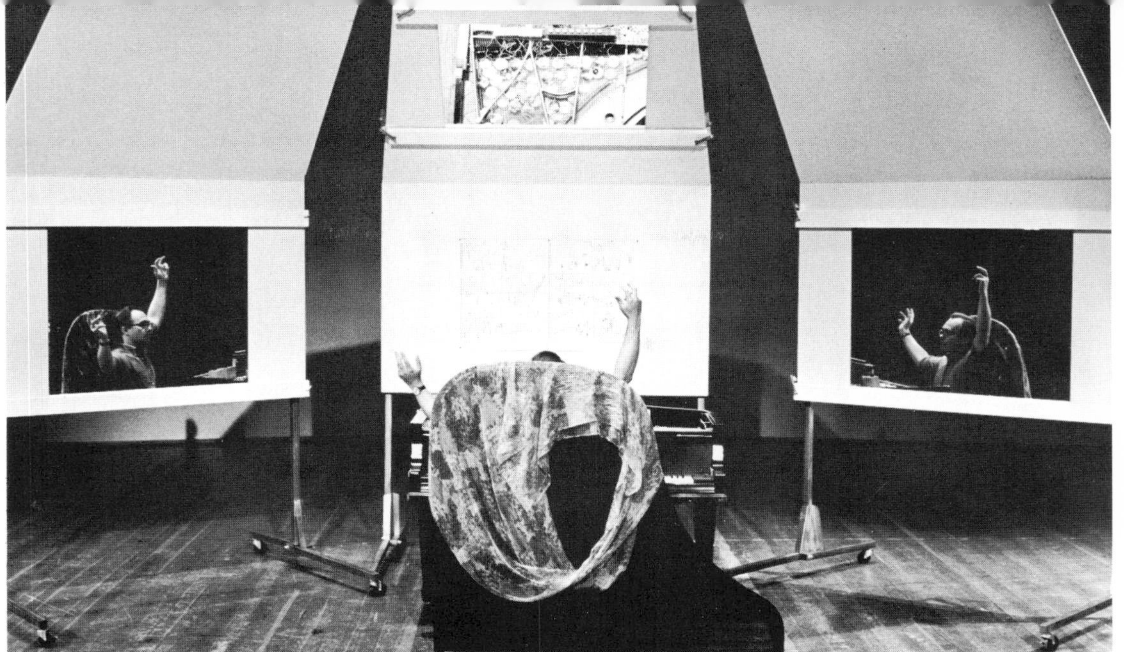

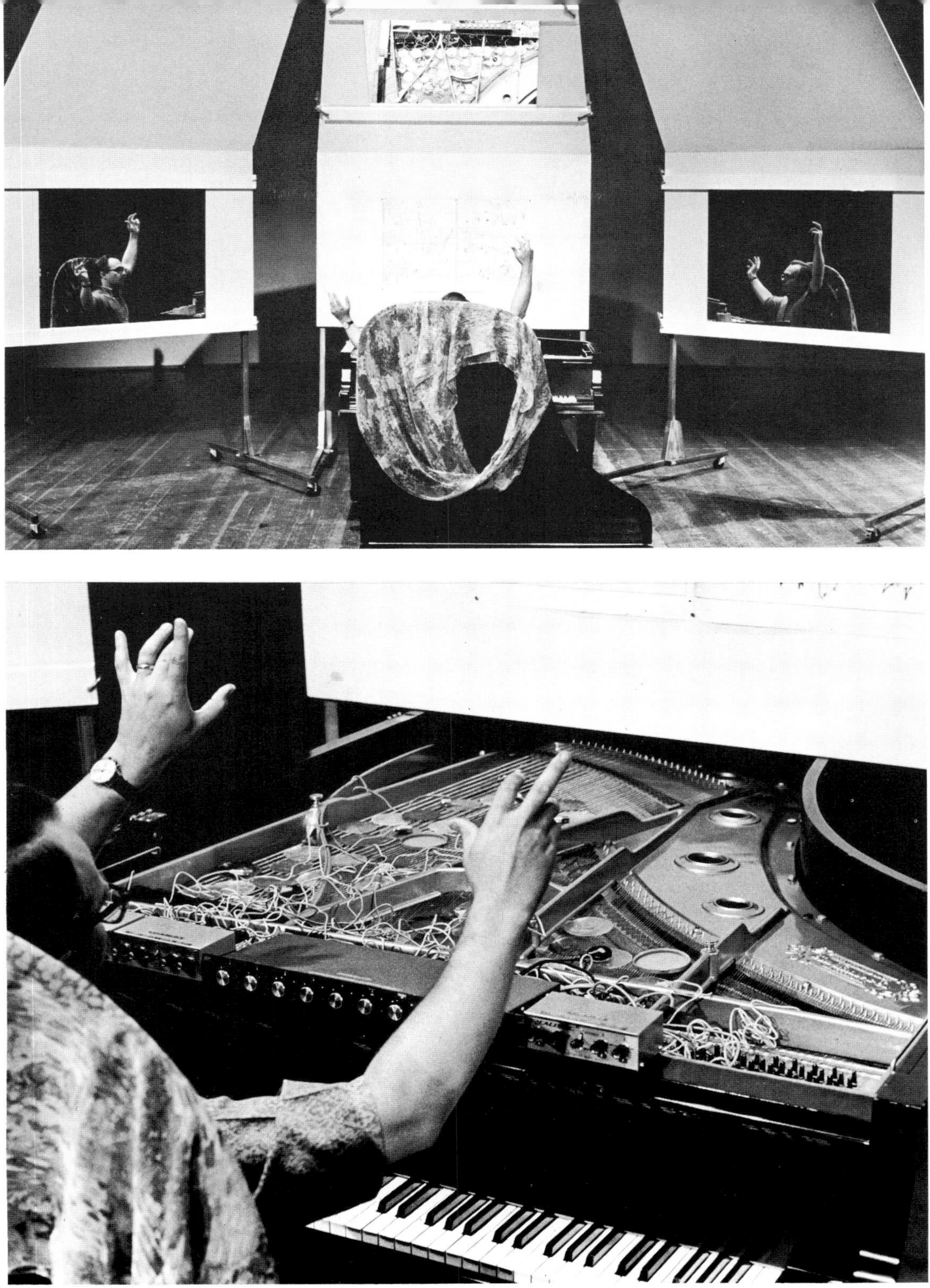

Ill. 26:1. ***A performance of*** **Accidents** ***by the composer, Larry Austin. Courtesy of David Freund.***

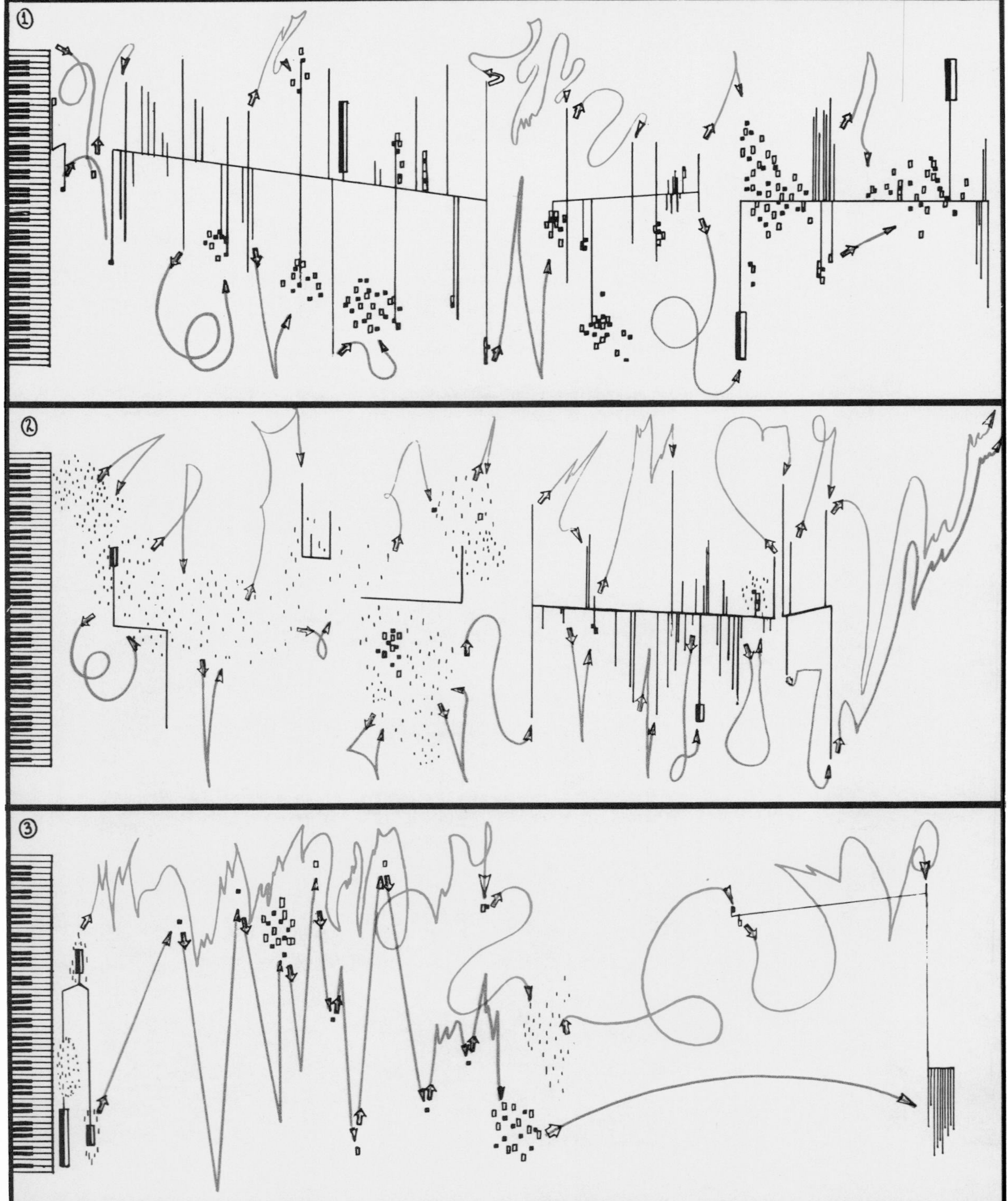
①
②
③

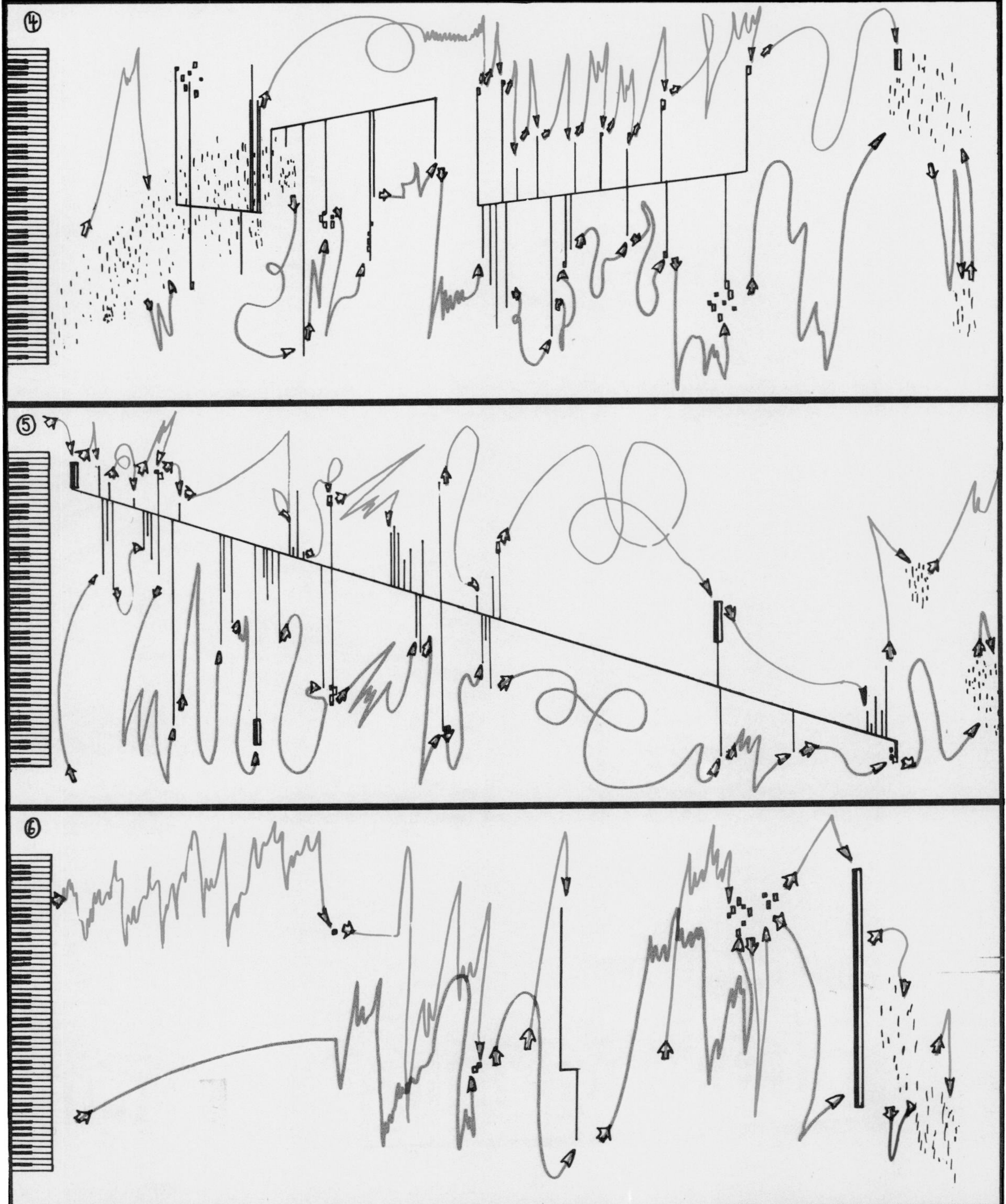

④
⑤
⑥

Ill. 26:2. *The piano used for* Accidents. *Courtesy of David Freund.*

(1) the sustaining pedal is fixed so that it is constantly engaged, all strings then vibrating freely;
(2) a number of shell wind chimes (or similarly light, thin, membranous materials) are placed over the strings so that most, if not all of the strings are in direct contact with the freely vibrating shells;
(3) a large number (at least 16) of contact microphones, guitar pickups, and cartridges are scattered over but not attached to the shells, so that they transmit the slightest vibration to as many as six but no less than two speakers spaced about the hall so that the sound seems not to come from the piano but from other places in the hall.

The dynamic range of the sounds can neither be controlled nor predicted. In general, however, this will depend on the strength of the sound of the accidents, the sensitivity of the electronic equipment, and, finally, the discretion of the player. The player should have an assistant controlling and varying the strength of the signals. Feedback is probable and should be exploited. It will be found that signals, once initiated, can be prolonged in this way and occasionally modulated by the next accident—and the next, etc.

The performer may choose one of two possibilities for the tape which accompanies the piece: (1) a tape storage system, wherein all accidents are "stored" and played back at strategic moments during the performance, or, (2) a prepared tape, available from the composer, which is played continuously during the performance. The taped sounds should be mixed with the live sounds.

Mirrors, Actions, and Projections

The piece should be carefully staged [see Ills. 26:1 and 26:2]. The piano keyboard faces the audience with the player seated with his back to the audience. Directly behind and attached to his chair is the piano lid, standing vertically so that only the top of the player's head and his upraised, gesturing arms can be seen. Draped attractively over the lid is some soft, luxurious, colorful material. At the other end of the piano stands the music and several large mirrors strategically placed so that the player's reflected visage can be seen from any point in the hall. A single powerful spotlight illuminates the area from behind the player so that sharp shadows are cast on the music by the player's gesturing hands. Choice of dress is left to the player.

Two actions are made by the player: (1) highly stylized, highly exaggerated motions of the hands and arms above the keyboard and visible to the audience, as indicated by the red (right hand) and the green (left hand) lines on the score, the arrows simply designating the relative direction of the gesture; (2) a new and always more menacing facial grimace with each successive *accident*.

Note: If electronic equipment is not available, the piece may be played without microphones, tape, and amplification.

SUMMARY: THE TWENTIETH CENTURY

To date, twentieth-century music has witnessed many trends and constant experimentation. The refinements, delicacy, and lush sonorities of Impressionism—a limited language—now appear only occasionally. The neo-Romanticism (actually not "neo" at all) of Strauss and Sibelius continues to some extent in the music of composers who feel that a complete break with the immediate past is unnecessary and ill-advised.

Neo-Classicism, a style advocated by a large group of eclectic composers, frequently depends on eighteenth-century form (suite, concerto) and technique (use of counterpoint), but its language is definitely of this century.

Dodecaphony began in the highly original works of Schoenberg, Webern, and Berg and has remained—through various transformations and mutations—one of the strongest influences on contemporary composers.

The avant-garde music created by imaginative and frequently very talented composers explores one radical aesthetic after another, offering the listener musical experiences—*musique concrète,* electronic music, aleatory music, and combinations of these media—that sometimes defy description.

This century has created new problems for the listener, for out of the many mixed styles and techniques employed by modern composers the listener must decide what he likes best and try to understand it. Modern emphasis on dissonance requires that the listener readjust his listening attitude: he can no longer expect that music will necessarily convey sadness or joy or some other human emotion or that it will be written only to create lyrical, emotional beauty; he must learn to approach contemporary music with the mind more than the emotions.

Today it is difficult for the listener to keep abreast of the composer. Until the present century he could usually follow the composer's intentions; he could analyze the music and thus better understand it. Now, particularly in serial and experimental music, he often finds it impossible to determine the music's design without having previously studied the score, and sometimes even professional musicians cannot understand modern works. Inevitably, a large part of the composer's intent is lost on his audience.

Some writers and critics are especially alarmed about the avant-garde and make little effort to conceal their feelings.

> It's Dada. It's sound for sound's sake. It's high camp. It's ear-grating and annoying. It's social commentary. It's infuriating. But is it music? Cage and his followers say yes. They invoke fearsome terms: cybernetics, game theory, Heisenberg, uncertainty, existentialism, DNA, the laser. Before these we are supposed to crouch and shudder. The Mage has spoken: John Cage, deadpan, in his wizard's robes, waving a wand with a *G* clef among runes that convey the mystery of scientific formulae.[33]

Some disenchanted listeners feel that the younger composers have left their audiences out of the musical experience entirely.

> These young musicians speak a language that was minted just last week. It is a language heavily indebted to modern physics and mathematics, those 20th Century equivalents of medieval religion and alchemy. Where two composers might be heard not long ago discussing music in terms of first theme, development, *ritornello,* coda, countersubject, and so forth, the cant words now are stochastic (predetermined) and aleatoric (chance), random and indeterminate, row and set, parameters and combinatoriality. Like any argot, this new language serves the dubious function of identifying the In group to its members, and the most modish concept can immediately become passé if the group suspects outsiders are about to grasp it. Electronic music, another important wing of the new music, has contributed such terms as white noise, dubbing, sine wave, tape loop, square wave, saw-tooth pitches and formants.[34]

This is of course a vastly one-sided picture; there are more sympathetic critics who view today's experimental composers with objectivity.

[33] "Does Anybody Need the Avant-Garde?," an article by Discus in *Harper's,* June 1966.

[34] "Serious Music: In Serious Trouble," an article by Donal J. Henahan in *Holiday,* March 1966.

Poseurs? Buffoons? Opportunists? One is tempted to say yes, until he considers the lessons of history. The critics wrote "crude . . . incomprehensible . . . ugly," when Beethoven's music was first played. A half-century later the same derision was heaped on Brahms and Wagner; Tchaikovsky and Puccini endured raging storms of critical scorn. Critics who found Wagner's melodies lacking would have gone home whistling all his tunes if they could have foreseen Alban Berg's *Wozzeck,* which now sounds comfy and old-hat beside the latest electronic tone-poem.[35]

This is the music of our time and we must attempt to comprehend it fully. Our most important contemporary composers approach their art very seriously. We in turn must approach the art of listening with special respect for today's music and with the realization that after all—and despite some derisive remarks to the contrary—it has been written for us, the listeners.

FOR DISCUSSION AND ASSIGNMENT

1. American musical history is only about 200 years old. That of Europe goes back many hundreds of years. Do you think that our contemporary music equals its European counterpart in quality? Does quality depend on a temporal factor or on other factors?
2. Do you think *musique concrète* and electronic music have a future? If so, will this future eventually eliminate live concerts?
3. From our survey it is obvious that there is a great quantity of American contemporary music, much of it seldom heard. What must be done to interest the average intelligent listener in the music of our time?
4. What style of contemporary music interests you most? Give your reasons.

FOR FURTHER READING

Barzun, Jacques. *Music in American Life.* Bloomington, Ind.: Indiana University Press, 1956. A Midland PB. This discerning essay deals with the present state and possible future of music in America.

Chase, Gilbert. *America's Music,* Revised Second Edition. New York: McGraw-Hill Book Co., Inc., 1966. Absolutely the finest book on this subject obtainable. In addition, Mr. Chase's skillful style makes the book a pleasure to read.

Howard, John Tasker, and George Kent Bellows. *A Short History of Music in America.* New York: Thomas Y. Crowell Co., 1957. PB. A readable, uncomplicated account of American music and its development. It provides a generally acceptable introduction, although it was originally published ten years ago and is therefore not up-to-date.

Machlis, Joseph. *American Composers of Our Time.* New York: Thomas Y. Crowell Co., 1963. A well-proportioned survey of American composers and their music.

———. *Introduction to Contemporary Music.* New York: W. W. Norton & Co., Inc., 1961. Although Mr. Machlis concentrates more on European composers, there is still much relevant material on American music to be found here.

[35] "Sound: But Is It Music?," an article by Alan Rich in *House Beautiful,* September 1966.

Mellers, Wilfrid. *Music in a New Found Land.* New York: Alfred A. Knopf, 1964. Subtitled "Themes and Developments in the History of American Music," this book traces America's progress in music. Professor Mellers is an Englishman who writes interestingly and informatively.

Note: Broadcast Music, Inc. (589 Fifth Avenue, New York City) publishes a quantity of composer brochures (brief biographies, press reviews, and catalogs of works), which may be obtained upon request.

Vistas Old and New | 27

> Written music is like handcuffs; and so is the pendulum in white-tie-and-tails up in the conductor's stand. Symphony means slavery in any jazzman's dictionary. Jazz and freedom are synonymous. . . . One-hundred-men-with-a-fuehrer, a music battalion hypnotized by a director's baton—that's no kind of a set-up for a man's inspired soul to shake loose and jump out of his instrument in a flood of carefree, truth-speaking, right-from-the-heart music.
>
> MEZZROW AND WOLFE
> *Really the Blues**

In the second part of this book we have traced the historical and stylistic development of Western classical and contemporary music from the known beginnings in Greece to the imaginative, often provocative music of the avant-garde—a development spanning more than 2,000 years.

Yet until now we have neglected some music. What of the music of the people, the folk music that has enriched every culture? What of the classical music of non-Western cultures, the exotic music from the Middle East and the Far East? And what of jazz, the music that has significantly influenced American life during the last half century? All these various types of music are historically important and intrinsically interesting. Although we cannot devote many pages to them in this book, it is essential to our musical experience that we at least have an introduction to them.

We feel that our present folk-song revival has given us new, refreshing music, yet folk music is most likely as old as language itself. Even jazz, that unique product of twentieth-century America, is a compound of other musical types—popular song, African tribal music, European music—that reach far back into history.

Non-occidental music, frequently defined simply as *exotic* music, provides an exception, for nothing about this vast repertoire seems contemporary. It proceeds as it has for centuries—dignified, mysterious, and ageless—yet at this

* Copyright 1946 by Random House, Inc. Reprinted by permission of the Harold Matson Company, Inc.

moment an increasing number of people are finding pleasure and meaning in this music from the East.

Folk music, jazz, and exotic music are all pertinent to the study of music appreciation; they are inherently worthwhile and enjoyable, and beyond that each has exercised a beneficial influence on the contemporary music written by European and American composers.

FOLK SONG

It may be argued that folk song should have been discussed earlier in the book, since there have been folk songs from time immemorial. The point is valid, and it is also true that many pre-twentieth-century composers—Haydn, Beethoven, Brahms, among others—showed more than a passing interest in folk music.

We discuss this type of music at this point because all folk music, both authentic and distilled, has become immensely popular within recent years, especially in the United States. Young and old alike sing it for pleasure and listen to it with obvious enjoyment. There are two reasons for including folk music in a music-appreciation text: first, within its own context it is meaningful music having a distinctive aesthetic; second, folk song has been and continues to be an inspirational source for many serious composers, particularly nationalist writers.

Our discussion of folk song will be noticeably brief, mostly due to the nature of the music itself. Since folk song is uncomplicated, its message reaches the listener directly and simply; no preparation is needed to understand and enjoy it. Basically, we should know what constitutes folk song and which types have survived. For practical purposes, we will concentrate on the English and American repertoires, where language poses no problem.

The *Century Dictionary* of 1889 defines folk song as "a song of the people; a song based on a legendary or historical event, or some incident of common life, the words and generally the music of which have originated among the common people, and are extensively used by them."

Funk and Wagnall's *New "Standard Dictionary"* (1960) states that the folk song is "a song or ballad originating and current among the common people, and illustrating the common life with its interests and enthusiasms as derived from legend or story; also a lyric poem on a popular or familiar theme in the style of such a ballad."

British folk-song collectors make a distinction between folk song (composer or composers unknown) and popular song. Unfortunately this difference is often ignored in the United States, where the term "folk song" applies not only to a genuine work produced by the folk mind but also to homely songs that have become widely accepted (the songs of Stephen Foster, for example) and to the "folk songs" that today's folk singers turn out so readily for popular consumption.

Generally speaking, true folk songs bear certain common characteristics. Their most prominent trait is strophic structure; that is, a folk song consists of several stanzas—with or without refrain—sung to one melody. The typical folk-song melody derives from a seven-tone scale—folk songs often have a modal character—although some are based on the pentatonic (five-tone) scale. Most

European and American folk melodies adhere to the concept of a regular metrical scheme and are, furthermore, strictly monodic. There is very little evidence of any traditional folk harmony.

Folk songs usually maintain a close relationship between words and music: musical and poetic lines coincide, and the music employs cadence points to fit the inflection of the text. On the whole, folk-song tunes are finer than their words, a fact suggesting that education is less essential in composing a tune than in writing a poem.

The words to some songs have often been corrupted by successive singers so that lines or expressions no longer make sense. Frequently obsolete, meaningless phrases appear in these texts, and sometimes the words have a religious significance that has been lost. Folk songs are not restricted to any traditional subjects. Mostly they pour out heartfelt emotions—love, sorrow, betrayal, mirth, anxiety, and the like. In every country some folk songs relate to specific occupations that they accompany—for instance, songs sung by railroad workers, mule drivers, field hands, miners, and lumber jacks. As the dictionary states, most folk songs describe "some incident of common life."

The most practical way to survey the American folk-song repertoire is to divide the songs into a few broad categories and mention a few examples from each. These categories are war songs, songs of occupation or work songs, songs of the homeless, spirituals, songs of protest, and frontier songs.

War Songs

Each time the United States has fought a war it has added new, pertinent folk songs to its folk repertoire. Many war songs go back to the American Revolution. Such a song is "Johnny Has Gone for a Soldier" (Ly 192),[1] which is based on an Irish song. One of our most beloved and durable folk songs, "Yankee Doodle" (Lx 23), originated with the British redcoats as a satire of the American militiaman. Later the Americans adopted it as a kind of unofficial national anthem.

The Civil War provoked poignant, emotional songs. "Goober Peas" (Lx 52) is an ironical rebel song about the rationing of chick-peas to the starving Southern troops. The most popular song to come out of the Civil War is the heart-rending "When Johnny Comes Marching Home" (Ly 196). Another fine text uses the same tune: "Johnny, I Hardly Knew Ye."

World War I songs—"Over There," "Pack Up Your Troubles in Your Old Kit Bag," "Johnny Get Your Gun," "Goodbye Broadway, Hello France"—are more like popular songs than folk songs, for songwriters at the time concentrated on patriotic ballads.

> There was relatively little singing in World War II, and the songs the soldiers sang were neither gay nor crusading and, though satirical, not very humorous. They picked up the Australian song "Waltzing Matilda," they borrowed a German commercial song "Lili Marlene" and made it a kind of folk song in a few months. . . .[2]

[1] "Ly" and "Lx" in this chapter refer to the folk-song collections by James F. Leisy and Alan Lomax (see Bibliography). Numbers refer to pages on which the songs may be found.

[2] Reprinted from *The Story of American Folk Song* by Russell Ames, p. 170. Copyright 1955 by Russell Ames, by permission of Grosset & Dunlap, Inc., the publisher.

Songs of Occupation

Cowboy Songs

To many, the most colorful work songs belong to the cowboy who roamed the Western range, spent his life under the skies, and helped to mold the character of the early frontier. When the unhurried, uninhibited style of the Western cowboy merged with the cruder hillbilly style of the Southern mountaineers, the mixture spawned our present-day country and Western popular-music repertoire.

During the years 1868–1871, range cowboys drove more than a million and a half cattle over the Chisholm trail, the most famous track to the Kansas railroads. "The Old Chisholm Trail" (Ly 249; Lx 106) succinctly pictures the cowboy's rugged life, and the song is said to have as many verses as the trail had miles.

One of the most famous cowboy songs is "The Streets of Laredo" (Ly 67; Lx 108), also known as "The Cowboy's Lament" and "The Dying Cowboy." This story line has been adapted for the blues song "The St. James Infirmary," as well as many spontaneous versions for different occupations: sailors, soldiers, etc. The original ballad idea is derived from an old racy British ballad called "The Unfortunate Rake." Our American cowboy version reflects the desolate thoughts of a lonely man who lives with death always nearby.

Realism and sentimentality enter into songs like "I Ride An Old Paint" or "I'm A-Ridin' Old Paint" (Ly 175; Lx 109), a favorite at Western get-togethers. The popular "Whoopee Ti Yi Yo" (Ly 358; Lx 107), a driver song, may be traced back to Ireland. And of course no discussion, however brief, could possibly omit what to some is the greatest of all cowboy songs, "Home on the Range" (Ly 164). As a matter of fact, it is not even a true cowboy song but a popular Western-style ballad that may have come from Kansas in the 1870s. Nonetheless, it is better known than most of the more authentic songs and is great fun for group singing.

Railroad Songs

As the railroads gradually expanded America's frontier, a substantial number of railroad songs developed. One of the finest narrates the story of the great folk hero "John Henry" (Ly 189; Lx 88), said to be the champion steel driver in the Big Bend Tunnel on the Chesapeake and Ohio Railroad in West Virginia. John Henry's contest with the steam drill (he died from sheer exhaustion) symbolized the workers' fight against automation and technological changes.

The lesser known "Drill, Ye Tarriers, Drill" (Ly 86) offers a tribute to the Irish tarriers who drilled and dynamited mountains to make tunnels for railroads. The song dates from the 1880s. A more modern example is the enormously popular railroad song "Casey Jones" (Lx 127). Jones was an engineer who was killed in a wreck on the Illinois Central Line, south of Memphis, in 1906. The original folk song was later adapted into a hit tune.

Sailors' Songs

American seamen faced a hard life in the early days: poor living conditions, iron discipline, and sometimes brutality. To lighten their heavy tasks and to forget their troubles, sailors sang chanteys. One of these, a hoisting and pulling song called "Whiskey Johnny" (Ly 353) both praises and condemns the habit of drinking, at the same time hinting that the captain might well offer his men a liquid reward. The famous "Blow the Man Down" (Ly 37) is a chantey relating to the arduous life of the men who manned the early packet ships, the blow in this case meaning "to knock" or "to strike."

"Shenandoah" (Ly 295), another song of the seas, takes its melody from an American inland song about a trader who courted the daughter of the Indian chief Shenandoah. Since the word itself is a corruption of the Iroquois name for the mountains on both sides of the Shenandoah Valley in Virginia, one of the many versions of this song expresses yearning for rolling hills and peaceful valleys. Sailors sang their version to whatever rhythm matched their heaving motions.

Songs of the Homeless

Even itinerants who had no definite work managed to create songs describing their happiness, nostalgia, or utter despair. The hobo, now a vanishing breed, fabricated his own peculiar brand of glamor. "Hallelujah I'm a Bum" (Lx 129) exalts freedom from social pressures and the joys of adventure, sung to the tune of that glorious old gospel song "Hallelujah, Thine the Glory."

In times past hoboes looking for apprentices to do their begging for them would try to induce poor boys to run away from home by telling them exaggerated tales about the joys of tramp life. To the same end, hoboes created fantasy songs to glorify these tall tales; one such song is "Big Rock Candy Mountain" (Ly 27; Lx 130), which we now think of as a children's song although it was once used to lure small boys into the hobo life. "Nine Hundred Miles" (Ly 240), a popular blues song of the open road, comes from the rich lore of Negro music. Possibly the railroad track here symbolizes the way to freedom for the slave, or perhaps the song is just another traveling ballad.

Many wanderers landed in jail, and prison songs constitute a distinctive folk-song category. The plaintive "Birmingham Jail" (Lx 118) may have originated among Negro prisoners in the deep South; its simple melody has a true folk-song ring. Prison work songs are also plentiful. Prisoners sang songs like "Stewball" (Lx 91), the tale of a miraculous horse who not only was fast but could talk, and let their axes or picks fall in unison. The prison song "Midnight Special" (Ly 230; Lx 125) is based on the legend that a prisoner would go free if the headlights of this train would shine on him through the bars.

Spirituals

For many people the Negro spirituals are the most distinctive and beautiful body of folk music. These fervent songs sprang from the heart of the enslaved

Negro, and most spoke of better days to come, freedom from the white man's tyranny, or glories to be enjoyed after death.

The Old Testament Hebrew leaders who had persisted to free their people became symbols of liberty to the Negro slaves, and they released their own oppressive sadness in happy songs extolling the great deeds of their symbolic heroes. "Joshua Fit the Battle of Jericho" (Ly 198) recounts the story of that city's capture in vivid rhythms. "Go Down Moses" (Ly 122; Lx 82), another freedom spiritual that has become a great classic, has many verses, including some probably borrowed from other spirituals. "Little David" (Lx 76) praises one of the greatest heroes in all Hebrew literature.

Many of these colorful songs might be called good-news spirituals, for they proclaim the power and glory of God. One favorite of the gospel singers is actually called "Good News" (Ly 131). The lively "Gospel Train" (Ly 133) lends itself beautifully to shouting and hand clapping. "Great Day" (Lx 83), a vivid folk portrayal of the Lord, Heaven, and Hell, is a staple revival hymn guaranteed to stir the congregation. The vision of God redeeming the oppressed on judgment day made "Didn't My Lord Deliver Daniel" (Lx 81) a satisfying comfort song.

Not all spirituals were optimistic. The lovely lament "Nobody Knows the Trouble I've Seen" (Ly 242; Lx 80) is a deeply emotional Negro hymn of tribulation.

Some spirituals contain enigmatic passages that at one time no doubt conveyed a symbolic meaning. Such is "All God's Children Got Shoes" (Ly 6), which is very likely a disguised freedom song. It is commonly assumed that "Kum Ba Ya" (Ly 209) was based on an African imitation of the words "come by here" spoken by the missionaries. The song became traditional in Africa, where it was "discovered" and brought to America. New verses keep turning up for this dignified little melody.

Songs of Protest

> From the earliest periods of American history the oppressed people forming the broad base of the social and economic pyramid have been singing of their discontent. What they have said has not always been pleasant, but it has always been worth listening to, if only as the expression of a people whose pride and expectation of a better life have traditionally been considered attributes of the American nation.[3]

The American Negro had every right to protest. Under slavery, he was looked on as inferior and treated accordingly. Once freed, he had to shift for himself, more often than not homeless, jobless, and untrained. Negro protest songs speak eloquently. One of the best tells about the steel driver "John Henry" (Ly 189; Lx 88), whose struggles against automation made his story legendary. Another famous song, the melancholy "Nobody Knows the Trouble I've Seen" (Ly 242; Lx 80) protests against the Negro's frustration and oppression.

Each crisis between labor and management inspired new protest songs, many of them sung to well-known tunes. The text of one of the most famous

[3] John Greenway, *American Folksongs of Protest* (New York: A. S. Barnes and Co., Inc., 1953), p. vii.

songs to come from the coal fields, "Which Side Are You On?" (Lx 139), fits the tune of the old Baptist hymn "Lay the Lily Low." Many new stanzas appeared as this song was taken over by protesting workers in other labor groups. In the nineteenth century, textile workers, including many women and children, sometimes were forced to work 75 hours a week for small pay. Their discontent produced songs like "The Winnsboro Cotton Mill Blues" (Ly 370).

In the 1930s the migrant workers protested their pitiful living conditions through song. "Blowin' Down the Road" or "Goin' Down the Road" (Lx 140) was sung by hundreds of farm workers as they shifted from one temporary job to another. The grim humor of "So Long" (Lx 141) only emphasizes the tragedy of the migrant life.

Protest songs are always with us. They are sung not only by the oppressed and abused but by those who have sympathy for the protestors. Racial inequity and the immorality of war are the dominant themes in today's protest songs, of which the civil rights song "We Shall Overcome" is a salient example.

Frontier Songs

The pioneers moved constantly, always pushing westward to enlarge their rapidly expanding frontier. Life was never easy on the homesteads or in the crude towns that mushroomed up with each new settlement, but these hardy people found pleasure and recreation in singing. They composed songs by the hundreds to fit every occasion in their lives and every important event in their era.

During the gold-rush days professional entertainers toured the numerous gold camps, hoping to get rich performing for the men. Since many of the first forty-niners had come from Pike County, Missouri, the entertainers would beguile them with sure-fire hits like "Sweet Betsy from Pike" (Ly 309; Lx 101), which good-naturedly complains about the hardships endured going west in a covered wagon.

Dance songs and party songs filled a great void in the small isolated communities. "Cindy" (Ly 58; Lx 69), a fiddling and dancing song, has always been a favorite among square-dance musicians. The lyrics poke fun at church-going, a protest possibly against the severe religious groups who frowned on dancing and fiddling. The popular "Skip to My Lou" (Ly 302) was a "play-party" or singing game (Lou here meaning sweetheart and thought to be derived from the Scottish *loo,* meaning love) and is still going strong in current folk circles. Since the play-party games used no musical accompaniment, they were acceptable to everyone. Participants sang the song as they went through their step patterns, and the spectators added rhythm by clapping and stamping their feet. Oklahoma's favorite play-party song was "Old Joe Clark" (Lx 70), a catchy dance tune with nonsense verses strictly for fun.

Some of the most interesting frontier songs dwell on love, courtship, and marriage. They are sometimes humorous and sometimes deadly serious. In the comedy song "Lolly Too Dum" (Ly 218; Lx 48), a mother worries over her teen-age daughter who wants a man; then once daughter is safely married, mother gets romantic ideas of her own. The song title appears throughout as a nonsense refrain.

Serious love songs often bemoan unrequited love or infidelity. "Black Is the Color of My True Love's Hair" (Ly 34) began as a girl's lament but in the twentieth century it changed to a man's complaint. Sung to the same tune as "Birmingham Jail," the well-known "Down in the Valley" (Ly 83) is especially effective in group singing. The refrain is said to relate to the misery of Southern mountain boys who have been forced to leave their fine mountain air to find work or go to jail in the valley. The verses constitute a love song.

The love song "Little Mohee" (Lx 27) descends from a British folk song about a whaleman and a Polynesian girl. In the American version the hero is a frontiersman and the heroine a Mohee (Mohican) Indian girl. The tune for this love song is also used for "Old Smokey," the lament of a backwoods girl deserted by her lover. "Careless Love" (Ly 54), a typical lament song, has become an American classic; it is a perennial favorite with campus singing groups and hillbilly bands.

The ups and downs of married life have always provided good folk-song material. "I Wish I Was Single Again" (Ly 177) warns the listener against marriage on the ground that it will bring nothing but woe; in the comic ballad "The Farmer's Curst Wife" (Lx 43), the wife is so shrewish that even the devil won't have her.

Some of the most dramatic folk songs are ballads describing murder, revenge, robbery, betrayal, and other gruesome tragedies, often with startling realism. The American ballad "Pretty Polly" (Lx 44) derives from an eighteenth-century English song about an innocent girl who is betrayed and murdered by her sweetheart. There are many American variations of another English murder ballad, "The Oxford Girl"; one is the "Banks of the Ohio" (Ly 20), in which a rejected lover graphically describes how he drowned the girl who refused to marry him.

Certainly one of the most famous murder songs is "Frankie and Johnny" (Ly 115; Lx 121), the protracted account of the shooting of a faithless lover by his woman, who is then condemned to die. In the murder ballad "Jesse James" (Ly 186; Lx 103) the legendary outlaw becomes a folk hero.

Frontier children may not have had many toys or fancy clothes but they had their own songs, many of which we still sing to our children. A delightful example is "Go Tell Aunt Rhody" (Ly 125), which is often changed to Aunt Nancy or any other aunt who might be interested in the demise of the old gray goose. "The Frog Went A-Courtin'" (Lx 61), a descendant of a sixteenth-century British ballad, can have as many stanzas as guests that the singer can think of to invite to the wedding celebration.

> The contemporary American folk song heritage is an expression of America's nature and character, its melting-pot culture, its diverse and dynamic qualities. As we go racing through the last half of the twentieth century, recovering from the greatest revival of conscious interest in folk music the world has ever known, we can't help but be aware of the countless blessings the movement has brought us. We've collected, preserved, and dished out (though frequently in too gross a serving) a folk song potpourri fine enough—and varied enough—to fit every taste. The diversity must have been inevitable from the beginning. The main body of songs and singing styles came originally from different and distinctive cultures—predominantly British and African. As an American culture and personality developed, the songs and singing styles became part of a new and dynamic native tradition—a living singing tradition that continues to change, to blend, and to grow.[4]

[4] From *The Folk Song Abecedary* by James F. Leisy, p. xii. Copyright © 1966 by Hawthorn Books, Inc. Published by Hawthorn Books, Inc., 70 Fifth Avenue, New York, New York. Reprinted by permission.

JAZZ

Folk song is a spontaneous, natural product created by ordinary people for their own pleasure and to entertain their friends. Thus by its very nature this music can be quickly understood and enjoyed. So it is with jazz. The necessarily short discussion that follows emphasizes the history and development of jazz, the nature of jazz, and some jazz techniques.

Everyone seems to have an opinion on what jazz is, but when it comes to the matter of a precise definition, only a few articulate observers have been able to describe it succinctly in terms acceptable and intelligible to the general public. One of the best definitions comes from Leroy Ostransky:

> Jazz is the comprehensive name for a variety of specific musical styles generally characterized by attempts at creative improvisation on a given theme (melodic or rhythmic), over a foundation of complex, steadily flowing rhythm (melodic or percussive) and European harmonies; although the various styles of jazz may on occasion overlap, a style is distinguished from other styles by a preponderance of those specific qualities peculiar to each style.[5]

As we know, improvisation is not new. Two thousand years ago, improvising on established melodies was a common practice among the Greeks. During the Middle Ages, singers improvised countermelodies against a given melody. Renaissance musicians accepted improvisation as a natural part of performance, and by the Baroque era it had become a fundamental part of performance. Thus improvisation has had a long and steady history. Jazz, a comparatively recent development in music, derives largely from the spontaneous improvisatory style inherent in all folk music.

> Jazz, then, is not a composer's art. The particular melody and harmonies which form the basis of a performance, improvised or arranged, are of secondary importance. Rather, jazz is the art of the performer, the performing ensemble, and the arranger. And the quality of the art is dependent upon their creative ideas.[6]

During performance the jazz player literally becomes a composer as he alters the set tune, keeping the basic melodic and harmonic outlines intact but embellishing the framework with variation. The possibilities are endless. Simultaneous improvisation can be an exciting experience for musicians and listeners: the various players in the ensemble listen to each other and converse in musical dialogue, all the while preserving harmonic unity. Such simultaneous improvisation produced the style known as Dixieland. Early Dixieland jazz is also called "New Orleans style," because it originated there; when jazz activity moved to Chicago, "Chicago style" developed; but for the general public the term "Dixieland" seems adequate to cover the earliest era of jazz.

Jazz is not all improvisation. In the 1930s the big bands—those of Artie Shaw, Glenn Miller, and the Dorseys—used many jazz "arrangements" (some jazz buffs might argue that this was no longer jazz), but their success still depended on the improvisatory talent and instinct of the bandsmen. The Benny Goodman

[5] Leroy Ostransky, *The Anatomy of Jazz* (Tacoma, Wash.: University Press, 1964), p. 45.

[6] Homer Ulrich, *Music: A Design for Listening* (New York: Harcourt, Brace and World, Inc., 1962), p. 449. Reprinted by permission.

Trio and Count Basie's group alternated between planned music and improvisation, and even some Dixieland bands based their improvisations on planned musical patterns.

Most people can enjoy jazz without preliminary preparation, but as with most art forms—and jazz *is* an art—full understanding and appreciation will come only if the listener has some knowledge of the different elements that make jazz. Even a brief description of these various jazz elements and a quick survey of the history of jazz should arouse admiration for this art, which has grown so rapidly in such a few decades.

Jazz is not jazz until some transformation or improvisation takes place. Usually the foundation for the improvisation is a popular song. The average popular tune has 32 measures and three-part form. The first eight measures, the *front strain,* are repeated. Then the middle eight measures—the *release* or *bridge*—intrude, followed by a repeat of the front strain. In a jazz interpretation of this popular tune, the performer (instrumentalist or vocalist) creates his version of the melodic line; he transforms both the rhythmic pattern and the note sequence of the tune but always attempts to retain its original identity.

One unique characteristic of this melodic line is the use of "blue" notes or a "blue" tonality. Such blue notes are actually quarter tones—pitches lying between the fixed half steps of the chromatic scale—below the third and seventh scale steps. Thus in *C* major, the blue notes lie between *E*♭ and *E,* and between *B*♭ and *B*. Although most instruments, including the voice, can accomplish these quarter tones or blue notes, the piano cannot. The pianist tries to compensate by fusing sonorities. In *C* major, for example, he will play the *E* and *E*♭ simultaneously; he does not of course produce the blue note, but he draws attention to these altered scale steps.

Standard jazz rhythm is fitted to $\frac{2}{4}$ or $\frac{4}{4}$ meter, because a steady rhythmic beat is important in jazz used for dancing. Now that so many people appreciate jazz as a listening experience, $\frac{3}{4}$, $\frac{5}{4}$, and other meters are not uncommon.

When a normally weak beat is accented or when a strong beat is omitted, *syncopation* occurs. Syncopation is often evident in classical music, too, but in jazz it is an integral stylistic feature. By superimposing syncopated rhythmic figures on a $\frac{2}{4}$ or $\frac{4}{4}$ meter, the performer can create intricate new sounds. Most dance rhythms depend on liberal syncopation.

Jazz developed from an oral tradition, and jazz tone colors resemble the unique quality of the Negro singing voice: rich, expressive, and wonderfully fluent in vibrato. Many instrumental sounds actually imitate a vocal line—for instance, the saxophone with its growls, slurs, and mute rasps. Besides this vocal characteristic, jazz has a percussive quality; musicians supplement the standard percussion group with flamboyant instruments such as bongo drums, Afro-Cuban maracas, miscellaneous cymbals, and the vibraphone.

Classic jazz is a blend of European and African musical cultures. In West Africa, music is a vital part of everyday life, a natural combination of drumming, singing, and dancing spontaneously interwoven with work, play, and social and religious ceremonies. Being a creative activity for all ages of the community, it helps to maintain the unity of the social group. The background of African music is rhythm, and the rhythmic language is much more complicated and hypnotic than any found in an average jazz piece.

Besides its rhythmic character, jazz borrows a technical procedure from African music: the call-and-response pattern, which is still found today in some evangelical Negro churches. Used frequently in jazz, the call-and-response is

notes for the various harmonic changes. Rhythm was supplied by tuba, banjo, and drums.

Ragtime flourished at the same time as Dixieland, from about 1896 to 1918. Although the early Dixieland bands did not use piano, sometimes a pianist was hired to entertain in lieu of a band. To compensate for the lack of supporting instruments, the pianist concentrated on developing a full sound at the keyboard. His right hand would carry the melody while the left hand played bass notes and chords. He specialized in syncopation: the left hand marked off a rather stolid $\frac{2}{4}$ meter; the right hand played eight beats during the same period but accented every third beat. This fancy syncopation probably gave the music its name: "ragtime," or "ragged time."

Most ragtime pieces have a form similar to that of the minuet with trio or the military march. Many rags were actually called marches.

The best and most renowned composer of rags for the piano was Scott Joplin, whose "Maple Leaf Rag" has been a durable success. Later some ragtime pianists formed orchestras and adapted the original piano style to an ensemble; a well-known example is Jelly Roll Morton and his Red Hot Peppers.

When Storyville, New Orleans' official red-light district, opened in 1897, many of its cabarets, honky-tonks, and gambling houses hired jazz musicians. Many musicians found work and New Orleans became the center of the rapidly growing jazz movement. Storyville and jazz both prospered until 1917, when the district was closed down, musicians lost their jobs, and jazz activity shifted to Chicago. During the 1920s, Chicago developed its own distinctive style of Dixieland jazz. The band itself changed during the twenties: a saxophone, double bass, and piano were added to the small ensemble of the early Dixieland era. This new band featured more solos by individual members, and each piece had a rather extended introduction and elaborate ending. The playing style also changed: the new music had frenetic drive and tension, a sharp contrast to the comparatively relaxed New Orleans music.

Even before the twenties Chicago had fine bands and superb jazz musicians. The outstanding Original Dixieland Jazz Band had arrived in Chicago in 1914, made a few records, and disbanded after a few weeks, but their records had a strong impact on other musicians. The fine cornetist Manuel Perez led another group, and Jelly Roll Morton's ensemble, which had moved to Chicago as early as 1910, continued to flourish. Big name performers included Joe Oliver, Louis Armstrong, Bix Beiderbecke, and Tommy and Jimmy Dorsey.

Chicago was a good piano town during the early twenties but after 1925 many expert pianists moved to New York. Then in the early thirties the depression struck the big jazz bands, which were too expensive to be hired. Many bands disbanded, and once again, as in the days of early ragtime, the pianist emerged as a single entertainer. The full keyboard style developed by the pianists of this era came to be known as "boogie-woogie," but in fact it was just another phase in the "barrelhouse" (after the lower-class drinking clubs) style of piano playing long familiar in New Orleans. Boogie-woogie piano style used an ostinato bass in a manner very like that of Henry Purcell and some of his English contemporaries. An eight-beat figure in the left hand was repeated measure after measure, ad infinitum. This figure consisted either of full chords or spread-out chord outlines played in "walking" fashion. The right hand was thus at liberty to improvise on the given melody.

The boogie-woogie virtuosos had a brief but lucrative era through the early forties. Early pianists like Jimmy Yancey, Pine Top Smith, and Meade Lux

Lewis gave the cue to later boogie-woogie experts like Cleo Brown and Earl Hines. Bandleaders like Lionel Hampton and Tommy Dorsey even succeeded in adapting the style for a jazz combo.

The period of the big, elaborate dance bands began in the middle thirties and lasted through World War II. These bands played written-out arrangements which allowed some leeway for improvised solos, and their musical style came to be known as "swing."

> Generally speaking, swing music was the answer to the American—and very human—love of bigness, for the formula of the big Harlem bands which had solved the difficult problem of how to assemble a large orchestra and still play hot jazz was adopted. At the same time, there was a real demand. With the repeal of Prohibition in 1933, jazz was brought out of the speak-easy. There was room to expand. The Depression was fading out as far as middle-class America was concerned, and a vociferous market sprang up among the college kids. They liked their music hot and their bands big. And they could pay for it.[11]

The general trend toward swing music was initiated by such bands as those of Fletcher Henderson, Duke Ellington, Don Redman, and others. Soon many bands were dispensing smooth, sonorous arrangements of standard hit tunes. Instead of the earlier intimate jazz ensembles consisting of five or six players, the swing band swelled to about 13 men, who were divided into three sections. The five-piece brass section and four-piece reed section manipulated the old call-and-response pattern with endless variety. The four-man rhythm section backed up the others with a steady—and at times overpowering—pulse.

For about ten years swing music and big swing bands dominated the entertainment world. Benny Goodman was probably the most publicized of the big bandleaders, but there were others with like talent and popularity—Duke Ellington, Glenn Miller, Lionel Hampton, Woody Herman, Artie Shaw, and Bob Crosby. Even William "Count" Basie built up his band during this period, a band "that gave depth and momentum to the whole swing era while planting the seeds that later gave birth to bop and the 'cool' school of jazz."[12]

While the swing music of the thirties thoroughly delighted listeners as well as dancers, the musicians wanted more chance for originality than they were permitted in the smooth arrangements used by the swing bands. Their revolt against the big bands and against the general commercialism in music ultimately led to "bop," a new style that completely won over some fans while it perplexed and even infuriated others. Bop (or "be-bop") music was marked by clashing dissonances, complex rhythms, and unrecognizable melodies. The word itself may derive from the Spanish *arriba,* the Afro-Cuban musician's equivalent for "go."

The great bop artist John "Dizzy" Gillespie, with his band and star soloists such as saxophonist Charlie "Bird" Parker and Chano Pozo, an extraordinary Cuban drummer, made highly original and at times extremely complex and rarified bop recordings.

Dedicated bop artists slowly worked out a new concept of jazz. Instead of improvising on a pop melody, they focused their skills on the harmonic framework, the chords supporting the tune. This treatment almost resulted in a whole new piece, not simply a new version of a popular tune, particularly since the tune was seldom if ever heard.

Although bop bands were relatively small, they accomplished a minor

[11] Stearns, pp. 140–141. Reprinted by permission.

[12] Stearns, p. 150. Reprinted by permission.

revolution in jazz. They worked something like this: the drummer used his equipment for accents and punctuation; the piano, guitar, and bass would play the customary chordal accompaniment to a tune; and soloists would improvise, not on the tune but by creating wild harmonies (ninths and augmented fourths) with the accompaniment instruments. When big bands tried this style, it was labeled "progressive jazz."

One of the more sophisticated events in jazz history occurred in 1949–1950 when trumpeter Miles Davis and a group of sensitive musicians made some recordings that came to be described as "cool." Their cool jazz had a restrained chamber-music quality that had little in common with the flamboyant bop sound. It was a conservative style that emphasized pastel colors through atypical instruments like the French horn, flute, oboe, and cello. This precisely scored music displaying contrapuntal textures, polyrhythms, and unusual meter signatures introduced new forms (such as the rondo and fugue) to jazz. During this cool phase (which diminished in the late fifties) jazz edged closer to classical music.

The jazz trends of the last ten years continue to show a classical influence. One recent offshoot of cool, known as "third-stream music," falls somewhere between classical music and jazz. As conceived by imaginative musicians like Dave Brubeck, third-stream music employs classical forms such as the fugue, canon, and theme and variations; in addition, polytonal and polymodal textures and irregular meters like $\frac{5}{4}$ often appear. Thus this new music attempts to combine traditional jazz and classical media into a single sound experience. Dave Brubeck's *Dialogues* for jazz combo and symphony orchestra and Rolf Liebermann's *Concerto* for jazz band and orchestra provide two excellent examples of third-stream music.

> On Nov. 17, 1959, a bearded prophet from Texas named Ornette Coleman carried his white plastic alto saxophone into New York's Five-Spot Café and blew the jazz world to pieces. The molten, unchained improvisation of Coleman and his waistcoated trio of young musicians confused many listeners and even infuriated many jazzmen. Some walked out in disgust. English critic Kenneth Tynan cried, "They have gone too far." But Leonard Bernstein leaped to the stand to embrace the new musicians, and advanced jazzmen such as conservatory-trained John Lewis proclaimed Coleman the apostle of a new age. The most violent, ambitious revolution in the history of jazz had begun.[13]

John Coltrane, Ornette Coleman, Cecil Taylor, Thelonious Monk—these are some of the names associated with the "New Thing," the term sometimes applied to present-day progressive jazz music. For some this style represents musical anarchy, for it seems to have unlimited freedom with rhythm, harmonic progressions, and even melodic continuity. If such a thing as improvised atonal music exists in the jazz world, this is it.

Today's progressive jazz is as surely a listening experience as is classical or contemporary music, and it demands equal concentration. It is specifically designed for listening, not dancing, and it appeals to a much smaller segment of society than did, say, Dixieland jazz.

But what of the other camp, those who dearly love jazz—or what they call jazz—but simply cannot accept the avant-garde variety? There is still plenty of music for them, of all kinds and styles. For example, folk-rock—a recent development in popular music—draws from blues, folk song, and western music to

[13] From an article entitled "The New Jazz," in *Newsweek* magazine, December 12, 1966.

achieve its appeal. An improvement over the loud and often monotonous rock-and-roll of the 1950s, this sound emphasizes the vocal element supported by a persistent rhythmic section and electric guitars. Composer-performers such as the Beatles and Bob Dylan have permanently influenced popular music with their highly poetic lyrics and often interesting melodies. Also, an instrumental group —such as Herb Alpert and the Tijuana Brass—frequently creates its own brand of jazz by adding a new "beat" or instrumental combination; such musicians have managed to give familiar tunes a fresh look without destroying their identity. These are only two of the many current musical styles that fit—however loosely—into the jazz category.

This survey of jazz would be incomplete without some mention of the jazz singer. Singing, which sparked the development of the Negro spiritual, has likewise supported every phase in the progress of jazz. After all, almost all jazz deals with improvisation on a tune, usually a popular *song*.

The earliest singers were Negro blues singers. One of the finest was Gertrude "Ma" Rainey, the nation's favorite blues singer in the mid-twenties. Her successor was Bessie Smith, who made hundreds of recordings (1923–1933) with the best bands—Henderson, Armstrong, Redman. During her first year of recording, her record sales reputedly reached the two million mark. Although more a straight pop vocalist like Lena Horne and Dinah Shore, the stage and screen actress Ethel Waters attracted countless fans in the early days.

The first important white jazz singer was Mildred Bailey, whose high, light voice set her apart from the ordinary jazz singer. The Negro singer Billie Holiday possessed an exceptional talent. She dispensed sensuous love songs in a highly characteristic manner, yet she also dearly loved semi-sacred songs.

Ella Fitzgerald, whose fine musicianship and vocal perfection have kept her at the top for many years, ranks with Bailey and Holiday in the roster of great jazz singers. And the versatile Peggy Lee can project a shouting blues or an almost whispered message in her songs.

Among the men, Leadbelly (Huddie Ledbetter) stands out as one of the first important jazz and blues singers. Accompanying himself on a twelve-string guitar, he could entertain with hundreds of songs—work songs, hollers, blues—some of which he learned during several terms in jail. Jelly Roll Morton, another early jazz great, dramatically recited lyrics to his own subtle piano accompaniment.

Leadbelly and Jelly Roll belong to jazz history, but Louis Armstrong is part of the living present. Although first a cornet and trumpet soloist, Armstrong has a unique raspy voice that has brought him additional fame as a singer. In 1925 he introduced jazz "scat" singing (singing on nonsense syllables).

Among the big names of the last decade or so, Ray Charles stands high on the list. Many pop singers, such as Frank Sinatra and the late Nat "King" Cole, successfully straddle the pop and jazz fields. Mel Tormé, who started as a crooner, is a particularly fine jazz vocalist. One of the all-time greats of jazz as well as pop singing is Bing Crosby, who uses his unusually good voice with skill and imagination.

The Influence of Jazz

True jazz constitutes a significant twentieth-century musical movement. Besides being an intrinsically interesting and unique contribution to American culture, it has definitely influenced serious contemporary composers in Europe, Latin America, and the United States.

Many European composers have been tempted to mix jazz techniques with their own styles, sometimes with good results and sometimes not. Maurice Ravel deftly handled elements from both popular dance music and jazz in his striking *L'enfant et les sortilèges,* but in his violin and piano sonata he misused the jazz factor. Another French composer, Darius Milhaud, adroitly assimilated a jazz vocabulary to create his admirable ballet *La création du monde*.

Ever since George Gershwin presented his opera *Porgy and Bess* and the still delightful *Rhapsody in Blue,* various twentieth-century American composers have been tempted to try jazz. Aaron Copland went through a jazz stage with *Four Piano Blues* and *Music for the Theater*. And Gunther Schuller, who is also an experienced jazz performer, draws simultaneously from classical and jazz materials for many of his works.

EXOTIC MUSIC

The music of the Western hemisphere has become such a traditional part of our culture that until recently we neglected most music from other cultures. Now that a wide variety of non-Western music is being recorded and East and West are exchanging their performing artists, we have increasing opportunities to hear music that we could previously only read about in music encyclopedias.

Exotic music—a general term applied to music outside the European tradition, which by extension includes the American tradition—may be folk, popular, classical, or religious music. Although exotic music is based chiefly on scale systems and rhythmic concepts foreign to our way of thinking, we can quite easily acquire a feeling for and partial understanding of the rich musical treasures available beyond our familiar traditions.

This musical category is vast. In Africa, where pagan, Moslem, and Christian cultures exist side by side, the traditional music covers a broad area; it might be the melodies played by a Negro xylophone orchestra, or a Moslem ballad, or a Coptic Christian chant. The Near East can boast of its rich, diverse folk music, for each country—Lebanon, Jordan, Syria, Israel, and others—possesses a distinctive corpus of indigenous songs and dances comparable to the finest Western repertoires.

Australia and the Pacific Islands offer yet another totally different ethnic experience. Australia's fascinating aboriginal music is a good example of music functioning as an integral factor of society and life. Music is also important in New Guinea's social and religious life, where native ensembles include a wide assortment of percussion, wind, and stringed instruments; polyphonic singing exists, but monophonic predominates.

Another chain of islands extends from Java through Borneo to the Philippines. Philippine music bears traces of the two dominant cultural forces in Philippine history—Spanish and Moslem. Indonesia's most outstanding and characteristic music centers around the *gamelan* (a generic term for orchestra).

The land bounded by Turkey on the east and China on the west is now known as the Soviet Southern and Asian Republics. Among the eight territories included in this general area, Georgia, Armenia, and Azerbaijan are most familiar to Westerners. There the major musical influences have come from the Persian and Arab cultures, notably evident in the choice of instruments. Long epic narratives sung without accompaniment by storytellers are a vital part of the vocal tradition.

The earliest known Indian music consists of hymns dating back 2,000 years before Christ, and it is possible that India has the oldest continuous vocal tradition in the world. The Indian raga, a highly complex but fascinating scalar-melody form, is now becoming increasingly familiar to Western listeners.

> The music of Southeast Asia [Burma, Singapore, Thailand, Cambodia, Laos, and Vietnam] today reflects a mixture of indigenous genius with various combinations of influences from four main external traditions: Indonesia, China, India, and, in more recent times, the West. Hybrid musics have bred further hybrids, so that today it is very difficult to separate the many interminglings and cross-influences. Southeast Asian music shows variation not only between each nation but also between geographical regions within each country.[14]

East Asia produces several distinctive kinds of music. To the Westerner, Tibet is synonymous with Lamaistic Buddhism, a religion in which the monks chant as they perform their rituals. Thus the mainstay of Tibetan religious music is chanting, usually with each priest seeking his own tonal level. Chanting can be accompanied by any of a variety of instruments; hand bells, cymbals, large two-headed drums, and the incredible copper trumpets from 5 to 20 feet long. In China, both folk music and court music have always enlivened the cultural life of that vast country, but the Westerner knows more about Chinese opera, a highly polished form encompassing dances, pantomimes, interludes, vocal recitatives, and arias. Some 300 different operatic varieties have been known to exist, many of which survive today.

The final group in this summary of exotic music comprises Northeast Asia and the Island Countries. Korean folk songs and dances are vibrant and exciting. Formosan music reveals a strong Chinese influence, although Japan and the West have also left ineradicable traces. Japan offers the most varied and stimulating musical experiences—in the Noh plays, the Kabuki theater, and the music of the popular koto.

Obviously we have simply skimmed the surface of the subject of exotic music. It would take years of study to understand the music of some of these countries; however, the music of India, Japan, and Indonesia is currently heard and discussed in the United States with enough frequency to warrant further explanation here.

India

Orchestral music never gained a sure foothold in India, where song is the basis of all music, even to the point of dictating the contours of purely instrumental pieces. It is this instrumental music—basically chamber-music types—that we Westerners find so attractive.

Two types of plucked string instruments are popular. The South Indian *vina* is a hollow bamboo tube with a gourd attached to the underside at both ends. It has seven strings: four are fretted, the other three are drones (strings with fixed pitch). The latest member of the vina family is the *sitar,* which has six or

[14] William P. Malm, *Music Cultures of the Pacific, the Near East, and Asia,* p. 88. © 1967. Reprinted by permission of Prentice-Hall, Inc., Englewood Cliffs, N.J.

Ill. 27:1. ***Concert of Indian music with sitar and tamburas. Courtesy of Institute of Ethnomusicology, University of California, Los Angeles.***

seven main strings (including two drones), with 20 movable frets, and an extensive number of sympathetic strings, tuned at the unison or octave. These secondary strings vibrate in consonance with notes struck on the main strings, giving a pleasant, unusual echo effect. Like the vina, the sitar has a gourd attached at each end to amplify the sound. On these instruments, the musicians play ornaments (pitch distortions) by pulling a string to one side.

The *tambura* has four metal strings but no frets; it is intended solely for a drone background (Ill. 27:1).

The *tabla,* a pair of drums, are played together. The semi-spherical left-hand drum has a brass body, and the cylindrical right-hand drum is made of wood. The tabla provide the rhythmical backbone of an ensemble.

Florid, exuberant music developed in northern India, where musical entertainments often took place at the courts and palaces. In the south, music retained its religious character, serving in the temples and avoiding emotional display. Today these two styles coexist and intermingle.

Classical Indian music is built on a system of ragas whose principles were formulated many centuries ago. A *raga* (meaning mood or tint) is actually a melody type having certain identifying characteristics: scale structure, note emphasis, frequency of certain notes and intervals, pitch range, ornaments, and melodic pattern. A musical composition consists of controlled improvisation on some raga. (The rhythmical component is known as *tala.*) Thus each piece uses a raga appropriate to its mood; there are ragas for different times of day and ragas associated with ceremonial occasions; some theory books describe as many as 1,000 ragas, of which about 300 can be put into practical application. Today's Indian musicians usually know around 50 ragas. To perform a raga generally takes from 20 minutes to well over an hour.

Indian music has exerted considerable influence on Western composers. A visit to French Indo-China and India prompted the French-born Albert Roussel (1869–1937) to write two major works, the orchestral *Evocations* and the opera-ballet *Padmâvati.* His compatriot Olivier Messiaen (*b.*1908) took inspiration from India when composing his symphony *Turangalîla.* In the early twentieth century Gustav Holst (1874–1934), attracted by Hindu epics, set to music four sets of hymns from the sacred Rig-Veda and composed the chamber opera *Savitri.*

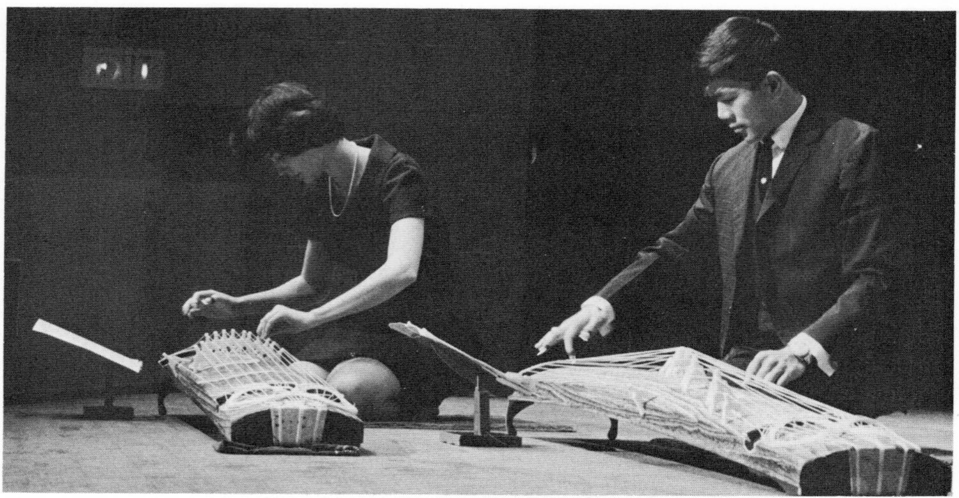

Ill. 27:2. ***Musicians playing the Japanese koto. Courtesy of Institute of Ethnomusicology, University of California, Los Angeles.***

Hindu culture has even invaded jazz; it is not uncommon to find jazz or even folk-rock groups employing exotic instruments (the Beatles have included the sitar in their recording ensemble).

Japan

Japan's most serious art form is the aristocratic Noh play, a theatrical medium that dates from the fourteenth century. It includes poetry, design, costume, dance, and music, and is essentially a music drama based on Buddhist ideals and concepts. Some actors are masked, and the play is highly stylized throughout. Noh vocal music consists of solo songs by the various actor-singers (either a recitative that hovers about one note or a kind of aria built on a melodic pattern, like the Indian raga) or unison singing by a chorus. It may or may not have an accompaniment. The classical instrumental accompaniment is provided by a flute and three drums; the three guitars now frequently encountered are a later addition.

The Kabuki theater is popular entertainment. Over 200 years old, it began as an all-female group but by tradition has become a medium for male actors only. It is basically a melodrama with popular Buddhist dances, accompanied by three kinds of music: on-stage ensemble, narrative music, and an off-stage musical group. The traditional Kabuki instruments are a flute, drums, gongs, bells, and a three-stringed guitar (*samisen*).

Japan's national musical instrument is the *koto* (Ill. 27:2), a thirteen-stringed zither used solo or for vocal accompaniment. It is 6½ feet long, and is played with ivory plectra attached to the thumb, index finger, and middle finger. Koto music, as well as other oriental music, is largely based on pentatonic (five-tone) scales, but one senses a constant tendency toward heptatonic (seven-tone) patterns in the music.

For a solo performance, the koto player traditionally plays variations of

Ill. 27:3. ***Gamelan concert. Courtesy of Institute of Ethnomusicology, University of California, Los Angeles.***

52 bars each. A short phrase of about five tones forms the basis of the composition; as this phrase is elaborated, it undergoes transposition and every conceivable type of variation. When used as an accompanying instrument, the koto follows the vocal line and maintains the rhythm when the voice sustains a tone. It may supply intervals—octaves, fifths, fourths, thirds, and seconds—to increase and strengthen the sonority.

Many Western composers' works have been inspired in a general way by Japan and its culture; Puccini's opera *Madame Butterfly* and Richard Strauss's *Japanese Festival Music* (1940) are two examples. A more direct influence is evident in Benjamin Britten's *Curlew River* (1964). This "parable for church performance" is based on a Japanese Noh play that the composer attended in Tokyo.

Indonesia

Southeast Asia is the center for the *gamelan,* a unique orchestral ensemble that accompanies dancing and drama, with either live actors or puppets, and that performs at important religious and secular ceremonies.

The Javanese gamelan dominates Indonesian classical music. The orchestra may consist of just a few instruments or more than 75. The typical gamelan (Ill. 27:3) has great instrumental variety: drums; tuned chime instruments like the xylophone, celesta, assorted gong-chimes, kettle gongs, and rattle chimes; single tuned gongs and untuned cymbals; flutes; and a two-stringed fiddle that serves as lead instrument (in some ensembles the drummer acts as leader).

Gamelan music is polyphonic; it is projected in numerous layers of sound created to adorn an initial basic melody. In general, gamelan music follows this pattern:

1. A basic melody similar to a cantus firmus or perhaps a raga pattern begins each piece in a rather deliberate, uncomplicated manner.
2. A special set of gongs divides the melody into a number of rhythmic segments.
3. Other instruments improvise, within certain limits, on the basic melody, thus generating many layers of different sounds.

Since a typical gamelan ensemble has a pitch range of from five to six octaves, the music has great variety. There are two basic playing styles: soft and loud. In addition, solo and unison-chorus singing is frequently added to the ensemble, especially for settings of Javanese classical poetry. In Bali, the main gong-chime instruments are found in pairs, one instrument in each pair being deliberately tuned slightly higher than the other. The resulting music has a distinctive shimmering quality.

The intriguing gamelan has exerted a noticeable influence on Western music and composers. It is very possible that when the Parisian Auguste Mustel designed the modern celesta, he derived his basic idea from a similar gamelan instrument. Claude Debussy was reportedly greatly impressed by a gamelan he heard at the Paris Exposition Universelle of 1889. And Benjamin Britten's ballet *The Prince of the Pagodas* (1957) gives such importance to chime instruments that it seems to be directly inspired by the gamelan.

FOR DISCUSSION AND ASSIGNMENT

1. Listen to portions from *A London Symphony* (Symphony No. 2) by Ralph Vaughan Williams. Does the symphony have an "English" sound? Could this result from Vaughan Williams' preoccupation with English folk song?
2. Listen to several recordings of the same folk song. Which do you prefer? Why? Does the singer you prefer necessarily have the best voice?
3. When you hear, via recordings, what course jazz has taken during the past 30 years, what do you predict for the future? Will jazz become intelligible to even fewer admirers?
4. As an art form, which era of jazz do you prefer and why?
5. In general, do you find Eastern music monotonous? Is there a great amount of repetition? Give your reasons for liking or disliking Eastern music.
6. Listen to "Laideronette, Empress of the Pagodas" from Maurice Ravel's *Mother Goose Suite*. This is obviously an example of exotic music. How is this exoticism achieved?

FOR FURTHER READING AND LISTENING

FOLK MUSIC

Ames, Russell. *The Story of American Folk Song*. New York: Grosset & Dunlap, 1960 (The Listener's Music Library). For the average layman, Mr. Ames' survey of folk song in the United States fills a definite need. It is informative, clearly written, and interesting.

Leisy, James F. *The Folk Song Abecedary*. New York: Hawthorne Books, Inc., 1966. This is probably the most complete, useful, informative, and accurate one-volume collection of folk songs in print. The book contains over 200 songs, both melody and words, together with commentary and discography.

Lomax, Alan, editor and compiler. *The Penguin Book of American Folk Songs.* Baltimore, Md.: Penguin Books, 1964. PB. Mr. Lomax needs no introduction to folk-song collectors. His book contains 111 folk songs of all types, together with commentary and piano arrangements.

Nettl, Bruno. *An Introduction to Folk Music in the United States.* Detroit, Michigan: Wayne State University Press, 1962. PB. Dr. Nettl's book approaches the folk song more from the analytical side than the narrative or historical viewpoint. For all its brevity, it provides a solid introduction to this aspect of music. There are copious musical examples.

———. *Folk and Traditional Music of the Western Continents.* Englewood Cliffs, N.J.: Prentice-Hall, Inc., 1965. A PB in the Prentice-Hall History of Music Series. This fine book is intended for the music student, the musician, and the musically knowledgeable layman. It discusses music of Europe, African music south of the Sahara, music of the American Indian, Negro folk music in the New World, and Western and Western-descended folk music in the Americas.

Sharp, Cecil J. *English Folk Song,* Fourth Edition, prepared by Maud Karpeles. Belmont, Calif.: Wadsworth Publishing Co., Inc., 1965. This is the standard general survey of the subject and should be read by anyone interested in English (and American) folk songs.

Vaughan Williams, Ralph. *National Music and Other Essays.* London: Oxford University Press, 1963. PB. The first 82 pages set out in vivid prose the composer's studied opinions concerning national music. The other essays in the book are also well worth reading.

Representative Recordings:

General:
- *Music of the World's Peoples* (10-Folk. 4504/8)

Western Europe and Great Britain:
- *Sussex Folk Songs and Ballads* (Folk. 3515)
- *Deutsche Volkslieder* (2-DGG. 004-157 to 004-160)
- *Folk Music of France* (Folk. 4414)
- *Folk Music of Italy* (2-Folk. 4520)
- *Flamenco Music of Andalusia* (Folk. 4437)
- *Songs and Dances of Spain* (3-West. 9802/4)

Eastern Europe:
- *Czech, Slovak and Moravian Folk Songs* (Monitor, MF 389)
- *Folk Music of Greece* (Folk. 4454)
- *Folk Songs of Hungary* (Folk. 4000)
- *Russian Folk Songs* (Van. 9023)

United States:
- *Anthology of American Folk Music* (6-Folk. 2951/3)
- *Library of Congress Recordings* (Woody Guthrie, 3-Elek. 271/2)
- *Music from the South* (10-Folk. 2650/9)
- *Negro Folk Music of Africa and America* (2-Folk. 4500)

JAZZ

Dexter, Dave. *The Jazz Story.* Englewood Cliffs, N.J.: Prentice-Hall, Inc., 1964. A panorama of jazz from 1890 to 1960. The book concentrates more on personalities than on the evolution of the music itself. As a supplement to the book, Columbia has issued a set of records with the same title.

Harris, Rex. *The Story of Jazz.* New York: Grosset & Dunlap, 1960 (The Listener's Music Library). This book is an abridgement of *Jazz,* first published in 1952 by Penguin Books (now out of print). It is quite brief but interesting and informative.

Hodeir, André. *Jazz: Its Evolution and Essence,* translated by David Noakes. New York: Grove Press, Inc., 1956. A Black Cat PB. An analytical study by an enthusiastic and perceptive critic. M. Hodeir is inclined to dwell at length on his particular favorites, both musicians and musical compositions.

———. *Toward Jazz,* translated by Noel Burch. New York: Grove Press, Inc., 1962. An Evergreen PB. In this sequel to the previous book, M. Hodeir's chapters are entitled: On Jazzmen, On Criticism, On Group Relations, On Works, Listening Notes, and Prospects of Jazz.

Ostransky, Leroy. *The Anatomy of Jazz.* Tacoma, Washington: University Press, 1964. PB. A clear and authoritative book. Its serious approach makes it a book especially worth reading.

Stearns, Marshall. *The Story of Jazz.* New York: The New American Library, 1958. A Mentor PB. This book has long been the standard introduction to the subject. Although not up-to-date, it still provides a good understanding of jazz for the layman.

Tanner, Paul, and Maurice Gerow. *A Study of Jazz.* Dubuque, Iowa: Wm. C. Brown Company, 1964. An analytical, brief study of jazz, this book traces the evolution of style. An LP record accompanies the volume.

Representative Recordings:

Encyclopedia of Jazz (4-Dec. DX-140)
History of Jazz: N.Y. Scene 1914–1945 (Folk. RF-3)
Introduction to Jazz (Dec. 8244)
Jazz (11-Folk. 2801/11)
Jazz Greats of Modern Times (U. Artists 3333)
Jazz Odyssey (9-Col. C3L 30, 32, 33)
Jazz Story (5-Cap. WEO-2109)
Original Sound of the 20's (3-Col. C3L-35)
What Is Jazz? (with Leonard Bernstein) (Col. CL-919)

EXOTIC MUSIC

Malm, William P. *Music Cultures of the Pacific, the Near East, and Asia.* Englewood Cliffs, N.J.: Prentice-Hall, Inc., 1967. A PB in the Prentice-Hall History of Music Series. The only book of its kind: a readable, informative, compact volume.

Robertson, Alec, and Denis Stevens, editors. *The Pelican History of Music,* Vol. 1. Baltimore, Md.: Penguin Books, 1960. A Pelican PB. The first section of this book—written by Peter Crossley-Holland—deals exclusively with non-Western music.

Wellesz, Egon, editor. *Ancient and Oriental Music,* Vol. 1 of *The New Oxford History of Music.* London: Oxford University Press, 1957. This book is intended for professional musicians and is a bit technical for the layman. However, it should prove valuable to the interested reader who wishes detailed information.

Representative Recordings:

Hawaiian Chant, Hula, and Music (Folk. 8750)
Music of Indonesia (2-Folk. 4537)
Arabic and Druse Music (Folk. 4480)
Classical Indian Music (Lon. 9282)
Classical Music of India (Nonesuch H-2014)
Folk Music of India (Col. KL-215)
India's Master Musician Ravi Shankar (World Pacific WP-1422)
Folk and Traditional Music of Burma (Folk. 4436)
Music of Thailand (Folk. 4463)
China's Instrumental Heritage (Lyrichord Lyr. 92)
Chinese Classical Masterpieces for the Pipa and Chin (Lyrichord Lyr. 82)
Chinese Classical Music (Lyrichord Lyr. 72)
Japan, The Ryukyus, Formosa and Korea (Col. KL-214)
The Koto Music of Japan (Nonesuch H-2005)

Index

List includes manufacturing concerns involved in the production of aircraft, major subassemblies and kits. Compilation of this list has been limited by the lack of comprehensive records and may not be all-inclusive.

• Company lifespans reflect years of actual, ongoing business activity. Production totals have, when recor[...]
• Sources: Company files, FAA reg[...] accounts and interviews.

S0-AXY-018

1940 1941 1942 1943 1944 1945 1946 1947 1948 1949 1950 1951 1952 1953 1954 1955 1956 1957 1958 1959 1960 1961 1962 1963 1964 1965 1966 1967 1968 1969 1970 1971 1972 1973 1974 1975 1976 1977 1978 1979 1980 1981 1982 1983 1984 1985 1986 198[...]

(1 aircraft)
(245 aircraft)
(3 aircraft)
(15 aircraft, 5,055 kits)
(50,650 aircraft)
(12,101 aircraft)
178,007 aircraft)
(1 aircraft)
(1,620 aircraft)
(3,316 aircraft)
(1 aircraft)
(232 aircraft)
(12 aircraft)
(145 aircraft)
(517 aircraft)
(18 aircraft, 300 kits)
(1,718 aircraft)
(1 aircraft)
(290 aircraft)
(59 aircraft)
(6,608 aircraft)
(40 airframes)
(68 kits/3 aircraft)
(1,725 kits/aircraft)
(36 aircraft)
(515 aircraft)
(599 aircraft)
(4-6 aircraft)
(5 aircraft)
(1 aircraft, 2 kits)
(2 aircraft)
(1 prototype aircraft)
(350 aircraft)

Overall production totals for Beech Aircraft Corporation and Cessna Aircraft Company include a very limited number of aircraft assembled, or constructed under licensed agreement in foreign countries.

• American Eagle Aircraft Company and Inland Aviation Company were originally located in Kansas City, Mo. before relocating to Kansas City, Kans. Aircraft Production numbers for these companies are listed with Kansas City totals listed first, followed by overall production totals that reflect production at both locations. Eg: (100/600 aircraft) American Eagle formed in Kansas City, Mo., in 1925; Inland Aviation Company, formed in Kansas City, Mo. in 1928.)

• The following Kansas companies operated as aircraft engine manufacturers: Blue Streak Motors, C. M. Mulkins Company, Poyer Motor Company, Self Aircraft Corporation, Quick Air Motors and Vanos Aircraft Corporation (All located in Wichita)

• Okay Aircraft Company and Brantly Helicopter Company were headquartered for a short time in Kansas; however, their manufacturing facilities were in Oklahoma.

• Charted timespans and production totals do not reflect periods that a founder spent experimenting/developing aircraft before the actual formation of a company (eg: timespans for Cessna would not include years prior to 1927.)

• Funk Aircraft Company of Coffeyville and the D.D. Funk Aviation Company of Salina were separate companies. Funk Aviation of Salina built the F-23A/B Crop Spraying aircraft based on the Fairchild M-62 (T-23) aircraft, while Funk Aircraft of Coffeyville produced the familiar Funk model F2B-85C Transport.

In Memory

of

Albert Stolfus and Jerome Brinkman

\- - -

Gayle Woods Gardner

A CENTURY OF AVIATION IN KANSAS

BORNE ON THE SOUTH WIND

BY FRANK JOSEPH ROWE AND CRAIG MINER

95_0121

This book is dedicated to my father,
Frank Joseph Rowe, M.D.
and to all those who have
contributed to the ongoing history
of Kansas Aviation

— Frank Rowe

PREFACE

The purpose of this book is simply stated. The state of Kansas has been perhaps the premier regional center for the development and production of aircraft since the first experiments with powered flight. The names Cessna and Beech, for example, both family names in the Wichita phone book, have become familiar and famous in flying circles. The state has been host to over 50 companies over the years, manufacturing everything from early unflyable contraptions, to popular lightplanes, to bombers and fighters. Within its 50 million acres have at times been produced about 60 percent of the Western world's general aviation aircraft. Yet, until now, there has been no comprehensive history of Kansas aviation.

Borne on the South Wind tracks, analyzes and illustrates the evolution and adaptation of a prairie industry quite unlike that of the traditional waving wheat. It provides perspective on the circumstances, people and plans that brought the state to its position of prominence by the 1920s, sustained it through the Depression, helped it boom as a major defense center during World War II, and kept it competitive in the jet age. And the story is hardly an exercise in nostalgia solely. What Kansas has done with aviation — beginning with nothing more than a few news stories and demonstration fliers — is a strategic development model for others. It is likely, also, that Kansas itself will build on its strengths, learn from its errors, and have a second century in aviation as remarkable as its first.

ACKNOWLEDGMENTS

Harry Adams, Aviation Data Service, Inc.
John F. Allen
Atchison (Kans.) Chamber of Commerce/Historical Museum
Norm Avery
Rick Baker, Kansas Museum of History
Virginia Baldwin
Rebecca Barber and John Nichols, Wyandotte County Historical Society
Jim Bede, Bede Jet Corporation
Mike Potts and Pat Zerbe, Beech Aircraft Corporation
David Blanton, Javelin Aircraft Company
Boeing Archives, Seattle
Paul Bowen
Alberta Brinkman
Steve Brown, Mid America Air Museum, Liberal
Mary Brunin, Rossville (Kans.) Public Library
John Burton and Carl Schuppel, Experimental Aircraft Association, Oshkosh, Wis.
Butler County Historical Society
Judy Chandler and Darren McGuire, Kansas Aviation Museum
Jack Clark
Crawford Auto-Aviation Museum/Western Reserve Historical Society
Scott Daymon and Frank Woods, Daywood Publishing
Gene DeGruson, Leonard H. Axe Special Collections, Pittsburg State University
Ted Eland, Piaggio Aviation, Inc.
FAA Regional offices, Wichita and Oklahoma City
FAA Department of Statistics, Washington, D.C.
General Aviation Manufacturers Association
Gordon German, Kansas Department of Commerce
Debra S. Giskie, city of Liberal, Kans.
Dan Hagedorn, National Air and Space Museum, Smithsonian Inst.
Candace A. Hargrove, General Motors Corporation, Fairfax Plant
Terry Harley, Girard (Kans.) Public Library
Cindy Hart, Kansas Secretary of State's office
Henry Ford Museum Archives
Jim Hephner
Lee Higdon
High Planes Museum of Goodland, Kans.
Dean Humphrey, Cessna Aircraft Company
Phil Michel, Cessna Aircraft Company
Kanhistique Magazine
Kansas City Public Library
Kansas State Historical Society
Frank Kehr, Silent Wings Museum, Texas
Mike Kelly, Special Collections, Wichita State University
Bob Maier
Bob McCall
SI McDonald
Randy Mertens
National Archives, regional branch
Newton (Kans.) Chamber of Commerce
Rex Norton
Marion Parker
Roland D. Parr
Dennis Pearce
Chuck Porter, Department of Defense Still Media Center
Pratt (Kans.) Chamber of Commerce
Pratt County Historical Society
Tom Prescott
Ken Rearwin
Royce Rearwin
William G. Robinson, Learjet Inc.
Jeff Miller, Learjet Inc.
Carolyn Russell, Boeing Wichita
Salina (Kans.) Chamber of Commerce
Nancy Scherbert, Kansas State Historical Society
Bob Schaefer
Randy Schlitter, Rans Company
Sedgwick County Historical Society
Don Simon
Erik Simonsen, North American Aviation Corporation
Ann Sindelar, Crawford Auto-Aviation Museum-Western Reserve Historical Society
Cliff Sones, American Bonanza Society
A Lee Spencer
Glenn Stearman
Staff Sgt. Mary K. Coln, Kansas Air National Guard
Robert Taylor, Antique Airplane Association
Minard Thompson
United States Air Force Museum, Wright Patterson Air Force Base, Ohio
U.S. Department of Commerce
Truman C. (Pappy) Weaver
Ken Weyand
Wichita (Kans.) Public Library
Wichita (Kans.) Chamber of Commerce
Donna Wise, Women's Aeronautical Association of Kansas
Dean Zongker

Thanks for consultation to:

John Davis
William Clark Ellington
Walt House
Edward H. Phillips
Steve Stelljes

Special thanks to:

Pat Rowe

Photographs from the Bob Pickett and the Edward N. Tihen Collection have been provided by the Kansas Aviation Museum, 3350 George Washington Boulevard, Wichita, Kansas 67210

NOTE:

As part of a continuing effort to document and preserve the heritage of Kansas aviation, the authors encourage all material (photographs, relics, memoirs, and other historical items) to be submitted for review and recording by the Kansas State Historical Society in Topeka as well as other statewide aeronautical museums and archives as noted in the acknowledgment section of this book.

CONTENTS

THE WHATCHIMACALLITS

"KANSAS SOMETIMES SEEMS TO HAVE MORE SKY THAN GROUND. SO MUCH SKY THAT PEOPLE WALK OUTSIDE AND NATURALLY LOOK UP. SO MUCH SKY THAT IT SEEMS AT TIMES TO OVERTAKE THE GROUND. SO MUCH SKY THAT IT ALMOST SEEMS TO INVITE DREAMERS AND EXPLORERS TO TEST THE LIMITS."
— ANONYMOUS

Once something has been done, however difficult or long in coming the breakthrough, repetitions and improvements quickly become commonplace. A stimulating vision like the age-old dream of flight, once implemented by practical demonstration and loosed into a fertile atmosphere, such as existed in early twentieth-century industrial America, spreads like wildfire into every hamlet and every innovative mind that can find an audience or a backer.

Wilbur and Orville Wright, who made and raced bicycles from their home in Dayton, Ohio, rode their fragile wood and fabric craft off its rail track and up into the winds at Kitty Hawk, N.C., on a cold December day in 1903. Within five years, the inspired amateurs would sell an airplane to the government. By 1909 in Goodland, Kans., a wind-swept outpost in the isolated northwest corner of a state just recovering from the worst drought, depression, and bout of political eccentricity in its history, there was talk of a locally produced helicopter.

As the Wrights had shown, small-town artisans had the sophistication and could raise the modest capital necessary to solve aeronautical problems of the time. Therefore it was no surprise that two mechanics employed by the Chicago, Rock Island, and Pacific Railway Company at Goodland, William J. Purvis and Charles A. Wilson, quit their jobs on the promise of rotary-winged aircraft. Their design was similar to one worked out by J. Newton Williams of Hammondsport, N.Y., in 1908, which in turn fit the ideas of Thomas Edison and, before him, Leonardo da Vinci about how an aircraft ought to work. The Goodland design had worked in dozens of small

VARIATION ON A WINDMILL

⇐ William Purvis and Charles Wilson stand by their marvelous rotary-winged aircraft in Goodland in 1909. Although it was a theoretically viable design, the two railway mechanics never had the time or money to work out the bugs.

Marion Parker

Kansas City Star

WILLIAM J. PURVIS
Purvis, a native of Illinois, arrived in Goodland in 1902. In 1909, while watching children play with whirligigs, he considered the possibility of building a larger, albeit highly modified, version. While posing his idea to his friend and future partner, he enthused: "All we've got to do is make it big enough to carry a man."

Kansas City Star

CHARLES A. WILSON
A native of Idaho and partner of William Purvis, the dapper Wilson recalled: "We made dozens of small models, and they all worked." Those successes fueled an addiction to flying that saw both Wilson and Purvis work as railway machinists at night and aircraft pioneers during the day.

models, and had reportedly managed in full-scale to create a gap between its wheels and the ground when hitched to the power take-off of a steam tractor borrowed from a local farmer. "We knew that if we could get the power it would go," said Wilson, reminiscing about it at his Kansas City home during the height of the World War II aviation boom in the state. "We saw it as a gyroplane that could land on a building or a small space of ground. We didn't want speed so much as we wanted maneuverability."

A tethered bounce might not have seemed impressive. And the design of the machine was enough to give pause to those strong on common sense and experience with Kansas wind, not to mention the state's "unimproved" landing fields. The pair planned to power their craft with two aluminum, 7 HP gas engines turning a spindly two and one-half inch vertical shaft nearly twenty feet long that would spin broad, counter-rotating, concave canvas blades (stiffened with the merest hint of bamboo doweling and guy wires) through an eighteen-foot radius. The whole thing weighed only 400 pounds, *sans* fearless aviator. Even storage was a problem: photos show the proud inventors in front of surely one of the tallest barn doors on record. The plane had, said one Goodland historian, "all the grace of a crippled praying mantis.

Those aesthetic and engineering problems did not discourage the air-minded local population any more than the fact that inventor and chief engineer Purvis, thirty-nine, had ended his formal education at age ten or that his partner, Wilson, was only twenty-two years old. During that summer of 1909, when the two were experimenting on a farm owned by Purvis, the activity drew crowds who delighted in spending their family weekends camped on the prairie watching the future unfold. To the technically uninformed, the description of how the machine would fly sounded impressive. The patent application filed in 1910 explained that after the machine was off the ground and at the desired altitude "swinging or tilting planes are provided at the opposite sides of the machine and extending outwardly therefrom. Each of these planes is mounted upon a transverse rockshaft carrying at its inner end a gear segment with which meshes a toothed rack or segment on the lower end of an operating lever, said lever having a suitable dog or latch to engage a rack, whereby it may be secured in a variety of adjusted positions, the construction and arrangement thus being such that the aeronaut may simultaneously adjust the plates to different angular positions in the same or opposite directions, at will."

Rube Goldberg could not have phrased it better. A reporter for the *Goodland Republic*, having viewed what he admitted was a "rude model" at a Thanksgiving Day demonstration in 1909, enthused that "its weight-sustaining feature cannot be questioned by anyone that has some knowledge of aerostatics." The gyroplane on that day was hitched to an external power

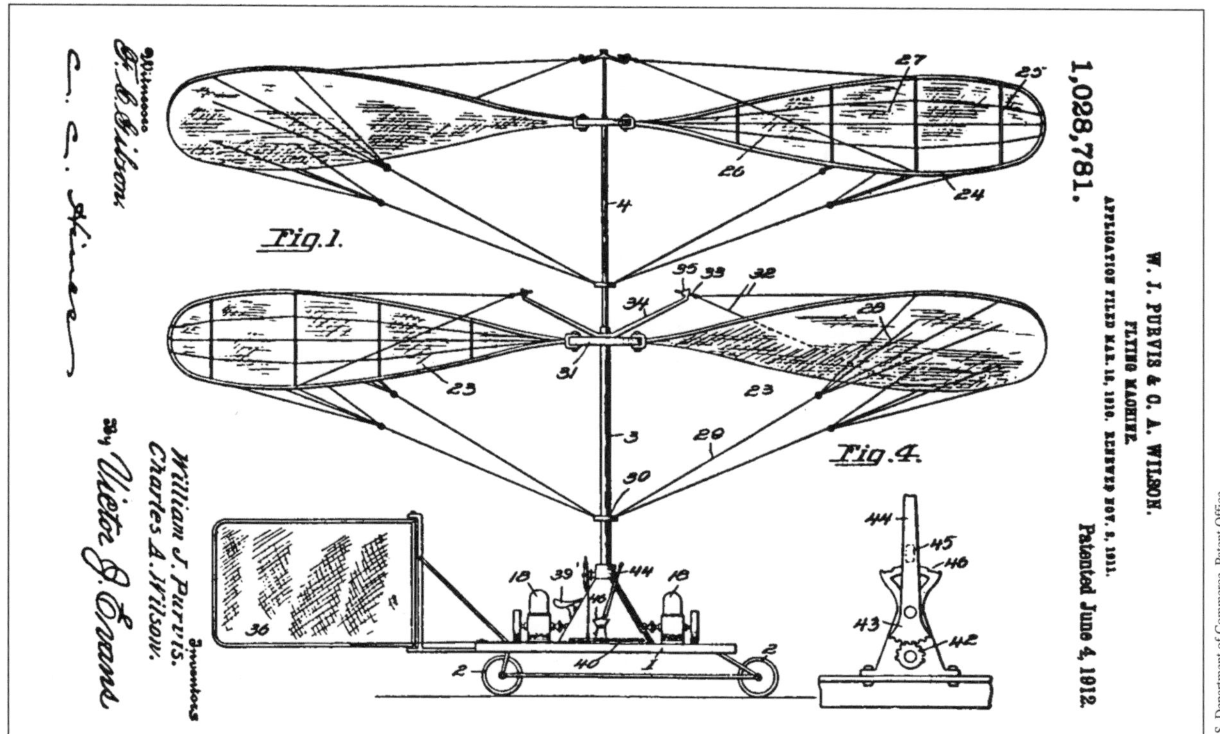

U.S. Department of Commerce, Patent Office

source and cabled to two large stones weighing a total of 500 pounds. When the power was applied, it was said that the motion of the rotors "perceptibly swayed the heavy ballast." Many were on hand that day to examine the "novel machine" and hear an explanation of its parts and the plans for it. "The writer refrains," said one journalistic expert, "from giving details that might jeopardize the owners' and inventors' interests, but will say this; it is unlike any other flying machine invented and constructed."

The proof of local backing came on the evening of December 1, 1909, when, at a meeting at the law offices of Calvert and Sparks, $30,000 in stock was authorized, and nineteen local men put down investments in the Goodland Aviation Company, of which Purvis and Wilson controlled 51 percent. There was great pride that these men, who "had to depend on their daily wages for support," had, during a year of hard work, come so far. "Goodland promises to become famous on account of the genius of some of its modest citizens and we believe the day is not far distant when the fame of these inventors will surpass all others, in regard to inventions of this character." It was, said the *Republic*, at least as good as the rain-making companies that earlier had given Goodland press coverage. "It can be said of the people they pull together."

The *Kansas City Star* in December 1909, gave the new "short grass flying machine" the better part of a page, complete with line illustrations of the

PURVIS/WILSON PATENT DRAWING

⇑ The 1909 Purvis-Wilson design for the Goodland Aviation Company was not just a fanciful curiosity. It is surprisingly similar to Louis Breguet and Rene Dorand's Gyroplane Labratoire, which flew in 1935. The first really practical helicopter, Sikorsky's VS-300 of 1939, abandoned the counter-rotating props in favor of a balancing tail rotor.

device and drawings of Wilson and Purvis. The slightly tongue-in-cheek article rejoiced that "inventive genius" was "neither dead nor dormant in western Kansas." Goodland was a real American place, the reporter thought, where "men's minds run in grooves of improvement and invention rather than toward art, literature, philosophy and religion." It should be fertile ground for the "embryonic Wrights" of western Kansas.

For a time things appeared promising. The fifty-pound, two-cylinder engines, which cost $800 each and were used to provide fail-safe dual power, were delivered from the G.H. Curtiss Manufacturing Company. One was placed on exhibit in the display window of the Goodland Clothing Company in March 1910. A test of the machine was expected within two months. That date was shortly moved back to July 4. As that date approached, the newspapers hedged by noting that the flying machine might only be exhibited and explained that day, not flown. On the Fourth of July, it failed to appear at all. Purvis said there was too much wind (it was, after all, summer in western Kansas). The celebration committee offered to furnish men enough to keep it from blowing over, but the inventor still refused. The newspaper laconically observed: "Mr. Purvis surely cannot expect much more support from the people of Goodland since his actions on the Fourth."

Purvis made a trip to St. Louis late that July seeking new engines, as he said that the Curtiss units were "entirely insufficient" to power the rotors. Tests with a 30 HP traction engine convinced the promoters that it would take an engine of between 40 and 50 HP "to do the stunt easily on the Goodland flying machine." Engines of this power, of course, did not weigh fifty pounds. In November 1910, Mrs. A.D. McIntyre of Goodland claimed she saw an aeroplane passing overhead matching the description of the "gyroscope" she had read about. After talking to the excited lady, a reporter rushed down to the Rock Island shops to see if the Purvis machine was there — it was. Purvis was making some changes, he said, and expected to test soon.

He never did. In the spring of 1911, Purvis sold his farm and left for the Ozark region of Missouri. The Goodland Aviation Company held its last meeting to dispose of its assets at auction and to dissolve the organization. Critics said that the gyroscope propeller was a good feature and might have provided for "poise in the air," but that Purvis' idea that the same rotors could be tilted to move the ship forward was a flawed concept.

What was left of the Purvis-Wilson flying machine project was auctioned in April 1911. A storage building went for $100, the engines went for less than $40 apiece, and the odds and ends were sold by lot. The obituary was brief: "The Goodland Aviation Company has collapsed very much like a balloon when punctured. They have gained some experience and lost some cash. Nobody complains and nobody blames."

Said Wilson years later: "You know how it is when you fail. You decide what you were doing wasn't your line. I haven't kept up with plane developments. I've stuck to the machine shop since." Harold Norton, a pilot who later built a replica of the Purvis-Wilson invention for a Goodland museum, commented that "the sorry part of it is, that if there hadn't been so much fun made of it — if there had been a little more money put into it and interest shown in it — they might have worked the bugs out of it."

Purvis, Wilson, and their enthusiastic backers belong to what might be called the "whatchimacallit" era of Kansas aviation — that heady period before 1911 when every aviation proposal in the state was original, extravagant, and unworkable. It was a time strong on vision and the entrepreneurial salesmanship that was already a Kansas tradition but short on experience and information from engineers elsewhere. People were especially quick to respond to promotions concerning flight because, though new as a practical possibility, the dream dated to the legend of Daedalus and Icarus. It had been said that Alexander the Great transported himself around on flying Griffins, steered by holding food above their heads. Renaissance readers thrilled to the spectacle of an evil necromancer hurling electric bolts at a female warrior while flying on a marvelous creature called a Hippogriff. Dragons and rocket birds were regular inhabitants of fiction, and da Vinci's drawings were but the earliest known survivors of thousands of serious paper plans for manned flying machines. By the early twentieth century, kites, windmills, gliders, parachutes, and balloons had brought the public tantalizingly close to the possibility of heavier-than-air flight. There was a veritable romance with aviation as an idea. Since heaven was somewhere above and angels flew, there was a widespread fancy that manned flight would change both society and human nature fundamentally and for the better. "Airmindedness" was close to evangelism in the public imagination.

Perhaps the best of it was that the Wrights had first achieved controlled, powered heavier-than-air flight and that the Langley Aerodrome, backed by the powerful Smithsonian Institution, had tumbled into the Potomac River. While the Wrights were not the tinkers that anti-intellectual Henry Ford liked to imagine they were, they were businesspeople and not eggheads. And they did achieve it all on a budget. Why not, therefore, Purvis and Wilson of Goodland, Kans., or Everyman of Anywhere, U.S.A.? No license was required to fly an airplane; no inspection was needed to build one.

Wichita aviation pioneer Emil Matthew Laird took off as a teenager in Chicago in a homemade contraption, and no one was more surprised than he to be airborne. Some would fail, but, as Otto Lilienthal had put it in the 1880s when his badly designed hang glider went into a stall and crashed, fatally injuring him: "Sacrifices must be made."

"Certain times or circumstances are necessary to validate most, if not all human aspirations," wrote Matthew Bruccoli. "The boy in the Florence of the Renaissance never hoped to become the Marshal of Abilene. Nor has it ever occurred to the Basuto tribesmen that there might be glory at the rear wheel of the Hook & Ladder." But Kansas, where historian Karl Becker sought "America double-distilled" by taking a stint at the university in Lawrence in 1910, was the heart of the civilization, where the elements coalesced to make it all happen and to focus the dreams of boys and men. The West had been different things to different eyes during its exploration, but around 1900 it went through an imaginative transformation that turned the Kansas of the mind's eye into a vast God-constructed virgin-prairie flying field, with room for error in all directions. High winds might be a problem but only after getting off the ground. The Kansas "whatchimacallits" were strange, but they were original — ones of a kind. And they showed promise for a future when air centers would not be made by copyists.

Purvis and Wilson's craft is thought to be the first rotary-winged aircraft ever patented, and was a serious predecessor to the workable helicopter, not perfected until the mid-1930s. Less could be claimed for a number of other early Kansas designs.

Actually Kansas did not wait around for the Wrights before beginning to talk about aviation projects in a specific, entrepreneurial manner. In 1885 Dr. S.L.N. Foote of Lebo, Kans., published an "Open Letter" claiming on the basis of a "rude model" to have invented a practical airplane. "Without a doubt," went a testimonial from the Emporia paper, "he has struck the key note to a perfect and safe mode of passing through the air, as we now pass over land and through the sea." Pages of names averred that it "could not fail." Foote himself advertised that with this device: "We, and not the Czar of Russia, shall become the world's dictators. … I know I have made the great discovery of modern times, and offer to divide the glory and gain with as many as I can." Foote claimed his model was the result of thirty years' study: "I have wooed the sciences with the midnight oil, and must still give it my guardian care, until it floats an accomplished beauty in mid-heaven and the world stands agape in admiration. Now peer through the thin veil that so feebly hides coming events, and no prophetic ken is required to see along the dusky horizon of years in the near future, multitudes of happy humans sportively darting through or around the silver edges of the clouds, or like migratory birds, fleecing from the biting breath of Boreas to the sunny isles of the southern seas."

While Foote said he cared nothing for money and would screen investors carefully for character and idealism, he would entertain deposits made in the Lebo bank for backing his company. Were it not for the careful collecting of the Kansas State Historical Society not even a single copy of

Roland Parr

STAR WARS, 1898

⇑ The Gabbey Airship, which originated in Rossville, was to have been propelled by revolving "screw parachutes." Each revolution of these devices was supposed to be the equivalent of the stroke of a bird's wing. The final version was to be 144 feet long, sixty-five feet wide and develop 150 HP, with the engine turning the screws through cables. It worked only in Dr. Robert S. Gabbey's imagination.

this promotional pamphlet would survive to mark Foote's enterprise. In short, nothing came of it.

A similar pamphlet documents the Gabbey Air-Ship Company of Rossville, Kans. The prospectus illustrated a most amazing flying device, looking for all the world like a UFO and sporting an American flag flying over smooth aerodynamics. A model had been built, and a patent filed in 1898 by Dr. Robert S. Gabbey, a sideburned physician in his mid-fifties, who, like Foote, thought that his scientific training as a physician qualified him to be an aeronautical engineer. His obituary in the *Rossville News* claimed hedgingly that he had many patents and that the *Scientific American* and other technical journals had accepted "his advanced theories on the perplexing problem (of flight) with due consideration of their plausibility and value." At any rate, he employed expert Kansas publicists.

Gabbey was said in the prospectus to have weighed innumerable birds and measured their wing surfaces, with the data incorporated into the design of a three-foot model. Subscriptions apparently came in slowly, if at all. It is uncertain whether the sixteen-foot model proposed as the next step was ever built, and Gabbey died shortly after the prospectus was issued.

More odd yet was the design of Frank Barnett of Kansas City, Kans., a cut of which was published in the *Kansas City Star* in 1897. It consisted of a large vertical vane mounted upright in the center of a wheeled undercarriage. From this vane projected a series of airfoils. Two propellers on each side of the machine were to provide locomotion. Barnett had exhibited a "machine for mechanical flight" as early as 1870 at the Iowa State Fair, along with his tomatoes and onions. He was laughed at by the best of them, including P.T. Barnum. Barnett admitted in 1908 that the Wrights had "greater means at their disposal than I had and undoubtedly with greater

KANSAS KITES

⇒ Set apart from the proponents of lighter-than-air gas airship designs were a band of pioneers espousing the use of kites with various means of propulsion. Frank Barnett of Kansas City, Kans., claimed, "The kite flyers of today will solve the airship problem, and the advent of the box kite will hasten it." His experiments took shape in a variety of paper models, as shown here.

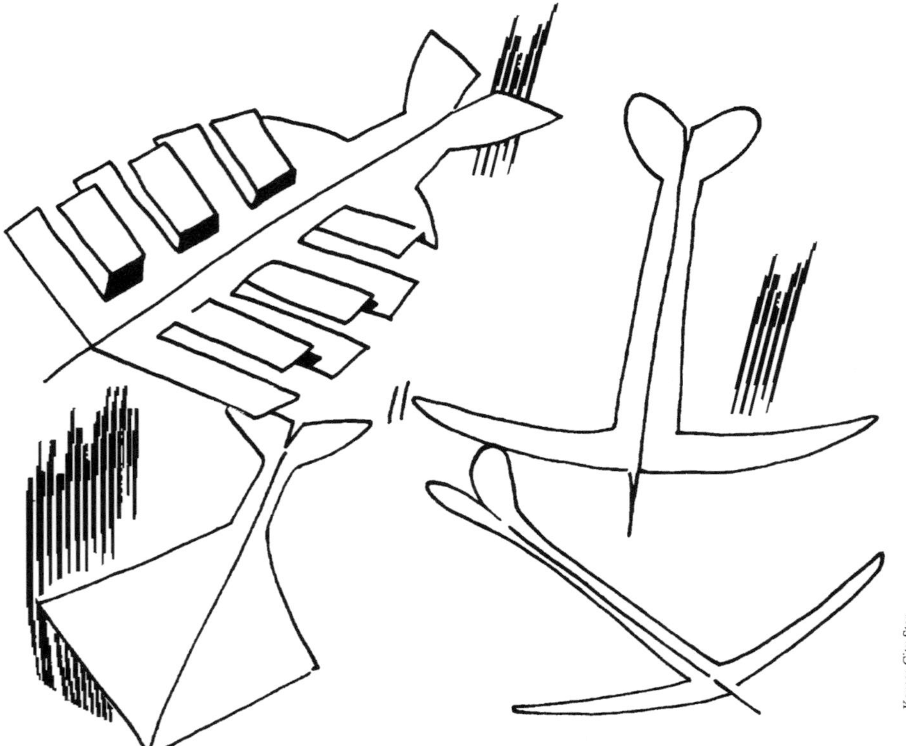

Kansas City Star

mechanical ability." But he contended that the principle was the same. It reminds one of the joke about a beaver contemplating Hoover Dam. "I didn't actually build it, " the animal says, "but it is based on an idea of mine."

Victor Murdock, son of the editor of the *Wichita Eagle,* attended an event in Chicago with Edison in 1891. His question, written out for the deaf inventor, was, "Will man ever fly?" Edison responded, "Yes, and in a heavier-than-air machine." The Wrights' achievement confirmed that, and speeded the pace of the Kansas claims, though at first the brothers' practical achievement made these designs no less exotic and original than before.

In 1900 Carl Dryden Browne promoted a commercial airplane factory at Freedom, Kans., a utopian community founded to advance the Labor Exchange movement, which imagined replacing money with labor checks. He said he had applied for a patent based on the "principle of rotary winged wheels." A small factory was erected, and Browne built a model, but was unable to perfect it. The factory closed in 1902, and the whole Freedom colony burned to the ground in 1905.

A.V. Weingarten of Leon, Kans., said in 1904 that he had built a two-foot-long airplane model that flew fine, even lifting 300 pounds of ballast, and he was scaling it up. Models often flew. The Wrights flew model planes as children, and several of Langley's Aerodromes flew in fairly large model versions, only to fail miserably at full-scale. Mrs. Weingarten, who had helped her husband by turning his lathe by hand for hours in his backyard workshop was said to have "collapsed out of pure joy (or from fatigue) when it was found that the machine would actually do what was expected of it." He had refused all of the many offers to buy his design, said the *Eagle*, that had come from capitalists as far away as New York and Washington, D.C. Even auto companies were supposedly interested, as they expected the airplane to replace the fledgling auto entirely. "The automobile," Weingarten said, "is a dirty machine and can never be perfected."

Weingarten's specifications were incredible. His next machine, he said, would weigh only 200 pounds and would be able to lift 600 pounds, or four adults. The accompanying drawing looked like a streamlined wooden railroad car attached to a grain auger — a true "whatchimacallit." The article in the *Eagle* was the first, last and only record of Weingarten in aviation history.

More bizarre still in appearance, as well as in purpose and promotion, was the device developed in Girard, Kans., by the Aerial Navigation Company of America. The inventor was Henry Laurens Call, a socialist lawyer and economist, and the initial purpose was to fly the considerable radical contingent in his little southeast Kansas town (J.A. Wayland's socialist

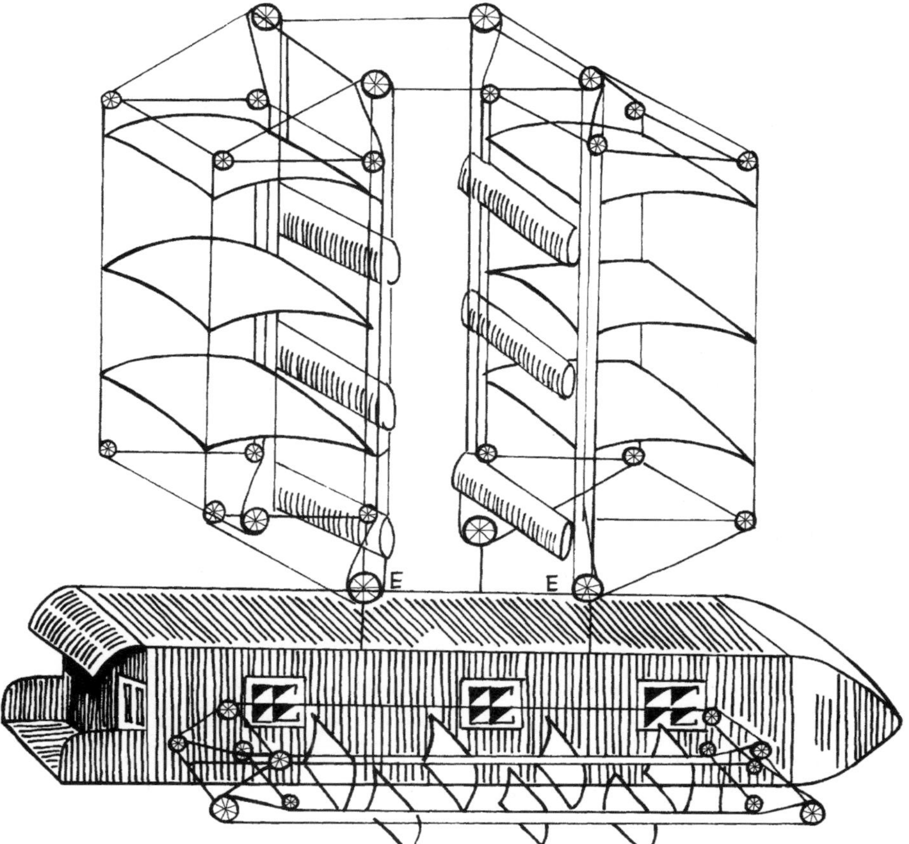

The Wichita Eagle

A FLYING GRAIN AUGER

⇐ After sixteen years of studying aerial navigation, A.V. Weingarten of Leon came up with this craft, which he claimed would carry 4 HP people, fly with a four horsepower engine and cost only $300 to build. "There's nothing about the contrivance that is even suggestive of a balloon," he wrote a reporter. "It is purely a flying machine." More machine, it might be added, than flying. To Weingarten it was elegant. "I cannot understand why I did not think of this system sooner," he said, "it is not only the simplest of any, but the most practical."

Gene DeGruson, Leonard H., Axe Special Collections, Pittsburg State University

A WOODPECKER-HEADED CREATION

⇑ The 1908 airplane of Henry L. Call of Girard, dubbed The Great Dream, had 2,000 square feet of canvas sail spread over a length of fifty feet and a height of twenty feet. When it was hauled along Forest Avenue in Girard toward a test site, a reporter said it looked "like a turkey gobbler with its wings clipped, who wants to fly the coop but can't."

newspaper *Appeal to Reason* was published there) to Chicago for the Socialist convention of 1908.

Had this mission been accomplished, the Girard group would have arrived in considerable style. The ship was an "amphibious" design, a combination automobile, aircraft, and boat. Local press coverage was sarcastic, noting that the purpose of the Call airplane was "to batter down tariff walls" or to establish a Socialist Aerial Navy to capture kings and queens. But, unlike many early projects, a full-sized version of this craft was completed, though too late for the convention. Tests were less than successful. First a wheel fell off. Later the engines would not start. Still later the machine got stuck on the runway, and on another test an assistant ran into the propeller and was killed. The best it ever did was to taxi at 10 MPH and that itself must have been quite a sight. "This," wrote one observer, "is no one-horse, one-man affair."

"The Call Airship," went a headline, "hasn't yet become addicted to the rising habit." But The *Girard Press* said the "woodpecker-headed creation" would surely be successful eventually, since everyone has seen both a house- and a horsefly. It labeled the project the *Whynot.*

Still, much was done. Over $30,000 was spent, enough, according to one estimate, to benefit Girard more than any other institution except the street railway. A factory was purchased (probably the first in Kansas devoted to aircraft), a flying school was established, two full-sized prototypes were built, and the weight was reduced to 1,500 pounds by the extensive use of aluminum in a kind of space frame. After extensive testing of the second prototype, Call decided that the engines were at fault and designed his own horizontally opposed, two-cylinder power plants, which he sold to others for additional revenue. However, although Call had studied math and physics, he ignored the Wrights' discoveries and took a basically unscientific approach. By 1911 he would change to a more conventional biplane design which rose as high as forty feet before crashing. Another crash of a monoplane design in 1912 ended his career, which had reached its high point, of nerve at least, with the earthbound journey of the grandiose Dream of 1908.

That ten-passenger baby buggy under a beach canopy cooled by fans was as curious as anything that had ever appeared in Kansas, or anywhere else. It was also the first Kansas-designed and built airplane to actually make an attempt to take off. And its failure was not for lack of trying: The company lost $85,000 on the venture, with many leading socialists as investors, before it declared bankruptcy in 1912. Henry Call's airship, wrote a Kansas City wag, was not the only thing in Girard "that is supposed to appeal to reason, but doesn't."

The Girard phenomenon was hardly the end of the unflyable originality of Kansans, though with the passage of time the flights of imagination were somewhat restrained by the growing body of practical experience in a few workable designs. A.E. Hunt's rotary flying machine, which vibrated itself to death without leaving the ground in 1912, was more incredible than the

Terry Harley, Girard Public Library

HENRY L. CALL ⇑

SOLID, BUT SLOW

⇓ Demonstrating a better grasp of blacksmithing than aeronautical engineering, A. E. Hunt entered the helicopter field with a machine that looked more like a carnival ride than a flying machine. It was dangerous on the ground and, luckily, remained there. But his work allowed Jetmore to be a part of the most up-to-date regional industry.

Virginia Baldwin

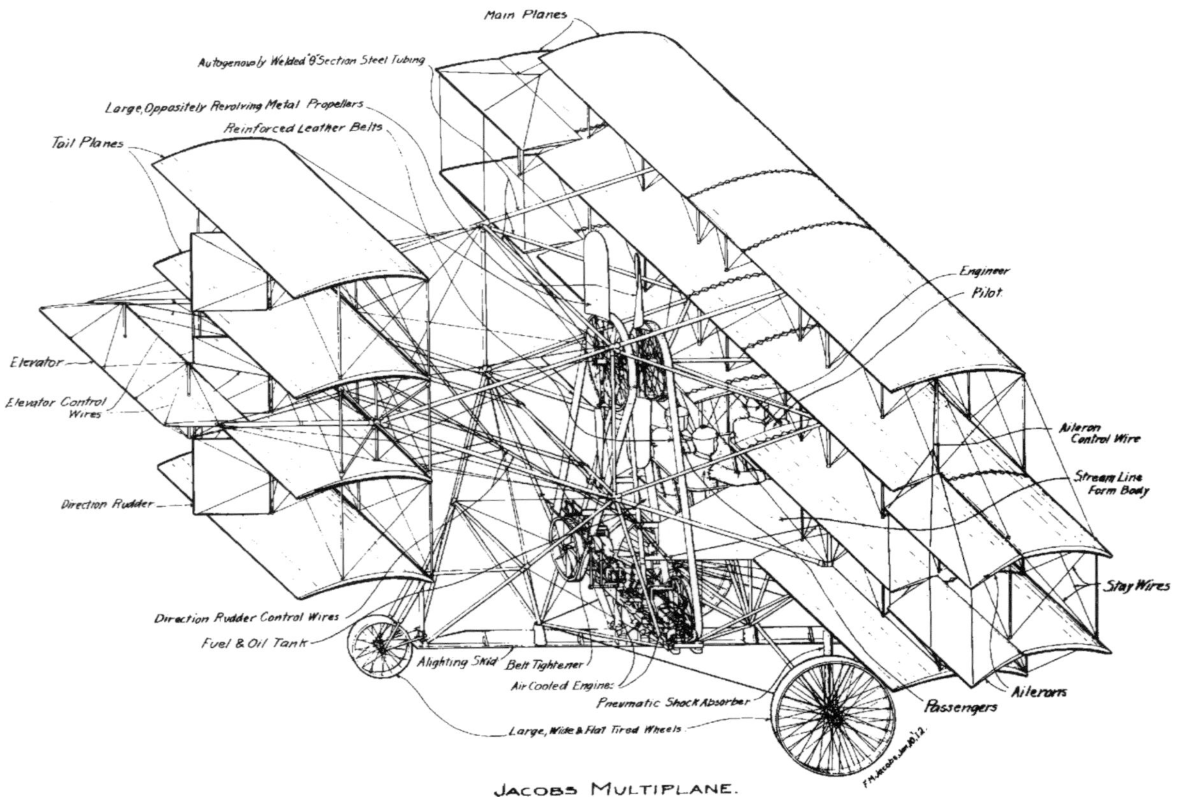

Alberta Brinkman

FREAK? ⇑ At the New York Aero Show in 1912, the appearance of the Jacobs Multiplane, built in Atchison, Kans., was likened to an "east-side tenement house." It never flew, but did make a good radio antenna, thanks to all of its wires and framework.

earlier Goodland helicopter prototype. It was constructed at Jetmore, Kans. — a west central Kansas community that made Goodland look like a metropolis — by a blacksmith who, in order to ensure its solidity, welded it up out of 4,000 to 5,000 pounds of angle iron. According to eyewitnesses, the machine when started up made an "awful noise" as the rotors, which resembled nothing so much as stock tanks on poles, began to turn in the wind. "I think he would have swallowed his pipe if it had taken off," laughed a friend of Hunt's.

Just as unusual in appearance was the Multiplane, built by H.W. Jacobs of Atchison, Kans. Reputed to have cost $18,000, and relying for lift on at least eight distinguishable wing surfaces towering above huge spoked wheels (four feet in diameter for landing in rough country with heavy loads), the Multiplane was to get its power from newly designed, air-cooled V-8 engines. The Multiplane, built as it was of "AirLight," a special steel "Theta section tubing … autogenously formed," would be, went the claim, safe, reliable, and easily assembled. It had a "non-capsizing, self-righting" action, demonstrated by dropping another one of those great models edgewise from a balloon a third of a mile up with no damage.

Jacobs announced his plans to the public in 1910 and tried a test flight with smaller engines than the design called for in 1912. The aircraft reportedly flew but could not gain altitude or turn quickly because of the lack of power. It showed enough promise, however, that it was shipped as an example of Kansas aircraft originality to the First Annual Aero Show, held in New York City in May to promote aviation. Doubtless, however, the comments of the New York papers, which called the Multiplane the "Freak Aircraft Feature of Aero Show," and a "Kansas man's conceit," were not pressed into clipping scrapbooks by the Jacobs family.

The Multiplane, shipped back to Atchison after the air show, was never reassembled. That summer Jacobs' younger brother, Frank, drowned when affected with a leg cramp while swimming with Henry. Jacobs received considerable money by selling patents on railway equipment to the Santa Fe Railway and that, combined with the loss of Frank, seemed to end his interest in aviation. He admitted that for him flying was purely a hobby and that he had developed the Multiplane to show that the monoplane design, such as Bleriot had used successfully to cross the English Channel, was fast but dangerous and to illustrate a craft that could carry heavy loads. "I became interested in the subject of airships merely because it's a branch of mechanics," Jacobs said. "I'm too busy in the service of a railroad's motive power and mechanical department to make aviation or the making of aerial crafts a

UMBRELLA-POWERED

⇓ Invented by Topeka resident General Vorhees, this airship featured a gas chamber for its primary lift. The inventor claimed that a series of umbrellas would provide motive power: "These umbrellas work up and down on an upright shaft and are so arranged that going up they open so as to let the air through, and close on the down pull so as to hold the air. These make an immense lifting power. A third umbrella, which is shown as extending below the ship (on a chain) is so adjusted so that can be thrown forward, and will pull the ship forward as it is retrieved."

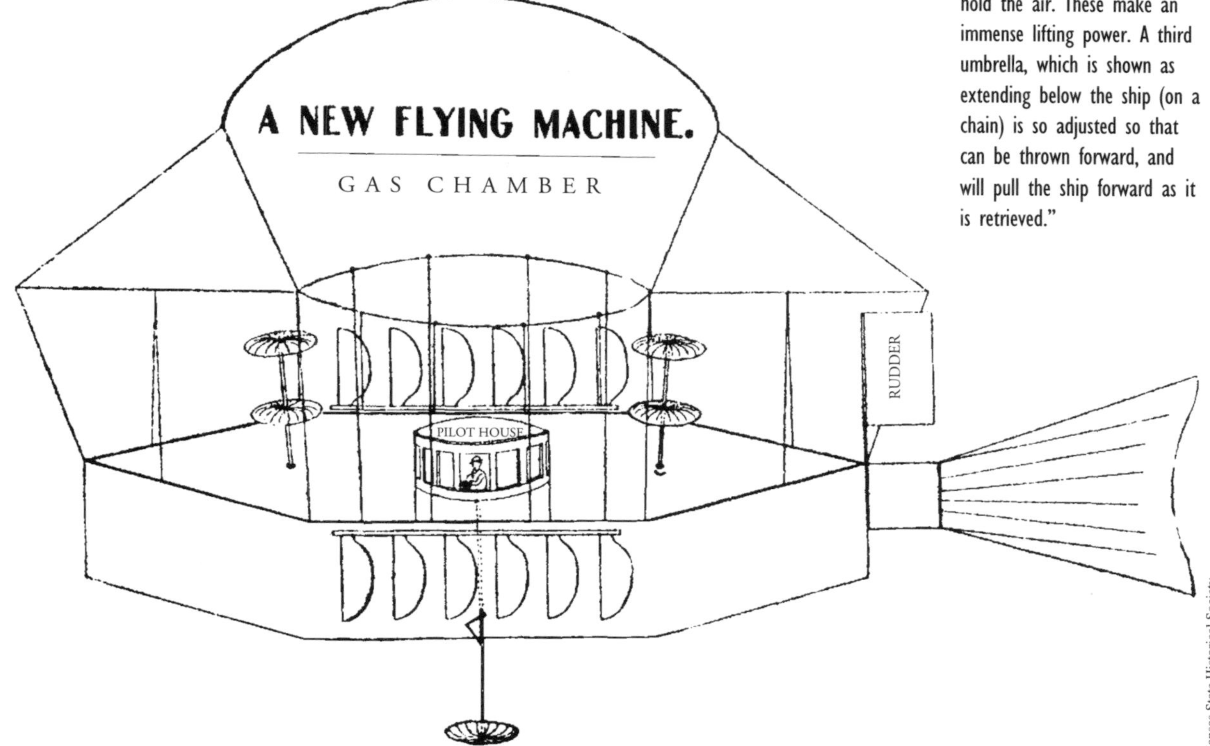

Kansas State Historical Society

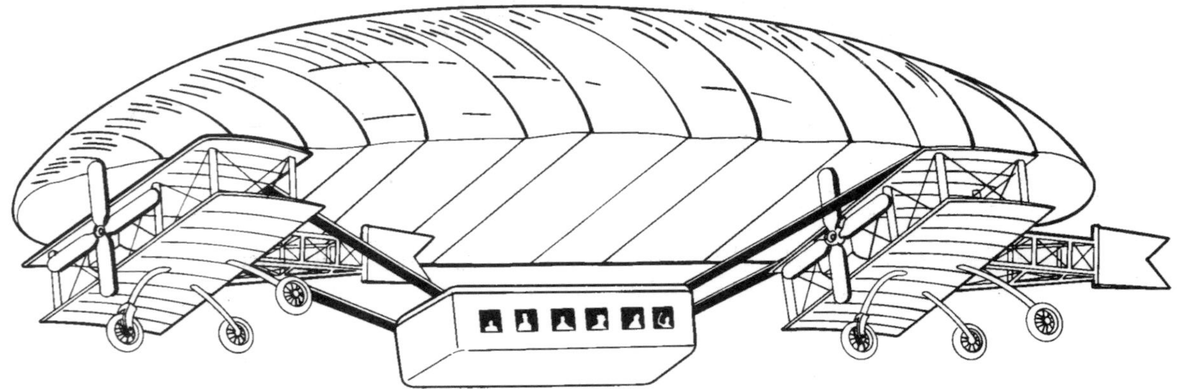
The Wichita Eagle

HAYWIRE HYBRID

⇑ Early aircraft projection was a game women could play, as Mrs. A. W. Jones of Wichita proved. Her 1914 offering for lengthy passenger travel included suspending a Pullman railway coach beneath a lighter-than-air craft "shaped like a fish cut longitudinally through the center." Conventional biplanes were to provide the forward motion, while the dirigible part of the design allowed for vertical takeoffs and landings as the airplane pilots coordinated their efforts via telephone.

profession. But there are great possibilities commercially in aviation. Fortunes have already been made with flying machines and more fortunes will be made." Henry Jacobs died in 1914. The V-8 engines for the Multiplane, when completed, were used to pump water and for other farm tasks. Recently two pieces of Theta tubing were found in use as survey stakes. Those and a 1912 brochure printed for the New York air show and rescued from a trash barrel, are all that is left of the Multiplane project.

The Hunt and Jacobs craft were true latter day "whatchimacallits." There were doubtless dozens of them, including a craft designed by Jacques Mueller, a German artist in Topeka, Kans., to decorate the murals at St. Joseph German Catholic Church. He announced in 1909 that he was building an airplane of brass tubing to be powered entirely without propellers, using a system of parachutes moving along the length of the plane on chains.

If Henry Ford could make a business out of a workshop project, so, by inference, could anyone. Maybe the latest of this individualistic breed was a hot-air craft designed in 1914 by a Wichita woman named Mrs. A.W. Jones. Her device, pictured in the *Eagle*, was a bag carried by two fairly conventional airplanes with coaches suspended beneath. "The new horizontal propellers," she said, "will also serve as a gyroscope, and will make it possible to turn the balloon in a moment's time by simply turning off the power from the front and back propellers on the right or left sides as may be demanded. A telephone should connect the two pilots. No landing fields will be required for individual machines of this type, since one could descend in his own back yard." Too good to be true — indeed, but in a wonderful Kansas tradition of confident projection.

17

WARPING THE GALE

"SEEING HIMSELF AN ATOM IN A SHROUD. MAN HEARS HIMSELF AN ENGINE IN A CLOUD."
— HART CRANE

If Kansans were eager to see a machine carrying a man and under directional control over their prairie, and undoubtedly they were, the first chances came from hybrid dirigible-style craft that were part balloon.

The earliest demonstration of "controlled" flight in Kansas was in a craft of the Knabenshue type. Roy Knabenshue had flown America's first successful dirigible at the St. Louis World's Fair in 1904, and cities around the country clamored for these craft to demonstrate at their fairs and exhibitions.

In August 1906, a Knabenshue ship called the *Eagle* arrived by train in Kansas City, Mo., along with its pilot, a Chicago electrician named Horace Wild. Its envelope was seventy-five feet long and sixteen feet in diameter and was made of varnished Japanese silk. The whole thing was powered by a 6 HP, two-cylinder engine that drove a front-mounted sixteen-foot propeller with blades made of fabric stretched over a spruce frame. At the rear was a canvas rudder, operated by a cord. Vertical control was achieved by Wild's walking back and forth over a spruce framework suspended below the bag to raise or lower the pitch of the prop — a hazardous undertaking indeed. Wild took off from Forest Park, in east Kansas City, several times and remained in the air for a few minutes each time. However, he never was able to reach downtown Kansas City, Mo., much less the Kansas border.

The next occasion for Kansans to see flight was in 1908 — the year of the failed Girard connection with the Socialist convention — at the Peerless Prophets Jubilee, a large fall street fair held in Wichita. The buyer from The George Innes Company in Wichita had seen flying demonstrated in New York by Knabenshue in a 150-foot-long dirigible powered by two 20 HP engines. It played well in the skyscraper canyons of New York, and on the advice of the buyer, $2,500 was raised in Wichita to transport a Knabenshue

AEROPLANE GOTHIC
⇐ Mr. and Mrs. Albin K. Longren of Topeka and Longren's 1911 flying machine in a typical Kansas airport setting of the period. The plane is noteworthy for its Hall-Scott V-8 engine, primitive aerodynamics, lack of safety features, and open-air cooling.

Kansas State Historical Society

craft to Kansas to cap the week-long October fair with a flight. Both local newspapers used the event as a chance to educate Wichitans about the fledgling U.S. aviation enterprise, and to create "airmindedness" in the residents.

The *Eagle* piece, "To Fly or Not to Fly" definitely favored "to fly." The Girard experiments, the editress thought, "have not yet been successful in the American interpretation of the word which infers (sic.) the qualifying adjective commercially." Perhaps the extreme claims for the future of aviation were overblown, but the staff at the *Eagle* definitely thought that flight would catch on because of the great enthusiasm it generated among people who observed in action even primitive machines. "No news item today interests more American people for a greater length of time and in a more absorbing way than does a report on an airship or flying machine exploit," the paper stated.

The rival *Wichita Beacon* published a five-part syndicated series on the status and possibilities of aviation authored by Frederic J. Haskin. The titles alone were exciting: "If Man Should Fly," "Ironclads in the Clouds," "The Overland Mail," "Freighters of the Air, "and "Aboard the Skyliner." "Although one of the aeroplanes of the Wright brothers lies a wreck at Fort Myer, Virginia, its duplicate is flying successfully at Le Mans, France," Haskins wrote. "The inventors are not discouraged. … After fifty centuries of effort, man seems at last to have conquered the air, and on the principle on which the Wright brothers have built their queer craft, they and other aviators will build and build again, until man shall fly some day as easily as the birds that he has envied and longed to emulate since the days of the cave dwellers." The airplane would revolutionize warfare, the series claimed, speed communication, and make the interchange of goods at a distance an affair for which there need be only hours of planning.

Knabenshue's ship, it turned out, demonstrated very little of that. The machine arrived, and quite an establishment for its care and feeding was created in and around a tent on Ackerman's Island, which at the time divided the Arkansas River into two channels at the downtown location where Douglas Avenue spanned it by bridge. The press had fun with the request for three tons of cast iron borings and thirty carboys of sulfuric acid from which the Knabenshue group would make its "high grade flying machine gas." The Jubilee ads promised that "the big attraction … will be the Knabenshue airship which will sail the air once every day during the week." The route was to be from the island, around the tall tower of Wichita's neo-Romanesque City Building, and back to the island — a round trip of about four blocks.

As it happened, failures to fly were announced about once a day. On October 12, when the first flight was scheduled, pilot Frank K. Goodale, a former scorecard salesman at the Toledo, Ohio, ball park, waited all day for

National Air and Space Museum, Smithsonian Institution (SI Neg. No. 75-7258)

the famous Kansas wind to die down. He considered a moonlight flight, but the breeze was still there at midnight. The same news came on the 14th. "Everybody's neck had an upward twist to it yesterday in hopes that the aviator would brave the elements and take a sail in spite of the wind, but the air kept moving at a greater rate of speed than eight miles an hour, so the performance is yet to be." By the 16th, with the fair closing down, and the airship still in its tent, the articles had a desperate tone. The flier agreed to stay, and fly on October 18. On that Sunday the wind still blew at more than 12 MPH most of the day. The airship was taken out of its tent and ascended into the air three times when the wind calmed. It rose as high as thirty feet. A large crowd watched what seemed to be a serious attempt to fly over the city late in the afternoon. The craft managed to cross the narrow river channel, allowing a photographer to snap a picture of it over the city. But the gas that had been in the bag all week was bad. The people departed with a promise of tomorrow.

In fact no serious flight was tried until Tuesday evening, by which time most spectators had stopped going to the island to watch. When it did happen, it was a disaster. "The Knabenshue airship," it was reported the next day, "lies in a shattered condition in the tent on Ackerman Island. Frank W. Goodale, the aviator, has a few body bruises, but otherwise is not injured." With the manager standing by, Goodale had started the engine the

A FLYING HAM

⇑ Jane's Aircraft Directory of 1909 said of the Knabenshue airship: "It has made several successful trips. The chief trouble seems to be lack of gas tightness." Indeed, at its 1908 flight attempt at Wichita, the craft was torn to shreds when the bag was whipped by the wind. Horizontal stability was achieved by the pilot's moving his weight along the spindly open undercarriage.

Kansas State Historical Society

MISFIRE

⇑ George Anderson died at the 1896 Miami County Fair at Paola after being fired from a cannon aboard a balloon at an altitude of 3,000 feet. His parachute opened, but the aviator was not wearing the customary safety belt attached to the parachute and lost his grip on it. Professor Bozarth of Missouri was paid $75 for the ascent, and the hapless Anderson was to receive $5. "As the body shot downward," went the day's account, "a cry of horror went up from the vast crowd that thronged the ground, and the day's pleasure was over for most of those who witnessed the terrible sight."

evening before "and with the prow pointing against the wind the vessel sailed upwards into the air. It reached a height of about fifty feet, when a sudden gust of wind carried the prow upwards, and to the few spectators it looked as though the gas bag would turn over. Goodale did not lose his nerve but swerved the course of the airship east and righted it, but just then another strong breeze blew the prow of the vessel downwards and it struck the whirling propeller. There was a snap and the big bag was ripped open and foul smelling gas could within a few minutes be detected within five blocks of the island." The remains of the airship, consisting mostly of many yards of torn Japanese silk, were shipped back to Knabenshue's headquarters in Toledo. The two promoters crept away, confessing that the technology for all-weather flight was lacking.

Wichitans were not altogether disappointed by the spectacle. It had been exciting thinking about watching a flight and actually seeing a man wrestling with a craft in the native zephyrs. They had learned from the newspaper articles surrounding the event. There was a postcard issued showing Knabenshue's airship superimposed on a photo of the City Building, just to illustrate what it might have looked like, had it worked as advertised.

There were flights of other dirigible hybrids, none very successful. Harry Ginter took his Stroebel Airship up in Topeka, Kans., in September 1911 and managed only a five-minute flight before ending up in a treetop. He wanted to fly around the Statehouse dome, but his rudder broke and so his machine came to an ignominious end.

More impressive among lighter-than-air craft operating in Kansas were the immense gas racing balloons that achieved impressive firsts in speed, distance and altitude between about 1910 and 1915. As the railway and the bicycle prepared people for the psychological changes involving speed and the individual control needed for automobile driving, balloons were a preparation for aviation.

Kansans were involved in ballooning early. B.J. Hobson, a Hutchinson, Kans., salt mine and foundry owner who moved to the state in 1872, was the designer and builder of the engines on what is thought to be the first dirigible built in the United States. The engines Hobson designed were steam, using a design by Rufus Porter, editor of *Scientific American.* The financing came partly from Congress. Unfortunately a few days before the test flight, a tornado struck Washington, D.C., and destroyed the craft.

Balloon ascents were a staple of state fairs and included both stunts and fatal accidents. As early as July 1869, there was a balloon ascension at Kansas City as part of the celebration of the opening of the railway bridge across the Missouri River. The pilot, H.H. Holman, flew his seventy-foot-

Wichita Public Library

PUSHED BY THE WINDS

⇐ The initial ascent from Wichita's Ackerman Island during the 1915 National Balloon Races. These race balloons used as much as 75,000 cubic feet of gas and were more than fifty feet across at their widest points. At lift-off, such balloons would carry 2,500 pounds of sand ballast, several crew members in a four-foot-by-five-foot basket, and provisions for the several days and hundreds of miles the craft might remain aloft.

high craft before 40,000 spectators, not one of whom would volunteer to be a passenger. Holman was a local jeweler who could see immense commercial potential. On a later flight, he scattered handbills advertising his shop over the countryside, and these attracted a flood of customers. In 1896 at the Miami County Fair in Paola, Kans., twenty-two-year-old George P. Anderson fell 3,000 feet to his death before shocked spectators from a balloon provided by a company in Missouri.

But accidents could do little to dampen interest. In 1910 Lillian S. Smith of New York became the first woman to go aloft in a balloon over Kansas, providing the perspective of a humanist, in contrast to the terse, almost astronaut-like comments of aviators and engineers, observations that too often were wholly unsatisfactory to people who yearned to know the sensations from the perspective of an ordinary person. Smith declared balloon flying to be "a splendid sport and … far ahead of any means of locomotion on earth."

"The ascent was so smooth," she wrote, "that I scarcely realized I was moving. When we were high in the air I saw both Lawrence and Topeka at the same time. They looked from that distance like little toy towns. I couldn't distinguish the trees. The earth looked as though it had been marked off into little squares, with the river like a silver thread on a green floor. When we went above the clouds I felt a slight deafness, but it lasted only a short while. We were immensely hungry and ate lunch a mile in the air. We alighted without a bit of jar, just missing a barbed wire fence. While I have enjoyed my visit in Kansas greatly, I have enjoyed this balloon trip more than anything else."

About a year later a reporter for the *Kansas State-Journal* went up aboard the balloon *Topeka I,* owned by the Western Aero Club, and gave an extensive description of the sensation: "Go out on your front lawn, crumple a piece of paper and drop it on the grass. Then tear up another sheet and sprinkle it around the crumpled mass. Stand back a few feet, squint your eyes and look at your handiwork. It will look much like the city of Topeka from a balloon." The fun of looking down, the man said, did away with all thought of fear. He loved the look of the Kaw River, the straight streets and section lines, and the tiny streetcars rolling near Washburn College. "Instead of feeling your basket flying over the country, the country flies under the basket. It is like sitting up on a pinnacle with the earth revolving beneath … Horses will chase a balloon as far as they can go. … Dogs will bark and howl. Roosters always crow their loudest. Rabbits will attempt to crawl into the ground and coyotes have several kinds of fits. Birds pay no attention."

Smith's and the *Journal* reporter's gentle experiences were not universal. On its very next trip, the balloon in which Smith had ridden passed

The Wichita Beacon

THE FRIENDLY SKIES

⇐ The kindly smiles on these cartoon balloons — with Wichita's symbol, the Peerless Princess of the Plains, riding atop the one on the left — suggested that the heavens were a welcome place for new technology. In fact, early trips were often wild rides amid high winds and storms, without any means of directional control.

through a storm, was carried away by winds, and landed 375 miles away in northwest Oklahoma — hardly an afternoon outing. *Topeka II* traveled 550 miles, from Kansas City to Minnesota, in October 1911 during the competition for the Lahm and Bennett Cups. The competition turned the crew of the *Topeka II* into "human icicles" as they were carried high by an overnight storm and sparked worry that they might have to ditch in the Great Lakes.

Such range was far beyond that of any other type of flying machine. The balloon provided a stable photo platform for the first aerial views of cities, while giving passengers a sense of pace and safety more acceptable to them than noisy wood and fabric concoctions. The trouble was in controlling the length and direction of a balloon flight.

Kansans missed no opportunities to promote ballooning. It was so popular that in 1910 a balloonists' trade union was formed, the Kansas City Aeronauts Local No. 1, with dues of 60 cents a month. An October 1911 meet, featuring nine large balloons, was part of the Kansas City Priests of Pallas carnival, First prize was $1,500. In the fall of 1915, Wichita hosted the

National Balloon Races. The Wichita Aero Club sponsored a $1.50-a-plate dinner, and the races attracted national publicity to a city that wanted very much to be identified with the nascent air business. The balloons took off from Island Park, site of the Knabenshue mishap, and some were expected to fly as far as 1,000 miles before landing. There was a local entry, *Wichita I.*

More than 14,000 people attended the fair over three days, partly to watch the beginning of the only balloon races in the United States that year and partly to see "motor madness" and aerial gymnastics with aircraft. There was a race between an automobile and an airplane at Speedway Park. Barney Oldfield, cigar and all, ran his 100 HP Fiat Cyclone against a biplane piloted by De Lloyd Thompson over a distance of five miles. The *Eagle* noted that Thompson was always the crowd favorite and that "often" he and his airplane actually won.

Unfortunately standard balloons went where the wind went, hardly useful for commercial travel. But for a time that was better than a Knabenshue dirigible or a fragile powered aircraft, which hardly went at all. After drifting over Oklahoma, the winning balloon in the 1915 races, *St. Louis I,* finally landed in Arkansas, 363 miles and over eighteen hours travel time from the start. The Kansas entry made it sixty-seven miles, landing near Winfield, Kans. These balloons were impressive to look at, too. The big distance-trophy balloons were more than fifty feet across at their widest points and could contain 75,000 cubic feet of gas. They carried as much as 2,500 pounds of sand as ballast, several crew members in a four-foot by five-foot basket, rope, instruments, and provisions for several days. The crews kept diaries of impressive adventures in the clouds, which were popular features in newspapers. It was real high adventure in a new sphere.

However, given the permanent hobby and exhibition nature of balloons, Kansas inventors and fliers stayed busy following up the promise of the Wright airplane. Cross-country flying in early craft imported into the state certainly did not compare with balloons, but flight's ultimate promise made it worth trying. Compared with balloon journeys, the first Kansas cross-country trips in aircraft were pitiful. The problem was the same as the Knabenshue ship had encountered in Wichita — wind.

In December 1909, Charles K. Hamilton, a member of the Curtiss exhibition team, put on a flying demonstration in a biplane at Overland Park, Kans. His visit was sponsored by W.B. Strang, president of a local electric trolley line, who may have paid Hamilton as much as $1,000 a day. He flew the same plane that Glen Curtiss had used to win the Gordon Bennett Cup at Rheims, France, earlier in the year, and he had just come from flights at St. Joseph, Mo., which were the first in a heavier-than-air machine west of the

DON'T SHOOT THE AVIATOR

IF YOU DO, SOMEONE WILL GET $1,000 FOR ARRESTING YOU

———

J.C. Mars Doesn't Care to Take Chances With Bullets and Air, Too – No Stops Scheduled Between Topeka and Here

———

If you are tempted to shoot at the aviator today, just to convince yourself that it really is a man – don't do it. J.C. Mars says there are sufficient dangers without being compelled to dodge bullets. He promises to do his very best to fly in a pleasing manner, and asks you not to make a target of him. To discourage persons who might want to take a shot at him, he has offered a reward of $1,000 for the arrest and conviction of anyone so doing. …

… "If a bullet from a rifle should strike the engine, most probably I would be burned up or else get my neck broken in the tumble. Hunters will have to quit considering everything in the air public targets," he said.

(from the Kansas City Star, 1910)

Mississippi River.

The craft was a pusher biplane with a wingspan of twenty-six feet, a front-mounted elevator, and mid-wing ailerons — not radically different from the Wright's first *Flyer.* The fabric covering was rubberized silk. There were numerous mishaps during the week that Hamilton stayed at Overland Park, but he flew controlled figure eights, and made one continuous flight of eighteen miles at a height of 500 feet, the best by an American aviator to that date. It was not officially entered as a record only because Hamilton had not been granted a pilot's license by the Aero Club of America.

Another early adventurer in heavier-than-air flight over Kansas was J.C. "Bud" Mars, a stunt man and also part of the Curtiss national demonstration team. In June 1910, he took off from Topeka in a Curtiss biplane called *Skylark* and flew! "Along the line of onlookers which numbered in the thousands," a newspaper commented, "the 'Skylark' sped with such ease and grace that the crowd was entranced and its enthusiasm had reached a high pitch by the time the aviator started to round the field a second time." Buffeted by the wind over Soldier Creek, Mars, swaying wildly, skimmed close to the ground and kept his craft under control until a Rock Island train roared by and sucked the air out from under him. Then he touched a wheel down on a muddy, newly plowed field, and *Skylark* turned turtle, with Mars pinned beneath it. "The spectators gave one long gasp, and Mrs. Mars exclaimed 'Oh mercy,' covering her face with her hands. Then the crowd fairly went wild for a moment." Militiamen from Manhattan, Kans., and Clay Center, Kans., held the surging mob back, and Mars got out with only a bruised knee and bumped head. He threw up his hands to wild cheers from an estimated 4,000 people who wanted to see him fly or die. Ten thousand people saw him make six flights on June 12, including his famous "Mars

MADMEN

⇑ There was considerable concern in the early days of Kansas aviation about the disruption and danger that low-flying planes might cause. Wichita passed an ordinance to outlaw low-level flight, and there was discussion on how to ticket violators. One official suggested anti-aircraft guns; another thought citations could be delivered via bow and arrow. This article suggests that frightened farmers might be tempted to dispense summary justice.

glide." "He thinks no more of taking an air flight than the ordinary man does of taking a ride in an automobile."

Topeka promoters had been disappointed that another Curtiss flier, Charles F. Willard, had left town without flying, but Mars went out of his way to provide a full show. On the last day of a week of demonstrations, he reached an altitude of 1,000 feet. Wrote a reporter: "No better demonstration of the wonderful capabilities of the machine, nor of the skill of its operator was desired by any person who watched." The sponsors lost $1,000 because of bad weather during much of the week but certainly stimulated great interest.

In a surprising encore, Mars announced on June 14 that he would attempt a cross-country flight to the Kansas City area. The distance, about fifty miles, might seem modest enough, but there were the prairie winds to contend with. The motivation was a $5,000 prize offered by Strang of Overland Park for the first person to achieve the flight. Mars' cross-country flight was said to be the first attempted in a low-power machine in Kansas. The 24 HP *Skylark* weighed 450 pounds. It was also reported to be the first cross-country flight of any kind attempted in the Middle West, though Hamilton's eighteen-mile hop of the year before must be considered.

Mars took off at 5:14 a.m. on June 15, accompanied by half a dozen cars full of mechanics and reporters. W.W. Webb, a local photographer, tried to take a picture, but it was too dark. The pilot ascended to 1,200 feet and for a time picked up a Rock Island passenger train, appearing to race above it. The plane then caught a down draft and missed crashing into the Kansas River by only fifty feet. The first leg lasted only nine miles. He missed a meadow and lighted in a cornfield, breaking several ribs on the aircraft. Upon taking off again, the engine again worked poorly, and on the second landing more ribs were broken and repaired with elm limbs. The next fifteen miles were covered in twenty-four minutes, and there, in the area of Midland, about twenty-seven miles east of Topeka and near the University of Kansas at Lawrence, he waited for the wind to improve. Squally winds worried him. "The idea of flying," he said, "is always to be where you can land safely. The best route is over flat country, where a place suitable for landing is always close."

That second leg, on which Mars outran all the chase cars and never dropped below a speed of 35 MPH (followers found him nonchalantly asleep under a tree), was the high point of the trip. Three attempts to get out of the Lawrence/Midland area failed. Passengers on a train, their faces pressed to every window, waved wildly as Mars circled, but finally the flight was called off for the day. "A day's struggle of human science and daring against nature ended tonight," said the Kansas City press, "with J.C. Mars, the aviator, defeated."

Mars thought about making a night flight the rest of the way (the spring

Tiben Collection, Kansas Aviation Museum

winds in Kansas regularly die at night), but his friends dissuaded him. "I was crazy to attempt a flight on a day like this," Mars said. "You don't feel the wind blowing strong down here, it isn't blowing much stronger a thousand feet above. I wish it were, if it were only blowing steadily. It has been blowing in fits and starts all morning. First I hit a dead calm. It's hard to go up in it, but I make good speed ahead. Then all of a sudden a 'puffy' gust comes up. It has been all I could do to right my machine several times. It seizes my planes before I can adjust them and swings the machine around. Just as I get to going fine against the wind and rising fast the wind dies down and I am left, hung in the air as it were. The choppy weather is the worst weather an aviator can have. I simply cannot fly longer in it." His description is familiar to any modern windsurfer who had fought a sail for control, exposed on a light board. But there was and is a great thrill in human struggles with natural forces at their most elemental. The twenty-seven mile flight, wrote a Topeka paper, was "spectacular in the extreme."

That was not quite the end of it. The machine was loaded onto a hay wagon and hauled into Lawrence. Mechanics worked on the engine all night by lantern light. However, a valve was broken and a local machinist could not make a new one until noon the next day. Mars, who had another show to do, decided to abandon the try, and had the craft put on a train. "I made a

WALNUT GROVE

⇑ Aviators who toured the Midwest did much to thrill and, at the same time, instill confidence in air travel. But Eugene Ely (one of four Curtiss aviators at Wichita's first air meet on May 4, 1911) was a poor prophet, predicting: "This generation won't see airplanes in common use. After awhile, the novelty will wear off, and people will stop going out of their way to see men fly. But the aeroplane won't become a common sight. Aviation is a great science, and it will be developed, not by the grandstanders who talk but by men who study it and experiment carefully. Not everyone can master the science of aviation, because not everyone can train his hand and brain to work together."

vow right then and there when I nearly dropped into the Kaw River at Calhoun Bluffs out of Topeka that I would have a big engine before I ever tackled another proposition like this. You think of a lot of things even if you are busy with the machine when you are going down and down. … If I can accomplish this feat with a 24-horsepower machine it will open all kinds of possibilities in flying. Then I will be honest, and admit I want to win that prize." Apparently, he did not go away empty-handed, as the fee for his Topeka exhibitions was reported to be $10,000.

The Curtiss contingent returned to Kansas the next year and demonstrated the rapidity with which advances were coming. The event was an air meet at Walnut Grove in northwest Wichita, held in May 1911, sponsored by O.A. Boyle, and featuring Curtiss aviators Eugene Ely, James J. Ward, C.C. Witmer and R.C. St. Henry. Advertising was extensive, special interurbans hauled spectators from surrounding towns, and automobiles crowded Arkansas Avenue ("a good sand road - NO MUD") to pay $1.25 admission to vie for places on high ground where the view was unobstructed. The strategy worked. Crowd estimates ran as high as 18,000, and the headline in the *Beacon* on the opening evening was "Wichita is Aviation Mad Today."

It was a time when world records might be broken at any local air meet and when there was every likelihood of a crash as well. "I hope you will not confound this highest type of men," wrote Boyle, "with the cheaper class of so-called birdmen, that show around the country on a few hours' notice." There was circling, gliding, simulated bomb dropping, a husband and wife flight by the newly-married teenaged Wards, and flights of record-setting altitudes. Interest was so great that national guardsman had to protect the planes, set up in tents, from being vandalized by souvenir hunters.

The Walnut Grove meet showed Kansans that airplanes were finally practical ("successful flights guaranteed" went the broadsides), and it showed them as well that their country was an ideal place for them. "There is plenty of room," said Witmer, a Kansan,"and I consider it ideal, and with perfect weather we will have as fine a meet as I have ever taken part in anywhere."

It was not perfect: 35 MPH winds gave Ely the "scare of his career." He had a 50 HP engine, which was "producing every pound of force it was capable of doing" while "the machine moved slowly and quivered like a leaf" in the gale. But local reaction was positive. The *Eagle* printed an entire aviation number, one of the earliest in the West. It contained a most perceptive editorial, pointing out that "it is human nature … that contemporary progress is as unreal to us as foreign lands, as unreal as things of the historic past, unless we see them with our own eyes. The aeroplane is unreal to Wichita … until we see it soar over our own local habitat. Then by such a first-event, the aeroplane is ours, and we are of the aeroplane age."

A *Beacon* reporter asked if there would come a time "within a reasonable period" when aerial navigation would be practical for regular transportation: "To predict the accomplishment of that feat is less presumptuous than it would have been twenty years ago to foretell the triumphs that are manifested in Wichita today. To move about at will in the air, directing the biplane hither and thither. … is surely a greater advance over the old balloon that followed the will of the wind, than would be the perfection of this biplane. … It is probable that the next ten years will develop machines as safe in the air as are boats at sea. The air will be full of them and accidents will be no more numerous than now occur on the railroad or upon the sea."

On the last day of the Walnut Grove meet, Ward ascended to 8,000 feet and made the longest, highest "and most daring feat of flying" ever attempted in Kansas. As he did it, Ely made a quick "commute" to Valley Center, north of Wichita, and back. A bevy of "sweet young things" lingered around the tents hoping to write their names on the wings as the planes were disassembled to be loaded back on railway cars.

By that fall Calbraith Perry Rodgers stopped in Kansas City, having flown there in a modified Wright B biplane called the *Vin Fiz,* after his soft-drink sponsor, from New York. He ignored warnings about the local air currents and toured the town by air. He then went on to the Pacific coast, breaking every record in the process and amazing even the Wrights. Within three months a transcontinental flight was made in the opposite direction, clearly eclipsing anything even the big racing balloons could do. The "dream of flight" was suddenly real.

Many claims have been made about the first Kansas-built airplane to fly successfully. These have been advanced, mostly by hometown boosters, with as much determination as the backers of a Massachusetts man who was supposed to have flown before the Wrights, or Brazilians who claim that Alberto Santos-Dumont invented aviation. All center on the 1909-11 period.

Probably the earliest Kansas claim involves Chester Melvin Vaniman of McPherson, who built a plane that flew successfully in Paris in 1909. This craft, a three-decker launched from rails, was described in the *Scientific American* of January 23, 1909. Vaniman, however, was living in Europe at the time of the achievement, so his Kansas home could not claim the feat.

The Bixler brothers of Hutchinson — John, Gould, Thurman and Earl — were at work on an airplane in 1910. Apparently it was an original, as a 1930s news account says that "the Bixler boys were strangers to aerodynamics in those days and leading edges and the buoyance of vacuums meant as little to them as the fourth-dimension." Their three-wheeled craft, piloted by John, is said to have risen "as high as a telephone pole" and flown for

Kansas State Historical Society

LONGREN BIPLANE

⇑ Glenn Curtiss' Golden Flyer pusher-type biplane found immediate favor among grass-roots aviators throughout the country, who borrowed or adapted its proven design. One such flier was A. K. Longren of Topeka. Shown is the earliest model of Longren's pusher-type aircraft. A later model (without a front boom assembly) is on display at the Kansas Museum of History.

about a quarter of a mile at a speed of 35 MPH. John Bixler went on to get a license from the Wright brothers and became involved in some documented flying exploits. However, that first flight is not clearly fixed in the record. The 1931 newspaper article describing it says it was the first airplane flight west of the Mississippi. That much, for certain, is not true. But as the first flight of a Kansas designed and built plane, the Bixlers are contenders.

In January 1910, there was a report in Wichita that a bank clerk named Merrifield Martling was building an airplane in a converted front room on the top floor of the Crawford Grand Theater downtown. "Though known to few people," the *Eagle* claimed he had been working for weeks by himself. "In style it resembles no biplane in particular, as he has taken the ideas of several different patterns in making his." A second Wichita man, A. Harrison, said in January 1910 that he had already built an airplane and made two flights. Most remarkably, he claimed that the power for the craft was himself, furnished through bicycle pedals driving a propeller. It was, one account said, "rather more of a monoplane than a biplane." Details were vague, witnesses non-existent, and the achievement highly unlikely.

Also in January 1910, it was reported that three University of Kansas civil engineering students, Harry Elliott, Paul Elliott and Gilbert Smith, had constructed an airplane combining features of the Santos Dumont and Bleriot monoplanes. They were in contact with Curtiss about engines for it, but there the trail disappears.

C.W. Parker of Abilene, Kans., who had considerable experience in manufacturing carousels, bought a Paulhan aircraft at an air show in Los Angeles in 1910. Parker told a Kansas City reporter that he was having the airplane shipped from Paris and would then duplicate it in commercial quantities in a Kansas factory: "There is no reason why I cannot build aeroplanes as well as any concern in the world and I intend to do it. The first one may be made in Abilene, but I expect to go at it in earnest when my new plant in Leavenworth is completed. The Central West is much in favor with the aviators. There was a strong feeling in Los Angeles for a meeting and races in Kansas City." Parker did not fear the Wrights' patents on the total design of the airplane (which were then being challenged in court), saying that he thought the federal government would soon annul all patents, as had been done in France. He had gotten a discount on the Paulhan airplane (list price $20,000) because of the advertising he could give it. He was sanguine about ever-larger craft that could carry explosives and bomb cities. "A large city could be destroyed in a night by such a craft."

In July 1910, Ed Ault, an employee of the McCarty Buggy & Carriage Works of Iola, Kans., was reported to be completing a biplane that had been under construction for three years. While it resembled a Wright or Curtiss, it was said to have several original features.

J.C. McCallum of Overland Park is said to have built and flown a biplane based on a Farman design in August 1910. It was reported to have a 70 HP engine and a wing that could be tilted in its entirety to change the angle in a turn, making tighter turns possible. However, very little is known about it.

Jacques Mueller, 29, whose chain-driven, parachute-powered idea of 1909 definitely belonged to the "whatchimacallit" class, built a monoplane dubbed the *Prairie Eagle* in 1910. He had moved from Topeka to Dorrance, Kans., sixty miles west of Salina. The *Eagle* was said by the contemporary press to be "the first monoplane to be manufactured in Kansas, perhaps in the United States." Although Mueller confessed that it was "a little different from most of the flying machines which have been exhibited in this country," he said "it will fly without any possible doubt." There is no evidence that it ever did.

Then there was James McCarty of Junction City, a twenty-one-year old, who constructed a plane in 1911 from a $2 set of plans ordered by mail. It was of the Santos-Dumont "Demoiselle" type, and was thought to be the smallest of its kind in the world — only a little over twenty-one feet long. McCarty had seen an airplane only once before he began building. The press was confident the craft would fly, but the only activity documented was an indoor engine test that sucked the wallpaper off the walls and ceiling of the young man's house.

Examples could be multiplied without resulting in a definitive list of Kansans who were working on aircraft around 1910. The vast majority of them had two things in common: Their designs never flew reliably and nothing significant came of their ideas. Any argument over firsts among this list has relatively little meaning.

Kansas State Historical Society

A.K. LONGREN

⇑ Practical flight and aircraft manufacture in Kansas originated in a field near Topeka in 1911, and the entrepreneur/engineer/pilot was Longren. He is not as well-known as other Kansas aviation pioneers largely because no major company developed bearing his name. But his contributions as a consultant to many companies were original and significant, and his role in convincing Kansans that flying could be a pragmatic business is unassailable.

There were two prominent exceptions: Clyde Cessna of Rago, Kans., and Wichita and A.K. Longren of Topeka. While neither started with an original design, they did assemble and fly Kansas airplanes before World War I. Both would become original aeronautical engineers and serious, consistent manufacturers and marketers of aircraft, thus laying the foundation for the state's future as an aviation center.

Although Cessna was a native Kansan and most of his air achievements were in Kansas, the fact that his first flights were made in Oklahoma, where he was living during a brief period he spent as an automobile dealer at Enid, and were accomplished in a kit plane manufactured in New York City, gives Longren priority at the gateway to the Kansas industry.

Albin Kasper Longren was born on a farm near Leonardville, Kans., in 1882. On September 2, 1911, he successfully flew a pusher biplane of his own manufacture, named the *Topeka I* (later renamed the *Dixie Flyer),* in a hay field at the Al Schmidt farm, seven and one-half miles southeast of Topeka. While his plane was essentially a clone of the pusher-type Curtiss Golden Flyer, Longren, first working alone, and then with some friends, had built it in Topeka beginning in the summer of 1910. It was an impressively large craft, thirty-nine feet in length and thirty-two feet from wing tip to wing tip, and was powered by a 60 HP, water-cooled Hall Scott V-8 engine. Some aspects were primitive: The fuel tank held only four gallons, and Longren's instruments amounted to a dollar watch fastened to the plane and a pocket barometer strapped to his wrist. But it unquestionably was a flier. That fall day in 1911, Longren, who had never flown either as pilot or passenger, made eight successful flights. Phil Eastman, the city editor of the *Topeka Daily Capital,* who observed at least one of these, said the plane flew six miles. Others have spoken of a fifteen-mile flight at altitudes of 1,000 feet and a trip over the crowd at the state fair. It was, at the least, more than a hop and more than an "ascension." His were sustained, controlled flights by a Kansan in an airplane designed and built in Kansas.

Longren commented when landing after one flight: "There wasn't a time that I didn't feel I had the bird under my control. I'm glad now to let the people of Topeka know what I've built." Asked why he had kept it a secret so long, he replied: "Well, I didn't want to make a lot of noise until I knew what I could do." How did it feel up there? "I didn't have time to tell. After the machine leaves the ground all thought of anything but making a good flight leaves me. You see I've wanted to do this so long that now it is possible I can't think of anything but doing it."

Longren's inspiration had been, of all things, the attempted Call flight of 1908 in Girard, which he had observed, as well as news of the daring cross-country flight of Glen Curtiss from Albany, N.Y., to New York City in

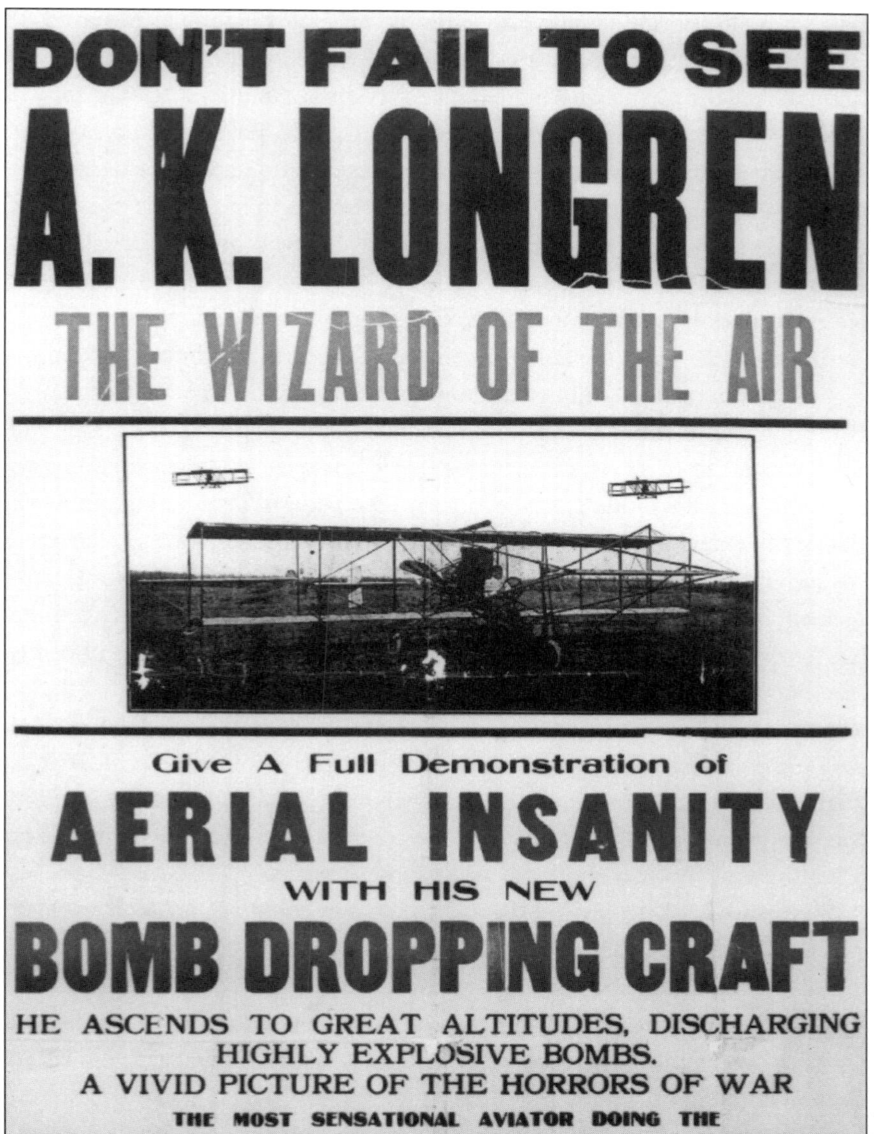

Kansas State Historical Society

PRAIRIE BARNSTORMERS

⇐ A.K. Longren and Clyde Cessna were among the most active of a "band of brothers" crisscrossing Kansas (usually navigating by following railroad tracks) from 1912 forward, demonstrating the capabilities of aircraft and providing rip-roaring entertainment at the same time. Such fliers were a feature of most every local fair and celebration of the period, and often, especially during and just after World War I, dropped flour "bombs." Sometimes these "bombings" took place before a show, and the "bombs" were filled with leaflets.

May 1910. Longren's financing and skills came from managing a machine and foundry company, as well as his activity in Longren Brothers Auto Sales and a correspondence course in mechanical engineering that he completed in 1911, just in time to take off in his airplane.

Longren's follow-up was immediate. He made further flights on September 4, 5, and 6, all without a crash. The next year he collected his

Bob Pickett Collection, Kansas Aviation Museum

A MASTER'S EXPRESSION
⇑ From his first experiments with the Silverwing monoplane to his 1930s race planes, Clyde Cessna was an original – as a designer, flier, financier, manufacturer, executive, and promoter. His cantilever monoplanes were clean, fast, efficient, and advanced. "The aviator is a genius," a reporter wrote about an early Cessna flight. "He made his machine, even the bolts that the machine contains."

first student and customer, Phil Billard, the son of Topeka Mayor J.B. Billard. On Noember. 17, 1912, Phil Billard flew over Topeka in his Longren pusher to realize "the height of aviation ambition." It was only a sixteen-minute trip, but Billard reached a height of 2,500 feet and was under perfect control, even stunting by circling around the Statehouse dome. His speed was estimated at 75 MPH as he roared from a flying field a mile south of Highland Park, over the Santa Fe railway shops, north to the Kansas River and back over the Statehouse and the business district. His only regret was that darkness fell before he could go farther. His enlarged gas tank would allow the plane to stay up two hours if weather and light permitted.

Those longer adventures came soon enough. On December 15, 1912, Billard was in the air for thirty minutes at a height of about 4,000 feet and flew a distance of thirty-seven miles. On Christmas Day the duration was forty minutes, the altitude 5,000 feet, and the pedestrians looking up many. Back at the hangar, he made a mock dive toward a friend in a car, recovered easily, and landed. H.L. Cook, secretary of the state fair association commented: "I have managed five or six aviation meets and have attended the big meets in Chicago, and I never saw a man have as perfect control of his machine as Billard had today." A friend agreed: "It was a beautiful flight. We have paid out our good money to see professional aviators fly here and they never did anything like Phil Billard did today. The people of Topeka ought to feel proud of him, especially when he flies over the city so that everybody can see him for nothing." There was more than a little Jayhawk pride showing through about the all-Kansas enterprise.

Naturally, all the luck in the Longren camp could not be good. In May 1913, Billard's engine stopped, throwing the craft into "a veritable dip of death," and a crash. The pilot was around the next day with his usual pluck. However, it did not cement relations with his father, who averred that he had not been won over to the support of aviation "especially when practiced by his son."

In September 1915, Longren had an accident during one of his many appearances at fairs. His plane stalled on takeoff on the last day of the Dickinson County fair and crashed into a departing automobile, breaking his leg, cutting his face badly, and causing internal injuries. The machine, the sixth manufactured by Longren and a new "tractor" type (with the propeller in front) was a total wreck. Longren soon added a lateral control device as a safety factor. But it did not keep him from hitting a cow while trying to land in a pasture in 1917, badly wrecking that airplane. The 1917 accident temporarily quashed the interest of Eastern investors in backing Longren's factory at Topeka and drove him to take a job at a munitions company in Denver. However, neither his flying and aircraft-building career, nor his res-

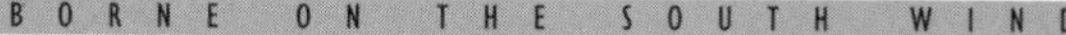

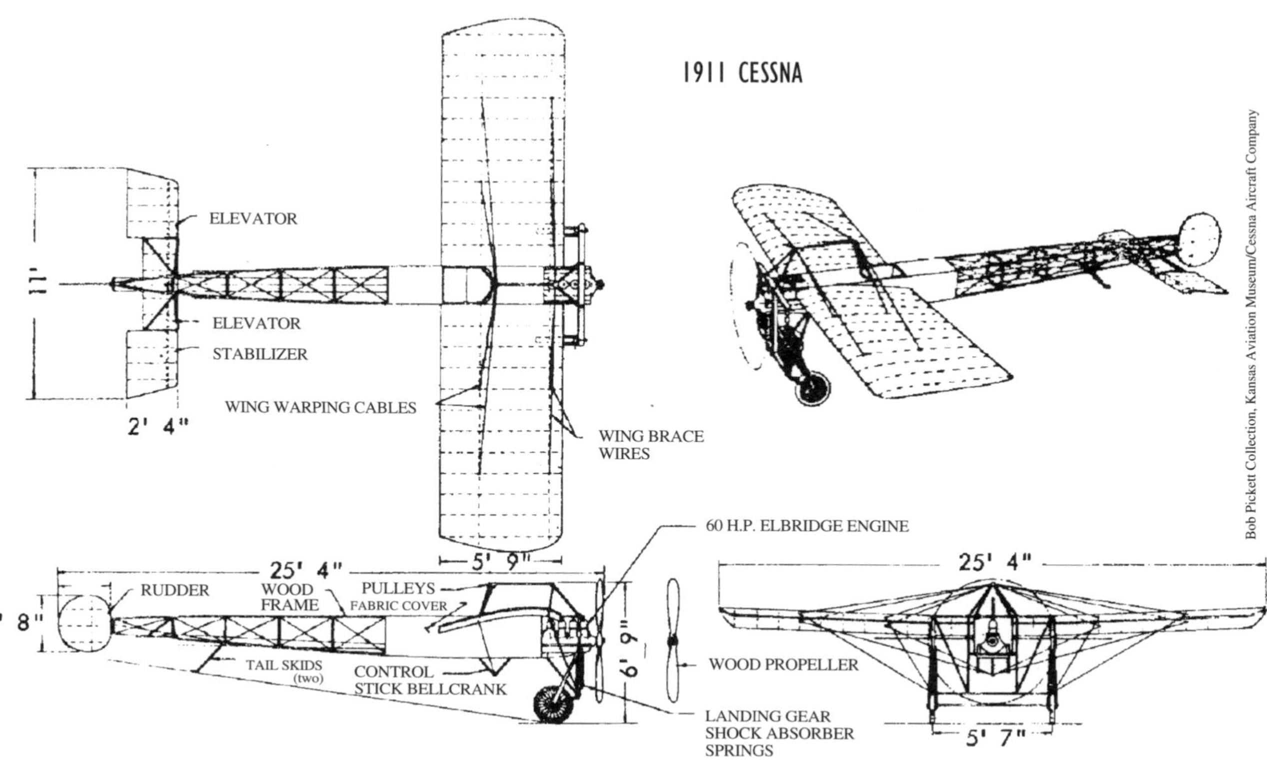

Bob Pickett Collection, Kansas Aviation Museum/Cessna Aircraft Company

idency in Kansas was interrupted for long. Longren was more than a visionary, more than a talker, and more than a barnstormer. He was a founder of the Kansas aviation establishment and its first credible member.

A nitpicker would disqualify Cessna in a contest with Longren over Kansas firsts. However Cessna flew successfully before Longren — in May 1911 — and his eventual influence on Kansas aviation was greater than that of the Topeka man. The company that would bear his name from the 1920s on would become the largest manufacturer of light-duty private aircraft in the world — a virtual household word among aviators everywhere. Cessna himself would be directly involved in promoting the company from his home in Kansas for twenty years.

Cessna had no formal training in engineering. He was a farmer with a knack for machines and an entrepreneurial bent. His wife, Europa, sewed fabric for his planes, and the residents of rural Kingman County, Kans., became familiar early with both the sound of a revving Anzani aircraft engine and the smell of the castor oil lubricant. Cessna was an early automobile owner and, like Longren, an automobile dealer. He followed the exploits of the first aviators closely, becoming particularly excited at the news of Louis Bleriot's crossing of the English Channel by air in July 1909.

SILVERWING

⇑ Like the Longren "Curtiss-type" machine, the Cessna "Bleriot-type" machine was not an original design, but it would establish a foothold for Clyde Cessna and his company. This aircraft became the parent of more than 178,000 Cessna airplanes. The name Silverwing can be attributed to the cloth used to cover the wings, which glistened with a light silver sheen.

The craft that accomplished the channel crossing was a monoplane, and Cessna fixed upon that design as the one that interested him most. The appeal was partly simplicity, but partly, too, it was cleaner aerodynamics resulting from fewer guy wires and struts, and the resulting increase in speed. There was little point in continuing to build airplanes that lost races with cars and trains, or that broke struts on rough landings, and Cessna foresaw that to move beyond the demonstration stage in aviation, the monoplane would have to be perfected.

On January 14, 1911, Cessna attended an air meet in Oklahoma City featuring Charles Hamilton in a biplane, and also Roland Garros in a Bleriot monoplane. Cessna talked to Garros about buying the Bleriot XI,, and probably learned from him about a kit, a copy of the Bleriot, available from the Queen Aeroplane Company in New York City. Cessna went to New York, worked on the monoplane assembly line for three weeks to learn all he could, and test flew the airplane with experienced pilots. He then bought a specially modified monoplane, named *Silverwing*, for the substantial price of $7,500 and had it shipped to Oklahoma.

That approach does not fit the mythological image of the local mechanic taking off on a wing and a prayer in a homemade contraption, but it made sense both from a scientific and business perspective. Even the Wright brothers, supposedly the quintessential small-timers, were sophisticated in mathematics and the science of aerodynamics and employed a careful and slow method to the solving of one problem after another. Cessna intended to make his expensive airplane pay, at first through demonstration flights and eventually through manufacturing and sales. That required considerable science and considerable responsibility.

Partisans of Longren delight to point out that Cessna, despite his lessons, did a whole lot more crashing than their man. And it is true. After much trouble with engines and several test flights, Cessna put on a public flight at the Salt Plains near Enid on June 18, 1911. That flight was successful but not nearly as impressive as the initial exhibition by Longren. Shortly after takeoff, the *Silverwing* dipped and hit the ground. The engine stopped and the propeller was broken. The Salt Plains were flat, which was an advantage, but the way the sun reflected off them made it difficult to judge altitude and made for some rough landings. Late in June, Cessna hit an updraft, causing the machine to climb quickly, and when he retarded the throttle, the Elbridge four-cylinder engine quit. This caused lateral control to be lost, and the subsequent crash badly damaged the plane. A July 4 flight was canceled when only $40 in admissions were raised. There was a two-mile demonstration on August 17, but it was not until September 10, about the time Longren was flying in Topeka, that Cessna flew before substantial numbers.

Bob Pickett Collection, Kansas Aviation Museum/Cessna Aircraft Company

OOPS!

⇑ Cessna's Silverwing monoplane survived this accident on the Salt Plains of Oklahoma on Sept. 13, 1911. Frail, yet efficient for its time, the monoplane would become a Cessna hallmark, although the Silverwing itself would require numerous modifications during several years of development to realize its potential. Of interest is the rope that was attached to keep the wreckage from being blown across the flats. This aircraft was rebuilt several times before being retired in 1913.

On September 13, during an attempted three-mile flight with a turnaround, there was another crash, with Cessna leaping out of the cockpit at the last second before impact. That crash cost Cessna more than $4,000 in booked exhibitions in addition to the damage to his plane. The complete rebuilding that was required forced Cessna into becoming a designer and a manufacturer, not just a flier.

It should be noted that early monoplanes, superficially resembling modern designs, were fragile and precarious. This was particularly true when they were steered by wing-warping, as was Cessna's craft. Warping was a Wright invention that turned an aircraft by using wires attached to the wings to bend (warp) the wing surfaces, as birds do. Not only did this require an extraordinarily light, and therefore breakable, wing structure, but it induced compressive loads and other misunderstood forces that caused the wings of monoplanes to buckle as engines grew more powerful and speeds increased. The basic airworthiness of the Queen Monoplane, on which Cessna's craft were based, came into serious question by 1910. The very guy wires intended to brace the monoplane wings introduced strains, while the basic wing design had a tendency to twist.

Cessna was lucky in the modest severity of his crashes. Harriet Quimby, who in April 1911 became the first woman to fly the English Channel, was killed three months after that feat in a monoplane. She took a passenger (a rather heavy man) out to the Boston Light, a twenty-mile trip over water, in her two-place Bleriot. Upon returning she took one more pass over the water, when the man apparently shifted, perhaps to yell something to her. The plane tipped, and he was dumped out, falling to his death in the muddy shallows. Unable to regain control with the loading change, Quimby herself suffered the same fate. The airplane settled quietly to the water with almost no damage, while shocked onlookers carried the crushed body of the aviatrix to shore. Ruth Law Oliver, a young flier who witnessed the tragedy, bought a Wright biplane. "The fact that she (Quimby) had been killed in a monoplane didn't scare me," she wrote. "I figured it was the monoplane's fault."

Cessna's own comments about his crashes reflect this difficulty. He said he was sure he would enjoy flying "after I get it learned." He noted that the monoplane was more difficult to handle than a biplane but that learning would be worthwhile. In December 1911, he made a seven-mile flight, landing in the same field from which he took off, without any damage or injury. That was an incontrovertible "true aerial flight." Improvements in an airplane that could begin to be called a "Cessna" came rapidly.

Over the next two years, Cessna was extremely active in flying for profit and also in crashing, repairing, and rebuilding airplanes. He formed a company, the Cessna Exhibition Company, and flew throughout Oklahoma and Kansas. He moved back to his farm near Adams in December 1913.

Local news items catch the flavor of the early Cessna flights. The *Norwich Herald*, the newspaper closest to Cessna's ancestral farm, picked up his activity in February 1913. On February 15, the newspaper reported, Cessna made a "beautiful flight" in his Bleriot monoplane from a meadow east of Norwich. On that occasion he flew six miles before a crowd of 1,400 people, considerably more than the total population of any of the towns nearby. "The streets of the town presented a holiday carnival appearance, and country and neighboring towns were represented by large delegations," the *Herald* reported. Cessna made a point of showing that the airplane could be useful for more than demonstrations, flying to see his parents at their nearby farm, and flying it to church on Sunday: "He is not bothered by bad roads or scary horses nor yet balking automobiles."

In March 3,000 people gathered quickly upon the arrival of Cessna's "bird," reminding the editor of "other days in Kingman in its early history when the crowds would assemble to witness balloon ascensions, but which ... would be postponed from day to day until the wind should go down and in numerous instances the matter would have to be called off entirely." The writer hoped that airplane flight would not be the joke that balloon ascents had become. The town of Harper booked Cessna for July 4, 1913, and billed

Frank Woods/Scott Daymon Collection

SHOW TIME

⥣ Pausing only long enough to oblige one of the many photo requests, Clyde Cessna readies for another of his aerial exhibitions at the 1915 Booster Day at Lost Springs. Many photo postcards such as this one were developed as souvenirs.

him as "the Kansas man who has gained nationwide fame as a bird man." He was in Nashville, Kans., late in August for the Harvest Home picnic. In September he was the top draw at the Wheat and Corn Jubilee at Stafford, Kans. At Stafford the monoplane and a balloon were in the air at the same time, a fascinating sight. Cessna gave a talk to the townspeople on aviation. That same month he performed at the Southwest Fair in Liberal, Kans. "He flies every day," the ad said. "No disappointments." Cessna did not arrive at these events with his airplane crated on a boxcar: He flew it in from his home.

Certainly people were impressed by what they saw and heard. Wrote a reporter: "The flights he made were not merely arising from the earth and fluttering in the air for a few seconds, but he circled at will over the country and made speed at the rate of about a mile a minute."

"His flying is not of the sensational type, but it satisfied the people, who stood and cheered him to the limit," commented another. "In his unassuming way Cessna has done much for aviation by taking away the 'fool killer' stunts and substituting 'on time' flight, regardless of weather conditions. He tells people he will fly at 4:30 p.m. and then he mounts into the air to show them he will."

Notable among Cessna's 1913 activities was an appearance and exhibition in Wichita during three days in October. His was not the first monoplane flight in the city. That distinction went to J. Hector Worden, who flew his French monoplane at Walnut Grove Park in May 1912. But Cessna added some promotion. A gimmick was a $5 reward for anyone who caught a football dropped from his plane at an elevation of 200 feet or $2.50 for the first to recover it. He spoke of the practicality of flying: "The fact that it used to make me so dizzy that I had to hold on tight to keep from falling off every time that I climbed up on a 35-foot windmill on the farm ought to be proof that any ordinary person can learn to fly. Flying is different than going up on top of a high building, where looking down makes a person dizzy." Cessna thought the fact that the world was "speed crazy" made aviation inevitable. Speed was dangerous on the ground, but quite safe in the air. While in Wichita, he also spoke to local people about a location for building aircraft, training fliers, and selling aircraft.

There was money in Wichita and, since the Walnut Grove meet of 1911, an enthusiasm about airplanes. The town was a significant jobbing center with good banking and communications facilities, and it had a considerable oversupply of industrial buildings left over from a failed boom during the 1880s. In one of these, the old Burton Car Works north of the city, the Jones 6 car was being manufactured. Wichita entrepreneurs were recovering from the 1890s depression, and the city was filled with honest workmen.

In 1914, Cessna got a six-cylinder Anzani radial engine. With it he could fly his second monoplane at 90 MPH. That summer he visited at least eleven towns and made twenty-five flights. The next year was better. On August 20, Cessna flew the 105 miles from Adams to Woodward, Okla., in one hour and fifty-five minutes. After 1912, Cessna built a new airplane every year at his farm, each one sleeker and faster than the one before. His vision was simple: "Speed is the only reason for flying."

By 1916, flying was well established as a native Kansas activity. Ruth Law, the famous aviatrix, "looped the loop," trailing sparks, over Wichita that year and did other aerobatics. During the same period Herman Wetzig of Junction City, who had been flying Curtiss airplanes at Kansas fairs since 1910, made two appearances a month throughout the Southwest. Wetzig's problem in making a profit was the industry problem: Flying was still entertainment and not a business, and its novelty was beginning to wear off. Mars could demand a $10,000 fee just to demonstrate flying in 1910, but by 1915 a Cessna or a Wetzig or even a Law could expect much less money and smaller crowds. It was time for the next steps toward standard production and paying customers, and those steps were taken in Kansas as early as any place in the country.

(Photo on facing page) Bob Pickett Collection, Kansas Aviation Museum

CESSNA MODEL AW

(1928)

THE THOMPSON TROPHY ⇒

Officially instituted in 1930 to replace the Thompson Cup, this gleaming trophy became the most coveted award in air racing during the 1930s and '40s for unlimited-horsepower speed events. Sponsored by the Thompson Products Company (producers of spark plugs) the ultimate event of the National Air Races originally consisted of a fifty-mile course. Charles Thompson, president of Thompson Products, had Walter Sinz design the regal trophy.

HOWARD DGA-6 ⇓

Although appearing somewhat ungainly for a 1930s racer, the big, barrel-chested Mr. Mulligan was designed to double as a high-altitude, non-stop, long distance racer for the Bendix Trophy and a low-level pylon racer for the Thompson Trophy. It captured both of these prestigious awards in 1935, an unprecedented accomplishment. Top speed was 292 MPH at 11,000 feet. Mr. Mulligan was destroyed after it shed a propeller blade over New Mexico in 1936 during the Bendix race. Shown is an exact replica.

"Anyone who rolled up to the starting line of the Thompson Trophy race, the most grueling air battle in peacetime history, had courage. There were no cowboys in that one."

– Andrew Elko, race fan

From the "September Champions," by Robert Hull, 1979

(left) The National Air and Space Museum, Smithsonian Institution Neg. No. 93-5513

(below) Experimental Aircraft Association (EAA), Jim Koepnick

(above) Beech Aircraft Corporation

"Now, don't say we are going to fly in the women's division of the Bendix. We are going to fly in *the* Bendix, are asking no consideration from anyone, and unless some of the other pilots do better flying and show better speed, we will win it. This Beechcraft will make that run in about fourteen hours and we will put it over the route."

– Louise Thaden, winner, Bendix Trophy, September 1936

From *The Wichita Eagle,* September 5, 1936

BEECH MODEL 17

⇑ Spacious, powerful and luxurious, the Beech Staggerwing biplanes were prestigious aircraft that made their mark on air racing in the 1930s and '40s. Louise Thaden and Blanche Noyes won the 1936 Bendix race in a Model C17R, and Jackie Cochran placed third in the 1937 Bendix while flying a Model D-17W. Typically seating four or five people in a mohair-trimmed cabin, Staggerwings came to be equipped with an array of radial engines. Seven hundred eighty-five were built by Beech, and four were assembled by Henry Seale of Dallas from parts built by Beech.

THE BENDIX TROPHY ⇐

Instituted in 1931, the Bendix Trophy was awarded to the winners of a cross-country speed dash that was part of the National Air Races. The races began on the West Coast and finished in Cleveland.

(right) The National Air and Space Museum, Smithsonian Institution Neg. No. 93-5512

(This page) Experimental Aircraft Association (EAA), Jim Koepnick

CESSNA UC-78 ⟹ Originally developed as an economy twin, the UC-78 (Utility/Cargo) was a military transport version of the Cessna Model T-50. Shown is a late war version on which, because of the Allies overwhelming aerial supremacy, silver paint was used instead of the customary olive drab camouflage.

BOEING MODEL N2S KAYDET ⇓ Originally designed by Harold Zipp and Jack Clark, the Boeing Model 75 Kaydet trainer became the best-known primary trainer of World War II. Almost universally called a Stearman, the roots of this trainer can be traced to the Stearman Model 70 built in 1933. After the Russian-built Antonov AN-2 and Polikarpov PO-2 biplanes, the Kaydet was produced in greater numbers than any other biplane. Shown is a U.S. version of the Model 75 trainer known the N2S.

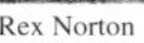
Rex Norton

Bob Pickett Collection, Kansas Aviation Museum

XA-38 GRIZZLY ⇑ Although only two flying prototypes were built as the war was winding down, the Beech attack bomber offered an overwhelming combination of firepower (including a 75mm automatic, nose-mounted cannon) and performance rivaling that of some of the better-known fighter aircraft.

PQ-14 TARGET AIRCRAFT ⇐ Culver Aircraft Company of Wichita built six models of target aircraft during World War II. Out of 2,644 target aircraft built by Culver, the company built 2,043 PQ-14s. The U.S. Army employed the PQ-14 for aerial and anti-aircraft gunnery training. This aircraft could be flown with one pilot while acting as a target for gun-camera-equipped fighters. A 150 HP Franklin six-cylinder engine powered this wooden aircraft up to speeds of 180 MPH.

Experimental Aircraft Association (EAA), Jim Koepnick

BEECH T-34B MENTOR ⇑ Designed in 1948 as an off-the-shelf high performance trainer, the Beech Model 45 Mentor won every competition in which it was entered as a training aircraft. The U.S. Air Force selected the T-34A as its official primary trainer in 1953, and the U.S. Navy picked the T-34B as its primary trainer in 1954. More than a dozen foreign nations employed the Mentor as part of their flight training programs.

CULVER CADET ⇒ Originally designed and built in Columbus, Ohio, production of the Cadet was moved to Wichita in 1940, where most Cadets were built. Production of this two-place sport aircraft, which sold for $2,475 in 1941, was halted for the duration of the war. However, its design was to serve as the basis for the PQ-8 series of target aircraft. Culver would follow up after the war with the Model V (for victory) until the company was closed in 1948. About 670 non-military Culvers were built in Kansas.

Experimental Aircraft Association (EAA), Carl Schuppel

Bob Pickett Collection, Kansas Aviation Museum

CESSNA 195A

⇐ Introduced in 1947 and in production through 1954, the Cessna 190 and 195 series of all-metal monoplanes provided outstanding comfort, robust performance, and eye-catching style. A total of 866 of the two models were built. Shown is a 1952 Model 195A, powered by a 245 HP Jacobs R-755-9 radial engine.

C-35 BONANZA ⇓ First flown in December 1945, the V-Tail Bonanza was in production until 1982. The unmistakable profile of its 33-degree V-tail would ensure that the Model 35 would remain a classic aircraft. Shown is a 1952 Model C35 Bonanza equipped with a 185 HP Continental engine, which could be flown at speeds as great as 190 MPH. This particular model sold for $18,990.

American Bonanza Society

Department of Defense, Still Media Record Center, Photo No. DF-ST-88-04694

BOEING B-52 STRATOFORTRESS

⇑ The B-52 was built from 1954 to 1962, and updated versions remain on active duty. Shown is a model B-52H, 102 of which were built in Wichita from 1959 to 1962. This model is similar to the B-52G, but has TF-33 Turbofan engines and a 20mm radar-directed tail gun.

CESSNA A-37B DRAGONFLY

⇒ Developed in 1967, the A-37B attack aircraft was used for ground combat support in Southeast Asia. The Dragonfly could be outfitted with napalm tanks, and 2.75-inch rockets as well as conventional bombs. A 7.62mm minigun provided awesome firepower for strafing. It could be pushed to 507 MPH, while offering in-flight refueling capabilities. A total of 577 were built.

Bob Pickett Collection, Kansas Aviation Museum/Cessna Aircraft Company

51

GREEN LIGHT ALOFT

"IT'S FINE TO SAIL THROUGH SPACE IN PERFECT AIR, SOOTHED TO SLUMBER BY THE PURR OF THE MOTOR. I NEVER EXPECT TO TRAVEL AT LENGTH AGAIN, EXCEPTING THROUGH THE MEDIUM OF AIRPLANES."
— JAKE MOELLENDICK

Longren and Cessna, the Kansas pioneers in practical local flight, were also the founders of the local commercial industry. At first it was on an extremely small scale, as was most U.S. aircraft manufacturing, with the exception of Curtiss, before the Great War.

Longren had a factory in Topeka at 611 Tenth Street, where it was said he not only built the airplanes Billard used but "other machines for wealthy (men) in this state and in Oklahoma." The volume is impossible to document, but was unquestionably very small. In 1917 Longren wanted to apply for a contract to build warplanes, but could not get backing from his hometown. He therefore went to Denver during World War I to work as chief aeronautical engineer on the construction of an aerial torpedo for warplanes operating in Europe. He did not return home to build airplanes in earnest until 1919.

His replacements were not in the same league. Ernest Greider, the eighteen-year-old son of a teacher at Topeka High School, was reported in 1916 to be constructing an airplane from an original design, confident that it would fly. William Kopseker of Topeka built an airplane with a thirty-foot wingspan based on the Barmont machine, which had attempted a flight from Paris to Warsaw, Poland, and crashed behind German lines in the war zone. Kopseker tried to fly it publicly, but the axle snapped. Although the *Topeka Journal* said that when his plane did fly "she'll be a revelation," nothing much came of his enterprise.

During this period, Cessna, like Longren, had a manufacturing operation, but one that could be called "commercial" only by broad definition. He moved his "plant" off his Kingman County farm and to the Jones 6 auto

DIRECT DRIVE

⇐ Clyde Cessna hand cranks the inertia starter of a nine-cylinder, 200 HP Wright Whirlwind J-4 radial engine. The aircraft shown is the Cessna-Roos Aircraft Company design Number 2. This was the typical method for starting high compression engines of the time, although a few aircraft used shotgun shells to provide the kick necessary to turn the crankshaft.

Bob Pickett Collection, Kansas Aviation Museum and Cessna Aircraft Company factory in North Wichita in 1916. However, no new company was formed, and there was no capital investment. George Sherwood, the production manager for J.J. Jones Motor Company and a representative of a group of Wichita businessmen who wanted Cessna to build airplanes and train pilots in their city, had persuaded him to move. He was given the use of Building I at the Jones plant and seventy-three acres adjacent to the works for a flying field. He flew over the city, entertained at the local Wheat Show that year, and gave tours of his new factory to local folks. His airplanes also became billboards. One had an ad for a local clothing store on the wing and another for the Jones "Light Six" car .

Cessna had hatched a promotional scheme, a cross-country flight from Wichita to New York City, which he planned to accomplish in 1917. The slogan at the building, where he continued to install machinery, was "From Wichita to New York," and he had two ships under way, the second a two-seater. He went to the National Aviation Congress in New York City in February 1917, bringing back both ideas and equipment. The operations were moved into Building H, where there was more room for expansion, and prospects looked promising. In June, Cessna enrolled five people in his flying school, and by summer his new single-place monoplane, the Comet (perhaps the first pure Cessna), was setting speed records for the region. The first airplane built *entirely* in Wichita was completed by Cessna at the Jones factory.

In April, the United States declared war on the Central Powers and formally entered World War I. That changed everything for U.S. and Kansas aviation. While the long-term effect was enormously beneficial, the short-term impact on U.S. aircraft manufacturing was highly negative.

After the war had broken out in Europe in 1914, there had been enormous advances in the design and capabilities of warplanes. So rapid had progress been that the 1914-style designs, such as the Bleriot monoplane upon which Cessna's models were based, were considered antiques — fragile "kites" that were useful at the front only for an observation function. There was an immense distance in design and deadliness between a Bleriot XI or a Nieuport 12 and a Spad XIII or a Fokker D VII, though only three or four years separated them.

When the United States entered the war in 1917, the aviation section of the Army Signal Corps had only fifty-five operational aircraft, none of them capable of the 120 MPH speeds and 20,000 foot altitudes that the latest 200 HP European fighters achieved regularly. U.S. Army aviators were trained in Curtiss JN-4s before going overseas and had to undergo extensive further training in France on high-performance craft before they could be assigned to combat pursuit groups.

Bob Pickett Collection, Kansas Aviation Museum/Cessna Aircraft Company

SIGNS OF THE TIME

⇑ Early aviators helped defray operating costs by advertising the goods and services of merchants. Jack Spines, a Wichita clothier, had his name and address (Spines – 111 W. Douglas) painted on the underside of the wing of this craft, the first Cessna monoplane completely built in Wichita. This photo, featuring members of the Beaver (Okla.) Booster Club, was taken during the fall of 1916.

For all these reasons, a strategic decision was made by the Allies to focus U.S. efforts on the production of engines — mostly bomber engines — and adapting them to European airframes. American engineers designed the Liberty engine, a water-cooled V-12 power plant with over 400 HP in some variations, and this was fitted to U.S.-made de Havilland DH-4s. That engine and the OX-5, a U.S. contribution of the same era, would mean that 1920s U.S. aircraft manufacturers could have a surplus of cheap and sophisticated engines to power their new designs. But for the moment it meant that all contracts to the United States were for engines and, except for some Curtiss designs for trainers, unarmed reconnaissance two-seaters and slow patrol flying boats, the nascent airframe manufacturing business was stifled for the duration. The French needed 4,000 engines a month, they said, and there was no need at all for antique U.S. aircraft. U.S. firms were in fact prevented by order of the War Department's Aircraft Production Board from developing new models on their own initiative for about a year after U.S. entry into the war.

Both Longren and Cessna made serious attempts to get war production contracts. Both failed. Cessna thought his new two-place ship would be ideal for reconnaissance, and he had plenty of space in the old railroad car plant to expand. He also offered to train pilots. The Army said that it would train its own pilots, and Cessna was not even able to complete his training of the five civilian candidates he had. Rationing of fuel, combined with the need for wheat and the lack of customers, so interfered with Cessna's aircraft business in 1917 that he returned to farming, putting his factory in mothballs.

The war ended late in 1918, and it seemed that the hype of aviation as *the* prototypical Jazz Age business began the next day. Partly it was stunts — from wing-walking to transcontinental, transoceanic, and around-the-world aerial endeavors — that drew the media. Perhaps the methodical stayed away from these as too much too soon, but to the public it was as though the Flying Circus of World War I, with its heroes and its daily drama, continued for a decade in the skies overhead. The climax of it all was the remarkable summer of 1927, when Charles Lindbergh's solo crossing of the Atlantic in late May was followed by the first non-stop flight to Hawaii, and then by a veritable troop of racers over the Pacific, where only months before no aircraft had ventured. It is easy to forget that the first nonstop flight across the Atlantic was actually in June 1919, when an open-cockpit Vickers Vimy biplane under the control of Englishmen John Alcock and Arthur Brown made the leap from Newfoundland to Ireland. En route they had to contend with a split exhaust pipe and carburetor icing. Their reward, £10,000 in prize money, was presented by Winston Churchill. Remarkably they were in a crowd of aviators attempting to do the same things, and their flight followed by less than a month the first flight across the Atlantic of any kind, taken in stages by Navy Curtiss NC-4, an American flying boat. In 1924, four Douglas World Cruisers, named for American cities, took off on an around-the-world flight, and, after multiple engine changes and 175 days en route, two made it. By that date, the U.S. Air Mail Service was running a regular transcontinental schedule in all weather across the country (the first short airmail route in New York state had been established in 1918), airlines were beginning to carry a few brave passengers, and miracles were almost to be expected.

Amid the excitement, there were tragedies galore — forgotten heroes like Charles Nungesser and Francois Coli, who disappeared without a trace in the *Oiseau Blanc* (White Bird) flying the Atlantic east to west in stormy weather just before Lindbergh took off, and the dozens of exhibitors or racers who died when their crafts disintegrated in attempting some new maneuver, or an old one tried once too often. But it was considered part of the price of a progress that must be rapid as well as sure. There were critics, certainly, who said too many were dying for nothing. There were those who claimed that it was already well-known that an engine would turn for enough hours that these endurance feats could theoretically be accomplished, and doing them brought safe and regular commercial flight closer no more quickly than had the more plodding ways of the cautious been respected. Yes, and there are historians who argue that railroads were unnecessary because the American West could have been served more cheaply by a system of canals. Without the public drama, and without the thrill of awaiting news of some miraculous flight almost as eagerly as if one were related to the pilot or actually in the cockpit, aircraft production might have been just another business. As it was, it gained a romance out of proportion to its profits, and it was upon this national air-mindedness that Kansas relied as it created one of the world's most concentrated aircraft manufacturing centers out of prairie, sky and enterprise.

A pivotal year for Wichita was 1919. Cessna was still on his farm, leaving the field temporarily to others. They were not long in coming. More than 10,000 men had been trained in the air services during the World War. Some never wanted to see an airplane again, but others were purchasing war surplus Canuck and Curtiss JN-4 (Jenny) wartime trainers and going into the barnstorming business. At first, they sold rides to small-town residents, and when that thrill faded, pilots performed ever more daring aerobatics at county fairs. "The rules were simple enough," wrote Martin Caidin in *Barnstorming*. "Landing fields were a gift of God and the sweat of a farmer's back, and part of the game was guessing about the low stumps or the ditches that you couldn't see. You played the wind by gosh and by guess, and you looked for cows with their rumps pretty much pointed in one general direction, for there's no better natural wind sock in the business than the tail end of a cow. ... It was flying, said some of the old-timers, the way that God intended man to fly. ... You came to know the sky by instinct and feel and smelling the weather almost as much as you did by studying the clouds and hunting for the signs splashed across the sky."

John Nevill, writing "The Story of Wichita" for *Aviation* magazine in 1930, asked the common question of how Wichita (whose population was about 100,000) had come to produce one-fourth of the commercial airplanes manufactured in the United States and could rival the efforts of New York, Detroit and Los Angeles The native Kansan's answer, he said, was direct. "One answer is topography. A second is geography. A third is climate. A fourth is air-mindedness, mentally, physically, and financially. A fifth, general 'go-getterism.'"

Wichitans had learned the force of the geographic destiny argument in their boom days in the 1880s, and by the 1920s the ego to go with the strong natural south wind, was returning to its native home. "They tell you in Wichita," Nevill noted, "that the city's aviation history began 'aeons and aeons ago when prehistoric seas subsided, leaving a vast mid-continental plain that was destined to become the largest natural airport in America.'"

Actually, while geographic centrality and stories about how Wichita and

Kansas were the only place to fly might play well with small boys and reporters, it took considerable and purposeful cultivation to draw investors and manufacturers to the Great Plains. Wichita, especially, was a master at that kind of ground-up promotion, partly from historical experience as the fastest-growing and most extremely active U.S. city of the 1880s and partly because the Plains were a progressive place, where spaces seemed to call for filling, where there was no dead weight of tradition, and where nothing ever fell into a local's lap by accident. The cultivation was partly quite secret: it involved wealthy Wichita businesspeople going out with promises of financing and finding and bringing manufacturers to Wichita, something they had been accustomed to doing since they attracted the railroad and the cattle trade in 1872. It was partly extremely public and involved the sponsoring of spectacles to create unwavering local support and undistracted focus on the single goal of attracting an air industry to town.

The creation of air-mindedness was always the first step. The aviation committee of the Wichita Chamber of Commerce decided early in 1919 to promote a specific Wichita landing field — a place to focus events and demonstrations and dispense repairs and gasoline. (An additional consideration was that a city had to have an "official" flying field before it could be considered a stop on the airmail routes). The field chosen belonged to J.J. Jones, the erstwhile automaker, and was located near 29th Street North along U.S. Route 81. This seventy-five acre field, on which Jones generously cut some perfectly good alfalfa so that planes could land, was acquired by the Chamber because the city government was not allowed by its own ordinances to purchase land outside the city limits, even had the City Commission been interested. It was dedicated in a stunning way by the Victory Liberty Loan Flying Circus on May 1.

The Flying Circus relied on war publicity to generate interest and to sell bonds to finish paying for the war. Large ads in local papers described war heroes with the headline "He Fought for You. The bonds he bought were written in Flanders mud." The circus was extremely colorful. There was a ship painted to resemble a fish — complete with scales, eyes and yawning mouth — and many had colorful squadron insignia. The entourage included seventy-five people, including several war aces, all of whom toured the country on a train of thirteen Pullman coaches. The enlisted people were members of the famous 163rd Aero Squadron, American Escadrille Lafayette, just returned from eighteen months at the front. There were demonstrations of the major warplanes — the French Spad, the English S.E. 5, the American Curtiss and the German Fokker D VII. There was mock combat "the same as was carried out over the lines in France." The city would be "bombed" with 20,000 copies of a "sky extra" of the *Eagle* in the hours preceding the event, and

Frank Woods/Scott Daymon Collection

attacks on the bombers by the enemy over Wichita were promised. It was, the circus people later said, the best piece of literature produced on their tour. Aerial photographs were to be taken of the city, which, it was advertised, would not only show individuals but the kind of cigars they were smoking. The entire state of Kansas was invited, and 100 special policemen were assigned to be certain the crowd did not get out of hand. "When the battle planes race over Wichita's buildings," a *Beacon* reporter wrote, "... with every cylinder of their high-speed and high-powered engines contributing to the continuous roar, the people of this city will be able to get something of the feeling of the way actual battle conditions were carried out."

The event itself exceeded every expectation, though heavy rains in the days preceding it made conditions less than ideal for flying. The crowd at the field itself was estimated at 25,000 to 50,000 people, while 75,000 more observed the planes from downtown as they swooped over. A favorite trick was to head directly at an automobile in the road until the car's occupants "were frightened almost speechless. Then with a sudden flit of the tail of the machine, it soared scores of feet above the car." The American Curtiss craft were the slowest of the group and were called by the fliers "trucks" — an observation not lost on potential Wichita manufacturers. While watching the Loan circus, Wichitans read in their local columns of the trans-Atlantic flight attempts then under way. They also had their pockets picked by anoth-

TURNING THE WORLD UPSIDE-DOWN

⇑ A Curtiss Jenny of the Angel-Burns Flying Circus performs over Garden City, shortly after World War I. Such outrageous stunts escalated in risk and inventiveness while capturing the imagination and dollars of a public whose expectations were unending. Several well-established flying circuses, such as the T-L-R (Tex Lagrone and Albert Reed) Flying Circus, the Garver Flying Circus, and the Angel-Burns Flying Circus, would often arrive in prairie towns shortly after the harvest, trying to take advantage of the available money and high spirits.

er variety of specialists, who worked the crowds to the extent of $1,000.

The *Eagle* editorialized the day after the event that there was "A Plane Lesson" in it. Open spaces close to Wichita were found by the fliers to be scarce, suggesting the need for a municipal landing field close to the business district. The pilots had shown the practicality of flying. "These youngsters who drove the battle planes spend their days performing hair-raising stunts. They seem to have no worries about it. Soon our own people will be coming and going in planes. Indeed, one Wichitan already has decided to abandon the crawling express trains and the creeping motorcars, because he cannot afford to waste time in getting about from one oil well to another. This conservative gentleman finds himself much embarrassed when he glides into his home town and has to alight out by Mt. Carmel or at Jones field, and get a taxi to take him home." It was suggested that everyone save the special edition of the newspaper so that at some future time when airplanes flew over the town in fleets, observers of the circus could tell their children about the first time airplanes in force were seen over the city.

The flying oil man the editorial mentioned was Jacob Melvin Moellendick. Lieutenant Earl Schaefer, later president of Boeing Wichita during World War II, flew up to Wichita from Fort Sill, Okla., late in May 1919. (Schaefer, a West Point graduate had listed as his three top choices for appointment: **1.** aviation **2.** aviation and **3.** aviation, and had made the Wichita flight, said to be the first active military aircraft to land there, without the knowledge of his superiors.) According to local lore, Schaefer flew Moellendick out to one of his wells. That was enough. Moellendick had made a fortune, as had many Wichitans, in the El Dorado oil field, a giant strike just east of the city that coincided exactly with the high prices and high demand of the war years. He was to devote his wealth entirely to aviation, and die in Wichita without enough money for his own funeral. True, he was abrasive, often drunk, and a great egotist, who had made enormous risks pay off by taking drilling contracts in El Dorado for "a piece of the hole." But he has been called the Father of Wichita Aviation, and he certainly deserves the title in many ways. He passionately loved air travel and the idea of its future, and made it his life. One man wrote in 1924: "Moellendick is simply out in the jungle, miles ahead of most mature men blazing away with a mental ax, his enthusiasm, his common sense and his fortune."

The El Dorado boom, along with general early twentieth-century local successes in such fields as broom-corn warehousing and marketing, meant that capital was available in town in the hands of entrepreneurial and somewhat technically oriented people for investment in the new field of aviation. The downtown was filling with new ten-story buildings in 1919, and the oil offices could quite well be supplemented by the headquarters of air companies.

There were organizations out in front of the public pushing. The

Chamber, which had united several local booster groups in 1917, established an aviation committee in November 1918 (three weeks after the signing of the Armistice) to confer with Washington about air routes that might include Wichita. The local newspapers, the *Eagle* particularly, worked hard for aviation. Marcellus Murdock, part of the *Eagle's* managing family, was an enthusiastic promoter of the airplane, and the *Eagle* became the first newspaper in the United States to own an airship. The paper called for Wichita to be first on the flying trails of the Southwest and suggested that if the city hesitated it would become a forgotten town site, just as had towns that missed the chance to attract a railroad when that industry was getting started.

Not all believed. Charles Driscoll, who wrote some of the puff editorials, remembered later that "in the spring of 1919 a Wichita newspaper was said to be making a fool of itself, repeating day after day that airplanes would soon be flying passengers and mail across the continent, and that Wichita should provide a landing field ... at public expense. I was the ... writer of the editorials that were causing my publisher no end of embarrassment in the marketplace and the country clubs. His friends taunted him with keeping a crazy editor on the job, and he relayed the opinions of the substantial citizenry to me."

Action followed the rhetoric quickly enough. Following the bond circus, in May and June, a fliers' club and two aircraft companies were formed in Wichita. The flier's club was organized to host Army Captain Eddie Rickenbacker when he came to the city for a lecture and to push for a municipal field. The two companies, the Wichita Aeroplane Service Company and the Wichita Aircraft Company, had broader goals.

The Wichita Aeroplane Service Company filed its charter on June 16, 1919, and was backed by A.A. Stratford, president of the Ponca Tent and Awning Company. Stratford was a friend of Lieutenant Leslie L. Petticord, who had 400 hours of flying time, mostly in the war, and was the actual operator. The company leased an eighty-acre tract at approximately 25th Street North and Hillside, about one-half mile north of Fairmount College, three and one-half miles northeast of downtown and just beyond the Wichita Park cemetery. It had a canvas hangar and was known as Stratford Field.

Income was to come from sales of Curtiss aircraft, the sale of $15 rides and contracting for stunt flying. At first the entire site was occupied by one Army surplus Curtiss Jenny. Shortly a second plane arrived, and within two days of opening thirty-one people had paid for rides. "He has established the first flying taxi business in the city," the *Eagle* said of Stratford, "and a lot of local history is being made on a grassy hill a little north of Fairmount College."

The Wichita Aircraft Company got its charter in July. Army Lieutenants J.B. Witt and E.J. Mason were the operators. Moellendick and several other

Wichita Public Library

VISIONARY

⇑ With production at the El Dorado oil fields reaching a peak of 80,000 barrels a day in 1918, many Kansans were accruing vast fortunes. One was Wichita oil man Jacob Melvin "Jake" Moellendick, one of general aviation's first venture capitalists. Moellendick fueled early aircraft operations with his own cash, nurturing young aircraft designers like E.M. Laird and Lloyd Stearman. While prone to fits of mismanagement, Moellendick's legacy is seen in the plants and offices of surviving Kansas aircraft companies.

Tihen Collection

MATTY

⇑ Emil Mathew "Matty" Laird's appearance in Kansas was brief, 1920 to 1923, but he left people talking. Laird shaped Wichita's commercial aircraft manufacturing tradition by hiring farmers and students, molding them into the workers that he and the state needed.

local businessmen, including hotel man George Sidhoff and contractor J.H. Turner, backed the company financially. Its plans included an air taxi service, a school for fliers, the construction of five hangars, and the establishment of an air passenger route between Wichita, Kansas City and Tulsa, Okla. It acquired a field also, this time within a mile of downtown. That shortly forced the Wichita Aeroplane Service Company to move its headquarters from Stratford Field to the McKnight Tract on East Douglas (now the location of Wichita East High School), only two miles from downtown. There was talk even of building landing fields on the tops of the new tall downtown buildings. The North Hillside field continued to be maintained and improved, and by fall had four hangars, a filling station, and a repair shop. Visiting pilots said it was the best landing field west of Dayton, Ohio.

A third group in Wichita, the Arnold Auto Company, got into the business by buying two Curtiss biplanes and offering them for taxi service. The auto agency sold them for $3,000 each, representing the first commercial aviation sale in Wichita and "a new era for commercializing flying machines in Kansas." The city wasn't yet the Air Capital of the World, but things looked promising. "The city with its wealth and its reputation for progress," wrote a close observer, "has appealed to men of the world of flight as an ideal point from which to pioneer the worthy enterprise of commercializing the airplane."

There was some hope and some fun with these companies and their facilities. Late in May 1919, Petticord took up the seven-, nine- and eleven-year-old sons of Stratford all at once, just to show how safe flying was. In August, Pete Wells, a seventy-seven-year-old man from Norwich, flew to Wichita with Petticord and, despite a crash from 100 feet while taking off from the McKnight field for the trip back, was delighted. The Civil War veteran had made the trip first by oxen and was enthused about this new transportation mode. "I've made the trip every other way," said Wells, looking at a reporter from behind his flying goggles, "and as I can't tell how soon I might begin to get old, I thought I'd better fly it while the flying was good. The trip was the finest experience of my life. We made it in 35 minutes and it used to take me all day to walk it." He said he was going to fly back as soon as Petticord got another plane.

"We are the first in the field in the state," ran a Wichita Aircraft Company ad that fall inviting people to drive out and examine the flying facilities. "Give ten minutes of your time for your city's benefit and your own."

The air infrastructure certainly advanced. As early as February 1919, the Chamber had built a concrete bull's-eye marker on the field at the Jones plant to attract airplanes. However seven DH-4 bombers of the U.S. air service squadron en route from Dallas to Boston late in May passed up Wichita

Walt House Collection

because there was no field safe for landing such heavy craft. Larger planes and faster planes, many commented, would take better fields. The field at Fairmount was some better, being "carpeted with sod," but there was still a call for a municipally owned field. "Wichita must look far into the future in planning facilities for airplane traffic. Private fields may some day be cut up and sold for residence and industrial purposes."

For all this talk and progress, neither of Wichita's pioneer companies prospered, and both were dissolved within a year. However, out of the ruins of one of them, the Wichita Aircraft Company, and a partnership with a very young airplane maker from Chicago, emerged one of the first commercially viable aircraft companies in the West.

Moellendick had become upset with the management of the Wichita Aircraft Company, and at the end of 1919 persuaded William Burke, a prosperous car dealer in Okmulgee, Okla., to move to Wichita to manage it. Burke made a trip to Chicago and while there visited with Emil M. "Matty" Laird, who was designing a three-place biplane. Burke had learned to fly at Rich Field in Waco, Texas, during World War I with Laird's good friend Buck Weaver and with a man named Walter Beech, who was to play no small role in Kansas aviation. Burke purchased an airplane (a two-place sport biplane called the Model S) from Laird early in 1919 and his considerable sales ability, applied at an air show in Chicago and followed up

PATRIARCH

⇑ Described as a cleaned-up Curtiss Jenny, the wood and wire-trussed Laird Swallow was the first Kansas aircraft to see serious production. It had a 17,000-foot ceiling, but its Curtiss OX-5 engine would have to strain for an hour with just a pilot aboard to reach 15,000 feet. Its main competition was from surplus Jennys and Standards. The Swallow's large wing area and low operational speed (86 MPH, tops) allowed many pilots to walk away from crashes. This Swallow belonged to the Lander, Moellendick & Cooper Drilling Company of Wichita. It was the first aircraft in the United States to be registered in accord with international conventions.

Kansas State Historical Society

HEAD AND SHOULDERS ABOVE THE COMPETITION

⇑ Towering over two E.M. Laird Airplane Company employees is Johan Aahson — a giant of a man at eight feet, nine inches and 503 pounds — who flew as a passenger in this Swallow in 1921. Aircraft companies employed spirited public-relations stunts to showcase the capabilities of their aircraft.

on a flight in a Jenny to an oil field near Wichita and to Oklahoma to test the market, persuaded Laird to move his factory to Wichita and to form a three-way partnership with him and Moellendick .

The deal was on a handshake, with no written documentation whatever. The corporate mission was not just an air taxi service and a landing field, but the manufacture and sale of a Wichita airplane. The factory was first located on the corner of Wichita and English streets downtown, behind the Wichita Forum building, in a former agricultural implement manufacturing plant. When finished, airplanes were hauled through the streets out to the old Stratford Field, renamed Laird Field. In May 1920, the concern became the E.M. Laird Airplane Company. It was the nursery of a legion of its like.

Laird was a fascinating man — about as mercurial in personality as Moellendick, and not always to the same ends. He was the son of a cabinet-maker, from whom he had learned woodworking, and, like so many boys, became interested in aviation by watching an early dirigible flight in Chicago

Walt House Collection

in 1910. After having put glider wings on his bicycle, he began making aircraft models, which he sold as Christmas presents for other boys. He and his friend Weaver, who accompanied him to Wichita, scaled up these models relying on Laird's drawings on butcher paper. In 1912, at sixteen, Laird, to his surprise, took off in a tiny monoplane. He immediately crashed. By 1915, however, his aircraft were advanced enough that he and Weaver barnstormed through five states in one of them, including Kansas.

The airplane they built in the little Wichita factory and assembled on the second floor of the Forum Building in 1920 was first called the Wichita Tractor — an unimaginative description of its forward prop. It was to be equipped with a war surplus OX-5 engine. Unfortunately the company purchased 50 new Curtiss OX-5 engines at $650 each from the factory, and were crushed to find that within a few months the U.S. government was selling them for $25 each. Laird lived in a small bachelor room at Victor and Hillside in Wichita, which cost him $4.50 a week, and drew a salary of $75 a week — a fortune for the time and place. He was glad to have Burke make the actual sales calls. Laird had broken his leg badly in an airplane accident and did not want to explain the circumstances of his limp to potential customers.

Laird spent much of his time early in 1920 trying to raise money from potential Wichita backers, without much success. Wichitans were morally behind it, he remembered later, but "lacked the vision to take the steps to provide the base from which to operate." He appeared before the Chamber and tried unsuccessfully to get it to take at least a lease on the California

1924 NEW SWALLOW

⇑ The successor to the Laird Swallow, the New Swallow set industry standards and was an instant success. About fifty planes were built between 1924 and 1926. Benefiting from Lloyd Stearman's architectural training, the New Swallow was a pleasing departure from bulky World War I-era trainers. Possessing an enclosed, hand-formed metal engine cowling; single bay wing design; and a split axle, the New Swallow was copied by many companies seeking to cash in on its success. This aircraft was in turn, the predecessor of the Super Swallow, designed by Charles Laird, in which tubular steel replaced the wood-trussed design of the New Swallow. Approximately fifty Super Swallows were built starting in 1926, to be followed by 250 1927 Swallows.

Section, the last full section of virgin prairie sod in the county (and eventually the site of the municipal airport) lying slightly southeast of the city. His appeal for risk capital was simple: "I told them I felt there was something on the horizon, but I couldn't predict whether it was going to be next year or five years or ten years ahead."

There was a test flight on April 8, 1920. The site was Laird Field and the pilot of the three-place, open, tandem-cockpit biplane was Laird himself. "It was a tense moment," said a reporter attending. "at 5:42 o'clock Thursday afternoon when E.M. Laird opened wide the throttle of the first airplane made in Wichita, and the untried ship headed into a light southeast wind." The flight was successful, and passengers were carried later in the day. The occasion also gave the airplane a better name. William Lassen, son of a local hotel promoter, was there and commented: "It flies just like a Swallow." The name became Swallow, and the airplane was marketed to those who wanted something better than a war-surplus Jenny.

It was certainly a relative success. It could carry a pilot, two passengers and baggage for more than 200 miles without landing. Most designers, the advertising said, responded to the need for more weight-hauling with a larger engine and more overhead. The Swallow made do with 90 HP and only a little over 1,000 pounds of weight empty. Orders for eleven planes came in quickly, and Moellendick called for production of twenty-five craft the first year. The company hired Lloyd Stearman, a young Kansas State Agricultural College architecture student who had returned to school after serving as a Navy pilot during World War I. Stearman adapted his skills to draw plans, and within a year would hire Beech and Weaver as pilot-salesmen. By May 1920, there was a rudimentary national distribution network, and thirty employees, including William Snook, who worked part-time while attending Fairmount College. In August, the factory was producing one airplane a week. By fall there were forty-five employees and plans for a new factory at Laird Field. Planes sold for $6,500 and probably about fifteen of them were in customers' hands by the end of 1920. This was a real firm.

Bob Pickett Collection, Kansas Aviation Museum/Cessna

HAULING THE MAIL

⇐ The 1926 Swallow Mailplane was essentially a 1924 New Swallow that had been converted by replacing the front cockpit with a mail compartment, increasing the wingspan by four feet, and replacing the stock 90 HP Curtiss OX-5 engine with a 160 HP Curtiss model C-6 engine. The first private contract carrier to carry the U.S. Mail was the Ford Motor Company (on February 15, 1926) using Ford-Stout cabin monoplanes as a part of Contract Air Mail (CAM) Routes Six and Seven. Ford's routes, as well as those of others, fed into the main New York-to-San Francisco line. Walter Varney, (who used six Swallow Mailplanes) became the second contract air mail carrier (CAM Route Five). However, Varney experienced inadequate cooling using the Curtiss C-6 engines in the desert environment. He replaced them with 200 HP Wright J-4 air-cooled radial engines as shown here.

Firsts followed firsts. The Swallow was advertised as the first commercial U.S. airplane, although the Curtiss Oriole is certainly a competitor for that honor. The first air express shipment to a Wichita company arrived at the Coleman Lamp Company in May 1920. A Swallow with Moellendick aboard aided law enforcement officers in catching an alleged murderer. The Aero Club of Kansas was formed in 1920, with Wichita as the headquarters and attraction of the airmail as its first goal. The first civil aircraft in the United States to be registered was a Swallow belonging to the Lander, Moellendick & Cooper Drilling Company. The date was the fall of 1922.

The Swallow played a great role in the success of the U.S. Air Mail. When the Kelley Act in 1926 made it possible for private contractors to carry airmail (it had previously been a monopoly of the U.S. Post Office), one of the first contractors was Varney Air Lines, and Varney used a fleet of six Swallow mail planes adapted from the standard model. The Wichita plant replaced the Curtiss OX-5 with a 160 HP Curtiss C-6 and increased the wingspan by four feet. Varney, with his isolated route from Elko, Nev., to Pasco, Wash., is credited with making the first consistent civil use of the air-cooled radial engine. Varney became a subsidiary of Boeing Air Transport, which in 1930 became United Air Lines. Thus the claim that United is the oldest continuously operating airline in the United States reaches back to Varney and Laird. The dean of U.S. aviation historians, Peter Bowers, writes that "Swallow was … the pioneer building of the post-World War I generation of private aircraft and introduced many new features that soon became the industry standards."

The Laird company lasted, but Laird himself left Wichita in 1923 after a final argument with Moellendick. The new factory, completed late in 1921, had been expensive, and Moellendick moved faster and more optimistically than Laird was comfortable with. When orders started coming in, Laird told an interviewer in 1930, "everybody went wild." According to that account: "The planning department, which is another way of saying Jake Moellendick, opened up the production throttle just as he would the main valve on one of his wells. … Eight hours a day became ten, then twelve, and then more. Employees, straining in their harness, began to grumble, but carried on."

A second factor in the departure of Laird was that the design of a seven-place, twin-engine airplane to sell to airlines had not gone well. There was serious interest from the Aerial Navigation and Engineering Company in Denver, the Roosevelt Air Line in New York City and the Larsen Aerial Navigation Company, which designated Wichita as a stopping point on a proposed route from New York to Mexico. But, after a maiden flight of the twin in 1921, and changes in engines from OX-5s to Libertys to Packards, the Air Limousine was still not right.

It was early to think about airlines, true, but the future was there to see for those who could extrapolate. It is one of the shortcomings of Wichita that it was never able to turn its great momentum in private aircraft into contracts for larger planes when airlines emerged in the late 1920s. The Farman F-60 Goliath passenger aircraft, the all-metal Junkers F-13, the Fokker F-II, and the U.S. transcontinental T-2 demonstrated clearly between 1920 and 1923 that airplanes could carry passengers and considerable weight over long distances on precise schedules. As early as August 1919, Aircraft Transport and Travel, Limited, was making daily passenger flights from London to Paris using modified de Havilland DH-9 bombers. It was simply a matter of making a coordinated business of it. However the Laird Limo was not the answer, and that airplane was either accidentally or deliberately destroyed in 1923 by Beech. One local story has it that he made a forced landing near Fairmount College, and asked Moellendick for further instructions. Moellendick replied, "Burn it." Beech did, and that ended that.

In any case, Laird returned to Chicago in 1923, after forty-three Swallows had been built and delivered, to develop his racing plane. Part of it surely was Moellendick's "disagreeable attitude." That was Weaver's explanation when he left in 1921 to go to Alliance, Ohio, where he built the successful Waco airplane. That was fundamentally what drove Beech and Stearman away in 1924 to found the Travel Air Manufacturing Company with Clyde Cessna. Stearman and Cessna shortly would themselves break away to form their own companies.

FAMILY TREE The evolution of Kansas into an aviation center can be traced to a combination of four factors: talent, money, promotion, and luck. A cadre of aircraft pioneers provided a foundation upon which the Kansas aviation industry was built. Shown are the companies that immediately descended from the E.M. Laird Company, which provided a foothold for a fledgling industry.

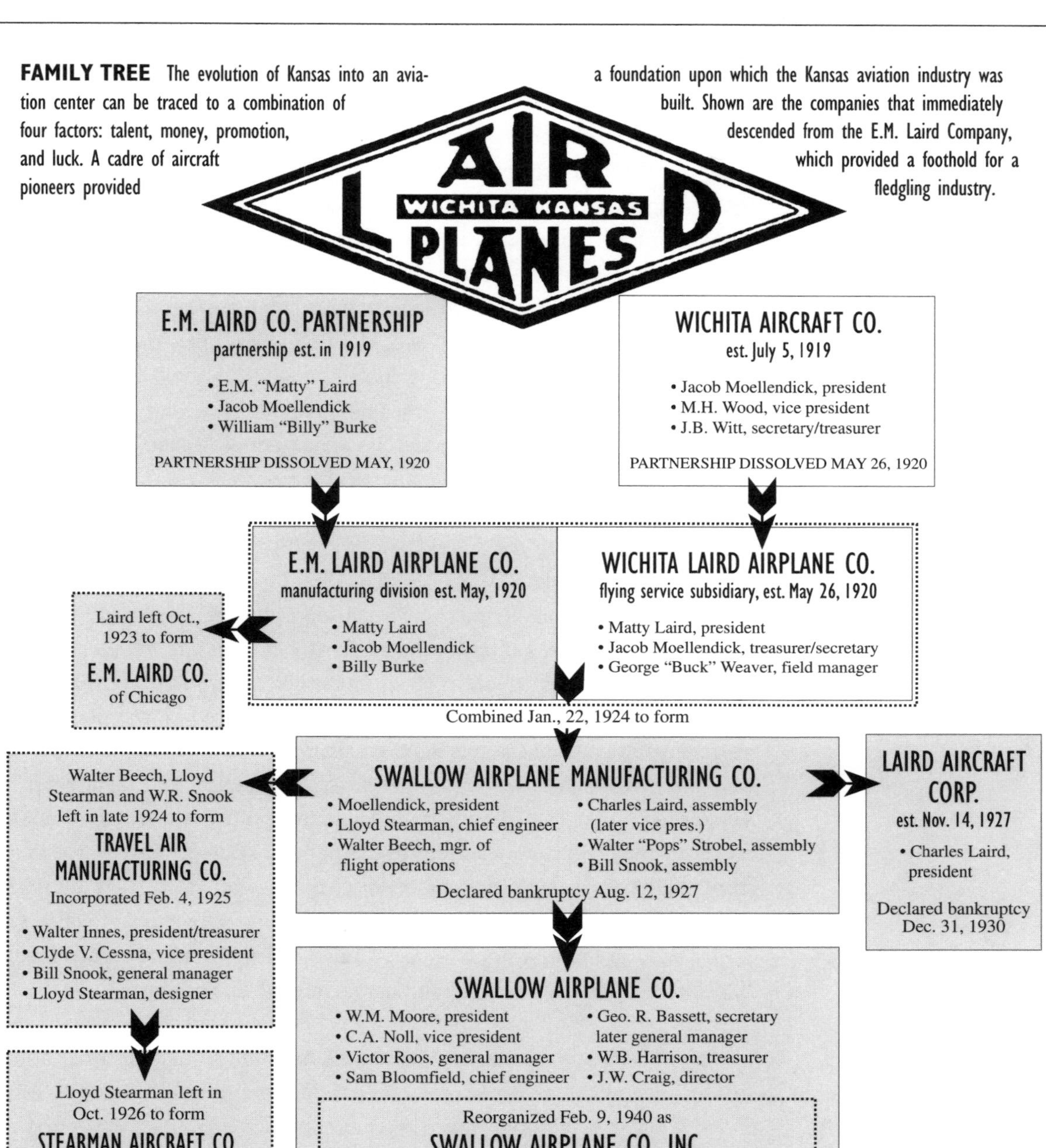

It can be argued that Moellendick's personality, combined with his stubbornness and overreaching ways, was among the best things that ever happened to Wichita and Kansas. It broke up the original crew, and each took his experience to a new company, where most worked out their successful history in Wichita itself, serving an ever-growing market. The diversity created strength and a "critical mass" that led to the city's national Air Capital status. And all the local companies could build on the association of the Laird name with the city and the wonderful publicity his early air race victories gave that odd-sounding Indian name of the Kansas town. Meanwhile the original company "under Jake Moellendick's open-pursed, but tight-gripped rule," continued as long as its backers' money lasted under the name Swallow Airplane Manufacturing Company.

Laird was philosophical about his departure. Moellendick had no sense of judgment, he said, and did not have the experience to make good judgments about aviation. Besides, Moellendick's oil income was dropping, the company was in deep debt, and Laird was all too well paid. "I mean things happen," Laird said in a 1978 interview, "and I guess, I think it probably was better in the long run for me too, because, under the conditions that I was working at that time, I'd have a lot higher blood pressure than I have now." He confessed, however, that it was fascinating, and, had it not been for the clash of personalities, he would have stayed. The crew at the plant worked seven days a week and nights, sometimes, in the early 1920s. "It was all so interesting work that we never thought of the clock." The local press was wonderful, "a big lift. They were anxious every day, not just for one story, but every day to have something in the paper (about) what was going on. I think that has been a big help in developing the whole area." As John Nevill put it: "Wichita had gained a foothold that subsequently enabled her to reach a lofty peak in the industry." By the time of Laird's death at eighty-seven in 1982, he had plenty of occasion to marvel at what he had started.

Wichita was unquestionably the bellwether for Kansas aviation in the early twenties, but it was not alone in the state in its advances. A census in 1921 listed twenty-one plane manufacturers in the state, and thirty-five Kansas counties had turned in reports to comply with a 1921 state law requiring the licensing of aircraft dealers and plants. When the U.S. Department of Commerce started regulating airplanes in 1926 and requiring type certificates, many of the backyard manufacturers, of course, disappeared, most of them deservedly.

"Pete" Hill became a partner in 1918 with Errett Williams and others in an airplane company in Arkansas City. The firm sponsored a barnstorming troupe, which for a time included Beech. It toured the country and repaired and sold several types of airplanes. Hill had a special interest in making flying as safe as possible, and in an attempt to cut out some of the "foolish, chance-taking," he and Williams wrote a Kansas aircraft law code similar to Department of Commerce rules that took effect later. "The Legislature didn't take so kindly the idea at first," Hill remembered a few years later, "but we soon changed that. We got a bunch of them to go into the Capitol dome, and then proceeded to show them just what it was that the code was intended to eliminate. We spun down on the dome, just missing it a few feet, dived on it, and pulled plenty of other stuff that made the lawmakers wonder if they were going to get out of that dome alive. And when they got back into the assembly, the code went through. It provided for pilot's licenses, just as the national code does today."

There was significant manufacturing activity in Topeka, with the return of Longren and the establishment of a concern in the spring of 1919. "The airplane will make more rapid progress in gaining public approval than has the automobile," Longren said. "I believe the one- and two-seater will prove the popular plane for general business and pleasure purposes." Longren proposed to sell stock all over Kansas and to equip a factory that would employ 150. In November 1919, the conversion of the former Topeka Woolen Mills was complete, and all was in readiness. However, while Topeka kept aviation interest high by establishing itself in 1919 as part of the airmail route, publicizing a cross-country flight from Topeka to Garden City, Kans., and even taking notice of an aerial wedding of a Hays, Kans., couple enroute to Kansas City, the Longren manufacturing project languished. The trial flights of the 500-pound Longren plane, called the Longren Fibre Sport Model AK, did not take place until late summer in 1921. Although a nationwide marketing organization was established for the ultralight airplane, and it was good-looking and won many contests, sales were not as brisk as were those of the Swallow. Longren closed his factory in the Oakland suburb of Topeka in 1924 and took bankruptcy for his company.

It took Topeka a time to feel regret, but eventually the townspeople began to think they had missed a wonderful opportunity offered by one of the two pioneer practical fliers and manufacturers in Kansas. Cessna took his time getting back into the business, but by the late 1920s, after a split with Beech, had his own successful company in Wichita. By then Longren no longer even lived in Topeka. The blame, in hindsight, fell to lack of financing — there was no Moellendick in the state capital — and to "public indifference." The *Topeka Journal* editorialized in 1927 that with Longren "the capital city lost its golden opportunity to become an airplane production center," and proved for certain that nothing grows in Kansas without care and cultivation.

Longren stayed in the industry working as a consultant for many companies, including Cessna Aircraft Company, and so his ideas, particularly those about light, strong fuselage structures for an inexpensive "people's plane" were not lost to Kansas.

The largest city touching the Sunflower State, Kansas City, Mo., entered the aircraft business relatively late, and its contribution was modest, at least compared with Wichita. Kansas City hosted the American Legion Air Meet on November 1, 1921, which drew a crowd of 45,000 people to watch thirteen planes in a 175-mile race around pylons. The city later was the production site of several famous custom-built racers. However serious aircraft production did not get going until 1925, when Ed Porterfield, formerly a Kansas City Ford dealer, started a flying school and factory that became the American Eagle Aircraft Corporation. In 1927, with new capital from a General Motors principal, the company built a brick factory building in Kansas City, Kans., across the street from Fairfax Airport. It built a Longren design, a folding-wing biplane, and prospered briefly, employing as many as 115 people. But a spate of fatal accidents with the spin-prone model A-101 was the beginning of the business's decline, and the Depression finished it. By the time American Eagle closed in 1932, it had manufactured about 500 airplanes.

Other Kansas City concerns were smaller. There was Rearwin, which in 1929 also constructed manufacturing facilities at Fairfax. Rearwin produced a fairly popular line of small airplanes of the 1930s, (Ken-Royce 2000, Junior, Sportster, Speedster and Cloudster), but by the 1940s the company was specializing mostly in engines. The Butler Blackhawk, designed by Waverly Stearman, which got a type certificate in 1929, was closely related to the Stearman airplane. That company hired Longren as a consultant for a time during 1930 and planned to produce a revolutionary Longren all-metal biplane. However, the Depression intervened, and Butler closed in 1931. Longren himself tried again with the Luscombe Phantom, an all-metal monoplane built at the Kansas City (Mo.) Municipal Airport in 1933, but production of that plane was soon moved to Trenton, N.J.

Kansas City became known more for the scratch-building of interesting prototypes, the cultivation of showmen and barnstormers like John K. "Tex" LaGrone, and the construction of one-offs and racers than for significant and long-lasting aircraft companies. It claimed four airplane factories and one glider factory in 1930, but the Inland Aviation Company, which manufactured the Inland Sport, and the Cook Glider factory barely qualified. The city occupied a stronger position in creating facilities to use its advantageous geographical position on the air routes. It had three airports in 1930. Municipal and Fairfax had quite good facilities, and Commercial Airways

Wichita Chamber of Commerce

BOOSTERISM

⇐ In 1928, the Wichita Kiwanis Club sponsored a contest to design a logo to be used in promoting Wichita as The Air Capital. Ted Young submitted the winning design, consisting of a circle with a sunflower that had sprouted wings. In the same year, the Aeronautical Chamber of Commerce lent credence to the city's claim, noting that 927 aircraft had been built in Wichita, compared with second-place New York state's 875 planes and third-place Ohio's 816.

Field, established in 1921 and one of the oldest commercial fields in the country, was on high ground and thus often fog-free. The city had invested $1.6 million in Municipal by that date. It had four runways, was a major airmail center, and was served by Transcontinental Air Transport, Southwest Air Fast Express, Western Air Express, National Air Transport, United States Airways, and Mid-Continent Air Express. Having a solid industrial base and trade position already in the 1920s, perhaps it was a little more complacent than Wichita about pushing the manufacturing end of a new industry.

To be fair, Wichita was a one-of-a-kind wonder in aviation, not only in Kansas, but nationally. Its Air Capital of The World moniker, emblazoned on a little shield and plastered on nearly everything made there in the late 1920s, was no exaggeration. By sheer force of numbers as more and more makers — most of them alums of Laird or long-time area residents — started factories, Wichita-built craft ended up in some feat of derring-do or demonstration of efficiency. That in turn created a larger market, longer hours for the plants and cheaper prices as volume production got under way. Wichita missed providing Lindbergh with a Travel Air called the "Spirit of Wichita" for his Trans-Atlantic flight in 1927, but it was not because he did not ask. And that was just about the only major aeronautical opportunity, other than building a true airliner, that Wichita missed. As the 1920s progressed, the names of Travel Air, Cessna, Stearman and a host of lesser lights were added to the Wichita pantheon and simultaneously to the forward part of the consciousness of the flying world.

The Liberty Loan Circus had its ever-improving successors in Wichita. Over the Decoration Day weekend in 1921, the Laird company sponsored an air derby, held on the California section and offering twelve prizes to be awarded at a dance at the Wintergarden sponsored by Moellendick. The best pilot overall received $20, and individual prizes were given for the best takeoffs and landings, spot landings, highest altitude, and twenty-mile races

PEOPLE OF THE SOUTH WIND

⇒ "The National Air Congress has done three things," said L.S. Seymour, president of the local chapter of the National Aeronautics Association in 1924. "It has brought the natural advantages of Wichita to the attention of leading aviators; it has shown the people that aviation has taken great strides the past few years; and it has proved excellent in the way of entertainment."

by class of aircraft. "This tournament," said Moellendick, "is held with the express purpose of demonstrating the safety and practicability of airplanes for the daily use of the businessman. We have intentionally omitted any reference to acrobatics as they have no value to commercial aviation."

Typically for Kansas there was a violent storm on the second day, and when spectators weren't rushing for cover, they entertained themselves mostly by watching the pilots try to protect their planes from being carried away. Because the field was too muddy for takeoffs anyway, all stayed for the dance, and there was a crowd the next day to see how fast the California section dried and whether there were any takeoff accidents. The *Eagle*, noticing that some minnows had been picked up on a parking lot, wondered if it had rained fish.

That was amateur stuff, however, compared with the National Air Congress of 1924 — a major national promotion. Two hundred local men got together and formed a local chapter of the National Aeronautical Association, which raised over $20,000 to attract the Congress. The heavily advertised event, presided over by "Princess Wichita" in flying helmet and goggles, was held on a Saturday and Sunday in mid-October — a time of the year when the weather is generally more favorable to spectators than the sometimes tornadic Kansas springs. Cash prizes of $10,000, along with a number of trophies donated by local merchants, drew more than 100 aircraft, representing all classes of military and civilian craft. The fighting planes had parts of their radiators incorporated in the wings and, it was promised that this, along with streamlined wire bracings, would "produce a shriek like a shell when the ship is clipping along at 170 or so miles an hour with full military equipment." From its start — with an "On to Wichita" race from the Dayton international air races — to its tragedy-marred finale, it was the most grandiose air show that the Great Plains had ever witnessed.

There was a little bit of everything that weekend. There were large, twin-engined Martin bombers that could carry a ton of weight at 100 MPH. There were Curtiss PW-8 pursuit planes. Even a blimp, the Army's TC-5, was there. Cessna arrived in a Swallow with an inscription on the fuselage: "11 years of flying without an accident. BUILT OWN SHIP AND FLEW WITHOUT INSTRUCTIONS IN 1910. BUILT AND FLOWN 8 PLANES. FLYING PROPERLY CONDUCTED IS SAFE." He brought with him his nephew, Dwane Wallace, who, at thirteen, could hardly have had better inspiration for the role he was to play in Kansas aviation. Every store in town closed at 1 p.m. on Friday to allow people to get out to see the arriving celebrities, and the sidewalks of the city were lined with flags to welcome the visiting fliers. The front-page headline on opening day in the *Eagle* was "Wichita the Capital City of Aviation World Today." And so, with only slight hyperbole, it was.

"Masters of the Air Furnish Thrills to Thousands," was emblazoned in large type Saturday. Laird airplanes stole the show that day. The Walter Innes Trophy, given by a local department-store owner, who also was a pilot and engine developer, to the fastest low-horsepower, two-seater performance, was won by Beech in his Swallow at 91.6 MPH. Second was Stearman in a Swallow, then came a Yackey Sport, followed by four more Swallows, one of them flown by Cessna. The Alvin Hinkel Trophy, given by another local department store owner for larger planes that raced over a fifty-mile course, was won by a foreigner, but Laird planes took the next three places.

Monday's headline had a different flavor: "Ruth Garver Plunges to Death as Son, 11, Looks On." Garver of Garver's Flying Circus had jumped from an airplane flying 1,000 feet above a crowd of 25,000, kicked as she tried to open her parachute, and then fell like a stone into a crowd of automobiles. Still the show went on. Garver's friend and fellow parachutist Mrs. Leavaughn Neville, who saw the whole thing from the airplane, could only comment with trembling hands: "It's a nerve-wracking business."

If the point was made about the real hazards in flying, the point of its promise also was driven home to Kansans in attendance at the Air Congress. According to C.M. Wanzer, president of the American Aeronautic Development Company of Cincinnati, Wichita had a large role in aviation's future. There would have to be a central point of distribution, and Wichita was ideal. From there would radiate air lines to all points of the compass. "At Wichita all passengers would meet and change planes for points of final destination and all mails would be trans-shipped. There would necessarily be located here great airship-yards for construction and repair of the fleet of sky buses that stopped here. Immense landing fields would be required."

Toward this end the National Air Congress was "a flying start." It was absolutely *the* subject of conversation on Wichita streets for a week, and the large crowds from all over Kansas learned not only something about aircraft but recognized "that the rolling prairies which are Kansas are waiting with open arms for the era of aviation. It is a small spark, but one which will fire the imagination of every honest-to-goodness Kansan." When Ruth Garver was buried in Attica, Kans., the Wednesday after the air show, Beech flew over in a Laird Swallow and dropped flowers.

Garver was no amateur. She had jumped many times before, and had packed her own parachute the day of her death. She and her husband, Karl, were part of the barnstorming phenomenon. Dozens of small-town newspapers in Kansas, Oklahoma, Missouri, Colorado, Texas, Nebraska, the Dakotas and even Mexico had since 1920 contained ads for the Garvers' "Extraordinary … Super-Sensational … Thrilling," and one might add death-defying, demonstrations of wing-walking, parachuting, airplane-to-airplane and automobile-to-airplane transfers. Unlike most troupes, which had JN-4 war-surplus planes, Garver and his partner, Clyde Horchem, mostly operated new Swallows. When an engine wore out, it was never repaired; Garver had on hand a large supply of cheap, surplus OX-5 engines. It was naturally believed that outfits such as Garver's Flying Circus would be a prime market for Kansas airframe manufacturers.

But these businesses were not long-lived nor were their principals. Karl Garver, who with his fleece-lined flying coat, white scarf, and jodhpurs

GARVER'S

FLYING CIRCUS

5 - AEROPLANES - 5

An Absolutely Top Notch Up-to-Date Attraction

Under Auspices

AMERICAN LEGION

A Spectacular Production of all the Dare-Devil Death-Defying Thrills Known to Craftsmen

A Wonderful Exhibition of Aerial Stunts and Novelties will be pres-nted by these Fearless Birdmen

Greatest Attraction of the Southwest **RUTH GARVER** **Champion Lady Parachute Jumper**

IN A THRILLING LEAP FROM PLANE

MARVELOUS DISPLAY OF DAYLIGHT FIREWORKS

PILOT GARVER

Unparalelled in Stunt Flying will present a full and unexcelled program consisting of 10 consecutive loops, 2000 foot Tail Spin, Immelman Turns, Barrel Rolls, Spirals, Falling Leaf, Ocean Waves, Etc.

PAUL DUNCAN

Champion Wing Walker

will walk on the wings of the Plane, stand on top through a maize of loops and tail spins, hang by his teeth, toes and one hand, from a trapeze, and do many other sensational stunts.

COME AND BOOST FOR THE LEGION BOYS

Wellington, Kansas, October 21, 1923

East on Lincoln to End of Street under the Bridge, and One Mile South, or One-Half mile East of Gaines Farm

FOLLOW THE BLAZED TRAIL—Red Arrow

Kansas State Historical Society

DIFFERENT WORLDS

⇐ Although handbills such as this one (A 1923 flier for Garver's Flying Circus) painted a world of daring adventure performed by dashing men and women, it was also a world of trials and hardships. Overhauling a cantankerous engine in blowing dust and 105-degree heat, while cleaning manure from the undersides of aircraft (farmers' pastures were the usual choice of landing fields), were images far from the minds of the crowds who went to see the daredevils.

tucked into laced knee-high boots looked every inch the barnstormer, would die of alcohol poisoning in Wichita in 1926. By that time his business was long gone. Bertha Horchem, the other circus wife and a former Wichita resident, had died in a crash in San Antonio, Texas, in March 1924, when the bottom left wing of her Swallow crumpled. Moellendick blamed that accident on rough treatment of the plane on the road and lack of proper repairs. Then came Ruth's fall. A month after that and one day after thrilling thousands at an air carnival in Oklahoma, Clyde Horchem unaccountably climbed out on the wing during a flight with a student, slipped and fell to eternity. Wayne Neville died flying the mail out of Kansas City in a storm

Ken Weyand Collection

UNEARTHLY OCCURRENCES

⇑ For six years starting in 1936, famous Midwestern barnstormer Ben Gregory thrilled audiences with an aerial act billed as the Ship from Mars. Gregory had modified his trimotor by removing the cabin seats and installing a 15,000-watt generator, which powered several searchlights and 250 feet of neon tubing that was attached to each side of the plane. When he combined the lighting with the craft's three smoke generators and other pyrotechnics, the airplane would scorch across the night sky, leaving a trail of smoke and flame as well as awestruck crowds. The act also drew love-struck couples, and Gregory reportedly performed ninety-six in-flight weddings.

while trying to demonstrate aircraft reliability .

But the barnstormers and the racers and the moving aerial circuses of which they were a part had an enormous impact on the consciousness of potential buyers and users of airplanes, especially in Kansas. For every meet the size of Wichita's National Air Congress, there were a dozen like the one at El Dorado in June 1923, which drew 5,000 people to a Kiwanis-sponsored air show. The Flying Garvers took people on rides and tried to outdo themselves in providing "heart-stopping" thrills before going to the next town and trying, before a crowd that had heard all about their tricks, to impress them anew.

Certainly these freewheeling gypsies took undue risks, many of which were literally dead-ends. Logic dictates that air development could have done without them. But the appearance of certain brands in air shows all over the country (Laird's pilots entered every one they could find) was good marketing, and often romance drives industry, at least in its early stages, as much as cool calculation. Barnstorming did demonstrate precision piloting and it did test the designs to their limits every day of the week. And it took small town residents out of the humdrum of rural routine. Caidin, in *Barnstorming,* describes a typical town entry this way: "The circus thunders overhead at a scant one hundred feet above the courthouse spire, and the wings loom hugely in the sky and the sound becomes a clattering rattle of thunder, like a locomotive rolling over and over down a hill. It's only the Cody Flying Circus, but the impact is tremendous and the natives react as if a flock of pterodactyls had suddenly been loosed among them from the ever-watchful north. Whittling freezes in mid-stroke, merchants dash outdoors and even the dogs spring dustily to their feet as the armada crashes by overhead."

The atmosphere was electric in the country and tense at the Laird factory, and the combination led to a special explosion of entrepreneurship in Wichita. At the end of 1924, with Laird gone, Stearman and Beech approached Moellendick with the idea of changing the Swallow's wood fuselage to a welded, metal-tubing space frame. Moellendick refused. The two kept working on their own and contacted Cessna over in the next county west to help them. Cessna agreed to join them in forming a new company to build the metal-frame aircraft and to put in significant capital. Between 1918, when he was forced out of the aircraft business by the war, and 1925 Cessna, in addition to working his own farm, had a custom threshing business that netted significant profits. He was to inject about $25,000 into the enterprise before banks would loan the new firm money. In January 1925, the three and a group of local backers formed Travel Air, Inc. with Innes as president and spokesman.

The Travel Air name has been since so eclipsed by Beech's own, that it is easy to underestimate how well-known Travel Air became during the 1920s. The *Woolaroc,* a Travel Air 5000 piloted by Art Goebel that flew to victory in the Dole Race to Hawaii in 1927, may be the most famous of the breed, but Travel Airs were a staple everywhere in the latter half of the decade. Like Laird, Travel Air's first factory was in downtown Wichita, at

STEARMAN MODEL LT-1

⇓ The LT-1, holder of Air Type Certificate Number 187, could transport four passengers and 500 pounds of airmail. Cargo was carried in a forty-cubic-foot forward compartment. The pilot was exposed to the elements in an aft cockpit — a customary design of the time. This LT-1, operated by Interstate Air Lines, was outfitted with a 525 HP Pratt & Whitney Hornet engine. The plane had a range of 690 miles and a cruising speed of 115 MPH.

Bob Pickett Collection, Kansas Aviation Museum

The Wichita Eagle

THE ORIGINAL BEECH

⇑ Although not an engineer, Walter Beech's skill as an aviator and salesman was a key to the advancement of the Swallow, Travel Air, and Beech Aircraft companies. His keen sense of promotion and market analysis would pave the way for many classic aircraft designs.

Bob Pickett Collection, Kansas Aviation Museum

THE ARCHITECT

⇑ Upon Matty Laird's departure from the Laird Airplane Company, the firm was re-established as the Swallow Aircraft Manufacturing Company, with twenty-three-year-old Lloyd Stearman as the chief engineer. Stearman would later work at Travel Air as a designer. In 1926, shaken by an accident in which he killed an airport bystander, Stearman left Wichita for California. He returned the next year, establishing the company that began production of his classic biplane.

535 West Douglas. In 1927 the company moved to the current Beech Aircraft Corporation location on East Central, where a flying field could be attached. The first Travel Air biplane, powered by an OX-5 engine, cost $3,500. That was a tidy sum, considering that war surplus planes in flying condition were available for $500. But the new company was banking on the day of the barnstormers and their hairline stunts in obsolete planes of fabric and glue quickly evolving into a commercial business, where thrills were not the point. And so it did. By the time of the move to the new factory in 1927, there was a regular public market in Travel Air stock, the company had delivered eighty biplanes, and it had a contract with National Air Transport for eight Cessna-designed Travel Air monoplanes, as well as feelers from Colonial Air Transport of Boston. It provided the Dole race winner that year and could have crossed the Atlantic with Lindbergh, too.

But there were defectors at Travel Air — pushed by the pressure and pulled by the opportunity and the challenge of going it alone. The first to leave was Stearman. He was upset by the death of Arkansas Valley Interurban president George Theis Jr., who was killed by the prop of Stearman's taxiing plane. For the moment, Stearman wanted to escape Wichita. In October 1926 he joined Fred Hoyt (a West Coast Travel Air dealer) and Mac Short to establish the Stearman Aircraft Company in Venice, Calif. Wichita business leaders, however, were not about to let a native son get away so easily. A local syndicate, including Harry Dillon and Walter Innes, Jr., raised $60,000 to encourage Stearman to move back, and they arranged space for him in the venerable old Burton Car Works/Bridgeport Machine Works/Jones 6/Cessna buildings on 35th Street North. He was back in Wichita building Stearman biplanes (the model C3B) in the fall of 1927 and in November 1930 built a new plant on South Oliver Street to specialize in constructing trainers for the military.

Cessna, although he became president of Travel Air and although the famous 5000 monoplane was largely his baby, was not a person easily contained in the same corporation with such a powerful personality as Beech. The 5000 was a luxury craft, and Cessna, the farmer, wanted a "flivver" monoplane with a full cantilever wing — something light, aerodynamic and cheap to operate. In January 1927 Cessna sold his Travel Air stock and built a monoplane called the *Phantom* in a workshop on West Douglas. With it he started the Cessna Aircraft Company (incorporated in 1927), first in partnership with Victor Roos and shortly, when Roos went to manage the Swallow Company, on his own. He and his son Eldon took Cessna quickly to a strong position in both sales and respect. The company's Model AW and BW, as well as its specialized racers, were technical marvels for the time, with chrome-molybdenum fuselages, light and small-displacement Anzani and

Bob Pickett Collection, Kansas Aviation Museum/Cessna Aircraft Company

STATIC TEST

⇑ Nearly eight tons of sandbags and workers are successfully applied to a Cessna cantilevered wing. This was a typical way to test the ability of a wing to survive in-flight loading. The Department of Commerce was a stickler for such tests, particularly in the case of strutless wings.

Warner radial engines, full cantilever wings without a strut in sight and a look of the future. They won awards, they won races, and they sold.

There were numerous other Wichita aircraft companies originating in the late 1920s — at least one of which, Mooney, is well-known and successful to this day in Texas — but the big four were definitely Swallow, Travel Air, Stearman, and Cessna.

Manufacturing methods were primitive by modern standards. "They gave us some blueprints, we made what tools we needed, and away we went," remembered a workman about the atmosphere at Stearman in the late 1920s. "The first jig fixtures we built were mostly bolted together. There was very little arc welding then. … I'd had about six months of experience at welding when I got the job. The foreman handed me a blueprint, told me to make 10 motor mounts, showed me the jig and walked off. I'd never even seen a blueprint. I didn't know what a finished motor mount looked like. But I got the job done in a couple of days and it was easier after that." At Cessna the controversial full-cantilever wings underwent static stress tests by piling sand bags on them. And of course there were the famous publicity photos showing a line of men standing on top of the high wing. At Cessna there were no titles but great autonomy and individual responsibility. Individual workers in charge of certain assemblies signed them personally with their initials. And while there were some problems when the static stresses of the shop became dynamic in the air (early Cessnas had a tendency for a sympathetic vibration to affect the ailerons at high speed and compro-

mise control), the craft worked well. Certainly the companies were perfectly positioned as manufacturers of modern, practical, and relatively inexpensive airplanes to meet demand from the business user, who was just then gaining the confidence to buy and fly, rather than just watch.

Wichita airplanes showed up everywhere it seemed. The *Eagle* had a regular column as early as 1921 headed "News of Those Who Use the Airplane Route in Their Day-by-Day business." Wichita, being far inland, was served only by railroads, which had the disadvantage of high rates, and autos, which were handicapped by bad roads. Airlines, air freight and airmail seemed the answer. In 1924, Moellendick and Beech covered 10,000 miles in ten days visiting air shows, winning races, and demonstrating their airplane. In 1926, the Swallow firm was shipping airplanes to Alaska, Brazil, and China.

Most needed was public confidence, something not aided by accident reports. A Wichita car salesman and his Texas pilot were killed in 1923 in a plane borrowed from William Lassen when the salesman became frightened during a flight, put his foot on the rudder guide, and froze. A Stearman salesman, Fred Hoyt, was lost in a forced landing over Utah and found frozen to death. A Wichita businessman was cut down by the prop of a taxiing airplane in front of his family.

Bert Jones of Wichita remembered carrying a gas can in a Swallow open cockpit to extend its range. When a downdraft bounced the gas can off its mount, pilot and passenger were sprayed with gasoline and watched the engine exhaust flame carefully for the rest of the trip. Such little inconveniences had to be dealt with.

One of the prominent ways of publicizing reliability was the Ford Reliability Tour, held between 1925 and 1931. Modeled after the Glidden auto tours that had begun in 1904, these long-distance demonstrations were to show people that aircraft were utilitarian vehicles and to encourage communities that wanted to get the publicity, and the crowds that resulted from being a tour stop, to establish modern airports.

Kansas planes were prominent in the air tour from the start. Travel Air dominated the first one, taking the first three places under an elaborate point

Bob Pickett Collection, Kansas Aviation Museum/Cessna Aircraft Company

WING WALKERS

⇑ This 1927 publicity photo, featuring seventeen men standing on the wing that would prove to be the flying testbed for the Cessna A-series aircraft, was a particularly persuasive way to demonstrate the strength of internally braced, or full-cantilevered, wing designs.

system related to the way an auto rally is run. A Swallow was fifth. Of seventeen planes in that first Ford tour, six were built in Wichita and a seventh by Laird, who had just left the state for Chicago.

That first tour did not go farther west than Kansas City. Later ones were more ambitious. In 1926 the tour went from Detroit through Chicago; Des Moines, Iowa; Wichita; Moline, Ill.; and Fort Wayne, Ind., before going back to its start at the Dearborn, Mich., headquarters of Ford. The winning plane was the one that carried the highest load relative to its power while moving at a good average speed. Beech won in a Travel Air 4000 at an average speed of 124.1 MPH, and Kansas planes were seventh, thirteenth and fourteenth. In 1927, "Wichita was a lunch stop, long enough to hear all about the frantic activity at Swallow and Travel Air where workmen were going round the clock to finish three ships in time for the Dole hop-off." Probably because of the focus on the Hawaii Dole race, there were few Wichita planes in the Tour in 1927. It was won by a Stinson SM-1. In 1928 the Tour went all the way to California, Oregon and Washington. That year the great attraction was an entrant with a Fairchild "cam" engine, which had the torque to swing a ten-foot propeller. The route was literally a lap of America, more than 6,000 miles. A Waco 10 won, and the field was full of Stinsons, Ryans, Bellancas, and Fairchilds but few Wichita names. Waco won first and second again in 1929 before the tour began winding down as interest lagged.

The reliability tour served its purpose for Kansas, and Wichita and Kansas City were nearly always on the route. At Wichita, the Ford Tour fliers landed at the Wichita Booster Club airfield next to the Travel Air plant on East Central. Beginning in 1929, the stop was the new municipal airport on

Henry Ford Museum and Greenfield Village Collection Photo No. 833.46791E

EDSEL FORD RELIABILITY TROPHY

⇑ Four feet high and made of gold and silver, the Edsel Ford Reliability Trophy cost Ford Motor Company more than $7,000. The publicity that a company could gain from doing well in the tour could be immeasurable. The stated purpose of the tour was "to end the dominance of the military and emphasis on thrills and stunt flying, (and) demonstrate the reliability of travel by air on a predetermined schedule regardless of intermediate ground facilities."

the California section operated by the Board of Park Commissioners. The hangar there had a big sign over the door: WICHITA THE AIR CAPITAL. No one laughed. Every flier on the tour already knew that.

Nineteen twenty-seven was an especially big year for Kansas aviation, as it was a kind of *annus mirabilis* for the whole industry.

Lindbergh, of course, was at its center. When the "Lone Eagle" made his New York-to-Paris flight late in May, it dominated the news. "Flying Fool is Alone" went the headline in the *Eagle* of May 21st. Of special local interest was the fact that in February, Lindbergh had negotiated for a Travel Air machine. Beech said at the time only that he had been offered a chance to build a monoplane for the trans-Atlantic competition and that his volume of business and backorders made it impossible. He had not mentioned the pilot's name. Like most people, he was unable to imagine what an impact that pilot and that contest would have on the public's imagination.

Lindbergh called his account of the flight *We*. He meant himself and his airplane as well as the hundreds of people involved in the design and construction of the airplane and its Wright Whirlwind engine, and all those who had advanced aviation from the time of the first tentative demonstrations fewer than twenty years earlier. The great appeal was that Lindbergh was a lone hero, an American type, but at the same time validated the achievements of the new science and technology bureaucracy. "Money Scorned by Ace," was one of the Kansas headlines in the days following. "Lindbergh Won't Tackle Pacific for Some Time," "None Like Him Since the War," "Yankee Honored by King" were some of the others. Lindbergh, who even talked about communing with spirits on his solitary night flight over the sea, was everything people wanted the demigods of the air to be. And they thought they could be that way, too, by the mere purchase of a fast metal monoplane, maybe from one of the Wichita factories.

Wichita was greatly pleased. Nearly a month after the flight, the *Eagle* was still running daily front page stories about Lindbergh. Naturally, there was enormous demand from all over the country for a visit from Lindbergh on his return to the United States, but Wichita, a town that "Slim" was most familiar with, had an edge in that department. The first hope was that Lindbergh would stop for lunch on July 10 if he were flying in the Ford Reliability Tour of that year. That was not to be, but Lindbergh came to Wichita in August. He presided over a dinner at the Lassen Hotel with 550 guests. Airplane models hung from the ceiling. He judged a boys' airplane contest, to the great joy of the winners. He was commissioned to consult on the design of the new Wichita Municipal Airport, and he had kind things to say about the city. "If Wichita continues as her past development has led

Bob Pickett Collection, Kansas Aviation Museum

THE EAGLE AND THE SWALLOW

⇐ As part of a forty-eight state tour sponsored by the Daniel Guggenheim Foundation, Charles Lindbergh visited Wichita (and posed for photographers in a Swallow) on August 18, 1927. About 75,000 people turned out to greet The Lone Eagle. Lindbergh noted: "I have long known Wichita. As does every other pilot. They know Wichita-built airplanes."

her," he told the crowd, "there is no reason why she shouldn't become the central airport of America." The thought that the good start in manufacturing would be supplemented by a central role on commercial air routes was a large stimulus indeed. Wrote a local reporter: "The town was already running bankfull with aviation and after a day with the Colonel everybody here is in favor of building dikes."

Lesser-known aviation events of 1927 involved Kansas more centrally than did Lindbergh's flight. The goal of flying non-stop to Hawaii, for example, while it involved a shorter distance that the New York to Paris feat, was a much more difficult navigational problem. An Army team in a Fokker C-2 monoplane with a 70-foot wingspan and three engines did it first late in June. Only two hours after that large plane departed from California, Ernest Smith and Charles Carter took off for Hawaii in a Travel Air. Ten minutes later they returned with the entire right part of the windshield missing.

Smith tried again in July with a replacement navigator, Emory Bronte. They were successful in making the first civilian flight to Hawaii and the first in a light, general-aviation airplane. That plane was the first Travel Air Model 5000 to come off the Wichita production line. The plane was somewhat customized. It had a Wright J-5 engine and a new advanced radio. Among the standard Travel Air features deleted for weight savings was "a cabin suction tube designed for the convenience of passengers adversely affected by air travel." Smith and Bronte made it in twenty-five hours and thirty-six minutes into a headwind, and landed between two breadfruit trees in Molokai on their last bit of fuel. It was a dramatic achievement and got well-deserved favorable publicity for pilots and airplane.

More publicity still came out of the Dole race, which took place in August, about the time of the Lindbergh visit to Wichita. Over $300,000 was

TRAVEL AIR MFG. CO. INC

Manufacturers of 'Travel-Air' Planes

WICHITA KANSAS

spent by competitors seeking $35,000 in prize money, and, for better or worse, the event included several Wichita-built airplanes. Beech was, as usual, strictly business. Arthur Goebel, who was to win the race, solicited funds nationwide to buy a Travel Air Model 5000 monoplane. But when at the last minute he came up $3,500 short, Travel Air refused to deliver. Goebel's attempt was saved only by the intervention of Frank Phillips of the Phillips Oil Company, who wanted to use the flight to advertise his aviation fuel and named the airplane *Woolaroc* after his ranch. Moellendick, at Swallow, was more taken by the romantic angle, and had his workers concentrating almost entirely, and to the detriment of the firm's other business, on the preparation of the Swallow *Dallas Spirit*, to be flown by William P. Erwin of that city with, it was first proposed, his nineteen-year-old wife as navigator.

Forty planes registered for the Dole event; fifteen put up the registration fee; and disasters and disqualification reduced the starters to eight. In addition to the two Wichita planes mentioned, there was another, the *Oklahoma*, also a Travel Air. Lloyds of London would not insure the airplanes, and gave the odds at four-to-one against any of the craft making it. The crowd of 20,000 that saw them off felt otherwise.

The results were mixed. *Woolaroc* proceeded without trouble and landed in the islands to a tumultuous reception. *Aloha*, a Breese monoplane, after some mid-Pacific delays for a navigation fix, was second. The rest was disaster. *El Encanto*, a Goddard monoplane, was wrecked on takeoff; *Oklahoma*, the second Travel Air, returned an hour after takeoff with an overheated engine. The *Pabco Pacific Flyer,* a Breese, could not get off the ground with its gas load after two tries. *Miss Doran*, a Buhl monoplane, returned to base with a plugged fuel line, then took off a second time to disappear forever over the Pacific. *The Golden Eagle*, a Lockheed Vega, took off but was also lost at sea in unknown circumstances.

Dallas Spirit was a variation on the tragic theme. It took off fine, but the crowd soon saw it returning, half its skeleton visible on the right side. A

Bob Pickett Collection, Kansas Aviation Museum/Beech Aircraft Company

window had come open and torn up the fabric. Repairs took too long to re-enter the race. Erwin was thinking of trying for the $25,000 Easterwood Prize for the first flight between Dallas and Hong Kong but instead volunteered, after ships had searched for two days for the missing *Golden Eagle* and *Miss Doran,* to try to locate them by air in *Dallas Spirit.* After a dramatic message in which he averred that he was the captain of his soul and did not fear death, Erwin and his Swallow took off and disappeared also. Particularly wrenching was that his radio worked perfectly, so listeners knew the exact speed and time of his fatal plunge from the moment he announced he was in a tail spin.

The Dole race was the final straw for Wichita's pioneer aircraft company. Moellendick was running on the ragged edge financially and personally, spending a fair amount of time in a sanitarium for treatment of alcoholism, and the gamble on the favorable publicity that might have come out of the race backfired. Actually, Swallow appears to have lost its gamble even before the disaster in the Pacific. The company applied for a receiver on August 12, before the Pacific racers took off, to defend itself from creditors' suits. The petition said the company had no working capital and could obtain no credit. Moellendick was fiercely loyal to Wichita and turned down offers

WOOLAROC

⇑ Designed by Lloyd Stearman and Clyde Cessna, the Travel Air Model 5000 (shown here with Walter Beech, left, and Dole race pilot Art Goebel) was intended to replace aging fleets of light transport planes such as the Curtiss Carrier Pigeon. The Model 5000 featured an engine and instrument-cluster module that could be removed and replaced in about 15 minutes, as well as a pilot's cupola for unobstructed viewing.

BUILDING A REPUTATION

⇒ Accredited by the U.S. Department of Commerce, the Braley Flying School was located adjacent to Wichita Municipal Airport. The school, one of the premier institutions in the country at the time, maintained its own 320-acre airport as well as an on-site factory (shown here in 1929) to build aircraft and provide aircraft-fabrication instruction. Students could live in the school's dormitories.

Bob Pickett Collection, Kansas Aviation Museum, Edgar B. Smith Collection

from several other cities to build him a factory and pay him a bonus to move. He said that he preferred Wichita above all other cities in the United States. But enthusiasm, in the face of neglected orders, was not enough.

Moellendick withdrew from the company's management. Later he said that after Erwin's ship was lost "it seemed that nothing mattered anymore." He went back to the oil fields with no success, and when Wichita's original aircraft pioneer died in 1940, he was penniless. Only contributions from businesspeople in the local industry he founded allowed him to have a private funeral rather than being buried by the county.

But the loss of the Swallow by no means signaled the beginning of a decline for Wichita. Its alumni were everywhere. A reporter for *Collier's* who visited Wichita in 1929 wrote: "Tradition is important in every craft. I'll wager you can't go into an airplane factory here or anyplace else in the country without stumbling onto a foreman who got his start in the old Swallow factory in Wichita."

Other Wichita factories were healthy. Goebel flew to Travel Air field in October 1927 in the famous *Woolaroc* to be greeted by crowds of well-wishers. The company had an order for every day of 1928, and the new factory was enormously busy. In January 1928, a Travel Air 5000 called *Peerless Princess,* after the nickname of its home city, tried unsuccessfully for the men's non-refueled endurance flight record. Stearman was turning its focus

Ken Weyand Collection

MODEL A-129

⇐ The A-129 was manufactured by American Eagle Aircraft Company of Kansas City, Kans. About 400 were built. Guiseppe Bellanca redesigned the "spin-proof" Model A-101, turning it into the A-129. First built in 1928, the A-129 accounted for the bulk of American Eagle's production. This particular plane is an early version, featuring extensive and costly machine finishing on the engine cowling and wheel covers.

Bob Pickett Collection, Kansas Aviation Museum, Edgar B. Smith Collection

JAYHAWK SESQUIPLANE

⇐ The Mars II Sesquiplane, built by Jayhawk Aircraft Company of Wichita, was touted as "Everyman's plane of the future." Produced in 1929, this aircraft featured wings that folded back to allow the airplane to be garaged, as well as full-span "flaperons." The term Sesquiplane (a biplane featuring a lower wing with substantially less span than the upper) was appropriate: The craft's upper wing had a span of thirty feet; the lower wing's span was nineteen feet, six inches. Only two were built.

Bob Pickett Collection, Kansas Aviation Museum, Edgar B. Smith Collection

STEARMAN C3MB

⇐ Powered by a nine-cylinder Wright J-5 Whirlwind engine that developed 220 HP, the Stearman Model C3MB was a star performer on airmail routes. The C3MB, developed by modifying and upgrading the company's C2B and C3B models, featured a thirty-three cubic-foot cargo hold instead of a front cockpit. Cruise speed was 112 MPH over a range of 560 miles.

to government sales with good results. Cessna was doing well with special racing planes, competing for the airline market with its model CW-6 and demonstrating the reliability and endurance of its products in every way possible. In 1929, a Cessna CPW-6 was prepared for Goebel to fly in the Los Angeles-to-Cleveland nonstop race. It was planned to use this same craft for an around-the-world flight departing from and returning to Wichita. Employing in-flight refueling, and assuming nothing went amiss with the plane's large 450 HP Pratt & Whitney Wasp engine, the idea was to cover the 20,000 miles in 300 hours of flying time.

By the end of the decade Wichita was the world leader in aviation production. It had at its peak sixteen aircraft-related factories, its own airline, thirteen flying schools, 1,600 acres of flying fields, and six aircraft engine plants. In 1929, it manufactured 1,000 airplanes, or 26 percent of the total U.S. production of commercial aircraft, and the companies expected to double that in the next year. A visitor to town noted that "the place is small enough so that the building of airplanes could interest a considerable part of its leading citizens and yet large enough to supply a sufficient number of skilled workmen. … It is logical that Wichita will continue to hold the position which it has established in the air industry."

Kansas followed Wichita's lead. For one thing, airports multiplied. Beginning in September 1927, Kansas City and Wichita were planning major airport expansions, and were landing sites for Transcontinental Air Express's addition of passenger and express service to its airmail routes. Suddenly, it was possible for a passenger traveling at night by rail and in the daytime by Ford tri-motor to commute across the country on a reasonably fast business schedule. Woody Hockaday of Wichita, who had been one of the nation's originators of published highway maps and marked highways, began to market the same service for the airways. A decent network of Kansas airports developed. Topeka, Lawrence and Coffeyville built fields in 1928 sufficient to handle the Ford airliners, and Garden City prepared its field to handle airplanes from Central Airlines of Wichita, which was proposing Wichita-to-Kansas City, Wichita-to-Denver and Wichita-to-Tulsa routes. It was proposed that Kansas should eventually have airports every thirty miles. "We have faced the task of pioneering the airplane project," a speaker at the opening of the Topeka airport said to a crowd of 4,000, "and now have to face the building program. The air route of today will be the trade route of tomorrow." Another speaker noted that the growth of civilization depended upon the way distance was conquered. "Today transportation is the medium of action in which everyone is taking part."

Air heroes often had a connection to Kansas other than the planes they flew. In June 1928, for example, Amelia Earhart, then of Boston, but born

Bob Pickett Collection, Kansas Aviation Museum, Edgar B. Smith Collection

1928 SWIFT SPORT

⥣ Built in Wichita by the Swift Aircraft Corporation, this "pathfinder" was used by the All-Kansas Air Tour to hunt for suitable landing fields (usually pastures or fairgrounds). Swift produced about a dozen Sports, including this one, which had a 125 HP Le Rhone rotary engine that had been converted to a stationary radial by Quick Air Motors of Wichita. Swift, which was started in 1927 by White Castle hamburger czar Walter Anderson, did not survive the Depression.

and reared in Atchison, Kans., became the first woman to fly the Atlantic, leading to an outsized contingent of Kansas women aviators dominating race headlines during the 1930s. The *Topeka Capital* headlined that Earhart "comes from sturdy Kansas pioneer stock." A photo of her, the press said, "shows her remarkable resemblance to Lindbergh." Ruth Haviland of Horton, Kans., who was a hostess at Fairfax Field in Kansas City and a well-known Kansas aviatrix, followed up on the Earhart spotlight by marrying a pilot the next year in the air in a seventeen-passenger plane that the couple had purchased for $25,000.

Kansas was hardly bashful about tooting its own horn. For years, the Wichita Board of Trade and Chamber of Commerce as a promotion sent something called the "Booster Train" all over the state to promote trade. It changed to automobiles in 1924, and in 1928 the event evolved into the All Kansas Air Tour. During the first week of April, a promotional party, including the governor, toured the state in a fleet of twenty-five airplanes "to spread the air gospel." Governor Ben Paulen characterized the tour as the biggest thing ever attempted in Kansas and said he knew of nothing in the United States that was its equivalent. His trip with the tour was also by far the longest ever taken by a Kansas governor by air, the previous record being held by the same governor when he flew the 130 miles from Topeka to Wichita for the Lindbergh dinner.

The tour itinerary was modest enough, but it was designed to have maximum effect and spectacle for each town visited. Marcellus Murdock, Wichita president of the National Aeronautic Association, spoke at each

CHARTING A NEW COURSE

⇒ Spreading the gospel of the Air Age, thirty aircraft carrying 100 dignitaries zipped around the state during the first All-Kansas Air Tour. It was estimated that at least 500,000 people turned out for the events and took part in the programs intended to promote new airport construction and enlist grass-roots support for the National Aeronautics Association.

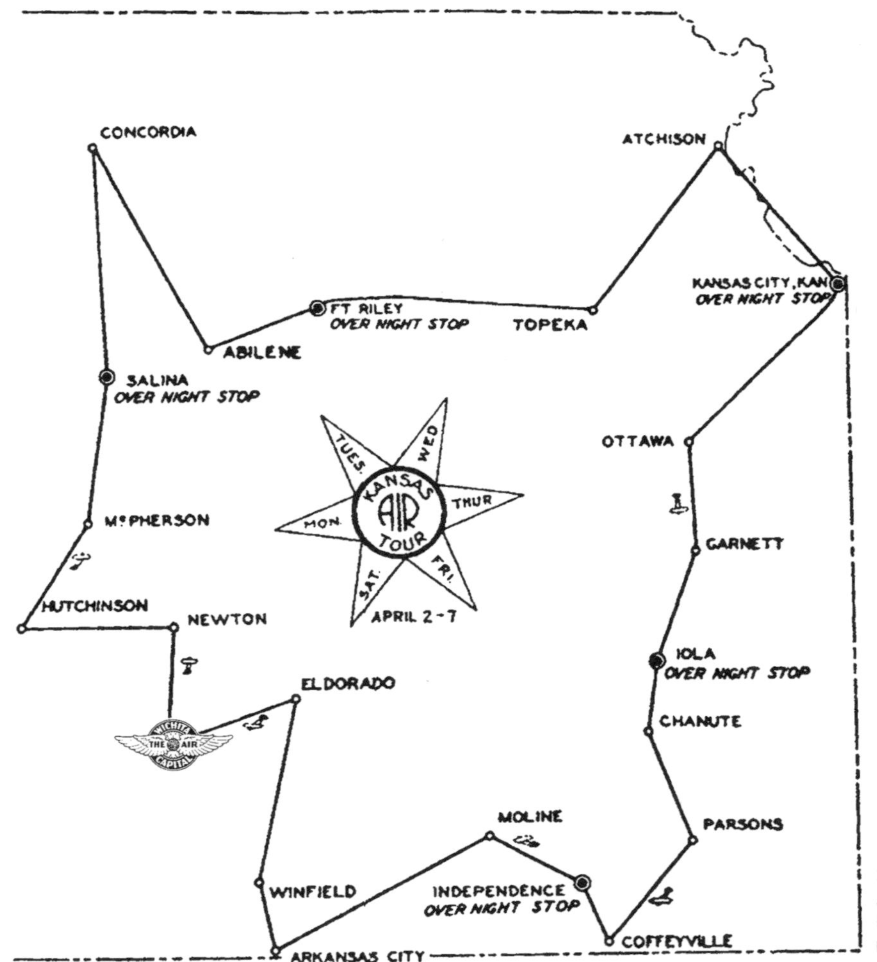

The Wichita Magazine

stop on the advantages of flying and was joined on the platform by a local man who was left with the message to promote in his area. About 35,000 people came in contact with the tour the first day. There were 8,000 at Newton to greet the planes, 7,000 at Hutchinson, and 10,000 at McPherson. Despite high winds and soggy fields, the planes landed safely with their load of political and business officials. They were delayed only once — by 60 MPH winds on the third day. "That Kansas rapidly is becoming air-minded was evidenced at every stop," a reporter noticed.

These were dramatic developments. Kansas had been through a major boom and bust cycle before in the late 1880s, but this time there seemed no end to the opportunity for regional growth through aviation manufacturing, marketing, and trade. The Wichita Air Capital logo with a Kansas sunflower sprouting wings was seen everywhere in the state as the symbol of a "New Era" economic miracle and a kind of spiritual awakening, too.

In February 1928, night airmail service was inaugurated in Wichita, adding a special feature to the airmail planes that had been coming to town via TAT since 1926. Night passenger service would soon follow, connecting Kansas with the romance of the Paris-to-Rome and Paris-to-Berlin flights then operating at night with deluxe sleeper airliners. The air was visualized as a new ocean, and Murdock is credited with coining a number of nautical terms, which stuck. He supposedly invented "airworth," and "port of call," though his word for "airsick" — "malduciel" — deservedly disappeared from the language. Like his father before him, he had a talent for capturing the excitement of a new business development in lush, romantic, "selling" prose. In a June 1928 editorial entitled "Marvels of Tomorrow," Murdock was at his best in describing a visit he made to see the new night airmail come and go:

> "A roar from the sky and a red and a green light aloft, port and starboard contributions from the ancient sea to the new air, announce the arrival of the mail plane. … Against the enveloping darkness the ground lights look, to the layman, feeble enough, and landing does not seem the careless gesture it appears to be in the daytime. The pilot brings the plane lower and over the field, swings back and reaches for the turf with caution. The pilot clambers out; those who service the machine are all over the overgrown owl in a jiffy; the mail is stowed away in the bird's stomach; the pilot, cushioned with the folded parachute, sinks into the pit; the propeller roars, the plane swings, still on the ground, in a gigantic gesture which instantly creates a highly localized but blinding dust storm, port and starboard lights are again aloft, the dust storm abates, the plane is gone and the thing is done. There is no lens through which man can fully define the future, but the night mail at Wichita Airport, better than any instrument yet invented, does give the searcher a peep into the marvels of tomorrow."

RACING AGAINST TIME

"THOSE WERE THE DAYS WHEN WE FLEW FOR SPORT, FOR THE THRILL OF BEING THE KINGPINS OF SPEED, TO WIN A MEDAL OR A TROPHY, FOR THE GREATER GLORY OF THE INDUSTRY, WHEN YOU STAKED YOUR NERVE AND YOUR LIFE AGAINST THE OTHER FELLOW FOR THE SHEER HELL OF COMPETITION." — PAUL GALLICO

The best short description of Kansas aviation in the 1930s is from Dickens: It was the best of times, and it was the worst of times.

Yes, the stock market crash in the fall of 1929 and the ensuing deep and long-lasting Depression shattered the dreams of volume sales, booming air capitals, and casual transcontinental travel that stimulated the Jazz Age. One after another, major aircraft conglomerates appointed receivers and struggled in bankruptcy. Kansas aircraft factories were invariably closed for a time, at least in the early 1930s, left in the care of lone watchmen. The projections were thrown out; buildings at airports were abandoned in mid-course; workers were laid off by the hundreds; executive perks disappeared; rhetoric came to earth with a crash.

Yet the 1930s is known among aviation industry historians as the "Golden Age," a mythical past filled with legendary virtue. The airplanes of that era, many built in Kansas, were, by all estimates, "classics"— a term reflecting a cluster of genii in engineering and design that paralleled the auditory delights of Mozart, Hayden and Beethoven. While soup lines formed and farmers were "tractored out" or dusted off their drought-stricken Kansas acres, the same state produced the Beech Model 17, popularly known as the Staggerwing, the Model 18 Twin, and the Cessna Airmaster series. While large companies failed, local Kansas entrepreneurs started their industry all over again, on a new basis, and with great success. While people made do with old cars and worn tires, they looked up from stadium seats at Cleveland or Miami or Los Angeles to watch gorgeous, powerful, and specialized air racers compete around pylon-marked courses or in cross-

HERO

⇐ In 1929, Doug Davis rocked the air-racing world by winning the Thompson Cup at the National Air Races in Cleveland in his Travel Air Model R. The plane heralded an era of phenomenal performance gains.

The Western Reserve Historical Society, Cleveland

country events for elaborate art deco trophies. It was the era of the Whirlwind and the Wasp, among the lightest and most sophisticated air-cooled, radial aircraft engines ever made. It was the "streamlined" decade for everything in the air, on the ground, or on the sea. It was the time of the first practical aircraft instrumentation and blind flying, transoceanic luxury dirigibles, gyroscopes, air-to-air refueling, and even a noisy little invention called the turbojet. Supercharged engines doubled the operational service ceiling of aircraft, improved aviation fuels allowed engine manufacturers to produce power plants of exceptional power-to-weight ratios, advanced methods of all metal construction improved airframes, controllable-pitch propellers provided efficient performance in both takeoff and cruise, improved aerodynamics upped speed and economy, and cabin design led to greatly improved comfort and security for passengers.

The unequal impact of the Depression was partly responsible. Those who had money could make it go far indeed. One could see Auburns, Cords, and Duesenbergs; streamlined aluminum trains; exotic fashions; and specialized jewelry, as well as campfires along U.S. Route 66. Partly it was mixed-circumstance. Oil was low-priced, but some of the biggest discoveries of all-time took place in the 1930s, and oil men needed fast airplanes to get to their wells and back. But partly it was fantasy. When a family spent its one night out, bought its one ticket, and went to the air races, its members did not want to see the airborne-equivalent of the Model T. It was encouraging during such hard times that somewhere there were no limits, that the stops were all out. It was wonderful to dream that some day that Staggerwing with the elegant interior and the immense engine could carry you at 200 MPH right out of the Depression and into the future.

The era started unequivocally strong. Wonder, it seemed, had followed wonder in the aviation field in the late 1920s. All of Wichita's native concerns had grown by bounds. Travel Air, for example, produced forty-six planes in 1926, 154 in 1927, 539 in 1928, and in the first six months of 1929 had delivered 307 planes valued at $2 million. It owned the 160-acre tract that had once been the Wichita Airport, employed 650 people on day and night shifts, and was headquartered in a new brick administration building. There was a boxing ring with night lighting for the entertainment of Travel Air employees. Wallace Beery, the famous movie comedian, had a special Travel Air built with a 420 HP engine, beginning a succession of visits by the rich and famous to Wichita to take delivery of airborne equivalents to their Duesenbergs. "Ten hours by plane from Los Angeles," wrote Wichita Magazine in the fall of 1929, "twenty-four hours by train-plane from New York City, a day from the Mexican border, and the same hour-mile ratio from most of the important cities of the country. Wichita is truly the crossroads of the air and the hub of the continent."

So successful were the Wichita firms that national concerns moved to purchase them. Travel Air became a part of Curtiss-Wright in August 1929, and Walter Beech moved to an executive office in St. Louis. Stearman became the second Wichita firm to go to a conglomerate when in that same month it was purchased by the United Aircraft and Transport Corporation. This giant was capitalized at $80 million, had assets of $250 million, and was backed by City Bank of New York. It included Boeing Airplane Company of Seattle, Chance Vought Corporation, Hamilton Aero Manufacturing Company, Hamilton Metalplane Company, Pratt & Whitney Aircraft Company, and Pacific Air Transport Company. Shortly, United Aircraft and Transport acquired National Air Transport, Varney Air Lines, and other air carriers to create the organization now known as United Air Lines. It even poured $1 million into an experimental factory in Burbank, Calif., run by John K. Northrop.

Of Wichita's Big Three, only Cessna remained independent. Yet, there were rumors of a merger with Swallow, and there was an offer from a Chicago firm to pay $2 million for Cessna if it could be moved to the Windy City. Cessna was included for some time in the United negotiations, and it was thought the conglomerate might take two of Wichita's aircraft factories in one swoop. Cessna did recapitalize and moved its location to the Franklin Road site associated with its great years. It thought, as did the others, that in the boom it must somehow grow or die.

The logic was compelling. Modernization seemed to dictate a transition from individual experimentation to corporate effort. Prosperous conditions made stocks and bonds easy to sell: Money flowed easily to financing schemes. "The reason we merged," said Stearman a few days after the United deal, "was because everybody else was merging. Besides, we thought we ought to give our stockholders a break."

There were clear local advantages. With the influx of capital, Stearman was able to move from the old and cramped Bridgeport Machine site and build a new $400,000 factory (now Boeing Wichita Plant No. 1) on South Oliver Street. The land surrounding this location would make a big difference when plans were being made for World War II bomber production and for the location of a huge War Department-financed factory. The immediate results were promising enough. In 1929, Stearman built and sold approximately $1 million worth of planes and made a net profit of over $65,000. From an initial investment in the company of $60,000 by Murdock; Walter Innes, Jr.; Howard Wheeler; J.O. Davidson; Henry J. Allen; and other prominent Wichitans, Stearman by the end of the decade had assets worth $450,000 and was debt-free. After the 1931 crash in the Flint Hills of Kansas of the Transcontinental and Western Air (later Trans World Airlines) Fokker airliner carrying Notre Dame football coach Knute Rockne, Stearman was able, thanks to the new money and facilities, to mount a serious effort to manufacture its twin-engined aluminum replacement. (The wreckage of the plane that had carried Rockne was stored in the Stearman hangar for a time.) The Stearman bid did not succeed, and the replacement plane became the DC (Douglas Commercial)-1, an aircraft whose successors, the DC-2 and DC-3, revolutionized air passenger travel, and whose manufacture would clearly have been a major coup for Kansas. Another distinct possibility was that parts of Northrop, which in its Alpha had one of the hottest airplanes of the 1930s, would be moved to Wichita by the United Organization. An Alpha was flown to Wichita by test pilot Eddie Allen in September 1931, and it was reported that manufacturing tools were ready to follow. The Northrop "Little Beta" airplane was moved to Wichita, and Stearman was asked to redesign and test new flaps for it.

A Northrop connection would have had immense impact. True, the top-down control in United led to the resignation of founder and chief designer Stearman in December 1930, but maybe the new age was not for the old local genius anyway.

Much else was cause for guarded optimism. In 1932, Ross Hadley made an around-the-world flight in a C-3B Stearman airplane. Meanwhile, workers making 50 cents an hour at Stearman, with maybe an occasional raise of 2.5 cents, raced their Fords and Chevrolets up and down the dirt road in front of the Stearman plant at shift changes and hoped for a better future.

There were similar changes at Travel Air. Beech no longer walked the plant floor, and designs were altered and renumbered, but for a brief moment the money poured in. In the first half of 1929, Travel Air had sales of over $2 million, and projections were for a tremendous increase with the merger. Travel Air stock, originally valued at $100 a share at its formation in 1924, was valued at the time of the merger at $4,000 a share. The governor of Kansas predicted that by 1933 Wichita alone would be producing 30,000 airplanes a year.

Actual production numbers in Wichita in 1933 were in the single digits. Cessna had closed its doors in 1931, and Travel Air in 1932. Stearman struggled along with a policy of "bidding on anything," but only the determination of Earl Schaefer, who visited United headquarters while ill to plead that the company not abandon the Wichita operation, kept the plant open. The Stearman company did develop its version of a classic, the Kaydet military trainer, and Schaefer, after a loan from the local First National Bank was called, refinanced the operation at the Fourth National Bank. Still things were tenuous. The great United conglomerate was forced in 1934 by New Deal policies to divest itself of its air transport companies and split up other parts of the company. One of the parts, Boeing, by then minus founder

William Boeing, came to own Stearman in September 1934, though the Wichita facility retained its separate name until 1941.

The new art deco terminal building at the Wichita Municipal Airport, called by some the "country club without dues," stood for some time abandoned and incomplete for lack of money on the California section. The building's elaborate entryway mural of Lindbergh's *Spirit* skirting the waves of the Atlantic appeared by that time to be a kind of cruel irony.

That a disaster of such magnitude could occur so quickly was perhaps something that Kansas, with its previous experience of boom and bust, could have imagined. But people do not expect disaster or plan for the worst. *Aviation* magazine pondered whether the aircraft market had reached a saturation point but concluded that this impression was more apparent than real. The secret to bringing aviation out of the Depression, it editorialized, was that old dream of mass production and the "privately owned or industrially owned plane." There needed to be such service that the pilot-owner never had to worry about the mechanical aspect of the airplane, and airplanes ought to be so easy to fly and so safe that insurance would be low and learning a breeze. Learning to fly ideally should be done in an afternoon, spin and stall accidents should become "literal impossibilities," vision should be better, and noise should go away. In fact those goals summarize much of what Kansas manufacturers tried to accomplish in the 1930s, and expresses basic hope in the industry that remains strong in the 1990s.

The automobile model was tempting. Why not the automobile of the air? The only trouble with these dreams is that one had to start with a bunch of closed factories and ruined enterprises. Wrote one wag in *Aero Digest*: "The witch-doctors, rain-makers, medicine men and nature-fakers are having an unusually busy season."

To simplify something complex, Kansas survived as an air center during the Depression with classy people and classic planes. When the chips were down, it was the locals who made things happen, because they had to.

Travel Air is a case in point. Beech, who had first come to Wichita as a hired pilot to fly over a Fairmount football game, returned to town in 1932 to see what he could do. Beech had thought about aircraft design since he had worked as a pilot with Pete Hill and Errett Williams in Arkansas City in 1920 and had helped design a "V" tail for the JN-4 Curtiss he flew. In 1932, he formed Beech Aircraft Company to revive the Travel Air tradition when that company, he had become convinced, was "just a toy in a giant corporation." Two years before, he had married Olive Ann Mellor, formerly his secretary at Travel Air, a woman who would eventually become company president. Given the challenge he and chief engineer Ted Wells faced, Beech deserved to have his name on the logo.

Bob Pickett. Collection, Kansas Aviation Museum/Beech Aircraft Corporation

A POWERFUL THIRST

⇑ A Beech Model A17F begins to take form on assembly lines leased from Cessna. Built between 1932 and 1934, this early Staggerwing featured either a 690 HP Wright R-1820-F11 radial engine or a 710 HP Wright R-1820-F3 radial engine. These power plants produced speeds as high as 225 MPH and gulped fuel at the rate of seventy gallons per hour.

The Kansas classic that came first from Beech was the Model 17 Staggerwing. It was an extraordinary plane by any standard but particularly surprising given the year of its first flight, 1932. The design goals were ambitious. The plane was to top 200 MPH and land at 60 MPH or less, a combination unprecedented at the time in non-racing craft. Beech had experience with racers, notably the Travel Air Model R monoplane (known to the press as the *Mystery Ship* or *Mystery S*) which set a pylon-racing lap record of nearly 230 MPH in 1929. But while there was resemblance in the new plane, the design was a clean sheet of paper.

To achieve the performance goals, Wells created a five-place biplane whose wings had a negative stagger. This stagger not only gave the airplane its popular name (the factory advertised it simply as the Beechcraft) but provided stability at all speeds, a superior viewing angle for the pilot, and safe, low-speed stall characteristics that have never been surpassed. The wing spars were steel tubing, when wood was standard for the era, the landing gear was panted, featuring partially retractable wheels, and the empennage was adjustable to give pitch trim. A thin Navy N-9 airfoil section was employed to give strength and good airflow, and the entire airplane was carefully streamlined (the extreme slant on the windshield, for instance, occasioned by the stagger of the top wing, gave it a modern look). Probably most prominent among the engineering and aesthetic features of the Staggerwing, however, was its engine, a 420 HP, nine-cylinder, 972-cubic-inch air-cooled Wright Whirlwind radial of enormous torque and presence. Without a sale in sight, Beech and Wells spared no expense to create the ultimate luxury and performance aircraft. The interior, as would become typical of Beech products, was first-class and won prizes for fit and finish at many air shows. The instrument panel, one of those seeming intangibles whose style makes such a difference to the owner who is looking at it, was a masterpiece of 1930s high-tech. It had gauges galore, carefully lettered porcelain buttons, lines of switches, beautifully cast and forged levers, pull-handles, and Lear-O-Scope electronics.

The Model 17 Staggerwing was a tail dragger, and it was cloth and dope-covered just like every other 1930s airplane. But its menacing look, even on the ground, set it immediately apart from anything else, and gives it still "enormous magnetic appeal." It was, says type historian Joseph Juptner, "the most outstanding example of aerodynamic novelty in this period. Fairly reeking with sophistication and daring, it is testimony indeed that Walter Beech and his associates had the fortitude to bypass convention and look far into the future." Staggerwing owners still fly their airplanes back to the factory on East Central in Wichita once every five years, and the gathering on the apron is, even now, a sight to behold. There is no question at all among aviation enthusiasts that it represents the ultimate biplane, with certain performance characteristics that have yet to be surpassed.

Spectacular as the product was, however, the initial effort at Beech Aircraft was tenuous as a business. After all, in 1932, when the Staggerwing was first flown, crude oil was 25 cents a barrel, wheat was 25 cents a bushel,

PACEMAKER

⇓ Walter Beech stands beside the first Staggerwing model to see serious production, the Model B17L. Produced from 1934 to 1936, the B17 series offered four different engines. (The B17L used a Jacobs L-4 radial engine of 225 HP, yielding a maximum speed of 175 MPH.) Retractable landing gear helped clean up aerodynamics. Forty-eight were produced at a price of $8,000.

The Wichita Eagle/Beech Aircraft Company

and General Motors stock was offered at $8 a share with no buyers. The Travel Air factory was not for sale, and had it been, Beech could not have afforded it. So he built the first Staggerwings with the help of a total work force of eight and the backing of some local businessmen at the Cessna plant on Pawnee Street (then Franklin Road), which had been closed a year earlier. Beech leased the Travel Air plant in 1934, and put his name on the building, before purchasing it for $150,000 in 1937. The first Model 17 sale was in July 1933 to the Loffland Brothers Oil Company of Tulsa, Okla. Another went to the Ethyl Corporation, painted in its corporate colors, the next year. But two sales over two years of corporate existence was not exactly the volume dream.

There were problems. The big engines of the A series (one had over 700 HP) overheated and used too much gas for anyone not in the fuel business. There were some airworthiness difficulties also, particularly with the vertical stabilizer. Then there was the matter that the plane cost $18,000 and there was a depression on. Nineteen Beechcrafts were built in 1934, but most were of the B17 series powered by a 225 HP engine and with other modifications addressed to the real market. Still, it was a remarkable plane in hard times and helped give Beech a $1 million sales year in 1938. In that year, the company sold fifty-nine Staggerwings to private owners, down a little from seventy-two the year before. The impossible dream had become a decent business.

The company wasted no time glorying in it. "Just a Freak," began a Beech ad in 1934. "That's what they said three years ago, when Walter Beech announced plans for a luxurious cabin airplane that would travel 200 MPH, and could be landed at ordinary airports. 'Some day, perhaps; not in our generation.' *But the first Beechcraft exceeded that speed.* … The early critics of the Beechcraft are now busy trying to imitate its many SUPERIOR FEATURES! The Beechcraft is out in front. … *and will stay there*!" Around a cut of the Staggerwing were stories of other "foolhardy" enterprises, from Fulton's steamboat to the Wrights and Lindbergh. The point was that old-fashioned entrepreneurship was alive and well in Kansas.

With its first classic hardly out of the hangar, Beech Aircraft created a second. The Model 18, while not as audacious as the Staggerwing, was an all-metal, split-tail, twin-engine monoplane that could hold six people in comfort and haul loads over long range for charter and feeder airlines. The core of the Model 18 was lightweight aluminum alloy. All exposed structures were carefully streamlined, and the wheels retracted into self-fairing nacelle and fuselage housings during flight. The design for the Model 18 was started in 1935, and the first flight, using two Wright 320 HP engines, was in January 1937.

Top speed was over 200 MPH, with a cruise of 192 MPH and a range of

The Wichita Eagle/Beech Aircraft Company

BEECH MODEL 18

⇐ This highly successful, light transport featured all-metal semi-monocoque construction and twin 320 HP Wright R-760-E2 radial engines. Similar in layout and design to the vaunted Lockheed Model 12, the Ted Wells-designed Beechcraft would span thirty-three years of production, during which time more than 7,104 were produced.

more than 1,000 miles with pilot, copilot and six passengers. Like the Model 17, the Model 18 had a low landing speed, less than 60 MPH. As a demonstration of efficiency and safety, one of the first Model 18s was flown fully loaded on a round trip from Philadelphia to New York on only one engine at cruising power, one prop totally stopped by a brake and the other in high pitch.

Model 18s, called by one magazine "Gray Flannel Fliers" or "Boardroom Bombers," operated on floats and skis in remote northern areas just as well as they provided visibility, panache, and the ultimate personal transport for Hollywood studios and their stars. As Richard Collins has put it, no one flew a Gee Bee racer to an important executive meeting. The Beech 18s and the Lockheed 12s of the 1930s could get those executives to meetings just as quickly, just as comfortably, and more flexibly than the airlines of the time. "The top-of-the-line, new business transport," wrote Collins, "was … the tireless Beech 18, carrying the boss through the weather at a reliable … 175 knots." During more than thirty-three years of production, in war and peace, and through many modifications (both by the factory and by outsiders "who rushed in like a Kansas cold front") the Model 18 was the workhorse, which along with the Model 17 racehorse, established Beechcraft as a household word among followers of aviation throughout the world.

One of the small group of engineers working for Wells on the Staggerwing modifications was Dwane Wallace, a recent aeronautical engineering graduate of the University of Wichita, and the nephew of Clyde Cessna. It probably grated on Wallace that Beech was making an airplane in Cessna's plant, and Cessna was not. And it was not long before Wallace and his brother, Dwight, did something about it. When Beech moved to the Travel Air plant in 1934, the Wallace brothers, through support from the holders of a majority of the stock, restarted the Cessna company in the firm's 1920s factory. Clyde Cessna and his son, Eldon, had been making racing planes, such as the CR-3 and custom jobs, like the C-3 monoplane, in a plant

DWANE WALLACE

that had belonged to the Mooney company during the palmy days of the 1920s. Eldon worked with Dwane Wallace on the first of the new projects before leaving for California. But, by and large, it was a new generation at Cessna. Wallace, the general manager, was 21 at the time of the takeover of Cessna and must have been one of the younger owner-managers of an aircraft plant in the nation. His salary was $100 a month to start, and he would remain at the company's helm for more than forty years, during which time the company manufactured over 170,000 airplanes, more than any other concern anywhere, ever.

Like Beech, the Cessna company against all odds created two 1930s classics, one a single and one a twin. And, like Beech, by cutting expenses to the bone (a visiting journalist once saw Wallace nearly alone in the plant personally painting the numbers on a plane for delivery), and through unity, spirit, and hard work, Cessna healed itself financially and established a sound position from which to grow after the Depression. Dwight Wallace watched the legal and accounting pitfalls, while Dwane did nearly everything else an executive staff was supposed to do and more. He was the test pilot, the race pilot, the traveling salesman, the personnel administrator, and the public relations department. It was said in the early days of the Depression that when Dwane returned from a race on a train rather than the airplane he left in, it was a cause for joy. It meant he had sold his race plane (which was only a slightly modified standard model), and the payroll could be met for the next few weeks.

At first it all depended on one plane, called simply the C-34 (Cessna, 1934 model). Like the A and B17 series Beechcrafts, it eventually got a popular and advertising moniker, and the models evolving from that 1934 Cessna are now reverently spoken of as Airmasters. Although related to the 1920s Cessna AW, the Airmaster was a significant advance. It had an economical engine, a 145 HP Warner Super Scarab radial, which, at 550 cubic inches was not physically small but had modest power and torque. Wallace's goal was not to make the C-34 outrace fighter planes or appeal in luxury fittings to movie stars, but rather to create an enormously efficient craft that would be usable for businesspeople who wanted no-nonsense flying capability every day for years running.

It was a high-wing monoplane, a design that gave fine visibility. The wing was a continuous cantilever structure, with not a strut in sight. The same was true of the empennage. It used the latest National Advisory Committee for Aeronautics airfoil for the wing and the latest cowling. Only the lack of retractable landing gear (Wallace did not like the pants that were first installed on the landing gear because they picked up dirt and diminished the utility, simplicity and beauty of the craft) kept the Airmaster from being as carefully aerodynamic as any craft in the sky. It cruised at 143 MPH, topped

The Wichita Eagle/Cessna Aircraft Company

out at 162 MPH, had a range of 550 miles on regular tanks, had a service ceiling of 18,900 feet. and returned fuel economy of five gallons per hour (a big-engined production Staggerwing typically burned nineteen gallons). It weighed a minuscule 1,220 pounds empty (one-third as much as a Model 17) and cost $4,985.

The prototype, NX12599, was painted solid blue, and was, when it rolled out in August 1934, a sight to behold. It had the rightness and inevitability typical of all good designs. It seemed to carry its thirty-three foot wings up forward, hunched on its shoulders, before narrowing dramatically in a long, graceful fuselage sweep, to flare again into broad surfaces at the tail. Stretched fabric over wood and bright-colored dope made possible an airy hand-crafted resonance in the airframe akin to the style of an early Italian harpsichord. There was a tension in the contrasts. From the rear, the C-34 looked like a model of a gull designed and built in a Renaissance workshop. From the front, the feeling was different. Looking at the blunt radial head on, or listening to the commotion and seeing blue smoke when the power plant caught, it more resembled a raging iron locomotive constructed in a sooty section of some industrial city — Beauty and the Beast. All the great 1930s machinery designs — the W124 Mercedes, the Auto Union streamliners, Donald Campbell's record-setting Bluebird boats – wore their mechanical origins on the surface, yet all achieved the status of technological art in a way that seems to have eluded later engineers. The C-34 Airmaster, like the Model 17 Staggerwing, looked right and was right for the time and for all time. That defines *classic*.

As the nation's economy improved during the late 1930s, Cessna built its classic twin. It was designated the T-50. Its popular name was the Bobcat. Presented to the board as a design in 1938, it first flew in the spring of 1939. The T-50 was a steel-tube fuselage faired with spruce and covered with fabric. It had a retractable landing gear, hydraulic brakes, and, by pro-

CESSNA C-34

⇑ The Cessna C-34 would eventually develop into one of several models to carry the Airmaster name. This four-place, high-winged cabin monoplane featured a seven-cylinder, 145 HP Warner radial engine that delivered a maximum speed of 162 MPH and offered a 550-mile range. The Airmaster series would win the title of World's Most Efficient Airplane in 1936. Forty-two C-34s were built. The price was $4,985.

REARWIN CLOUDSTER

⇒ This roomy, three-place monoplane had excellent cross-country capabilities and was employed successfully as an instrument trainer by Pan American Airways. The Model 8090 was powered by a Ken-Royce 90 HP radial engine, and the Model 8135 used a Ken-Royce 120 HP radial engine. The Cloudster, introduced in 1938, was built at Fairfax Airport in Kansas City, Kans. About 124 were built.

Bob Pickett Collection, Kansas Aviation Museum

KAYDET

⇒ This classic biplane evolved from the Stearman C series. The Kaydet (Boeing Model 75) was produced in quantities that far outstripped any other biplane in the western world. Considered to be an antique even when it was first produced, the Kaydet's robust airframe was perfect for absorbing the rigors of pilot training.

Boeing Aircraft Company

duction time, two 225 HP, seven-cylinder Jacobs engines. It was no Model 18 in luxury, but it had a similar range (1,000 miles), and was designed to be an alternative to the Lockheed 12 and Beechcraft 18 at a smaller size and price. The T-50 cost $30,000. Model 18s sold for more than $63,000. Both the Model 18 and the T-50 were to serve as wartime trainers — the Model 18 variants as AT-7s, AT-10s, AT-11s. Most Bobcats were known as AT-17s.

Stearman's claim to a classic was unquestionably the Boeing Model 75 Kaydet. The prototype, the Model 70 (based on Stearman's Model 6) was first built late in 1933. It flew in World War II as the PT-13, PT-17, PT-18, PT-27 and N2S for the Army and Navy. More than 60,000 air cadets learned to fly in it before production ceased in 1945. After the war more than 4,000 Kaydets, available then for a few hundred dollars, were turned into crop-dusters and air show aerobatic machines, and they seemed to last and last. In 1975 an estimated 2,000 of the 8,584 Kaydet variants built were still flying.

The Kaydet wasn't as dramatic an achievement as the Beech and

Cessna offerings. It was a biplane with an unshrouded engine, an open, tandem cockpit, with all the struts and wires typical of a 1920s design. It was heavily reinforced, particularly in the undercarriage, to bear the landings of novice pilots, and was somewhat a slug. It cruised at barely over 100 MPH, and could operate no higher than 12,000 feet, using the full 220 HP of its Lycoming R-680 engine sucking fuel to get there. But it was the first Wichita airplane to achieve substantial sales to the military, an important market, and it established Boeing's Wichita division as a military specialist, while transoceanic, passenger-carrying Clippers were being built and tested on the waters near company headquarters in Seattle. This established momentum for Wichita, which was to be important through the B-29, B-47, and B-52 production years of World War II, Korea, and the Cold War. So it must be said that, for a unique combination of reasons, the stubby, tough, little Kaydet is a 1930s Kansas classic in its own right.

These made up the prairie front range, the blockbusters, but there were others — a sort of outpouring of regional creativity in response to national crisis. One particular category coming out of Kansas was designed to fill the obvious niche of absolute bare-bones flying machines. The Rearwin models, built at Fairfax in Kansas City, fit. That company had a bare-minimum monoplane called the Rearwin Jr., powered by a 30 HP engine and in production until 1932. Later the Sportster and Speedster models went slightly upscale with a 70 HP radial. These airplanes sold for around $2,000 and $3,000, respectively. But they had plenty of competition just in Kansas City. The Porterfield, originally a shop project of the Aviation Club of Wyandotte High School in Kansas City, Kans., was tested on the Kansas

BARE BONES

⇓ A new type of aircraft emerged during the Depression: the ultralight. Initially selling for $995, this 500-pound American Eagle Eaglet was typical of the breed. The one-place Model A-130, which was built in 1930, was equipped with a 25 HP Cleone two-cycle engine. Kansas production of the Eaglet culminated in the Model B-31, which employed a 45 HP Szekely engine and had seating for two people. As many as ninety Eaglets were produced in Kansas City, Kans., by the American Eagle-Lincoln Aircraft Company. Shown is a Model A-230.

Frank Woods/Scott Daymon Collection

Bob Pickett Collection, Kansas Aviation Museum/Cessna Aircraft Company

A PRODUCT FOR HARD TIMES

⇑ Designed by Eldon Cessna, Clyde's son, the CG-2 glider was one of the crafts designed to help get the company through the Depression. About eighty-four CG-2s were built between December 1929 and September 1931. Shown is a CG-2 being launched by two teams of men using shock cords to boost the glider into the air.

side, and the American Eaglet was built there.

The Eaglet qualified as an ultralight — really a powered monoplane glider. Introduced in 1930, it was a single-seater that could carry one passenger under "favorable conditions." It had a two-cylinder, two-cycle 25 HP engine and weighed less than 500 pounds empty. The plane was described as "as simple as it could be, within the acceptable limits of the prevailing state of the art." It sold for $995 and was "strictly a fair-weather bird."

Because these airplanes were neither very useful nor very safe, low price alone did not attract many buyers. However, there was one more step that the person who wanted desperately to fly — but could not afford to — could take. Cessna was one of several manufacturers who offered a primary glider. Cessna's was called the CG-2 and sold in the early 1930s for $400. One could buy a kit from several manufacturers for $100 to $200. Even then the planes were often too expensive for individuals, and Cessna had an offer that anyone who organized a club that raised $300 could get a discount on a glider picked up at the factory.

During the 1930s, primary gliders were never as popular in the United States as in Europe. In Europe they were used for straight downhill glides, but in this country people tried to fly them like airplanes, with poor results and bad publicity for gliding.

Every flight was an adventure. The pilot sat in front of the craft and had nothing between himself and the horizon for optical reference to determine if he were straight and level. Launch was usually by shock cord, often snapping the glider into the air with a rush after a pull by a car. They were "aerodynamic nightmares," often held together by one-sixteenth-inch wires and usually piloted by complete novices. Such a craft at an altitude of 400 feet (to which it could be catapulted) was a frightening prospect. Yet while these gliders virtually disappeared from the market by 1940, they were the first flying experiences for many and the only one for a few.

The ultralights and the gliders have been regarded in hindsight as dead ends. However, the experimentation that went on with the ultimate, simple flying machine in response to the 1930s economic crisis became useful again in the 1990s, with regular aircraft again priced out of the means of most. The ultralight movement of the 1990s, benefiting from composites and lightweight engines, might look back to the Rearwin, the Porterfield, the American Eaglet, the Braley Skysport, the Cook primary glider, the Roydon, and the Cessna CG-2 as their visionary progenitors. So it may be too early to declare that these tiny Kansas planes are to be barred from the classic category.

The Depression era clearly was a time of breakthroughs for aviation. While the "family car of the air" never quite became reality, unprecedented safety, reliability and acceptance became characteristics of industry products. The Pratt & Whitney Wasp Jr. radial that went into some Staggerwings, for instance, would run 1,500 hours between major overhauls — durability that made the thirty-five hour continuous run of Lindbergh's Whirlwind, a miracle only a few years earlier, seem insignificant. And, according to most sources, the bottom of the economic slide was reached in 1933, after which there was a slow improvement in the private, airline, and military markets. In 1936, 700 people were employed in the aircraft industry in Wichita, and the payroll of $750,000 was the highest "since the boom days." Beech went from ten employees in 1933 to 250 in 1938, before the war boom had much

PRIDE OF THE PLAINS

⇓ Located on 640 acres of prime Kansas grassland, the $250,000 Wichita Municipal Airport was, at one time, one of the five busiest air terminals in the country. Begun in 1929 and dedicated March 31, 1935, the Glenn Thomas-designed Administration Building incorporated art deco motifs. The last commercial flight took off from Wichita Municipal in 1954. The building is on the National Register of Historic Places and serves as the home of the Kansas Aviation Museum.

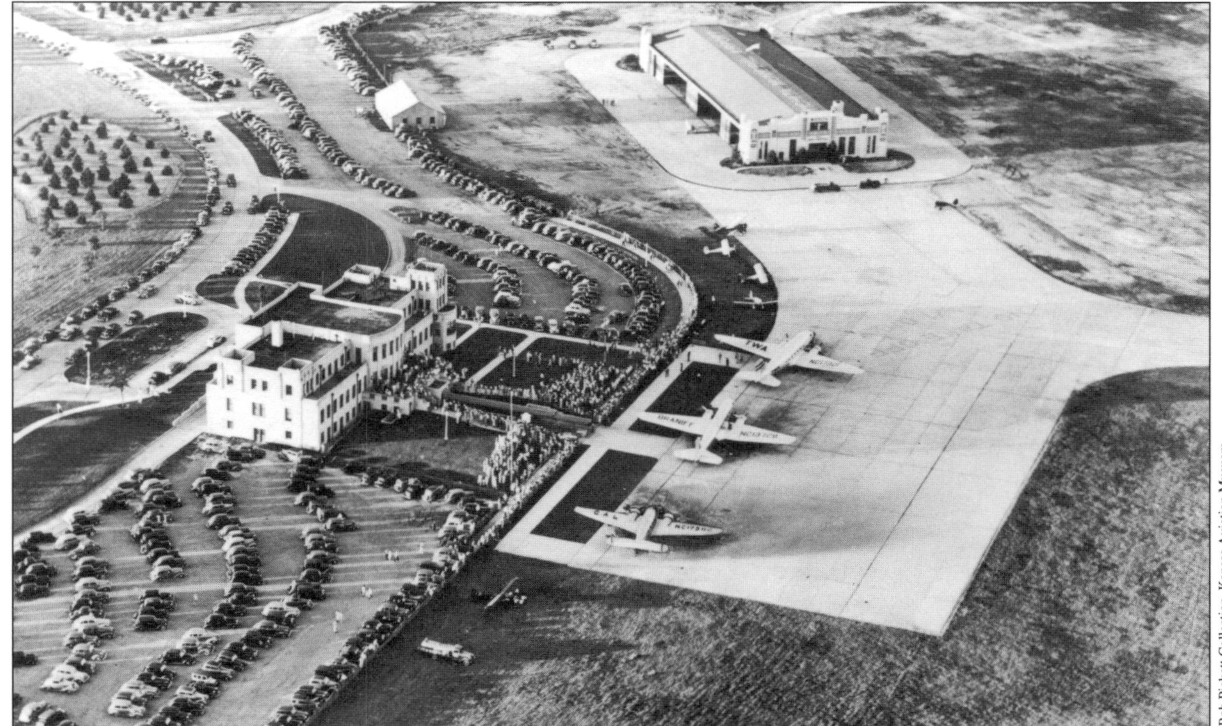

Bob Pickett Collection, Kansas Aviation Musuem

Wyandotte County Historical Society

CROWN JEWEL

⇑ A classic example of 1930s design, loosely patterned after the better train stations of the day, the terminal building at Fairfax Airport in Kansas City, Kans., featured an orchestra balcony, where musicians would play to help soothe the nerves of air travelers. The building was razed in 1987 to make way for an expansion of a General Motors plant.

of an effect.

Indicative, perhaps, of the era's optimism, were Kansas airports. The impressive Wichita Municipal Airport became a gem. Set in the California section's unbroken prairie sod, which made landings for tail-draggers easy, the airport had been established six miles southeast of the center of town in 1928. The Wichita Board of Park Commissioners had the foundation for a hangar laid and the runways marked and fenced by June 1929. However, completion of the striking administration building was delayed by the Depression (airport revenues declined from $236,000 in 1930 to $81,000 in 1931) and not accomplished until 1935. The paving of the runways was a Works Progress Administration (WPA) New Deal project, something that Republican Kansas got little of. Richard Robbins, president of Transcontinental & Western Air, which by 1934 was landing its new DC-2 airliners at Wichita as a stop on the transcontinental route, wrote the Wichita City Commission in 1933 complaining that Kansas' aviation facilities were not what they used to be: "You might be interested to know that many of the thousands of passengers who pass through your Airport have read or heard of your slogan 'Wichita, the Air Capital of the World.' When these passengers find an improvised and unattractive waiting room in the corner of a hangar they are somewhat puzzled in trying to determine the basis of this claim. This is especially true as these travelers know of the accommodations furnished by other cities throughout the country which make no particular claims to their foresight."

Kansas City likewise was a major air crossroads and struggled to remain competitive in services. Fairfax Airport on the Kansas side of the state line and Municipal Airport on the Missouri side both handled heavy Midlands air traffic. "Clear back to the days of ox trains," a reporter wrote, "Kansas City always has held a strong geographical advantage over all the other points of the Middle-West in transportation and modes of travel."

However, it was noted that safety, more than location, determined the air hubs, and Kansas City had to prevail in competition for facilities. The Woods Brothers Corporation of Kansas City owned land suitable for an airport and invested the capital necessary to make Fairfax a premier facility. In 1933 it was fully lighted and had three runways, the longest being 7,000 feet. There were spotlights to allow night landings, and its communication equipment included telephone, telegraph, and radio service. There were five passenger and express transport lines landing there with twenty-four planes arriving and departing daily, as well as eight airmail arrivals. As with Wichita, not only was every service available, but a board of architects and a landscape group ensured that the airport, with its significant surrounding land, was a place of beauty and pride and a pleasant gateway to the municipal area. It helped, too, that Fairfax had a major natural gas discovery on its property, which in 1930 was producing 22 million cubic feet a day from fourteen wells. The only blot on the facility's sterling reputation was the grisly crash of a Central Airlines plane there that year, which killed five, rocked the industry, threatened Walter Beech's and Travel Air's attempt to enter the airline business by backing Central, and led to the beginnings of federal regulation of airlines.

Wichita's airport was also much beautified by the Park Board through plantings all along the diagonal that led to it from downtown and throughout the curving drives on the grounds. No 1930s traveler, with luxurious train

FAIRFAX AIRPORT

⇓ This 1930 photo shows, in numerical order, **1.** two Curtiss-Wright Aircraft Company sales hangars, **2.** the Universal Aviation Corporation (later used by Rearwin Airplanes), **3.** the Porterfield Flying School, **4.** the American Eagle Aircraft Company, **5.** a general-purpose hangar, **6.** a double hangar used by the Eddie Fisher Flying School, **7.** the Fairfax Terminal Building, **8.** the Inland Aviation Company and Rearwin Airplane Company building, and **9.** Mercury Aircraft Corporation (later used as a part of the Rearwin Airplane works). **10.** Located just below the Kansas City skyline on the Missouri side of the river is the site of New Richard's Field, which became Kansas City Municipal Airport before evolving into Kansas City Downtown Airport.

Wyandotte County Historical Society

Wyandotte County Historical Society

ALL-PURPOSE

⇑ At the ground-breaking ceremonies for the Curtiss hangars at Fairfax Airport, a biplane was used to pull a plow — a stunt that no doubt reassured tractor manufacturers everywhere.

service as an option, would put up with the cattle car shuffling that has come to be regularly endured at airport hubs. Ironically, no matter how much Wichita emphasized its central location in the country, its aviation background, and its square-mile prairie landing field, it was increasingly bypassed in air routes and did not become a major manufacturer of airline machinery. The great advantage of the California section in Wichita for the early Transcontinental Air Transport rail-air trips, for which it was a fuel stop, was that the Fokker and Ford trimotors had limited cross-wind landing capabilities, and so the large, undifferentiated sod field gave maximum flexibility. One of the first Ford trimotors on TAT's transcontinental route in 1929 was named *City of Wichita*. But TAT made Kansas City Municipal, not Wichita Municipal, its hub and service headquarters for the area, and Wichita became a fuel stop, on the order of Waynoka, Okla., Clovis, N. Mex., or Winslow, Ariz. In 1930, TAT merged with Western Air Express, creating Transcontinental and Western Air. That same year, the rail-air combination, which allowed passengers to sleep in a Pullman at night rather than risking unmarked skyways, was abandoned, as were many of the stops. On October 25, 1930, a TWA plane made its first all-air transcontinental flight in 36 hours. The overnight stop was Kansas City.

Transcontinental travel was, of course, not the only reason for Kansas airports. There were regional feeder lines tried between Kansas City and Wichita that included a feeder run by Southwest Airways between Tulsa and Salina, Kans., with a stop at Wichita, and a Central Air Lines route between Wichita and Tulsa. These were never very successful, because an automobile trip took only a little more time and cost less on short routes. More important to airport development was government largesse. In the late 1930s, the WPA and Public Works Administration (PWA) had airport improvement as one of their primary relief employment objectives. Also, the government wanted to build an air transportation system equivalent to the highway system, with fixed base operators at nearly every village and an electronic beacon/radio network linking the whole. Two hundred WPA workers got started in 1937 on a $287,000 airport project in Topeka. The PWA spent over $200,000 in 1938 on a new passenger terminal at Kansas City Municipal Airport.

Certainly the Kansas airports of the 1930s, large and small, were places of recreation and excitement. They had a social prominence that was in some ways as unexpected as had been the interest during the 19th century in taking walks in cemeteries — those places being the best landscaped and pleasantest retreats in the developing industrial cities. The Kansas airport was a place outside the municipality by some distance — a nice summer drive away. Cool breezes swept the runways and roads, and it was free

CROSSROADS OF THE NATION

⇓ As reported in an obviously biased article in the August 1929 issue of Wichita Magazine, all airways led to Kansas. The publication touted Kansas, and Wichita in particular, as being destined for a position in air transportation. "Ten hours by plane from Los Angeles, twenty hours by plane-train from New York, a day from the Mexican border, and the same hour-mile ratio from most of the important cities of the country."

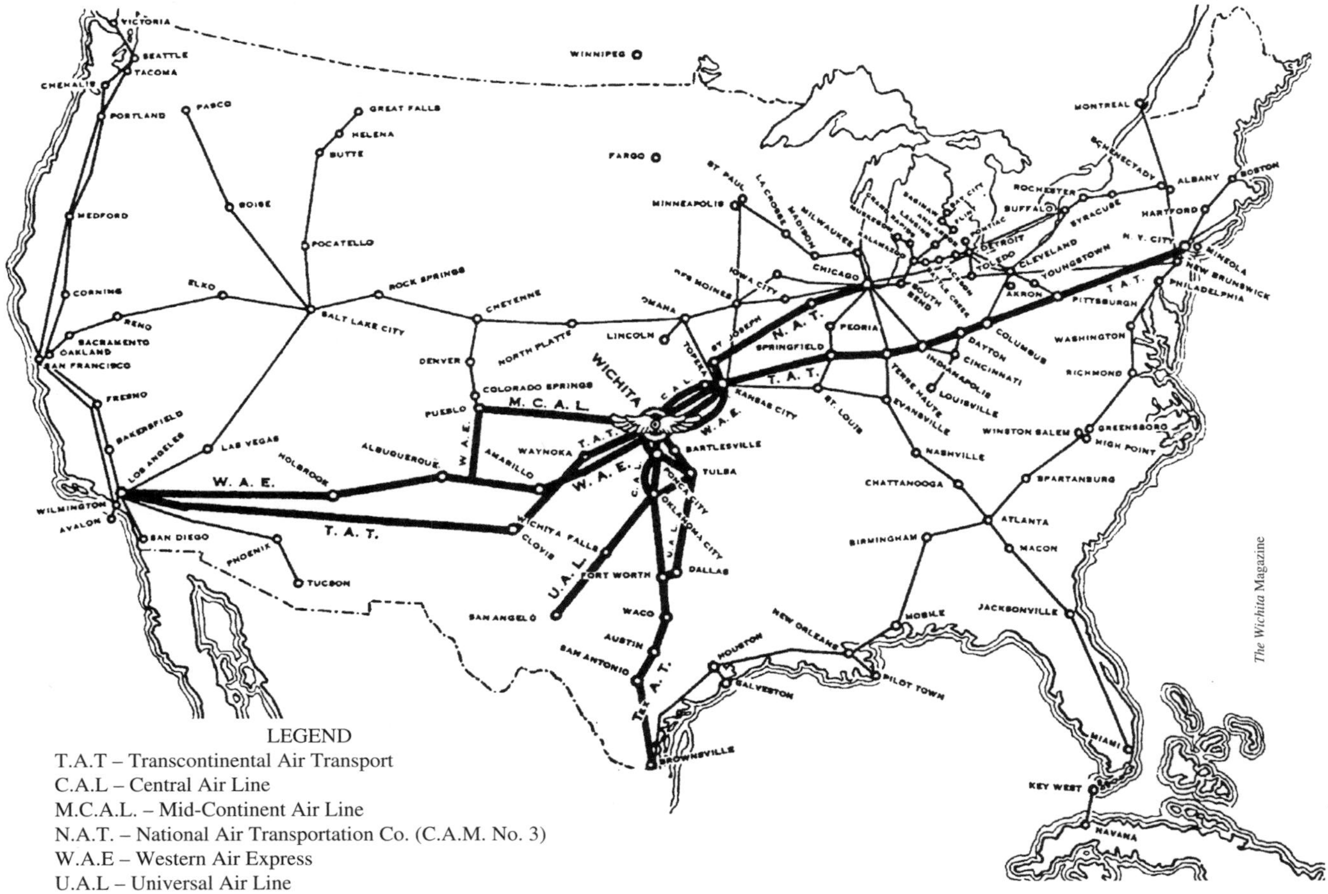

The Wichita Magazine

The Western Reserve Historical Society, Cleveland

AERONAUTICAL RODEO

⇑ Rotated among the cities of Cleveland, Chicago, and Los Angeles, the National Air Races originally played to packed houses over a run of more than ten days during the last week in August and the first week in September.

entertainment to watch the airliners land and perhaps catch a glimpse of some famous personality alighting for a few minutes at the terminal building on the way to one of the coasts. The original transcontinental one-way fare for rail-air service on TAT could be over $400, depending on train accommodations, and the air service itself was 16 cents a mile, about double the rate of first-class fares right after World War II. TAT lost money. However, the fare ensured that not just anybody was aboard those airplanes.

Wichita's airport had a huge spotlight to guide airliners in at night. The atmosphere there was described by a WPA writer: "In the nocturnal hours the airport becomes an abode of romance superseding the public parks. The local contingent of the legion of youth motors to the spot in droves. A swain and his lady-bird are nonchalantly parked in a Chevvie coupe beside a swain and his lady-bird parked in a V-8. They loiter, they linger amid the fragrance of a rose-bower, their serenade to be broken presently by the roar of a pair of twin-motors as a giant air-liner swoops down and pulls up within the glare of floodlights to empty its human cargo. The intent crowd in the gallery lining the enclosure murmur with a ripple of excitement as a fluttering figure steps out to promenade — a Hollywood star bound either east or west, with a satellite in her train. ... She treads upon native prairie terrain where gophers were burrowing only a few years before, and an occasional harmless bull snake crawled to keep rodents from being too utterly prolific. Suave and glamorous under the flame of lights, she flickers like that butterfly that she is on the silver-sheet, re-enters the cabin, and flies away to light again either at Kansas City or Albuquerque, depending upon which way the winds of fortune blow her."

The airliners themselves, one article said, were so solid that one should not have the slightest worry sitting in the aluminum and wicker passenger seat. Metal implied sturdiness, and one had only to look at "the metal propellers, the bulging tires of the landing gear," the Pratt & Whitney Wasp engines, the array of instruments in the pilots' compartment (tachometers, altimeter, temperature gauges, shut-off cocks), to know there was nothing that could go wrong. Things did go wrong of course. In the crash near Bazaar, Kans., that killed Rockne, there were no instruments that could deal adequately with a Kansas thunderstorm. Pieces of those wicker and aluminum chairs were spread all over the pasture along with the bodies of the passengers. Still, the psychological, technological, and economic appeal of the "time collapsing commercial bird" was tremendous. TWA spanned the continent west and east, New York to Los Angeles, noted a reporter in 1937. Braniff Airways connected the Great Lakes with the Gulf of Mexico, Chicago to Brownsville, Texas. At Los Angeles, TWA passengers could board Pan American Airways' Clippers for Hawaii, the Philippines, and the Far East. At New York, they could go by Pan Am and Imperial Airways to Bermuda and on to Europe. From Brownsville they could board airplanes for Central and South America. And the place where all these lines crossed was somewhere in Kansas. The thought was wonderful. "Years of familiarity have not dulled its power to excite thoughts of romance and strange beauty."

These thoughts were probably excited most, however, by air racing. Air racing in an unlimited, awesome style — never possible before or since — was a central feature of aviation consciousness in the 1930s and a key element both in marketing new commercial ships and in developing the experimental, envelope-pushing craft that would be the basis for the Allied fighters of the Second World War. The pylon races for the Thompson Trophy at the National Air Races of the 1930s were a far cry from the previous decade's air circuses.

Yes, aircraft now have higher performance, but, except perhaps for a once-a-year momentary pass at the Experimental Aircraft Association meet at Oshkosh, Wis., or a dip of the Blue Angels over a local football stadium, we do not expect to see state-of-the-art fighters and bombers over residential areas at treetop level, and certainly not competing in earnest with others of their type at the outside range of their performance capabilities. But in the 1930s, that was precisely what people expected to see, and did see, when the unlimited "specials" raced around pylons over Cleveland or cross-country at speeds and g-forces well beyond the best current fighter planes, sharing the spotlight and the public enthusiasm with the Beechcrafts, Cessnas, and Inland Sports (planes built in Kansas City, Kans.) from Kansas. Heroes with the kind

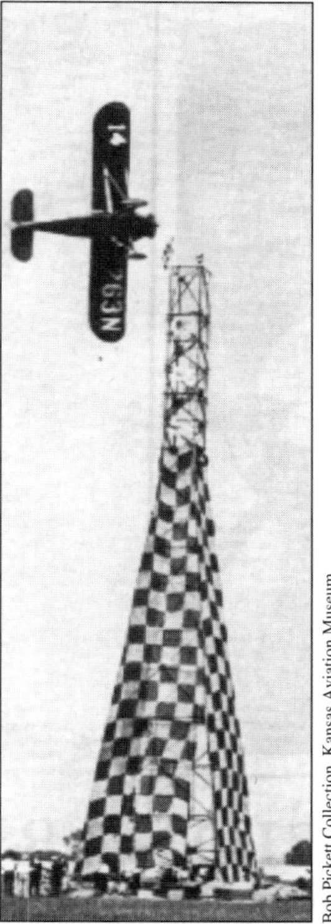

Bob Pickett Collection, Kansas Aviation Museum

PYLON POLISHERS

⇑ Sprints by planes (such as this Inland Sport) around closed courses marked by thirty- to fifty-foot-high pylons were spectacular sights. The pylons used in early events were manned by a crew of three. One judge stood in the center of the pylon and looked directly up through a series of sight-rings to determine if a racer had committed an infraction by cutting a corner too close. A second official was positioned outboard of the pylon to check for position infractions, and a third man was located on top of the pylon to wave a violations flag, forcing a pilot to return and re-circle the pylon.

INLAND SPORT MODEL S-300

⇒ Based on a 1927 design by Dewey Bonebrake, the Inland Sport was put into production by Arthur Hargrave in 1929. The Sport was a parasol-winged monoplane featuring side-by-side seating for two, which eliminated the traditional problem of shifting centers of gravity that accompanied tandem seating. In spite of a neat overall design and good performance, sales of Inland Sports suffered because their introduction coincided with the start of the Depression.

National Air and Space Museum, Smithsonian Institution (SI Neg. No. A-542)

of public relations and endorsement pull of modern-day professional sports stars were created overnight when they carried home one of the extravagant art-deco silver trophies associated with the major air racing events.

In 1913, the speed record for aircraft was 126.59 MPH, set in pursuit of the Gordon Bennett Aviation Cup. The Pulitzer Trophy, which from 1920 to 1925 was given in conjunction with the National Air Races upped that speed record to 248.975 MPH. The Pulitzer was replaced at the National Air Races between 1930 and 1939 by the Thompson Trophy, given by Charles E. Thompson, an industrialist from Cleveland, where the races were generally held. Thompson Trophy racers regularly exceeded a 250 MPH average over Cleveland suburbs on a wrenching fifteen-mile closed course around pylons. Then there were the Bendix Cup, a transcontinental race held from 1931 to 1939, and the Schneider Trophy, the premier race in the world for seaplanes, and maybe for any planes. The Schneider races, held from 1919 to 1931 and sponsored by French businessman Jacques Schneider, involved government sponsorship, enormous costs, and dazzling speed. Manufacturers built special models just for the Schneider, creating such marvels as the British Supermarine (the predecessor of the wartime Spitfire fighter) and the Italian Macchi-Castoldi MC.72. The latter, completed in 1931 for the seaplane races, was powered by a Fiat A.S. 6, a twenty-four cylinder, liquid-cooled engine developing 2,800 HP. A year before, a Staggerwing had set the commercial world buzzing with a top speed of more than 200 MPH. The Macchi-Castoldi on the seaborne race circuit was capable of straight-line speeds of 440.681 MPH, though it was obviously not suited for pylon turns. The U.S. government withdrew from funding or sponsorship of the Schneider races in 1926 and the Pulitzer races in 1929, (the year the private entry Travel Air Model R trounced government fighters), on the grounds that in poor economic times the costs were obscene. Some felt that attitude was short-range thinking, but, in general, private sponsors took up the slack, and the development, along with the entertainment, continued.

These were the showcase races, but there were many other venues and types of contests and shows. Some, like the Ford Reliability Tours, emphasized efficiency. Others focused on short-field performance or construction quality. The All-American Air Maneuvers, held in Miami, divided racers by engine displacement, as did events like the *Detroit News* awards for the most efficient aircraft. Therefore, such events would draw everything from tiny Taylorcrafts to unlimited racers with more than 1,000 HP.

The 1936 Miami maneuvers provide one example of how much press Kansas got at such events. That year a Cessna C-34, piloted by Dwane Wallace, won the silver Argentine trophy, valued at $2,000, and a $350 cash prize in the 550-cubic-inch displacement pylon race. He averaged more than 156 MPH on the five laps (a milestone of one mile an hour per horsepower) around a very tight five-mile pylon course. Wallace also won the Detroit News Trophy, given for the best score on a series of tests including cruising fuel economy, barrier takeoff and landing, private-owner features, and cost

BUILDING A LEGEND

⇓ Dwane Wallace receives the Argentine Trophy awarded at the 1936 Miami All-American Air Races. His Cessna C-34 outdistanced all competitors over a five-mile course, and he won $350 for finishing first.

Bob Pickett Collection, Kansas Aviation Museum/Cessna Aircraft Company

Bob Pickett Collection, Kansas Aviation Museum/Cessna Aircraft Company

BETTY BROWNING

⇑ This Kansas Citian captured the 1936 Amelia Earhart Trophy at the Los Angeles National Air Races, piloting her Cessna C-34 over a twenty-five mile course to win $675.

efficiency. That victory allowed the Airmaster series to be advertised as "The World's Most Efficient Airplane." Betty Browning of Kansas City, who had just won the Amelia Earhart trophy in the women's class at the National Air Races in Los Angeles, used the same airplane to fly exhibitions at Miami. She was to have been joined by Wichitan Louise Thaden, who had become famous by winning the Bendix Trophy that year against all comers, male and female, in a production Staggerwing. But Thaden was grounded by weather on the flight southeast and missed her event. Kansas Citian Bill Ong in a C-17B Staggerwing won the 850-cubic-inch displacement class. A Staggerwing from Dallas came in second. The maneuvers ended with a race to Cuba, where the fliers were entertained. A Miami newspaper editor was in wonder at the whole thing: "It is a mighty age. … It is full of the romance of achievement and the disabilities of defeat. But at no time have there been deeds to stir humanity more than at present."

These air races were an entire phenomenon, complete with dances, clowns, and elaborate artistic trophies. The trophy that Wallace won in Miami was given by A.H. Silva, a sportsman from Argentina then residing in the United States. The trophy for the 200-cubic-inch displacement class at Miami was made of silver and crystal by Cartier of New York and financed by the government of the Dominican Republic. The Gordon Bennett trophy depicted a woman holding a biplane overhead; the Earhart trophy was similar. The Bendix trophy was an art-deco extravaganza, featuring a demigod and an airplane conquering the globe, while the Thompson was an immense stylized winged man with mountains, sea, and sun above and below. The sculptor on that one was told by the sponsor: "Now I don't want a nude woman waving a flag. Every trophy you see these days is of a nude woman sitting up there with her ass in the wind. I don't want any of that." He did, however, want to be part of the aura that surrounded the races. While they lasted, the races and the exploits of Wallace, Browning, Thaden, Roscoe Turner with his trademark lion cub, Steven Wittman, Jimmie and Mae Haizlip, Harold Neumann, Jimmy Doolittle, Tony LeVier, Benny Howard, and a host of others showed a lot of people that not everything about the Depression was depressing.

Truman C. Weaver Collection

THE VICTOR

⇐ Harold Neumann, receives the Greve Trophy from L.W. Greve after winning Event Number Three at the National Air Races in Cleveland on September 1, 1935. Neumann pocketed $4,000 for piloting Benny Howard's 489-cubic-inch Menasco-powered aircraft to victory, averaging 207.292 MPH.

It was the airplanes, however, particularly the custom-built models that appeared at these races, that attracted the most attention at the time and were the most significant as time passed. Kansas, of course, was well represented by production models, and it was also well-represented among the specials.

Matty Laird, who had left Wichita in a huff but was much associated with Kansas in his early career, built numerous successful racing planes in the 1930s. Probably the most famous was the Laird LC-DW-500 Super Solution biplane, which was built in 1931, had 535 HP and a top speed of 265 MPH. With it Doolittle won the Bendix Trophy and broke the transcontinental speed record in 1931. Several of the modifications on the airplane were made at the Swallow plant, with which Laird maintained a close connection, and at the Christopher Brothers company, also in Wichita. Also of

The Western Reserve Historical Society, Cleveland

OUTFITTED FOR SPEED

⇒ Pilots like Captain Frank Hawks, shown with a Travel Air R, dressed carefully to ward off the effects of flying open-cockpit planes at high altitudes and speeds of over 200 MPH. Some early aviators used whale grease and various gadgets to stem the debilitating effects of the cold.

Bob Pickett Collection, Kansas Aviation Museum/Cessna Aircraft Company

MYSTERY SHIP

⇑ Designed by Herb Rawdon and Walter Burnham, the Travel Air Model R crushed a field of eleven competitors at the 1929 National Air Races in Cleveland. Powered by a 420 HP Wright J6-9 radial engine, the Mystery Ship's top speed was 235 MPH. Although not the world's fastest aircraft in 1929 (the Supermarine Model S-6 held that distinction), its effect on the industry was revolutionary.

note was the LC-DW-300 Solution, which in 1930 became the only biplane to win the Thompson trophy. Later Turner won the Thompson Trophy in the Laird-Turner L-RT Meteor, built in 1937. That craft had over 1,000 HP and a top speed exceeding 300 MPH.

The Travel Air Model R Mystery Ship came directly from Kansas, and had great racing success in the late 1920s and early 1930s. It was a sensation when a privately entered Model R (generally called by the press the Mystery S), piloted by Doug Davis, beat all the fighter planes at the free-for all event at the 1929 Cleveland National Air Races. He posted a speed of 194.9 MPH, the highest achieved by a commercial plane to that time, and Beech intended to sell it as a sportster to the public. During his court-martial, General Billy Mitchell asked pointedly why a lightplane company in Wichita "could build an airplane for peanuts that could so utterly destroy the best fighters the military had to offer."

And it had great appeal. "Breathes there a modeler," commented one fan magazine, "who has never built a Mystery Ship … or at least copied its red and black paint scheme on another design?" Another Mystery Ship, in the hands of a customer, Texaco, established more than 200 speed records in the United States and Europe with corporate pilot Frank Hawks at the controls. He broke transcontinental U.S. records both ways, established many intercity records and then, in 1931, took the plane (dubbed *Texaco 13*) on a 20,000-mile European tour to show it was hardly a one-sprint specialized racer. The Model R, with 420 HP, could exceed 235 MPH and operated reliably in day-to-day use. Its configuration became the basis for innumerable

LOUISE THADEN

⇒ One of the premier aviatrixes of the 1930s, Thaden gained national prominence by winning the 1929 Santa Monica-to-Cleveland Women's Derby, piloting a Travel Air Model D4000 Speed Wing.

The Western Reserve Historical Society, Cleveland

successful 1930s racers, notably the Gee Bee sports planes and racers, the Wedell-Williams racers, the Boeing P-26, and the Ryan ST. Not bad for something designed by Herb Rawdon and Walter Burnham at their homes in Wichita and built in a screened-off section of the Travel Air plant.

Staggerwing victories have been alluded to. The Bendix victory in 1936 was achieved by Thaden at an average speed of only 165 MPH, going west to east against strong head winds and into violent weather, and after the near-fatal crash of race leader Benny Howard in the Southwestern desert. Olive Ann Beech was eager to see success by a woman in air racing, and Vincent Bendix had offered a $2,500 prize for the first woman to finish the race. However, it was not expected that women would finish first and second in airplanes not specially designed for racing (second-place Laura Ingalls flew a Lockheed Orion). The blue Sherwin-Williams Model 17 that Thaden flew was an object of great pride in Kansas. Bill Ong was successful with the Staggerwing not only at Miami, but in the Mile-High Air races at Denver in 1936. In 1937, Jacqueline Cochrane took third-place in the Bendix race in a Model 17, and the same plane came in fourth the next two years.

Cessna did well in various racing venues with the C-34 and its successors. Clyde Cessna also built custom racing planes in the early 1930s independent of the company. These were built on the racing tradition established with the "A" racer in 1927 and with the CPW-6, which was designed in 1929 as a two-place endurance racer. He and his son, Eldon, built a supercharged plane called the GC-1 in 1930 to contest the 5,541-mile Cirrus All-American Derby, with prize money of $25,000. It was sponsored in the race by a group of Oklahoma businessmen, and was named *Miss Blackwell.* Engine trouble in the event meant it won only one leg of the race, but it did place fourth at the Chicago National Air Races that year in the 1,000 cubic-inch event (good, considering its displacement was only 310 cubic inches but supercharged). The Cessnas built another plane for the National Air races that year, the GC-2 Racer. It was sponsored by Walter Anderson, the owner of the White Castle hamburger chain, which originated in Wichita. Ong and Mae Haizlip flew it. She finished second in the women's free-for-all event and Ong placed second in the 450- and 650-cubic-inch events and third in the 800-cubic-inch category. In 1932, Roy Liggett of Omaha, Nebr., entered the National Air Races in Cleveland in a design designated CR-2 and called *Miss Wanda*. By 1933 the same plane won the Col. Green Cup race in Miami. For the 1933 American Air Races, Art Davis flew the CR-2 and Johnny Livingston a new design, the CR-3.

The CR-3 was the fastest and most famous racer built by Cessna, and in many ways the most amazing. It had a 145 HP Warner engine much like the one in the Airmaster. In it, Livingston set a world speed record for aircraft with engines of less than 500 cubic inches displacement: 237.4 MPH aver-

The Western Reserve Historical Society

BLANCHE NOYES

⇑ Co-pilot and navigator aboard the Beech Staggerwing that won the 1936 Bendix Trophy, Noyes (with Louise Thaden) bested a field made up of four women's teams and three men's teams. Taking off from Bennett Field in New York, the two landed in Los Angeles fourteen hours and fifty-four minutes later. Wichita was their only fuel stop.

MISS WANDA

⇓ Eldon Cessna and Garland Peed designed this bright red, fully cantilevered mid-wing racer. Named after Cessna's sister, the CR-2 was a modified CR-1 that originally featured a 422-cubic-inch, 125 HP Warner radial engine. That power plant was later replaced with a 145 HP Warner. The retractable landing gear and full NACA-cowled engine provided superior streamlining.

Truman C. Weaver Collection

Truman C. Weaver Collection

SLIM

⇑ In sharp contrast to the massive, radial-engined racers of the day were the slim-waisted, bullet-like racers that sported smaller displacement in-line engines. Built on the premise that a smaller, lighter aircraft would be able to cut through the air more easily, the planes were competitive with much larger and more powerful opponents. Examples of such lightweights were Benny Howard's DGA-4 Mike and DGA-5 Ike. Powered by 485-cubic-inch Menasco Buccaneer engines, these bantam racers won many races at speeds of more than 200 MPH.

age around pylons, with a fast lap of 242.35. In a straight line, Livingston reached 255 MPH and thought he could make 300 MPH with a few aerodynamic changes. Before that could be done, however, the CR-3's string of 1933 victories ended at Columbus, Ohio, when the gear failed to go down, Livingston bailed out over country fields, and the racer dove straight into the ground at a speed estimated at 400 MPH. That same year, the *Miss Wanda* crashed when a piece of the cowling flew off at 175 MPH, hit the wing and broke it off near the root. Liggett was killed in that crash, which his good friend Clyde Cessna witnessed. These events, and their deeply disturbing effect on Cessna put an end to his design of racing planes and his active involvement in aviation.

Kansas had a role as well in providing the airplanes of Ben O. Howard, one of the best-known and successful of the 1930s racers. Designed by Howard himself, his planes were mostly constructed and tested at Fairfax Airport. Howard used rented space at the old American Eagle plant. Joe Jacobson, Neumann, and Ong, Howard's most successful pilots, were Kansas Citians. Howard himself was a pilot for Robertson Air Lines out of St. Louis, flying a mail plane on a route with a stop in Kansas City, where he became acquainted with the Fairfax facilities.

Howard's first design of note was DGA-3 (Damned Good Airplane-3), called *Pete*. DGA-2 had been used by a bootlegger in the mid-1920s, but the speed of the basic design suggested an air racer. *Pete* was a departure from the unlimited air racers. It had a 90 HP Wright Gypsy engine of 326 cubic inches and was extremely tight (uncomfortable) and light. It was only one-quarter the size of some of its competitors but took five firsts and two thirds at the 1930 National Air Races, including a win in the 1,000-cubic-inch event and third in the Thompson Trophy race. In 1933 he appeared with *Mike* and *Ike* (DGA-4 and DGA-5), two nearly identical planes that were slightly larger than *Pete*, but like that plane low-winged, wire-braced monoplanes with minimal frontal area and light weight. *Mike* took four firsts, two seconds, two thirds, and one fourth at the National Air Races in 1933. So dominant was Howard in 1935 that the National Air Races that year were called by the press the Benny Howard National Air Races. His new plane — DGA-6, *Mr. Mulligan* — a cabin monoplane with an 830 HP Pratt & Whitney Wasp engine and a top speed of 292 MPH — won the Thompson, Bendix and Greve trophies that year, while *Mike* dominated the 550-cubic-inch class. Howard's crash in the 1936 Bendix race was perhaps the only thing that could have ended his experimentation.

For a time air racing had a direct effect on commercial and military applications. Howard's DGA-8 commercial ship, which was built in Chicago and patterned on *Mr. Mulligan,* is an example. The Cessna and Beech racers often were very nearly the same planes that anyone could buy. Heroes of the air races — Haizlip, Wedell, Turner, Earhart — were frequent visitors to the Wichita airport, and the results of air races, particularly when there was even a remote Kansas connection, were front-page news in the regional press. The Schneider race planes virtually became the high-performance fighters of World War II, and great innovative race planes, like the Caudron C460, which showed up from France in 1934 with a speed of more than 300 MPH using a six-cylinder engine in a light airframe, were epiphanies to the industry. However, the racers increasingly became specialized. The famous Gee Bee series of Super Sportsters won several Thompson trophies but were extremely dangerous and very nearly unflyable under ordinary conditions.

The Western Reserve Historical Collection, Cleveland

THE HAIZLIPS

⇑ The husband-and-wife team of Jim and Mary was one of the most successful duos of the 1930s. They flew some of the era's most sophisticated planes, including Wedell-Williams and Gee Bee racers. Mary's successes included a first-place finish in an Inland Sport in the women's 500-cubic-inch race during the 1930 National Air Races. She also won races while flying Travel Air biplanes.

Don C. Wigton Collection, NASM Acquisition No. Q-969-22, National Air and Space Museum, Smithsonian Institution (SI Neg. No. 75-2940)

KING OF THE HILL

⇐ The only aircraft to win both the Bendix and Thompson trophies in the same year, Benny Howard's DGA-6 Mr. Mulligan, ruled air racing in 1935. It overwhelmed the field in the Bendix Race, even though pilots Benny Howard and Gordon Israel forgot to retract the flaps during one leg of the race. Its 1,344-cubic-inch Pratt and Whitney Wasp Senior radial engine was modified to achieve 830 HP.

MOVERS

⇒ Designer Benny Howard, right, and pilot Harold Neumann often combined their talents to drub racing competitors. "The Lord wanted me to be a pilot, and I just kept charging," said Neumann, who eventually logged nearly 30,000 hours in the air.

The Western Reserve Historical Society, Cleveland

Then there was the dark side — the grisly crashes and the disappearances as advances were pushed too far and too fast. Earhart disappeared somewhere over the Pacific in 1937 in the midst of enormous publicity and in the wake of a return to her hometown of Atchison for a "noisy tribute." Her spirit had been infectious, and the nation wanted to believe that she was fully in control. "I always weigh the results before I start on any flight," she said. "If they are worthwhile I try my best to accomplish them. If they're not, I don't even try to worry through it. ... Hamlet would not have made a good aviator." But the "female Lindbergh" proved all too mortal, and her airplane all too insignificant at the far reaches of irrational nature. Although she became a legend, there were few potential aircraft users or passengers who wanted to join her.

Racing, too, had its tragic underside. The Gee Bee killed a brace of pilots, and the Thompson Trophy came to an end as the traditional finale of the National Air Races when Odom crashed his highly modified P-51 Mustang into a house during the 1949 event. A housewife whose body had to be dug up in pieces from under the tiles of the bathroom where she was standing when the engine hit her did not exactly fit the boyhood dreams of Roscoe Turner's Flying Circus.

Kansas more than survived the 1930s as an air center, but it missed some opportunities. The greatest ferment in these United States today," said a speaker at the banquet forming the Kansas State Aviation Association in 1938. "Never was there a time so propitious for the development of aviation. At no time has aviation moved backward. It continuously moves forward." Prophetically Murdock said at that meeting: "Until this country wakes up to the importance of airplanes in national defense it is as helpless as the pioneer who didn't learn how to use the flintlock." However, there was a great deal of "calling of the roll" of Kansas aviation greats and too little of the old-fashioned promotional ability.

Nevertheless, Kansas was positioned perfectly at the outbreak of World War II to become a major center for the production and testing of military aircraft. Through a near miracle of business acumen and self-promotion, it had maintained its 1920s dominance through hard times, had adjusted to the "streamlined" 1930s, and was prepared to watch closely for the right chance as its prime industry again underwent the rapid change that was its legacy. After a generation of bootstrap success, Kansas finally was to receive an enormous boost from conditions completely external to the cycles of the prairie.

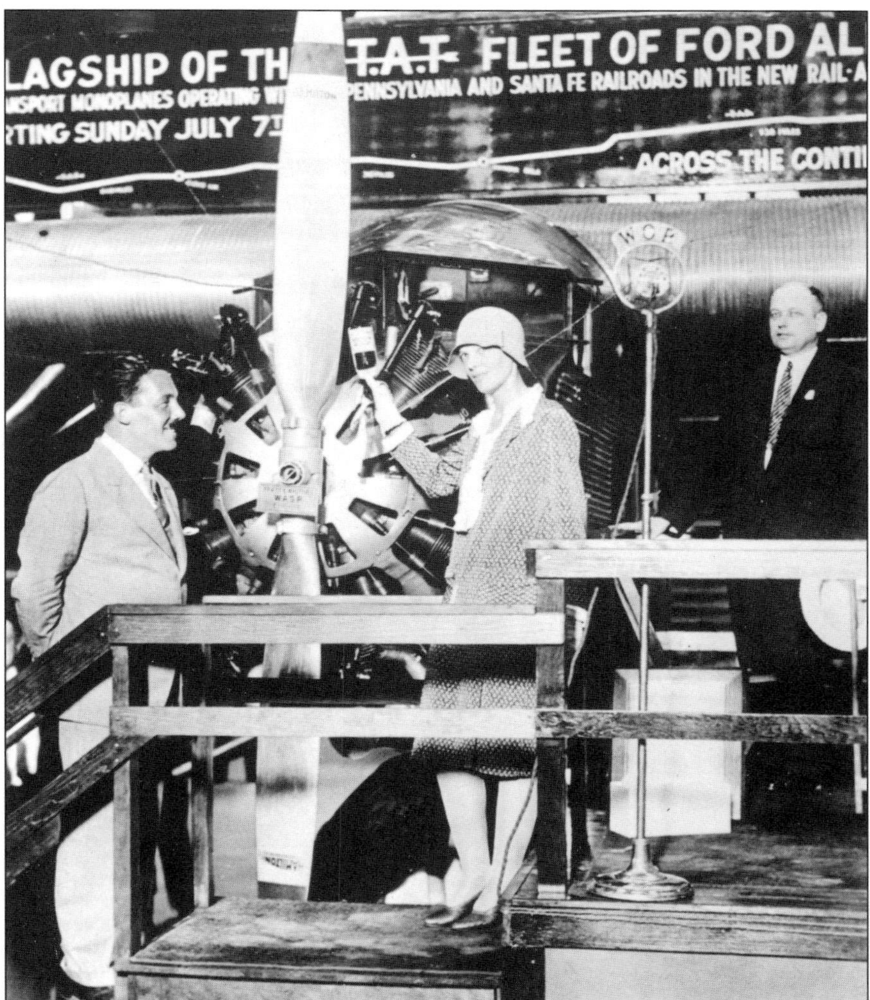

Ken Weyand Collection

AMELIA

⇐ Amelia Earhart's fame often came close to rivaling Lindbergh's. She was flooded with requests to endorse a wide variety of products. On July 7, 1929, she was photographed with Grover Whelan in New York City at the inauguration ceremonies of the TAT 48 Hour Air/Rail Coast-to-Coast service. This transcontinental route operated until October 1930, when newly formed TWA started cross-country air service. Urged on by her husband, George Putnam, Earhart maintained an extremely aggressive schedule of appearances like this one in order to ensure a lasting high profile to the public.

THE BATTLE OF KANSAS

"YOU WOULDN'T KNOW YOUR POOR OLD BLEEDING KANSAS OF DAYS AGONE. SHE HAS SPROUTED WINGS."
— EARL SCHAEFER

The Luftwaffe and Wehrmacht Blitzkrieg overwhelmed Poland in 1939 and brought the Western Alliances into the Second World War. More surprising yet was the fall of France in 1940, and the dominant role of speed, on the ground and especially in the air, which crushed in a matter of weeks what was thought to be one of the world's most powerful military forces. The French Maginot defense lines were useless against German aircraft and lightly armored but fast and expertly deployed Panzers. Stuka dive bombers rained ruin from the air, while the Messerschmitt 109 German fighters, with their twelve-cylinder Daimler-Benz engines and 350 MPH speed, were equaled in the air only by a relatively small corps of Hurricanes and Spitfires in soon-to-be-besieged Britain.

Lindbergh had visited Germany in the late 1930s to examine its air forces. He looked over the Messerschmitts, the Focke Wulfs, the Junkers, and the Heinkels, and doubtless heard rumors of rocketry and jet propulsion. His conclusion was that the United States should avoid war with Germany at nearly any cost. Lindbergh's activity with the America First group of isolationists cost him much of his popularity during the war hysteria of the early 1940s, but in the context of the times, and not accounting for the remarkable progress and focus of the U.S. aircraft industry during the next few years, his position appeared defensible. Using available historical data, a rational planner might well have concluded that fielding an air force to defeat the Germans was not very likely. Still less of a chance existed to face on equal terms the aircraft made by Mitsubishi, Kawasaki, Kawanishi, and Nakajima that became factors after December 1941. And air power was only a piece of the threat to the United States and the Western way of life.

ARMED AND READY
⇐ The business end of a twin .50-caliber Bendix dorsal turret gun platform of the type installed on B-25 Mitchell bombers built in Kansas City, Kans.

National Air and Space Museum, Smithsonian Institution (SI Neg. No. A 542)

Mistakes May Mask Sabotage

The war has taken a new turn, a second front has been established. This means trouble for Hitler and possibly trouble for Beechcraft. ... Greater becomes the need for the axis to sabotage American industry, and attempts are being made and will increase in number and effort.

There is always someone willing to play a Benedict Arnold. ... Report all suspicions to your Plant Protection Department. Do not aid in covering the mistakes of others – mistakes in aviation mean death to many.

Remember the German government is using American-born and naturalized subjects to carry on this work. Each will be thoroughly Americanized and provided with phony identifications.

A good plan is to watch everyone – the saboteur will eventually slip and expose himself, so be on your guard ... protect your country, your fellow workmen and your job.

The Beech Log, Beech Aircraft Corporation

A WORD TO THE WISE

⥣ Appearing in a 1942 edition of the Beech employee news magazine, this warning about the potential for sabotage was taken seriously. Armed guards roamed the plant day and night, and a canine corps helped keep the ground secure. Few cases of actual sabotage were documented, but two employees at the North American plant at Fairfax Airport were reportedly removed from the plant after reports surfaced of chewing gum being placed in B-25 fuel tanks.

"In retrospect," wrote a student of air power in these times, "Germany's defeat in World War II seems incredible."

Crisis, however, strengthens those it does not destroy. In 1939, $300 million was appropriated for the expansion of the U.S. Army Air Corps. Naturally when thinking of air-defense production centers, Kansas came to mind. It was in the center of the country, isolated from the East Coast, where German U-boats prowled within easy view of U.S. cities, and from the West Coast, which experienced blackouts, Japanese balloon attacks, and internment camps by 1942. Kansas had a relatively homogeneous population, with an especially low percentage of Asians, and its rural-based work ethic, as well as the adaptability of the regional labor force to aircraft production, had been demonstrated through two decades.

In 1940, Wichita aircraft leaders were briefed in Washington just before President Franklin Roosevelt made his public call for the rapid manufacture of 50,000 aircraft to buttress U.S. readiness. They were shocked at the magnitude of the call. Earl Schaefer of Boeing Wichita tried to explain to leaders on Capitol Hill that there was more to building an airplane than they could imagine. It was not enough to send cash and a purchase order for fighting planes and to expect him to construct "a giant cookie cutter and stamp the units out." The best compromise he could get from Washington, however, was to reduce the 50,000-a-year goal to 18,000 by April 1, 1942, and to maintain an 18,000 plane-a-year capacity thereafter — still a very tall order. In the entire history of powered flight, the United States had designed and manufactured fewer than 45,000 airplanes. Yet between 1938 and 1940, world governments placed orders for 45,000 planes from U.S. factories to be delivered within two years.

Production was not the whole of it either. When the Luftwaffe flew into Poland, it relied on twenty years of training and planning for that specific mission and was backed by a capacity for producing aircraft and combat crews unequaled anywhere in the world. It had 1,000 bombers and 1,050 fighters available for the strike on Poland at a time when the United States had 489 fighters and 728 bombers. Only twenty-two of the latter were B-17s, the latest model. Most planes contained in that count were obsolete or not in operational condition. Hap Arnold and Ira Eaker, two Army generals, explained in the 1941 book *Winged Warfare* why Germany was a favorite to win. Appropriately and typically, Arnold was then put in charge of U.S. production to make sure his scenario did not come to pass.

By September 1940, Wichita aircraft plants had $20 million in orders — four times the business they had a year earlier. Employment in the aircraft plants jumped to 13,000 that year and would be 60,000 before war's end, nearly doubling Sedgwick County's population within five years. By the end of 1940, Wichita's aircraft plants had an order backlog equal to the total value of the city's manufacturing in 1937. Boeing Wichita was working multiple shifts with a payroll of $150,000 a month and a backlog of $11 million in government orders. Beech had added 70,000 square feet of space and had plans to expand by 183,000 square feet. Cessna had increased its space by 60 percent. Production began to be estimated by pounds of airframe rather than units. "And the factory executives lean forward to whisper — 'it's only the beginning,'" wrote a wire-service reporter.

It was a huge effort. Skilled workmen (soon to be "workers" as women became over 50 percent of the labor force) were scarce, as was materiel. Trained pilots were hard to find. In 1939, there were only seventeen Army air bases and four depots in the continental United States, graduating fewer than 300 pilots a year. The objective was increased to 1,200 fliers a year before the end of 1939, to 7,000 a year in June 1940, to 12,000 a year in July 1940, and to 30,000 a year in February 1941 — 100 times the rate of two years earlier. By the time the War Training Service ended in mid-1944, it had trained 430,000 student pilots at 1,132 schools. Airfields were constructed across Kansas and the country simultaneously with the craft that were to fill them. Employment burgeoned. It was estimated that in the summer of 1941 Kansas had 25,000 aircraft workers, though it had never previously had more than 3,500. Arnold reported: "It was not unusual to find a training field with dozens of planes flying above it, bulldozers on the ground finishing earth work, cement mixers turning out concrete for runways yet to be built, and men in the open still clearing brush from what had been grazing land."

All sorts of new mass-production techniques were pioneered in Wichita to cut the normal lead time on new models. Similarly, construction companies set records in building new plants, financing and constructing housing for a flood of workers, and moving rapidly from design to testing in various degrees of secrecy. As George Trombold, Boeing Wichita's personnel director at the time, put it: "Just adjusting to this required a tremendous cooperative effort of everybody and all elements of the community, the city government, the service industries." Schaefer told a group of Wichita businessmen that defense contracting would transform an agricultural town to a factory town quickly and that habits of community life would have to change radically. Along with those changes across the nation, monthly production of military aircraft jumped from 402 in April 1940 to 2,464 in December 1941.

The effect felt in Kansas was out of proportion to the rest of the country, in Wichita out of proportion to the rest of Kansas, and at the Boeing Wichita plant out of proportion to anywhere else in Wichita.

The Wichita Eagle/Boeing Aircraft Company

J. EARL SCHAEFER

⇑ Born June 11, 1893, Schaefer dedicated his life to establishing Boeing Wichita and shaping its contributions to aviation. When he graduated from the U.S. Military Academy at West Point in 1917, Schaefer gave his preferences for assignment as "**1.** Aviation, **2.** Aviation, **3.** Aviation." He served as general manager of Boeing Wichita from 1938 to 1959.

The first priority was training aircraft, and to meet it Boeing expanded its plant (soon to be designated Plant I) at a cost of over $184,000, completing the expansion in November 1940. During the process, the ante was upped several times. The original trainer contract called for 480 Kaydet biplanes to be delivered on a tight schedule — a rate of twenty-five planes a month. But within weeks, the request was for thirty planes. By July 1940, the quota was sixty a month, and Schaefer was worried about the psychological effect on his workers, because the military was not able to pick up the planes and ferry them out as quickly as they were being built. This production was accomplished with 766 employees, compared with the nearly 30,000 that the facility would have at its wartime peak. These workers had to make a rapid transition from Depression-era care for every dollar and every piece to "breathless haste" and an intense focus on rapid production, whatever the cost.

Trainers adapted from existing commercial models, however, were far from the whole story in national wartime aircraft production. The largest boost for Wichita — the thing that made boom and stress into absolute pandemonium and unprecedented, revolutionary change— was the decision to focus production of the secret B-29 Superfortress bomber at Wichita. This required the War Department's constructing an immense plant next to the old Stearman facilities, and it required housing, people, supplies, and logistical control many levels beyond the early production miracles.

The standard U.S. long-range bomber of the time, the B-17, was authorized in 1934 and had been in limited production at the Boeing plant in Seattle since 1935. It was a capable airplane, particularly for the relatively short-range work that was to be required in Europe. The prototype, weighing 32,432 pounds, had a bomb capacity of 4,800 pounds, a ferry range of 3,010 miles, and a top speed of 236 MPH. It was powered by four Pratt & Whitney 750 HP Hornet engines, although production models had Wright R-1820 Cyclone engines with 1,000 to 1,200 HP. Eventually all these capabilities were much increased. The B model's top speed was 292 MPH, the C's and D's was 323 MPH, and the G's was 310 MPH. The G model weighed more than 48,000 pounds, and could carry 6,500 pounds of bombs 3,750 miles. It was a craft roughly equivalent to the British Lancaster or the Consolidated B-24 Liberator.

Such planes were dwarfed by the B-29, which was authorized in February 1940. The minimum requirement was for a 5,333-mile range and an all-around performance considerably superior to the B-17. The airplane would have a wingspan of more than 140 feet, a weight of 140,000 pounds, a bomb capacity of 20,000 pounds, a top speed of 360 MPH, and a ferry range of 5,830 miles. It was to be powered by four, eighteen-cylinder, 2,200

Beech Aircraft Corporation

HP Wright Twin Cyclones. The height of the tail would be twenty-seven feet, nine inches. Its flaps were to be larger than any ever put on an airplane — larger than the wings of many fighters.

Arnold, William Knudsen, and other leaders of the U.S. air effort visited Wichita in August 1940 to see whether the Air Capital was all it was said to be and left satisfied that it was the place to center the B-29 project. It was said also that General K.B. Wolfe, head of the B-29 program, hated Seattle's weather and said that testing could move faster in Kansas skies. When the contract was let for the new Boeing Plant II (to envelop the smaller Plant II facility, which was itself not then completed) in October 1940, there was no mention of the production of a super bomber. The official explanation was that the space was to produce greater numbers of Kaydets and possibly to do more B-17E subcontracting work.

JUST FOR PRACTICE

⇑ Equipped with a Norden bombsight and as many as ten 100-pound practice bombs, the Beech AT-11 honed the skills of thousands of Allied bombardiers. During training missions, the AT-11 carried three students and two instructors. A total of 1,582 AT-11 Kansans were built. Powered by 450 HP Pratt & Whitney radials, the plane's maximum speed was 215 MPH.

It was soon clear that something very big was happening at the site. Ground was broken in June 1941, and in November it was occupied though not fully complete. Full completion came in January 1943, and the first production B-29 rolled out on April 19. By February 1945, the 1,000th Wichita B-29 had been produced, far more than at any other production site. By that time the equivalent of more than 10,000 Kaydets had been sold (8,431 as complete airplanes, the rest as spare parts), mostly at Plant I. Production at its peak was 4.2 B-29s and nine Kaydets every working day. Boeing's net profit for fiscal 1944 was $4.1 million, compared with a loss of $2.6 million for the first six months of 1939.

The statistics of size and scope as well as rate of change were impressive. Schaefer admitted that the size of the new construction was hard to grasp. Plant II cost $27 million and contained $20 million worth of tools and fixtures. There were 3 million square feet, or about 65 acres, of production and storage space. The steel trusses spanning the final assembly bays at Plant II were the largest ever fabricated: 300 feet long and 128 tons each. There was enough concrete in the Wichita plant addition to pave a thirty-five-foot-wide highway between Wichita and Winfield, fifty miles to the south. The warehouses alone would house 110 regulation basketball courts and the monthly electric bill was more than $35,000. Water was used at a rate of 36 million gallons a month, gas at more than 65 million cubic feet a month. An average of 68,645 calls a day came through the Boeing Wichita switchboard during the war. The Boeing Wichita cafeteria was, by 1941, the biggest restaurant in Kansas, serving 15,000 meals a day, costing 28 cents each. Every day, 5,000 pounds of meat, 3,500 pounds of potatoes and 1,250 homemade pies were delivered.

The Austin Company of Cleveland was the contractor on Plant II, and its wartime construction record was remarkable even in a time of construction miracles. It had built a forty-one-acre bomber plant for Boeing Seattle, a virtual twin of this new one in Wichita, in less than 12 months. The speed was helped by standardization. Wide distribution aisles flanked warehouses on either side of the production area to expedite handling by powered and hand trucks, with a minimum of cross traffic. Every aisle had a street name, as well as a number designation. People could, for instance, be directed to Broadway in a facility that was virtually a city. Stainless steel, aluminum alloy, and other aircraft metals in the form of sheets, tubing, and bar stock found their way to a lofty primary shop where shears, brakes, hydraulic presses, drop hammers, and nonferrous heat-treating furnaces were located, or to the machine shop and welding department. Materials in process flowed through heat-treating, plating, and painting departments in ventilated rooms and toward wide assembly bays. Subassembly shops were often located

Bob Pickett Collection, Kansas Aviation Museum/Boeing Aircraft Company

above the main shops, and all production flowed and was integrated using large monorail bridge cranes operating over the entire assembly area that held huge bomber parts "like so many jackstraws as they progress from storage balconies through jigs to the final positions where bombers are finished and engines mounted in place." It was the ultimate in coordinated mass production and materiel flow, a skill that U.S. workers, managers, and suppliers had been honing for 75 years.

It was not just the unprecedented size and power of the B-29 that presented construction problems. It was an innovative plane in many ways. There was an ingenious "three bubble system" of pressurization, and all sorts of structural and power problems had to be worked out. The wing was an experimental airfoil that would support nearly twice the weight per square foot of area as a B-17 wing. Regularly during production, subcontractors would be flown to Wichita to brainstorm day and night on some modification during twenty-four-hour periods of "orderly confusion." Once it was a crash program to get the bomb-bay doors to open in one-fifth of a

HEAVY LIFTING

⇑ The scale of manufacturing operations required to produce the B-29 was clearly evident at the assembly station in which the seventeen-ton center wing sections were joined to bomb-bay sections.

second, so there would be no advance warning to the enemy of a bomb run. Then there was the gun-control system used on some B-29s. It was designed by General Electric and allowed the ship to fly unescorted. Once a change had to be made in a gunfire-interrupter mechanism, and that required insertion of a cam. Modifications took place during a blizzard, and many tests were done by flashlight illumination outdoors.

For that matter, the controller itself was a radically new device. It was found that the inevitable jerking in the gun sight as a gunner tracked his target had to be compensated for by programmed instructions to the machine. An electrical connection of gyroscopes and springs had to be invented to feed information to the computer. During firing tests alone, one engineer fired 500,000 rounds of ammunition during 400 hours in the air.

Another famous fix came when 1,200 mechanics were pulled from the assembly line to work on the open-air apron in bitterly cold weather, making changes inside the wings of partially completed B-29s.

Still another involved a problem with electrical plugs used in connecting the more than ten miles of wiring in each plane. The plugs worked in pre-assembly tests but not in flight. The units had to be disassembled and more than half a million connections resoldered — a job that took 40,000 hours.

Such events were collectively called the "modification blitz" and were in some ways as miserable as war itself, albeit minus the shooting. "We didn't get much sleep," said a veteran of the modification struggle. "We worked as many hours as we could stand up, then took over someone else's bed."

Sandwiched around the hectic testing and modifying was the actual production, which had to achieve sufficient numbers to be of use in the conflict. (To hedge its bets, the Army also had awarded bomber development contracts to Consolidated for the XB-32, to Douglas for its XB-31, and to Lockheed for its XB-30. Only the B-32 went into production.) As an example of the cost-be-damned attitude that was taken on the B-29, a 1944 military statement pointed out that the first prototype, with all the development that went into it, had cost $3,392,396.90. In hindsight, it seems inexpensive. On May 17, 1941, over a year and a half before the first test flight of the prototype, and months before Pearl Harbor, the military ordered 250 B-29s. Before the prototype XB-29 had even been thoroughly tested by Boeing test pilot Edmond "Eddie" Allen, the Army ordered 990 of them — ten to be delivered in 1942, 450 in 1943, and 530 in 1944. Never in the history of U.S. military procurement had such orders been placed in the absence of competition or testing. Pressure was so great that there was no time to fix drawings when an engineering change was needed. "I saw engineers make sketches on the cuffs of their shirt sleeves," said an eyewitness, "and then they'd give the shirt to someone else to copy."

Bob Pickett Collection, Kansas Aviation Museum

HUSH-HUSH

⇐ Culver Aircraft Corporation of Wichita was one of very few aircraft manufacturers to operate under a complete blanket of secrecy for the entire war. It was not until October 1945 that it was revealed that the company had built the Model PQ-8 and PQ-14 series of target aircraft. This PQ-8 was powered by a 90 HP Franklin four-cylinder engine and had a maximum speed of 110 MPH.

Every change was a production problem: The XB-29 prototypes had sixteen engine changes and twenty-two carburetor changes during the first twenty-seven hours of test flying. In 1943, with 1,600 of the planes on order, a test pilot died in the prototype. Because production was so central, so pressed and so problematical — and because the bulk of it was in Wichita — the struggle with the B-29, and by implication the other vital air production activity in the state, has been called by historians "The Battle of Kansas."

Other wartime aircraft activity in Wichita was less imposing but hugely significant. Some small local manufacturers, like Rawdon Brothers, suffered from the shutdown of civilian sales as well as the overwhelming competition in training aircraft, only to re-emerge after the war. Some, like Collier, were defeated by the unfortunate timing of their origin. Others adapted to military production. Culver Aircraft Company, for instance became a prime manufacturer of radio-controlled target drones adapted from its efficient, small, prewar commercial model, the Cadet. The company moved to Wichita from Columbus, Ohio, in 1940, settled into 93,000 square feet of space at the Bridgeport site, where Cessna's first production had been in 1915, employed 300, and produced 2,644 target drones and a large number of propellers during the conflict. Culver survived the war to introduce its "Victory" model low-winged monoplane, and built about 400 of them.

Beech and Cessna were so well established that there was no question they would have a large wartime role.

Lieutenant Colonel Dwight Eisenhower, then chief of staff of the U.S. military mission to the Philippines, visited Beech in 1938 to inspect a Model 18 that had been purchased by the Philippine Army Air Corps for aerial photography. It was the first of many Model 18s that would be modified for World War II service. Walter Beech had been aware of the model's capabili-

"E"

⇒ Awarded for excellence in wartime production, Beech, Boeing Wichita, Cessna, and Culver were among the 3 percent of U.S. war manufacturers to win the Army-Navy "E" award five straight times. North American Aviation of Kansas City, Kans., would attain the distinction twice.

The Wichita Eagle

ty and had his company participate in the U.S. Army Air Corps evaluation competition at Wright Field in 1939. By the start of the war, Model 18 sales were thirty-nine, including an order from the Chinese government. Beech began at that time to outfit five airplanes with gun turrets and bomb racks. Following an inspection tour in 1941, Arnold ordered 150 similar units. Eventually Beech would produce about 7,400 twins for military use during the war. To give some idea of the degree of change, consider that between 1935 and 1940, Beech manufactured 308 commercial and forty military airplanes. From 1940 to 1945, it manufactured only twenty-two civilian craft. The AT-10, another twin, made up a good portion of the wartime production. Because of supply shortages, it was made entirely of plywood except for the cowlings and cockpit enclosures (Culver targets and Cessna trainers also utilized plywood in their construction). In addition, the company manufactured over 1,600 sets of wings for the Douglas A-26 Invader attack bomber, manufactured large numbers of propellers, recycled surplus materials through a subsidiary, and designed, built, and tested a combat aircraft called the XA-38 Grizzly. Like Boeing and Cessna, Beech received the Army-Navy "E" production awards for outstanding services, earning it five consecutive times. Walt Disney created a special symbol, the Beechcraft Busy Bee for the company, and the little character with the riveter was emblazoned on badges worn by outstanding employees.

As with Boeing, the financial and operational results were striking. Even in 1948, after the war boom was past, Beech reported a ten-to-one increase in deliveries compared with 1940, an employment three times as large, a tripling of wages, an 800 percent increase in plant space, and twenty-two times as much taxes paid. It is to the company's credit that it maintained so much of its wartime gain in the postwar years, but the war provided it the breakthrough momentum. The federal Reconstruction Finance Corporation, for example, lent Beech over $13.5 million late in 1940. Wichita did its part

BUSY BEE

⇓ Created by Walt Disney especially for Beech Aircraft Corporation, the Beechcraft Busy Bee was a symbol of merit and honor for employees during the war. This was the first Disney character especially created for an industrial organization.

The Beech Log, Beech Aircraft Corporation

The Wyandotte County Historical Society

MITCHELL

⇐ This B-25J bomber, fresh off the assembly lines at Fairfax Airport, was armed with twelve .50-caliber machine guns and could haul 6,000 pounds of bombs. Powered by two 1,700 HP Wright R-2600-92 engines, the B-25J was flown by a crew of five or six.

Pickett Collection, Kansas Aviation Musuem

CG-4A GLIDER

⇐ Designed by the Waco Company of Troy, Ohio, the CG-4A combat transport glider was built by sixteen U.S. companies. Cessna subcontracted to build 1,500 CG-4A-CEs, of which 750 were completed (assembled in the aisles of Boeing Wichita's Plant II). CG-4As were used in airborne assaults in Burma, France, Holland, and Sicily. Costing about $25,000 each, the CG-4A normally carried two crew members and thirteen infantrymen. While quite basic in appearance, the CG-4A required over 70,000 parts for manufacture.

also. A new sewer line was built to serve the plant, and approximately $600,000 was invested in access roads to the factory. By 1941 Beech had 5,300 employees who, a reporter said, were "welded into a productive machine so efficient and complex as to be perplexing to the layman." There were 8,000 parts in a Beechcraft, many purchased from dozens of small Wichita machine shops and many made inside the plant — all of which had to come together on a strict schedule. Each shift knew exactly where to start when taking over from the other, and the plant's two 2,500-ton hydraulic presses were never idle. Perhaps all this coordination, and an accompanying moratorium on strikes, was related to a picture of an aircraft gunner hung in the Beech lobby with the caption: "Don't let this man down."

Cessna had a slower start on the federal contracts. Its first large order, for a modified T-50 twin for military use (500 planes, 200 extra engines),

Beech Aircraft Corporation

GRIZZLY

⥣ Only two flying prototypes of this Beechcraft Model 28 (military designation XA-38 Destroyer) were built. Intended to fulfill a role of "airborne artillery," the Grizzly was built around a 75mm nose-mounted cannon that could fire twenty rounds in twenty-four seconds. Powered by two supercharged, water-injected Wright Duplex Cyclone radials of 2,200 HP each (the same engines used on the B-29), the plane had a top speed of 375 MPH.

came from Canada, where the plane was designated the Crane. The financing to build it in volume was local, coming from Fourth National Bank. Quickly, however, the U.S. government began ordering, too, under the designation AT-8 and later AT-17 and UC-78. The plywood Cessna trainer was popularly called the Bobcat or the Bamboo Bomber. Cessna had 200 employees early in 1940. A year later it was hiring 200 a month, and by the spring of 1941, it had 1,500 employees. "This supercharged aviation activity is something new to Kansans," wrote the *Eagle*. "Every Sunday hundreds of motorists drive the seven miles from town to watch huge and somewhat incongruous appearing factories going up on the rolling plains."

The expanded Cessna plant designed its own cargo plane, the C-106, which, like Beech's Grizzly, did not get into production. It was also a subcontractor, along with other Wichita plants such as Coleman, and built B-29 subassemblies. Cessna made about 1,500 vertical stabilizers, rudders, heat exchangers, instrument panels, dorsal fairings, elevators, leading edges for wings, and rubber pedals for the B-29.

In all, Cessna contributed 6,111 aircraft to the war effort, mostly twins, but also 750 troop-carrying CG-4A-CE gliders. Its motto was "Quality trainers in Quantity." A U.S. flag was placed in every department, and the wartime spirit was expressed by Wallace, who said, "Our job is one of great responsibility, where everyone must gladly shoulder his just share — in this conviction there must be no doubt." By the beginning of 1942, Cessna was ordered, as Boeing had been earlier, to go on a seven-day-a-week, twenty-four-hour-a-day production schedule for the duration of the war. A Cessna branch factory was built at Hutchinson, fifty miles northwest of Wichita.

That 108,000-square-foot factory was erected and in operation within 30 days of its start.

In an emergency such as the war, the effect of production and training needs were spread all over Kansas. Commonwealth Aircraft Incorporated at Fairfax Airport in Kansas City, a successor firm to Rearwin, had a contract for Waco gliders and produced nearly 1,500 of them, becoming the nation's second-largest producer of combat gliders. Funk Aircraft, run by Howard and Joe Funk in Coffeyville, kept its little enterprise going by building AT-10 parts. And the war couldn't stop the production of "whatchimacallits" in the state. Rex Maneval, a chicken hatcher from Frankfort, Kans., built a helicopter in 1941 that flew while tied to the ground and illustrated that counter-rotating blades could work.

More important was the use of Kansas as a branch manufacturing site for the B-25. North American Aviation built a 1 million-square-foot factory adjoining Fairfax Airport in 1941, designed to use automotive-assembly techniques to construct Mitchell medium bombers. North American's Inglewood, Calif., plant suffered from a labor shortage and was already at 1 million square feet itself — thus the second location inland. The Kansas City factory, which consisted of six buildings spread over eighty-five acres, cost $10 million and was built by the Army Corps of Engineers and paid for by the War Department. The plant was of the "blackout" type, and it was said its sandy roof, aluminum painted steel walls, and buff concrete blended with the surroundings so as to make it almost invisible to a plane flying as low as 500 feet. In addition, North American leased space in General Motors' Chevrolet plant, the International Harvester Company plant, and several other local factories.

Production began in Kansas City in 1941. The most widely produced version was the B-25J-NC, of which 4,318 were rolled out between 1943 and 1945 (total B-25 production was 9,815 planes). The inland facility worked so well that in July 1944 the entire production of Mitchells was transferred to Kansas City, allowing the Inglewood plant to concentrate on the output of P-51 Mustangs, which were badly needed in Europe as long-range fighter escorts.

Manufacturing was not the whole of it for the state either. There was training to be considered, and there had to be airfields upon which to test and service the myriad new aircraft. All over Kansas in the 1990s are the remains of large airfield installations, some now dedicated to industrial use in whole or in part but often ghostly and rotting reminders of the 1940s crisis. Major Army airfields were created at Coffeyville (1942-46), Dodge City (1942-45), Kansas City (1942-50), Topeka (1942-present), Garden City (1942-47), Great Bend (1942-45), Herington (1942-47), Independence (1941-48), Liberal (1943-45), Wichita (1942-present), Pratt (1942-45),

Salina (1942-65), Winfield/Arkansas City (1942-53), and Ellis County (1942-46). Naval air stations sprouted at Hutchinson (1943-46 and 1952-59) and Olathe (1942-1970). At least one civilian air training school in Kansas, McFarland Flying Service in Pittsburg, trained military pilots under a stop-gap program, called the Civil Pilot Training Program, designed to utilize all training possible facilities.

The missions of these fields varied. Coffeyville, for instance, concentrated on training photo-reconnaissance pilots. Dodge City was to provide transition training on the B-26 Marauder, to break the idea that it was a dangerous plane. Fairfax specialized in ferrying the B-25s made at the North American plant there. Forbes, outside Topeka, trained bombardment specialists. Liberal trained for the B-24. Garden City boasted the smallest community college in the nation with a course in aviation. Significant numbers of people were stationed at these fields. Dodge City trained over 2,000 — a considerable strain on a small town — while Liberal, also a small town in western Kansas, graduated 4,468 four-engine commanders and 1,025 pre-transition pilots. Extensive barracks, runways, hangars, and administrative buildings were constructed at these sites on the same frantic schedule and during the same time in 1941 and 1942 that there was such pressure to build manufacturing plants. The National Public Housing Administration sometimes brought in trailers to accommodate families temporarily, and, as was true in the manufacturing centers, the Federal Housing Administration through local building firms financed the construction of temporary low-rent homes. The frenetic pace of building had its downside, though. Even historic landmarks, such as a house in Johnson County that had been a landmark on the Santa Fe Trail, were razed to make room for the building boom.

The engineering, flying, and physical training at these bases was highly concentrated. At Liberal, the mission was to become proficient as a commander of four-engine aircraft. The program involved 105 hours of flying, fifteen hours of Link trainer time, 146 hours of technical instruction, dozens of hours of physical training, and twenty-six hours of bomb approach, ground school, trainer, and flight missions. Each student was scheduled to fly five hours every other day. When weather interfered, they performed maintenance work. On alternate days came the technical training. The greatest problem, particularly at the western Kansas bases, was maintenance of the aircraft. Student pilots are notoriously hard on airplanes, and the bombers flown at many of these places were designed for long-range missions and relatively infrequent landings, not for the kind of use they got in training. Replacement parts were therefore needed more often than usual, and the training bases did not have priority for shipment of parts. This was complicated by inadequate and inexperienced personnel, and the Kansas weather. A historian of the

The Wyandotte County Historical Society

TURNING UP THE HEAT

⇑ B-25 Mitchells poured out of North American's Fairfax plant at a peak rate of thirteen aircraft a day. A total of 2,290 B-25Ds and 4,318 B-25Js were built in Kansas City, Kans., accounting for 67 percent of all B-25s produced during World War II.

Liberal base noted that "a man cannot do satisfactory maintenance with a wind of 30 to 40 miles per hour in freezing weather."

Given these drawbacks, the performance of the Kansas Army airfields is remarkable. It is a picture for the fevered imagination to envision a place like Walker Air Field in Ellis County, with no town of more than a few hundred people within a radius of 100 miles (and therefore virtually zero recreational opportunities) being home by 1944 to nearly 6,000 people, where the mammoth B-29s utilized the 10,000 foot runways that the flat prairie topography allowed to be built with little grading.

In addition to the airfields, there was an enormous educational effort in Kansas, focused at Wichita High School East, to train skilled aircraft-plant workers, particularly riveters, sheet metal workers, and welders. One of the early pieces of national publicity on the Kansas boom, an article by Shelby Cullom Davis in the January 1941 issue of *Current History and Forum*

Mid-America Air Museum

PLAINS OUTPOST

⇑ Sixteen Army and two Navy training bases were located in Kansas during the war. One of the Air Corps fields was near Liberal. It covered 1,946 acres and cost $8 million to build. Approximately one-fourth of all U.S. B-24 Liberator commanders passed through the program in Liberal during its twenty-seven months of operation.

magazine, issue spoke about "a 62-million-dollar tornado in a town of 120,000 — more national contracts per capita than any other established inland community in the United States. A tornado that is sweeping men off the Kansas prairies into Wichita. … It's just too fabulous." Davis observed that "aircraft training schools are springing up overnight in vacant garages and facilities for instruction in welding and riveting are coming into being miraculously. Vocational schools are running 24 hours a day." The attitude of Wichita, the author said, was to plan for success and thus force it. When asked why aviation should center in Wichita, the city's leaders responded by asking why the greatest violin of all time, the Stradivarius, had been designed in the little Italian town of Cremona.

Local educators had seen the coming need for a large labor force early, and about the time of the Munich crisis in 1938 decided to install a sheet metal department at East High. There were already courses in mechanical drawing, woodworking, electricity, printing, and auto mechanics. In April 1939 officers of the three major aircraft plants went to J.C. Woodin, supervisor of industrial education, and asked for the assistance of the public school system. This appealed to Woodin, whose motto was: "You can make things happen." And it appealed to L.W. Brooks, the principal of East, and L.W. Mayberry, the superintendent of Wichita's schools. At first the courses were available only to high school students, but shortly they were thrown open in the evening to people who wanted to work in the factories. With Mayberry's approval, the sheet metal, woodworking, and machine shops of the schools were opened three hours each, three nights a week and on Saturday for eight hours. By that summer, the facilities were open all week and every night. Kansas farm people were particularly mechanically apt. By the time a national emergency was declared, the school had already turned out 500 mechanics.

Two similar, albeit private, schools were also in operation during the late 1930s and early 1940s. There was the Great Plains Aviation School on North Hillside at the old Swallow factory and the Swallow Airplane Company Airplane and Mechanics School at Lincoln and Washington streets, at the former site of the Supreme Propeller Factory.

The schools let the industry call some of the shots. If a personnel manager at a plant thought an applicant could be trained in eight weeks, that person was automatically accepted for a probationary tryout at the school. When the National Defense Training Act was signed in 1940, East High was the first school in the country to go into it at full speed. Enrollment immediately jumped from 290 to 600, and a welding division was added. By 1941, East High was "a veritable factory," training students twenty-four hours a day in three shifts of seven and one-half hours each, and employing sixty-one teachers just for the aircraft vocational program. Each week it graduated fifty people who were ready to work. Local businesspeople raised $15,000 to buy the school new equipment rather than waiting for a government appropriation. The plants themselves started apprenticeship programs, where young men between eighteen and twenty-two could work with journeymen at 40 cents an hour, supplemented by school vocational training. During the war, the National Defense School operated by the Wichita Board of Education trained 28,000 workers, most of them Kansans. In addition, the factories sent 36,000 employees to the schools for instruction, and these people took an aggregate of 53,000 courses. The *Current History* article concluded: "Wichitans are meeting the new emergency in the same 'bound to win' spirit that has characterized their past. ... For thousands Wichita is becoming a town in which dreams of success suddenly become realizable. ... The zoo has acquired its first tiger. ... But no boom would have come near Kansas' dust bowl had not plenty of vision and hard work and planning gone before. Wichita is about to reap the harvest where there had been flat monotony, drouth and many a whirlwind."

Of course, housing was a problem everywhere in Kansas, as people were moved into production and training centers not only from around the state but from around the nation. The cantonment section at the Coffeyville Army Air Field contained sixty-seven enlisted men's barracks, twenty-five cadet barracks, three WAC barracks, eighteen officers' quarters, eight mess halls, a guard house, a commissary, thirteen warehouses, eleven administration buildings, twelve supply rooms, a post headquarters building, a finance building, a post-engineer building, six operations buildings, one fire station, one telephone building, and a signal office building. And that did not include the training section, the recreation and welfare section, and an extensive hospital.

In Wichita, entire federally sponsored cities appeared nearly instantly. Roosevelt declared Wichita one of 146 "defense areas," where homes could be financed through the Federal Housing Administration with no down payment. In addition, the federal government announced in 1941 that it would build homes in Wichita to accommodate defense workers, through the Federal Public Housing Authority, at an average cost of $3,500. The major concentrations built in 1942 and 1943 were Hilltop Manor (population 5,000), Beechwood (2,500), Wichita Trailer Park (1,300), and Planeview (20,000). Certainly housing was needed. For the first 400 units at Hilltop, there were 1,100 applications.

Planeview, which adjoined Boeing, was surely the most interesting as well as the largest of these Kansas planned communities. It was controversial partly because of the sameness of its curvilinear streets and the inexpensive and aesthetically unappealing identical units. Some of the so-called demountables were manufactured housing with asbestos siding, constructed at the Southern Mill Manufacturing company in Tulsa. The village did have the virtue of being near the plant, thus relieving an unbearable traffic problem that had arisen during the era of rationing of gasoline and tires. But some local residents feared juvenile delinquency in its one-class streets and its enormous (1,400-student) high school. (The ugly subject of prostitution by "victory girls" came up). Even more than that, people wondered what would become of it once the war was over, and whether it would become an unsightly slum.

Others saw it as a wonderful experiment in integration and cooperation, a model for suburban communities of the future. Sidewalks and parking were carefully planned. Streets built to aircraft-runway standards connected the living units and the commercial area. Playgrounds and parks were interspersed; there was a 1 million-gallon reservoir for water pressure and fire protection, and utilities were well provided for. Nearly everything required was within walking distance, including all-night stores and day care — doing away entirely, in a very modern way, with the need to go downtown to shop. Residents denied that it was a lower-class tract, and pointed to 225 occupations represented. The Associated Press called it a "miracle city."

The fears ultimately prevailed, leading to demands that the war housing be torn down by the federal government after the war. Much of it was. Only small parts remain in the 1990s. Many of the buildings were never intended to outlast the conflict. And Wichita's basic conservatism, along with the fears of the real estate people about the subsidized competition, played a role. "Wichita has had no experience with government housing projects," the *Eagle* wrote in 1941. Perhaps real estate agents' negativism was partly due to the $3 million in building permits issued in the town during 1940, an all-time record. Total building in Wichita in 1941, public and private, was over 3,200 units. Although it seemed to many a waste to destroy these federal houses, they did serve an emergency purpose, and the rise and fall of

The Wichita Eagle

war housing was only a fraction of the waste and expense that went into the terrific modification of American life as it had been lived.

Sometimes it seemed everything had changed. There were security guards at plant gates and on factory floors. Fifty-four buses provided commuter service, some of them covering 500 miles a day from towns within a seventy-mile radius of Wichita and arriving three times at day at shift changes. The plants organized enormous recreational programs. At Boeing there were fifty-six bowling teams in 1942 and fifty departmental teams in the basketball league. The company constructed a nine-hole golf course, two ten-

PLAN OF PLANEVIEW

⇑ Planeview, a federal public housing project, was the largest settlement for wartime workers in Wichita. Consisting of duplexes, triplexes and single family homes, 4,382 units housed a population of 20,000, making Planeview the seventh-largest city in Kansas. The average rent was $32 a month.

The Wichita Eagle/Boeing Aircraft Company

BOEING PORT AUTHORITY

⇑ With a wartime peak employment of 29,795 workers, Boeing Wichita (along with other manufacturers) started a bus service to try to conserve gasoline and rubber as well as relieve traffic congestion. As organized by Emergency Transportation Incorporated, bus service to Boeing Wichita operated three times a day and served towns within seventy miles.

nis courts, and badminton, horseshoe, croquet and shuffleboard facilities. The Cessna employees' club had its own building, which included a gym and a lounge with pool and a snack bar. The Beech employees' club sponsored dinner dances, and the city of Wichita remodeled the Rose room of the Forum Building, mostly with federal money, for the expanded work force.

A local woman, Kunigunde Duncan, wrote an evocative piece for the *New York Herald Tribune* in May 1942 on the atmosphere. "A magic boom has descended upon Wichita," she wrote, "like a chamber of commerce dream come true. … When a community expands so suddenly, living conditions are upset. There are too many people in stores, on buses, at the bank, gas, water and electricity pay windows. It takes forever to get nothing done. There are too many traffic tangles and accidents, too few lodgings for airplane workers, too few seats in school rooms. There is an increase in crime, and streets are now trash-laden. It is a headache to try to telephone." Wichita was filled with "hot-flops," so-called because beds were slept in there for three shifts with never a chance to cool. Much of the housing was new. "Every available lot was used, every urban acreage turned into new and shiny-paved streets of boxlike bright-roofed bungalows, row houses, apartments, trailer courts." Motor drone was an all day and most of the night presence. "Traffic signal change has been increased to thirty-two seconds to get sidewalk crowds across safely, and around every filling station is a ring of trailers in which new arrivals await a demountable house, fabricated to the stage where you can get tired little children to bed."

Small businesses thrived, and subcontractors seemed to appear almost daily. More than $100 million in parts, subassemblies and tooling were accepted by Beech from subcontractors during the war out of $425 million in total parts made. Observers were always shocked at the small size of the company's machine shop, but overhead was kept low by depending on the small, decentralized businesses spread through Wichita and Kansas. At the peak of the war work, Beech subcontractors employed nearly 10,000 people and used 1.5 million square feet of floor space on Beech contracts.

This feature was striking to a writer covering "War in the Heart of Kansas" for *Colliers* in November 1942. He visited a former concrete shop in Wichita where wing painting was going on in the yard under electric bulbs strung overhead. "The word you hear oftenest in Wichita," he wrote, "is the word 'deal.' Everything there from the weather to the state of the nation is a deal. ... Perhaps it is natural that this new development, wholesale decentralization, should appear most clearly in Wichita." Different companies did it differently. Some trained subcontractors and supervised their operations, others supplied material and advice but gave free rein to the imagination and initiative of subcontractors. "The thing that strikes you at the moment, the thing that almost stops your breath, is the sight of one section of the country completely mobilized, of industry taken into the home, into garages and basements, of shops improved out of oil-well equipment, of overage tools lovingly restored to perfection, of elderly men working long hours, working after hours. ... America at work offers a thousand aspects. The one you catch sight of in the machine shops, big and little, of Wichita is not to be overlooked."

There were broader social changes, too. In 1942, women working in the Wichita airplane factories were forbidden from wearing dresses and, for safety reasons, limited to simple blouses, slacks and coats. By that time, it was noted that the "defensette" contingent was "really beginning to be something to reckon with, not just look at, around the plants." Wichita plants had had a few female workers since Lillian Whipple went to work at Earl Schaefer's office at Stearman in 1927, so it was not the cultural shock that it was when women started working at Ford Motor Company, which had previously had a solid rule against employing them. Given that the

WICHITA EAGLE EDITORIAL CARTOON,
⇒ Sunday January 24, 1943

The Wichita Eagle

plants wanted only draft-exempt men with 3-A Selective Service classifications and at least two direct dependents, it was inevitable that women should form a substantial part of the work force. But it was something new to see a woman outfitted in a war industry. "These new women in war industry lean over their torches," said a reporter, "temporarily setting aside the touches of femininity that man has associated with them for generations. But with their 'jeans' over overalls, goggles, heavy gloves, and hair tucked under kerchief, they are attending their objectives — filling an important job in the war program." They were on the sports teams at the plants as well as at the dances, and their "social and recreational habits … are as modern and streamlined as the airplane."

Rosie the Riveter often got up at 4 a.m., put on her work clothes at home, dropped off her sleepy children at day care and, on arriving at work, put a turban over her hair. She was treated without distinction and took pride in the job. "It is not hard to imagine," wrote an observer, "some youngster in 1985, telling his school chums that 'my grandmother helped build the planes we used to whip the Japs away back in 1943.'"

It was clear that the end of the war would not end this sexual revolution. One cartoon showed a giant-sized woman in coveralls with a lunch bucket and an envelope in her pocket reading "Her Own Man's Size Pay Envelope" leaving the farm for the factory. A tiny man was calling, "But remember you got to come right back as soon as the war is over." The giant said, "Oh yeah?" and the caption read: "Somebody else let a Genie out of a Bottle Once Too." The only bar to the most skilled jobs was experience. "Personnel men say they draw no lines, and that if some girl shows up with 10 years' experience running a 25,000-ton hydraulic press, can stand the work and knows her business, they would not turn her down just because she wears a dress and patronizes beauty parlors on her time off."

AT HER OFFICE

⇓ To accommodate the women who would make up 50 percent of the wartime work force, manufacturers modified equipment – adding rails, counterbalances, roller tracks, and other improvements – so it could be operated with less muscle. Plant workers typically worked ten-hour days and got every other weekend off.

Boeing Aircraft Company

One aspect of the war effort in which Kansas took special pride was the local origin of most of its aircraft plant executives. The Beeches were an example. Dwane and Dwight Wallace at Cessna were another. Earl Schaefer, head of Boeing Wichita, was a native son who had sold newspapers and jerked sodas in Wichita as a boy.

There was also pride in pointing to the size of the warplane industry centered at Wichita. Of the thirteen states in the Midwest procurement district, only Wichita and St. Louis had airplane plants before the war. By 1944, there were great aircraft factories, engine plants, and modification centers at Kansas City; Omaha; Dallas-Fort Worth, Texas; Oklahoma City; Tul-sa; New Orleans, La.; Denver; and Cheyenne, Wyo. They manufactured thirty types of airplanes and employed several hundred thousand workers, many of whom had been housewives a few years earlier. In 1942, the value of the planes and parts turned out by these plants exceeded $3.7 billion, more than the output of the U.S. auto industry in its biggest year, 1941. In 1943, the plants doubled that, and they doubled it again in 1944. Administration of the district was headquartered in Wichita at the Municipal Airport administration building. Brigadier General Ray G. Harris was the district supervisor.

There was considerable spin-off to Kansas. Wichita led the nation in the dollar value of war contracts awarded per capita. The $2 billion in orders were too much even for 60,000 Wichita workers. It was estimated early in 1944 that Wichita's Big Three aircraft plants had subcontracted $71,416,468 of work to Kansas firms of a total of $182,851,717.

Wichitans and Kansans can be excused for thinking this was no accident. Beech Aircraft issued a statement claiming that "Wichita achieved this distinction because of the initiative, energy, and cooperative spirit of its people. From the beginning of the defense program, Wichitans backed up their prime contractors by providing housing, transportation, training schools, and other vital facilities. They cheerfully accepted dislocation of their accustomed habits and ways of living, and flocked to the production lines by the thousands. These acts enabled the prime contractors of Wichita to do their jobs on schedule and thus attracted more and more war contracts until the present achievement was attained." Nearly 26,300 military aircraft emerged from Wichita plants between 1940 and 1945, and production in the rest of Kansas pushed the state's wartime total to approximately 34,500 planes.

No individual company record in Kansas was more impressive during the war than that of Boeing Wichita. Although the division missed producing the most famous B-29, the *Enola Gay,* which dropped the atomic bomb on Hiroshima (It was made in Omaha), Wichita made 44 percent of all B-29s built, and more of them (1,644) were built in Wichita than anywhere else. Wichitans took the "deepest pride" in the news of the first attack of the B-

The Wichita Eagle/Beech Aircraft Company

TURNING THE TIDES OF WAR

⇑ Ten years after they founded Beech Aircraft Corporation, Olive Ann and Walter Beech found themselves the owners of a company that had become largely a military contractor, specializing in the production of twin-engine trainers.

29s on Japan in June 1944, and the fact that the first planes in it were Wichita-made.

But even those working at the plant had not been completely familiar with the plane because of to tight secrecy and security. Therefore in October 1944, when the B-29 was at last put on public view locally, 50,000 Wichitans lined up one Sunday to see it. They passed through the Boeing gates at a rate of 100 a minute "to view at close range the B-29 Superfortress and to gain a first-hand impression of the tremendous operations involved in building it." It was wonderful, they thought, that such a thing could be done by ordinary people, 50 percent of them women. "Who makes this intricate piece of air-borne destruction?" a Kansas City reporter wrote. "At this particular plant it seems to be the farmer, the farmer's wife and the folks from town."

There was every indication that production in Wichita and Kansas would not only continue at a high level, but increase if the war in Europe or Asia were extended. There seemed no clear limits on the productive capacity of the Midlands, at least none that were about to be reached in 1945. As late as October 1944, Boeing Wichita got authorization to proceed with the procurement of materials for 700 additional B-29s, the fourth major order.

SUPERFORTRESS

⇒ Originally designed to bomb Germany from U.S. bases, the B-29 was primarily used against Japan, seeing its first action in June 1944. In addition to being the heaviest plane of its time, it was the first pressurized bomber, used the most powerful radial engines, and possessed the highest degree of wing loading.

Boeing Aircraft Company

Schaefer noted: "This places even greater importance on the idea that no matter when victory is achieved in Europe, Wichita's assignment is in the Pacific. Our job will not be finished until Japan is finished."

Still, things were changing. In June 1945, though production of B-29s had not diminished, employment in Wichita aircraft plants was down to 38,000 from the peak of 60,000 in December 1943. In June 1945, there were 17,916 at Boeing, 10,200 at Beech, 2,467 at Cessna, 612 at Culver and 6,805 at subcontractors. Local aircraft payrolls remained at $9 million a month. By comparison, it had been estimated that in 1939 — after the military buildup had begun to have an effect locally — about 1,400 were employed in the aircraft industry in Wichita, that the industry had a capacity of between 450 and 500 craft a year, and that the turnover in money attributable to it was $4.5 million annually.

Bob Pickett Collection, Kansas Aviation Museum/Boeing Aircraft Company

A CONTRAST IN STYLES

⇑ During February 1945, the last Kaydet and the 1,000th Wichita-built B-29 were rolled out of the factory. Contributed by employees in a spontaneous expression of generosity, the B-29 bore on its aluminum skin $10,343.68 in coins and currency as a donation to the Infantile Paralysis Foundation. On the Kaydet was an additional $218.85 for the fight against polio. Although the sign on the Kaydet says it was the 10,346th (and last) built, it was actually the 8,431st.

But in August 1945, thanks to a new weapon dropped from a B-29, Japan was finished and so was the Battle of Kansas. The church bell that rang at Boeing Wichita every time a B-29 rolled out (and then additionally once a shift so the enemy would not know how many planes were being produced) was silenced. Layoffs were rapid all over Kansas, and plants that had been humming months, even days before appeared tomblike. It was a particular psychological shock to move from a crisis to complete inactivity. Sixteen thousand people received pink slips at Boeing Wichita in one day. "We worked 10 hour days, seven days a week, with every other weekend off," said a Boeing worker. "I never thought anything about it." The contrast was hard: "All the unfinished airplanes (were) rolled out, and were broken up and hauled away. I remember looking out the window and seeing those carloads of parts — these airplanes had equipment in them, all the instruments and everything, they didn't take anything out. It was hard to look out the window and see all those things chopped up like that. Then one morning everybody in the whole group got pink slips." By the time the Army officially announced the suspension of B-29 production in September 1945, Boeing Wichita had only 5,000 employees. That was immediately cut to 2,500, and by 1946, it was 1,388. Boeing formally terminated its lease with the government on Plant II, and the Reconstruction Finance Corporation

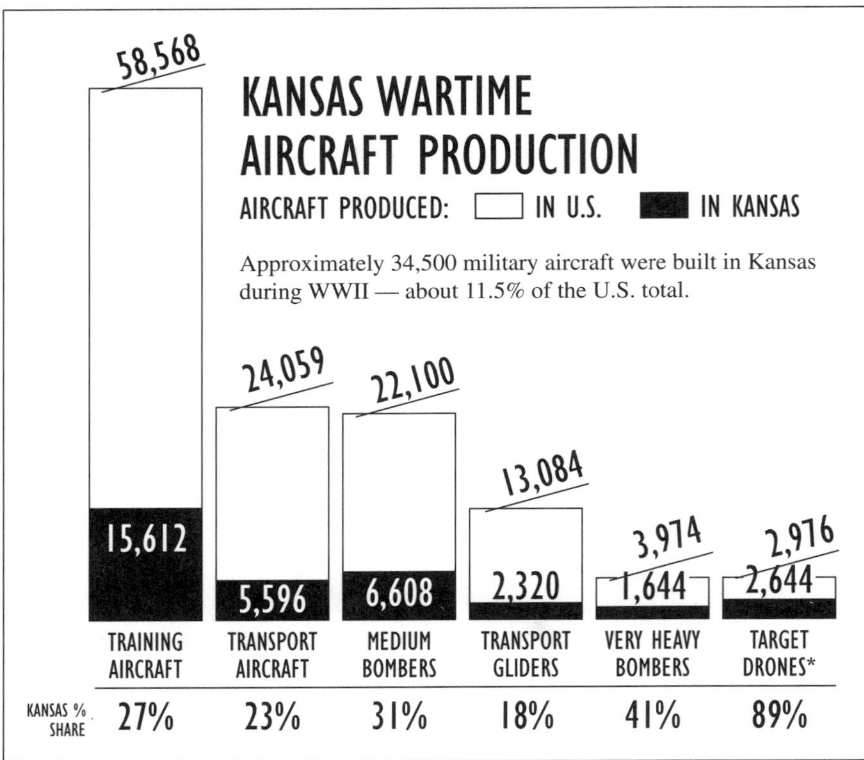

Sources: Statistical Service of Aircraft Industries Association of America; U.S. Army Air Forces Office of Statistical Control, *The Aircraft Yearbook for 1946*, Lanciar Publishers, Inc.

* Man-carrying remote control

advertised it as warehouse space. In the summer of 1947, just as a Boeing jet bomber prototype called the XB-47 was making test flights in Seattle, Plant II was offered for sale.

The cutback was, at the very least, an economic challenge. Wichita especially tried to imagine what to do with its vast capacity in facilities and the trained personnel that suddenly seemed entirely excess. Cessna had been advertising its postwar all-metal "Family Car of the Air" throughout the conflict, and with its smaller plant and work force it seemed possible that it might sustain itself in aviation. For the other plants, the picture was bleaker.

Schaefer toured Plant II with a reporter in September 1945. Sixteen Superforts in various stages of completion were shoved up near a door to be loaded on rail cars for scrap. He said he was glad the war was over but wondered not only "What of Boeing?" but "What of Wichita?" Some of the city's war housing, he said, was "little better than stylized slums," and there was no telling how much of the increased population could be retained. Yet returning to a prewar environment did not seem feasible either. For one thing, the city's infrastructure, financed by bonds dependent on a future tax base, was now geared for a metropolitan area of 200,000, not the 100,000 of the late 1930s. For another, the war workers who had moved there wanted to stay, and many of the women who had jobs during the war did not want to give them up.

In effect, Wichita and Kansas faced again the kind of severe business cycle that had been dealt with successfully after the 1920s boom turned to Depression. As was the case then, the external support evaporated. The region was left with its own people and resources, and with the aviation opportunities that its former momentum and success might give it. "Before there are wings for war," went an ad congratulating Boeing, "there are forces at work to make them. Excellence of American design has been proved; the skill of American craftsmen has been demonstrated; the genius of American organization recognized by the world. In modern war, we are combining these basic elements of superiority, an outstanding example being in the production of machines and materiel for aerial combat." A record of having built nearly 44 percent of the primary type trainers (13 other plants nationwide combined were turning out the remaining 56 percent and nearly half of the B-29 bombers used in World War II justified a little hyperbole. But it was not rhetoric that would sustain the Kansas aviation payroll or keep much of wartime Wichita from becoming as abandoned, ghostly, and nostalgic as western Kansas' Army airfields.

157

THE WORLD CALLS

"DIVORCED FROM MY AIRPLANE I AM AN ORDINARY MAN, AND A USELESS ONE — A TRAINER WITHOUT A HORSE, A SCULPTOR WITHOUT MARBLE, A PRIEST WITHOUT A GOD. WITHOUT AN AIRPLANE I AM A LONELY CONSUMER OF HAMBURGERS, THE FELLOW IN LINE AT A CASH REGISTER, SHOPPING CART LADEN WITH ORANGES AND CEREAL AND QUARTS OF MILK. A BROWN-HAIRED FELLOW WHO IS STRUGGLING AGAINST PITILESS ODDS TO MASTER THE GUITAR." — RICHARD BACH

The war was a watershed worldwide, particularly in technology. But it affected everything from general lifestyle expectations to business methods. The very term "prewar" implies in things mechanical something wooden or upright or vacuum-tubed or in some other way 20th-century antediluvian. And although perhaps the culture shock in the post-atom-bomb world was not quite as great as with the destruction of the Proud Tower of Edwardian class security following World War I, there are plenty of sociologists who maintain that the links from the atomic age back across the 1940s conflict were few and the generation gap ponderous.

There was great anticipation in 1946 that the truly "modern" was on the verge of arrival and that at last there would be the political stability for Americans to fully enjoy economic prosperity. The 1950s were a time of ranch homes in the suburbs, new cars with yearly model changes, "brinkmanship" and "massive retaliation" in U.S. foreign policy, rock 'n' roll, and the genuine prospect of a personal flying machine for everyman.

The dream of personal flight and of the sort of demigod status it was imagined would result had existed for many years. An old woman had once gone up to Lindbergh and asked him how much he would charge to fly her to heaven and leave her there. But the rapid developments in aircraft in World War II, combined with the large numbers of returning veterans with a knowledge of planes and flying, the expanded plant facilities and trained work forces around the country, and the federal commitment to create a national radio-navigation system, led to serious speculation that mass pro-

LIFT-OFF

⇐ In order to compensate for the high wing loading and slow rate of acceleration of early B-47s, eighteen rockets were used to fling the aircraft into the air. Located in the sides of the aft fuselage, each rocket produced approximately 1,000 pounds of thrust. In combination with the plane's six engines, 42,000 pounds of thrust could be generated on takeoff.

Bob Pickett Collection, Kansas Aviation Museum/Boeing Aircraft Company duction and sales were about to come to the aircraft business.

Among the things that sustained hope and interest during the long war were regular articles with titles like "Flying in the Future" (1938) and "Will You Fly Your Own Plane After the War?" (1945). The popular press imagined that not only would nearly everyone fly a safe, easy-to-control personal airplane after the war, but that this development would change society for the better. Louise Thaden said that sex discrimination would be impossible in the air. Science magazines showed "flying flivvers" in peoples' garages and helicopters atop their modern ranch homes. A 1951 *Popular Mechanics* article claimed that the airplane would "create the countryside" as the auto had created the suburb. Workers would at day's end be "rising like homing birds" to fly to cool mountain retreats, and the average family could expect to take extensive vacations every weekend. Fred Weick's Ercoupe was promoted as a two-seat, all-metal plane that was "foolproof," and there were Autogyros that were supposed to land in a backyard and be rearranged in minutes to drive the highways as a car. The new planes would use auto engines and cost little more than a Plymouth.

In 1945 the *Saturday Evening Post* took a survey. It showed that 32 percent of the U.S. population wanted to own a plane after the war, and 7 percent actively planned to buy one. That would represent 3 million definite purchases and a potential for sales of 15 million craft. A government estimate, which was said to be ultraconservative, was that 400,000 airplanes could be sold immediately after the war. One in three car dealers expected they would be selling airplanes by the late 1940s. In 1946 Americans actually bought 33,254 airplanes, five times more than in any previous year. *Flying* magazine in December 1946 listed forty-six aircraft models, built by thirty-four companies. In 1945 Macy's in New York added the Ercoupe to its inventory. Elevator operators stopping on the fifth floor would announce: "Ladies' girdles, gentlemen's socks, airplanes, and household appliances."

Kansas participated in the hype — particularly Cessna. The Airmaster had been a first step, because it emphasized utility, and Cessna controlled a number of Longren patents for mass producing an all-metal single-engine craft. Cessna mounted a major public relations campaign beginning in the fall of 1941, when Wallace announced the company's "family car of the air" plan for maintaining production after the war through a straight-line plant operation similar to auto assembly. Wallace told Fulton Lewis, Jr. on a radio program in 1942 that "if war were to end tomorrow, we would put this plane on the market just as quickly as an automobile manufacturer could 'tool up' his factory for a new yearly model." Airplanes would relieve congestion on the highways. Cessna participated in 1943 in the organization of a Personal Plane Manufacturers Association to promote the national infrastructure that expansion of flying would require. It suggested a "skyway" plan using marking pylons developed by an employee. It placed full-page ads in *Colliers, Saturday Evening Post,* and *Country Gentlemen*, as well as trade journals, showing farmers and professors flying airplanes. The captions were compelling. "Things are looking up in Wichita for young folks nowadays." "Texas won't be much bigger than Rhode Island ... when you're driving a Cessna car of the air."

Certainly the Cessna 120/140 and the Beechcraft Bonanza, to name just two of the postwar Kansas classics that emerged to create as well as exploit this supposed market, were remarkable in price and performance, in safety and style. However, the boom was neither spectacular nor long-lasting. From a high in 1946, the market dropped by half in 1947 and by another half the year after that. By 1950, serious talk about mass flying had ended.

Although the expected miracle was a flop, another kind of miracle did occur. The Kansas aircraft industry, which had survived the Depression and met the expansion challenges of the war, not only adjusted to the postwar return to private selling but began marketing its new products worldwide in unprecedented volume. Only by comparison with the fevered dreams of the flying flivver were small-plane sales a failure; compared with anything general aviation had ever done before, it was revolutionary. The names Beech, Cessna and Boeing — long familiar among the limited flying fraternity, airshow patrons, and readers of war news — became familiar to businesspeople, airline patrons, and military watchers worldwide during the 1950s. A distant stranger's knowledge of Wichita history might have included gunfighters and cattle drovers; but the mention of the city after the 1950s would almost surely and nearly anywhere bring to mind some connection with aircraft.

That it would be so was anything but obvious as World War II ended. The fate of the four Wichita aircraft manufacturing companies (Beech, Boeing, Cessna and Culver) and the city's 100 aviation subcontractors was highly uncertain. A 1944 survey of the 55,000 workers then employed in the aircraft plants of Wichita revealed that 34 percent of them would either leave town or would not work after the war. Two-thirds, however, wanted to stay and work in Wichita after the war ended, though only half the men and a quarter of the women imagined that their occupation would be shop work, much less aviation manufacturing. The Chamber of Commerce predicted a substantial expansion in other types of businesses that could use this skilled labor pool and absorb the 60 percent wartime increase in Wichita's population.

The initial response of the aircraft plants to what they considered a position of overexpansion in employees and physical space was to seek other products that could be manufactured by aircraft workers and marketed by the companies. As Jack Gaty of Beech put it, the companies had a history of being able to adjust to change, had new aircraft in the works, enjoyed a fine reputation for quality products, had adequate finances, and had built a remarkably efficient organization during the war. "All Beechcrafters should remember," Gaty told employees, "that there is no simple and easy method of navigation through such a period of reconversion and that our course is being affected by many factors beyond our control and that navigation must be pursued by dead reckoning and from point to point like that of an airplane flying around local thunderstorms along its course."

During the war, the company had built a volume that would have taken more than 300 years to construct and deliver at the rate of production existing in 1940. So it made sense that confidence existed to handle other challenges. One promising trend was international marketing. The first Beech deliveries overseas took place in 1946 when airplanes were flown to Cairo, Egypt, by way of South America for use by the Egyptian airline. Cessna also opened overseas markets. This was symbolic of the belief that "the world is our market." Gaty summarized by saying that "if we fail to make a howling success out of the year 1946 it can only be because our organization has deteriorated. Our review of the past indicates no reason to suspect such deterioration. It is believed that all of us can be confident that the same people, all of us, who created our past reputation can uphold and even improve it in the future."

At the end of the war, Beech had only one seriously marketable airplane, the Model 18 twin. Although the company had upgraded it (as the D18S), and claimed it was "strictly modern," the design was from 1936, and there were shortages in the engines that powered it. The Staggerwing, brought to its ultimate form in the Model G17S, was considered too expensive ($29,000), and its parts and subassemblies did not lend themselves to mass production. Parts and assemblies for twenty new Staggerwings were completed in 1946, but the postwar production line in this model never got started. "Ordinary business judgment and prudence dictated that the management of your company should act with the utmost energy to develop new models of aircraft," went the Annual Report for 1946. However, this prototype development and testing, which in light of the complete suppression of civilian design imposed by the government on defense contractors during the war, had to be from scratch, meant, in the absence of other interim products, that the stockholders would sustain heavy losses as research and development expenses mounted without compensating airplane sales.

Beech therefore proposed at the close of the war several new non-aviation products, which could be stopgaps if the new airplanes succeeded or could change the direction of the company fundamentally if they did not.

Bob Pickett Collection, Kansas Aviation Museum/ Cessna Aircraft Company

WAVES OF WINGS

⇐ Anticipating a tremendous boom in postwar private flying, manufacturers geared up to respond to the lucrative market. Cessna sought to capture its piece of the market with its popular 140. In 1946, builders shipped about 35,000 planes. Piper and Aeronca were the industry leaders, each with shipments of about 7,500 craft. Cessna held third place with 3,559 planes delivered. By the next year, deliveries had dipped to 15,594 airplanes, and the slump of 1948 was nearly at hand.

One successful stopgap was a Beech subsidiary known as Material Distributors Incorporated. MDI bought and sold surplus materials and obtained scarce materials for itself, the government, and other manufacturers. It liquidated millions of dollars worth of government-owned surpluses and allowed the buyers of these to re-enter the civilian market more quickly. That business, however, was very short-lived. MDI made a net profit of $153,032.68 in 1946 while the parent company lost over $1 million. However, MDI disappeared in 1947 because of the complete liquidation of government stores.

More promising for the long run was the sale of engineering skill through the marketing of parts such as the Beechcraft controllable propeller and domestic and overseas spare-parts sales, as well as acting as a subcontractor in order to hold the Beech production team together. A division was established to solicit orders, and items actually produced included vending machines, components for home refrigerators and dishwashers, pie pans, and fuel tanks for other aircraft. In 1949, a $1 million contract was signed for the complete manufacture of several thousand Great American Farm corn pickers, built for a manufacturer in Chicago. "Thus," wrote the company magazine, "Wichita, long known as the 'Air Capital of the United States,' receives national recognition for its industrial manufacturing abilities, and this new 'industry within an industry' is striking proof of the wide versatility of an aircraft manufacturer that is known the world over for its aircraft."

Bob Pickett Collection, Kansas Aviation Museum/Beech Aircraft Corporation

BEECH 4WD

⇑ Although postwar orders for Bonanzas demanded Beech's full manufacturing capabilities, in 1946 the company thought the Plainsman automobile might be a way of expanding and diversifying its product line. Providing ample room for six, the 2,200-pound four-door sedan offered an array of features while utilizing a unique four-wheel-drive system.

Perhaps the most interesting projects were those built not at all, or only in prototype form. Company engineers completed a design study in 1946 for an automobile called the Plainsman, which was to be built at the Beech factory. Among its unusual features were four-wheel electric drive, which eliminated transmission, clutch, drive shaft, differential and rear axle; an air-cooled, horizontally opposed aircraft-type engine coupled to the electric drive generator; air spring suspension; aluminum body and frame; a telephone as standard equipment; and crash protection by rubber and leather pads. A full-scale mockup was built, and although the advertising said it had "sleek, clean lines," it resembled the contemporary Hudson or the Tucker in its late art deco ugliness. It also was high-priced. The target had been $4,000 to $5,000 initially, but in 1948 it was estimated it would cost at least twice that if produced, making it one of the world's most expensive cars. Although the motoring press thought there might be a niche among "those with enough money to gratify even expensive whims" for the kind of advanced road vehicle that could be built by aviation technicians not overly concerned with cost or mass sales, Beech abandoned the Plainsman as its aircraft business improved.

A second and more famous dream project was Buckminster Fuller's Dymaxion "Dwelling Machine." Fuller, one of the most innovative thinkers in the country, designed metal circular houses hung around a central pole having self-contained utility systems that could make their owners independent of climate and politics. The houses could be disassembled, packed in a shipping tube and moved by helicopter anytime the owner wished. The project was disclosed to the public late in 1944, when it was announced that a prototype house was under construction at the Beech plant in Wichita. Gaty said: "While aircraft manufacturing is unsuitable for the production of conventional prefabricated houses, we have great hopes that Fuller's dwelling machines may be the answer." He denied that Beech had committed absolutely to producing the homes but did note that the U.S. market for homes during the ten-year period following the close of the war was estimated at 1 million per year and that the largest number ever produced in a year in the past using traditional methods was 300,000. In 1946 it was said that the project was moving along favorably and that interest had been shown by several branches of the government and several private groups. It would give the company "an opportunity to render a public service as well as to provide additional jobs," but the possibilities could "be evaluated only as circumstances develop and time passes."

The most optimistic projections were for 50,000 Dymaxion Dwelling Machines. However, neither Beech nor anyone else produced them in volume. It is questionable whether the technology existed to make the home function as intended, at least in Kansas. But it remains as a fascinating example of a technological and social "might have been."

Cessna did not investigate anything as elaborate as a car or a house. However, it did manufacture furniture, hydraulics, and aluminum lockers.

HOME ON THE RANGE

⇓ The Dymaxion Dwelling Machine was designed to solve the postwar housing crisis. A one-story, hemispherical design thirty-six feet in diameter, it offered 1,017 square feet of floor space divided into a combined living and dining room, a kitchen, two bathrooms, two bedrooms, and an entrance hall. Beech anticipated selling the homes for $6,500.

The Wichita Eagle/Beech Aircraft Company

THE WEATHERED LOOK

⇒ A Cessna technician inspects furniture for wear during durability testing. After World War II, Cessna's non-aircraft-related product line included furniture, hydraulics for farm machinery, and aluminum lockers. The company's furniture sales in 1948 amounted to nearly $7 million. Chairs and stools were manufactured in Wichita; tables and bureaus were assembled in Hutchinson.

Bob Pickett Collection, Kansas Aviation Museum/Cessna Aircraft Company

BOEING BROUGHAM

⇓ Not to be left out of the postwar rush to offer product diversity, Boeing researched and designed this cab-forward automobile. Other than this rakish patent sketch, no serious attempts were made to develop this automotive curiosity.

Boeing Archives, Seattle

Furniture was the largest contributor to the bottom line, with sales of nearly $4 million in 1949. Cessna got a contract with the Army's Quartermaster Corps in 1947 to build furniture using aircraft metal fabrication techniques. Construction was mostly metal, with a fungus-resistant veneer of walnut plywood finished in such a sturdy way that the company left desks and chairs out in a parking lot all winter to test them. Cessna made bedroom bureaus, dressing tables, dining room sideboards, two types of dining tables, chairs, chiffoniers, pivot-top tables, and desks. It eventually manufactured 40,000 pieces and was for a time one of the nation's leading furniture manufacturers, in volume at least. When its military contract ran out, the company tried to market the pieces commercially through Marshall Field's in Chicago. "The furniture is definitely modernistic," an ad said, "with its square corners and wheat colored appearance." *House Beautiful* magazine spoke of the products' "Gibraltar-like" construction. However, the market in furniture apparently tended toward aesthetic rather than industrial considerations. Cessna ceased manufacturing furniture in 1951 because of low sales, materiel shortages, and reconversion to aircraft. The last of the inventory was sold at wholesale prices to employees and friends.

Boeing Wichita, it was said, had "roots imbedded firmly in the soil of Kansas" and would remain "an integral part of the industrial life" of Wichita. But, its postwar job outlook was especially discouraging. Boeing obtained a patent for a teardrop-shaped automobile — so modern that it incorporated a "cab-forward" design with the driver over the front wheels. However the company never seriously considered producing it. The Seattle management toyed too with the idea of a Boeing lightplane. The Model 200 Scout (military designations XL-15 and YL-15) was designed at Wichita in 1946, and twelve were built for the Army. The craft had a 40-foot wingspan,

Bob Pickett Collection, Kansas Aviation Museum/Boeing Aircfat Company

L-15 ⇐ Powered by a 125 HP Lycoming engine, the Boeing Scout was intended to be used as an observation platform to allow Army ground forces to spot troop movements, direct fire support, and lay communications lines. It was noteworthy for the panoramic view afforded the observer, who sat facing the rear. The L-15 had a range of 250 miles and a maximum speed of 104 MPH. Only twelve were built, and most of them were used by the U.S. Fish and Wildlife Service in Alaska.

Bob Pickett Collection, Kansas Aviation Museum/Boeing Aircraft Company

SPECIAL DELIVERY

⇑ The Boeing Model L-15 Scout aircraft could be easily dismantled and transported. Designed and built by Boeing Wichita in 1947, this versatile aircraft could be towed like a trailer or loaded into a C-97 cargo transport aircraft for rapid, long-range deployment.

HIGH TECH BICYCLE

⇓ Sporting the latest aircraft technology, these Stearman bicycles were intended to be a transition bike for preteens. A V-belt drive transmitted power to rear wheels.

The Kansas State Historical Society

was capable of a 95 MPH cruising speed with a service ceiling of 15,000 feet, and weighed 1,509 pounds empty. It had fine visibility and could fly for long periods at low speed. But the experience of McDonnell Aircraft Corporation, North American, and others successful in the military field suggested that a transition to general aviation was anything but automatic given the low overhead and fierce competition from those accustomed to it. Mostly, it appeared that the Wichita facility would be occupied in helping build airliners based on the B-29, (the Model 377 Stratocruiser was the one at hand), and would need to be satisfied with a much reduced payroll.

Small Kansas aircraft companies were in a similar situation. Glenn Stearman owned Ariel Aircraft Company of Coffeyville. Unable to sell airplanes immediately after the war, he built approximately 200 children's bicycles. Like the Beech car and the Cessna furniture, these showed considerable engineering skill and manufacturing talent. They used a magnesium casting and were driven by a V-belt instead of a chain.

The prediction by government experts was that the aircraft industry nationally would be reduced in 1946 to 4 percent of its wartime peak employment. Beech, therefore, was glad to retain an average of 40 percent of its peak wartime employees, with other Kansas companies boasting a similar record. A proposed Beech-Cessna merger in 1945 did not go through, and both companies grew independently. When the government proposed in the early 1950s that Wichita be designated a "critical area" to receive special economic help, its aircraft manufacturers strenuously rejected the designation and worked ceaselessly not to merit it. "Wichita always has solved its own problems with a minimum of outside help," went the business response. "It established quite a reputation in that respect during the war. The city certainly doesn't want to lose that reputation now just because a few citizens have gotten excited. If this is declared a critical area, it will mean government controls. That is something this area always has opposed. It will mean no more military contracts either for Wichita or Kansas."

By 1954, the city would employ 45,000 in aircraft manufacturing and 20,500 in manufacturing parts. Boeing Wichita would be back to its wartime peak of 30,000 employees, and more than $1 billion worth of aircraft would be produced in the state. In 1958, when the U.S. private aviation fleet of 66,000 exceeded the number of planes in the U.S. and Soviet air forces combined, there were articles paralleling those in the 1920s calling Wichita "The Detroit of the Small-Plane Age." Photo spreads in major magazines showed swept-wing jet bombers lined up on the apron at Boeing Wichita for delivery to Strategic Air Command bases all over the world.

What had happened between the "critical" period of corn-pickers and

A SMALL CITY

⇓ The Wichita division of Boeing developed into the largest manufacturing facility in Kansas. This 1955 aerial photo shows the 447 acres where about 30,000 people worked.

Boeing Aircraft Company

dining room tables and the era of Kansas world aviation leadership was a tale of entrepreneurship and invention as impressive as the one that brought the state through the Depression to its peak as a defense center during the war.

As in the 1930s, it began with a series of classics.

The Cessna 120 was a two-place, fabric-covered, aluminum-structured, high-wing monoplane that, at a 1946 sales price of $2,695, came as close to being the family car of the air as anything built. Its 85 HP, four-cylinder engine would propel it at a steady 100 MPH with auto-like economy, and its construction of 24ST, a hard aluminum alloy, promised hard service with less maintenance. The Model 140 was a more expensive version of the same concept. These airplanes had a simple but sturdy wide, one-piece, vanadium-steel leaf-spring landing gear. They could handle descent-rate misestimates by beginning pilots, and absorb shock without the complication and expense of the many moving parts in a traditional landing gear. Their broad stance avoided many ground loops (when the tail came around on landing) — the bane of tail-dragger pilots. In the spring of 1946, nationally syndicated cartoon artist Zack Mosley put hero Smilin' Jack in a Cessna 140 named *Miss Wichita Winnie*. A more tangible measure of popularity was in sales. Rival Luscombe Airplane Corporation of Trenton, N.J., was unable to compete with the 140, and the company went bankrupt in 1949.

"It is our objective," wrote a columnist in the company magazine, "to provide excellent and safe planes with a maximum of utility and do this at the lowest price possible. ... We are selling America on the importance of using more airplanes, and we are very much stronger in this market than most of our competitors." In December 1946, Cessna built nearly as many small planes as all its competitors put together, the beginning of a long period as the world's highest-volume aircraft producer. It had by that time established a fine series of distributorships and outlets in Canada, Mexico, Brazil, Venezuela, Argentina, Belgium, Sweden, and South Africa. Production of 120s and 140s was about thirty airplanes a day. Dealers were invited to come to the factory, listen to an inspiring speech by Wallace, and then fly away in new Cessnas. They did so with enthusiasm, and in great numbers.

Cessna completed its line with the luxury 190 and 195, which were powered by an old-style radial engine and looked like a large, updated Airmaster, and the 170, a four-place plane with a horizontally-opposed six-cylinder engine and a service ceiling of over 15,000 feet. The 190 and 195 were introduced in 1947 and the 170 in 1948. The 170 started at $5,475, but by the peak year of its production, 1952, when 1,108 were made, it cost more than $7,000. In 1956 came the 172 Skyhawk, which replaced the tail-dragger configuration of the 170 with a tricycle landing gear — a design that made it easier for most beginning pilots to steer a plane on the ground. In

Bob Pickett Collection, Kansas Aviation Museum/Cessna

1953 came the Model 180 and its companion, the 182 Skylane, which offered higher performance at a higher price (nearly $13,000). The 180 advertised "living room comfort," and the 182's tricycle gear was dubbed "Land-O-Matic — the patented feature that revolutionizes flying." In 1960 the Model 210 Centurion was introduced. It would eventually be offered in turbocharged and pressurized models capable of extremely high performance. In the luxury field, Cessna marketed, beginning in 1954, its 310 twin, a sleek, all metal-ship that made the old T-50 Bobcat seem primitive. A 310 was the real star of the early television program "Sky King," in which Grant Kirby used his *Songbird* to catch the bad guys.

The Cessna philosophy was to offer good performance-to-price ratio in ultrasafe, reliable, no-nonsense utility aircraft. As was typical of auto marketing, Cessna's full line provided various steps for people who wanted more performance or convenience without having to spend too much extra or move into something unfamiliar.

The Beech postwar general aviation classic was the V-tail Bonanza, an airplane substantially different in philosophy and execution than any Cessna. Introduced in 1947, the Model 35 had a variable-pitch propeller, a cantilever low wing, a range of 750 miles, fully-retractable tricycle landing gear, and a host of features that exuded quality — all of which came at a price, both in money and handling ease. The tail was absolutely distinctive at any airport,

PICTURE OF PROSPERITY

⇑ Benefiting from the competitive rivalry between Cessna and Luscombe for the postwar two-place trainer market, the Cessna Model 140A emerged as a sales leader. Its most noteworthy feature was a spring steel landing gear developed by Steve Wittman, the famous racing pilot. Produced from 1949 to 1951, the 140A cost between $3,495 and $3,695. The 140's tapered all-metal wing would become a Cessna hallmark.

Bob Pickett Collection, Kansas Aviation Museum/Beech

V-TAIL

⇑ First flown December 22, 1945, the Beech Model 35 Bonanza would become one of the most easily recognized personal aircraft ever built. The four-place, all-metal monoplane combined a degree of comfort usually associated with expensive automobiles with 180 MPH performance. The V-tail concept, successfully developed during the 1930s by Polish aeronautical designer M. Georges Rudlicki, effectively combined the rudder and elevators. Shown is a 1950 Model B-35, which sold for $11,975.

and the Bonanza anticipated in many ways the appeal of the Japanese luxury car of the 1990s by offering style, extensive standard equipment, and a fit and finish level far above competing aircraft in its price range. At an initial price of just over $7,000, it had full IFR navigation equipment, all-metal construction, large mufflers, a smooth six-cylinder engine that produced full-cruising power at only 2,050 RPM, a built-in cabin loudspeaker, a luggage compartment that loaded waist-high and held 120 pounds, a Beech-designed ventilation system, individual ash trays and sun shades, full carpeting, and all-wool upholstery.

When a businessman got out of his luxury car, he did not have to suffer the indignity of traveling in an expensive airplane that seemed tacky by comparison. A Bonanza was a personal device, a little difficult to fly in turbulence or if one was unskilled. But with a cruising speed of 175 MPH, it was unparalleled among small singles in performance. It cost one-third as much as the ultimate postwar Staggerwing and the claim was that, although it was expensive at the outset, it was designed to last 2 million miles without unusual maintenance.

As though to highlight the durability claim, in 1949 Bill Odom flew one, euphonically named *Waikiki Beech,* non-stop from Honolulu to Teterboro, N.J. — 5,273 miles — with complete reliability and at a total fuel cost of $75. It was an all-time aviation record set by a true production airplane, and it made the Bonanza instantly famous. "When they say 'Where is the postwar airplane?'" Odom quipped after his flight, "I'll point to the *Waikiki Beech* and say, 'There it is.'"

As with the Cessna 170, the basic Bonanza was a long-lasting, flexible, and hugely successful design. By 1955 it cost $24,300, had a fuel-injected engine and cruised at 190 MPH with a top speed of 210 MPH. V-tail Bonanzas were built into the 1980s. The basic airframe, with a more traditional tail (occasioned by questions about the lighter structure's stability in dives) was being built in the 1990s, with 300 HP piston-engine, twin-engine, and turboprop variations. It holds the record for length of continuous production of an aircraft model.

Hangar fliers all over the world have had years of entertainment debating the respective merits of the Beech and Cessna postwar philosophies, centering more than anything else on the virtues of high-wing vs. low-wing design. The truth is that both worked and found loyal customers. Beech and Cessna together sold nearly $20 million worth of general aviation airplanes in 1947, and Cessna was one of two aircraft companies in the country (Stinson was the other) to show a profit that year. A total of 1,209 Bonanzas went out the door in 1947, and Wichita as a whole delivered 3,599 completed airplanes, more than any other city in the United States.

The companies got more publicity than their chief executive officers. Dwane Wallace, partly because of his own shyness and the company's name, lived somewhat in the shadow of his uncle, Clyde Cessna, even though it was Wallace who was at the helm during the manufacture of most of the models and examples that made Cessna the best-selling aircraft in the world. Olive Ann Beech, who took the reins following the death of her husband in 1950, though well-recognized from the start as a rare example of a female executive in the aircraft field, was less well-known for the inside details of the industrial miracles she wrought while raising two daughters. She feared pub-

Wichita State University, Special Collections, Ablah Libary

OLIVE ANN BEECH

⇑ Born September 25, 1903, Olive Ann Mellor grew up in Waverly, Kans. In 1924, she became Travel Air's twelfth employee. She rose from bookkeeper to office manager before becoming secretary to Walter Beech, whom she would marry on February 24, 1930. In 1940, Walter was struck by illness and hospitalized for nearly a year, and Olive Ann guided the company through its wartime expansion.

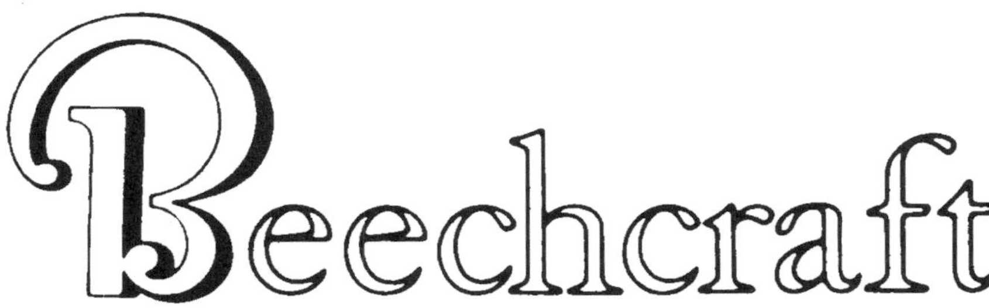

Bob Pickett Collection, Kansas Aviation Museum

VINTAGE TRANSPORTATION

⇑ Introduced in September 1945, the stubby Culver Model V (for victory) generated plenty of curiosity but few sales. Designed for the amateur pilot, the Model V's most notable feature was the Simpli-Fly flight-control system, which was designed to make flying less demanding. About 400 Victory models were built. The upturned elliptical wingtips provided the Model V with added stability and contributed to a unique silhouette. The price was $3,589.

lic speaking and cameras, and once told a reporter that her official and brief company biography contained all she was ever likely to reveal about her role in the company. Wallace and Beech were oriented toward the future, often the near future. Their task and exclusive focus was keeping the plants, which had taken so much exertion and risk to build, running.

While Cessna and Beech dominated the general aviation field among Kansas companies, they were not alone in the state after the war. There was, for example, the Mooney Mite M-18-L, built by Al and Art Mooney in Wichita from 1947 until the company moved to Kerrville, Texas, in 1953. Mooney was formed by former employees and executives of the defunct Culver (Al Mooney had designed the Culver Cadet) and tried to carry on that company's low-price philosophy. The Mite was a true everyman's sport plane, with power from a 25 HP Crosley automobile engine that made it, it was claimed, the lowest cost transportation for one person by any means then known. It sold initially for less than $2,000, and to save weight and cost did without an electrical system and used a Simpli-Fly hand-cranked mechanism to control flaps and trim simultaneously. Like other manufacturers, however, Mooney found there was little market for minimal aviation, and as the company moved its craft upscale it ran into formidable competition. Mooney made about 290 Mites in Wichita. The Mooney from Kerrville remains a popular airplane in the 1990s, but its high performance and high cost are quite a contrast to its origins.

Another Kansas experiment in lightplanes was the Helio Courier, which was first manufactured in Pittsburg, although it had its corporate headquarters on the East Coast. Its prominent feature was a very short landing and take-off requirement — less than 75 yards — occasioned by an ability to fly fully controlled as slow as 30 MPH. It was thought this would be useful for executives landing at plant sites, government border patrols, and agricultural inspections. The company was founded in 1948 by Dr. Lynn Bollinger of the Harvard Graduate School of Business Administration and Professor Otto Koppen of the Massachusetts Institute of Technology, and the first four-seat prototype flew in 1949. Regular production began in 1955, and recalled for some the dreams occasioned by the Call airship of 1908 in nearby Girard. The Helioplane was sometimes referred to as a "tennis court" airplane because of its ability to use small fields, and with the moniker "litter bug," it did significant duty on CIA secret missions during the Vietnam War. Helios were manufactured at Pittsburg, with some interruptions, into the 1980s.

Smaller firms abounded. Fairchild Aircraft, headquartered in Hagerstown, Md., established a personal plane division in 1947 with a factory at the former Army base at Strother Field near Winfield and advertised a four-place personal airplane using its experience in building primary trainers during the war. Production never got under way, but it was significant that

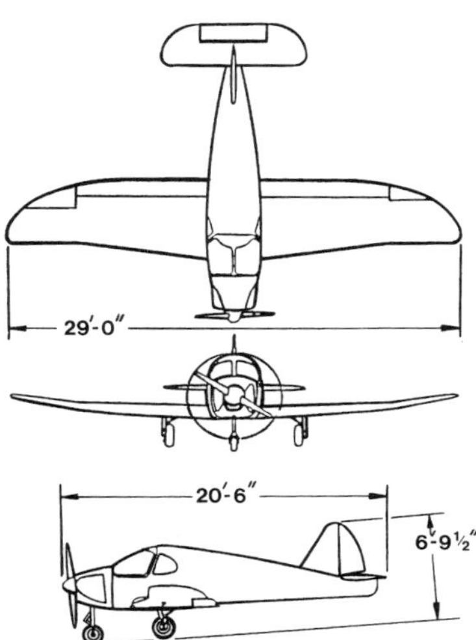

CULVER MODEL V

⇑ Powered by an 85 HP continental C-85-12J engine and claiming an empty weight of 1,033 pounds, the Model V could achieve 135 MPH with a range of 625 miles. The price was $3,589. Designer Al Mooney would go on to design the Mooney Mite.

(This page) Bob Pickett Collection, Kansas Aviation Musuem

MOONEY MITE

⇐ With part-time labor and low manufacturing overhead, the Mooney Mite was an attempt to provide a low-cost, one-place personal sport airplane for the masses. Formed by C.G. Yankey and Al W. Mooney, the Mooney Aircraft Company of Wichita introduced the Model M-18 in 1948.

TENNIS COURT SPECIAL

⇒ The Helio Courier, America's first STOL (short take-off and landing) aircraft, may not have landed on many tennis courts, but it could land in a distance equal to three lengths of the airplane. More than 500 Helio aircraft were manufactured from 1955 to 1984 by Mid-States Manufacturing Company of Pittsburg. Shown is an early Helio Courier, typically powered by a 260 HP Lycoming GO-435-C2B2 engine and costing about $30,000.

Experimental Aircraft Association/Jim Koepnick

BOARDROOM BOMBER

⇒ A few businesses emerged after the war solely dedicated to turning surplus military aircraft into executive transports. Among them was Rock Island Aircraft of Hutchinson. Operating between 1958 and 1963, the company produced the Monarch 26, a conversion of the Douglas A-26 Invader. The 400 MPH plane featured picture windows, a galley, a lavatory, and six sleeper chairs. The planes sold for as much as $250,000.

Bob Pickett Collection, Kansas Aviation Museum

again Kansas was the site selected. Rawdon Brothers Aircraft in Wichita produced an aerial spray plane in 1950, which was marketed internationally by Beech. Kansas led the nation in the number of farms taking advantage of aerial spraying, so the regional market was considerable. The aircraft division of Rock Island Oil & Refining Company was backed by Wichita's Koch family and located at the Municipal Airport in Hutchinson. Rock Island's specialty was turning military surplus Douglas A-26 Invader piston-engined bombers into executive aircraft. Its product, the Monarch 26, had a range of 2,000 miles. Although its operating costs were formidable, it filled a niche. The basic conversion, which was picked up by several other companies around the country, sold well between 1958 and 1963 and, together with a number of other high-powered, war-surplus conversions, established the market for the corporate jets that were to come.

Kansas' "whatchimacallit" spirit was still healthy, as was demonstrated by the career of the Seibel helicopter. Charles M. Seibel of Wichita designed and built a helicopter of radically different and simpler design in 1947 — a model that he thought could be sold for between $5,000 and $10,000 (figures as low as $3,000 were mentioned), rather than the $25,000 or more that helicopters of the time typically cost. He also thought it could be flown without extensive special training. Lateral and longitudinal control were obtained by moving the center of gravity during flight through the shifting of the forward portion of the fuselage where the pilot sat, thus avoiding the usual complicated pitch changes in the rotor mechanism. The helicopter had a patented, simplified clutch to vary the pitch of the rotor blade, and automobile parts were used extensively to save money. The first flight, with Seibel as the pilot, was also the first time the designer had ever flown an aircraft of any kind, demonstrating its simplicity.

Seibel, compared in the press to Henry Ford, was not a rude mechanic. After graduating from Wichita East High School in 1938, he had been awarded bachelor's and master's degrees at the California Institute of Technology and worked five years as a helicopter engineer with Bell Aircraft Corporation. He held a job as aerodynamicist with Boeing Wichita, but the helicopter was a project done solely on his own time and with backing from friends and associates. For a 27-year-old, it was a startling innovation. In 1948, Wichita backers formed a $150,000 corporation to build the copter, and Seibel quit his job at Boeing to devote full time to it. In 1950, the Seibel S-4A flew before 2,000 spectators, including the governor of Kansas. With a helicopter-design history dating to the Goodland experiments of 1909, it now seemed Kansas had a keeper in the air.

FILLING A NICHE

⇓ Originally constructed in Akron, Ohio, in 1939, the Funk monoplane was built in three models until the Slump of 1948, when the market was saturated and the government slashed flight training under the GI Bill. Initially equipped with a highly modified Ford four-cylinder engine, later models would use engines from Continental and Lycoming. Joe and Howard Funk moved back to their hometown of Coffeyville in 1941 and set up production facilities in South Coffeyville, Okla. Approximately 230 Funks were built after the relocation.

Walt House Collection

In 1952, Cessna purchased the company, renamed the craft the CH-1, and hired Seibel to head a helicopter division. In 1955, the CH-1 set a helicopter speed record of 122 MPH at sea level and achieved a hovering ceiling of 15,000 feet. It got national publicity by landing on top of Pike's Peak that summer and was approved by the FAA for IFR weather. *Air Facts* magazine predicted that the helicopter might compete with the Cessna 180: "It is possible that zero speed will also start moving like hot cakes, too, when the mechanical arthritis which plagues the machine is cured." The CH-1B set a world altitude record of over 30,000 feet in 1957. Deliveries of the Cessna Skyhook helicopter began in 1961 at a price of $79,960 (a far cry from early predictions), but production was terminated in 1963 because of declining sales and a worrisome series of test accidents. Only twenty-nine CH-1C production models were made.

The trend in general aviation was clear. Aircraft that had once been for daredevils and rich men — the aerial equivalent of the wooden sailboat — were expensive appliances in the postwar world, in daily use by oil men, doctors, and ranchers, if not casual vacationers. The personal or general aviation airplane in which Wichita specialized represented only 18 percent of total airplane production in 1949, but it was a substantial market and represented the most significant marketing and training challenge in the field. "I believe in today's airplane," wrote Wallace in 1950. "We have an outstanding forward step in transportation, and what we need to do most is simply demonstrate in the safest and most effective manner how valuable this new tool is for those who travel and to demonstrate this in such a way that efficiently run companies cannot overlook the airplane as a money-making tool in this business." Business executives began to see fine color ads in *National Geographic* for the Bonanza and could ponder the slogan: "The world is small when you fly a Beechcraft."

The next step was airports, avionics, and simplified flying procedures for greater safety and convenience. Blanche Noyes, a former air racer who was director of air marketing for the Civil Aeronautics Authority, stopped in Kansas on a flying survey in 1946 to suggest that the state needed an aviation commission and a mission to improve air navigation within its borders. She complained that hangar space at Topeka's Phil Billard Airport had always been inadequate and that modern pilots like her did not like to leave their planes staked out, exposed to the weather where people could climb on them. "Unless ports like this get more hangars and give better service, pilots will start going into the larger cities such as Kansas City."

The opinion of women mattered. Nadine Ramsey, daughter of the owner of Wichita's Lassen Hotel, had just picked up a shopping bargain in the form of a war surplus P-38 Lightning fighter. She bought the plane for $1,250 in Kingman, Ariz., from the War Assets Corporation and was

The Kansas State Historical Society

POOR MAN'S HELICOPTER

⇑ Using a truck differential, an automotive clutch, and other odds and ends, Charles M. Seibel produced the S-3 helicopter in his cellar. Powered by a 65 HP air-cooled Franklin engine, the craft's maximum speed was 90 MPH.

observed flying the plane away at something close to 400 MPH. Women were part of the Kansas Flying Farmers' Club, which toured the state that year. In 1951 the Kansas chapter of the Ninety-Niners, an all-female flier's group, received its charter. Women were moving into the cockpit and the boardrooms, and were not willing to accept the rough and ready, dare-the-elements-in-a-white-scarf, taxi-in-the-mud model of what air transportation should be.

Across the state came news of new airports, the kind of news that had last made local headlines during the 1920s. In 1946 a man in Salina created something called Sky Village in a wheat field west of town. Zula Bennington Greene, a *Topeka Capital* columnist whose by-line was Peggy of the Flint Hills, described it as "as fresh and engaging as a new day" for the modern air tourist. It was only 80 years earlier, she noted, that the Butterfield stagecoaches had rumbled over the site where people now could get meals, a room, service for their airplanes, and flying lessons all without grabbing a ride to town. Odd-looking but effective VHF radio towers sprouted. Private flying services appeared in most Kansas towns, and the Wichita Rent-a-Plane company, with its Bonanza rentals, and the Aero Flying Services U-Fly-It system struggled with the insurance companies to try to make aircraft more immediately available.

Federal aid to airports through the Federal Airport Development Act was immense, though not quite up to the national defense subsidy that went to the interstate highway system during the 1950s. Topeka created a second airport, Huntoon, in 1946. There was new airport construction that year in the Kansas towns of Phillipsburg, Syracuse, Lyons, Hugoton, Smith Center, Dodge City, Oberlin, Pratt, Oswego, Independence, Great Bend, Burdett, Bucklin, Elkhart, and Stafford — many of these very small towns — to welcome small planes. In 1947, the CAA announced that $1.3 million in federal airport money would be distributed for thirty-five airport projects throughout the state. Winfield and Arkansas City in 1947 dedicated Strother Field, midway between the towns, before a crowd of 10,000. Governor Frank Carlson said on that occasion that "with the many natural advantages we have, Kansas should become the hub of the national and international air transportation system. We have a strategic location, ideal climatic conditions, and a terrain which permits construction of all types of airports at the least possible cost. With all these advantages plus the large airplane industry and the rapid development of an adequate system of airports the future of Kansas aviation seems assured."

It seemed for a time this might occur. Federal money continued to be available, and towns repeated their 19th century habit of pushing to get on a transportation line as a means to survival and prosperity. There were 158 airport sites slated for improvement in 1949, and there was a serious political bid to be the location for the Air Force Academy, rumored to be budgeted at $175 million. However, one airport project of that year, the upgrading of Fairfax in Kansas City for the use of Trans World Airlines, reflected the concentration of air traffic at relatively few major cities catering to commercial rather than general aviation craft. The two Kansas Cities agreed to joint operation of Fairfax, which was in Kansas, and the metropolitan area took great pride in TWA's overhaul base, where airliners headed for destinations all over the world after being repaired and serviced. The TWA stock department had 90,000 parts. There was nearly 400,000 square feet of hangar space, where 800 Kansas City workers took responsibility for 122 TWA transports flying 32,000 miles of routes. Just as the existence of Boeing Plant II in Wichita was to give the Air Capital the upper hand in attracting military contracts, the facilities at Fairfax, constructed to build B-25s during the war, gave that site clear momentum .

The commercial hub system was in an embryonic stage, but development was as steady as the move toward upscale private craft and away from the Mooney Mites of the world. It was not necessarily inevitable, but it did seem to reflect the market as tested. Still, the enormous improvements at hundreds of local airports, combined with the national radio navigation system, made the small personal airplane a useful instrument for those who

Bob Pickett Collection, Kansas Aviation Museum/Boeing Aircraft Company

could afford it. And that kept Kansas manufacturers busy, no matter how much they may have wished to cash in on airline business as well.

In addition to general and commercial aviation, however, there was another major and highly lucrative sector of the flying business to consider — the military. In the 1950s, Boeing Wichita, with a running start from its B-29 work during the war, would play a major role.

The key to Boeing's military contracting success after the war was the B-47 Stratojet bomber. The design number at Boeing was Model 450, and the craft was filled with new ideas. The most visible were wings swept back at a 35 degree angle and engines suspended in pods under them — an appearance that has become so universally familiar in its civilian descendants that it is hard to remember that such elements were once brand-new and controversial features. The first prototypes were ugly, and the lovely final design, with its fighter-like bubble cockpit and natural aluminum finish, was so underpowered, and acceleration was so lacking, that it had to use a dramatic but cumbersome rocket assist on takeoff. But in time it became a classic.

STRATOJET

⇑ Distinguished by an extended nose, the Boeing RB-47E was the reconnaissance version of the Air Force bomber. Roughly one out of every three B-47Es built in Wichita was an RB-47E. Powered by six General Electric J47 engines, producing 7,200 pounds of thrust each, the aircraft could achieve a maximum speed of more than 600 MPH and achieve a service ceiling of 40,000 feet. In all, Boeing produced 1,390 B-47 variants.

The XB-47 first flew in 1947, and in July 1948 the decision was made that production of it should center in Wichita despite Boeing President William Allen's low opinion of Kansas' scenery and climate. One argument was that Russian bombers could reach Seattle more easily than Kansas. It was a $3 million airplane, the most expensive Boeing had ever built, and the designers were grateful that the transistor had been invented in time for use in the complex avionics and other electronic systems. The first models used 1,000 vacuum tubes and, partly for that reason, required enough air conditioning to cool five five-room homes.

General Curtis LeMay was uncertain that a jet, especially one that could carry only a single atomic bomb, was the right vehicle for the Strategic Air Command's worldwide mission in the unfolding Cold War. The B-47 was a medium bomber, and LeMay advocated heavy bombers. But the proof was in the pudding. The B-47 had its faults, notably outboard engine failures resulting in asymmetrical thrust, which pilots had only two seconds to correct before an accident was nearly inevitable. But for all its faults, it dominated its competitors — the B-29 upgrades, the Convair B-36 and XB-46 — and more radical possibilities for strategic defense, such as the Northrup XB-35 piston and XB-49 jet flying wings. The B-47 set two transatlantic speed records in the 650 MPH range, was the first jet to fly over the North Pole, and in 1954 flew 21,000 miles non-stop using refueling to give the Air Force long-range strike power.

Of the 2,040 B-47s that were produced, Boeing Wichita built 1,390 before production ended in 1956. Lockheed and Douglas built the rest, except for two orphans made by Boeing Seattle. Before the plane's retirement and rapid scrapping in the mid-1960s, many were calling it the most significant aircraft conceived and produced in the postwar era. "Let's not belittle the B-29," an early B-47 pilot exclaimed. "It's a fine job, and there's plenty of work for it yet. But moving from a B-29 to a B-47 is about like stepping from a 1914 flivver to a 1951 Cadillac." Perhaps the best thing about the B-47 was that it was the basis for the B-52, a true balance-of-power weapon.

The impact of the B-47 on Wichita was immediate and significant. The population of the city began to rise in 1947 for the first time since the war, and by 1950 equaled its wartime peak. Early in 1948, the government took title to Boeing Wichita Plant II from the War Assets Administration. Boeing was shortly doing B-29 and B-50 modifications. In September 1948 local newspapers carried ads for workers to build the B-47. When the prototype XB-47 flew to Wichita from Seattle in June 1949, there were traffic jams on Oliver Street as Wichitans flocked to see it. By 1950, B-47 production in Wichita was under way, with Beech, Cessna and Coleman producing parts for it. In 1951, thirty-six local firms had B-47 subcontracts worth $72 million.

Just then the Korean War broke out — a boost for the Kansas aviation industry, however unfortunate in other ways. Wrote the *Topeka Capital* in 1950: "The huge aircraft factories of Kansas are preparing to spread their production wings to build implements of war for the military and the second chapter of an amazing story of wartime plane production may soon be written in the golden pages of America's aeronautical album." The war clearly did more in Kansas than step up demand for the B-47, though that step up, combined with a record 50 inches of rain in Wichita in 1951 that drenched unfinished jets sitting outside, was problem enough.

Beech leased the old World War II air bases at Herington and Liberal, where it manufactured a jet-engine starter unit and rebuilt and modernized Model 18s, among other jobs. These leases obviated costly expansion of the main plants in Wichita to meet what might be temporary wartime demand. The company sold the military the Model 45 Mentor (military designation T-34), a modification of the Bonanza that it had been unable to market successfully as a trainer before the conflict. There were T-34s built at the reopened Fuji plant in Japan, and there were models eventually powered by Allison engines, although the plane's active service life with the Air Force ended in 1961 with the switch to jet trainers. The severe demands of military service, highlighted by one testing accident in which a pilot hit a power line over the Royal Gorge in Colorado and brought the Mentor home, was good advertising for the durability of the commercial Bonanza. During the war Beech also designed but did not produce the T-36A, a 300 MPH twin that was to be used as a bomber trainer. Additional products included jettisonable fuel tanks, napalm tanks, and complete sets of wings for Lockheed jet trainers and fighters. In December 1952, the company had 13,418 employees, nearly equal to its World War II peak.

Cessna in 1950 received a $5 million contract, the result of a competition among its prototype and those from Piper Aircraft Corporation, Taylorcraft, and TEMCO for the manufacture of 400 two-place, light observation planes for the Army. Cessna's L-19, soon known as the Bird Dog, was designed for maximum visibility, could takeoff and land in less than 600 feet and weighed no more than 1,200 pounds. During the Korean War, an experimental model fitted by Boeing with a 210 HP turboprop established an altitude record for its class of 37,063 feet. The Bird Dog gave sterling service as late as the Vietnam era. The Army bought more than 3,000. In addition to this special airplane, which used 170 wings and a number of other standard parts, stock Cessna 172s, with the designation T-41, and 310s, designation FL-27A/U-3A, were used for military pilot training.

But more stunning than these was the development and first flight in

1954 of the Cessna Model 318, military designation T-37. Fondly called the Tweety Bird because of the high-pitched-whine of its turbojets (which some said sounded like "a 4,000 pound dog whistle") and more respectfully known as the Dragonfly, the T-37 was a versatile, rugged, and incidentally beautiful entry for Cessna into the jet field. This side-by-side trainer was produced from 1954 to 1977, and the 1,272 copies were incredibly long-lived and efficient in training service. An A-37 derivative even saw combat in Vietnam.

The T-37 was the first specialized jet trainer. The Air Force had been using the Lockheed T-33, which was really an F-80 Shooting Star fighter modified to seat two in tandem, not an economical or practical solution to its training needs. The T-33, for instance, weighed 16,000 pounds, while the Tweety Bird, at 5,600 pounds, weighed hardly more than an American car of the period. When test pilot Bob Hagen landed the T-37 after its first test flight, he commented: "I think she's going to be a real sweet airplane." She was indeed.

The Cessna entry won the contract over fifteen other design proposals from eight manufacturers. It was the only one using twin engines — 900-pound thrust jets designed by a French company — and its acceptance over more conventional designs indicated the perceived quality both of the product and its Wichita manufacturer. The aerodynamics, interestingly, had been tested at the University of Wichita wind tunnel, as Wichita designs had been since the university became a municipal college in 1926. The wide-track landing gear and wonderful visibility were only two of the features that endeared the plane to student pilots. "Wichita designers and engineers have been in the forefront in the industry since its pioneering days," wrote the *Wichita Beacon* in 1953, "and the result is a general acceptance of the product. Military planes, while in some respects 'seasonal' production, are in themselves builders of good will for peacetime markets. All of the many thousands of men who fly the military planes made here will remember, when they return to civilian life, the makers of the planes. Military contracts, too, are positive assertions of the fact that when such commitments decline, the same confidence in quality of fabrication will be transferred to the output of other goods." And the military development had as much potential direct commercial application for Cessna as the B-47 obviously did for Boeing. Utilizing 200,000 hours of flying experience by mostly new pilots with the design, Cessna in 1959 built a mock-up of a four-place business jet, the Model 407, based on the T-37. Wallace said it could "foreseeably be the forerunner of a modern commercial fleet in the next five to ten years."

As the Cessna L-19 contract was announced in 1950, it was learned, too, that General Motors would build Republic Aviation Corporation's F-84F

General Motors Corporation, Fairfax

Thunderstreak fighter for the Air Force, a part of the old North American plant at Fairfax in Kansas City, which was then being used for assembly of Buick, Oldsmobile, and Pontiac cars. Less famous perhaps than the F-86 Sabre, the F-84 was the first jet fighter designed to carry atomic weapons and to be refueled while airborne. It became the fighter-bomber workhorse of the Korean War. The production change that necessitated moving the production lines from Republic's Farmingdale, N.Y., factory was the switch to swept wings on the F series. Almost 600 F-84Fs were produced in Kansas City before production ended in 1957. Like Beech's lease of the Herington and Liberal air bases and Boeing's use of Plant II, the lease of the old North American plant provided GM with the advantage of having to pay for a facility that was actually owned by the U.S. government only so long as the company had a use for it.

The old B-25 plant at Fairfax had some unique characteristics that made

NOT YOUR FATHER'S OLDSMOBILE

⇐ Flush with cash, General Motors could hog the postwar media spotlight with products like the F-84 Thunderjet. The F-84F ground-support fighter-bomber was in such high demand that an additional assembly line was started in Kansas City, Kans., where GM produced 599 F-84Fs. Possessing a 40-degree swept wing, the F-84F was powered by a Wright J65 engine that produced as much as 7,800 pounds of thrust to power the plane to a top speed of 685 MPH.

for an unusual production plan. A two-level assembly process had been developed for the B-25, allowing the fuselage to be built at the floor level while the wing and tail assemblies moved along an upper-level line. Because demand for cars remained high during the Korean War, automobiles continued to be assembled on the upper level of the plant while F-84s were constructed on the lower level, all using the same workers. GM executives thought this might help regularize the ebb and flow in hiring that came with the ups and downs of military demand. There were problems with this complex production line, including the realization that manufacturing skills were not as interchangeable between cars and airplanes as first thought. Cars of the 1950s were built to loose tolerances and "were sometimes sledge-hammered to fit," whereas the F-84F was a 690 MPH fighter that had to be manufactured to very close tolerances. Additionally, the factory had no windows, was in a floodplain that put it under 13 feet of water during the great Kansas floods of 1951 and 1952, and experienced other morale-sapping difficulties. Perhaps these were not the only reasons the F-84F was the last airplane built in Kansas City, but they may have contributed.

Wichita's Korean War hero, Jimmy Jabara, flew an F-86 Sabre, and he really frosted the cake of the town's Korean War boom. In 1951 Jabara, the the son of a Lebanese grocer, became the first U.S. jet ace by downing his fifth MiG-15 near the Yalu River in Korea.

The city he returned to for a parade to kick off his publicity tour was as much of a boom town as it had been during World War II. The Municipal Airport had become so surrounded by Boeing test activity and the beginnings of a new Air Force Base (to be named after the local McConnell brothers of World War II flying fame) that the federal government bought the airport for $9 million, which allowed the city to build a new airport on the west side of town. McConnell Air Force Base, which had originated as a bid for the Air Force Academy, became a major training base for B-47 pilots. Like all government projects, once under way, it had considerable momentum and continued to be a major factor in the Wichita economy, later serving as a base for F-105 Thunderchiefs, F-4 Phantoms, and B-1B bombers. It was said that having a training site for B-47 pilots right across the street from the plant where the airplanes were built would give a year's head start in combat readiness. Meanwhile the whole town, "mother-nest of Uncle Sam's phenomenal jet-bomber," was "literally bustlin' with pride, excitement, and payroll money." Local residents called the Boeing building, under heavy guard all the time, the "little Pentagon"— a place where the payroll doubled in a year. The ripple effect of Boeing's defense dollars was tremendous. In Kansas alone, Boeing in 1951 placed $90 million in subcontracts among firms building parts and components. Only six cities in the

Bob Pickett Collection, Kansas Aviation Museum/Boeing Aircraft Company

STRATOFORTRESS

⇑ Weighing in at 488,000 pounds and capable of carrying 60,000 pounds of weapons, the B-52 series of strategic bombers symbolized U.S. air power as wielded by the Strategic Air Command. Although the first models were built in Seattle, Wichita would eventually manufacture 63 percent of the bombers. Shown is the first Wichita-built B-52D during its inaugural flight June 4, 1956.

state in 1951 were larger than the work force at Boeing Wichita.

During the short time that Boeing shared the Municipal Airport, the air-traveling public got a glimpse of all this glamour. Speed and distance records galore for the B-47 originated in Wichita, and any resident could glimpse lines of the bombers, looking, one man said, like competition swimmers poised for the start, on runways and in immense hangars south of the city. An Idaho grocer flying east was eating in the old Wichita airport's excellent Dobbs House restaurant one day in 1951 when he "gawked awe-stricken (and spilled some soup from a spoon) when a great 47 landed and slowed rapidly as a spreading white parachute erupted from its slender tail." A Boeing employee at the table hardly looked up and told the man it was routine in this town.

"Where the Chisholm Trail once passed the conflux of the Big and Little Arkansas Rivers," wrote a columnist in *Barrons*, "there is Wichita, Kansas, a one-time cow town, now yanked into national importance and a booming future by the coming of the air age." The B-47 had some faults, the journalist thought, but it was a miracle that it was brought to production so quickly. "Six years ago the B-47 was little more than some scattered blueprints. Following World War II the Boeing Wichita factory, now crammed with $45,000,000 of machinery and worked by 21,000 men and women, was stripped and silent save for the flutter of sparrow's wings." It was a "tremendous intricate act of industrial organization," and the writer hoped that the generals and politicians "who inherit these marvels will have the wisdom to know how to use what an obscure Providence puts in their hands."

The B-52 Stratofortress project got its start in a telephone conversation and a feverish planning weekend in a Dayton hotel room in 1948, shortly after Wichita got the go-ahead for B-47 production. The first flight was in Seattle on April 15, 1952, only a few months before the U.S. exploded its first hydrogen bomb. To illustrate the pace at which the company dashed into the future, at a Boeing directors' meeting on April 22, not only did the management plan production for the B-52, it authorized the Dash 80 airliner (eventually to be known as the 707), and discussed a supersonic bomber known as the XB-59, which, despite Mach 2 speed, eventually lost out to the Convair B-58 Hustler.

The B-52 was not produced in numbers as large as the B-47; it did not have to be. There were 744 total. Of these, 467, or 63 percent, were built in Wichita, beginning with the B-52D model in 1956, when Wichita finished its last B-47. The rest, mostly early versions, were made in Seattle, where the craft had been designed and tested. Even during the testing, however, there was a Kansas connection: Alvin Melvin "Tex" Johnson, the test pilot, was a native of the Sunflower State. The airplane easily overcame its only real prototype competition, a jet version of the Convair B-36 called the YB-60, and its service has been in every way extraordinary.

In January 1957, three B-52Bs flew around the world nonstop using Boeing-built KC-87 tankers for refueling. It was the B-52 that carried the North-American X-15 rocket plane aloft on its many record flights; and it was the B-52, equipped to launch several generations of missiles, that was the heavy-bombing workhorse in wars from Vietnam to the Persian Gulf. Before the B-52, it was unheard of for a bomber to have a service life of 40 years, but during the mid-1990s there were plans for continuing to use it. The plane became such an icon that in 1957 a Kansas-built B-52 flanked by F-104 Starfighters appeared on a U.S. stamp issued to commemorate the Air Force. Aviation writer John Zimmerman noted that some called it "the most brilliant design ever conceived." It was an intercontinental plane "which would be swift, high flying and capable of carrying within its light metal frame death and destruction of so vast a nature as to leave the potential enemy in awe."

Although the B-47 has been called "the indispensable forerunner" of the B-52, the latter was far more impressive. Like its predecessor, the B-52 was innovative and a big risk. The government ordered 13 B-52As, at a cost of $29 million each, sight unseen, in February 1951. On the average over its ten-year production run, B-52s cost the Air Force about $6 million apiece,

Bob Pickett Collection, Kansas Aviation Museum/Beech Aircraft Corporation

PRACTICE MAKES PERFECT

⇐ Developed in 1955 for the Navy, the Beech KDB-1 was the first of several propeller- and jet-powered target drones. Also available as a reconnaissance airplane, the KDB-1 could operate at 40,000 feet and achieve a maximum speed of 350 MPH.

twice the B-47's price tag. It was twice as heavy, but just as fast and had a 10,000-foot higher ceiling. Perhaps most important, it could carry four hydrogen bombs. The B-52D had an unrefueled range of 10,000 miles, a combat ceiling of 47,000 feet, a gross weight of 450,000 pounds, a 48-foot-high tail, a wing area of 4,000 square feet, a length of over 156 feet, a bomb load of 64,000 pounds, a top speed of 660 MPH, and a fuel capacity of almost 50,000 gallons. A brand-new jet-engine design, the J-57 from Pratt & Whitney, increased thrust enormously (to 9,000 pounds of thrust from each engine on B-52As to 17,000 pounds each — nearly as much as all six engines on the B-47 — on the 1961 B-52Hs) to haul all this hardware into the sky. Modifications to airframe, engines, electronics, and weapons systems were constant as the mission changed, and Wichita was kept busy working on B-52s long after the last one was manufactured in 1962. The B-47 and B-52 were in the "not invented here" class for Kansas, no matter the local production record, but in small general aviation airplanes Wichita and the region did it all by the mid-1950s. The aviation press in 1955 was declaring that the mass market in airplanes had arrived — perhaps not quite as massive as the immediate postwar predictions but substantial, regular, and utilizing an aerial vehicle of considerable sophistication and utility. A report in *Aviation Age* on the Cessna 310, for example, noted that with a top speed of 220 MPH and a range of 1,000 miles the airplane could get one to places more conveniently than anything else. "Cessna has been building good airplanes since Clyde Cessna put his first one together in a farmyard back in 1911. One or two have been great airplanes, that kind that stay in the hearts and minds of pilots long after the last one has been built. Such a one was the old Airmaster. And if the indications prove out, such a one will be the new twin-engine 310. ... It has a certain flair that quickens your anticipation of the flight to come."

Leighton Collins, in *Air Facts,* pointed out something more subtle about the 310. It was the product, not of a "band of brothers" waiting for air race trophies so they could draw a paycheck, but of a unionized factory participating in a large, somewhat bureaucratized and worldwide business. Beech and Cessna signed their first contracts with the Machinists union in 1940, and Boeing in 1943. Boeing had its first strike in 1948. "The day of one-man airplanes is about over," Collins wrote. "You can see Dwane Wallace, for instance, in the Cessna Airmaster, but only part of him in the 310." The latter model was a team effort that cost as much as $4 million in development costs alone. It had to sell, and there was every chance it would. A government report predicted that business flying, which was 3.9 million hours in 1954, would be 5.7 million in 1960 and 7.2 million in 1965, while pleasure flying by 1965 would reach 2.6 million hours.

The Experimental Aircraft Association in the 1990s recognized a category of aircraft called Contemporary Age, circa 1956-60, based on the idea that "1955 was in many respects the approximate end of one era and the beginning of another. With just a few notable exceptions, 1955 saw the end of many aircraft design cycles that had begun in the 1930s or immediately after World War II and the beginning of a new wave of lightplane designs, new avionics ... and even a new federal agency to regulate aviation." That new age, it was said in 1992, was the one small planes are yet in. In military aviation it was certainly the beginning of something called "aerospace." The Soviet Union's launch of Sputnik in 1957 symbolized a change of focus and perception that was seminal. In the late 1950s, Wichita's Big Three began designing rocket targets and guided missiles. In general aviation, everyone had to think of jets and turboprops, new liability for aircraft safety, environmental concerns, price escalation, and a host of other changes.

As this transition began, Kansas was in an excellent position, having dominated several aspects of the postwar recovery years in private aviation, while keeping a solid place in the military, if not so much in the growing airline field. A 1956 headline in the *Lawrence Journal-World* pointed out "Kansas Firms Build Biggest U.S. Jet, Most Light Planes." The state's aviation firms in that year had a combined annual payroll of $176 million and a backlog of $100 million. Beech and Cessna that year made 72 percent (in terms of dollars) of the light commercial airplanes sold in the United States, and did considerable military business. The Model 73 Beech jet, called the world's smallest jet plane, joined the Cessna T-37 in the small jet class. The next year Cessna and Beech together produced more than half the nation's business planes, turning out 1,377 units, selling for $34 million, in just five months. The only other real players in this field were Piper and the Aero Design & Engineering Company. Cessna's Wallace, however, spoke of a "saturated market" for the 172/182 models that made up 75 percent of his company's output and emphasized that it was unwise to rest on one's laurels.

Certainly the variety and choice had been revolutionized since the war. In 1958, Beech and Cessna between them offered twelve different models priced from $7,000 to $210,000. Beech led in total business with 1957 sales of $104 million, 66 percent of them to the military, but Cessna was the world's largest private-plane maker in volume, with commercial sales of 2,489 planes worth $33 million and total sales of $70 million. Kansas itself, with a relatively small population, was tenth among the states in number of civilian aircraft licensed to its residents, with 1,923 registered in 1959. "Beech and Cessna," wrote a journalist, "have learned that the U.S. businessman will pay handsomely to fly the right plane at the right price."

As though further to mark a transition, a sort of maturity began to be perceived in the Kansas aviation business in the 1950s. No longer was it seen as an upstart industry but rather as something with a legacy, a heritage that was almost hoary with tradition. In 1954, Clyde Cessna died at the farm, where he had built his first monoplanes in the teens. His passing was important enough to rate a telegram from President Eisenhower, and the flyover at the rural cemetery where he was buried was a missing-man formation of screaming military jets. Two years later, Mrs. E.L. Nicholson, a retired schoolteacher living in Oklahoma saw a photo in the *Eagle* magazine of A.E. Hunt's Jetmore helicopter of 1910. "Can it be 46 years?," she wrote the editor. She recalled that her class had been dismissed for a carnival in which the main event was to be the ascension of Hunt's ungainly craft. "All day we watched for the spectacular event to occur. We would wander away for a few minutes to ride the merry-go-round or buy a bag of peanuts, but we kept one eye focused on the plane. I can't recall whether or not we were disappointed in Mr. Hunt's failure to make good his promise. Probably not, for after all, hadn't the new-fangled device given us a holiday from school, a trip to the city, a carnival and a meal at a restaurant? It didn't take much to thrill a bunch of kids in those days." About the time that Nicholson was watching that "whatchimacallit" in Jetmore, Lloyd Stearman was at an air show in Wichita. In 1956 a school in Wichita was named after him. A great deal had happened in one lifetime.

(on facing page) Bede Jet Corporation

JIM BEDE WITH A BD-5B MICRO KIT

Bede Jet Corporation

BD-5 DEMONSTRATION TEAM

⇑ Originally retailing for $2,100 in 1972, the BD-5B kit version of the Micro pusher-prop aircraft generated tremendous interest. Weighing close to 600 pounds and powered by a Xenoah three-cylinder, two-cycle engine, the BD-5 could exceed 200 MPH. Complete aircraft were to be marketed as the BD-5D, and a jet-powered version was listed as the model BD-5J. Although operations at the Newton, facility ceased in 1977, BD-5 Micros are still a crowd pleaser at air shows.

CESSNA AG HUSKY

⇒ Cessna produced several crop-dusting and aerial spraying variants of its Model 188. Shown is a 1980 Ag-Husky equipped with a 310 HP turbocharged engine and a 280-gallon hopper tank. Almost 4,000 Model 188s were built.

Bob Pickett Collection, Kansas Aviation Museum/Cessna Aircraft Company

Bob Pickett Collection, Kansas Aviation Museum/Cessna Aircraft Company

CESSNA MODEL 310 ⇐ Since its introduction in 1954, the Model 310 has established itself as Cessna's best selling twin-engine aircraft, with 5,447 civil and military versions built by the time production halted in 1982. A 1960 Model 310D, the Songbird II, had a starring role in the television series "Sky King." Shown is a 1976 Model 310 R, powered by 285 HP Continental 10-520 engines. It sold for $138,500.

PRESCOTT PUSHER ⇓ First flown in 1985, the four-place Prescott Pusher was marketed as a home-built kit, selling for $36,000, minus engine and instruments. Powered by a 180 hp Lycoming 0-360 engine, it could achieve a top speed of 212 mph. Thirty-three component mini-kits made up the complete craft, from a trim kit selling for $275, to the fuselage kit selling for $5,000. Featuring gull-winged doors and a futuristic shape, sixty-eight kits were sold before the company folded in 1988.

Experimental Aircraft Association, Jim Koepnick

Beech Aircraft Corporation/Paul Bowen Photography

BEECH MODEL 2000A STARSHIP

⇑ First flown in 1983 as an 85 percent, proof-of-concept aircraft, the Starship was developed to succeed the King Air line of business turboprops. Shown is a Model 2000A, which can travel as far as 1,787 miles, with a maximum speed of 386 MPH. The selling prices was $4.4 million.

BOEING MODEL 737 ASSEMBLY

⇒ In support of Boeing Seattle's commercial airplane operations, Boeing Wichita has built many parts and assemblies for the company's airliners. About 75 percent of the short-range 737 is built in Wichita. More than 2,500 737s have been manufactured, making it the most popular jet airliner ever built. Shown are model 737-300 and 737-400 fuselage sections being readied for rail shipment to Seattle for final assembly.

Boeing Aircraft Company

Bob Pickett Collection, Kansas Aviation Museum/Cessna Aircraft Company

CESSNA MODEL 172 SKYHAWK

⇐ Almost 35,000 of the venerable Skyhawks were built between 1956 and 1986, making the Model 172 the best-selling, single-engine civilian aircraft ever. Shown is a 1973 Model 172M, which sold for $20,750.

LEARJET MODEL 35A

⇓ Carrying as many as eight passengers, the Learjet Model 35A is capable of flying non-stop over transcontinental distances. Powered by two Garrett TFE-731-2-2B turbofan engines, with 3,500 pounds of thrust each, the 35A can cruise at 529 mph. The Model 35A set an around-the-world speed record in 1983 of 50 hours, 22 minutes and 42 seconds.

Learjet, Inc.

Cessna Aircraft Company, Paul Bowen Photography

CESSNA CITATION II ⇑ With sales of more than 2,000 Citations since the model was introduced in 1971, Cessna has dominated its portion of the business-jet market. Shown is a 1985 Cessna Citation II, which seats eight passengers and two pilots. The Citation II has accounted for most Citation sales, with over 660 aircraft sold.

THE COLLIER TROPHY

⇒ In 1985, the prestigious Robert J. Collier Trophy was awarded to Russ Meyer and the Cessna Aircraft Company for the outstanding safety record of its Citation fleet of business jets. This award is given annually by the National Aeronautics Association for the "greatest achievement in aeronautics and astronautics in America." The Collier had not been awarded to a general aviation airplane since 1911, when Glenn Curtiss won with his hydro-aeroplane.

Cessna Aircraft Company

"We felt there was a gap between the turboprops and the existing jets. There was nothing between 300 and 500 miles an hour. A lot of people said 'Who needs another jet?' They couldn't see the market we were really aiming at."

– James Taylor, Cessna Citation program director, October 1973

(facing page) Piaggio Aviation, Inc., Paul Bowen Photography

PIAGGIO P-180 AVANTI

Cessna Aircraft Company

CESSNA CITATION X

⇑ Expected to enter service by mid-1995, this high-speed, long-range (3,800 miles) business jet made its first flight in December 1993. Priced at about $12.8 million, the Citation X can seat as many as twelve passengers. Shown is a computer-generated top view of the Citation X at speed.

RANS MODEL S-11 PURSUIT

⇒ The Model S-11 Pursuit project began in 1987 as a study in lifting-body (blended wing) designs. Over 80 percent of lift is achieved by the aircraft's body, with its wings acting as boosters. Powered by an 80 HP, four-cycle Rotax engine, the single-place Pursuit can achieve a maximum speed of 225 MPH. A 180 hp, two-place 300 MPH version is being considered.

The Experimental Aircraft Association (EAA), Carl Schuppel

CHANGEMASTERS

"SOME MEN ENJOY GOLF, OTHERS SPORTS CARS. FOR ME, THE BEST OF LIFE IS THE EXERCISE OF INGENUITY — IN DESIGN, IN FINANCE, IN FLYING, IN BUSINESS. THAT IS EXACTLY WHAT I'M DOING IN WICHITA" — BILL LEAR

The 1960s and 1970s were characterized by extraordinary business and regulatory changes, even for an industry that saw rapid change as a near-standard condition. The space race, with its opportunities and pitfalls in a new type of government contracting; record high interest rates and rationing of bank loans; the emergence of purely recreational aircraft; undeclared wars; rapidly changing federal tax incentives and disincentives relating to aviation; the re-emergence of a kit-airplane industry; and burgeoning product-liability costs following unprecedented court awards were only a few of the trends. Paralleling these were the technological changes brought about by the acceptance and wide use of jet engines, even on relatively small business aircraft; the introduction of entirely new lightweight aircraft-construction materials; and the revolution in avionics, traffic control, and design and manufacturing control methods brought about by the transistor, the integrated chip, and the computer.

As an old-line producer, Kansas might have been expected to rest on its laurels and be left behind. But the most important lessons it had learned during its whiplash history was the necessity for flexibility and that success had to be earned again every day and every year. The Kansas firms that remained operating in the 1990s were clearly survivors. The company names and the buildings might have been the same as those used during the 1960s, but the firms were smaller and more efficient, and able to respond more quickly to market opportunities. Although volume decreased as time passed, and the airplane for everyman receded further into the museum category, earnings — with a few cyclical exceptions — remained good thanks to the profit on high-end business jets and turboprops. Of course, God is in the details.

WILLIAM P. LEAR, SR.
⇐ Born June 26, 1902, in Hannibal, Mo., entrepreneur Bill Lear built a business jet of such performance and appeal that the public would use the name "Lear Jet" interchangeably with the term "business jet."

As symbolic a latter-day Kansas industry event as any was the stunning arrival in Wichita of William P. Lear and his Lear Jet Company in 1962.

Lear was 60 when he arrived in Wichita but had not given a thought to retiring. He got his cocky attitude (if he wasn't born with it) watching airmail pilots during the 1920s deal with the infirmities of war-surplus DH-4s. And from those observations came a determination to apply his inventive genius to making life easier and more efficient for pilots. He began flying in 1925 at Tulsa in a Lincoln Sport, built from a kit and powered with an Anzani engine, which he was forced to rebuild. His innovations in electronics, both in aviation and home entertainment, were legion. He invented AC-DC converters, noise filters, a wire recorder, car and aircraft radios, the Lear-O-Scope aircraft direction finder, a remarkable electric cowl flap control system that virtually replaced hydraulic controls during World War II, an autopilot, the eight-track stereo tape system, and more — making money on some devices and surviving the rest with confidence intact. In the 1950s, he won the Collier Trophy for aviation achievement, received an honorary doctorate in engineering, and earned a fortune. Before his stormy life was over, he would pour millions into a steam car and the Lear Fan aircraft design.

But perhaps the climax of his genius, and most satisfying accomplishment to him, was the complete and stunning Lear Jet executive transport. It is the achievement that will most likely be associated with his name and style as long as entrepreneurs are talked of. "Under Bill," wrote one of his

THE SWISS CONNECTION

⇓ Featuring a wing design that closely approximated the type that Bill Lear was searching for, the Swiss-built P-16 single-seat ground-attack fighter served as the starting point for the first Learjet. Only five Model P-16s were built before the Swiss government canceled the project. Shown is a fully armed P-16-04 Mark III, which flew in July 1959.

Learjet, Inc.

Learjet, Inc.

executives, "it was unthinkable to do other than to advance the state of the art. He expected it. It was routine. Once we got over the shock of doing the impossible weekly, it was a great deal of fun. … Bill stirred men's blood."

Lear began experimenting with corporate transports during the 1950s, when the Air Force gave him an outdated Lockheed Lodestar to use as a test bed for the autopilot and blind-landing system that his company was manufacturing for the military. He overhauled the engines, changed the interior, and made an executive transport out of it. He sold it to Fairchild Corporation and bought two more Lodestars for modification into Learstars. He added staff for the project, beginning with Gordon Israel, who had worked on Benny Howard's racers in the 1930s, and eventually including Hank Waring, who had worked for Cessna developing the T-37 jet trainer. Under their guidance the Learstar distanced itself more and more from its source craft. It became a veritable hot rod, with a cruising speed of 300 MPH and a range of 3,800 miles— both records for twin-engine private transports.

In 1955, with the expensive Learstar moving slowly in the market, Lear moved his family to Switzerland to start work on an entirely new craft in isolation and with the help of Swiss engineers. His personal airplane at the time was a Cessna 310 equipped with Lear ADF, autopilot, automatic approach coupler, transmitter and receiver, which he took pride in flying and landing anywhere – including Moscow at the height of the Cold War – and in any weather.

The result of his Swiss experiments was the Lear Jet, based on ideas from prototype planes as diverse as the U.S. Marvel turboprop and the Swiss Air Force P-16 fighter. He panned the existing Lockheed JetStar and Rockwell Sabreliner executive jets, calling them "royal barges," and promised that his craft would be the first designed from the start specifically

LIFE IN THE FAST LANE

⇑ The early Learjets were extremely fast by early-1960s standards. The Model 24 was powered by two GE CJ610-4 turbojets providing 2,850 pounds of thrust each. The plane could achieve a maximum speed of 564 MPH and could even be coaxed to exceed 600 MPH in certain situations. Seating as many as six passengers, the Lear Jet Model 24 could fly as far as 1,700 miles before refueling.

for businessmen and that it would outperform all competitors. Performance was everything. "If you want to take a walk, go to Central Park," he said. "You can't stand up in a Cadillac, either." "A rest room is an admission you're spending too much time getting where you want to go." He said he could sell 600 of these compact craft, and his critics hooted. Lear might have been a genius, but few thought he could sustain a stable business.

In 1962, having sold all his stock in his diversified company, Lear decided to bring his jet-aircraft business back to the United States and mounted a competition among three cities — Grand Rapids, Mich., Dayton and Wichita — to be its headquarters. The announcement that Wichita had won was made in dramatic fashion at an air show in June of that year. Lear figured that the per-pound cost of airframe construction was less in the Air Capital than anywhere else in the world. The city also helped mightily. It offered to raise $1.2 million in industrial revenue bonds (its first such offering) for a Lear plant adjoining the Wichita airport and purchased sixty-four acres for the facility. Lear proposed to build 400,000 square feet of manufacturing space and employ 1,200 people initially. Somewhat to the surprise and chagrin of the Swiss, he had 500 tons of equipment moved from Europe to Wichita. He shipped his wife, Moya, to the Plains, too, though at first it was a shocking transition for her from the amenities of Geneva. The SAAC (Swiss American Aviation Corporation) 23 became the Lear Jet 23.

Before the doubting eyes of his Wichita competitors and local bankers, Lear did something that had been thought to be impossible. He skipped the prototype stage and went into production tooling, fully intending to sell Lear Jet No. 1.

Cessna had done a market survey that concluded that businessmen would continue to prefer piston-engine planes. Beech had decided that the turboprop was the answer. Only Lear and the Aero Commander Company were willing to stake their fortunes on a small jet (Lear's target was under 12,500 pounds) costing substantially less than the $1 million-plus of the Sabreliner and JetStar. "The trick is," said Lear, "to discern a market before there is any proof that one exists." He controlled everything at the plant and seemed to have uncanny instincts — driven, said biographer Richard Rashke, "by a vision of beauty and simplicity in which every part sang harmony." Lear calculated that with his wealth he could spent a thousand dollars a day until he was a hundred. "But one way to condemn me to the most awful suffering would be to say: 'Lear, you have to go sit on the beach.' "

On October 7, 1963, test pilot Bob Hagen flew the first Lear Jet. It looked great and performed wonderfully. As local radio stations broadcast the news, air-minded Wichitans snarled airport traffic to watch it land. There were tears in the eyes of some of the engineers as the first flight ended, but Lear was quite calm. He had flown it in his mind so many times, he said, that

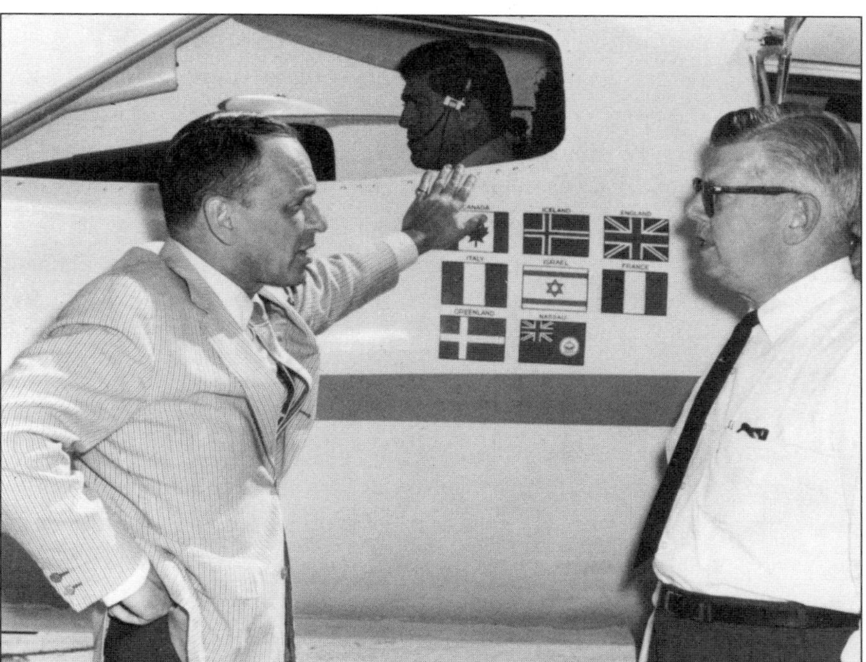

Learjet, Inc.

SUPERSTARS

⇐ The sleek and racy looks of the Lear Jet captured the fancy of many celebrities, among them Frank Sinatra, the Smothers Brothers, Danny Kaye, Bob Cummings, Paul Harvey, Richard Nixon, and George Peppard. The comings and goings of the stars resulted in the Lear Jet factory being called Hollywood East.

he was not surprised that it worked. He went directly on to developing the eight-track stereo while sending a standard production Lear Jet on an around-the-world flight that set innumerable speed and reliability records.

By the spring of 1966, the company had delivered more than 100 Lear Jets representing sales of more than $38 million. During the preceding eight months, profits had exceeded $3.5 million. Suddenly those who had laughed at Lear were forecasting that more than 3,000 business jets would be in operation by 1975, and Lear Jet would sell 40 percent of them, or 120 planes a year. Not all of those predictions came true. Lear's company had some poor years in the late 1960s after the initial excitement wore off. But in 1966, the man who popularized the business jet was producing half of all such planes and contributing more than $1 million a month to the Wichita economy in payroll and purchases.

Lear never learned what could not be done. From the time he told Paul Galvin of Motorola in 1924 that he could build and market a car radio (without the government's regulating it out of existence because it might distract the driver), Lear pushed into things and made them happen. His forward style applied in financial and social matters as well as technical. When Olive Ann Beech, who was part of Wichita's prestigious Metropolitan Council, opposed Lear's coming to her city, Lear named a beach he owned on Sardinia "Olive Ann Beach" and, according to a biographer "committed an act of personal defilement on it," as he promised one of his Wichita backers he would. Crude, but original. "Quit thinking," he would say to his ruminating engineers, "and try something."

The Lear Jet was a latter-day Kansas classic, comparable to the Staggerwing and the Airmaster in its influence. In a 1965 test, it climbed to 40,000 feet in seven minutes and twenty-one seconds, a new business-jet record. And it did so while flying on a Lear autopilot in inclement weather with seven people aboard. In 1968, the Model 25 lowered that to six minutes, 19 seconds. Pilots who had jockeyed all sorts of military jets claimed that the Lear outperformed all of them at lower altitudes. It weighed 12,500 pounds, as promised, and it cost, at least for a short time, $500,000, as promised. With its more-than-adequate 2,850-pound-thrust General Electric CJ610-1 turbojet engines, it could cruise at 561 MPH as low as 25,000 feet. It was approved for altitudes as high as 51,000 feet, the first civil aircraft to be allowed to fly that high. It was also the first plane to have winglets on production models and the first commercial jet known to have been involved in combat: An Argentine Lear Jet was shot down in the Falklands War. Although it was not really the first business jet, (there were others, six of which went into production, including the JetStar, the Sabreliner, and the Jet Commander that Lear so detested), the Lear Jet made such a spectacular impact that many magazines have since identified Lear as "the father of the corporate jet." It revolutionized the economics of business flying, and corporate pilots and accountants regularly said so.

Partly too, as with all classics, it possessed sheer beauty, the right looks. Lear Jet N802L, the second built, has a prominent place in the Smithsonian's National Air and Space Museum, partly because of its importance in aviation history, and partly because the striking, go-fast looks of "Bill Lear's Beauty from the Kansas Cornfields" so perfectly symbolize the changes of the 1960s.

In 1967, after some serious negotiations with Beech concerning a buyout, Lear sold his company to Gates Rubber and moved on to his steam car and the Lear Fan. His jet-manufacturing concern, however, remained in Wichita, adding models, known from then on as Learjets, to the original close-fitting 23.

While Lear drew the headlines during the 1960s, the rest of Kansas aviation hardly dozed. Boeing's B-52 and airliner modification programs; Mid-States Manufacturing's Helioplane; Cessna's T-37; and targets, missiles and drones enough to move Beech to create an entire division in 1956 for pilotless and classified aircraft at Boulder, Colo., continued as a major money draw in Kansas.

The decade was a curious mixture of tradition and future shock. Johnny Livingston, the prewar air racer of Cessna's CR craft and the model for Richard Bach's philosophical avian flier in the 1970 best-seller *Jonathan*

Livingston Seagull, visited Wichita in 1959 and was overjoyed to have lived long enough to fly the Cessna T-37 jet and Beech's proposed MS-760 commercial jet. The members of the state's new OX-5 club could mix nostalgia with observation of the mid-1960s production by Boeing Wichita of more than 90 percent of the hardware for the first-stage booster of the Saturn rocket that would help land Americans on the moon at the end of the decade. While publicizing its Model 18 as the oldest continuously produced business airplane, Beech was marketing not only the Model 18's direct replacement, the Queen Air, but an all-new turboprop-powered fifteen-seat commuter plane for small airlines — the Model 99. Beech's airliner did not look as impressive as the venerable DC-3, but it had a 24 percent greater capacity in ton-miles and operated at half the cost. When, in 1967, test pilot Dave Blanton flew a restored Travel Air 2000 biplane over the factory where it was born, the workers and executives had only a moment to consider the past lest the future get away from them. The deaths of the Kansas air industry pioneers — Walter Beech and Clyde Cessna in the early 1950s, R.A. Rearwin at 91 in 1969, Lloyd Stearman at 76 in 1975, Matty Laird at 87 in 1982, J. Earl Schaefer at 85 in 1978 — passed with hardly more than standard obituary notices, and little attempt had been made to collect their memories for posterity. In fact Kansas aerobatic ace Harold Krier, though still active in the 1960s, was probably better known in Washington, D.C., where his picture hung in the Smithsonian, than in his native state. Still, the fact that the local aircraft companies would never fully back an air museum, which was perennially suggested for Wichita, might not be a characteristic that boded wholly ill. Their people's minds were on other things — things that paid.

Although the nature of the market had changed, non-military aircraft production continued to be dominated nationally and worldwide in the 1960s and 1970s by Beech and Cessna. Dwane Wallace of Cessna predicted at the outset of "the Soaring Sixties" that the decade would be one of opportunity for Kansas that would exceed all that had come before — a period during which his company had sold 40,000 planes. "There are only 550 airports in the United States served by commercial airlines," Wallace said. "But there are some 7,000 airports — and many hundreds of other landing strips — which can be used by smaller airplanes. Besides, the airlines never seem to leave when you want to go. Surface transportation is not getting faster in most points." And there was the fact that as other forms of transportation, particularly passenger trains, disappeared, commercial air travel became increasingly congested and unpleasant. "Those who flew," wrote Joseph Corn, "endured the same bureaucratic hassles, and suffered the same personal inconveniences common to those old-fashioned and often detested modes of earthly travel." Even the sensory joys of the earlier days of flight

Bob Pickett Collection, Kansas Aviation Museum/ Beech Aircraft Corporation

SUPER KING AIR

⇑ Powered by two 850 HP Pratt & Whitney PT6A-41 engines, the Beech Model 200 not only became Beech's flagship but has been the turboprop of choice in corporate flight departments. Introduced in 1973, the Super King Air's most distinctive features are its large T-tail and increased wingspan. The cabin of the best-selling plane provides seating for as many as eight people. Shown is Beech's demonstrator ship, the Free Enterprise.

were gone when on autopilot in a pressurized tube far above the scenery and the weather. Flying a lightplane of one's own, Wallace said, would avoid inconvenience and deprivation and would be a powerful attraction. He had been a good prophet before, predicting in 1950 that Cessna would be doing $100 million a year in business by 1960, when the actual figure turned out to be $105 million.

Just as it might be a shock to learn that the height of Kansas oil and gas production came in the 1970s, so it is that many are surprised to learn that more new aircraft models and variations were introduced by Kansas companies in the 1960s and 1970s than ever before. The Beech genealogy chart gets thick with variations of the Bonanza, including turbocharged, aerobatic, and turboprop models; the Model 95 Travel Air twin (reviving the earlier company name); variations of the inexpensive Musketeer Sport; versions of the popular Beechcraft Baron twin, the Duke, Debonair, Queen Air, and King Air (which were to fill that high-performance, small-business aircraft slot that Lear leapfrogged); the Model 99; the Skipper trainer; and the Model 76 Duchess twin, with its counter-rotating props. By 1970, 10,000 Model 35 Bonanzas had been sold. In 1982, Beech extended the Super King Air to produce the Model 1900 airliner for use by the ever-increasing number of commuter airlines.

King Airs were a kind of institution unto themselves in this period. When the first Beechcraft King Air 90 was delivered in 1964, few could have predicted its overwhelming acceptance or that over the next twelve years there would be 1,300 King Air deliveries and five distinct variations of the airplane. The prototype made a thirty-eight-country demonstration tour, and seemed to impress all who saw it, even when compared with such seemingly more futuristic planes as the Learjet. When the first King Air came off the production line, there was a $28 million backlog of orders for it. It became "the backbone of executive travel in the '60s." In 1984, twenty years into the model's history, the King Airs accounted for half the planes delivered in their class.

Owners of Beechcrafts were virtually the world business establishment. Volkswagen A.G.,, for example, which did well with its own classic, the Beetle, was a multiple King Air owner. The J.P. Stevens Company had five Model 18s and, later, five King Airs. Walt Disney Productions used a King Air. Art Linkletter was a customer and good friend of Olive Ann Beech. The LBJ Company in Austin, Texas, operated a Queen Air 80 before its owner began getting around in a Boeing 707 called Air Force One. When Arthur Godfrey took delivery of a Beechcraft Baron D55 in 1969, it marked forty years of association between him and the company. He had learned to fly in 1929 in an OX-5 powered Travel Air and had owned three of the company's

TRIED AND TRUE

⇓ Introduced in 1961, the Beech Baron line of light piston-engine twins was a response to the success of the Cessna Model 310. So far, more than 5,000 Barons have been sold. Shown is a Model E55 fitted with two Continental IO-520-C engines that produce 285 HP and provide a maximum speed of 230 MPH. The relatively spacious cabin can seat six.

Bob Pickett Collection, Kansas Aviation Museum/Beech Aircraft Corporation

Bob Pickett Collection, Kansas Aviation Museum/Cessna Aircraft Company

GOLDEN EAGLE

⇑ The best-selling piston twin among the 400 series of aircraft, the Cessna Model 421 was first sold in 1967. Nearly 2,000 were built during its fifteen-year production run. Shown is a 1973 Model 421B that featured a pressurized cabin and seating for six. Powered by two 375 HP Continental GTS10-520-H engines, the 421B could fly at 260 MPH. It sold for $188,000.

planes in between. Beech planes were flown by astronauts and movie stars, and each delivery (early on always with Olive Ann Beech standing for a photograph beside the famous buyer) brought publicity for Kansas.

Cessna likewise developed and sold airplanes in the 1960s and 1970s at a record pace, though in a pattern skewed more to the high end and profits than to the low end and absolute volume. The 210 soldiered on and became ever-more sophisticated, including turbocharged and pressurized options. The 320 twin and its variants replaced the venerable 310, while the 400 series, culminating in the 421 Golden Eagle series and Turbo Prop 441 Conquest, boasted pressurization, a cruise speed of more than 250 MPH, and a price exceeding $150,000. Still, the 421 was half the price of a King Air and filled a niche.

Production continued apace on the tried and true singles. Purchases in 1959 and 1962 of French companies around Rheims gave Cessna more presence in Europe, and Cessna Argentina S.A.I.C, established in 1961, put an anchor in South America and augmented the assembly of singles in Colombia. The company used Strother Field regularly for overflow production during the 1970s boom. Venerable designs, such as the Skylane, continued to sell. The 1979 version of what old-time aviators had once sniffed at as the "training wheels" model, had a turbocharger and retractable landing gear and could climb at 1,000 feet a minute to 20,000 feet, where one settled down to 200 MPH. Of course this came at a price — $50,000 for a 1978 Skylane and $106,000 for the 1986 version, compared with the $13,000 1956 plane.

These were improvements — evolution. But there was also innovation of a fundamental sort at Cessna. The Model 336-337 Skymaster was a case in point. The Skymaster was a twin with the second engine oriented as a pusher, directly in line with the front engine and positioned between twin tail booms. The great danger of a conventional twin was loss of control if an engine was lost, resulting in sudden, unbalanced thrust. With this 1961 design, the loss of an engine was an inconvenience that reduced performance but did not modify centerline power or endanger stability.

The daring of the design and its basic soundness won kudos from the experts, and the Super Skymaster was named Plane of the Year for 1966 by the editors of *Plane and Pilot*. It was less successful with buyers, however. Its appearance was one drawback. It was said to look like that famous beast in Dr. Doolittle stories called the Push-Me, Pull You. Aviation writer Leighton Collins remembered that "people kind of laughed at the thing. It looked like an egg beater and was an unconventional airplane." A second factor was cost. In its 337 version, the Skymaster was a high-performance, retractable-gear plane that was more expensive than similar-performance airplanes such as the Piper Comanche and Beech Baron twins, and was somewhat noisy. Cessna buyers were not used to paying more, nor were they accustomed to being radically different. Safety did not sell, and production of the 337 ended in 1983. Even so, more than 2,000 were sold.

Bob Pickett Collection, Kansas Aviation Museum/Cessna Aircraft Company

THE WORLD'S MOST POPULAR AIRPLANE

⇐ The Cessna Model 172 Skyhawk — which first appeared in the mid-1950s, along with its stablemate, the 182 — was built to compete with the Piper PA-22 Tri-Pacer, the top-selling private plane from 1952 to 1956. When production ended in 1986, almost 35,000 examples had been built. Shown is a 1976 Model 172M powered by a 150 HP Lycoming D-320E2D engine, which powered the plane to 140 MPH. It cost $20,750.

A second, longer-lasting, and more influential Cessna innovation of the period was the Citation. The lesson of the Learjet was hardly definitive, and Beech was still shying away from jets. Cessna studied the market for ten years before announcing its 500 series in 1968. The airplane first was called the Fanjet 500 and later the Citation, after the famous racehorse. In many ways it was a direct contrast to the ground-breaking Lear 24. The Lear was a hot rod, while the Citation's performance was often criticized as hardly jetlike. The Lear was raucous (its original Garrett engine, an observer said, was nearly as noisy as a T-37), while the Cessna, organized around the new Pratt & Whitney JT5D-1 turbofan engine, was quiet — the goal was "the quietest airplane ever built" — and ultra-smooth. It was a relatively simple engine, too, with simple turbines, great reliability, modest maintenance expense, and good fuel economy. The airplane provided walking-around room to carry six in comfort at a price ($695,000 in 1972) that undercut considerably (generally by about half) its competition. In addition, it could land on shorter fields than many other jets.

But there were drawbacks. Early sales were slow, and a host of naysayers and second-guessers opened up on the Citation and its major backer, Wallace. It did not have swept wings, and its blunt nose, large, high-browed windshield, and hunched-forward pod engines made its appearance odd — "platypus-looking," someone said. Its speed didn't exceed 400 MPH, about 100 MPH slower than the competition and 150 MPH off the early pace of the Lear Jet. Wags called it a Near Jet. Another problem was with the dealer

SKYMASTER

⇓ Conceived as the safest twin available, the Cessna Model 336/337 Skymaster series was designed to compete with the Piper Twin Comanche. About 2,500 Skymasters were built between 1963 and 1983, making it Cessna's second-largest selling twin. By using one engine to pull and another to push, asymmetrical thrust problems were eliminated when only one engine was working.

Bob Pickett Collection, Kansas Aviation Museum/Cessna Aircraft Company

Bob Pickett Collection, Kansas Aviation Museum/Cessna Aircraft Company

organization. The new jet was not marketed through the regular Cessna network but directly through the factory. Marketing director James Taylor, in trying to appeal to the wealthier types who bought business jets, offended some of the populist old-line salespeople affiliated with the "everyman" company. In a push to get some early sales, Citations were deeply discounted to famous people, and that did not sit well, either.

The most public attack was an article in *Forbes* magazine April 1, 1972, entitled "The Perils of Positive Thinking." "Old Dwane Wallace is an optimistic fly-boy," wrote the reporter. "Always was, always will be." Ask him about the jet and "a smile creases his leathery face: 'Shutting down the jet program (and writing off about $7.6 million in tooling costs) is the furthest thing from my mind. I still say we'll sell 1,000 jets in ten years. … You watch and see." The magazine noted that such optimism could blind. Six months after the first demonstration flight, Cessna had sold only fifteen jets and was deep in the red on the project. Wallace's response to that was "I'm not losing any sleep over it. Are you with me?"

Of course, Cessna had over forty models and commanded 53 percent of the market, so it was not dependent on any one plane. But it did need to estab-

A NEW BREED

⇑ Although slow out of the gate, Cessna would eventually capture more than 60 percent of the market for light- to medium-sized business jets. Cessna's goal in 1968 was to target the upscale turboprop market with a small jet that was simple to build and affordable to maintain. The first flight of the Cessna Fanjet 500 took place Sept. 15, 1969. Through the efforts of Cessna marketing chief James Taylor, the Fanjet 500 was rechristened Citation.

lish a direction for the future, and that future did not seem to be in light singles. The Citation was designed for the niche between the big turboprops and the smallest business jets. "It was to be a sort of flying Ford Mustang," Forbes said, but it did not seem to be working. Gates Learjet's latest model cost $160,000 more but carried eight people farther and faster. And in the preceding six months Learjet had sold twenty-two jets vs. Cessna's fifteen. Beech's King Air, at $644,000, was going out the door at six a month, and Mitsubishi's MU-2 was doing well also, indicating strongly that maybe the focus on the large turboprop was the right one. Wallace believed in the plane, but was intuition and will enough? "All he needs," *Forbes* concluded, "is a scarf around his neck and the Red Baron in his sights. Trouble is the longer sales stay down, the more he sounds like an old-time Wichita barnstormer flying by the seat of his pants."

But it did work. By 1978, the Citation had become the best-selling business jet in history, and by 1979 it was selling at the rate of more than 100 planes a year, a level that made Wallace's prediction good. Of course it had evolved, and the price had gone up. The Citation III of 1979 had swept-wings, spoilers, even Garrett engines. The Cessna jet cost nearly $1 million in 1977 and $2.5 million ten years later. There was no denying, however, that the instinct and the concept was right. Over time the Citation became ever more important to the company as changes in the market and the regulatory environment reduced the number of other models offered for sale.

Boeing Wichita's history, while representing steady and profitable sales and military contracting, might seem less dramatic but for one thing — the Supersonic Transport (SST) project. Boeing had been dreaming of a supersonic passenger plane since 1957 and imagined one that would do Mach 2.7 (more than 1,900 MPH), carry 250 passengers, and be made of titanium. Boeing presented a mockup to the media in 1966 and estimated the planes would cost $11 million each. Lockheed had a competing design with a double delta wing. A Soviet SST flew in 1968, and so did the Concorde prototype developed in Europe. However, the U.S. program, which might have had considerable impact on Kansas, was mistimed and seen as too expensive and environmentally menacing. After Boeing had spent 8.5 million man-hours on design and $1 billion on development, the SST project died in 1971. With it died a Wichita role in design tooling and fabrication, which on the two prototypes authorized in 1970 alone would have amounted to $20 million. Had the 300 planes projected ever been built, the impact would have been immense.

Modification work at Boeing Wichita, however, both on B-52s and on the company's airliners, as well as construction of subassemblies of those airliners, kept it prosperous. Wichita in 1975 was building major structural

Bob Pickett Collection, Kansas Aviation Museum/Cessna Aircraft Company

PAR FOR THE COURSE
⇐ Cessna and Beech enjoyed catering to the occasional celebrity and basking in the publicity that accompanied high-profile sales. Here Russ Meyer of Cessna hands over the keys to a 1976 Cessna Citation I to golfer Arnold Palmer.

components for the 707, 727, 737, and 747 airliners, as well as parts for Boeing's CH-47 helicopter. The division was active in conversions of planes from passenger to cargo hauling. By 1979 there was talk of Boeing Wichita employment returning to the record levels of World War II. Early in the 1980s, Wichita's major role in the construction of the B-1B bomber increased activity further.

Mixed success was typical of entrepreneurship, and it was certain on balance that the mid-1970s were a wonderful economic time for the Kansas aircraft industry. The state remained air-minded. In 1970, it had more than twice as many aircraft per 10,000 people as the U.S. average and the seventh-highest ratio of aircraft to population in the nation. In 1974, Kansas produced nearly 70 percent of all business, general aviation, and utility aircraft in the free world and was exporting 30 percent of its planes overseas. Cessna had 14,500 employees in Kansas. Sales for fiscal 1974 were $416 million, a record, and up $44 million over the previous year. That went up 20 percent the next year, during which Cessna delivered its 100,000th single-engine aircraft, its 1,000th Golden Eagle twin and its 250th Citation, all records in each class. Beech had $241 million in sales — $42 million in August alone. It made major expansions in manufacturing facilities at its Salina plant, where it had 50,000 square feet of space to manufacture Barons. Gates Learjet, which had hired 500 people in 1974, was running at a $100 million-a-year sales clip. Boeing Wichita employed 10,600 workers, up 3,000 in a year. "I think when you look at the aircraft exports and the grain exports," an industry insider said, "that describing Kansas as a kind of Japan on the Great Plains would be pretty accurate. We are surely pulling our share." That share, despite the energy crisis, was $182 million in aircraft exports. Arab countries, with their oil income, were buying heavily, and only the Soviet bloc lagged. A man at Beech commented on that: "They haven't learned what a light aircraft can do for them yet. ... But they'll learn. And when they learn, they'll probably come to us."

TRAINING WHEELS

⇓ Innovations abounded in the BD-5 series of aircraft, not only in the plane's design but also in the remarkable approach the company took to dual instruction. Here a BD-5 aircraft is attached to a pickup using an articulating framework. The student pilot in the airplane and the instructor in the truck communicated by radio. As the truck sped down the runway, the aircraft would reach a height of ten feet, allowing the BD-5 to bank and yaw up to 10 degrees.

The big numbers, as always, were in Wichita and with the Big Three. But the rest of Kansas was active, albeit on a smaller scale as it ever had been. The "whatchimacallit" people were vigorous and far more successful at getting their inventions into the air and acquiring backing from daring capitalists than had been the case early in the century.

For example, there was James R. Bede. While some of his frustrated kitplane customers might like to treat him to an old-fashioned lynching, Bede's designs were innovative and attracted much more attention than the products of most small shops. He has been called "one of aviation's most prolific —

The Wichita Eagle

and controversial — designer-developers," and both claims were true.

In 1971 a Kansan driving by Delmar Hostetler's farm near Harper could read a sign that said: "Bede Aircraft Experimental Shop — No Admittance." Inside was the prototype of an airplane — the BD-5 — for which 900 orders had been received before it ever flew. By the end of the year, after the first BD-5 test flight at Hutchinson, there were 2,000 orders, with a $200 deposit on each. By 1973, when the first production model started testing at the Newton airport, there were 4,300 orders. Customers included Barry Goldwater and author Bach.

The specifications, appearance, price, and sales pitch for this airplane were unquestionably spectacular. *Popular Science* for August 1973 headlined its cover picture of the canopied, pusher-prop powered composite microplane with three simple, riveting phrases: "200+ miles per hour, 38 miles per gallon, under $3,000." The craft weighed less than 600 pounds with pilot and fuel, and was powered by a two-cylinder, 40 HP snowmobile engine that cruised at 6,500 RPM and sounded like a "baby banshee." It was claimed to have a range of 1,215 miles nonstop. It was said that it could be treated to a top overhaul in less than ten minutes for $300. It had two sets of wings for different purposes and was supposed to be easy to build.

Bede admitted that he could not prove all the claims immediately, and there was a question of whether a builder of the kit could get the craft FAA certified once completed, but the plane did fly (with regular problems), and it was terrifically exciting. As *Flying* magazine put it, "thoughts of flying the sleek, bullet-shaped aircraft ... stimulated the imagination of nearly everyone who had heard of the program." Many thousands all over the world paid $5 for information kits.

The concept was translated into a fine ad: "Join tomorrow's generation today and own a personal aircraft that cruises at 202 MPH on 40 HP — for just $2,100 base price, complete! This fully aerobatic, high performance home-built aircraft is the result of years of development and incorporates a whole new design concept with modern engineering breakthroughs. ... Using simple tools, you can build the BD-5 in your home workshop or basement." The BD-5D, advertised in 1974 for $4,400 was still "Another plane you can afford to love from Bede Aircraft." No question there was truth in the statement: "This may be your only chance to own a plane." And there was great historic passion in the thought of the everyman airplane, which seemed to be fading so fast from the offerings of the major companies. "It's a dream airplane come true."

There was reason for hope. Although some engineers laughed at the Bede concept, and some marketers viewed his sales hype with "cold contempt," the same people had snickered at Lear and Cessna. Bede's operation

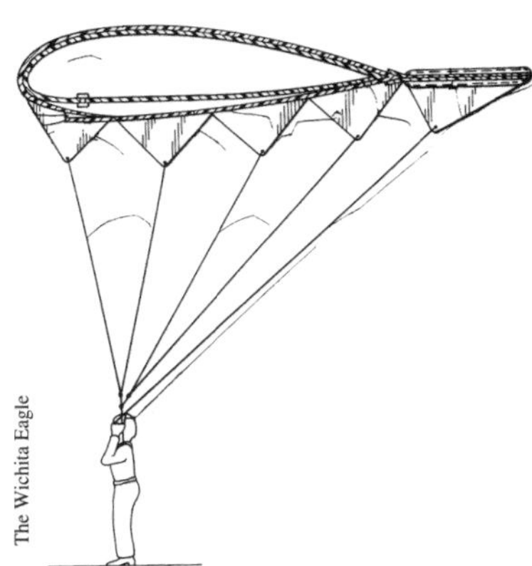

The Wichita Eagle

BASIC TRANSPORTATION

⇑ In a last-ditch attempt to salvage his BD-5 project, Jim Bede developed this version of elementary flight, called the Bede Wing. Part parachute, part blimp, part aircraft, and part hang-glider, it was to have been marketed to recreational thrill seekers. Designed to sell for about $1,500, the helium-filled airfoil (built by Playtex) was a truly modular approach to affordable flight. Powered and unpowered models were conceived. Three prototypes were reportedly built.

was more than a post office box, and he had built successful, if flawed airplanes in the past. The BD-2, for instance, a powered sailplane characterized by one magazine as a "mechanical albatross and hangar queen," did not fly around the world nonstop as proposed but, piloted by Bede, did exceed a number of distance and duration records, including the mark of 8,854.3 miles set by a B-29. Bede had been pursuing his dream since 1964, when, as a graduate of Wichita State University still in his 20s, he promoted, though never produced, the BD-1 as the first lightplane to be bonded together with epoxies rather than rivets and offering a swing-out engine for easy maintenance. His BD-4 was a four-place job with fold-back wings and a host of other unique features. Not the least of the BD-5's innovations was a wrist-operated side-stick controller to avoid gross arm movements.

Doubters abounded. "James R. Bede," wrote a Kansas reporter in 1972, "is a modern-day dauntless Don Quixote who looks more like Sancho Panza and may in fact turn out to be victorious St. George instead. He'd rather like to be St. George. … But there are those who suspect he's the dragon."

Bede himself reveled in his reputation of having replaced Lear as the "undisputed *enfant terrible* of the airplane business" and was undeterred by errors. "Guys who play baseball," he said, "will come up, and seven out of ten times, they don't hit the ball — and people say, 'What a fantastic ballplayer.' But when I say, 'I'm going to fly around the world,' and then go out and fly seventy hours, they say, 'See, he didn't do it.' If I'd said I was gonna fly fifty hours, they'd have thought it was great." The conventional industry, he said, had a collective "warped mind." His best people did not have degrees, and he thought a design engineer with more than five years' experience in conventional aircraft was ruined for what he wanted them to do. His development director in 1972 was a 29-year-old member of the Experimental Aircraft Association and composite-construction enthusiast named Burt Rutan. Rutan eventually designed the famous *Voyager,* which was enshrined in the Smithsonian after making the "impossible" non-stop around-the-world flight in 1986 that Bede had proposed with similar design concepts in 1969. And it would be Rutan who put the experimental kitplane builders into the commercial limelight in the early 1980s with his design of the radical Beech Starship, complete with epoxy-bonded composite structure and pusher props, a la BD-5.

Bede did not make it big — not yet anyway. Despite promotion of an inflatable wing that was to power the first under-1,000 pound jet aircraft (his eighteenth patent) and the promise of a $29,000 "poor man's jet" to be built at a new $5 million plant in Kansas, the assets of Bede Aircraft at Newton were sold for $21,000 in a sheriff's sale in 1978. The Federal Trade Commission concluded that the 10,000 people who bought or ordered $50

John F. Allen

million in planes from Bede "were misled and deceived." According to the agency, no production engines or drive systems existed that met the company's specifications on performance, reliability, and safety for the BD-5.

Bede was discouraged but not depressed. Nearly 100 people had successfully completed BD-4 kits. He said the BD-5 failed because the engine manufacturer did not deliver as promised — and he could correct that. He had done many things. He had discovered a huge market that no one had known was there, and he had developed a new airplane at a low cost. "We could have failed just the way others have," Bede said, but at least this failure was productive. "I'm very close to the end of the mountain — I'm not there yet — and I honest to goodness don't see any reason to give up. I'm quite confident we'll get there." Of the BD-5, which looked like an overgrown motorcycle and originally had a rope-pull starter and hand-cranked landing gear, he said simply, "It's just a little bit magical."

Bede was not the only small and innovative Kansas aircraft company in the 1970s, though it was the most well-known. Merkel Airplane Company in Wichita sold an aerobatic biplane called the Merkel Mark II, which had evolved out of a master's thesis on lightplanes and first flew in 1973. Alon Incorporated of McPherson took over Fred Weick's Aircoupe safety airplane design in 1963. The Alon A-2 Aircoupe sold for $4,100 at first, increasing to $7,825 by the end of Kansas production in 1967. A total of 245 examples came from the McPherson plant before Alon merged with Mooney. Mooney tried but failed to market the plane as the Mooney Cadet. It was the end of a long experiment, with over 5,000 of the "foolproof" planes sold since 1940. Dave Blanton, who had often been visible over the years as a modifier of special-purpose airplanes, founded the Javelin Aircraft Company in Wichita

SAFETY FIRST

⇑ One of several aircraft designed to be foolproof, the Aircoupe was manufactured in Kansas for a brief period during the 1960s. Designed not to stall, the Aircoupe featured a control system that dispensed with conventional rudder pedals. Spiraling interest rates and stifling competition from Cessna's Model 150 (which sold for about $7,000, compared with $9,000 for an Aircoupe) led to a decision by Alon Incorporated of McPherson to sell out to Mooney Aircraft of Kerrville, Texas.

in 1953. During the 1960s he developed a retrostyle biplane called the Wichawk, aimed at the home-built market. Essentially it was a three-quarter-scale Stearman, a 1934 design. The new version first flew in 1971 and had considerable appeal. Blanton was about as outspoken as Bede or Lear, and was a considerable booster of Wichita and Kansas. His track record as a designer and restorer, including a stint working on the BD-4, was generally impressive, and in 1976, 72 percent of those who had ordered plans had Javelin Wichawks under construction. "Having fabricated every single piece of my Wichawk," said builder Jim Crawford, "I can truthfully say that it is one of the best designed homebuilts in the country." Another Kansas retroplane was the Great Lakes Trainer, a 1929 design produced by hand with modern materials in Wichita at the rate of two kits a week by the mid-1970s. "We may never be as big as Boeing or other aircraft industry giants," said owner Doug Champlain. "But I believe when it comes to quality, our name will always rank among the best."

Kansas innovation in the air was not limited by any means to the commercial or semi-commercial. In 1970 a one-time insurance salesman named Charles Grimm built a kit helicopter with a 113 HP engine that he hoped would carry him over the prairie at 75 MPH. The next year, Joe Funk of Coffeyville attracted attention in an entirely open, steel-tubed pusher craft called a Breezy. Ervest Lehl and Glen Zumwalt of Wichita State Univer-

WICHAWK

⇓ This fully aerobatic biplane has been one of the most successful and appealing of all kit-built airplanes. Configured after a three-quarter-scale Stearman trainer, the prototype was powered by a 180 HP Lycoming four-cylinder engine, but other engines could be installed. Plans for the Wichawk, which was designed by David D. Blanton of Javelin Aircraft Company of Wichita, have sold for $125. Partial kits are also available.

Dave Blanton Collection

Bob Pickett Collection, Kansas Aviation Museum

sity's aeronautical engineering department were promoting an "air train," designed to run at 300 MPH by jet power along an elevated rail. "People were getting tired of wheeled vehicles," said Lehl, "but they still were scared of airplanes. I decided that nothing short of flying at ground level was going to make everyone happy."

The garage and warehouse builders, the small manufacturers, the major plungers, the corporate evolutionists, the dreamers, the copyists, along with the design, production, and marketing innovators of the 1960s and 1970s were a powerful combination of entrepreneurship on all fronts. And that was a Kansas tradition. Change was a stimulus still, and crisis was a challenge in the crosswinds over the Plains.

A BLAST FROM THE PAST

⇐ Originally designed in 1928 by the Great Lakes Aircraft Corporation of Cleveland, this ragwing's timeless design has attracted an enthusiastic following. Originally designated the Model 2T-1A, this aircraft became a very popular sport trainer during the 1930s and could attain 110 MPH. Production eventually landed in the Midwest, with the majority of its airframe being built in Wichita and final assembly taking place in Enid, Okla.

PURSUIT

ONCE MORE

"THIS WAS SOMETHING NEXT TO GOD TO BE ABLE TO BUILD A PLANE. I SAW THAT GROWING UP IN MY TEENS AND I FELT THE BUZZ, THE FEEL, THE HUM WHEN YOU WALK INTO A FACTORY AND KNOW THAT SOMETHING WONDERFUL IS BEING CREATED."

— RANDY SCHLITTER

Hidden amid all the prosperity of the 1970s — the doubling of licensed U.S. pilots to 800,000 and increased use of general-aviation airplanes by commuter airlines — there were transitions in major Kansas aircraft plants that marked the passing of a second era in the state's industry.

Early in 1968, Olive Ann Beech turned over the presidency of Beech Aircraft to her nephew, Frank Hedrick. By 1978, Hedrick was sixty-eight and Beech seventy-five. This suggested another set of management changes soon, despite a statement by Beech to Art Linkletter that "they'll have to carry me out." There was not too much left for Beech to achieve. She was regularly listed among America's Top 10 Women in Big Business by *Fortune* magazine, had won every aviation award, was included in all the halls of fame, and had company stock worth more than $20 million. At her company she was treated as a "near deity" and confessed, "I do about what I please now." It was suggested that a merger might "eliminate the probable personal agony of Mrs. Beech and Hedrick having to name successors to run the firm so closely identified with their lives."

The same was true of Wallace at Cessna, especially after his late-life "baby," the Citation, proved its mettle in the market. In 1975, Russell Meyer, Jr., forty-two, was named board chairman and chief executive officer, replacing Wallace, who had been at the helm for forty-one years. Like Beech, Wallace had largely avoided the media and the limelight, and was temperamentally incapable of the grandiosity of a Lear or Bede. But, like Beech, Wallace was a near legend in his company, town, and country, having built a closed concern surrounded by the Dust Bowl into a firm that

THE NEXT GENERATION
⇐ Randy Schlitter, the founder of the Rans Company of Hays, has built more than 1,700 sport and ultralight aircraft kits since deciding to pass up a career in rock 'n' roll. Schlitter wants to expand his product line to include turbine- and jet-powered craft.

Rans Company

employed 13,000 people worldwide, had 1,000 dealerships and had constructed more airplanes (55 percent of all general-aviation planes in 1975) than its next several competitors combined. It was a difficult record and style to follow, though Meyer, a Yale University and Harvard Law School graduate and Air Force and Marine pilot, was handpicked to do it.

At Lear, too, management was aging even as the company enjoyed record sales. Harry Combs had been president since 1971, but he turned sixty-five in 1978. Learjet was being mentioned seriously as a plum for acquisition by another outside firm.

Boeing, which estimated that its sales in 1979 would top $8 billion, up 55 percent from a year earlier, was large enough that the Kansas end of it was a tail connected to a very powerful dog. It employed more than 13,000 in Wichita that year, planned a $200 million investment in facilities expansion locally, and had a backlog of orders worth more than $15 billion for its popular commercial aircraft, which the Wichita operation, now focused in Plant II, shared.

Moya Lear, who was trying to finish the Lear Fan 2100 (plans for which had been pasted on the wall of Bill Lear's hospital room when he died in 1978) found that no Wichita plants were interested in building it, mostly because they were so busy with other things. Some testing of the Lear Fan was later done at Learjet but, as Moya Lear put it, Wichita companies were just too "fat" to take it on. The eventual $250 million in development money for the Lear Fan would go elsewhere.

Given high earnings, good prospects, and management either aging, in transition, or separated from majority stock ownership, takeover talk abounded. Cessna's stock jumped several times in the summer of 1979, amid such rumors. But the first definite news of fundamental corporate change in Wichita's aviation establishment came from Beech. In October 1979 the company announced it would merge with the Raytheon Co., a manufacturer of missiles, electronics, and consumer appliances. There were assurances that the plant would remain where it was, as would the management and the mission. However, it was the effective end of the family managed aircraft firm, a tradition dating back to Clyde Cessna's move to the Burton Car Works buildings in 1916. What would happen to the airmindedness of the community future operations was uncertain.

Before any merger rumor became reality at Cessna, the company staggered and suffered significantly in one of those cyclical downturns characteristic of the industry. Beginning in 1979, there were problems with the tail of the Cessna Conquest, a ten-passenger, pressurized turboprop that the company had heralded as the "airplane of the '80s," grounding it, and causing costly delays.

BOEING WICHITA COMMERCIAL AIRPLANE PROGRAMS

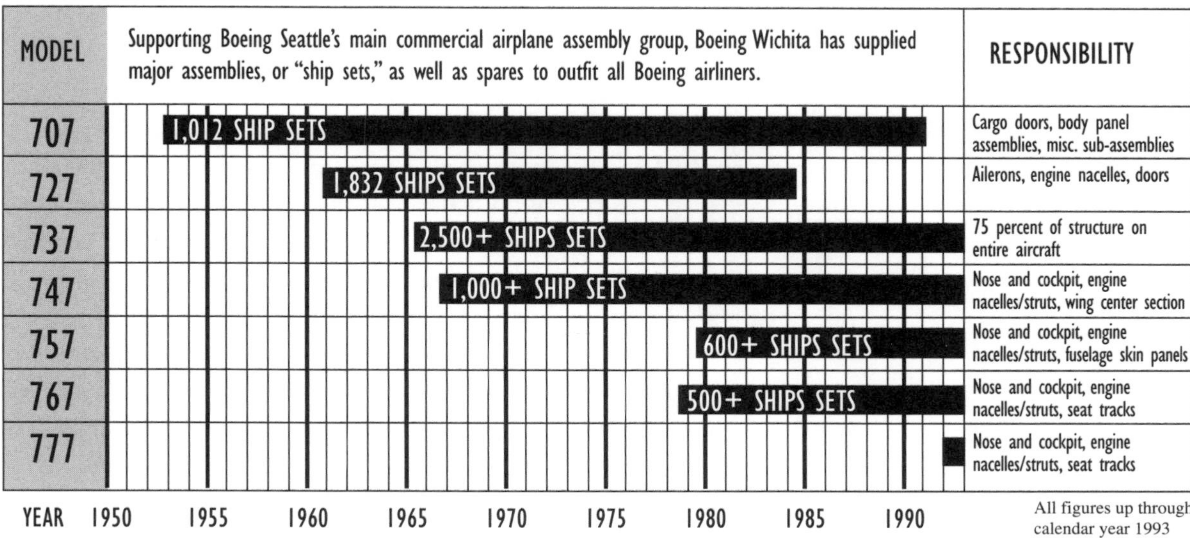

All figures up through calendar year 1993

In 1982 Kansas unemployment reached 5.1 percent, and all the Wichita planemakers, including Boeing, were laying off workers. Beech laid off 2,500 people between mid-1981 and the spring of 1982, and Cessna let 3,045 workers go indefinitely and 1,700 temporarily. It was the continuation of a trend that saw Kansas aviation employment fall from 18,050 in 1979 to 12,922 in 1981. Partial shutdowns and lengthened vacations became common. Earnings slid everywhere. Boeing's were down 58 percent in the spring quarter of 1982, and Cessna's dropped to $1.7 million, down from $19.4 million a year earlier. Meyer said the company was responding "to perhaps the most challenging economic environment we have ever encountered." It began leasing airplanes that it could not sell, boosted prices on its single-engine models, and still, in April 1983, reported a $1.2 million loss, only the second in its history. Cessna was hardly alone. Beech sales fell 50 percent in the final quarter of 1982, ending ten consecutive years of increased sales.

When, late in 1983, General Dynamics Corporation began to buy large amounts of Cessna stock (it would complete its acquisition in 1986), and it became obvious that Wichita's last independent lightplane producer would be independent no more, it appeared to some to be more a salvage operation than a merger with a "white knight." Adding to the corporate uncertainty, more than 800 Cessna dealers filed a class-action lawsuit the next year claiming $93 million in damages based on discriminatory discounting, an amount equivalent to more than half of the company's estimated working capital.

All the older Wichita companies, especially Cessna, because of its volume, would suffer from the Tax Equity and Fiscal Responsibility Act of 1982, which levied a federal tax on general aviation fuel; larger liability awards against manufacturers; and a series of other hits, such as the 1991 luxury tax on airplanes. Headlines about the regional industry employed phrases like "Cloud Looms."

The financial crisis, combined with the mergers, accelerated what might have been a more gentle management transition away from the Kansas family tradition. In May 1982, Raytheon replaced the top three managers at Beech — Beech, Hedrick and Ed Burns — and Beech left the board. She emphasized that Raytheon had been chosen from among 3,500 merger prospects, ten of which had been carefully studied. And to the end she remained both the "boss" and the "lady" in strictly separate categories. "I never concerned myself with what people thought of me," she said. "If I had, I'd have been pretty noisy. And not nearly so successful. Or mysterious." In January 1983 Wallace, then seventy-one, abruptly left the board of Cessna. The *Eagle* tried mightily to get to the bottom of things, but had to settle for a vague explanation from one of the company's directors, who said it was "just a matter of personal dispute." The source of the rift mattered less than Wallace's leaving. His departure, coupled with Beech's, clearly marked the end of a memorable, even romantic, period.

Learjet laid off 1,000 in the fall of 1984, almost a third of its Wichita work force. The company moved some operations to Tucson, Ariz., in 1985 and regularly threatened to move the rest. The same year, Beech closed its plant at Liberal, with the facilities eventually becoming an air museum. Even Boeing, with its billion-dollar airliner orders, was forced to start accepting used-jetliner trade-ins. Wichita was no longer, as the media had become fond of saying, a "pocket of prosperity."

What happened next was what always had happened in the Kansas aviation business: The challenge bred an imaginative response in new ships and new methods, and the adaptations brought the companies back.

Just as the 1980s takeovers were reminiscent of the same phenomenon at the turn of the 1930s, and just as the financial downturn of 1983 harkened back to the Depression of 1933, new models came forth to spur sales and inspire headlines. This time the crisis was not so severe as to close the plants, and there was no return to management by local families, but the new airplanes were as significant and as daring as earlier.

Boeing Wichita worked on airliners and spacecraft, but most of the work came from modifications of 747s and subassemblies for craft that had been developed and first rolled out in Seattle. Building 2,500 737 fuselages and 1,000 747 cockpits was no small achievement, but many hankered for the days when entire airplanes were built at Boeing Wichita. A modest exception was the KC-135R tanker, rolled out in Wichita in 1982, the first new model introduced at the plant since the B-52H twenty-four years earlier.

The Boeing marching band, which had accompanied rollouts during World War II was missing, but there was a gathering of workers and lineup of politicians at the lectern.

Even so, calling the KC-135R a new model was stretching things, because the basic plane had been flying for two decades. However, little thrills accompanied the modification of Air Force One in 1988 and the restoration of a B-47E for exhibit, bringing back the tight security and publicity that the Wichita operation had once enjoyed. But it was largely business — big business — as usual. Boeing Wichita President Lionel Alford said in a 1982 speech that he almost introduced himself as "re-engining" because he had been working at that so hard for so long. Boeing had its bread and butter, and Wichita was not its headquarters. It continued to provide huge employment and economic impact within the state but not the pizzazz that some of the smaller, less profitable, and more threatened concerns did in their struggle for survival in the 1980s.

Cessna did much with its Citation — so much that it became nearly a new airplane. The first flight of the Citation II was in January 1977. It had a

ADDING IT ALL UP

⇓ Since final go-ahead was received in February 1965 for 737 subassembly production, over 2,500 Wichita-built sections have been produced. Accounting for over 75 percent of the entire aircraft's structure, Wichita-built sections of the 737 twin-jet, short-range airliner are shown in this illustration as darkened areas. The 737 has proven to be the most popular airliner in history.

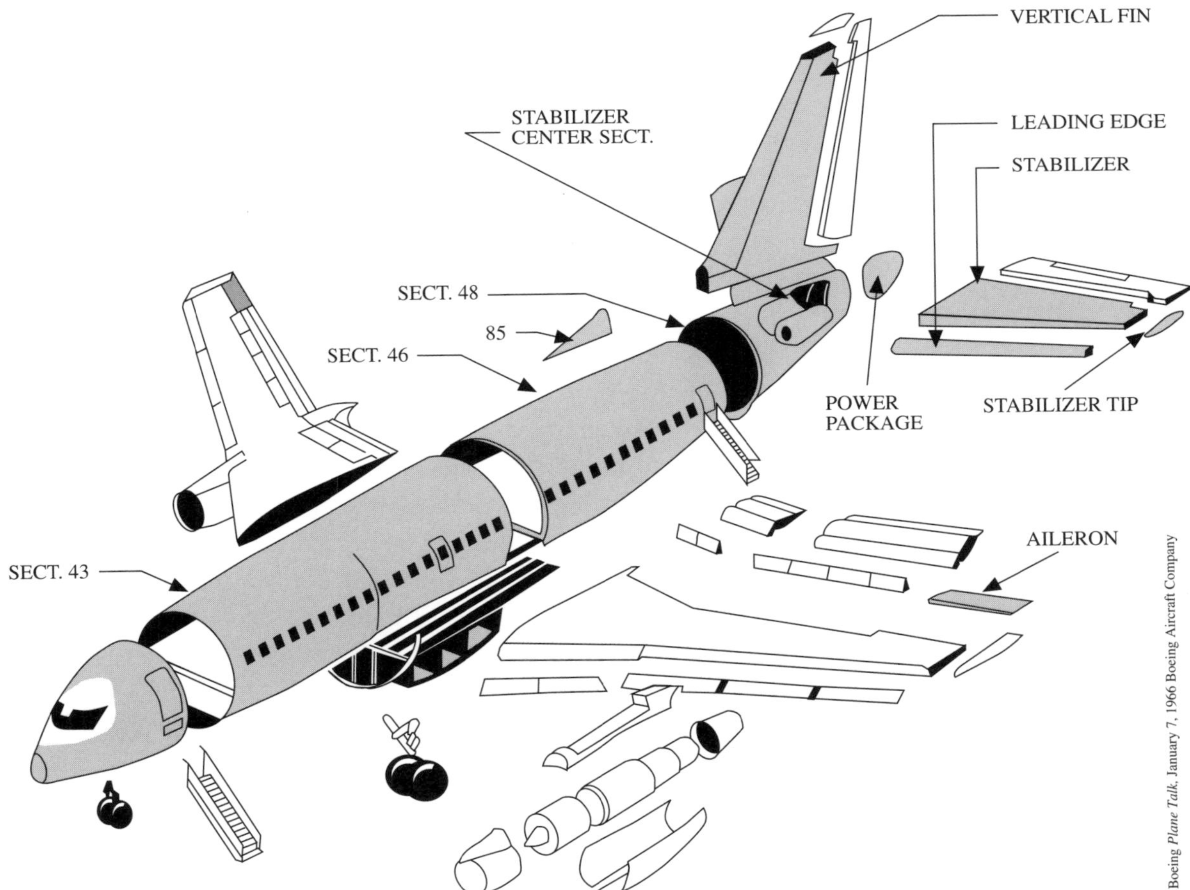

Boeing *Plane Talk*, January 7, 1966 Boeing Aircraft Company

Boeing Aircraft Company

AIR FORCE ONE

⇑ Working seven days a week for months inside a closely guarded hangar, Boeing Wichita workers modified two 747 jetliners for use by U.S. presidents. The $250 million project included installing more than 100 telephones, sixteen TVs, eleven videocassette recorders and seven bathrooms in each plane. Capable of flying at 640 MPH, with a range of 8,000 miles, both 747s can be refueled in flight. The planes were delivered in 1990.

stretched fuselage, more fuel capacity, and increased takeoff thrust. During 1979, 112 were built. That year, too, the Model 650 Citation III, with a 25-degree swept wing and a price of over $6 million, was added. In 1984, golfer Arnold Palmer became the first customer to take delivery. By 1993 the luxury Citation VI and Citation VII had evolved, and the Model 525 entry-level CitationJet had been added. The Citation VII seated thirteen, could fly at 51,000 feet and had range and speed to match any competitor. Meanwhile, the Model 525 CitationJet harked back to the line's original concept by being priced lower than most turboprops and outdoing them in maintenance and fuel costs. There continued to be a mix of small and large, swept- and straight-wing Citations in production simultaneously. The Citation II, for instance, was still being produced in 1992, and the first flight of the Citation X, capable of flying from New York to Los Angeles nonstop in less than four hours, took place in December 1993, giving a line of six Citations from which to choose. With a cruising speed of 528 MPH, there were no jokes (as there had been with early Citations) about birds overtaking a Citation X. And it was still a bargain of sorts. "If it were priced at $25 million," went the ad copy, this jet would be considered remarkable. But, at $12.5 million, the Citation X is nothing short of phenomenal." By mid-1993, more than 2,000 Citations had been delivered, making it the best-selling business jet of all time.

In 1981, among otherwise grim news, Cessna opened a $5.5 million Citation service and support center at Wichita Mid-Continent Airport. That building, Meyer said, and a new Citation III assembly facility "reflect our commitment to Kansas. We like Wichita. It has been a good partnership over the years."

Another bright spot for Cessna was the Model 208 Caravan, a powerful, large (52-foot wingspan and 12-foot long cargo area), single-engine turboprop with great lifting capacity that first flew in 1982. It became popular with the growing package-express services and with the government for State Department special missions because of its economy, reliability in hard service, and relative simplicity. It could carry 3,000 pounds of cargo. Its Pratt & Whitney PT6 engine could run seemingly forever on almost any kind of fuel. And it was the only single-engine aircraft approved for mail service. Like the old Airmaster series, the Caravan was adaptable to modification with floats and special equipment for Arctic and other remote-area duty.

But as Meyer put it in a 1988 interview, Cessna had never gone for the

CITATION X

⇓ Powered by two Allison GMA 3007C turbofans producing 6,000 pounds of thrust each, Cessna's Model 750 is the world's fastest production business jet, with a top speed of Mach 0.9 (about 600 MPH). The Citation X can accommodate a crew of two and as many as twelve passengers. The price of the plane, the first copies of which are to be delivered in 1995, is about $13 million.

Cessna Aircraft Company

Bob Pickett Collection, Kansas Aviation Museum/Cessna Aircraft Company

CESSNA CARAVAN
⇓ The Model 208/208B was seen as a replacement for the aging fleets of de Havilland Otters and Beavers. Capable of transporting more than a ton and a half – and featuring eight doors to load and unload the freight – the Caravan provides good service on unimproved fields. A passenger version capable of carrying fourteen people is available. Shown is a Super Cargomaster, powered by a 675 SHP Pratt & Whitney PT6A engine.

radical departure but rather for steady improvement and excellent function. By 1988, the company had sold 176,000 airplanes and was committed to support all of them. Even if changes in the way liability insurance is priced were to put Cessna back into the piston-single market, it would not necessarily have to be with something radical. The old designs were a bit like the bicycle. One could mess with it a lot and add great cost and not contribute much to what had become a tremendously efficient and cost-effective machine. "We can spend an enormous amount of money — $80 to $100 million — and the result that you get is little better than what is already in hand," Meyer noted. "I don't buy the continued criticism that the 1985 172 was no different from a 1956 172. Not true. It doesn't look very different but ... a lot ... of items were changed."

That was somewhat the way Beech had always looked at things, too. The company was slow with jets, and consistently seemed to prefer the upscale, roomy and economical turboprop, along the lines of the King Air and Super King Air. As early as 1955 it had acquired the rights to build the Morane-Saulinier MS 760 French jet, which would hold four in a pressurized cabin, fly 410 MPH on twin engines, and looked a great deal like the Cessna T-37. But like the T-37 it was either too early or inappropriate for the market. Another early experiment was the Model 73 Jet Mentor, developed in 1955 as a basic jet trainer. It lost the military competition to the Cessna T-37, and only one was built. There was a deal with the British firm Hawker-Siddley in 1969 through which Beech marketed the BH 125 in North America in a modest way. Beech's own, more radical, three-jet design, dubbed PD-339, reached the design-drawings stage in 1983 but was never produced, partly because it appeared at a time of severe recession and cutbacks in the industry. Beech did not enter the jet field again until 1986, when it adapted the Mitsubishi Diamond series seven-passenger craft and sold it (with Beech interior modifications) for over $3 million as the Beechjet. It compared favorably with its major competitors, the Cessna Citation II and the Gates Learjet 35A. Those competitors, of course, were entirely made in Wichita, not just assembled and modified.

Those were defensive measures, but there is every evidence that most of Beech's enthusiasm was not in leased jet designs but in its own in-house project, the highly advanced, turboprop Model 2000 Starship. The Starship, whatever its ultimate sales, certainly will take its place among great Kansas classics and innovative departures. It was a particularly unusual step for Beech, which, a newspaper said in 1983, had not had a "major new aircraft design" since the V-tail Bonanza. When the advertising for the Starship referred to the "Dawn of a New Era," it was not hype.

Of course, pusher aircraft made of composites and bonded with adhesives had been experimented with in small volume among home-builders and kit-makers like Bede. And the high-tech materials, combined with computer-generated aerodynamic designs, had begun to be applied to all kinds of industrial products, from bicycles to boats. But the Starship was different — in size, in mission, and in corporate commitment. It was planned to be the opening of an entire line of composite airplanes for Beech, including a small, single-engine replacement for the Bonanza, originally called the Model 81 POC.

BEECHJET

⇓ Purchased by Beech Aircraft Corporation in 1986, the Mitsubishi Diamond series of business jets was renamed the Model 400 Beechjet. The seven-passenger jet is powered by two Pratt & Whitney JT-15D-5 engines producing 2,900 pounds of thrust with a maximum speed of 530 MPH. In 1990, the Air Force selected a military version, the T-1A Jayhawk, as the winner of the $1.3 billion Tanker Transport Trainer System contract.

Bob Pickett Collection, Kansas Aviation Museum/Cessna Aircraft Company

The Starship's appearance was spectacular. Like the Staggerwing in the 1930s, it made its owners the center of attention at any airport, and now as then, some owners liked that better than others. It first flew as an 85 percent proof-of-concept vehicle built by Rutan's Scaled Composites Company in 1983, and three full-scale prototypes were flying during type certification in 1987. Although ultimate performance fell short of business jets, the plane had a host of innovative features: a glass flight deck featuring fourteen monitor screens; variable geometry; vertical tipsails; multibus electrical system; fully automatic, electronically controlled pressurization; and close-mounted pusher engines that minimized thrust asymmetry under single-engine conditions as well as noise and vibration in the cabin. It even had a front canard, which, along with its pusher props, made it resemble the Wright brother's first plane at least in its most basic configuration.

Its functional attractions were many. It had a speed of 405 MPH, a 41,000-foot cruising altitude, and seating for as many as ten, and it used 25 percent less fuel than a comparable jet. The Starship was the result of a five-year development program designed to replace the King Air with a similarly comfortable and economical turboprop of higher performance. Initial designs were more conventional in appearance. But mounting a larger engine at the front made the craft noisier, while the necessary extra soundproofing made it heavier. Thus in some ways the radical appearance, which reflected Rutan's involvement, was the ultimate in practicality. By the time the plane was introduced, the Starship design program was at least a $300 million investment for Beech and one that had required 2,000 man-years to solve various problems. Its production involved the design of approximately 12,000 new tools and the reservation and construction of a half-million square feet of space at the Wichita plant, partly financed by city and county industrial revenue bonds. At one time, there were 250 engineers working on the project.

Composite construction made more efficient aerodynamics possible. The desired performance was obtained using two proven 1,000 SHP PT-6A-67 Pratt & Whitney turboprops. The sandwich of Nomex honeycomb between carbon-fiber and Kevlar skins formed a rivetless shape and resisted corrosion while providing strength and a 19 percent weight saving over aluminum. Titanium was used at joints for extra strength. Special paint was necessary to make sure the epoxy resin didn't soften in the hot sun. The craft gained significant speed on the King Air 300 at any altitude while sacrificing nothing in size. The wing was naturally stall resistant, and its shape provided a good location for fuel close to the center of gravity, thus avoiding the center of gravity and trim problems that might occur otherwise.

Reaction was favorable. Reporters called the plane "a serious rival to

The Wichita Eagle/Beech Aircraft Corporation

STAR-CROSSED CLASSIC

⇑ Marketed as the world's first all-composite business turboprop, the Beech Starship underwent a series of redesigns because of certification requirements that ultimately restricted its performance and desirability. Shown is a Model 2000A, powered by two 1,200 SHP Pratt & Whitney PT6A-67A turboprops. The price for the plane ultimately reached $4.4 million.

Luke Skywalker's *Star Wars'* fighter in appearance," and Beech executive Linden Blue's early statement that it would start "a family of airplanes ... which will lead the industry for the next 20 years," seemed within the range of possibility. It won the 1991 New Product Award from the National Society of Professional Engineers. At the Paris Air Show in 1987, the plane attracted shoppers such as Prince Fahd and Prince Khalid of Saudi Arabia.

Yet there were questions about marketability. The Starship cost $3.5 million initially. Its competition, the King Air 300 and Piper Cheyenne 400LS, sold for hundreds of thousands less, putting the plane in nearly the same price category as the Beechjet and Citation II. By the early 1990s the base price reached $4.4 million, and the company claimed it was still losing money on each plane it sold. During the FAA certification process, the craft gained weight (about 2,000 pounds) and fuel economy fell. There was tension between the factory and Rutan. Beech bought his Scaled Composites Company, then sold it back to him. It destroyed the proof-of-concept prototype rather than giving it to the Experimental Aircraft Association Museum, which badly wanted it. It appeared that the touted joining of the homebuilders and the corporate suits was not everything it was cracked up to be. Even the improved Starship 2000A had a range of only 1,787 miles and reduced passenger space to six to meet the original performance goals. One aviation consultant noted that the plane was being forced to compete in a slow market with used jets that provided more performance for the same money.

By the fall of 1993, forty-seven Starships had been completed but only sixteen delivered, despite every effort in advertising and special lease arrangements. At that point, manufacturing of the Starship ended, perhaps forever. The market had spoken, and Kansas aircraft makers had always understood that voice. Said Beech President Jack Braly: "The marketplace really needs to demand the airplane or we have to stop building them. ... You can't go on building one airplane a month forever." By the time of its demise, research and development costs on this great gamble had, by some estimates, reached nearly $1 billion.

During this period of market contraction, though, Wichita's air-mindedness continued to draw out-of-state, even out-of-country dreamers and entrepreneurs, any one of which might be the next Lear. The Italian aerospace company Piaggio, for example, seriously studied building its advanced, delta-finned P-180 Avanti in Wichita, after entering a development partnership with Gates Learjet that ended in 1986. For some time, Piaggio built all cockpit and cabin sections in Wichita, shipping them to Italy for final assembly. However, in 1993, the firm was teetering on the verge of bankruptcy, and the U.S. expansion had been largely abandoned. But there were ever new rumors. Maybe Toyota would build a plane, and it could be lured to Kansas. And if it were, it could make a huge difference. Who knows?

As always, Kansas continued late in the 20th century to generate a great deal of aviation activity independent of the major companies. The Rans Company in Hays created the Rans S-11 Pursuit, with which company head Randy Schlitter won the Outstanding Individual Light Aircraft Manufacturer Award at the EAA Oshkosh Air Show in 1992. By using lifting-body technology, in which the fuselage becomes a part of the wing design, Rans was able to effectively use composite construction. "We think over a period of ... years," Schlitter said, "we'll see some fantastic performance out of aircraft that look a lot different than the planes we fly today." The S-11 qualified on that score, especially from the rear. Schlitter was hardly out of his twenties in 1992 but had grown up in Kansas and with airplanes. The childhood experiences that caused him to become a manufacturer were the flights he and his dad, a fixed-base operator, would make to Wichita to pick up parts. "What a wonderful place that was. Here was this factory with hundreds of people making noise, pounding aluminum. ... There's a definite hum in an airplane factory that severely infected me at an early age." He was absorbing in those visits not only the look and the feel but the momentum and the tradition of Kansas aviation, and it had crept into his blood. By the early 1990s, the company produced kits for a whole line of small aircraft — the Coyote I and II, the S-7 Courier, the S-10 Sakota, the ultralight S-12 and S-14 Airailes, and the S-9 Chaos, in addition to the Pursuit. There was a "sail trike," harking

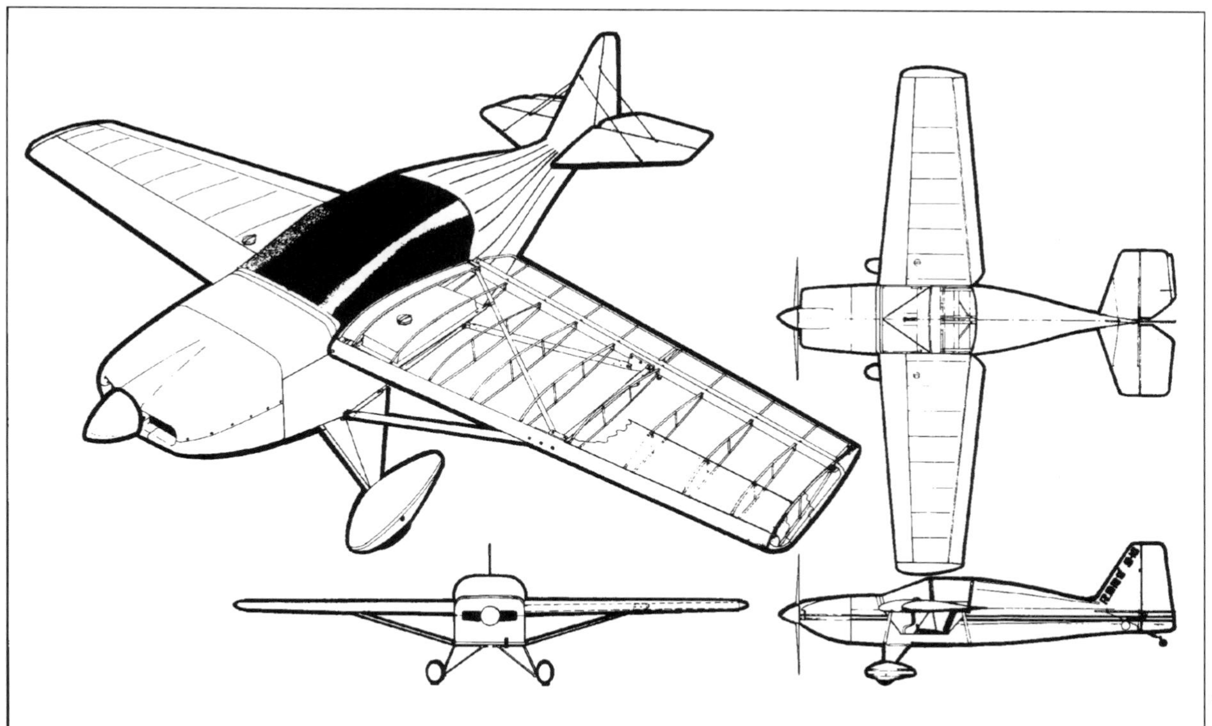

Rans Company

back to the wind wagons of early Kansas. And as a sideline, Rans made and marketed a successful recumbent bicycle, reproducing the combination of products the Wright brothers had made in Dayton, Ohio, once upon a time.

In Johnson City, Kans., there was the Smith propjet. Flown for the first time in 1982, the Smith was a high-performance, six-seat, turboprop single-engine business aircraft. As with Schlitter, those analyzing Smith's motivation put in a large dose of Kansas. "The wind blows hard most days in west Kansas," wrote a columnist for *Flying*. "The land is absolutely flat, and unless the dust is blowing you can see for 50 miles. It's a good thing, too, because it's a long way between towns and between neighbors. People learn to be self-sufficient or they don't last long. Mike Smith is a product of the Great Plains. He has spent his life solving problems in the most direct fashion because there was no other way." Smith bought a P-51 Mustang fighter in 1971 in pieces, put it together, and used it for personal travel. He then went into the business of restoring and maintaining war birds, and finally designed and produced a successor of his own. In 1984, a Bonanza owned by Smith claimed two trans-Atlantic speed records. Smith, a former crop-duster and "thunderstorm buster," commented, "We're going to give the big boys a little run here, and even if nothing comes of it, at least we tried."

Joe Tong of Lecompton, one of the Kansas Territory's early capitals, built ultralights and in 1983 made a transcontinental flight in his under 300-

HIGH PLAINS KIT PLANE

⇑ First flown in January 1988, the Model S-10 Sakota is typical of the sporting kits available from the Rans Company. Powered by a 65 HP Rotax Model 582 engine, the plane can reach 130 MPH. The base price for a 1993 S-10 kit was $13,300.

PRESCOTT AERONAUTICAL CORPORATION

pound craft, setting several records, including fastest transcontinental flight, for the class. "I'm kinda looking at this thing much the same way Lindbergh must have seen," he said. "I'm aiming to set a record and pioneer a new form of aviation."

In January 1983, a scale model of a plane called the Prescott Pusher was flown in Wichita, and in 1985 a full-scale prototype, designed entirely on a computer drafting system, was tested. Though 5,000 prospects were lined up by advertising a selling price of $36,500, initial sales were dismal, and one of the company founders resigned. Sixty-four people purchased kits, and there were total capital expenditures of over $5 million, but the great barrier of commercial viability was not breached.

Still, the four-place homebuilt Pusher "looked like nothing else from Wichita" and pushed the envelope into what one magazine called "unconventional values" — "no production airplane would dare look like this." The Pusher had gull-wing doors, tiny wings, a single prop directly at its rear, and "more glass than a chandelier." It interested such heavy hitters as former Beech President Linden Blue, who invested in the company and was its chairman for a time. Like the Starship, the pusher design reduced vibration to a tingle, and more than a few were impressed by test rides out of Jabara Airport. Developers Tom Prescott and Stan Blankenship, again men as young and ambitious as the developers of the early Goodland helicopter, predicted that someday and with some airplane, a new breed would come to dominate the small-airplane end of the market while the old line companies, which were quickly abandoning single-engine entry-level planes, concentrated on the higher-priced turboprops and business jets. "You know, " said a western Kansas Cessna dealer, "not a week goes by that someone doesn't come in and say, 'What have you got under $20,000? What have you got

A DIFFERENT APPROACH

⇓ Intended for sale primarily to Third World countries (with eventual kit distribution in the United States), the Skyhawk Air Jet Rotor Helicopter was to have been powered by a 420 HP gas turbine engine. Compressed air would feed through the rotor blades and exit through the blade tips to propel the four-place, 750-pound helicopter at 140 MPH. The manufacturing venture, which operated out of Liberal, was sunk by financial problems.

City of Liberal

Learjet, Inc.

MODEL 60

⥣ A product designed to recapture market share, this $8.3 million, medium-range transcontinental business jet (based upon the Model 55C and Model 31A) is Learjet's largest offering. Powered by two Pratt and Whitney PW305 engines generating 4,600 pounds of thrust, the Model 60 will accommodate a crew of two and six to nine passengers while flying at 533 MPH.

under $18,000? What have you got under $15,000?" And those questions still stimulated the young thinkers and doers of the state.

Yet another local variation was the Skyhawk helicopter. The company that built it was founded in 1984, with backing from a Cessna dealer in Turkey and with a small group of employees in Liberal. Advertised as "The Simple Machine Whose Time Has Come," the Skyhawk worked on an air-jet rotor principle. The design eliminated the requirement for the primary and secondary mechanical drive trains that powered the main and tail rotors of conventional choppers. It used compressed air flowing through hollow rotor blades to drive the rotor.

In 1993 the Star Kraft Company was proposing building a twin in Olathe, designed by engineers who owned a printing and engineering firm in Fort Scott, Kans. Luscombe Aircraft was proposing to build a single certified in 1948 at the Parsons airport.

And of course there was still Bede, whom one magazine called "the indefatigable aeronautical engineer." Maybe he feared returning to Kansas, but he drew sixty reporters to the Mojave Desert in the spring of 1992 for the first flight of his BD-10 jet. Again he was receiving deposits, building kits, making spectacular if brief flights, and talking. "You're going to get there three times faster," he told reporters, "and you're going to have to learn how to flip those knobs real fast as you go through one VOR after another." Then a pause, and a laugh. "All right, all right," he said. "I exaggerate."

Exaggeration or no, there was plenty of historical momentum, plenty of imagination, and plenty of ongoing achievement in Kansas aviation at all levels and for all markets as the turn of the millennium approached and the industry's first century drew to a close. Wichita executives were in Washington pushing for changes in liability law, promising that the moment it happened Cessna, at least, would go back into the single-engine piston-powered, everyman airplane business that it had abandoned in 1986 after producing 90,000 such planes over forty years.

This book, though it is a celebration of the Kansas heritage in aviation, is by no means a monument to a purely historical phenomenon. The corporate changes continue. Learjet, after an incredible series of buyout rumors, a three-year period in which no complete planes were made in Wichita, and yearly losses amounting to as much as $20 million, in 1990 became part of Bombardier, a Montreal firm that also purchased Canadair. In 1992, Cessna, where composite manufacturing capability was being developed and experimental Starship-like planes were being spotted, changed hands again, this time going to Textron, Inc. of Providence, R.I. Textron, one reporter said, was "the quintessential conglomerate," with businesses ranging from golf carts to watchbands to insurance.

Some of the second-generation Kansas aviation giants, honored with every possible trophy, award, and hall of fame plaque there was, died — Dwane Wallace in 1989, Olive Ann Beech in 1993. But there were others of different style but equal drive and imagination to face different challenges. The prestigious Collier trophy, for example, was won by Cessna in 1986 for the safety record of the Citation fleet — the first time it had ever been awarded to a member of the general-aviation industry.

General aviation's future contained a familiar mix of promise and problems, combined with a few new twists. There were 17,000 airports in the United States, few of which were served by scheduled airlines and twenty-eight of which handled 75 percent of the airlines flights. For those to whom time and efficiency mattered, the small general-aviation aircraft could hardly be beat. The number of pilots and the number of new pilots being trained was falling off slowly, but active pilots were more active and better trained than ever. New-plane sales in the utility category were off, but used-plane sales and sales of repair parts were at an all-time high. Liability insurance costs to manufacturers, which had averaged $51 per plane in 1962 and $2,111 in 1972, reached $70,000 in 1985. Weather, cost, and the perceived difficulty and danger of flying a small plane remained barriers, but new technology – such as the Global Positioning System for navigation, upgraded compact radios, and data-link radar and positioning maps that were practical and inexpensive – promised to help in that field. Control technology promised again to bring about the absolutely safe commercial and private plane. It was said of Boeing's new airliner, the 777, that it took a crew of two: a human and a dog. The dog was to bite the human if he touched anything.

However short the Kansas industry has fallen of its greatest dreams, its actual performance has been a wonder. Cessna is a case in point. Its commercial production before 1945 was 463 airplanes. During the war it produced more than 6,000 planes for the military. In 1951, its production amounted to 551 planes per year — more than it had produced in its first twenty years. By 1973, that annual production figure was 7,252. It peaked in 1977 at 8,839, and in 1992 produced 140 expensive airplanes. By 1992, Cessna had made 177,841 airplanes. For Kansas as a whole during the first century of its aircraft industry, about 266,500 airplanes were produced. No other state in the nation and, as far as is known, no other country in the western world came close in volume, economic impact, or variety. Where else, outside a specialized air show, would one be likely to see a B-1B bomber, a Beech Starship, and a Staggerwing in the same field of view except in Wichita?

The Kansas Air Century was only a century, but what a century for technology! Borne on, in, and by the ever-present south wind, the Sunflower State's entrepreneurs crafted in wood, steel, aluminum, and composites realized dreams, rationalized visions, miracles in practice. Such an achievement was in tune with the tradition and character of the state and its determined progressives, who viewed the sky as well as the sweeping horizons as tablets to write large human achievements upon. It remains to inspire, stimulate, and inform — never to limit or overawe — Kansas residents and businesspeople of the future. No place is so inland or outlawed, this history says, that it may not, by the efforts of great folks, be a setting for great deeds.

FOR FURTHER READING

Much of the research for this book was done in primary sources or relatively obscure magazines which would not likely be easily available to the general reader. However, there are some excellent books that will supplement *Borne on the South Wind,* both for the Kansas story and the national context. Among these are:

Angelucci, Enzo.	*Rand McNally Encyclopedia of Military Aircraft. World Encyclopedia of Civil Aircraft.*
Avery, N.L.	*B-25 Mitchell, the Magnificent Medium*
Bauer, Eugene.	*Boeing in Peace and War*
Berry, Peter.	*Beechcraft Staggerwing*
Boesen, Victor.	*They Said It Couldn't Be Done: The Incredible Story of Bill Lear*
Bowers, Peter.	"Yesterday's Wings," retrospective aviation series appearing in *The AOPA Pilot*
Boyne, Walter.	*Boeing B-52: A Documentary History*
Caidin, Martin.	*Barnstorming*
Christy, Joe.	*American Aviation: An Illustrated History*
Corn, Joseph.	*The Winged Gospel: America's Romance with Aviation, 1900-1950*
Crouch, Tom	*A Dream of Wings: Americans and the Airplane, 1875-1905*
Farris, Mary.	*The Short Happy Life of the Kansas Flying Machine*
Forden, Leslie.	*The Ford Air Tours 1925-1931*
Hart, Clive.	*The Dream of Flight: Aeronautics from Classical Times to the Rennaisance*
Hull, Robert.	*September Champions: The Story of America's Air Racing Pioneers*
Huntington, Roger.	*Thompson Trophy Racers: The Pilots and Planes of America's Air Racing Glory Days 1929-49*
Hutchinson, Robert	*Jane's, All the World's Aircraft*
Hutig, Jack.	*1927: Summer of Eagles*
Juptner, Joseph.	*U.S. Civil Aircraft,* Volumes one throught eight
Leary, William.	*Aerial Pioneers: The U.S. Air Mail Service 1918-1927*
McDaniel, William.	*Beech: Four Decades of Aeronautical and Aerospace Achievement*
Miner, Craig.	*Wichita: The Magic City*
Mingo, Howard	*Aircraft Year Book,* The. Lanciar Publishers, Inc.
Mosley, Leonard.	*Lindbergh: A Biography*
Nevill, John.	"The Story of Wichita," Aviation (Sept., 1930)
O'Neil, Paul.	*Barnstormers and Speed Kings*
Peacock, Lindsay.	*Boeing B-47 Stratojet*
Phillips, Ed.	*Beechcraft: Staggerwing to Starship*
Phillips, Ed.	*Cessna: A Masters Expression*
Phillips, Ed.	*Travel Air: Wings Over the Prairie*
Plehinger, Russell.	*Marathon Flyers*
Porter, Donald.	*The Cessna Citations*
Rashke, Richard.	*Stormy Genius: The Life of Aviation's Bill Lear*
Redding, Robert and Yenne Bill.	*Boeing: Planemaker to the World*
Rolfe, Douglas.	*Airplanes of the World*
Schmidt, S.H. and Weaver, Truman.	*The Golden Age of Air Racing Pre-1940*
Serling, Robert.	*Legend and Legacy: The Story of Boeing and Its People*
Shamburger, Page.	*Command the Horizon*
Smith, Robert.	*Staggerwing: Story of the Classic Beechcraft Biplane*
Stoff, Joshua.	*The Thunder Factory: An Illustrated History of the Republic Aviation Corporation*
Van Meter, Sondra.	"The Primary Contribution of E.M. Laird to the Aviation Industry of Wichita" (M.A. Thesis, University of Wichita, 1962)
Weyand, Ken	"Aviation History in Greater Kansas City.' By the editors of Historic Aviation Magazine
Wichita Eagle, The	"Aviation Pioneers' 1987 — a compliation of a 41-part series which began in October, 1984.
Zimmerman, John.	*Aerospace: The Wichita Perspective*

INDEX